PEARSON ALWAYS LEARNING

Business Applications of Social Responsibility, Volume II

Third Edition

Compiled by Donna Sockell, Ph.D., Francy Milner, J.D.
and Kevin McMahon.

Cover Art: Courtesy of Digital Visions/Getty Images.

Pearson Learning Solutions, 501 Boylston Street, Suite 900, Boston, MA 02116
A Pearson Education Company
www.pearsoned.com

Printed in the United States of America

1 2 3 4 5 6 7 8 9 10 V0CR 16 15 14 13 12 11

000200010270768442

BW/OP

ISBN 10: 1-256-33825-7
ISBN 13: 978-1-256-33825-3

Copyright Acknowlegements

Grateful acknowledgment is made to the following sources for permission to reprint material copyrighted or controlled by them:

"Principles of Corporate Government 2005," by Business Roundtable (November 2005), by permission of Business Roundtable Institute for Corporate Ethics.

"Oh Lord Won't You Buy Me a Mercedes-Benz?": How Compensation Practices are Undermining the Credibility of Executive Leaders," by Jay A. Conger, reprinted from *The Quest for Moral Leaders* (2005), by permission of Edward Elgar Publishing Company.

"In the Money: A Special Report on Executive Pay," reprinted by permission from *The Economist*, January 20, 2007, by permission of The Economist Newspaper Ltd.

"Shared Goals," by Shelly Banjo, reprinted from *The Wall Street Journal*, April 14, 2008, by permission of Dow Jones & Company Inc.

"Boards Flex Their Pay Muscles," by Joann Lublin, reprinted by permission from *The Wall Street Journal*, April 14, 2008.

"New Rule on Proxies Puts Heat on Firms," by Joann S Lublin, reprinted from *The Wall Street Journal* August 22, 2010.

"New Law Has an Effect on Executive Pay," by David Nicklaus, reprinted from *Stltoday.com*, January 7, 2011.

"Home Depot's CEO Cleans Up," by Brian Grow, reprinted by permission from *Business Week*, January 15, 2007.

"Shareholders to Home Depot Chief: You're Chicken," by Parija Bhathagar, reprinted from *Money.cnn.com* April 14, 2008, Cable News Network, a Time Warner Company.

"Out at Home Depot," by Brian Grow, reprinted by permission from *Business Week*, January 9, 2007.

"Robert Nardelli Named CEO of Chrysler," by Katie Benner, reprinted from *Money.cnn.com*, Aug. 6, 2007, Cable News Network, a Time Warner Company.

"Consumer Product Safety Act of 1972," by Burton S. Kaliski, reprinted from *Encyclopedia of Business and Finance*, Cengage Learning.

"Salmonella Outbreak Fuels Food-Safety Efforts," by Jane Zhang, reprinted from *The Wall Street Journal*, 2009, by permission of Dow Jones & Company Inc.

"Business and Its External Exchanges: Ecology and Consumers," by Manuel Velasquez, reprinted from *Business Ethics: Concepts and Cases*, 2006, by permission of Prentice-Hall, Inc.

"Pinto Fires," by Dennis A Gioia, reprinted from *Managing Business Ethics*, by permission of John Wiley & Sons, Inc.

"Coke Sued for Fraudulent Claims on Obesity—Promoting "Vitamin Water"," January 15, 2009, Center for Science in the Public Interest.

"Lawsuit Over Deceptive Vitamin Water Claims to Proceed," July 23, 2010, Center for Science in the Public Interest.

"Letter to David Vladeck Re: Deceptive Advertising of "Vitamin Water"," by Sally Greenberg, February 2, 2011, National Consumers League.

"Law and Ethics," by Jeff Richards, reprinted from *Texas Advertising: University of Texas at Austin* by permission of The University of Texas at Austin, Advertising Department.

"How Advertising Practitioners View Ethics: Moral Muteness, Moral Myopia, and Moral Imagination," by Minette Drumwright and Patrick Murphy, reprinted from *Journal of Advertising* (summer 2004), by permission of Journal of Advertising.

"Veteran Marketer Promotes a New Kind of Selling," by Suzanne Vranica, reprinted from *The Wall Street Journal*, 2008, by permission of Dow Jones & Company Inc.

"We'd Rather Not Know," by Robert B Reich, reprinted from *A Templeton Conversation: Does the Free Market Corrode Moral Character?* (2008), John Templeton Foundation.

"Predatory Lending Practices," reprinted from *National Association of Consumer Advocates (NACA).*

"Faces of Foreclosure: A Loan Choice Proved Costly," by Dawn Wotapka, reprinted from *The Wall Street Journal*, December 29, 2010, Dow Jones & Company Inc.

"Subprime Lending and Marketing: From Payday to Title Loans," by Marianne Jennings, reprinted from *Business Ethics Case Studies and Selected Readings* (2009), Cengage Learning.

"Foreclosure Exposure: A Study of Racial and Income Disparities in Home Mortgage Lending in 172 American Cities," by Association of Community Organizations for Reform Now (September 5, 2007), ACORN.

"Bank of America in Settlement Worth Over $8 Billion," by Ruth Simon, reprinted from *The Wall Street Journal* 2008, by permission of Dow Jones & Company Inc.

"U.S. News: Housing Bill Relies on Banks to Take Loan Losses; Lawmakers Pressure Lenders to Pitch in to Curb Foreclosures," by Damian Paletta, reprinted from *The Wall Street Journal*, 2008, by permission of Dow Jones & Company Inc.

"Federal Laws Prohibiting Job Discrimination," reprinted from *The U.S. Equal Employment Opportunity Commission.*

"Diversity and Discrimination," by Joseph DesJardins, reprinted from *An Introduction to Business Ethics* (2005), by permission of McGraw-Hill Companies.

"Texaco: The Jelly Bean Diversity Fiasco," by Marianne M Jennings, reprinted from *Case Studies in Business Ethics* (2005), Venture Literary.

"Planning Can Help Reduce Exposure to Layoff-Related Suits," by Glen Doherty, reprinted from *Boston Business Journal* (2002).

"When Downsizing is Unethical," by William Roth, reprinted from *Ethics in the Workplace* (2005), by permission of Prentice-Hall, Inc.

"Short-Circuited: Cutting Jobs as Corporate Strategy," reprinted from *Compass Bank-Wharton* (2007), by permission of The Wharton School, University of Pennsylvania.

"Recalculating the Cost of Big Layoffs," by Scott Thurm, reprinted from *The Wall Street Journal*, May 5, 2010, Dow Jones & Company Inc.

"The Role of Business Ethics in Employee Engagement," by Tom Monahan, reprinted from *Ethisphere* (November 4, 2009), Ethisphere Institute.

"Pinnacle Brands: A Strike Puts Employees Up to Bat," by Gillian Gynn, reprinted from *Perspectives in Business Ethics* (2005), by permission of Crain Communications.

"Wal-Mart's Women," by Manuel Velasquez, reprinted from *Business Ethics: Concepts and Cases* (2006), by permission of Prentice-Hall, Inc.

"Supreme Court Will Consider Wal-Mart Challenge to Class-Action Suit," by Jess Bravin; Ann Zimmerman, reprinted from *The Wall Street Journal*, December 7, 2010, Dow Jones & Company Inc.

"Wall Street's Disappearing Women," by Anita Raghavan, reprinted from *Forbes*, 2009, by permission of Forbes.com.

"Beyond Greening: Strategies for a Sustainable World," by Stuart Hart, reprinted from *Harvard Business Review* (January-February 1997), Harvard Business School Publishing.

"A Road Map for Natural Capitalism," by Amory B Lovins; L. Hunter Lovins; Paul Hawken, reprinted from *Harvard Business Review* (1999), Harvard Business School Publishing.

"Timeline: BP's Woes," reprinted from *The Wall Street Journal*, January 16, 2007, by permission of Dow Jones & Company Inc.

"Oil Gushes Into Arctic Ocean from BP Pipeline," by Leonard Doyle, reprinted by permission from *The Independent/UK*, March 12, 2006.

"It's Not Easy Being Green," by Paul Roberts, reprinted by permission from *Mother Jones* (November-December 2006).

"At Exxon, Making the Case for Oil," by Jad Mouawad, reprinted from *The New York Times*, 2008, by permission of The New York Times Company.

"White House Probe Blames BP, Industry in Gulf Blast," by Steven Power; Ben Casselman, reprinted from *The Wall Street Journal*, January 6, 2011, Dow Jones & Company Inc.

"As CEO Hayward Remade BP, Safety, Cost Drives Slashed," by Guy Chazan; Benoit Faucon, Ben Casselman, reprinted from *The Wall Street Journal*, Dow Jones & Company Inc.

"BP's Safety Drive Faces Rough Road," by Guy Chazan, reprinted from *The Wall Street Journal*, February 1, 2011, Dow Jones & Company Inc.

"Business and NGOs: Reaching for a Longer Spoon," reprinted from *The Economist*, June 3, 2010, by permission of The Economist Newspaper Ltd.

"BP Offers Financial Aid to Station Owners," by Naureen S Malik, reprinted from *The Wall Street Journal*, June 29, 2010, Dow Jones & Company Inc.

"Briefing: Green America," reprinted from *The Economist*, January 27, 2007, The Economist Newspaper Ltd.

"A Free Economy is a Clean Economy: How Free Markets Improve the Environment," by Ben Lieberman, reprinted from *2011 Index of Economic Freedom*, Heritage Foundation.

"Time for a Smarter Approach to Global Warming," by Bjorn Lomberg, reprinted from *The Wall Street Journal: Opinion Page*, December 19, 2009, Dow Jones & Company Inc.

"Does Helping the Planet Hurt the Poor?" by Peter Singer, reprinted from *Business News & Financial News-The Wall Street Journal*, Dow Jones & Company Inc.

"Does Helping the Planet Hurt the Poor?" by Bjørn Lomborg, reprinted from *The Wall Street Journal*, January 22, 2011, Dow Jones & Company Inc.

"Cancun Climate Summit Avoids the Cost Question," by Jeffrey Ball, reprinted from *The Wall Street Journal*, December 13, 2010, Dow Jones & Company Inc.

"David Schoenbrod and Richard B. Stewart: The Waxman-Markey Cap and Trade Bill is a Fraud," by David Schoenbrod; Richard B. Stewart, reprinted from *Business News & Financial News-The Wall Street Journal*, August 24, 2009, Dow Jones & Company Inc.

"Chilling Effect," by John Fund, reprinted from *The Wall Street Journal*, February 25, 2008, by permission of Dow Jones & Company Inc.

"Cleaning Up: A Special Report of Business and Climate Change," reprinted from *The Economist*, 2007, by permission of Economist Newspaper Ltd.

"CEO's Can Have a 'Huge Impact' on Climate Change," by Jeff Swartz, reprinted from *The Wall Street Journal*, 2008, by permission of Dow Jones & Company Inc.

Excerpts from "Today's Climate-Change Report," reprinted from *The Wall Street Journal*, by permission of Dow Jones & Company Inc.

"Exxon Softens Climate-Change Stance," by Jeffrey Ball, reprinted from *The Wall Street Journal*, January 11, 2007, by permission of Dow Jones & Company Inc.

"What is Long Term Wealth?" by Steven Lydenberg, reprinted from *Corporations and the Public Interest: Guiding the Invisible Hand* (2005), by permission of Berrett-Koehler Publishers Inc.

"Teaming Up to Brand and Bond: Timberland Partners with City Year, SOS, and Skills USA," reprinted by permission from The Center for Corporate Citizenship at Boston College.

"2008 Disability Status Report," by Cornell University, Cornell University Press.

"The Americans With Disabilities Act," by Susan Campbell; Matt Rita.

"An Entrepreneurial Approach to Welfare to Work Programs," by Carolyn Brown, reprinted from *CELCEE Digest*, 1999, by permission of Ewing Marion Kauffman Foundation.

"Is It All About the Brownies-Taking Less as Opposed to Giving Back," by Beth Parish, reprinted from *ICOSA* by permission of ICOSA Magazine.

"In Defense of International Sweatshops," by Ian Maitland, reprinted from *British Academy of Management Annual Conference Proceedings* (September 1997), by permission of Cengage Learning.

"Can Multinational Corporations Protect Workers Rights?" by Auret Van Heerden and Dorothee Baumann, reprinted from *Fair Labor Association* (October 2000), by permission of Fair Labor Association.

"The Long Road to Sustainability," reprinted from *The Economist*, September 23, 2010, by permission of Economist Newspaper Ltd.

"Building the Right Model for Business in China," by Jeff Schwartz, reprinted by permission from *Fastcompany.com*, July 13, 2009.

"Microfinance's Success Sets Off a Debate in Mexico," by Elizabeth Malkin, reprinted from *The New York Times*, April 5, 2008, by permission of The New York Times Company.

"Frequently Asked Questions and Microfinance Glossary," reprinted from *International Year of Microcredit* (2005), UN Capital Development Fund.

"Reimagining Microfinance," by Alex Counts, reprinted by permission from *Standford Social Innovation Review* (summer 2008).

"Time to Take the Credit," reprinted from *The Economist*, March 15, 2007, by permission of Economist Newspaper Ltd.

"Microlenders, Honored with Nobel, Are Struggling," by Vikas Bajaj, reprinted from *The New York Times*, January 5, 2011, The New York Times Company.

"Suicides in India Revealing How Men Made a Mess of Microcredit," by Yoolim Lee and Ruth David (December 28, 2010), Bloomberg Press.

"CGAP The Client Protection Principles in Micro-finance," Consultative Group to Assist the Poor.

"Moral Courage Checklist," reprinted from *Moral Courage* (2005), HarperCollins.

"Values in Tension: Ethics Away from home," by Thomas Donaldson, reprinted from *Harvard Business Review on Corporate Ethics* (November 2005), Harvard Business School Publishing.

CONTENTS

Part Six: Stakeholder Influence: A Principled or a Pragmatic Approach: Obligations and Beyond 3

Part Six (A): An Overview of Corporate Governance 5
Business Roundtable 7
Introduction to Sarbanes-Oxley **29**
Leading From the Boardroom **43**

Part Six (B): Shareholders 55
Executive Compensation Principles and Commentary **57**
"Oh Lord, Won't You Buy Me A Mercedes-Benz": How Compensation Practice are Undermining the Credibility of Executive Leaders **65**
In the Money: A Special Report on Executive Pay **81**
Shared Goals **89**
Boards Flex Their Pay Muscle **93**
New Rule on Proxies Puts Heat on Firms **99**
New Law Has An Effect on Executive Pay **103**
Questions on Readings for Part Six (B) **107**

Case #4: Executive Pay Abuses? The Case of Robert Nardelli **109**
Home Depot's CEO Cleans Up **111**
Shareholders to Home Depot Chief: You're Chicken **115**
Out at Home Depot **117**
Robert Nardelli Named CEO of Chrysler **123**

Part Six (C): Consumers 125
Consumer Product Safety Act of 1972 **127**
Salmonella Outbreak Fuels Food-Safety Efforts **129**
Business Ethics: Concepts and Cases **133**
The Contract View **156**
The Due Care View **157**
The Social Costs/Strict Liability View **158**
Coke Sued for Fraudulent Claims on Obesity—Promoting "Vitamin Water" **159**
Lawsuit Over Deceptive Vitamin Water Claims to Proceed **161**
Letter to David Vladeck: Re: Deceptive Advertising of "vitaminwater" **163**
Case: Pinto Fires **167**
Questions on Readings for Part Six (C) 1 of 2 **171**
Law and Ethics **173**
How Advertising Practitioners View Ethics **183**
Veteran Marketer Promotes a New Kind of Selling **213**
We'd Rather Not Know **217**
Can and Does Consumer Activism Make a Difference: What is the Impact of Consumers as Stakeholders?* **219**
Questions on Readings for Part Six (C) 2 of 2 **221**

Case #5: Subprime Mortgages & Predatory Lending **223**
Subprime Mortgages and Predatory Lending: Introduction/Overview **225**
Predatory Lending Practices **229**
Faces of Foreclosure: A Loan Choice Proved Costly **231**
Subprime Lending and Marketing: From Payday to Title Loans **233**
Foreclosure Exposure: A Study of Racial and Income Disparities in Home Mortgage Lending in 172 American Cities **237**
Bank of America in Settlement Worth Over $8 Billion **249**
U.S. News: Housing Bill relies on Banks to Take Loan Losses; Lawmakers Pressure Lenders to Pitch in to Curb Foreclosures **253**

Part Six (D): Employees: Discrimination and Layoffs 255
Federal Laws Prohibiting Job Discrimination **257**
Diversity and Discrimination **269**
Texaco: The Jelly Bean Diversity Fiasco **283**
Questions on Readings for Part Six (D) 1 of 2 **293**
Planning can Help Reduce Exposure to Layoff-Related Lawsuits **295**
When Downsizing is Unethical **299**
Short-Circuited: Cutting Jobs as Corporate Strategy **309**
Recalculating the Cost of Big Layoffs **315**
The Role of Business Ethics in Employee Engagement **319**
Pinnacle Brands: A Strike Puts Employees Up to Bat **321**
Can and Does Employee Activism Make a Difference? **326**
Questions on Readings for Part Six (D) 2 of 2 **327**

Case # 6: Wal-Mart and Wall Street Women **329**
Wal-Mart's Women **331**
Supreme Court Will Consider Wal-Mart Challenge to Class-Action Suit **339**
Wall Street's Disappearing Women **341**

Part Six (E): Environment and a Modern Approach to Sustainability 349

Part Six (E) (I): Environment—General Issues 351

Beyond Greening: Strategies for a Sustainable World **353**
A Road Map for Natural Capitalism **367**
Questions on Readings for Part Six (E) (I) **380**

Case #7: BP & Deepwater Horizon **381**

Timeline: BP's Woes **383**
Oil Gushes into Arctic Ocean From BP Pipeline **387**
It's Not Easy Being Green **389**
At Exxon, Making the Case for Oil **391**

White House Probe Blames BP, Industry in Gulf Blast **399**
As CEO Hayward Remade BP, Safety, Cost Drives Clashed **403**
BP's Safety Drive Faces Rough Road **409**
Business and NGOs: Reaching for a Longer Spoon **415**
BP Offers Financial Aid to Station Owners **419**
Our Values: About BP **421**

Part Six (E) (II): The Global Environment—Climate Change 423
Briefing: Green America **425**
A Free Economy is a Clean Economy: How Free Markets Improve the Environment **431**
Time for a Smarter Approach to Global Warming **439**
Does Helping the Planet Hurt the Poor? by Peter Singer **443**
Does Helping the Planet Hurt the Poor? by Bjørn Lomborg **447**
U.N. Climate Talks End **451**
The Cap-and-Trade Bait and Switch **453**
Chilling Effect **455**
Cleaning Up: A Special Report of Business and Climate Change **457**
CEOs Can Have a 'Huge Impact' on Climate Change **467**
Excerpts from "Today's Climate-Change Report" **469**
Exxon Softens Climate-Change Stance **471**
Can and Does Environmental Activism Make a Difference? **474**
Questions on Readings for Part Six (E) (II) **476**

Part Six (F): The Community: Local and Global 477
Corporations and the Public Interest: Guiding the Invisible Hand **479**
Teaming Up to Brand and Bond Timberland Partners with City Year, SOS, and SKILLSUSA **491**

Case #8: Oklahoma League for the Blind (New View) and Greyston Bakery **501**
New View (Formerly the Oklahoma League for the Blind): Introduction/Overview **503**
The 2008 Disability Status Report **505**
- Employment **508**
- Annual Earnings (Full-Time/Full-Year Workers) **509**
- Poverty **511**
- Education **512**

The Americans with Disabilities Act **513**
An Entrepreneurial Approach to Welfare to Work Programs **519**
Is it All About the Brownies? **523**
In Defense of International Sweatshops **527**
Can Multinational Corporations Protect Workers Rights? **535**
The Long Road to Sustainability **543**
Building the Right Model for Business in China **547**
Can and Does Community Activism Make a Difference **549**
Questions on Readings for Part Six (F) **551**

Case #9: The Future of Microfinance: The Accion International Model v. The Grameen Bank Model **553**
Microfinance's Success Sets Off a Debate in Mexico **555**
Frequently Asked Questions and Microfinance Glossary **559**
Reimagining Microfinance **563**
Microfinance: Time to Take the Credit **573**
Microlenders, Honored with Nobel, Are Struggling **575**
Suicides in India Revealing How Men Made a Mess of Microcredit **579**

The Client Protection Principles in Microfinance **587**

Part Seven: Values Revisited: Enter Courage 589
Moral Courage Checklist **591**
Values in Tension: Ethics Away from Home **593**
New Ethics in the Office **607**
Get Aggressive About Passivity **609**
The Courage to Be Moral **611**
Hotlines Helpful for Blowing the Whistle **617**
Questions on Readings for Part Seven **621**

Case #10: Whistle Blowing **623**
Critics Blow Whistle on Law **625**
Merck to Pay $650 Million in Medicaid Settlement **627**
2nd WSJ Update: Merck Settle Sales, Marketing Probes **631**
Merck Whistleblower Wins $68M Award **635**
The Curious Case of Lehman's Whistleblower **637**
The Lehman Whistleblower's Letter **641**

Part Eight: Values and a Job: Building a Culture or Finding a Fit: The Role of Conscience 645
50 Codes of Conduct Benchmarked **647**
Beyond the Code: Inspiring Ethical Conduct **651**
Making the Tough Call **653**
Ethics and Organizational Culture **657**
Pinto Fires and Personal Ethics: A Script Analysis of Missed Opportunities **659**
Questions on Readings for Part Eight **673**

CENTER FOR EDUCATION ON SOCIAL RESPONSIBILITY

Foreword

It is with sincere gratitude that we wish to acknowledge the assistance of the Instructors and Staff of the Center for Education in Social Responsibility (CESR). Their commitment to values-driven education is evidenced in the classroom, this textbook and the continued growth of CESR. We also acknowledge the invaluable assistance of Chelsea Kiyabu and Nick Mooney. These two outstanding students provided invaluable research, sourced relevant articles on individual cases and updated key portions of the text.

Donna Sockell
Francy Milner
Kevin McMahon
May 25, 2011

VOLUME II

CENTER FOR EDUCATION ON SOCIAL RESPONSIBILITY

PART SIX

STAKEHOLDER INFLUENCE: A PRINCIPLED OR A PRAGMATIC APPROACH: OBLIGATIONS AND BEYOND

Business Roundtables' Guiding Principles

1. The Board of Directors' Job is to oversee management.
2. Management's job is to operate the company ethically and effectively.
3. Management must produce complete financial statements.
4. Board oversees Oversee Independent auditing firm.
5. The Board shapes corporate governance and selects qualified Board candidates.
6. The Board oversees CEO and senior management compensation and compensation policies.
7. The Board responds to shareholder concerns.
8. The corporation must deal fairly with employees, customers, suppliers and all constituencies.
9. Both the Board and management must focus on generating long-term shareholder value.

Specific Duties of the Board of Directors

1. Plan for management development and succession.
2. Oversee and understand corporation's strategic plans and monitor the implementation of those plans.
3. Understand and approve operating plans and annual budgets.
4. Focus on clarity and integrity of financial statements.
5. Review and approve significant corporate actions as required by state law (election of officers, dividend declaration, major transactions).
6. Review management's plans for resiliency (risk assessment and management).
7. Nominate directors and committee members.
8. Oversee ethical and legal compliance.

Duties of the CEO and Senior Management

1. Operate corporation and apprise Board.
2. Strategic planning.
3. Develop operating plans and budgets.
4. Select qualified management and establish organization structure.
5. Identify and manage risks.
6. Accurate and transparent financial reporting and disclosure (responsible for the integrity of the financial reporting system), evaluate internal controls over financial reporting and disclosure, certifying accuracy.

CENTER FOR EDUCATION ON SOCIAL RESPONSIBILITY

PART SIX (A)

AN OVERVIEW OF CORPORATE GOVERNANCE

BUSINESS ROUNDTABLE

FOREWORD AND INTRODUCTION

Business Roundtable is recognized as an authoritative voice on matters affecting American business corporations and, as such, has a keen interest in corporate governance. Business Roundtable is an association of chief executive officers of leading corporations with a combined workforce of more than 10 million employees and $4 trillion in annual revenues. The chief executives are committed to advocating public policies that foster vigorous economic growth, a dynamic global economy, and the well-trained and productive U.S. workforce essential for future competitiveness.

Since May 2002, when Business Roundtable issued its *Principles of Corporate Governance,* U.S. public corporations have witnessed fundamental and accelerated changes in the area of corporate governance, beginning with the passage of the Sarbanes-Oxley Act of 2002 and continuing with the adoption of strengthened listing standards by the securities markets. We note that many of the best practices recommended in the principles are now embedded in the Sarbanes-Oxley Act and in securities market listing standards.

Following the publication of *Principles of Corporate Governance* (May 2002), Business Roundtable issued *Executive Compensation: Principles and Commentary* (November 2003), *The Nominating Process and Corporate Governance Committees: Principles and Commentary* (April 2004), and *Guidelines for Shareholder-Director Communications* (May 2005). Other publications from Business Roundtable that have addressed corporate governance include *Statement on Corporate Governance* (September 1997), *Executive Compensation/Share Ownership* (March 1992), *Corporate Governance and American Competitiveness* (March 1990), *Statement on Corporate Responsibility* (October 1981), and *The Role and Composition of the Board of Directors of the Large Publicly Owned Corporation* (January 1978).

Business Roundtable continues to believe, as we noted in *Principles of Corporate Governance* (2002), that the United States has the best corporate governance, financial reporting and securities markets systems in the world. These systems work because of the adoption of best practices by public companies within a framework of laws and regulations.

Given the fundamental nature of the changes that have occurred during the past several years in the framework of laws and regulations related to corporate governance, as well as in best practices, Business Roundtable believes it is appropriate, once again, to restate our guiding principles of corporate governance. Although applicable legal requirements and securities market listing standards establish minimum requirements, these principles, we believe, should help guide the ongoing advancement of corporate governance practices and, thus, advance the ability of public corporations to compete, create jobs and generate economic growth.

Business Roundtable supports the following guiding principles:

First, the paramount duty of the board of directors of a public corporation is to select a chief executive officer and to oversee the CEO and senior management in the competent and ethical operation of the corporation on a day-to-day basis.

Second, it is the responsibility of management to operate the corporation in an effective and ethical manner to produce value for shareholders. Senior management is expected to know how the corporation earns its income and what risks the corporation is undertaking in the course of carrying out its business. The CEO and board of directors should set a "tone at the top" that establishes a culture of legal compliance and integrity. Management and directors should never put personal interests ahead of or in conflict with the interests of the corporation.

Third, it is the responsibility of management, under the oversight of the audit committee and the board, to produce financial statements that fairly present the financial condition and results of operations of the corporation and to make the timely disclosures investors need to assess the financial and business soundness and risks of the corporation.

Fourth, it is the responsibility of the board, through its audit committee, to engage an independent accounting firm to audit the financial statements prepared by management, issue an opinion that those statements are fairly stated in accordance with Generally Accepted Accounting Principles and oversee the corporation's relationship with the outside auditor.

Fifth, it is the responsibility of the board, through its corporate governance committee, to play a leadership role in shaping the corporate governance of the corporation. The corporate governance committee also should select and recommend to the board qualified director candidates for election by the corporation's shareholders.

Sixth, it is the responsibility of the board, through its compensation committee, to adopt and oversee the implementation of compensation policies, establish goals for performance-based compensation, and determine the compensation of the CEO and senior management.

Seventh, it is the responsibility of the board to respond appropriately to shareholders' concerns.

Eighth, it is the responsibility of the corporation to deal with its employees, customers, suppliers and other constituencies in a fair and equitable manner.

These responsibilities and others are critical to the functioning of the modern public corporation and the integrity of the public markets. No law or regulation alone can be a substitute for the voluntary adherence to these principles by corporate directors and management.

Business Roundtable continues to believe that corporate governance should be enhanced through conscientious and forward-looking action by a business community that focuses on generating long-term shareholder value with the highest degree of integrity.

The principles discussed here are intended to assist corporate management and boards of directors in their individual efforts to implement best practices of corporate governance, as well as to serve as guideposts for the public dialogue on evolving governance standards.

KEY CORPORATE ACTORS

Effective corporate governance requires a clear understanding of the respective roles of the board and senior management and of their relationships with others in the corporate structure. The relationships of the board and management with shareholders should be characterized by candor; their relationships with employees should be characterized by fairness; their relationships with the communities in which they operate should be characterized by good citizenship; and their relationships with government should be characterized by a commitment to compliance.

The board of directors has the important role of overseeing management performance on behalf of shareholders. Its primary duties are to select and oversee a well-qualified and ethical chief executive officer who, with senior management, runs the corporation on a daily basis and to monitor management's performance and adherence to corporate and ethical standards. Effective corporate directors are diligent monitors, but not managers, of business operations.

Senior management, led by the CEO, is responsible for running the day-to-day operations of the corporation and properly informing the board of the status of these operations. Management's responsibilities include strategic planning, risk management and financial reporting.

Shareholders are not involved in the day-to-day management of corporate operations but have the right to elect representatives (directors) to look out for their interests and to receive the information they need to make investment and voting decisions. The board should be responsive to communications from shareholders and should address issues of concern to shareholders.

Effective corporate governance requires a proactive, focused state of mind on the part of directors, the CEO and senior management, all of whom must be committed to business success through the maintenance of the highest standards of responsibility and ethics. Although there are a number of legal and regulatory requirements that must be met, good governance is far more than a "check-the box" list of minimum board and management policies and duties. Even the most thoughtful and well-drafted policies and procedures are destined to fail if directors and management are not committed to enforcing them in practice. A good corporate governance structure is a working system for principled goal setting, effective decision making, and appropriate monitoring of compliance and performance. Through this vibrant and responsive structure, the CEO, the senior management team and the board of directors can interact effectively and respond quickly and appropriately to changing circumstances, within a framework of solid corporate values, to provide enduring value to the shareholders who invest in the enterprise.

THE ROLES OF THE BOARD OF DIRECTORS AND MANAGEMENT

An effective system of corporate governance provides the framework within which the board and management address their respective responsibilities.

The Board of Directors

- The business of a corporation is managed under the direction of the corporation's board. The board delegates to the CEO—and through the CEO to other senior management—the authority and responsibility for managing the everyday affairs of the corporation. Directors monitor management on behalf of the corporation's shareholders.
- Making decisions regarding the selection, compensation and evaluation of a well-qualified and ethical CEO is the single most important function of the board. The board also appoints or approves other members of the senior management team.
- Directors bring to the corporation a range of experience, knowledge and judgment. Directors should not represent the interests of particular constituencies.
- Effective directors maintain an attitude of constructive skepticism; they ask incisive, probing questions and require accurate, honest answers; they act with integrity and diligence; and they demonstrate a commitment to the corporation, its business plans and long-term shareholder value.
- In performing its oversight function, the board is entitled to rely on the advice, reports and opinions of management, counsel, auditors and expert advisers. The board should assess the qualifications of those it relies on and hold managers and advisers accountable. The board should ask questions and obtain answers about the processes used by managers and the corporation's advisers to reach their decisions and recommendations, as well as about the substance of the advice and reports received by the board. When appropriate, the board and its committees should seek independent advice.

- Given the board's oversight role, shareholders and other constituencies can reasonably expect that directors will exercise vigorous and diligent oversight of a corporation's affairs. However, they should not expect the board to micromanage the corporation's business by performing or duplicating the tasks of the CEO and senior management team.
- The board's oversight function carries with it a number of specific responsibilities in addition to that of selecting and overseeing the CEO. These responsibilities include:
  - *Planning for management development and succession.* The board should oversee the corporation's plans for developing senior management personnel and plan for CEO and senior management succession. When appropriate, the board should replace the CEO or other members of senior management.
  - *Understanding, reviewing and monitoring the implementation of the corporation's strategic plans.* The board has responsibility for overseeing and understanding the corporation's strategic plans from their inception through their development and execution by management. Once the board reviews a strategic plan, it should regularly monitor implementation of the plan to determine whether it is being implemented effectively and whether changes are needed. The board also should ensure that the corporation's incentive compensation program is aligned with the corporation's strategic plan.
  - *Understanding and approving annual operating plans and budgets.* The board is responsible for understanding, approving and overseeing the corporation's annual operating plans and for reviewing the annual budgets presented by management. The board should monitor implementation of the annual plans to assess whether they are being implemented effectively and within the limits of approved budgets.
  - *Focusing on the integrity and clarity of the corporation's financial statements and financial reporting.* The board, assisted by its audit committee, should be satisfied that the financial statements and other disclosures prepared by management accurately present the corporation's financial condition and results of operations to shareholders and that they do so in an understandable manner. To achieve accuracy and clarity, the board, through its audit committee, should have an understanding of the corporation's financial statements, including why the accounting principles critical to the corporation's business were chosen, what key judgments and estimates were made by management, and how the choice of principles and the making of these judgments and estimates affect the reported financial results of the corporation.
  - *Advising management on significant issues facing the corporation.* Directors can offer management a wealth of experience and a wide range of perspectives. They provide advice and counsel to management in formal board and committee meetings, and they are available for informal consultation with the CEO and senior management.

- *Reviewing and approving significant corporate actions.* As required by state corporate law, the board reviews and approves specific corporate actions, such as the election of executive officers, the declaration of dividends and (as appropriate) the implementation of major transactions. The board and senior management should have a clear understanding of what level or types of decisions require specific board approval.
- *Reviewing management's plans for business resiliency.* As part of its oversight function, the board should designate senior management who will be responsible for business resiliency. The board should periodically review management's plans to address this issue. Business resiliency can include such items as business risk assessment and management, business continuity, physical and cyber security, and emergency communications.
- *Nominating directors and committee members and overseeing effective corporate governance.* It is the responsibility of the board, through its corporate governance committee, to nominate directors and committee members and oversee the composition, independence, structure, practices and evaluation of the board and its committees.
- *Overseeing legal and ethical compliance.* The board should set a "tone at the top" that establishes the corporation's commitment to integrity and legal compliance. The board should oversee the corporation's compliance program relating to legal and ethical conduct. In this regard, the board should be knowledgeable about the corporation's compliance program and should be satisfied that the program is effective in preventing and deterring violations. The board should pay particular attention to conflicts of interest, including related party transactions.

The CEO and Management

- It is the responsibility of the CEO and senior management, under the CEO's direction, to operate the corporation in an effective and ethical manner. As part of its operational responsibility, senior management is charged with:

- *Operating the corporation.* The CEO and senior management run the corporation's day-to-day business operations. With a thorough understanding of how the corporation operates and earns its income, they carry out the corporation's strategic objectives within the annual operating plans and budgets, which are reviewed and approved by the board. In making decisions about the corporation's business operations, the CEO considers the long-term interests of the corporation and its shareholders and necessarily relies on the input and advice of others, including senior management and outside advisers. The CEO keeps the board apprised of significant developments regarding the corporation's business operations.
- *Strategic planning.* The CEO and senior management generally take the lead in strategic planning. They identify and develop strategic plans for the corporation; present those plans to the board; implement the plans once board review is completed; and recommend and carry out changes to the plans as necessary.

- *Annual operating plans and budgets.* With the corporation's overall strategic plans in mind, senior management develops annual operating plans and budgets for the corporation and presents the plans and budgets to the board. Once the board has reviewed and approved the plans and budgets, the management team implements the annual operating plans and budgets.
- *Selecting qualified management, and establishing an effective organizational structure.* Senior management is responsible for selecting qualified management and implementing an organizational structure that is efficient and appropriate for the corporation's particular circumstances.
- *Identifying and managing risks.* Senior management identifies and manages the risks that the corporation undertakes in the course of carrying out its business. It also manages the corporation's overall risk profile.
- *Accurate and transparent financial reporting and disclosures.* Senior management is responsible for the integrity of the corporation's financial reporting system and the accurate and timely preparation of the corporation's financial statements and related disclosures in accordance with Generally Accepted Accounting Principles and in compliance with applicable laws and regulations. It is senior management's responsibility—under the direction of the CEO and the corporation's principal financial officer—to establish, maintain and periodically evaluate the corporation's internal controls over financial reporting and the corporation's disclosure controls and procedures. In accordance with applicable law and regulations, the CEO and the corporation's principal financial officer also are responsible for certifying the accuracy and completeness of the corporation's financial statements and the effectiveness of the corporation's internal and disclosure controls.

- The CEO and senior management are responsible for operating the corporation in an ethical manner. They should never put individual, personal interests before those of the corporation or its shareholders. Business Roundtable believes that when carrying out this function, corporations should have:
  - *A CEO of integrity.* The CEO should be a person of integrity who takes responsibility for the corporation adhering to the highest ethical standards.
  - *A strong, ethical "tone at the top."* The CEO and senior management should set a "tone at the top" that establishes a culture of legal compliance and integrity communicated to personnel at all levels of the corporation.
  - *An effective compliance program.* Senior management should take responsibility for implementing and managing an effective compliance program relating to legal and ethical conduct. As part of its compliance program, a corporation should have a code of conduct with effective reporting and enforcement mechanisms. Employees should have a means of seeking guidance and alerting management and the board about

potential or actual misconduct without fear of retribution, and violations of the code should be addressed promptly and effectively.

HOW THE BOARD PERFORMS ITS OVERSIGHT FUNCTION

Publicly owned corporations employ diverse approaches to board structure and operations within the parameters of applicable legal requirements and securities market listing standards. Although no one structure is right for every corporation, Business Roundtable believes that the corporate governance "best practices" set forth in the following sections provide an effective approach for corporations to follow.

Board Composition and Leadership

- Boards of directors of large, publicly owned corporations vary in size from industry to industry and from corporation to corporation. In determining board size, directors should consider the nature, size and complexity of the corporation as well as its stage of development. The experiences of many Business Roundtable members suggest that smaller boards often are more cohesive and work more effectively than larger boards.
- Business Roundtable believes that having directors with relevant business and industry experience is beneficial to the board as a whole. Directors with this experience can provide a useful perspective on significant risks and competitive advantages and an understanding of the challenges facing the business. A diversity of backgrounds and experience, consistent with the corporation's needs, also is important to the overall composition of the board. Because the corporation's need for particular backgrounds and experience may change over time, the board should monitor the mix of skills and experience that directors bring to the board against established board membership criteria to assess, at each stage in the life of the corporation, whether the board has the necessary tools to perform its oversight function effectively.
- The board of a publicly owned corporation should have a substantial degree of independence from management. Board independence depends not only on directors' individual relationships but also on the board's overall attitude toward management. Providing objective independent judgment is at the core of the board's oversight function, and the board's composition should reflect this principle.
- A substantial majority of directors of the board of a publicly owned corporation should be independent, both in fact and appearance, as determined by the board. In accordance with the listing standards of the major securities markets, the board should make an affirmative determination as to the independence of each director annually and should have a process in place for making these determinations.

- *Definition of "independence."* An independent director should not have any relationships with the corporation or its management—whether business, employment, charitable or personal—that may impair, or appear to impair, the director's ability to exercise independent judgment. The listing standards of the major securities markets define "independence" and enumerate specific relationships (such as employment with the corporation or its outside auditor) that preclude a director from being considered independent.
- *Assessing independence.* The board should approve standards for determining directors' independence, taking into account the requirements of the federal securities laws, securities market listing standards, and the views of institutional investors and other relevant groups. These standards should be set forth in the corporation's corporate governance principles. When considering whether a director is independent, the board should consider not only whether the director has any of the relationships covered by the board's independence standards but also whether the director has any other relationships, either directly or indirectly, with the corporation, senior management or other board members that could affect the director's actual or perceived independence.
- *Relationships with not-for-profit organizations.* The board's director independence standards should include standards for assessing directors' relationships with not-for-profit organizations that receive support from the corporation. In applying these standards, the board should take into account the size of the corporation's contributions and the nature of directors' relationships to the recipient organizations. Independence issues are most likely to arise when a director is an employee of the not-for-profit organization and when a substantial portion of the organization's funding comes from the corporation. It also may be appropriate to consider contributions from a corporation's foundation to organizations with which a director is affiliated.

- Most American corporations have been well served by a structure in which the CEO also serves as chairman of the board. The CEO serves as a bridge between management and the board, ensuring that both act with a common purpose. The decision concerning whether the CEO also should serve as chairman of the board often is part of the succession planning process, and the board should make that decision in light of the corporation's facts and circumstances.
- Although no one structure is right for every corporation, it is critical that the board has independent leadership. Some boards have found it useful to separate the roles of CEO and chairman of the board. Alternatively, there is a growing trend for boards to appoint a "lead"or "presiding" director. A lead director generally advises on board meeting schedules and agendas, chairs executive sessions of the board, oversees the flow of information to the board, and serves as a liaison between the independent directors and the CEO. The lead director also may play a key role in overseeing performance evaluations of the CEO and the board, be available for communication with shareholders, and lead the board in crisis situations.

- Still other boards have designated an independent director to preside over the executive sessions of a board's independent or nonmanagement directors that are required by securities market listing standards. Depending on the corporation, the so-called presiding director also may perform some or all of the other functions performed by the lead director.

Board Organization

- Virtually all boards of directors of large, publicly owned corporations operate using committees to assist them. A committee structure permits the board to address key areas in more depth than may be possible in a full board meeting.
- Decisions about committee membership and chairs should be made by the full board based on recommendations from the corporate governance committee. Consideration should be given to whether periodic rotation of committee memberships and chairs would provide fresh perspectives and enhance directors' familiarity with different aspects of the corporation's business, consistent with applicable listing standards.
- Committees should apprise the full board of their activities on a regular basis. Processes should be developed and monitored for keeping the board informed through oral or written reports. For example, some corporations provide minutes of committee meetings to all members of the board.
- Business Roundtable believes that the functions generally performed by the audit, compensation and corporate governance committees are central to effective corporate governance. The listing standards of the major securities markets require corporations to have an audit committee that performs specific functions, and many corporations also are required to have committees that oversee executive compensation, director nominations and corporate governance matters. Business Roundtable does not believe that a particular committee structure is essential for all corporations. What is important is that key issues are addressed effectively by the independent members of the board. Thus, the references below to the functions performed by particular committees are not intended to preclude corporations from allocating these functions differently, consistent with applicable listing standards.
- Additional committees, such as finance or risk management committees, also may be used. Some corporations find it useful to establish committees to examine special problems or opportunities in greater depth than would otherwise be feasible.
- The responsibilities of each committee and the qualifications required for committee membership should be clearly defined and set out in a written charter that is approved by the board and publicly available. Each committee should review its charter annually and recommend changes to the board as appropriate.

- A more detailed discussion of particular committee functions appears in Business Roundtable's *Executive Compensation: Principles and Commentary* (November 2003) and *The Nominating Process and Corporate Governance Committees: Principles and Commentary* (April 2004).

Audit Committee

- Every publicly owned corporation should have an audit committee of at least three members, who should all be independent directors.
- Audit committees typically consist of three to five members. The listing standards of the major securities markets require that all members of the audit committee qualify as independent directors under applicable listing standards, subject to limited exceptions, and that they meet additional, heightened independence criteria.
- Audit committee members should meet minimum financial literacy standards, as required by the listing standards of the major securities markets, and at least one member of the audit committee should be an audit committee financial expert, as determined by the board in accordance with regulations of the Securities and Exchange Commission. Just as important is the ability of audit committee members, as with all directors, to understand the corporation's business and risk profile and to apply their business experience and judgment with an independent and critical eye to the issues for which the committee is responsible.
- With the significant responsibilities imposed on audit committees under applicable law, regulations and listing standards, consideration should be given to whether it is appropriate to limit the number of public company audit committees on which a corporation's audit committee members may serve. Some boards have adopted policies that audit committee members may not serve on the audit committees of more than three public corporations, in accordance with applicable securities market listing standards. Policies may permit exceptions to this limit when the corporation's board determines that the simultaneous service would not affect an individual's ability to serve effectively on the corporation's audit committee.
- The audit committee is responsible for supervising the corporation's relationship with its outside auditor. In performing this responsibility, the primary functions of the audit committee include:
  - *Retaining the auditor and approving in advance the terms of the annual audit engagement.* The selection of the outside auditor should involve an annual due diligence process in which the audit committee reviews the qualifications, work product, independence and reputation of the outside auditor and the performance of key members of the audit team. The committee should be mindful of the schedule, mandated by applicable law

and regulations, for rotating the engagement and concurring partners and should begin the process of reviewing new partners sufficiently in advance of required rotations. The audit committee also should consider periodically whether it is appropriate for the corporation to change its outside auditor. The audit committee should base its decisions about selecting and possibly changing the outside auditor on its assessment of what is likely to lead to more effective audits. In retaining the auditor, the audit committee should oversee the process of negotiating the annual audit engagement letter and should scrutinize the terms of the engagement carefully.

- *Overseeing the independence of the outside auditor.* The audit committee should maintain an ongoing, open dialogue with the outside auditor about independence issues. The committee should consider its overall approach to using the outside auditor as a service provider and identify those services, beyond the annual audit engagement, that the outside auditor can provide to the corporation consistent with applicable law and regulations and with maintaining independence. In pre-approving all non-audit services to be provided by the outside auditor, as required by applicable law and regulations, the audit committee should decide whether to adopt a pre-approval policy or approve services on an engagement-by-engagement basis.

- The audit committee also is responsible for overseeing the corporation's financial reporting process. The audit committee should review and discuss the corporation's annual financial statements with management and the outside auditor and should review the corporation's quarterly financial statements and related earnings press releases prior to issuance. As part of its reviews, the audit committee should review and discuss with management and the outside auditor the corporation's critical accounting policies, the quality of accounting judgments and estimates made by management, and any material written communications between the outside auditor and management.
- The audit committee should understand and be familiar with the corporation's system of internal controls over financial reporting and its disclosure controls and procedures, including the processes for producing the certifications required of the CEO and principal financial officer, and the audit committee should be comfortable that the corporation has appropriate controls in place. On a periodic basis, the committee should review with both the internal and outside auditors, as well as with management, the corporation's procedures for maintaining and evaluating the effectiveness of these systems. The committee should be promptly notified of any significant deficiencies or material weaknesses in internal controls and kept informed about the steps and timetable for correcting them.
- Unless the full board or another committee does so, the audit committee should oversee the corporation's program that addresses compliance with ethical and legal standards and important corporate policies, including the corporation's code of conduct and the mechanisms it has in place for employees to report compliance issues. In accordance with

applicable legal requirements, the audit committee should establish procedures for receiving and handling complaints and concerns related to accounting, internal accounting controls and auditing issues, and the committee should evaluate these procedures periodically and revise them as appropriate. The audit committee should be briefed regularly on the status of outstanding compliance issues, including concerns submitted through the committee's procedures for handling accounting and related concerns, and it should receive prompt notification of any significant compliance issues.

- The audit committee should understand the corporation's risk profile and oversee its risk assessment and risk management practices.
- The audit committee should oversee the corporation's internal audit function, including reviewing the scope of the internal audit plan, reports submitted by the internal audit staff and management's response, and the appointment and replacement of the senior internal auditing executive.
- The audit committee should implement a policy covering the hiring of personnel who previously worked for the corporation's outside auditor. At a minimum, this policy should incorporate the "cooling off" period mandated by applicable law and regulations.
- Audit committee meetings should be held frequently enough to allow the committee to monitor the corporation's financial reporting appropriately. Meetings should be scheduled with enough time to permit and encourage active discussions with management and the internal and outside auditors. The audit committee should meet privately with each of the internal and outside auditors and management on a regular basis, and in any event at least quarterly, and communicate with them between meetings as necessary. The audit committee also should hold private sessions with the corporation's chief legal officer on a regular basis to facilitate the communication of concerns regarding legal compliance matters and significant legal contingencies. The audit committee also may determine that it is appropriate to hold private sessions with other parties, such as outside counsel, from time to time.

Corporate Governance Committee

- Every publicly owned corporation should have a committee composed solely of independent directors that addresses director nominations and corporate governance matters.
- The corporate governance committee (often combined with or referred to as a nominating committee) should have at least three members and should be composed solely of independent directors.
- The corporate governance committee recommends director nominees to the full board and the corporation's shareholders; oversees the composition, structure, operation and evaluation of the board and its committees; and plays a leadership role in shaping the

corporate governance of the corporation. Depending on how the board has allocated responsibilities among its committees, the corporate governance committee also may oversee the compensation of the board if the compensation committee does not do so, or the two committees may share oversight responsibility for this area.

- In performing the core function of recommending nominees to the board, the corporate governance committee should establish criteria for board and committee membership and recommend these criteria to the board for approval. Based on these criteria, the committee should identify director candidates, review their qualifications and any potential conflicts with the corporation's interests, and recommend candidates to the board. The committee also should assess the contributions of current directors in connection with their renomination.
- In identifying director candidates, the corporate governance committee should take a proactive approach by soliciting ideas for potential candidates from a variety of sources. The committee should have the authority to retain search firms as appropriate to assist it in identifying candidates and should develop a process for considering shareholder recommendations for board nominees. Although it is appropriate for the CEO to meet with board candidates, the final responsibility for selecting director nominees should rest with the corporate governance committee and the board.
- The corporate governance committee should monitor and safeguard the independence of the board. An important function of a corporate governance committee, related to its core function of recommending nominees to the board, is to see that a substantial majority of the directors on the board meet appropriate standards of independence that are consistent with securities market listing standards and to see that these directors are independent in both fact and appearance. The corporate governance committee should develop and recommend standards of independence to the board, assess the independence of directors in light of these standards, and make recommendations to the board regarding determinations of director independence. In addition, the committee should be notified promptly of any change in a director's circumstances that may affect the director's independence.
- The corporate governance committee also recommends directors for appointment to committees of the board. The committee should periodically review the board's committee structure and annually recommend candidates for membership on the board's committees. The committee should see that the key board committees, including the audit, compensation and corporation governance committees, are composed of directors who meet applicable independence and qualification standards.
- The corporate governance committee should oversee the effective functioning of the board. The committee should review the board's policies relating to meeting schedules and agendas and the corporation's processes for providing information to the board. The corporate governance committee should assess the reporting channels through which the

board receives information and see that the board obtains appropriately detailed information in a timely fashion.

- The corporate governance committee should develop and recommend to the board a set of corporate governance principles, review them annually, and recommend changes to the board as appropriate. The corporation's corporate governance principles should be publicly available and should address, at a minimum, board leadership, qualifications for directors (including independence standards), director responsibilities, the structure and functioning of board committees, board access to management and advisers, director compensation, director orientation and continuing education, board evaluations, and management succession.
- The corporate governance committee should oversee the evaluation of the board and its committees. Specifics concerning the evaluation process are discussed under "Board and Committee Evaluation."

Compensation Committee

- Every publicly owned corporation should have a committee composed solely of independent directors that addresses compensation issues.
- The compensation committee should have at least three members and should be composed solely of independent directors. All committee members should have sufficient knowledge of executive compensation and related issues to perform their duties effectively.
- The compensation committee's responsibilities include overseeing the corporation's overall compensation structure, policies and programs; establishing or recommending to the board performance goals and objectives for the CEO and other members of senior management; and establishing or recommending to the independent directors compensation for the CEO and senior management. The compensation committee should see that the corporation's compensation policies reflect the core principle of pay for performance and should establish meaningful goals for performance-based compensation.
- The compensation committee should have the authority to retain compensation consultants, counsel and other advisers to provide the committee with independent advice.
- The compensation committee should understand all aspects of an executive's compensation package and should review and understand the maximum pay-out due under multiple scenarios (such as retirement, termination with or without cause, and severance in connection with business combinations or the sale of a business).
- The compensation committee should require senior management to build and maintain significant continuing equity investment in the corporation. The committee should establish requirements that senior management acquire and hold a meaningful amount of the corporation's stock. The committee also should consider whether to require senior

management to hold for a period of time a specified amount of stock earned through incentive-based awards.

- In addition to reviewing and setting compensation for senior management, the compensation committee should look more broadly at the overall compensation structure of the enterprise to determine that it establishes appropriate incentives for management and employees at all levels. The committee should consider carefully and understand the incentives created by different forms of compensation. Incentives should further the corporation's long-term strategic plan and be consistent with the culture of the corporation and the overall goal of enhancing enduring shareholder value.
- Executive compensation should directly link the interests of senior management, both individually and as a team, to the long-term interests of shareholders. It should include significant performance-based criteria related to long-term shareholder value and should reflect upside potential and downside risk.
- The compensation committee should consider whether the benefits and perquisites provided to senior management are proportional to the contributions made by management.
- The compensation committee should oversee the corporation's disclosures with respect to executive compensation. In particular, the committee should use the compensation committee report included in the corporation's annual proxy statement to provide shareholders with meaningful and understandable information about the corporation's executive compensation practices.

Board Operations

- Serving on a board requires significant time and attention on the part of directors. Directors must participate in board meetings, review relevant materials, serve on board committees, and prepare for meetings and discussions with management. They must spend the time needed and meet as frequently as necessary to properly discharge their responsibilities. The appropriate number of hours to be spent by a director on his or her duties and the frequency and length of board meetings depend largely on the complexity of the corporation and its operations. Longer meetings may permit directors to explore key issues in depth, whereas shorter but more frequent meetings may help directors stay up-to-date on emerging corporate trends and business and regulatory developments. When arranging a meeting schedule for the board, each corporation should consider the nature and complexity of its operations and transactions, as well as its business and regulatory environment.
- Directors should receive incentives to focus on long-term shareholder value. Including equity as part of directors' compensation helps align the interests of directors with those of the corporation's shareholders. Accordingly, a meaningful portion of a director's compensation

should be in the form of long-term equity. In this regard, corporations increasingly are providing the long-term equity component of directors' compensation in the form of restricted stock, rather than stock options, to better align directors' interests with those of shareholders. Corporations should establish a requirement that directors acquire a meaningful amount of the corporation's stock and hold that stock for as long as they remain on the board.

- Business Roundtable does not endorse a specific limitation on the number of directorships an individual may hold. However, service on too many boards can interfere with an individual's ability to satisfy his or her responsibilities, either as a member of senior management or as a director. Before accepting an additional board position, a director should consider whether the acceptance of a new directorship will compromise the ability to perform present responsibilities. It also is good practice for directors to notify the chair of the corporate governance committee for each board on which they serve before accepting a seat on the board of another corporation. Some corporations require the prior approval of the corporate governance committee. Similarly, the corporation should establish a process to review senior management service on other boards prior to acceptance.
- The board's independent or nonmanagement directors should have the opportunity to meet regularly in executive session, outside the presence of the CEO and any other management directors, in accordance with applicable listing standards.
  - Time for an executive session should be placed on the agenda for every regularly scheduled board meeting.
  - To maximize the effectiveness of executive sessions, there should be follow-up with the CEO and other appropriate members of senior management.
- Many board responsibilities may be delegated to committees to permit directors to address key areas in more depth. Regardless of whether the board grants plenary power to its committees with respect to particular issues or prefers to take recommendations from its committees, committees should keep the full board informed of their activities. Corporations benefit greatly from the collective wisdom of the entire board acting as a deliberative body, and the interaction between committees and the full board should reflect this principle.
- The board's agenda must be carefully planned yet flexible enough to accommodate emergencies and unexpected developments. The chairman of the board should work with the lead director (when the corporation has one) in setting the agenda and should be responsive to individual directors' requests to add items to the agenda and open to suggestions for improving the agenda. It is important that the agenda and meeting schedule permit adequate time for discussion and a healthy give-and-take between board members and management.
- Board agendas should be structured to allow time for open discussion. Board members should have full access to senior management.

- The board must have accurate, complete information to do its job; the quality of information received by the board directly affects its ability to perform its oversight function effectively. Directors should receive and review information from a variety of sources, including management, board committees, outside experts, auditor presentations, and analyst and media reports. The board should be provided with information before board and committee meetings, with sufficient time to review and reflect on key issues and to request supplemental information as necessary.
- Corporations should have an orientation process for new directors that is designed to familiarize them with the corporation's business, industry and corporate governance practices. Common practices include briefings from senior management, on-site visits to the corporation's facilities, informal meetings with other directors and written materials. Corporations also should encourage directors to take advantage of educational opportunities on an ongoing basis to enable them to better perform their duties and to keep informed about developments in areas such as the corporation's industry, corporate governance and director responsibilities.
- Where appropriate, boards and board committees should seek advice from outside advisers independent of management with respect to matters within their responsibility. For example, there may be technical aspects of the corporation's business—such as risk assessment and risk management—or conflict of interest situations for which the board or a committee determines that additional expert advice would be useful. Similarly, many compensation committees engage their own compensation consultants. The board and its committees should have the authority to select and retain advisers and approve the terms of their retention and fees.

Management Development and Succession

- Long-term planning for CEO and senior management development and succession is one of the board's most important functions. The board, its corporate governance committee or another committee of independent directors should identify and regularly update the qualities and characteristics necessary for an effective CEO. With these principles in mind, the board or committee should periodically monitor and review the development and progression of potential internal candidates against these standards.
- Emergency succession planning also is critical. Working with the CEO, the board or committee should see that plans are in place for contingencies such as the departure, death or disability of the CEO or other members of senior management to facilitate the transition to both interim and longer-term leadership in the event of an untimely vacancy.
- Under the oversight of an independent committee or the lead director, the board should annually review the performance of the CEO and participate with the CEO in the evaluation of members of senior management. All nonmanagement members of the board

should participate with the CEO in senior management evaluations. The results of the CEO's evaluation should be promptly communicated to the CEO in executive session by representatives of the independent directors and used by the compensation committee or board in determining the CEO's compensation.

Board and Committee Evaluation

- The board should have an effective mechanism for evaluating performance on a continuing basis. Meaningful board evaluation requires an assessment of the effectiveness of the full board, the operations of board committees and the contributions of individual directors.
  - For some companies, securities market listing standards now require that the board and its audit, compensation and corporate governance committees conduct annual evaluations. Regardless of whether an evaluation is required, the performance of the full board should be evaluated annually, as should the performance of its committees. The board should use the annual self-evaluation to assess whether it is following the procedures necessary to function effectively. Each board committee should conduct an annual self-evaluation to assess its effectiveness, and the results of this evaluation should be reported to the full board.
  - The board should have a process for evaluating whether the individuals sitting on the board bring the skills and expertise appropriate for the corporation and how they work as a group. Board positions should not be regarded as permanent. Directors should serve only so long as they add value to the board, and a director's ability to continue to contribute to the board should be examined by the corporate governance committee each time the director is considered for renomination.
- Planning for the departure of directors and the designation of new board members is essential. The board should plan ahead for changes in membership, and it should have written criteria for director candidates that should be re-evaluated periodically. The board also should establish procedures for the retirement or replacement of board members. These procedures may, for example, include a mandatory retirement age, a term limit and/or a requirement that directors who change their primary employment tender a board resignation, providing an opportunity for the governance committee to consider the desirability of their continued service on the board.

RELATIONSHIPS WITH SHAREHOLDERS AND OTHER CONSTITUENCIES

Corporations are often said to have obligations to shareholders and other constituencies, including employees, the communities in which they do business and government, but these obligations are best viewed as part of the paramount duty to optimize long-term shareholder value. Business Roundtable believes that shareholder value is enhanced when a corporation treats its employees well, serves its customers well, fosters good relationships with suppliers, maintains an effective compliance program and strong corporate governance practices, and has a reputation for civic responsibility.

Shareholders and Investors

- Corporations have a responsibility to communicate effectively and candidly with shareholders. The goal of shareholder communications should be to help shareholders understand the business, risk profile, financial condition and operating performance of the corporation and the board's corporate governance practices.
- Corporations communicate with investors and other constituencies not only in proxy statements, annual and other reports, and formal shareholder meetings, but in many other ways as well. All of these communications should provide consistency, clarity and candor.
- Corporations should have effective procedures for shareholders to communicate with the board and for directors to respond to shareholder concerns. The board, or an independent committee such as the corporate governance committee, should establish, oversee and regularly review and update these procedures as appropriate.
  - The board should respond in a timely manner to substantive communications from shareholders, and when appropriate, directors should meet with shareholders regarding issues of concern.
- A corporation's procedures for shareholder communications and its governance practices should be readily available to shareholders. Information about the board's structure and operations, committee composition and responsibilities, corporate governance principles, and codes of ethics should be widely disseminated to shareholders.
- The board should be notified of shareholder proposals, and the board or its corporate governance committee should oversee the corporation's response to these proposals.
- Directors should attend the corporation's annual meeting of shareholders, and the corporation should have a policy requiring attendance absent unusual circumstances. Time at the annual meeting should be set aside for shareholders to submit questions and for management or directors to respond to those questions.
- The board should seriously consider issues raised by shareholder proposals that receive substantial support and should communicate its response to proposals to the shareholder-proponents and to all shareholders.
- The board should respond appropriately when a director nominee receives a significant "withhold" or "against" vote with respect to his or her election to the board. The corporate governance committee should assess the reasons for the vote and recommend to the board

the action to be taken with respect to the vote, which should be communicated to the corporation's shareholders.

- In planning communications with shareholders and investors, corporations should consider:
  - *Candor.* Directors and management should never mislead or misinform shareholders about the corporation's operations or financial condition.
  - *Need for timely disclosure.* In an age of instant communication, corporations increasingly are disclosing significant information closer to the time when it arises and becomes available. Business Roundtable supports prompt disclosure of significant developments.
  - *Use of technology.* Technology makes communicating quicker, easier and less expensive. Corporations should take advantage of technological advances to enhance the dissemination of information to shareholders and employees.
  - *Ultimate goal of shareholder communications.* Whatever the substance of the communication, the corporation's ultimate goal should be to furnish information that is honest, intelligible, meaningful, timely and broadly disseminated and that gives investors a realistic picture of the corporation's financial condition and results of operations through the eyes of management.

Employees

- It is in a corporation's best interest to treat employees fairly and equitably.
- Corporations should have in place policies and practices that provide employees with compensation, including benefits, that is appropriate given the nature of the corporation's business and employees' job responsibilities and geographic locations.
- When corporations offer retirement, health care, insurance and other benefit plans, employees should be fully informed of the terms of those plans.
- Corporations should have in place and publicize mechanisms for employees to seek guidance and to alert management and the board about potential or actual misconduct without fear of retribution.
- Corporations should communicate honestly with their employees about corporate operations and financial performance.

Communities

- Corporations have obligations to be good citizens of the local, national and international communities in which they do business. Failure to meet these obligations can result in damage to the corporation, both in immediate economic terms and in longer-term reputational value.

- A corporation should be a good citizen and contribute to the communities in which it operates by making charitable contributions and encouraging its directors, managers and employees to form relationships with those communities. A corporation also should be active in promoting awareness of health, safety and environmental issues, including any issues that relate to the specific types of business in which the corporation is engaged.

Government

- Corporations, like all citizens, must act within the law. The penalties for serious violations of law can be extremely severe, even life-threatening, for corporations. Compliance is not only appropriate—it is essential. Management should take reasonable steps to develop, implement and maintain an effective legal compliance program, and the board should be knowledgeable about and oversee the program, including periodically reviewing the program to gain reasonable assurance that it is effective in deterring and preventing misconduct.
- Corporations have an important perspective to contribute to the public policy dialogue and should be actively involved in discussions about the development, enactment and revision of the laws and regulations that affect their businesses and the communities in which they operate and their employees reside.

INTRODUCTION TO SARBANES-OXLEY

Kenneth Goodpaster

The Sarbanes-Oxley Act was signed into law by President George W. Bush on July 30, 2002. The act is named after Senator Paul E. Sarbanes (D-Maryland) and Representative Michael R. Oxley (R-Ohio), who helped shape the bill's content and guided it through Congress.

Sarbanes-Oxley was passed as a legislative response to the accounting scandals that began to surface in late 2001. This is suggested by the summary description of the House version of the bill: "An Act to protect investors by improving the accuracy and reliability of corporate disclosures made pursuant to securities laws, and for other purposes." Remarks by President Bush at the bill's signing further underscored its link to the legal and ethical failures at firms like Enron, Tyco, and WorldCom:

> America's system of free enterprise . . . is not a jungle in which only the unscrupulous survive or a financial free-for-all guided by greed. The fundamentals of a free market—buying and selling, saving and investing-require clear rules and confidence in basic fairness. . . .
>
> The only risks, the only fair risks are based on honest information. Tricking an investor into taking a risk is theft by another name. . . . Those who break the rules tarnish a great economic system that provides opportunity for all. Their actions hurt workers who committed their lives to building the company that hired them. Their actions hurt investors and retirees who placed their faith in the promise of growth and integrity. For the sake of our free economy, those who break the law, break the rules of fairness, those who are dishonest, however wealthy or successful they may be, must pay a price.[1]

The act was shaped over the course of little more than a year. The seeds of the law were sown in hearings chaired by Oxley prior to the scandals on the question of Wall Street analyst independence.[2] Hearings on legislation intended to address broader corporate misconduct began in December 2001.[3] By April 2002 the House had passed a modest reform bill sponsored by Oxley; however, a stronger bill emerged in the Senate under Sarbanes's leadership, and House members embraced its tougher stance as the list of companies caught in questionable practices lengthened.[4] The act became the occasion for legislators to adopt measures that had been floating before Congress for years. For example, Sarbanes-Oxley creates an accounting oversight board, a concept first introduced in draft legislation during the 1970s.[5]

Sarbanes-Oxley applies directly to companies that are publicly traded in the United States, that is, all corporate issuers of securities registered under the Securities and Exchange Act of 1934. It touches a number of corporate roles and practices that contributed to the scandals of 2001–02. This note briefly describes the principal provisions of the law. It emphasizes critical mandates for audit committees, public accounting firms, senior executives, corporate directors, corporate financial disclosures, securities analysts, and attorneys. It highlights sections of the act that strengthen legal safeguards for whistle-blowers and penalties for corporate misconduct. It also considers the implications of Sarbanes-Oxley for non-U.S. companies and privately held firms. Finally, it documents reactions to the act which emerged over the course of its first year.

AN EXPANDED ROLE FOR THE AUDIT COMMITTEE

Sarbanes-Oxley (SOx) expands the role of the audit committee of a company's board of directors. The act limits audit committee membership to independent directors. Under SOx, board members are considered independent if they receive no compensation from the company other than for their board duties, and they have no other affiliations with the company or its subsidiaries. In addition, the law requires a company to disclose whether its audit committee contains at least one "financial expert," as defined by the Securities and Exchange Commission (SEC). The definition identifies five competencies a committee member must possess to qualify for this status (Exhibit 1). The SEC rule recognizes these competencies can be acquired in a variety of ways; however, it suggests that they are preferably the product of experience, not merely education. If a company's audit committee does not include a qualified financial expert, SOx compels it to explain why.

SOx charges the audit committee with supervision of the company's external auditor, including (1) appointing the audit firm, (2) overseeing its activities, and (3) determining its compensation. The act empowers the audit committee to hire any external advisors or consultants needed to fulfill its responsibilities. The company is obligated to compensate the audit firm and other advisers at the level set by the committee. SOx also requires the audit committee to establish procedures to handle complaints about accounting and audit matters, including anonymous complaints from employees.

A CHANGING CONTEXT FOR AUDITORS

The new law has wide-ranging implications for public accounting firms. To protect investors' interests and to help rebuild public confidence, Sarbanes-Oxley established an independent, non-governmental board to oversee public company audits. The board, called the Public Company Accounting Oversight Board (PCAOB), is responsible for establishing audit and attestation standards for auditors. All public accounting firms that prepare audit reports for corporations issuing securities in the United States are required to register with the board. The PCAOB also is charged with assessing how well public accountants comply with the act and with establishing disciplinary procedures and rules.

SOx introduced three directives intended to mitigate potential conflicts of interest for auditors. First, it prohibits auditors from providing certain services to their audit clients. These services are summarized in Exhibit 2. Second, the act prohibits audit firms from serving any company whose chief executive officer, chief financial officer, chief accounting officer, or controller was employed by the firm within the previous 12 months. Third, it requires auditors to rotate the lead partner and reviewing partner assigned to each client every five years. Nonlead auditors must be rotated every seven years.

SOx mandates specific topics on which an external auditor must report to the audit committee. These include (1) all critical company accounting policies; (2) any alternative treatments of financial information under generally accepted accounting principles (GAAP) discussed with management and their ramifications; (3) the auditor's preferred accounting treatment; and (4) any disagreements encountered with management on financial representations. Auditors also must disclose all other material written communications between management and themselves.

NEW EXECUTIVE RESPONSIBILITIES AND RESTRICTIONS

Sarbanes-Oxley created new responsibilities for senior executives of publicly traded companies. Chief executive officers and chief financial officers must henceforth certify six conditions for each quarterly and annual report. These conditions are described in Exhibit 3. Executives who certify a financial report knowing that it is inaccurate can be fined up to $1 million and imprisoned for up to ten years. If an executive does this willfully—that is, to intentionally and deliberately misrepresent the company's position—the maximum penalties increase to $5 million and 20 years.

Failure to comply with federal financial reporting requirements can result in monetary forfeitures by executives. For example, if a company's reporting failure is the result of misconduct and a restatement is required, its CEO and CFO must return bonuses and other incentive-based pay they received during the 12 months following the erroneous statement's release. They also must relinquish all profits realized from sales of company securities during that same period.[6]

SOx prohibits company officers and directors, or anyone working under their supervision, from fraudulently influencing, coercing, manipulating, or misleading public or certified accountants engaged in an audit. It also prohibits officers and directors from buying, selling, or transferring securities acquired as a consequence of their employment during pension blackout periods.[7] Finally, the act forbids companies from making loans to executives and directors. An exemption is granted to consumer credit organizations, if the loans are of a type generally available to the public and the terms are market rate, that is, no more favorable than those offered to other customers.

MANDATED DISCLOSURES

Sarbanes-Oxley requires new disclosures in annual and quarterly reports. For example, it mandates disclosure of unconsolidated entities and all off–balance sheet transactions, arrangements, and obligations that have, or are reasonably likely to have, a material impact upon the firm's current or future financial condition. These disclosures must appear in a specially captioned section within "management's discussion and analysis."[8] The firm also must provide a tabular overview of certain known contractual obligations, including long-term debt, capital lease obligations, operating leases, and unconditional purchase obligations.

Companies also must clarify their use of financial measures that do not conform to GAAP requirements. These metrics, commonly described as "pro forma," increasingly have been employed by companies to place their performance in the best possible light. SOx defines a non-GAAP measure as a numerical metric of a company's historical or future financial performance, financial position, or cash flow that *excludes* amounts *included* in a comparable GAAP measure, or *includes* amounts *excluded* from a comparable GAAP measure. Metrics that fall within this definition include adjusted earnings measures or liquidity measures, for example, earnings before interest, tax, depreciation, and amortization (EBITDA). When a company publicly discloses material information that includes a non-GAAP measure, SOx requires (1) an accompanying presentation of the most directly comparable financial measure calculated and presented in accordance with GAAP and (2) a reconciliation of the differences between the non-GAAP measure and the "best-fit" GAAP measure. The act also details additional requirements and restrictions that apply when pro forma measures are utilized in SEC filings.

To complement certifications made by the chief executive and chief financial officers, a company's annual report must explicitly address its internal control structure. Specifically, the report must state management's responsibility for establishing and maintaining adequate internal controls and financial reporting procedures. It also must include an evaluation of the effectiveness of these controls as of the end of the most recent fiscal year. Furthermore, the firm's auditor must attest to assertions made by management in this evaluation.

SOx also requires publicly held corporations to disclose whether they have a "code of ethics" that applies to their chief executive officer, chief financial officer, and chief accounting officer.

The SEC defines a code of ethics as a set of written standards designed to deter wrongdoing and promote:

- Ethical conduct, including the ethical handling of real or apparent conflicts of interest.
- Full, fair, accurate, timely, and understandable filings and public communications.
- Compliance with applicable laws and regulations.
- Prompt internal reporting of code violations.
- Accountability for adherence to the code.

Companies that have adopted a code must reveal any subsequent amendments or waivers of its requirements. Companies that do not have such a code must disclose this fact and explain why one has not been adopted.

SOx also requires firms to accelerate their reporting. For example, it requires companies to report the stock transactions of directors, officers, and principal shareholders (i.e., those who own more than 10 percent of the firm) within two business days of their execution date. The previous reporting deadline for such transactions was ten days following the end of the month in which they occurred. More broadly, the act requires publicly held companies to report "on a rapid and current basis" additional information concerning material changes in the firm's financial position or operations. Such information is to be disclosed "in plain English," supplemented by trend data, quantitative information, and qualitative explanations which the SEC deems necessary for the protection of investors and the public interest.

NEW OBLIGATIONS FOR ANALYSTS AND ATTORNEYS

Sarbanes-Oxley details new responsibilities for securities analysts. Under the legislation, research analysts are now required to certify that the views expressed within their reports reflect their personal assessments. Furthermore, analysts must disclose whether they received compensation or other payments for expressing the recommendations and views detailed within their research reports. They must make a similar certification on a quarterly basis concerning views expressed in public appearances.

SOx also establishes standards for attorneys. It requires both in-house and outside counsel to report evidence of material violations of securities laws, or breaches of fiduciary duty, to the company's chief legal counsel or chief executive officer. If an appropriate response is not forthcoming, the attorney is required to bring the evidence to the audit committee of the firm's board of directors or to the full board itself.

In January 2003, the SEC extended the comment period on a controversial mandate for lawyers that appeared in the initial draft of implementation rules, the so-called "noisy withdrawal." This provision would have required attorneys to quit and inform the SEC if company directors failed to take appropriate action on their notification of a securities law violation. Critics complained that this requirement would undermine attorney-client confidentiality. While not abandoning the "noisy withdrawal" concept, the SEC proposed alternative approaches to implementation. For example, rather than requiring an individual to report his or her withdrawal, the company itself might be compelled to disclose it, or to disclose the attorney's written notice that he or she has found the company's response deficient. As of mid-2004, a final ruling on this matter had not been announced.

STRENGTHENED PROTECTIONS AND CRIMINAL PROVISIONS

Sarbanes-Oxley strengthens legal protections for whistle-blowers while increasing penalties for fraud and other criminal behaviors. The act closes a significant loophole in the Victim and Witness Protection Act of 1982. Specifically, it prohibits companies from firing or discriminating against employees who lawfully inform their supervisors, a federal agency, or Congress about actions they reasonably believe constitute fraud. This proscription of *workplace* retaliation supplements the legal safeguards against *violent* retaliation established by the 1982 statute. Violators may be imprisoned for up to ten years and subject to fines.

SOx creates two new felonies. The first penalizes those who knowingly alter, destroy, or falsify records for the purpose of impeding federal investigations or bankruptcy proceedings with up to 20 years' imprisonment and fines. Furthermore, the act obliges public accountants to keep audit records for five years after the close of the fiscal period for which the audit was conducted. A knowing and willful violation of this requirement is punishable by imprisonment for up to five years and fines.

SOx also authorizes the SEC to bar violators of the antifraud provisions of securities laws from serving as officers or directors of public corporations. It enables the SEC to implement these exclusions as a remedy within its own administrative proceedings, supplementing the Commission's existing power to seek them in court. Past court interpretations have significantly limited the SEC's ability to obtain bars. SOx reduces the level of proof required to demonstrate that an individual is unfit to serve as an officer or director, making it easier for the Commission to impose this sanction.

IMPLICATIONS FOR NON-U.S. COMPANIES

Sarbanes-Oxley applies to all companies that issue securities under U.S. federal securities statutes, whether headquartered within the United States or not. Thus, in addition to U.S.-based firms, approximately 1,300 foreign firms from 59 countries fall under the law's jurisdiction.[9]

Reactions from this quarter were swift. Some foreign companies that had previously contemplated offering securities in the U.S. market reconsidered in light of the conflicts they believed SOx created. For example, in October 2002 Porsche AG announced it would not list its shares on the New York Stock Exchange. A company press release identified the passage of SOx as the "critical factor" for this decision and singled out CEO and CFO certification of financial statements for criticism. Recounting the process Porsche uses to prepare, review, and approve its financial reports, the release concluded that "any special treatment of the Chairman of the Board of Management [i.e., Porsche's CEO] and the Director of Finance would be illogical because of the intricate network within the decision-making process; it would be irreconcilable with current German law."[10]

By late 2002, the SEC found itself subjected to intense lobbying by foreign companies pressing for exemptions from SOx. In remarks to an association of German firms, SEC Commissioner Paul Atkins summarized the regulatory body's obligations and its approach to conflicts between the act and the laws of other nations:

> Sarbanes-Oxley generally makes no distinction between U.S. and non-U.S. [securities] issuers. The Act does not provide any specific authority to exempt non-U.S. issuers from its reach. The Act leaves it to the SEC to determine where and how to apply the Act's provisions to foreign companies. The SEC is well aware that new U.S. requirements may come into conflict with requirements on non-U.S. issuers. As we move forward to implement Sarbanes-Oxley, we have tried and we will continue to try to balance our responsibility to comply with the Act's mandate with the need to make reasonable accommodations to our non-U.S. issuers.[11]

In January 2003 the SEC proposed rules addressing several of these conflicts. The proposal recognized that some non-U.S. corporate governance practices—in many cases prescribed by home country laws—were consistent with the act's spirit even though they violated its letter. Furthermore, the proposal suggested specific practices that the SEC could accommodate. For example, the commission signaled that it would permit non-management employees of German firms to serve as audit committee members, even though they fail to meet SOx's independence test. The SEC also indicated it would allow shareholders of foreign companies to appoint outside auditors, despite the fact that the act assigns this duty to audit committees.

European responses to these rules were positive. However, by April a new flashpoint had emerged, namely, the question of whether auditors headquartered outside the United States would be required to register with the PCAOB. During a public hearing held on April 1, Charles Niemeier, the acting chair of the PCAOB, stated that "the U.S. markets now involve companies and auditors that are not in the United States. . . . We believe registration is extremely important for us to be able to fulfill our mandate."[12] European officials voiced concern about the impact on European accounting firms, particularly in light of Sarbanes-Oxley's mandate that public accountants retain audit records, a stipulation that could conflict with European Union confidentiality laws.

In late April, the PCAOB announced it would extend the registration deadline for non-U.S. auditors to April 2004. However, this concession failed to mollify EU officials, who threatened to enact regulations for non-EU auditors. At the same time, the EU moved to strengthen its own standards for auditing and corporate governance, in reaction to both U.S. initiatives and the February 2003 scandal at Ahold, a Dutch retailer. Reflecting on these developments, Gregor Pozniak, deputy secretary general of the Federation of European Stock Exchanges, observed that "a response to recent corporate developments in the United States and Europe was necessary," and the EU action "increases the chance of mutual recognition from the United States."[13]

THE EFFECT ON PRIVATE COMPANIES

Sarbanes-Oxley's prescriptions are reshaping corporate governance expectations. Hence, while the act does not apply directly to privately held firms, they will encounter its effects. Private companies may initially feel the law's influence through business partners who insist on compliance with specific dimensions of SOx as a condition for commencing, continuing, or expanding a relationship:

- Lenders may require the installation of independent directors and an independent audit committee prior to approving a loan.
- Insurers may require executives to certify financial statements before issuing or renewing liability coverage for the company's directors and officers.
- Prospective investors in a private security placement may insist on audited financials, assurances of auditor and audit committee independence, and disclosures of "insider transactions" before investing their funds.

The act's mandates are immediately relevant to private companies considering a public offering. Such businesses must carefully integrate the implementation of SOx's requirements into their public placement strategy. Yet compliance with the law can offer advantages even to private firms that do not intend to issue equity publicly. One corporate advisor summarized these benefits:

> By taking action now to comply voluntarily with many of these requirements, larger private companies. . . can reap rewards associated with third party approvals and improved internal controls and governance, while at the same time reducing their litigation exposure. In addition, investors and acquirers may be willing to pay a premium to invest in or buy companies with sound corporate governance practices. The administrative cost—in time and dollars—associated with undertaking such actions will in most cases be outweighed by these benefits.[14]

At a minimum, the law can provide private firms with a model for corporate governance. Thus, Martyn R. Redgrave, chief financial officer of the Minneapolis-based Carlson Companies, described his approach to its provisions:

> The standard I have applied is that if we find the rules relative to current practices would increase transparency or awareness, we are in favor of them. . . . [But] we're not going to sweep through our entire global system to do what is required of public companies. We're using it as a new benchmark against which we measure ourselves, and we have a lot of it in place.[15]

Ultimately, SOx may impact private companies through direct governmental action. State authorities could extend regulations modeled after the act directly to private firms, as well as hospitals and nonprofit organizations. Such parallel legislation was already evident in early 2003, when the legislatures of California and New Jersey passed laws limiting the services public accounting firms could sell to publicly *and* privately held clients.

RESPONSES TO SARBANES-OXLEY

Soon after Sarbanes-Oxley was signed, a number of criticisms were leveled at the act. Some critics contended that the new law was insufficiently demanding of corporate executives. Others complained that the legislation had been drafted and enacted too quickly to adequately address the complexities of corporate governance in a global economy. Still others focused on the specific rules developed by the SEC. Corporate advocates denounced the rules as unnecessarily costly and onerous, while investor advocates charged that the rules had grown soft under pressure from special interests, particularly the accounting and legal professions. Surveying these reactions, one commentator concluded that "[i]n the end, it's safe to say that no one came away unscathed. . . . The question now is whether corporations, accountants, [and] lawyers. . . will have time to digest these rules and regain investor trust through their actions or whether these rules will be the source of more violations that undermine that trust."[16]

What was clear in the immediate aftermath of the law's passage is that SOx confronted business leaders with a new set of governance expectations. John Stout, a partner at the Minneapolis law firm of Fredrikson & Byron and a veteran adviser of corporate boards, summarized its impact this way: "What's being created here are some practice standards. I don't know if they're the best practice standards, but they're better practice standards."[17]

The promulgation of SOx sparked considerable corporate activity. A survey released by Pricewater-houseCoopers in March 2003 indicated that 84 percent of large U.S. multinational corporations had changed their control and compliance practices in the wake of the new law.[18] The survey also showed that executives credited SOx with providing a formalized framework for corporate governance and control. Roughly one-third of the executives surveyed view SOx as a good first step towards rebuilding public confidence in the financial markets; however, only 9 percent consider the act an adequate response to the problems of accounting and financial reporting.

A study released in April 2003 by the law firm Foley & Lardner attempted to quantify the cost of efforts aimed at meeting the requirements of the new corporate governance environment.[19] According to this report, senior managers of middle-market ("midcap") companies expected costs directly associated with being publicly traded to rise approximately 90 percent, from $1.3 to $2.5 million annually, as a result of the new mandates emanating from SOx, the SEC, and stock exchanges.[20] Costs for large midmarket and Fortune 500 companies likely would be three to five times higher in dollar terms; however, as the Foley-Lardner study noted, the resource base of the larger firms enabled them to absorb such increase more readily. One commentator bemoaned the impact of these costs upon smaller, entrepreneurial organizations:

> Unfortunately, these are dollars that will not go into research and development or increasing productivity of the workforce. This means, among other things, that public companies in this country will have to assess this radically increased cost structure in terms of the benefits provided. The benefits are going to be negligible for those companies that do not access the capital markets on a regular, perhaps even annual, basis. In other words, small, innovative, emerging growth companies that do not regularly seek equity capital through public offerings will find the cost of maintaining public status prohibitive.[21]

In contrast, some observers believed it was still too early to assess the act's strengths and weaknesses. For example, Warren Neel, the head of the University of Tennessee's Center for Corporate Governance, remarked in July 2003 that while his center is preparing to evaluate the bill's impact, it had found a "dearth of data largely because major parts of the bill's 68 sections aren't even in effect yet."[22]

Others have pointed to the limitations of *law* as a way of promoting fundamental change within corporations. For example, Dawn Marie Driscoll criticized SOx as an "underwhelming" initiative that failed to address the root cause of corporate misconduct:

> The reason is simple: the business scandals of the past year were caused by inattention to ethics and values. You can't legislate an ethical corporate culture, a diligent board of directors or senior executives with integrity. . . .
>
> When Enron, Tyco, WorldCom and others came to light, Congressmen acted like Captain Renault in the movie Casablanca: "shocked, shocked" that financial scandals may have resulted from legislative loopholes passed a few years earlier, from accounting reforms buried in legislative limbo and from an underfunded SEC. Unwilling to go home to the voters and

> say, "Capitalism is not risk-free," they needed to pass some laws that would make everyone feel better.
>
> Capitalism is not risk-free, but it must not be ethics-free. Our capital market structure is built on trust. . . . There is no law or requirement that can be passed that will mandate, "Do a good job." But economic and political leaders of integrity could have stood up and, like the little child who exposed the Emperor, said, "The folks who were responsible for those business scandals were not business leaders of integrity. There is no shortcut or quick fix to that."[23]

Frank Brown, the global leader of Pricewater-houseCoopers' Assurance and Business Advisory Services, echoed Driscoll's concern about the limited ability of law to influence a firm's moral culture. "Rules, standards, and frameworks can only do so much," he noted, "it will take demonstrated commitment to transparency, accountability, and integrity to restore public trust."[24]

CONCLUSION

A *Forbes* article published to commemorate the first anniversary of the law's signing noted that "nobody thinks Sarbanes-Oxley will be an instant fix."[25] The law was the consequence of a "focusing moment" on corporate governance, the business scandals of 2001–02. Its standards underscore board and executive accountability for corporate conduct and financial disclosures. It also demonstrated the willingness of government to step in when the professions—in this case, the accounting and legal professions—failed to effectively regulate themselves. But while the Sarbanes-Oxley Act of 2002 represented a step toward improved corporate governance, by the summer of 2003 it remained unclear just how significant an advance it was, and whether some adjustment of its mandates was required to better balance the law's costs and benefits. It also remained unclear whether the SEC rule-making process could adequately reconcile Sarbanes-Oxley's requirements with the increasingly global nature of the capital markets.

For practitioners, the most cogent dimension of the debate over Sarbanes-Oxley was the criticism emphasizing that the scandals of 2001–02 resulted as much from *moral* failure as *legal* failure. They served as a helpful reminder that an exclusive focus upon legal compliance would ultimately prove inadequate to protecting a company from the breakdowns that undermined Enron, Tyco, and WorldCom. Laws and regulations can change behaviors by adjusting incentives and sanctions; however, they have a difficult time reaching the fundamental ethical values that operate within a firm. Hence, corporate directors and executives must complement their Sarbanes-Oxley compliance effort with work designed to create, institutionalize, and sustain a robust culture of conscience.

Exhibit 1 The SEC Definition of a Financial Expert

Section 407 of the Sarbanes-Oxley Act requires the audit committee of publicly traded companies to include at least one member who qualifies as a financial expert under rules promulgated by the Securities and Exchange Commission (SEC). The competencies required for this status include:

- An understanding of generally accepted accounting principles (GAAP) and financial statement
- The ability to assess the application of GAAP in connection with accounting for estimates, accruals, and reserves.
- Experience preparing, auditing, analyzing, or evaluating financial statements that display a complexity comparable to the company's statements, or experience supervising individuals engaged in such activities.
- An understanding of internal controls and financial reporting procedures.
- An understanding of audit committee functions.

Exhibit 2 Nonaudit Services Prohibited by the Sarbanes-Oxley Act

Section 201 of the Sarbanes-Oxley Act prohibits public accounting firms from providing the following services to their audit clients:

- Bookkeeping, or other services related to the accounting records or financial statements of the audit client.
- Financial information systems design and implementation.
- Appraisal or valuation services, fairness opinions, or contribution-in-kind reports.
- Actuarial services.
- Internal audit outsourcing services.
- Management functions or human resources.
- Broker or dealer, investment adviser, or investment banking services.
- Legal services and expert services unrelated to the audit.
- Any other service that the Public Company Accounting Oversight Board determines, by regulation, is impermissible.

Exhibit 3 CEO and CFO Certifications

Section 302 of the Sarbanes-Oxley Act requires a company's chief executive officer and chief financial officer to certify in their company's quarterly and annual reports that:

1. They have reviewed the report.
2. To the best of their knowledge, the report neither omits material facts nor contains misleading or inaccurate information.
3. To the best of their knowledge, the report fairly presents the company's financial position, including operating results and cash flows.
4. They are responsible for establishing and maintaining the company's internal controls; the internal controls have been designed, established, and maintained for the purpose of providing material information to them about the company and its subsidiaries; they have evaluated and reported on the effectiveness of these controls within 90 days of the report's filing; and they have disclosed in the report their conclusions about the controls' effectiveness.
5. They have disclosed to the audit committee and auditors all material weaknesses or deficiencies in the design or operation of the internal control system; and they have disclosed all fraud, material or not, involving any individual who plays a significant role in the internal control system.
6. They have disclosed within the report whether any changes to the internal controls that could appreciably affect their effectiveness were implemented subsequent to the date of the evaluation, including corrections of significant or material weaknesses.

NOTES

1. *Weekly Compilation of Presidential Documents*, 5 Aug. 2002.
2. Michael Schroeder, "Cleaner Living, No Easy Riches," *The Wall Street Journal* 22 July 2003: C7.
3. Allison Fass, "One Year Later, the Impact of Sarbanes Oxley," *Forbes.com* 22 July 2003, 1 Aug. 2003 (forbes.com/2003/07/22/cz_af_0722sarbanes.html).
4. Schroeder, C7.
5. Fass.
6. Sarbanes-Oxley also authorizes federal courts to impose financial penalties upon corporations as well as individual executives, for the purpose of granting "any equitable relief that may be appropriate or necessary for the benefit of investors" (Section 305).
7. A "pension blackout period" is a length of time during which the participants in a company's pension plan may neither sell shares of the company's stock present in their individual accounts, nor purchase additional shares.
8. "Management's discussion and analysis" is a required section in annual and quarterly reports that explains major changes in the firm's income statement, capital resources, and liquidity.

9. Paul S. Atkins, "Liabilities of German Companies and the Members of their Executive Boards under the Sarbanes-Oxley Act of 2002," Deutsches Aktieninstitut 4 Feb. 2003 (www.sec.gov/news/speech/spch020403psa.htm).
10. Porsche Press Release, 16 Oct 2002.
11. Atkins, 4.
12. Carrie Johnson, "Accounting Panel, SEC Back Registry for Foreign Auditors," Washingtonpost.com 1 Apr. 2003, 23 May 2003 (www.washingtonpost.com/ac2/wp-dyn/A62762-2003May31).
13. Originally found at "EU to strengthen corporate oversight," *CNNMoney* 21 May 2003, 23 May 2003 (cnnmoney.printthis.clickability.com/pt/cpt?action=cpt&expire=&urlID=...).
14. Andrew G. Humphrey, "The Effect of Sarbanes-Oxley on Private Companies," *Faegre & Benson LLP Legal Updates* Mar. 2003 (www.faegre.com/articles/article_838.asp).
15. Matt Murray, "Private Companies Also Feel Pressure to Clean Up Acts," *The Wall Street Journal* 22 July 2003: B7.
16. Tim Reason, "Did the SEC Gut Sarbanes-Oxley?" *CFO.com* 1 Mar. 2003, 30 May 2003 (www.cfo.com/printarticle/0,5317,8843)/C,OO.html).
17. Susan Feyder, "Veteran Advisor Makes Sense of Congress' Corporate Reform," *Minneapolis Star-Tribune* 27 July 2002: D1.
18. PricewaterhouseCoopers LLP, "Sarbanes-Oxley Act Requires Changes in Corporate Control, Compliance, According to PricewaterhouseCoopers Survey of Senior Executives," 24 Mar. 2003 (www.faegre.com/articles/article_838.asp).
19. Lance Jon Kimmel and Steven W. Vazquez, "The Increased Financial and Non-financial Cost of Staying Public," 2003 National Directors Institute 23 Apr. 2003. Full report available upon request from Foley & Lardner, www.foleylardner.com.
20. Eighty percent of the increase was attributable to higher costs for D&O insurance, audit fees, legal fees, board compensation and compliance personnel.
21. Pierce A. McNally, "Too Much Cost, Too Few Benefits," *Minneapolis Star Tribune* 21 Sept. 2003: D4.
22. Michael Schroeder, "Cleaner Living, No Easy Riches," *The Wall Street Journal* 22 July 2003: Cl.
23. Dawn Marie Driscoll, "Sarbanes-Oxley: Pardon Me If I'm Underwhelmed," *Ethics Matters* Feb. 2003 (ecampus.bentley.edu/dept/cbe/newsletter/jannewsletter/SOx_Issue_1.pdf).
24. PricewaterhouseCoopers LLP.
25. Fass.

LEADING FROM THE BOARDROOM

Directors can reclaim their agendas and refocus on the work of leadership. Here's how.

Jay W. Lorsch and Robert C. Clark

Jay W. Lorsch (jlorsch@hbs,edu) is the Louis E. Kirstein Professor of Human Relations at Harvard Business School in Boston. Robert C. Clark (clark@law.harvard.edu) is the Harvard University Distinguished Service Professor at Harvard Law School in Cambridge, Massachusetts.

It's no exaggeration to say that the governance of companies has moved from the inner sanctum of the boardroom to the white-hot spotlight of public discourse. More is demanded these days from independent directors: They're expected to ensure their firms' compliance with an ever-evolving set of regulations, head off executive wrongdoing at the pass, and appease shareholders' and Wall Street's never-ending hunger for positive short-term results.

As directors have become more hands-on with compliance, they've become more hands-off with long-range planning, exposing shareholders to another kind of risk.

Directors seem to be rising to this challenge. They're more serious, they're working harder, and in most cases governance reform appears to have given them real power to oversee management's actions. As a result, corporate boards have taken big steps forward in the past decade. But having to operate in a post-Enron world has also produced some negative and unintended consequences for boards—the most critical one being directors' inability to be leaders who focus on ensuring the long-term success of their companies.

Major public companies are important engines of economic prosperity, and boards have a paramount obligation to see that these national assets thrive. As historian Alfred D. Chandler, Jr., pointed out, the decline and ultimate failure of once-great companies has been a historical fact. But such decline is not inevitable. Rather, it results when corporate leaders (CEOs and directors alike) don't anticipate and deal with the long-term threats facing their companies.

By necessity, boards are working overtime to comply with Sarbanes-Oxley and other relatively new reporting requirements. To keep pace, they're overemphasizing committee work instead of harnessing the intellectual power of the whole board to deal with complex matters. Instead of working collaboratively with management, they're creating or perpetuating dysfunctional relationships that cast directors as corporate police who enforce rules and trace managers' missteps, rather than guides who help managers choose the right path.

Further, boards' long-standing focus on quarterly results has intensified. This emphasis on the short term has repercussions. (See Robert H. Hayes and William J. Abernathy's "Managing Our Way to Economic Decline," HBR July–August 1980.) In March 2007 the U.S. Chamber of Commerce, one of the world's largest business federations, with about 3 million members, even went so far as to recommend that companies move away from posting quarterly earnings guidance. The thinking was that such reports inevitably put the squeeze on boards and on CEOs—whose average tenures during the past decade have shrunk even as their pay packages have increased—to take the quickest route to results, not necessarily the path to long-term success. The knee-jerk reaction of most boards when confronted with corporate decline over several quarters has been to remove the CEO and search for a replacement—often from outside, since boards frequently fail to ensure internal management continuity.

Boards can and must do better at balancing their function as compliance officers with their function as shapers of the future. From their places around the table, directors must steer themselves and the company's management team toward farsighted strategic and financial thinking and succession planning. Certainly it is management's responsibility to develop and implement strategy, but the board must use a long-range lens when requesting and vetting senior leaders' proposals—encouraging the top team to raise its game even when things are going well and challenging it to respond creatively when threats or problems emerge.

Independent directors cannot be expected to understand all the details of their companies' performance successes or failures, but they can and should be able to stay focused on long-term trends and the impact of those trends on their companies. In short, they must learn to lead from the boardroom.

In the following pages, we'll provide some advice for doing just that. We'll explore the changed environment directors are operating in, what they need to do to regain control of their agendas, and what it looks like when directors take the lead in critical, forward-looking discussions about finance, strategy, and talent development.

COMING UP SHORT

Last year a board we're familiar with created a strategy committee of the five directors who had the most knowledge about the company's industry. The idea was that the committee would work closely with management to study the likely evolution of the industry and the company's position in it. The team's mandate was to come back to the full board with some long-term strategy recommendations, ones that management wholeheartedly supported. For six months, the members of the committee labored; they collected information and met frequently, by themselves and with senior leaders at the company. The result? A plan for containing costs and growing revenues—over a mere two years. Obviously, the plan was focused neither on significant changes in strategy nor on the long term, yet the full board did not seem particularly bothered by that fact. There are several reasons why this board and those of plenty of other struggling public companies are coming up short—or short-term, as the case may be.

More Focus on Compliance Means Longer Agendas

New regulations have increased directors' workloads, yet the amount of time they have together to do their jobs hasn't changed. The average board, even at a very large company, meets only five or six times a year, for just over a day each time. Board agendas, meanwhile, are overflowing with governance matters—compliance, accounting, legal, and shareholder-related issues—all of them important, all clearly of concern at the board level, but none of them germane to leadership or strategy. Since the introduction of Sabanes-Oxley, in 2002, for instance, the time required for audit committee meetings has at least doubled. This, in turn, has increased the time the whole board spends on accounting and financial-reporting matters.

Despite the added demands, most boards are stuck in a time warp, conducting their affairs pretty much as they always have: the same number and length of meetings, the same committees,

and the same patterns of interaction among directors and between directors and management. Their response to new compliance requirements has been to stuff 10 pounds of content into a five-pound bag. The directors' committee work usually cannot be completed in the allotted time, and their discussions often end up being truncated or spilling over into hastily arranged teleconferences. Agenda items that might address future concerns get short shrift. Directors put their heads down and push ahead; they do not step back and ask themselves how to change their processes and procedures to accomplish more.

Boards' Relationship with Management has Changed

Directors typically have relied on senior management for most of their information about the company. After all, the directors aren't—and don't want to be—as immersed in the minutiae of their organizations as management is. From the directors' perspective, the CEO and his or her team should have the latitude and responsibility to run the company the way they see fit, with the board providing high-level guidance. Because of their current focus on compliance, however, directors find themselves in the very role they have long tried to avoid—that of micromanager, probing the senior team's actions, taking less for granted, looking more closely at proposals and reports to be certain that management's behaviors are free of malfeasance and illegalities. To us, the irony here is that as directors have become more hands-on in the area of compliance, they've become more hands-off in the area of long-range planning, which exposes shareholders to another—potentially greater—kind of risk.

The Pressure for Immediate, Measurable Results is Still There in Spades

The obsession with quarterly earnings impedes boards' ability to plan for the long term. Some business leaders argue that all their companies need are short-term goals and results. After all, the long term is made up of a series of short-term accomplishments, they point out. We strongly disagree. We've been on boards where directors and management were so absorbed with quarterly earnings or fast-track product launches that they were slow to recognize trends that ultimately created problems for their organizations—disruptive technologies in their industries, for instance, or new competitors from emerging markets.

If companies are to succeed in the global economy, their directors and top executives need to have a clear view of where they want their organizations to be in five or 10 years. Most directors will say they squeeze some time into their meetings to discuss what they call "strategic matters." In most cases, however, they're actually talking tactics: They're answering questions like "How did we do last quarter?" and "What do we need to do differently in the next three months?" The metrics considered are almost always financial, because that is a language that directors with different backgrounds share and can converse in knowledgeably. Strategic capabilities such as technology or marketing often get only limited attention. When the company's ultimate destination is always just 90 days away, neither the board nor the senior managers will have the time or incentive to draft explicit and well-articulated long-term organizational goals.

Admittedly, today's public companies are growing bigger and more complex—and it has become more of a challenge for directors to keep up with various facets of their businesses and industries. It may be unrealistic, for example, to expect the independent director of an automobile manufacturer to know the details of a new engine technology. But that director should be able to, say, understand the implications of the large pension and health care obligations of the company, or participate in talks about the company's global brand strategies—should we expand in India, and if so, should we outsource or find a JV partner?—or conduct regular reviews of competitive intelligence. Directors similarly should be able to reasonably discuss issues of talent development and succession. Sadly, this is more the exception than the rule in most boardrooms.

TAKING THE LONG VIEW

Most directors will say they squeeze some time into their meetings to discuss what they call "strategic matters." In most cases, however, they're actually talking tactics.

In assuming leadership of their companies' long-term destiny, boards first need to be clear with themselves and with management about the complementary roles each side must play. Each group must be realistic about what it has the time and knowledge to do on its own. Different boards and management teams will define their roles differently, of course, according to company circumstances. In general, however, the setup will look familiar—but with an emphasis on the long term: Management will develop and propose long-range plans, and the board will react to these proposals and debate among itself (and with management) their validity and wisdom.

Second, since directors are forced by law and regulations to get into the weeds on compliance, they'll have to be smarter about staying out of the weeds as much as possible when considering strategic issues. Instead of worrying about coming up to speed on the fine details of the business, they should exercise their broad knowledge and accumulated wisdom about a range of relevant business domains: finance, strategy, marketing, technology, and the like. It is precisely their 10,000-foot view that allows boards to more easily identify trends and threats on the horizon.

Third, directors must not only be intelligent, well-informed, highly interactive audiences for management, but also push management to address the company's future. Boards have the power to approve plans and proposals, they can change the top management of companies, and they are unavoidable—they must be reported to regularly. Boards, therefore have an effective platform from which to evangelize for the long term—that is, to deliberately engage senior managers in discussions about critical future concerns and to signal that those issues are priorities.

And fourth, the directors must encourage leadership not just from the boardroom but within it. There has been a long-running debate in U.S. companies about whether the top executives at organizations should continue to assume the roles of both CEO and chairman of the board. It's hard to argue with the premise that separating the jobs can strengthen independent leadership in the boardroom. But a survey we conducted in 2005 of directors of *Fortune* 200 companies suggests that boardroom effectiveness has less to do with formal structure than with the quality of the directors themselves and how they interact. (See the sidebar "The Real Signs of a Strong Board.")

Legally, boards are groups of peers, with collective rather than individual responsibility, but the most effective ones include multiple directors willing to don the leadership mantle when it comes to particular issues, no matter what their titles are. Sometimes a committee chair can be the catalyst for improvement. Sometimes a plain-vanilla director, seeing the need to get the ball rolling on an issue, takes the initiative. In the case of the strategy committee we mentioned earlier, a director who wasn't on the committee pointed out the lack of long-term focus in the group's proposal and the need for a more farsighted look. (What's our plan for 10 years out, not just two?) Initially, the other board members ignored his comments, particularly the directors who had been on the committee and worked so hard on the recommendations. But the dissident director persisted with his arguments, and eventually the board concluded that a longer-term strategic plan was in order.

As the example suggests, it's just as critical for individual directors to speak up and ask tough questions as it is for the board as a collective. Yet such leadership is rarely realized because it poses an overt challenge to the board's basic modus operandi and because any conflict consumes a precious resource—the directors' time together to discuss and reach decisions.

WHEN THE BOARD REASSERTS ITS LEADERSHIP

Once directors accept the need for more consideration of the long term, they can allocate their time more efficiently—meeting compliance standards but also buying back hours to go over future-focused concerns. Let's take a closer look at what happens when the board assumes a more active leadership role.

Defining the Long Term

This process has to start with a common understanding between directors and senior management about how far out the "long term" goes. All too often, boards will think their discussions about a discrete transaction—an acquisition or a divestiture, for instance—constitute consideration of the company's long-term strategy and finances. In fact, that is rarely the case. An individual company's definition of the long term will depend on how confident directors and management teams are in their ability to project several years into the future with reasonable accuracy. Industry activity may be a factor: It can be difficult to make far-reaching predictions in industries in which there are frequent technological or product innovations or low barriers to entry (for instance, internet-based businesses). Conversely, it may be easier to forecast events further into the future in industries where innovation is less frequent and dramatic and demand is tied to population growth (consumer products and household goods).

THE REAL SIGNS OF A STRONG BOARD

The intention of shareholder activism is to improve corporate governance, but in fact, it has very little effect on how well boards do their jobs. A survey we conducted in 2005 of directors of *Fortune* 200 companies suggests they do not believe that many criteria used by ISS Governance Services (formerly Institutional Shareholder Services) and other ratings agencies to assess board performance have much to do with board effectiveness.

We asked the directors their opinions about 52 of the so-called indicators of effective corporate governance favored by ratings agencies—which included many check-the-box factors such as the appointment of a lead or presiding director and compliance with relatively new stock exchange requirements. The directors didn't find much value in those factors. Instead, they gave more credence to criteria that related to the quality of board composition, talents, and processes. Three of the most highly rated factors concerned the specific background, knowledge, and abilities of directors—"Is there understanding among board members on the key drivers of the company's business?" and "Is there understanding among board members on appropriate metrics of corporate performance?" and "Is the mix of experience and backgrounds of directors appropriate to the company's business(es)?"

Also among the highest-rated factors were specific activities or processes—for instance, did the board have manageable agendas and allocate time appropriately at meetings, so management could present information but have adequate time left for discussion and decision making? And did the board disseminate information to directors before meetings, so they could consider the issues at hand and prepare ahead of time?

Among the less-favored factors were those related to publicly visible characteristics—whether the board was large, whether it limited independent directors' involvement to a small number of other boards, whether it separated the positions of chairman and chief executive, whether it set a mandatory retirement age for directors, and whether it required director education programs. Such indicators trumpeted by the ratings agencies were treated with great skepticism by the directors surveyed—yet the search for talismanic indicators of quality continues.

Taking the Lead in Finance Discussions

Directors must get serious about their role in ensuring the development of the next generation of senior leaders at their organizations.

Once the time frame has been determined, the board and management must create a set of financial goals for the long term—for example, clearly articulated expectations for revenue and profit growth, returns on assets or investments, cash flows, and debt-to-equity ratios, as well as dividend and share-repurchase policies. Those measures will in turn help determine the company's strategic direction. Such objectives will also reflect to the public how the board intends to allocate the wealth the company creates.

As we mentioned earlier, management in most instances will actually draft the financial goals and the means for achieving them. But boards must help determine whether the senior team is creating the right capital structure. The important point here is that directors should spend less time on quarterly earnings and more time on financial infrastructure—delving into questions about, say, the cost of capital or the debt-to-equity balance that the company is wrestling with.

Taking the Lead in Strategy Discussions

Once the board and management have crafted explicit financial goals, they need to turn their attention to how the company will hit those targets. Specifically, the directors must step back from fighting fires and consider how management's view of the future squares with their own broader, higher-altitude views.

Board retreats provide a good setting for this. The board and management at Philips Electronics hold an annual two-to three-day retreat—uninterrupted time devoted to discussing the company's direction for the next several years. There is time for management and the board to interact, certainly, but time is also set aside for director-only sessions, which encourage open and frank discussions and draw out knowledge and insights in an uninhibited way. It was such discussions, for example, that led Philips in 2006 to exit the semiconductor business, a segment in which it was losing ground, and focus more heavily on medical technology—in particular, on the quickly growing market for home health care.

Everyone involved in such retreats should understand that these getaways aren't the only time to look ahead: "Strategy time" should be set aside at most, if not all, board meetings. Such time must remain sacrosanct, interrupted only for dire emergencies. The focus of management's proposals and boardroom discussions should be on the long-term logic, not the short-term implications. The two parties must systematically examine the company's competitive advantages and opportunities through several long-range lenses—industry trends, geographies, brands, IP, talent, labor contracts, and product and operational costs.

Any agreed-upon strategic plans should be reassessed regularly—not to fit management with a straitjacket but to help directors and senior executives understand whether factors have emerged that may require a shift in priorities or a move in another direction. Time should be reserved at each board meeting for such reassessments. The board of a software company we observed successfully followed this practice: The firm had acquired a smaller rival in the hopes of capitalizing on the former competitor's promising new product. Within months of the acquisition, the product met with such enthusiastic customer response that the board pressed management to raise its revenue and profit goals for this new business over the next several years.

Like Rome, new strategies aren't built in a day. We've found that shaping (or reshaping) strategies for the long term is a process that takes place over multiple board meetings. But we wonder how many directors have participated in such lengthy exercises—too few, we fear.

Taking the Lead in Developing Talent

Directors must also get serious about their role in ensuring the development of the next generation of senior leaders at their organizations—that is, creating a deep bench of potential successors to the CEO and other top executives. When agendas become overcrowded, talent development and CEO succession are among the easiest topics to ignore or at least defer, even while directors recognize the importance of having the right people at the top.

A few years ago, a midsize company we observed had a successful CEO who was three years away from the mandatory retirement age. The directors began to discuss informally how to approach the situation and decided to put the process of identifying a successor on the board's agenda. Unfortunately, when the time arrived to address this agenda item, the board and management were immersed in deliberations about a possible acquisition. Over the next 18 months, the succession issue was put on the agenda at each board meeting. Every time, a more pressing issue arose. With only a little over a year left until the CEO was slated to step down, the directors finally began active talks about this topic. By then, they had a severe problem: The CEO was an adamant supporter of an internal candidate for succession with whom the board felt uncomfortable. After a couple of hastily arranged discussions among themselves, the independent directors insisted that a search firm be retained to look outside. The CEO was opposed and continued to argue for his choice. Soon he began to insist that the succession decision was his alone, while the directors argued it was theirs. In the end, the board brought in an outsider, but the retiring CEO left in anger and frustration, which had a negative impact on the other members of the C-suite.

As this example illustrates, independent directors need to be particularly hands-on when it is time to select a new CEO. While most companies have a clear policy about the retirement age for their CEOs, the transition can still be a tricky one to navigate. CEOs, of course, don't want directors to believe anyone can replace them; they may downplay internal candidates' readiness to take over and overstate the lack of leadership talent available outside the organization. To counteract these tactics, boards must come to a firm agreement with their CEOs—from the earliest days of their relationship—about when the chief executive will step down and how and when the board will find a successor. Specifically, there must be a few directors who build trust with the CEO so they can talk candidly with him about his personal situation—what he is planning to do after his retirement, how he can best help his successor, and how he can exit gracefully. In some cases, a few of the directors themselves may have gone through a retirement process and can share their experiences with the CEO.

Directors often have only a superficial knowledge of the up-and-coming talent in their companies. Acquaintances are made at board dinners, and this social chitchat becomes the primary means by which directors are supposed to assess the strengths and weaknesses of the managers before them for promotion. This is hardly adequate. Directors need to devote more time to their companies' emerging leaders. A good way to start is periodic on-site visits by the directors—something that is done by board members at GE, where directors meet younger executives on their own turf and observe how they work with their subordinates. GE's directors also meet with and address rising talent during development programs at the company's Crotonville training facility and sometimes invite high potentials to make presentations at GE board meetings.

The board should also hold the CEO and the company's human resources director accountable for at least an annual in-depth review of the company's top management bench: What does the CEO think of these executives? How is this cadre of managers being developed, and are

"Instead of *cubicles* we call them *interconnected productivity centers*"

there potential successors for each of them? As they must do with their strategy and finance discussions, boards must carefully protect the time set aside to discuss talent—probably not at every meeting but often enough so that directors have some knowledge about the high potentials on the company roster.

. . .

The basic argument for boards' intense focus on compliance is to prevent the loss of shareholder value that corporate misdeeds create. But the argument for strong leadership from boards is even more compelling. Without it, there may be even greater destruction of shareholder value as companies go into decline. Obviously, whatever changes boards choose to make to achieve a longer-term perspective, they cannot abandon or even diminish their attention to compliance. Current laws and regulations require it, and shareholders and the public expect it—and will continue to demand it. But boards cannot afford to become so mired in it that they lose their way and fail to live up to their larger obligation: to help their companies grow and prosper, not just in the next quarter but in the next decade and beyond.

CENTER FOR EDUCATION ON SOCIAL RESPONSIBILITY

PART SIX (B)

SHAREHOLDERS

EXECUTIVE COMPENSATION PRINCIPLES AND COMMENTARY

PRINCIPLES AND COMMENTARY

Principles of Executive Compensation

1. Executive compensation should be closely aligned with the long-term interests of shareholders and with corporate goals and strategies. It should include significant performance-based criteria related to longterm shareholder value and should reflect upside potential and downside risk.

2. Compensation of the CEO and other top executives should be determined entirely by independent directors, either as a compensation committee or together with the other independent directors based on the committee's recommendations.

3. The compensation committee should understand all aspects of executive compensation and should review the maximum payout and all benefits under executive compensation arrangements. The compensation committee should understand the maximum payout and consequences under multiple scenarios, including retirement, termination with or without cause, and severance in connection with business combinations or sale of the business.

4. The compensation committee should require executives to build and maintain significant continuing equity investment in the corporation.

5. The compensation committee should have independent, experienced expertise available to provide advice on executive compensation arrangements and plans. The compensation committee should oversee consultants to ensure that they do not have conflicts that would limit their ability to provide independent advice.

6. The compensation committee should oversee its corporation's executive compensation programs to see that they are in compliance with applicable laws and regulations and aligned with best practices.

7. Corporations should provide complete, accurate, understandable and timely disclosure to shareholders concerning all elements of executive compensation and the factors underlying executive compensation policies and decisions.

Introduction

Business Roundtable, an association of CEOs of 160 leading corporations, is committed to policies and actions that stimulate economic growth and foster investor confidence and public trust in businesses. Roundtable CEOs take seriously their responsibilities to improve corporate governance and promote the highest standards of accountability and ethical behavior.

Business Roundtable CEOs lead companies with more than $4.5 trillion in annual revenues and more than 10 million employees. Member companies comprise nearly a third of the total value of the U.S. stock market, collectively returned more than $110 billion in dividends to shareholders and the economy in 2005, and represent nearly a third of all corporate income taxes paid to the federal government. The CEOs advocate public policies that encourage economic growth in the United States and across the world and have been leaders in developing the well-trained and productive U.S. workforce essential for future competitiveness.

For the past three decades, compensation has played an increasingly significant role in attracting, retaining and motivating executive officers and employees at all levels. In March 1992, when Business Roundtable released Executive Compensation/Share Ownership, we noted the intense interest in compensation paid to corporate executives. The stock market boom of the late 1990s and the corporate failures in the early part of this decade have heightened the focus on executive compensation. Moreover, there has been a growing concern among investors and the public that pay has not always been commensurate with performance, with a perception that some executives have reaped substantial financial rewards even at times of declining stock prices and large losses to employees and shareholders. Roundtable CEOs share that concern and believe that executive compensation should be clearly linked to company performance.

Since the publication of our executive compensation principles, there has been continuing scrutiny of executive compensation and developments relating to compensation committees. Major securities markets have adopted listing standards that require compensation committees' or independent directors' oversight of executive compensation, along with prescribed minimum responsibilities for compensation committees.

Given the ongoing development of best practices in executive compensation, Business Roundtable is updating our principles of executive compensation. In addition, the Roundtable urges all corporations to make their compensation policies and practices as responsible and transparent as possible.

Compensation should serve the objectives of a corporation's business. Accordingly, the structure and components of an appropriate executive compensation program will vary widely among corporations due to such factors as a corporation's size, industry, competitive challenges and culture. Nevertheless, the executive compensation program of every publicly owned corporation should adhere to two fundamental characteristics. First, it should reflect the core principle of pay for results. Although this concept is not new, it means that a corporation's executive compensation program not only rewards success, but also incorporates a meaningful element of risk. Additionally, it should reflect the performance of the corporation, not just the stock market in general. Second, the executive compensation program of every publicly traded corporation should be established and overseen by a committee comprised solely of independent directors who, among other things, set the goals and objectives for executive compensation and determine whether those goals and objectives have been achieved. In doing so, compensation committees should be aware of all aspects of their corporation's executive compensation and see that the compensation arrangements are in the best interests of shareholders.

Building on these characteristics as a foundation, Business Roundtable has developed seven interrelated principles to serve as best practices for the design, implementation and oversight of executive compensation programs at publicly held corporations.

We urge all corporations and their compensation committees to consider these practices as they develop and implement executive compensation arrangements.

Commentary on Executive Compensation Principles

1. Executive compensation should be closely aligned with the long-term interests of shareholders and with corporate goals and strategies. It should include significant performance-based criteria related to long-term shareholder value and should reflect upside potential and downside risk.

- Compensation is a primary tool for attracting and retaining the highly qualified individuals necessary for a corporation to succeed in a competitive world economy. The board of directors is responsible for adopting and overseeing the implementation of compensation policies that support the corporation's ability to compete successfully in the marketplace.

- Executive compensation should directly link the interests of executive officers, both individually and as a team, to the long-term interests of shareholders. Equity-based compensation can be effective in accomplishing this objective. Establishing a meaningful link between executive officer and shareholder interests requires careful consideration of the incentives created by different forms of compensation.

- Compensation committees and boards of directors should establish meaningful goals for performance-based compensation; payment should be tied to the achievement of those goals. A failure to meet performance goals should reduce or eliminate payments.

- Once performance goals have been established, corporations should adhere to them. A corporation should not adjust previously established targets or reprice options prior to the end of a performance measurement period or the options' term simply because it appears that results for that period or term may fall short of the goals.

- In setting performance goals, corporations should look beyond short-term market value changes and focus on metrics related to long-term shareholder value creation. Compensation plans should further both the near-term objectives and the corporation's long-term strategy, and they should be consistent with the culture of the corporation and the overall goal of enhancing sustainable shareholder value. They should avoid windfalls due solely to general stock market performance.

- In setting performance measures, consideration should be given to a variety of performance metrics, both qualitative and quantitative. These metrics should not be tied solely to the corporation's short-term stock price. Examples of quantitative metrics that may be used include such items as cash and debt management, cost containment, dividends and earnings per share, labor relations, margins, market share, mergers and acquisitions, return on equity, revenue and profit growth, sale of assets, stock price, and significant reorganizations. Qualitative metrics include such items as community relations, crisis response, customer satisfaction, employee development and relations, ethics and a culture of integrity, leadership, legal compliance, product quality, succession planning, and workforce diversity. In addition, consideration of performance relative to peer groups as well as absolute performance may be appropriate measures.

- Performance-based incentives should reflect both business and individual accomplishments. Incentives should be tied not only to the corporation's operating results, but also to the executive's distinctive leadership in managing the corporation effectively and ethically, which creates long-term value for shareholders.
- A meaningful portion of executive compensation should be performance based, thereby incorporating a greater element of downside risk into compensation arrangements. This can be accomplished, for example, by linking the granting or vesting of equity compensation to the achievement of meaningful performance targets, including a meaningful vesting period. Performance-based or performance-vested stock options, performance share units, or stock appreciation rights that are payable in the corporation's stock or cash — only if targets are met — put equity-based compensation "at risk" and link pay to performance.
- Restricted stock can be an alternative or supplement to stock options and other equity-based compensation. Although restricted stock can be an appropriate and effective retention device, it also can be more effective as a long-term incentive if it is paid or vests based on the achievement of specified performance targets.
- Performance-based incentives often will measure accomplishments over several years. For example, in a year when the corporation experiences declining financial results, the CEO may receive performance-based compensation keyed to a previously established multi-year target. Similarly, gains realized from option exercises and stock sales in a given year may be the result of options granted over many years and several years' appreciation in the underlying stock. Corporations should take steps to enhance investor understanding of the relationship between pay and performance by providing meaningful disclosure about this relationship in the corporation's Compensation Discussion and Analysis (CD&A).

2. Compensation of the CEO and other top executives should be determined entirely by independent directors, either as a compensation committee or together with the other independent directors based on the committee's recommendations.

- Directors who sit on a compensation committee should be independent in both fact and appearance. Committee members should have, and be perceived to have, the ability to exercise independent judgment free from any relationship or influence that could appear to compromise their ability to approach compensation issues decisively and independently.
- In recommending directors to serve on the compensation committee, the corporate governance/nominating committee should consider the following:
  - A diversity of professional backgrounds is important to the effective functioning of a compensation committee.

- Periodic rotation of members and the chair can bring fresh perspectives to the compensation committee.
- All members of the committee should have sufficient knowledge of executive compensation and related issues to perform their responsibilities effectively. In-depth orientation should be provided to new committee members, and all committee members should be encouraged to participate in continuing education programs related to executive compensation.

- The particular duties and responsibilities that are delegated to the compensation committee will depend on the corporation and should be set forth in the committee's written charter. At a minimum, the duties and responsibilities of the compensation committee should include:
    - Overseeing the corporation's overall compensation structure, policies and programs;
    - Reviewing and approving corporate goals and objectives relating to executive compensation;
    - Evaluating executive officers' performance in light of those goals and objectives;
    - Determining and approving (either as a committee or together with the other independent directors) executive officers' compensation level based on this evaluation; and
    - Setting or making recommendations to the board with respect to executive compensation and compensation plans.
- The compensation committee should play an integral role in the preparation of the CD&A to be included in a corporation's proxy statement or annual report, and it should see that the CD&A effectively explains the material aspects of the corporation's compensation objectives and the factors underlying executive compensation decisions. The compensation committee also must indicate in its committee report whether it has reviewed and discussed the CD&A with management and recommended to the board that the CD&A be included in the corporation's proxy statement or annual report.
- The compensation committee should perform an annual evaluation of its performance and review the adequacy of the committee's charter. In light of this review, the compensation committee should consider appropriate changes in its practices and recommend any necessary changes in its charter to the board.
- Corporations should consider having compensation committee chairs speak for the corporation on executive compensation matters and be available at annual meetings to address executive compensation.

3. The compensation committee should understand all aspects of executive compensation and should review the maximum payout and all benefits under executive compensation arrangements. The compensation committee should understand the maximum payout and consequences under multiple scenarios, including retirement, termination with or without cause, and severance in connection with business combinations or sale of the business.

- The compensation committee should fully understand all the benefits and consequences to the executive and the costs to the corporation of the compensation arrangement under various circumstances, including under a range of economic results and severance scenarios. The committee should understand how the various elements of cash and noncash compensation, including benefits, deferred compensation arrangements and supplemental retirement benefits, are allocated and work together. In addition, the committee should understand the accounting and tax aspects of different types of arrangements. Executive compensation arrangements should not be unduly complex.
- The compensation committee should be aware of all elements of the compensation of each executive officer; there should be no surprises. This may be facilitated by the use of tally sheets, which should include all forms of compensation.
- In structuring a compensation arrangement, consideration should be given to whether the amount and mix of compensation is reasonable, appropriate and fair in light of the roles, responsibilities and performance of the individual, the corporation's circumstances and overall compensation structure, and the need to attract and retain high-quality executive officers.
- The committee should consider building into executive compensation agreements the right to review and consider changes at appropriate time intervals. When a compensation arrangement is modified, the committee should assess and understand how the change will affect the overall compensation of an executive officer.
- Particular attention should be paid to severance arrangements and to all benefits provided to executive officers in connection with termination of employment. Corporations should review such arrangements on a regular basis. They should not offer excessive severance packages that reward executives who have not met performance goals and objectives during the term of their employment. Employment contracts, if any, should clearly articulate the consequences of termination and the circumstances in which an executive can be terminated for cause.

4. The compensation committee should require executives to build and maintain significant continuing equity investment in the corporation.

- The compensation committee should establish requirements that executive officers and members of the board of directors acquire and hold a meaningful amount of the corporation's stock to align executive and director interests with the interests of shareholders.
- Stock retention requirements can foster a long-term stake in the corporation among executive officers. The compensation committee should require that executive officers hold a specified amount of the stock for a period of time until they meet the corporation's stock ownership guidelines or until they leave the corporation.
- To minimize questions and possible concerns about the propriety of particular stock trades, corporations should make available to executive officers and directors prearranged trading plans to the extent they determine to sell some portion of their stock. When executive officers and directors enter into such trading plans, they should be disclosed.

5. The compensation committee should have independent, experienced expertise available to provide advice on executive compensation arrangements and plans. The compensation committee should oversee consultants to ensure that they do not have conflicts that would limit their ability to provide independent advice.

- The compensation committee should have the authority to retain compensation consultants, counsel and other outside experts in compensation matters to provide the committee with independent advice for performing its responsibilities. Nevertheless, decisions with respect to executive compensation are the ultimate responsibility of the compensation committee and the the board.
- The compensation committee should retain and oversee any compensation consultants hired to assist with executive compensation matters, approve the terms of their retention and fees, and evaluate their performance. In doing so, the committee should consider any other work that the consultants may perform for the corporation and whether such work has any impact on the advice provided to the compensation committee. The compensation committee should consider whether it should preapprove any other work the consultant does for the corporation.
- The compensation committee should use information from a variety of sources in determining compensation levels. The committee should resist an over-reliance on surveys and other statistical analyses in determining compensation levels. Although such information can be used as a tool, company-specific factors should be given significant weight in determining Executive Compensation: Principles and Commentary 11 executive compensation. In addition, the compensation committee should carefully examine the composition of any peer groups used in considering executive compensation and consider, among other things, the performance of the other corporations included in the peer group.
- The compensation committee should retain independent counsel that reports directly to the committee to assist in negotiation of the CEO contract and benefits and to assist the committee in addressing its other responsibilities as appropriate.

6. The compensation committee should oversee its corporation's executive compensation programs to see that they are in compliance with applicable laws and regulations and aligned with best practices.

- The compensation committee should assess whether executive compensation programs are consistent with the corporation's goals and strategies.
- The compensation committee should review on an ongoing basis its policies and practices with respect to the granting of stock options and other forms of equity compensation to see that they are in accord with state corporate law, Securities and Exchange Commission (SEC) rules, accounting standards, Internal Revenue Service regulations, and any other applicable requirements. The committee should be sensitive to the timing of such grants (e.g., no "back dating") and maintain consistent practices.
- Corporations should consider adopting policies and/or provisions in compensation plans or agreements that permit them to seek the return of bonuses and equity compensation

from executive officers in the event of a financial restatement or fraud resulting from an executive's misconduct or fraudulent activity.

- The compensation committee should carefully examine executive perquisites and determine whether they are appropriate and in the interest of shareholders. If not, the corporation should not bear the cost of personal expenses.
- Benefits granted to executive officers should not be safeguarded to a greater extent than regular employee benefits.
- Corporations should be sensitive to the appearance of executive compensation practices, and special attention should be given to such controversial practices as:
  - Tax gross-ups and supplemental retirement plans beyond those provided to other employees and
  - Preferential investment or above-market interest for deferred compensation.

7. Corporations should provide complete, accurate, understandable and timely disclosure to shareholders concerning all elements of executive compensation and the factors underlying executive compensation policies and decisions.

- Disclosure about executive compensation should be transparent and understandable to shareholders and in plain English. Corporations should disclose the terms of executive officer employment arrangements when they are entered into or materially changed. Disclosure about a corporation's executive compensation arrangements, as a whole, should address not only the form and amount of executive compensation (including projections of future benefits), but also the interaction of the different elements of compensation, the economic impact of the compensation (such as any dilution resulting from stock options) on the corporation and its shareholders, the material factors underlying compensation policies and decisions, why specific elements of compensation were awarded, and the relationship of executive compensation to corporate goals and strategy.
- Corporations also should disclose the criteria used in performance-based awards to executives and the measurement methods used to determine whether those criteria have been met, unless disclosure of the criteria involves the disclosure of trade secrets or confidential information that could cause competitive harm.
- As required by SEC rules, the CD&A included in the proxy statement or annual report should provide shareholders an explanation of all material elements of compensation for executive officers. The CD&A should include information explaining the objectives of the compensation program, what the compensation program is designed to award, and how each element fits into the corporation's overall compensation objectives and affects other elements.
- Corporations should use the CD&A to provide shareholders with meaningful and understandable disclosure about their executive compensation philosophy, policies and practices; the factors that the compensation committee and the board consider in making compensation decisions; and the relationship between executive compensation and corporate performance.

"OH LORD, WON'T YOU BUY ME A MERCEDES-BENZ": HOW COMPENSATION PRACTICES ARE UNDERMINING THE CREDIBILITY OF EXECUTIVE LEADERS

Jay A. Conger

The singer Janis Joplin penned a song entitled "Oh Lord, Won't You Buy Me a Mercedes Benz" in which she playfully implores God to provide her with a number of the extravagant niceties in life. There is a striking parallel between the attitude and desire conveyed in this song and those of executives of America's publicly traded corporations when it comes to their own compensation. For more than a decade, the news headlines have highlighted the fact that executives have been largely successful in getting most of what they want: "Crony Capitalism," "A Decade of Executive Excess: The 1990s," and "CEO Compensation: Time for Reform." These headlines and their stories chronicle a trend in the business world to reward senior business leaders with excessive levels of compensation. For example, the median CEO compensation of a majority sample of Fortune 500 companies in 2003 was $7.1 million. Those in the Fortune 100 averaged $12.2 million. In 2002, the average US CEO earned 282 times what the average employee did. This compares to a ratio of 42 to one in 1980.[1] But these are average figures. At the extreme end of the spectrum, there is Larry Gulp, CEO of Danaher, who received $53 million in 2003 compensation or Steve Jobs, CEO of Apple Computer, who took home $74.8 million.[2] In essence, compensation at the top continues to be excessive and has even become corrupt in some firms. As a byproduct, it is not uncommon to find executives possessing an entitlement mentality that far exceeds the bounds of reasonable rewards for performance. These excessive payouts do more harm than good—undermining the credibility of executive leaders and reinforcing incentives for many executives to manage the financial performance of their firms for the short term rather than for long-term growth and value.

The two-decade bull market of the 1980s and 1990s fueled the recent compensation boom and brought media attention to executives at well known companies like Enron, WorldCom, and Disney for their exorbitant pay packages. The "poster boy," however, of this era was one Dennis Kozlowski, former chairman and CEO of Tyco International, an industrial conglomerate. Under Mr Kozlowski's leadership, a former government laboratory with $3 billion in revenues was transformed into a $36 billion conglomerate and Wall Street darling. His compensation mirrored the spectacular growth in his firm. In 1992, his salary stood at $950,000. By 1997, total compensation had jumped to $26 million. Then one year later it reached $70 million. By 2000, his compensation package was some $137 million. Indicted for evading state taxes on personal purchases of multi-million dollar artwork, he would later be charged under a second indictment with defrauding Tyco of more than $300 million. According to court filings in 1998, he charged Tyco International for $52,334 in wine, $96,943 in flowers, $155,067 in clothing, and $72,042 in jewelry. He hosted a $2.1 million birthday party for his wife of which some $1 million was paid by Tyco according to court records. In 2000, without consulting his board, he decided to "forgive" a large portion of a personal relocation loan which included $19.4 million for the purchase of his home and land in Florida.[3] Kozlowski's sense of entitlement had no apparent bounds.

The critical question of course is whether executives like Kozlowski represent a small handful of individuals or the tip of a far larger iceberg encompassing the corporate world. In other words, was he one of a few bad apples among corporate chieftains or is the apple barrel itself rotten? As Kim Clark, dean of the Harvard Business School, argues, how one answers this question profoundly determines what can and should be done to address executive compensation abuses. For example, if the conclusion is that a small number of executives are at fault, then the solution is fairly straightforward: prosecute the "bad apples," fine and jail them, and hope that punishment and publicity will curb the inclinations of the remaining bad ones. If the barrel is the real problem, then the solutions must be far more systematic and widespread. They must involve revamping corporate governance and boardroom oversight as well as instituting new regulations and tax codes.[4] My experience in boardrooms and in the world of business tells me that the barrel itself has a serious degree of rot. In this chapter, I will discuss the forces that have been undermining the integrity of that barrel and offer suggestions as to how we might mend executive compensation and restore credibility to executive leadership in the process.

As a caveat, this is a very difficult barrel to mend. The problem is a recurrent one. Numerous attempts to remedy it have had very limited success. To illustrate its long history, we can look back to 1929 when Eugene Grace, CEO of Bethlehem Steel, received an annual salary of $12,000 which in those times was considered a great deal of money. That same year, because of the performance of the company, he was awarded a bonus of $1.2 million—a truly remarkable and groundbreaking sum for a professional manager. As a result, became the first millionarie of a publicly traded company in American history.[5] Before that time, business people who became millionaires were entrepreneurs, the builders of companies; individuals such as DuPont, Vanderbilt, Rockefeller rather than professional managers. By the first half of the twentieth century, however, entrepreneurial builders were no longer leading many of the nation's largest companies—the very firms they had built. Rather the leadership of these firms was in the hands of professional managers. The exuberant stock market of the 1920s had encouraged rewards based on stock performance (a striking parallel to the 1990s), and Grace at Bethlehem Steel became one of the most prominent beneficiaries. That said, it is not until 1933 (in the midst of the Great Depression) that the issue of executive compensation created a genuine firestorm. In that year, George Washington Hill, who was the head of American Tobacco, received a bonus of $1.3 million. The shareholders took him to court over what they perceived as excessive pay. It was the first lawsuit over CEO pay. The Supreme Court decided that pay could be subject to judicial review at public companies.[6] This set in motion the first regulations concerning CEO compensation. As an outcome, CEO pay had to be approved at the company's shareholders' meetings. As we have witnessed over the last decade, this safeguard, however, proved to have limited efficacy.

HOW AND WHY THE EXECUTIVE COMPENSATION BARREL DEVELOPED A PERENNIAL PROBLEM WITH ROT

The executive compensation barrel is a complex one made of many planks which are subject to an array of forces. One of the most powerful forces that historically causes "barrel rot" is a booming equity market. For example, the equity markets of the roaring 20s and 90s both induced excessive levels of executive compensation. A more durable and fundamental contributor is the capitalist orientation of the United States. America is at its heart a society built around the notion of individual achievement and reward with a strong emphasis on acquiring personal wealth as a measure of one's success. This is apparent even among the youngest members of society. In the annual survey of freshman college students conducted by UCLA, one question asked of the incoming freshman across the country is "what are your priorities as a young person?" In 2003, 74 percent of all freshmen responded "to be financially successful." The only survey item which was ranked more highly is "to raise family."[7]

But there are other equally weighty contributors which make it difficult for the barrel's integrity to withstand the pressure of the first two forces. The most influential of these include: (1) the nature of corporate boards and their relationship with the CEO, (2) fundamental shifts in compensation practices over the last two decades, (3) our tendency to romance the influence of the CEO role, (4) executive narcissism and an accompanying sense of entitlement and (5) public conceptions of the purpose of corporations. We will start with the first of these—the corporate boardroom-where safeguards should have been in place.

Boardroom Leadership

In most US corporations, the chief executive officer is the de facto leader of the boardroom. The CEO's authority is further reinforced by the fact that most CEOs also hold the position of board chairman. In other words, formal leadership rests entirely in their hands. This is due in large part to the natural advantages of their position. As CEO, they have far greater access to current and comprehensive information about the state of the company than other board members. In contrast, the typical director's knowledge about company affairs is extremely limited given their part-time role and their status as outsiders. Most directors are all too aware of this gap in their own understanding and therefore often concede authority to the CEO. In addition, most directors see their first role as providing oversight. This belief is fostered by the fact that most board directors of publicly traded companies are CEOs themselves, and they share in an etiquette that suggests restraint from aggressively challenging or from meddling too deeply into the details of a fellow CEO's business. These dynamics encourage directors under most circumstances to defer to the CEO's judgment. As a result, the CEO normally determines the agenda for meetings and controls much of the information that directors receive.[8] The CEO often selects who sits on the board and who is a member of the board's committees. While new government regulations and governance practices are being introduced to counter such outcomes, only in the last few years are they having an impact. Outside of a serious decline in company performance or a scandal, CEOs continue to "lead" most boardrooms.

In the case of executive compensation, the dilemma with the "CEO model" of board leadership is that it lacks an effective system of checks and balances. If a CEO feels quite strongly that he and his executive team deserve a certain pay package, his strong leadership position ensures a high probability of receiving that package. Given that most board members today are CEOs, the board is further prejudiced towards the award of generous pay packages based often on an implicit notion of reciprocity: the "I'll-scratch-your-back-if-you'll-scratch-mine" principle. [9] Moreover, a study by Governance Metric International reveals that one out of every twelve public traded corporations has a CEO who sits on the board of another company led by a member of his own board of directors.[10] Since the stakes are high given the large sums of money involved in executive compensation and directors' personal ties to the CEO, executive compensation decisions can encourage collusive behavior in the boardroom. Directors may have an explicit or implicit agreement to give the executive team positive evaluations and in return high levels of compensation. Even in situations where directors take the task of evaluating the compensation of the executive team in a rigorous and objective manner, there is another factor that leads them to make favorable compensation decisions. Their compensation assessments depend heavily upon the outside world—in other words, boardroom compensation committees have largely outsourced decision-making.

The Outsourcing of Compensation

Today, compensation decisions for corporate executives are made by the board of directors and the board's compensation committee. That said, the actual evaluation of CEO performance and compensation decisions have been largely outsourced to the market and to consultants. During the bull market of the 1990s, boards and CEOs came to believe that particularly CEO performance should be evaluated by a shareholder value model. In other words, the growth rate of the company's market capitalization or its share price appreciation represented the best measure of company performance and in turn a reflection on the capabilities of a firm's executives. As a result, compensation packages began to include larger and larger stock benefits. In the early 1990s, for example, only approximately 8 percent of a Fortune 500 CEO pay package was in equities. By the end of the 1990s, this percentage hit 66 percent, in other words two-thirds on average of the pay of a CEO of a large publicly traded company was in some form of stock compensation.[11]

In addition, board compensation committees increasingly turned to outsiders for compensation guidance—individuals called compensation consultants. The rationale was a simple one. They could provide benchmark compensation data for executives in comparable companies. The problem was that the consultants came from firms that provided other services beyond compensation advice to their client companies. Their firms also provided executive recruiting, auditing, pension advice, and consulting services. The potential for serious conflict of interest problems arose. For example, executive recruiting firms have a key relationship with the CEO of many firms. How could they declare that their client, the CEO, needed to take a far more modest pay increase without jeopardizing their mainstream recruiting business? A similar predicament is faced by accounting and human resources consulting firms who provide compensation advice. Millions of dollars in lucrative contract work in auditing and consulting are also provided to the same client. A less than attractive compensation proposal for the company's top decision-makers might make the auditing and consulting practices of competitors look far more attractive. As a result, compensation consultants face the age old predicament "Why bite the hand that feeds you." This dependence presumably encourages a built-in bias towards proposing attractive compensation packages for the top decision-makers. As Kim Clark has argued, the use of external consultants in essence has created the Lake Wobegon effect—"in Lake Wobegon, everyone is above average."[12]

In addition, the compensation consultants and the boardroom compensation committees most commonly employ the use of peer groups and competitive benchmarking to determine what is a "fair market" executive compensation package. In 1992, the SEC instituted a new requirement in which publicly held companies had to report how much their CEOs were paid. While the intention was to create greater transparency around executive pay, this requirement also created a transparent peer group for the benchmarking of compensation.[13] In this case, the peer group employed by the compensation consultants was executives in companies within the same industry and of a similar size. What most boards attempt to do is to keep executive compensation at par or above the median level of the industry peer group. This benchmarking, however, is further contributing to compensation excesses. For example, research discovered that CEOs who are paid below the median level in total compensation of their peer group received pay increases that are twice as large relative to the raises received by CEOs who are paid above the median of their peers.[14] These raises were not only greater in percentage terms but also in absolute dollars. The researchers further discovered that large compensation increases for executives paid below the median of their peer group occurred even when their companies had, on average, worse accounting and stock price performance than their peers.

Romanticizing of the CEO Role

Organizational members, the public, and the media are subject to a psychological phenomenon which is known as "The Romance of Leadership." This well documented phenomenon reveals that human beings desire to attribute much of the control of an organization to a single individual—that being the senior-most leader. Whether or not this individual is actually in control is irrelevant. We simply want to believe they are. The popular hero myths of society further reinforce this stereotype with their emphasis on a single actor who triumphs over daunting challenges.

As Jim Meindl and his colleagues have pointed out, this "romancing" phenomenon is the product of the fact that most organizational events involve multiple determinants and therefore are too complex and difficult to fully comprehend.[15] Members of an organization and interested outsiders, however, want to make sense of this complexity. Because senior leaders are the most visible and have a formal position of authority, there is a strong tendency to attribute the cause of organizational outcomes directly to their actions. In other leadership research, Gary Yukl points out that this process of attribution also reflects societal biases towards explaining outcomes in terms of the rational actions of human beings in contrast to random events or larger forces.[16] Underpinning this belief is the assumption that organizations are themselves largely rational, goal-oriented systems that are seeking to meet the needs of their members and society. Individuals in senior leadership positions come to symbolize the controlling or guiding forces behind this promise of the organization. This in turn encourages organizational members to overemphasize the personal characteristics of their leader and to minimize the situational factors when searching for explanations of outcomes.[17]

This phenomenon of "romancing" is particularly apparent in the press, in business books, and in the financial community where there is a singular focus on the statements and actions of CEOs to explain the successful performance of companies. The dynamic of romancing CEO leadership became particularly pronounced in the 1990s when a large number of "celebrity CEOs" appeared—from Jeff Bezos of Amazon to John Chambers of Cisco to Herb Kelleher of Southwest Airlines to Jack Welch of General Electric. While this attribution does not capture the reality that hundreds or thousands of individuals are actually managing and leading complex organizations, it serves to skew executive compensation decisions. After all, if the organization, the financial community, and the media deeply hold an assumption that a single individual in the CEO role can profoundly influence the performance of an organization, there should be no hesitation in ensuring that person is handsomely compensated. It is imperative to keep them highly motivated and to ensure they remain with the firm rather than depart to a competitor.

Executive Narcissism and Entitlement

At the top of corporations, it is not uncommon to find individuals who are highly narcissistic. Michael Maccoby even argues that there has been a pronounced change in the personality of today's senior business leaders towards greater narcissism.[18] Executives tend to be strongly ambitious and achievement-oriented individuals—qualities lending themselves to a strongly narcissistic personality. This generation of executives is accustomed to a great deal of attention from the media and Wall Street feeding into a sense of self-importance. Narcissists in general fall prey to the romancing of leadership assuming that they are indeed "leading" the enterprise and that much of the firm's success can be directly attributed to their actions. Highly narcissistic individuals also tend to have an intense competitive drive constantly benchmarking everything and everyone.[19] These qualities reveal themselves in executive compensation. For example, it is not uncommon to hear executives rationalize their pay packages by comparing them to those of sports figures or entertainment celebrities who receive multi-million dollar pay contracts. They argue that their own contributions as business leaders overseeing organizations that are providing essential goods and services for the public are far more important than those of the celebrities. Therefore they deserve comparable if not higher rewards. As highly competitive individuals, executives often rationalize their pay and perks using the "equity theory" of compensation, which is most evident in the benchmarking of peer groups. So, for example, they might argue "Eugene Grace of Bethlehem Steel received a $1.2 million stock payout this year. My company is just as big, and so I deserve $1.2 million. Actually I think I'm better than he is, I probably deserve $1.5 million." For instance, I am aware of other executives who rationalize their perks as imperatives to the successful performance of their job. One CEO argued that she required a personal chef as an essential perk. She explained that she did not have time to go down to the cafeteria on the first floor of the building given the demands on her time. Her use of a personal chef would ensure that her day was spent more efficiently. Moreover, as the CEO, she was so valuable that any chance of food poisoning needed to be minimized. By having a chef she could control the quality of her food as well as control her diet and therefore her health.

Dennis Kozlowski, the former CEO of Tyco, was asked why he considered certain personal expenses as ones that he could deduct from the company. He had a very simple rationalization—"We were all about growth. It took thirty-seven million dollars in expenses to affect our earnings even by one percent." James Steward commented "This [rationalization] became a recurring theme: no matter how expensive (his expenditures on company perks) in absolute terms, the costs were insignificant as a percentage of Tyco's revenues and profits."[20]

Notions of the Public Corporation

Throughout the twentieth century, there have been two distinct but conflicting conceptualizations of the public corporation. One is the *property conception*; the other is the *social entity conception*.[21] Under the property conception, the corporation is the private property of the owners or shareholders. Corporate directors are agents of the owners, and it is their role to dutifully advance the financial aims of the "owners." The corporation's purpose is to enrich shareholders. In sharp contrast, the conception of the corporation as a social entity treats the organization as an institution with multiple constituencies. The corporation is no longer simply a private entity responsible solely to its owners but rather it is accountable to the public. It not only serves its community but also has an obligation to act as a model corporate citizen.

Throughout the nineteenth as well as the early and late twentieth century, the property conception has been the dominant conception of the corporation. A pivotal law case, the 1919 Michigan Supreme Court, *Dodge v. Ford Motor Co.* case, epitomized this viewpoint.[22] In their capacity as shareholders, the Dodge brothers had sued the Ford Motor Company arguing that the corporation did not have shareholder welfare as its principal concern. The impetus for the suit was a decision by Henry Ford to suspend indefinitely dividend payments and instead to reinvest some $58 million in company profits so that the company could lower the price of products and to expand the company's business. While Mr Ford had argued that the purpose of a corporation was to produce good products inexpensively, to provide employment, and only "incidentally to make money," the Dodge brothers contested this viewpoint arguing that the shareholders were the owners of the enterprise and that they were entitled to a portion of the accumulated profits. The Michigan Supreme Court sided with the Dodge brothers and ordered Ford to restore the dividends. Underlying its decision, the court highlighted a principal assumption: "A business corporation is organized and carried on primarily for the profit of the stockholders. The powers of the directors are to be employed for that end."[23]

The social entity conception of the corporation first appears in the late nineteenth century with the emergence of the modern business enterprise. At that time, the "owners" of the modern corporation were increasingly outside investors (rather than the entrepreneurial founders) who could and did, easily and at little cost, move funds from company to company.[24] In addition, they were fragmented, which simply reinforced the fact that it was easier to sell than to intervene when top management was ineffective. As control of the corporation shifted towards professional managers, the expertise and freedom of this group to act were soon seen as critical ingredients in shaping the success of the modern day business enterprise. It was felt that the investment maximizing aims of shareholders should take a back seat to the seemingly longer term, value creation aims of professional management. While the contributors of capital were due an attractive rate of return on their investment, there were other constituents to serve—customers, employees, and the community. No longer were directors solely beholden to shareholders but rather they had to balance with management the frequently conflicting claims of the corporation's many constituencies. In turn, the board of directors' duties went beyond "assuring investors a fair return, to include a duty of loyalty in some sense to all those interested in or affected by the corporation."[25]

One can imagine that under the social entity conception, executive compensation would be strongly moderated by a need to distribute company wealth more widely to the employees and the community and to reinvest in the firm. It would be difficult to imagine a CEO paying him or herself excessive amounts of pay since the primary metric or rationale for pay does not rest upon shareholder value. Hoarding large sums of money for oneself would not comfortably align with an organization whose mission is a larger social purpose.

While the property and social entity notions of the corporation have co-existed without a great deal of debate for most of the twentieth century, the takeover movement of the 1980s pushed board directors towards the property conception.[26] For example, when most if not all of the shareholders wished to sell control of the company, whose interests were the directors to promote and protect—shareholders or management? How could a board member turn down a hostile cash tender offer when investors saw it as a wise return on their investment? After all, how could directors turn down a significant financial gain for investors using arguments that future returns might be better?[27] Directors soon found themselves in conflict over their allegiances. The takeover environment had created a situation where it was extremely difficult for directors to convince shareholders that realizing an immediate, substantial profit on their investment was a bad idea. The property conception regained the upper hand. Shareholder value became the central mantra in many boardrooms.

In the 1990s, however, the tug-of-war was intensified when there was a sharp divergence between the decisions of the court and shifts in the market place. Setting the precedent, the Delaware Supreme Court in the *Time Warner* case decided that corporate directors could indeed take actions that prevented shareholders from realizing an immediate high premium offer if they are acting in pursuit of goals aimed at the corporation's long-term welfare.[28] In essence, the judgment implicitly recognized the social entity conception. Following this decision, legislative acts were passed in 28 jurisdictions in the late 1980s that in one form or another authorized a board of directors to weigh the interests of all stakeholders in their decision-making.[29] The states of Connecticut, Indiana, and Pennsylvania were especially clear in stating that directors were not obligated to give a controlling effect to any one constituency or interest. Maximizing the financial interests of shareholders was not the only core duty of a corporate director; rather directors and senior managers had to walk a tight-wire between their responsibility to investors in the form of stock market performance and to the employees and community in terms of social responsibilities.[30]

Despite this favorable legal environment, the concentrations of power in today's institutional shareholders and a highly competitive global economy have continued to exert an enormous pull on directors—pulling them towards their obligations to investors. No similar pressures remind them of the obligation to other stakeholders. As a result, most directors of publicly traded companies see shareholder value rather than social responsibility as their primary performance metric. Moreover, shareholder value can be easily and "objectively" measured by returns on equity valuations. This is not the case with contributions to a "social community" where the notion of "returns" are far more elusive in their measurement. As a result, the property conception remains the dominant one in America today. As a consequence, this paradigm of the corporation can to a large extent explain why executives and their boards in the 1980s and 1990s pegged executive compensation to shareholder returns. This in turn encouraged the exorbitant pay packages of those decades.

HOW WE CAN STRENGTHEN THE INTEGRITY OF THE EXECUTIVE COMPENSATION BARREL

Any attempt at building greater integrity in the executive compensation barrel will require a multi-pronged approach. For example, it will not be enough to rely on the self-policing efforts of boards themselves or on a set of government regulations. Moreover, compensation excess will likely be a recurring problem whenever booming equity markets appear. The temptation to profit from a boom is always great. Individuals and organizations have an enormous capacity to be "creative" when it comes to finding loopholes around existing rules and regulations or creating new means to profit from "good times." Greed is an indomitable human force, and capitalist societies are by their ideology reluctant to place serious constraints on the rights of individuals to amass wealth. That said, there have been a number of recent proposals and initiatives that can help to strengthen the integrity of the compensation barrel and restore credibility to the executive leadership of public corporations. These include: (1) full disclosure of actual compensation packages, (2) changes in the tax code, (3) changes in compensation practices themselves, and (4) shared leadership in the boardroom. We begin with the issue of transparency and the full disclosure of compensation.

Transparency for Outside Shareholders

Part of the dilemma for shareholders outside of the executive suite is a lack of detailed information on the actual compensation packages of company executives. Therefore one remedy to rein in excessive compensation would be to make that information completely transparent. Shareholders could then decide at annual meetings whether they approved of proposed compensation packages or not. In a recent *Wall Street Journal* article, Arthur Levitt, a former chairman of the SEC, offered a number of strong recommendations that could transform what is today a still opaque process into one where shareholders and the financial community could make highly informed judgments about the fairness of executive pay packages.[31] A significant first step would be for boards to disclose other forms of compensation which have been disguised to date. The use of corporate jets and automobiles, club memberships, loans, and retirement packages all need to be disclosed to shareholders. Current SEC rules do not require corporations to reveal whether compensation is performance-based and if it is, what the performance triggers are. These need to be made transparent. If the metrics for performance are changed by the board, these should be considered a critical event and therefore be fully disclosed. Levitt has suggested that corporations provide shareholders with a table that includes all benefits including perks highlighting their actual monetary value, deferred compensation, retirement benefits, and then a column that discloses the total value of compensation. These data would also be benchmarked against the same compensation metrics of their peers in the industry. If the compensation relative to performance is greater than peers, the board compensation committee would be required to provide a written justification for the difference.

Changes in the Tax Code

One vehicle to influence executive compensation through government intervention is through changes in the tax code. The current code permits corporations to deduct a "reasonable allowance for salaries and other compensation." There is no definition, however, of what constitutes "reasonable." In essence, corporations are deducting fully executive salaries, benefits, and perks as normal business expenses. There was an attempt to close this loophole through legislation in the early 1990s that capped the deductibility of executive compensation to a maximum of $1 million. But the law only capped non-performance-based salaries and so corporations passed resolutions making compensation above $1 million "performance-based" with the bulk of this in stock options and bonuses linked to performance. In 2003, new accounting regulations were passed which require that mega-grants of stock options be expensed on income statements starting in 2004. As a result, a number of public corporations such as Microsoft have dispensed completely with stock options. The Financial Accounting Standards Board has issued a new accounting standard for stock options which is supported by the Securities and Exchange Commission. This standard requires after June of 2005 that most US publicly-traded companies treat all options granted to employees as compensation expenses.[32]

That said, other forms of compensation—salaries, bonuses, restricted stock, long term payout, and assorted perks—have not come under regulatory scrutiny. As a matter of fact, the most popular alternative to stock options which are grants of restricted stock increased by 17.3 percent in 2003 to a median of $2 million at Fortune 500 companies.[33] The SEC itself has not required any major improvements in executive compensation disclosure.

Changes in Compensation Practices

As evident in this chapter, the most hotly debated dimension of the executive pay package has centered on the disbursement of stock or stock options. For example, as noted earlier, the bull market of the 1990s encouraged the widespread use of stock options as an essential part of the executive compensation package. On the one hand, this form of compensation makes great intuitive sense. After all, shareholder returns are measurable and appear to reflect the overall performance of the corporation. That said, what does compensation in equity-based rewards actually foster in terms of executive behavior?

Roger Martin of the University of Toronto argues that stock compensation by itself encourages executives to raise expectations about future, not actual, earnings since these expectations directly lead to higher stock prices. As Martin points out, there are several ways in which managers can build earnings expectations. The slowest and more difficult is to increase real earnings. The most expedient is for the CEO or CFO to hype expectations to the financial community—a popular tactic in the late 1990s. Since the fall of Enron and WorldCom, this tactic, however, has become more difficult to deploy. Wall Street is more skeptical, and financial analysts are under greater pressure to resist such hype. An additional way to inflate earnings expectations is to deploy aggressive accounting to "create" greater earnings—by filling the distribution channels to boost sales or reducing reserves for bad receivables. WorldCom, itself, supposedly classified some $7 billion in expenses as assets. A string of acquisitions can also stimulate earnings growth.[34]

Given this dilemma, Martin has proposed that boards consider abolishing stock-based compensation and in its place substitute bonuses based on real earnings. At a minimum, boards could retain stock options but ensure that they have longer vesting periods.

When it comes to stock options and rewards, Kevin Murphy notes that incentives based on options do *not* mimic the incentives of actual stock ownership despite an intuitive perception that they might.[35] They encourage only stock-price appreciation rather than total shareholder returns since total returns include dividends. Executives rewarded with options have strong incentives to avoid dividends and to prefer share repurchases. Options also have a tendency to encourage riskier investments which could dramatically increase the firm's share value. Lastly, stock options lose their incentive value when the stock price falls below the exercise price and the executive sees little chance of exercising their options. This outcome is often used as justification for repricings of options whenever there are share-price declines. In reality, stock options are at best a weak surrogate for total shareholder returns. That said, if options are employed, a more effective way to link them to share price performance would be to set their exercise price above the market price when they are issued. For example, IBM has issued its top 300 executives options with exercise prices 10 percent above the market price of the firm's stock. In the past, the company had issued them at market price.[36]

In the ideal case, companies would simply self-impose stricter compensation requirements rather than have their hands forced by changes in tax codes or government regulations. For example, in 2003, General Electric instituted a tough pay-for-performance pay plan for its CEO Jeffrey Immelt. He was granted 250,000 "performance share units" (each unit is equivalent to a share of stock in value) which at the time had a market value of $7.5 million. He receives half of them if he is able to grow GE's total shareholder return so that it meets or beats the S&P 500's returns between 2003 and 2007. He receives the other half if he grows GE's operating cash flow by 10 percent a year during that same period.[37]

In addition to the compensation of the executives themselves, any reform in current practices would need to address board director compensation. In research by Donal Byard and Ying Li on executive pay, it was discovered that a heavier reliance on stock options as compensation for independent board directors more tightly aligned their behavior to the interests of top management rather than shareholders.[38] For example, they found that the granting of options involved greater timing opportunism when directors on the compensation committee received a greater proportion of stock options in their compensation package. Timing opportunism involves the ability to profit relatively quickly from the granting of options by issuing them either just before positive news or just after bad news. This problem is compounded by the fact that a significant percentage of director compensation is now in stock options. It may be time to return to director compensation without options, or else option arrangements that are structured to preclude timing opportunism. For example, timing opportunism might be addressed by spreading option grants to the CEO over the course of a year in equal monthly installments versus the current practice of a single grant once a year.[39]

Lastly, it is important to reconsider the "performance standards" that are employed for compensation decisions. For example, the primary determinant for bonuses is accounting profits. However, as Kevin Murphy notes, there are two dilemmas with this metric. Accounting profits are inherently backward-looking and short term. Executives can enhance accounting profits with actions that harm the long-term profitability of the firm. For example, they may cut R&D spending or manipulate profits shifting earnings across periods or adjustments in accruals. Performance standards based on budgets or prior-year performance can create additional problems. It is possible to "sandbag" the budget process or simply promote incremental performance improvements to beat last year's performance. Generally speaking, external performance standards are more objective measures—for example standards based on the cost of capital or standards based on the performance of an industry peer group.[40]

Boardroom Leadership Remedies

Though the idea of a separate or non-executive boardroom chair has been circulating around for at least a decade, only a small minority of companies have adopted the idea. The slow inroads made by the practice suggest strong resistance to the idea. This, however, has not stopped governance commissions and activist pension funds from promoting the idea. In its study of board best practices, the Blue Ribbon commission on Director Professionalism, a prestigious 28-member group created by the National Association of Corporate Directors and headed by noted governance specialist Ira Millstein, concluded: "Boards should consider formally designating a non-executive chairman or other independent board leader." An equally high-profile group, the Committee on Corporate Governance in Canada, sponsored by the Toronto Stock Exchange, made a similar recommendation: "In our view, the board should be able to function independently of management . . . Perhaps the simplest means for implementing this guideline is for the board to appoint a strong non-executive chair of the board whose principal responsibility is managing the board of directors."[41]

The Principal arguments in favor of a separate on non-executive chair have to do with enhancing the ability of the board to monitor the CEO's performance and leadership. It is assumed that directors will feel more at ease to raise challenges to the CEO if the board is led by a fellow director. In addition, fund managers often assume that a CEO seeks first to serve themselves and secondarily the shareholders. A non-executive chair whose mandate is to enhance shareholder value is less likely to be compromised.

There is one important caveat to this suggestion. If the separate board chair is *a former CEO* of the firm, then there is not a genuine independent and objective counter-balance to the CEO since the chairperson is most likely to have chosen the CEO him/herself. A CEO whose board chair is the company's former CEO describes the dilemma:

> If he [the board chair] has been involved in selecting the new guy to be CEO as was true in my case, the chair is in a kind of funny position of not being able to be critical of the new guy for some time. He's got to preserve the honeymoon aspect of it. If a new guy comes in and wants to change anything, there is also the unavoidable explicit criticism of the old guy insofar as how he did things. There is an awkward tension set up between the new guy and the old guy that results in an awful lot of senatorial dancing around the issue of why these problems existed before and why the old guy didn't do anything about them. If the new guy comes in and wants to dramatically change direction, he has the old guy who is lurking there either biting his tongue or, heaven forbid, arguing with him about it. If the new guy wants to kill some of the pet projects of old guy, it is an awkward situation. Personally, I believe the retiring CEO is "in the way" in the simplest of terms and should go out gracefully. If the new CEO wants to call on the wisdom of the retired CEO he is certainly free to do that without the old guy being on the board.[42]

It is important, therefore, that the board chair not be someone who is the former CEO. As importantly, it must be an individual who is highly admired by the directors themselves and who has the self-confidence and industry knowledge to take a leadership role especially during times of trouble. They must also be someone who can be dedicated to following both the company and the industry closely. In addition, the non-executive chairperson should not hold board directorships elsewhere give the role's potentially high demands. Nor should the company's CEO sit on the chair's board if the chair him/herself is a CEO. In general, however, standing CEOs of other companies are not appropriate given the normal demands on their time as a standing CEO of another organization. With this from of counter-balancing board leadership, the system of "checks and balances" is further reinforced when it comes to abuses in the area of executive compensation.

CONCLUSION

In the ideal world, boards would take it upon themselves to impose stricter means of both evaluating and rewarding executive compensation. Government regulations also need to play a role in the process. Sarbanes Oxley is one such step in that direction. Finally, shareholders must become more active participants or at the least overseers of executive compensation practices. Pension funds with their longer term investment horizons and large holdings in individual companies have the greatest incentive to reshape executive compensation. One would also hope that executives would themselves come to appreciate how perceptions of excessive compensation have hurt their own credibility as leaders. A greater degree of restraint on their part will go a long way to enhance public perceptions. There is some reason to be hopeful. A recent survey of 2004 compensation data for CEOs of large US companies shows a rise of just 5 percent compared with increases of 7.2 percent in 2003 and 10 percent in 2002.[43] This is very promising news in light of the fact that 2004 appears to be one of the most profitable years for US corporations. Moreover, there is a continued shift away from option schemes towards restricted stock awards. We may be in a transition period at the end of which executive compensation levels may come back to earth.

NOTES

1. Boyle, M. (2004), 2003 Executive Compensation, *Fortune*, vol. 149, issue 9, page 123, May 3.
2. Ibid.
3. Steward, J. (2003), Spend! Spend! Spend!, *The New Yorker*, Feb. 17 and 24, pp. 132-47.
4. Clark, K. (2003), At the Center of the Corporate Scandal: Where Do We Go from Here? Presentation to the National Press Club, Feb. 26.
5. Arbogast, G., Grundig, J., Peirano, L., and Dayton, T. (2002), CEO Compensation Versus Performance: A Qualitative Analysis, paper presented to the Academy of Business Disciplines, Fort Myers Beach, FL, November.
6. Ibid.
7. Walcott, J. (2004) Today's College Freshmen Party Less, Volunteer More. Christian Science Monitor, online edition retrieved from http://www.csmonitor.com/2004/0203/p14s01-legn.htm
8. Conger, J.A., Lawler, E.E., and Finegold, D. (2001), *Corporate Boards: New Strategies for Adding Value at the Top*, San Francisco, CA: Jossey-Bass.

9. Binmore, K. (1994), *Playing Fair*, Cambridge, MA and London: The MIT Press.
10. Levitt, A. (2004), Money, Money, Money, *The Wall Street Journal*, Nov. 22, p. A14.
11. Clark, op. cit.
12. Ibid.
13. Arbogast, G., et al., op. cit., p. 3.
14. Bizjak, J.M., Lemmon, M.L., and Naveen, L. (2000), Has the Use of Peer Groups Contributed to Higher Levels of Executive Compensation? Working Paper, Department of Finance, Portland State University.
15. Meindl, J.R., Ehrlich, S.B. and Dukerich, J.M. (1985), The Romance of Leadership, *Administrative Science Quarterly*, 30, 521–51.
16. Yukl, G. (1994), *Leadership in Organizations* (3rd edn), Englewood Cliffs, NJ: Prentice Hall.
17. Meindl et al., op. cit.
18. Maccoby, M. (2000), Narcissistic Leaders: The Incredible Pros, the Inevitable Cons, *Harvard Business Review*, Jan-Feb, pp. 69–77.
19. Ibid. p. 75.
20. Steward, J. (2003), p. 137.
21. Allen, W.T. (1992, April 13), Our Schizophrenic Conception of the Business Corporation, Paper presented to the Samuel and Ronnie Heyman Center on Corporate Governance, Cardozo School of Law, Yeshiva University, New York, Published in *The Cardozo Law Review*, 1992, 14, 261 and retrieved from electronic database.
22. Ibid.
23. Ibid.
24. Ibid.
25. Ibid.
26. Ibid.
27. Ibid.
28. Ibid.
29. Ibid.
30. Ibid.
31. Levitt, A. (2004), Money, Money, Money, *Wall Street Journal*, Nov. 22, page A14.
32. *Financial Times* (2004), Tougher Options, December 20, p. 16.
33. Boyle, M., op. cit.
34. Martin, R. (January 1, 2003), Taking Stock, *Harvard Business Review*, p. 34.
35. Murphy, K. (1999), Executive Compensation, Working Paper, Marshall School of Business, University of Southern California, p. 18.
36. *Financial Times* (2004), op. cit., p. 16.
37. Boyle, M. (2004), 2003 Executive Compensation Report, *Fortune*, May 3, vol. 149, issue 9, p. 123.
38. Morgenson, G. (2004), Are Options Seducing Directors Too?, *New York Times*, Dec. 12, p. 1 (section 3).
39. Ibid., p. 4.
40. Murphy, K., op. cit.
41. Conger, Lawler, and Finegold, op. cit.
42. Ibid.
43. Roberts, D. (2004), Chief Executives Stem Rises in Their Salaries to Avoid Embarrassment, *Financial Times*, Dec. 13, p. 1.

IN THE MONEY: A SPECIAL REPORT ON EXECUTIVE PAY

from *The Economist*

IN THE MONEY

Executives have enjoyed an astonishing pay bonanza. Edward Carr explains why most of them deserved it.

Right and left, Americans and Europeans, stockmarket investors and antiglobalisation campaigners all share one belief: top managers pay themselves too much. The evidence seems to bear them out. For almost half a century the ratio of top executives' pay to median earnings was as smooth as a boardroom table. Then, starting in America in the 1980s and a few years later elsewhere, this ratio began to increase before taking off exponentially and peaking around the turn of the millennium (see chart 1 later in this article). At that point the worker on an American shop floor was earning in a year roughly what his boss on the top floor took home each evening.

Most people think they know what lay behind this. Greedy chief executives, abetted by weak, sycophantic boards, gorged themselves at the expense of savers—more often than not the very pension and mutual-fund investors who, as workers, had seen their salaries and benefit packages fail to grow.

To add to the grievance, many executives did not seem to deserve such rewards. Extraordinary pay for great performance is fine, it is routinely said. But many executives have been paid a fortune for presiding over mediocrity. The Corporate Library, an American corporate-governance consultancy, last year identified 11 large and well known but poorly governed companies, including AT&T, Merck and Time Warner, where the chief executive had been paid at least $15m a year for two successive years even as the company's shares had underperformed. Robert Nardelli received a $210m pay-off when he lost his job earlier this month even though the shares of his company, Home Depot, fell slightly during his six years in charge. Carly Fiorina, ejected from Hewlett-Packard almost $180m better off—including a severance payment of $21.6m—after a lacklustre tenure as chief executive, let it be known in her autobiography that money was not important to her. Not everyone believed her.

Unappreciated

No wonder the standing of executives has fallen so low. A poll for Bloomberg and the *Los Angeles Times* last year found that 80% of Americans thought executives were overpaid. Even those sympathetic to business are unsympathetic to its leaders. In a second-year class at Harvard Business School quizzed by Ira Kay, head of the compensation practice at Watson Wyatt, a consultancy, two-thirds of the students were critical of bosses' pay. In a survey, Mr Kay discovered that fully 90% of institutional investors—ie, companies' owners—thought executives were "dramatically overpaid". So did 60% of their directors. That is quite a confession, given that directors are the very people who decide how much managers should earn.

But the diatribe against executives is mistaken. Poor governance alone cannot readily explain some of the most striking features of pay over the past few years. To dwell on the undoubted failures of governance is to gloss over the economic and corporate shifts that have been the main causes of the extraordinary rise in top managers' earning power.

National pay schemes vary greatly, and America remains ahead of, and more extreme than, other countries. (That, together with the superior quality of American data and the research they support, is why much of the material in this report is drawn from the United States.) But over the past decade all markets have displayed the same pattern: widening gaps between managers and workers and greater emphasis on long-term incentives. It is hard to see how this could have been caused by universally poor governance across so many different systems.

The chief mistake of the past 15 years was the granting of too many share options to too many people on terms that were too generous. That was costly and unwarranted, but it stemmed more from foolish accounting and tax policies supercharged by bull-market mania than from a sinister plot hatched in the executive suite.

This is not to deny the abuses and downright crookery that have marred executive pay. Even now, dozens of senior managers are under investigation for "backdating" their share options—illegally manipulating the timing of grants to increase the likelihood of a payment. Nor is it to assert that all is right in the boardroom. Indeed, the case for reform is strong.

It is, however, to argue that popular opinion is wrong. The lion's share of the executives' bonanza was deserved—in the sense that shareholders got value for the money they handed over. Those sums on the whole bought and motivated the talent that managed businesses during the recent golden age of productivity growth and profits. Many managers have done extremely well over the past few years; but so, too, have most shareholders.

Between 1993 and 2003 the total pay of the top five executives in the Standard & Poor's 1,500, which accounts for roughly 80% of listed American companies by value, amounted to some $350 billion, according to Lucian Bebchuk and Yaniv Grinstein, of Harvard and Cornell Universities. The share of earnings consumed by those people's pay rose from 5.2% in the first five years of that period to 8.1% in the second five. And this is without counting the value of pensions, which can boost the total by as much as a third.

That is a lot of money, to be sure—though not quite as much as it sometimes seems. The "average" pay that is often quoted, and which is used as the basis for comparison with the "average worker", is the arithmetic mean. Chart 1 on the next page, from a different study, shows the average earnings of the top three executives all the way back to the 1930s. Whereas mean pay at the peak was 320 times average earnings, the median pay was "only" 120 times. In 2000–03 their mean annual pay was $8.5m and the median $4.1m. The median is a better measure than the mean because the mean for those top three is skewed by a few huge payments, often to company founders or family managers who are not standard executives.

Although overpaying a chief executive on its own is unlikely to bankrupt a company, there are other reasons to care about top pay. One is incentives. The role of pay is not to get executives to work harder (most are workaholics already, toiling towards an appointment with the heart surgeon), but to recruit good managers and get them to take difficult decisions. Shutting a subsidiary, sacrificing a pet project or forgoing a tempting acquisition is not much fun. Without the spur of high pay managers tend to avoid such things.

Pay is also outsiders' most visible test of a board's capacity to monitor a company's executives. Mr Bebchuk, a fierce critic of the developments of the past few years, declares that "pay is not isolated: it is a classic board function important beyond just dollars." If he is right that boards are unable to control pay, then poor governance is leaving managers free to use the company's assets for their own benefit. Excessive pay "undermines the notion that we can trust investment to managers and directors", says Nell Minow, head of the Corporate Library. It becomes the justification for wide-ranging governance reform.

Lastly, executive pay is the most controversial aspect of the increasing inequality that has appeared over the past couple of decades. As the topmost echelon appears to be capturing a huge share of new wealth, everyone else's wages have barely shifted. This would be disruptive even if managers were felt to deserve what they are paid. It would be explosive if high pay continued to be seen as a swindle. Ultimately, businesses function with the blessing of workers, shareholders, customers and voters. If business leaders are universally seen as immoral and grasping, cynicism and mistrust will flourish and choke enterprise. Jeb Bush, a Republican former governor of Florida and no enemy of business, gave warning last year that "if the rewards for CEOs and their teams become extraordinarily high with no link to performance, then it undermines people's confidence in capitalism."

Across the rich economies, governments have begun to demand disclosure of pay and new corporate-governance codes. In America's Congress Charles Grassley, a Republican and former head of the Senate committee on finance, is calling for boards to "do their job" instead of being "in hock" to managers. Barney Frank, the new Democratic head of the House financial-services committee, is likely to introduce a bill on pay.

All this makes business people extremely nervous. The difficulty is that they find it hard to discuss pay. (Imagine the talking point: "I am worth $100m because . . .") Their case is seldom heard or examined. But "it is a societal problem," says Jay Lorsch, of Harvard Business School. "If the business community doesn't do something, we are going to get more pressure from the federal government—and we don't want that."

The arguments about pay are subtle and complex. They start with that moment in the 1980s when the long-established relationship between workers' and managers' pay began to break down. What could explain such a turning point?

THE STOCKPOT

The story of pay is largely the story of share options

As head of RJR Nabisco in the 1980s, Ross Johnson used the corporate jet for his pet dog, listed as "G. Shepherd" on the passenger list. He employed maids on the company account and put sports stars on the payroll. Such were the trappings of power for the imperial chief executive before raiders stormed the citadel.

Private-equity outfits such as Kohlberg Kravis Roberts (KKR) changed all that. By rising up against inefficiency and waste in the corporations of the 1980s, they started the ideas that led to today's pattern of pay.

At the time the raiders were condemned for their greed. Looking back, however, what stands out is their largesse. They paid huge premiums on listed-company valuations. KKR, for instance, offered RJR's shareholders $12 billion more than their company's stockmarket value of $13 billion. Shortly before the KKR bid Mr Johnson was featured in *Fortune* magazine as a paragon of corporate leadership. The bid was a brutal demonstration of how the supposedly best had fallen short.

Buy-outs were a solution to a failing that has plagued the public limited company. One way to think of managers is as "agents" paid by the shareholders, who own the company, to act as stewards on their behalf. Agents do not share the same interests as the principals who employ them. They may, for instance, seek to use the company's assets for their own private benefit and shirk unpleasant decisions. So the corporation has devised mechanisms to mitigate these "agency costs". Managers agree with owners to submit themselves to auditors, to answer to boards and to take part of their pay in the form of bonuses. All these things help to ensure that they act more in owners' interests.

But the system had its flaws. By the 1970s boards had become the creatures of management. There was minimal disclosure. Shareholders found it expensive to enforce their wishes. Rather than spending money to control wayward executives, they sold the shares and moved on, leaving managers almost unmonitored.

Free to spend other people's money, managers and directors squandered it. Instead of returning cash to shareholders, they kept it in the company. Businesses such as RJR typically spent too much money on pet projects, ill-advised diversification, obsolete operations, extravagant indulgences and pointless research.

The raiders' antidote was ingenious. By loading up the company with debt that needed servicing, the buy-out firms in effect took the decision about what to do with free cashflow away from managers and restored it to the capital markets. By taking the company private, they returned control of the board to the owners. And—what matters here—by motivating and monitoring managers, they got them to take tough, commercially astute decisions.

This analysis was articulated by, among others, Michael Jensen, an American academic, in a series of brilliant articles later gathered into a couple of books. The lessons were eagerly embraced by listed-company investors looking to emulate the raiders' results. Executives had been paid like bureaucrats, not just in that they were more or less given a job for life, but also because they were rewarded mostly for making their companies bigger rather than more profitable. Whereas executives in public companies earned about $3 for each extra $1,000 of profits, managers in the buy-out firms earned $64, according to Steven Kaplan, now of the University of Chicago.

In a world transformed by Ronald Reagan and Margaret Thatcher, it was time to pay managers more like entrepreneurs. The share option, until then chiefly a way of avoiding tax, began to be used as a device to make managers think like owners. Because an option confers the right to buy a share at a set price, it should motivate the manager to push the share price as far above that threshold as possible. A share, in theory, is the present value of all of a company's future dividends, so the long-term value of the company will go up. As it turned out—and as this report will explain later—this elegant solution to short-termism created its own set of problems. But it certainly motivated managers to try to maximise profits.

Options were handed out in astonishing quantities. Indeed, the story behind the growth of pay in the 1990s is really the story of the option. In 1992 S&P 500 companies issued options worth $11 billion. At its peak in 2000 the number reached $119 billion, though by 2002 it had fallen back to $71 billion (all in 2002 dollars).

Survival of the fittest

The new spirit of "shareholder value", as it became known, has brought about a change in the job of chief executive. For a start it has steadily become more precarious. Between 1992 and 1997, according to Mr Kaplan and Bernadette Minton, of Ohio State University, chief executives could expect to last about eight years in the job. Between 1998 and 2005 that fell to six years, and executives from underperforming firms were more likely to have been booted out by boards. The National Association of Corporate Directors and Mercer Delta, a change consultancy, looked at the replacement of 163 chief executives between 2002 and the first half of 2005 and found that a quarter of them were "non-routine"—meaning that the chief executive had been forced out or poached.

The growing tendency to jettison the chief executive may be one reason why boards have increasingly been searching outside the company for a replacement. According to Kevin Murphy, of the University of Southern California, that now happens in about one-third of such searches, compared with only 10% in the 1970s.

In addition, businesses seem to be placing a higher value on general management skills and relatively less on managers' special knowledge of their own company. That is the conclusion of Carola Frydman, of the Sloan School of Management at the Massachusetts Institute of Technology, who with Raven Saks, of the Federal Reserve, did the research on which the chart in the previous article was based. Ms Frydman found that senior executives these days have worked in more firms, have a broader experience within each company and tend to have joined the firm they lead later in their careers. (Business-school professors are also quick to point out that ever more bosses have MBAs.)

All this amounts to a new deal between chief executives and their companies, says Alan Johnson, a pay consultant who specialises in financial services. The job has become "Darwinian", he says. Chief executives are under pressure. They know that if the board does not like them they are out. In turn, executives have become more selfish and less loyal to their companies.

That deal changes the nature of executive pay. Managers will need compensating for taking on the increased risk of losing their job and the shorter tenure that goes with it. The same applies to the risk of losing their job and the shorter tenure that goes with it. The same applies to the risk of taking on options, which are less valuable than cash because they are illiquid and not certain to pay out. Pay will also tend to be inflated by the growth in an outside market for executive talent. When your present employer is the only company likely to offer you a top job, it has a big say in your remuneration. The more other companies are bidding for your talents, the more you can demand. Ask Alan Mulally, wooed away from Boeing last year by Ford, which was in need of a saviour and prepared to pay a saviour's wage.

These changes were magnified by the bull market and in turn probably helped to feed it. Talk about the "entrepreneurial executive" was nothing more than rhetoric, because managers did not actually put their own capital at risk. But it became seductive in those heady years when options-fuelled start-ups were changing the world and the old economy was desperate to prove that it, too, could "get it".

The bull market did more than just increase share values: it also created a source of new demand for executives. Diane Doubleday, a pay consultant at Mercer, recalls how companies in the 1990s struggled to hire talent and keep it. George Shaheen's decision to quit his job as head of Andersen Consulting and join Webvan seems almost quaint now, if only because the dotcom grocer has long since been consigned to the great shopping trolley in the sky. But at the time it sent a shiver through corporate America.

All the while another more general force was pushing up executive pay. As the average firm size increases, so each company must pay its top executives more. When managers control more assets, they can make more of a difference to absolute profits. Hence, in a competitive market full of bigger companies, boards will be prepared to spend more on talent. Using a schematic mathematical model, two American-based European economists, Xavier Gabaix and Augustin Landier, concluded that the sixfold increase in the size of American firms between 1980 and 2003 may account for much of the sixfold increase in managers' pay during that period. Tiny differences between the abilities of top managers could explain large differences in pay. Chart 2, from another study, shows how in historical terms the level of pay is still relatively low in relation to the size of companies.

Had executives exploited lax governance to cash in, you would expect them to have done far better than high-flyers in other professions. Going by Social Security data, executives of non-financial companies represented 20% of the 30,000 or so Americans with the biggest incomes in 1994. But in spite of the huge increase in their pay over the following ten years, executives made up only slightly more of that group in 2004, according to Mr Kaplan and Josh Rauh, also from the University of Chicago. The results from tax-return data indicated a larger increase in the number of executives among the very richest Americans. But even then, the authors conclude, the growing prosperity of the very rich cannot be explained by the growing prosperity of executives alone: other high-flying groups were rapidly getting richer, too. There are fewer rich lawyers than rich executives, but in the decade to 2004 the lawyers joined the richest group at a faster rate. So, too, with financiers, who are both more numerous than they were and more numerous than high-earning executives.

In fact, the typical chief executive of an S&P 500 company, who earned just under $7m in 2005, according to the Corporate Library, must think he is in the wrong job. According to Mr Johnson, the pay consultant, senior investment bankers stood to earn bonuses of $20m-25m in 2006 and top traders $40m-50m. To qualify for Institutional Investor's *Alpha* magazine rankings of the top 25 hedge-fund managers in 2005, you had to earn $130m.

Metering merit

Yet if the level of typical pay is within the bounds set by other professions, what about the pattern? After all, the main idea of the shareholder-value movement was that pay should depend on the company's financial performance.

For an answer, look at a second study by Messrs Kaplan and Rauh. They assembled several groups of companies with similar-sized assets (to allow for the fact that pay depends partly on a company's size) and, within each size-group, sorted the chief executives into ten pay classes. They then took all the executives from the top class in each group and compared their companies' share-price performance with that of their competitors; ditto for the second-to-top class, and so on. Chart 3 on the previous page shows a clear relationship between pay and performance.

Given that managers receive such a large part of their pay in shares, perhaps that should come as no surprise. But it is often suggested that the value of executives' option packages bears no relation to their performance. One reason for this may be a confusion between a manager's target pay and what he actually ends up with. Remember that options have no fixed value: their worth depends on how the share price at the time of the sale compares with the strike price. So assessing the value of someone's options on the day they are granted involves guessing what the underlying shares will one day be sold for, and that number may be quite different from the price actually achieved several years later. If the company has prospered, the options could be worth more than expected; if it has struggled, they may have no value at all. Watson Wyatt found that successful and unsuccessful firms alike grant long-term incentives such as options. However, managers of the top companies ultimately earn three times as much as managers of the laggards.

To sum up the argument so far: executive pay reached an inflection point in the 1980s, when attacks from raiders prompted companies to use options to motivate the chief executive to make profits, punish failure with dismissal and value general management skills more highly. This corresponded with a period of outstanding prosperity in which both top executives and other high-flyers did extremely well. But that story is incomplete. And the more closely you look at what really goes on inside boardrooms, the more incomplete it seems.

SHARED GOALS

Shelly Banjo

Everybody agrees: Top executives should own stock in their own company. The trick is how to get them to do that.

In the early 1990s, companies began establishing guidelines for ownership of their shares by top executives. The idea was simple: to help align the managers' interests with those of shareholders and give executives a powerful incentive to improve performance.

"Like motherhood and apple pie, share ownership gives investors a positive feeling," says Steven Van Putten, the East region practice leader of Watson Wyatt Worldwide Inc.'s executive-compensation consulting practice.

But even as more companies establish such guidelines, many continue to wrestle with how to ensure compliance by executives who may be wary of investing too much of their personal capital in one company, even if it is their own employer.

A number of companies threaten to penalize executives who don't achieve targeted stock-ownership levels within a certain period. However, such rules tend not to be strictly enforced, and some compensation experts argue that penalties can strain the relationship between a company and its executives. In a new twist, a handful of employers are instead offering incentives—in the form of cash or additional shares—to encourage executives to achieve stock-ownership goals.

According to Equilar Inc., a Redwood Shores, Calif., executive-compensation research firm, about three-quarters of Fortune 250 companies surveyed in 2006 had executive stock-ownership guidelines. Typically, the guidelines require or strongly encourage chief executives and other senior managers to invest between one and 10 times their annual base salary in their company's stock, within three to five years of employment. Others establish a fixed number of shares or a dollar amount as the target.

MAKING THEM PAY

Many companies have established procedures to force executives to reach their targets. According to Equilar, nearly one-third of the Fortune 250 companies with ownership guidelines require executives to hold all or a portion of the shares acquired in any stock awards or from the exercise of stock options until they reach required stock-ownership levels—or at least for a specified period beyond the exercise or vesting date of the shares. Some companies require cash incentive payments such as annual bonuses to be dedicated to buying company shares until the target is met.

At Pittsburgh-based chemicals company PPG Industries Inc., officers are expected to meet ownership requirements within five years of taking a position, absent unusual circumstances. If executives miss their target, they must receive 20% of their annual cash bonus in the form of PPG common stock until they meet the guidelines. In addition, those shares can't be sold for a period of two to five years, depending on the level of stock ownership of the executive.

According to PPG's 2007 proxy statement, 20%, or about $97,000, of Senior Vice President J. Rich Alexander's annual incentive award for 2006 was paid out in 1,420 shares on Feb. 28, 2007. Mr. Alexander has been an officer at the company since 2002 and a senior vice president since May 2005. "This is part of our program . . . and a good way to keep executives engaged and motivated for the success of the company," Mr. Alexander said through a company spokesman.

REWARDING PURCHASES

Other companies have begun to try another approach: rewarding executives who meet or exceed their targeted holdings, especially if they are able to reach them early.

At Sunoco Inc., for example, executives who exceed their stock-ownership targets are eligible to receive their performance-based stock awards in cash. Dominion Resources Inc., a utility based in Richmond, Va., takes a more proactive approach. To help executives achieve their target holdings, Dominion matches 25% of their purchases of the utility's shares—if the executives participate in the company's "Tool Kit" programs for stock purchases. These programs allow executives to exchange annual bonuses for shares or acquire shares directly from the company rather than going through a broker.

Tom Wohlfarth, chief accounting officer at Dominion Resources, says the company's stock-ownership guidelines help "officers get in the game." He became an officer in 2004, and in 2006 he started putting $2,000 a month toward purchasing Dominion shares. In 2007, he was promoted to senior vice president and now must acquire an additional 10,000 shares in three to five years, for a total of 20,000 shares. "I'm starting to get close now," he says. "I hope to achieve that in the next year or so."

Mr. Wohlfarth says incentives are better than penalties for encouraging stock purchases, because what companies "really want is somebody to have a positive attitude toward reaching the guidelines and feel this is a team effort," rather than being in fear they might be punished.

Some companies provide matching stock when executives hit their targets. At San Francisco-based PG&E Corp., when executives invest toward their annual ownership milestone the company rewards them with shares totaling 20% of their investment. Executives who buy more than the targeted amount of PG&E shares are rewarded with stock totaling 30% of the amount by which they exceed the annual target. These additional shares are subject to certain holding requirements.

Limited Brands Inc., a retailer based in Columbus, Ohio, combines penalties and incentives. Executives who fail to hit their ownership target are required to receive at least 15% of incentive payments such as year-end bonuses in the form of Limited Brands shares. But executives who choose to take more than the minimum amount of incentive payments in shares (up to 25%) are rewarded with a stock grant equal to 25% of the additional amount.

The stock awards issued by Limited Brands work in a couple of ways. First, they give executives an incentive to increase their ownership of the company. But they also encourage executives to stay with the company, because the shares don't vest for three years. If the recipients leave the company before then, they don't get the stock awards.

Some compensation experts say, however, that such incentives must be awarded in the context of an executive's overall compensation package. "Any incentive to accumulate stock must be offset in some other area of compensation," says George Paulin, chairman and chief executive of executive-compensation consulting firm Frederic W. Cook & Co. If not, incentives will just provide additional compensation for something executives already should be doing to boost their ownership of the company.

—Ms. Banjo is a staff reporter for The Wall Street Journal in South Brunswick, N.J.

BOARDS FLEX THEIR PAY MUSCLES

Joann S. Lublin

Directors are increasingly exercising more clout in setting CEO compensation. And in some cases, the boss is actually feeling a little pain.

Dorrit Bern, chief executive of Charming Shoppes Inc., recently signed a new employment contract that she found less charming than her three prior pacts.

The latest agreement dropped $154,760 of annual perquisites, including the Philadelphia apartment and weekend flights to Chicago that Ms. Bern had enjoyed since arriving in 1995. She also lost the $1 million signing bonus she had received with previous contracts, as well as the right for the contract to automatically renew on the same terms without negotiation. In addition, Charming Shoppes pegged more of her equity grants to performance—picking a tough external measure for the first time.

The revamped package, which took effect Feb. 1, "is more closely aligned to the interests of our shareholders," says Kathy Hudson, who is chairwoman of the board's compensation panel at Charming Shoppes, a women's apparel retailer based in Bensalem, Pa.

But Ms. Bern wasn't pleased. "She wanted directors to simply extend her old agreement," one individual close to the situation remembers. Ms. Bern "won't have a comment" about her new contract, a spokeswoman says.

Directors, facing unprecedented pressure from investors, lawmakers and regulators, are increasingly cutting back the pay-setting power of CEOs. Board compensation committees are retaining their own lawyers, holding frequent executive sessions and evaluating management more rigorously.

The result? Bold boards are killing practices long popular among big bosses, such as retention grants of restricted shares, generous exit rewards and "gross-ups" to cover the taxes that executives have to pay for certain benefits.

A growing number of compensation committees limit corporate chiefs' control over pay decisions because "we understand it is an obligation we have to shareholders," says E.J. "Sandy" Sanderson, Jr., chairman of the pay panel at Science Applications International Corp.

DON'T CRY YET

Still, dissident stockholders and governance experts say, aggressive boards determined to rein in management's clout and rewards remain the exception rather than the rule. Pay committees too often "take away with one hand and give back with the other," says Nell Minow, co-founder of the Corporate Library, a corporate-governance research firm in Portland, Maine. She believes that Hewlett-Packard Co. typifies this ambivalence.

Shareholders of the computer and printer maker last year approved a resolution urging that directors link "a significant portion" of executives' equity grants to challenging performance targets. Heeding the nonbinding vote, the H-P board soon replaced plain-vanilla restricted shares and stock options with restricted-stock units tied to performance. The units won't pay off in three years unless H-P hits its cash-flow goals and shareholder returns outpace a broad market measure.

But directors gave themselves an escape hatch. They may offer equity without performance triggers "in individual cases," the latest H-P proxy statement says. "The board is considering such a special incentive for the CEO" before April 30, the proxy adds. H-P spokesman Robert Sherbin declined to comment.

"It's always going to be a tug of war when you are asking executives to give up compensation 'must haves,'" says Janet Clarke, head of the compensation committee for Asbury Automotive Group Inc. and ExpressJet Holdings Inc. "Dealing with CEOs over pay often gets very emotional."

Compensation committee leaders like her feel torn between pleasing investors and pleasing the top brass. "You don't want to rubber-stamp management's recommendations," Ms. Clarke says. Yet "if you don't do the right thing in rewarding your executives, they can go elsewhere."

LEGAL ADVISER

Asbury's pay panel receives help walking that fine line from an attorney, James D.C. Barrall, who runs the global executive compensation and benefits practice at Latham & Watkins LLP in Los Angeles. He had never worked for the car-dealer chain before he began serving the committee in 2006.

Mr. Barrall telephonically attends about a third of the panel's face-to-face meetings and the executive sessions without management that always follow. A pay panel lacking an independent legal adviser "is like going out in winter without a coat on," Ms. Clarke says.

Asbury committee members enlisted Mr. Barrall's assistance after management resisted directors' efforts to nix a potentially lucrative management proposal in February. Senior officials wanted to remove limits on selling their restricted stock if they retired after reaching a certain age and length of service. The pay panel opposed creating a blanket policy in which "anybody can leave and get their money," Ms. Clarke says. But "management was pretty insistent."

So, she sought Mr. Barrall's advice. He warned the move would force executives to pay income taxes for those shares on their age/service target date even if they didn't retire then. Ms. Clarke believes several would have accepted the extra tax bite in exchange for the accelerated vesting. But the lawyer's warning made the committee's turndown more palatable for management. "It took the exclamation point off our 'No,'" Ms. Clarke says.

Mr. Barrall played an equally useful role at eFunds Corp., where a similar setup threatened the pay panel's ability to keep CEO Paul Walsh. Under a companywide policy, the 58-year-old leader could have cashed in all of his options and restricted-stock units by retiring last September, his fifth anniversary with the provider of transaction-processing and risk-management services.

"It didn't make a lot of sense" for Mr. Walsh's equity to vest so soon, Mr. Barrall says. He recalls warning several directors as they considered a sizable retention grant for the CEO in February 2007.

Mr. Walsh says he considered the accelerated-vesting policy "a great deal" until two former chief executives on the compensation committee confronted him. "You have every right to demand that that [policy] remain in place," they told him. "But we will resign from the board of directors . . . because there is no way to retain you." Mr. Walsh agreed to relinquish the early-retirement sweetener.

Doing so didn't retain the eFunds chief, however. Fidelity National Information Services Inc. eliminated his position after it acquired eFunds last September, according to Mr. Walsh. He says he collected severance that was three times his annual salary and targeted bonus—a total of about $4.3 million.

Other compensation committees take greater control by becoming more involved in evaluating key senior executives before they hand them bigger bucks. The pay panel at Science Applications International, a government-services contractor known as SAIC, requires Chief Executive Kenneth C. Dahlberg to give an oral report card every year about the strengths and weaknesses of his lieutenants. The performance reviews even cover his executive assistant.

'HOW'S HE DOING?'

In addition, Mr. Dahlberg's annual bonus partly reflects feedback that pairs of compensation-committee members glean during interviews with each of his direct reports, according to Mr. Sanderson, the committee chairman. He says the panel members typically ask, "How is Ken doing? What is going well? What areas need improving?"

The SAIC pay panel occasionally pushes even further in putting Mr. Dahlberg's associates under the microscope. Soon after Mr. Dahlberg took command in November 2003, members obtained his written assessment of an underperforming colleague. They wanted to make sure the evaluation had spelled out improvement steps, Mr. Sanderson says, who adds that the subordinate "ended up leaving the company." Mr. Dahlberg declines to comment.

Another way boards flex their muscle is by amassing a wider array of objective data before approving executives' pay goals. Tapping compensation advisers with no other business ties bolsters this effort. For the first time, about a dozen pay panels recently asked independent consultant Jack Dolmat-Connell to compare management predictions of future financial performance with investment analysts' outlook for those companies.

Directors needed to know whether "what the company was expecting to do was in line with those external forecasts," says Mr. Dolmat-Connell, head of DolmatConnell & Partners Inc. in Waltham, Mass. A mismatch arose at a small medical-device maker, prompting its pay panel to award senior executives fewer options and restricted shares this winter than the CEO had sought, he says.

The chief squawked. Pay-panel members "told him he could go play with his marbles elsewhere," Mr. Dolmat-Connell says. "He left a bit chastened."

Compensation committees "need to stand up and do their job" without fear of management's reaction, says Robert Womack, who is chairman of the pay panel for Commercial Metals Co., a producer and recycler of steel and metal products. "We should be driving the executive-compensation train."

Mr. Womack believes he did just that in dealing with the ticklish issue of peer groups. Under 2006 disclosure rules, proxies must describe and name peer companies that boards use to gauge pay competitiveness while creating compensation plans. But management often persuades pay panels to pick competitors that will justify juicier deals.

THE RIGHT PEERS

Assisted by pay experts from Ernst & Young LLP, Mr. Womack and fellow pay-panel members replaced a steel-industry index with a peer group in 2006. Management, advised by a different consulting firm, proposed putting rival Alcoa Inc. on the board's list. Directors refused. "Alcoa was more into engineered products" and much bigger than Commercial Metals, Mr. Womack says.

His committee now targets top executives' base salaries at the 40th percentile of the market within its peer group—down from roughly the 60th percentile before, according to Mr. Womack. "If everybody pays above the 50th percentile, that causes ratcheting," he says.

One upshot? "The committee decided not to increase the salaries of approximately half of the company's senior executives" this fiscal year, ending Aug. 31, its latest proxy says. Among those affected was CEO Murray R. McClean—though his salary did climb to $600,000 from $475,000 upon his promotion in September 2006. He declines to comment.

Some newly assertive pay panels also are cracking down on severance pay for high-level managers. Last year, the SAIC compensation committee reduced the amount of severance promised its 14 top executives following a takeover from three times their salaries and target bonuses to 2.5 times.

At the same time, the panel canceled severance coverage for any officer whose title or duties changes. One executive affected by that decision retired in April 2007, the month he turned 57. Losing his guaranteed severance "probably didn't excite him," Mr. Sanderson says. But "we as a committee want to maintain control over severance-protection agreements."

Such actions illustrate how profoundly power over executive-compensation decisions "has moved away from the CEO," says Paul Hodgson, a senior research associate for the Corporate Library. On the other hand, he cautions, autocratic chiefs of certain big businesses "are still calling the shots on pay."

—Ms. Lublin, the management news editor for The Wall Street Journal in New York, served as contributing editor of this report.

Write to Joann S. Lublin at joann.lublin

In the tables on chief-executive pay in Monday's Journal Report on CEO compensation, "2005-2007 Company TSR" is an annualized three-year total return for each company's stock during fiscal years 2005-2007. The article on the survey methodology that accompanied the tables didn't indicate that figures for this category were annualized.

NEW RULE ON PROXIES PUTS HEAT ON FIRMS

By JOANN S. LUBLIN

Certain big businesses that angered investors this year may find themselves under more pressure next year.

The reason: Stockholders are gaining greater clout to elect corporate directors. On Wednesday, the Securities and Exchange Commission is expected to finalize a "proxy access" rule allowing large investors to nominate their own board candidates using companies' ballots.

Currently, shareholders who want to install their own directors must bear the costs of winning support from other investors. Such proxy fights can cost millions of dollars to pay for proxy solicitors, lawyers and printing and mailing costs. The new rule would largely reduce that cost by letting shareholders put their own nominees in the proxy next to the company's selections.

Proponents contend proxy access would hold directors more accountable by dramatically altering the board-selection process. Under the proposed change, investors with a 3% stake for at least two years will be able to propose nominees starting in 2011, people close to the situation say.

"Proxy access is a new and powerful tool that can be used by shareholder activists to improve underperforming boards," says Michael Garland, an official of CtW Investment Group, an arm of labor union federation Change to Win.

He and other activists say they have yet to pick companies where they will pursue directorships through proxy access. But they're making assessments based on several criteria.

Major institutional investors probably will target big companies with narrow re-elections of some directors, ignored corporate-governance changes approved by stockholders, exhibited weak management succession or rewarded top brass handsomely despite poor results, activists and proxy advisors predict.

Big companies that fall into at least one of those categories include Hewlett-Packard Co., Massey Energy Co., Dell Inc., Abercrombie & Fitch Co., Chesapeake Energy Co. and Nabors Industries Ltd.

All except H-P saw significant opposition to some directors face during their 2010 annual meetings. H-P board members face a investor backlash for giving former Chief Executive Mark Hurd a sizable exit package after forcing him out Aug. 6. An H-P spokeswoman for the technology giant declined to comment.

At Massey, a coal company under fire since an April mine explosion killed 29 men, a coalition of public pension funds urged the ouster of three board members at its May annual meeting. The trio narrowly retained their seats.

CtW Investment Group this spring sought the removal of Don Blankenship, longtime chairman and CEO of Massey.

Retired Navy Adm. Bobby R. Inman, the lead independent director, says he subsequently conferred with more than a dozen institutional investors about overhauling its governance practices.

Massey board members embraced several suggested changes and named two new outside members this month. Mr. Inman is considering individuals proposed by investors for additional seats.

"We have really moved to try to meet every high governance standard that we could find," he explains. "I am not worried about proxy access."

Some critics say Mr. Inman should worry. Massey already "is on the short list of companies that could see proxy access nominees in 2011," observes Mr. Garland of CtW Investment Group. This spring, CtW sought the removal of Don Blankenship, Massey's long-time chairman and CEO. Shareholders will assess whether the board changes "impact the company's leadership and behavior," Mr. Garland continues.

Michael Dell, chairman, CEO and the biggest shareholder of Dell, suffered a surprise setback when 25.1% of votes at the Aug. 12 annual meeting opposed his re-election to the board.

Two labor groups campaigned for his defeat. They cited a recent SEC suit alleging a pattern of accounting manipulations and growing payments from chip giant Intel Corp. that called into question Dell's apparent financial success from 2002 to 2006. Mr. Dell agreed to pay a $4 million fine without admitting or denying wrongdoing.

Related News

The End of Management

Lisa Lindsley, director of capital strategies for the American Federation of State, County and Municipal Employees union, said Dell directors should consider replacing Mr. Dell as chairman and changing outside auditors. She thinks Dell "definitely has the potential" to become a proxy-access target.

The computer maker's board doesn't anticipate altering Mr. Dell's chairmanship and supports his continued leadership, a company spokesman has said.

During Abercrombie's annual meeting in June, investors in the teen retailer defeated a long-term pay plan and nearly blocked the re-election of two members of the board compensation committee.

"Abercrombie officials are dealing with issues reflected in the meeting results, and will continue communicating with many large shareholders about those issues ahead of the 2011 annual meeting," says Ronald A. Robins Jr., Abercrombie's general counsel. He doesn't anticipate the new proxy-access rule "will have any effect" on next year's meeting.

At Chesapeake, two directors encountered strong re-election opposition at its June annual meeting. The natural-gas producer last year had ignored a successful but nonbinding shareholder resolution favoring annual election of board members, citing the industry's volatility. The three-year terms for directors make it hard for outsiders to push for change.

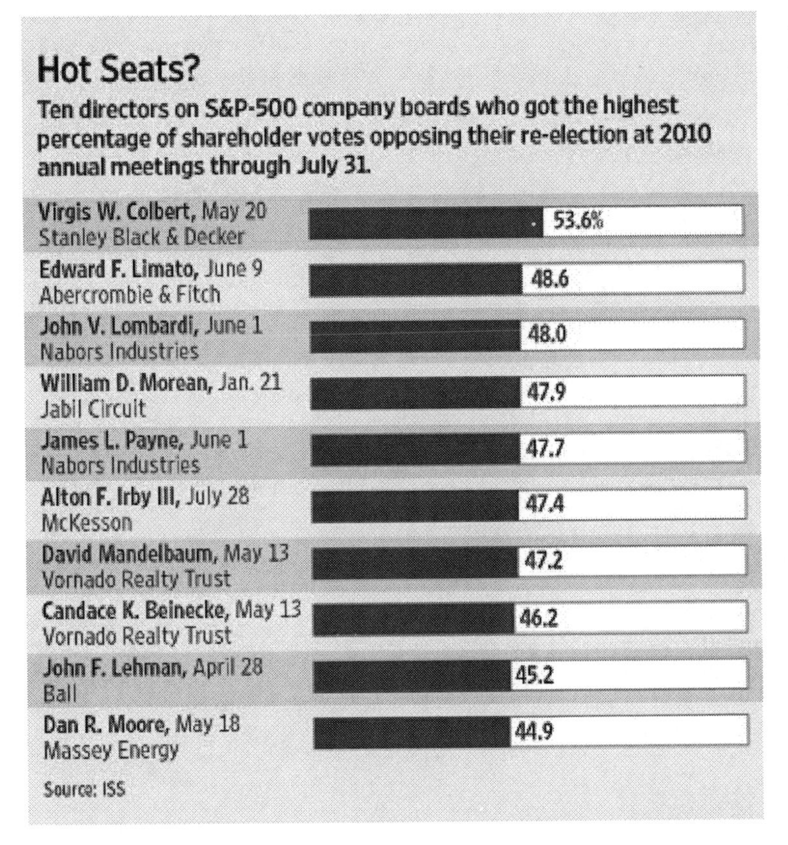

Investors had berated the Chesapeake board for approving a $112.5 million compensation package for Chief Executive Aubrey K. McClendon in 2008, a year when its shares fell 59%.

Independent directors recently chose their first lead director, and Mr. McClendon is forging deeper ties with activist stockholders, according to Marc Rome, Chesapeake's assistant corporate secretary. That's why he doubts the company will be the target of a proxy access campaign next year.

Anne Sheehan, director of corporate governance for California State Teachers' Retirement System, disagrees.

Chesapeake executives' investor outreach represents a positive move but for now, "they would be on our watch list" for a possible proxy-access contest. The public-pension fund owns about two million Chesapeake shares.

Nabors also saw two directors barely re-elected this year. Last year, the Houston oil-drilling concern cut its CEO's rich death benefit to $100 million. Some shareholders had attacked such "golden coffins" as a waste of company assets. A Nabors spokesman didn't return calls seeking comment.

NEW LAW HAS AN EFFECT ON EXECUTIVE PAY

DAVID NICKLAUS

FRIDAY, JANUARY 7, 2011 12:00 AM

Maybe you think Emerson Chief Executive David Farr deserved every penny of his $24.8 million pay package last year. Or perhaps that Monsanto's Hugh Grant was overpaid at $13.2 million.

In the past, your opinion didn't really matter, even if you owned shares in the company. But this year, every publicly traded company in America must ask shareholders what they think of the bosses' pay package.

The "say on pay" votes, which are required by the new Dodd-Frank banking law, are strictly advisory; the board of directors can ignore them if it wants to. They do, however, give shareholders a powerful new way to express their discontent with top brass.

Moreover, the mere prospect of having to defend pay practices is already causing some boards to do things differently. A survey by consulting firm Towers Watson found that 48 percent of companies were adjusting their pay-setting process in anticipation of the votes.

In most cases, the main change is to explain things better. Instead of reciting the dry legalese of the CEO's contract, companies are trying to summarize key pay policies in plain English.

Towers Watson also found that many boards are trying to strengthen the link between pay and performance and are thinking about changing "high visibility" things like perquisites and severance packages.

A protest vote by someone who owns 100 shares may not register on the corporate seismograph, but boards don't like to risk the displeasure of big mutual funds and pension funds. For those institutions, the ballot issue provides important new leverage.

"The say-on-pay proposal is really a communication mechanism that we think will be more effective than what has been available in the past, which was just to vote 'no' on directors," says Carol Bowie, head of compensation research development at ISS-MSCI, which advises large shareholders on how to vote.

Say-on-pay isn't a completely new phenomenon. Banks that received federal bailout money were required to hold such votes last year. Many other companies did so voluntarily, or in response to a push from shareholder groups.

Bowie says her firm recommends a "no" vote about 20 percent of the time. At three companies — Occidental Petroleum, Motorola and Keycorp, a Cleveland bank — the nos were in the majority last year.

At the very least, such a defeat is embarrassing for top management. When a majority of shareholders thinks you're overpaid, it's definitely not a sign of job security.

Even when the pay proposal passes, Towers Watson's James Kroll notes, the board probably doesn't want it to be by a narrow margin.

Nearly half of companies told pollsters that they didn't know what a successful outcome would be. Among executives who had thought about it, an 80 percent "yes" vote would make them comfortable.

A second proposal on this year's ballots will ask shareholders whether they want to conduct "say on pay" votes annually, every two years or every three years.

The boards of Emerson, Esco Technologies, Laclede Group and Monsanto, which are among the first St. Louis companies to consider the issue, are recommending a vote every three years. Monsanto says that would be enough time for the company to "thoughtfully respond to share-owners' sentiments."

ISS-MSCI, on the other hand, wants the pay vote to happen every year. Bowie says it should be part of the annual corporate routine, like re-electing directors and ratifying the audit firm.

Companies may find the votes uncomfortable at first, she says, but if they're really listening to their shareholders, they should have nothing to be afraid of.

Can and Does Shareholder Activism Make a Difference? What is the Impact of Shareholders as Stakeholders?*

1) Proxy Resolutions. Among the basic rights of shareholders is the right to propose a resolution for the proxy statement if they hold $2000 or more in stock. But the company need not include a resolution if it is concerned with "ordinary business," which is left to corporate managers. Even if activist shareholders win the battle, convincing the Securities and Exchange Commission that a resolution belongs in the company's proxy statement because it is outside "ordinary business," and if the resolution is approved by a majority of the shareholders, it is still non-binding.

In recent years shareholders have filed more public interest proxy resolutions, putting pressure on boards to change corporate policies and practices on such matters as global labor standards, equal employment, human rights and environmental policy. Such resolutions can, at minimum, attract media attention and potentially "shame" a corporation into making a proposed change. To avoid adverse publicity, some firms have agreed to change a policy in exchange for the withdrawal of the resolution.

Since 1991, executive compensation has become the subject of shareholder proposals and today is this is the most common shareholder resolution. The Wall Street Journal reported that in just the first three months of 2007, investors had submitted 281 shareholder resolutions over executive pay, compared to just 173 proposed in all of 2006.

In response to these pressures, some members of boards of directors are beginning to reach out to shareholders, giving them a channel to air their grievances about matters like corporate governance and executive pay. In doing so, they must be careful not to violate U.S. rules about selective disclosure of corporate information.

In 2010, the Securities and Exchange Commission was expected to finalize a rule that would allow investors to nominate their own board candidates using companies' ballots. 'Proxy access' would eliminate the high costs shareholders are required to pay to put nominees in the proxy. The new rule will allow investors owning at least 3% of outstanding shares for at least 2 years to propose nominees. By changing the process of board selection, the directors are expected to be held more accountable. The proxy access rule may be revised but is expected to be put into effect in 2012.

2) Other informal mechanisms: Because of the attention brought by shareholder resolutions, the effectiveness of withhold campaigns, and the ability of shareholders to collectivize and communicate with managers and each other with the assistance of technology (internet message boards, for example), many "underperforming" CEO's have lost their jobs. Shareholder activists have also used these mechanisms to influence policy on issues such as discrimination, environmental protection and monitoring of supply chains.

3) Legal Action: Shareholders can sue individual directors or member of the audit committee, or even the whole board, for providing misleading information on financial matters or social issues.

4) Investment in "Socially Responsible Funds" (SRI): Impact on Social Policy. In 2005 there were approximately 800 SRI funds worldwide and the number of such funds has been growing steadily. According to David Vogel, in *Market for Virtue,* the percentage of investors who are social investors is small and a firm's inclusion in an SRI portfolio does not seem to have an impact on its share price.

- Net effect? Shareholders have more influence on narrow issues such as executive pay, but companies still have wide latitude to act.

Summary based, in part, on "Investors: The Role of Informal Pressures" from *Market for Virtue* by David Vogel.

http://jimhamiltonblog.blogspot.com/2011/01/sec-brief-defends-proxy-access-rule.html

http://tcbblogs.org/governance/2011/04/19/on-first-read-expect-proxy-access-to-be-retooled-for-2012/

Lublin, Joann S. "Rule Lets Investors Elbow In on Boards - WSJ.com." Business News & Financial News - The Wall Street Journal - Wsj.com. 22 Aug. 2010. Web. <http://online.wsj.com/article/SB10001424052748704488404575441411083702370.html>.

Questions on Readings for Part Six (B)

What are the legal requirements boards and senior management have in dealing with shareholders?

Do they have any legal requirements related to executive pay?

What are the moral obligations the board and senior management have in dealing with shareholders?

Do they have any moral obligations related to executive pay?

What are the reasons one could give to support the view that executives are (or are not) highly overpaid?

Why haven't boards of directors constrained executive pay?

What could be done to control executive pay?

What role does/should government play in executive compensation?

What impact or influence have shareholders had on business decisions, including those related to executive pay?

CENTER FOR EDUCATION ON SOCIAL RESPONSIBILITY

CASE #4:

EXECUTIVE PAY ABUSES? THE CASE OF ROBERT NARDELLI

HOME DEPOT'S CEO CLEANS UP

Brian Grow

CEO Robert Nardelli is a rarity among managers of major corporations: $3 million of his annual bonus is guaranteed

It's been a flush five years for Home Depot Chief Executive Robert Nardelli. Since he took the helm of the Atlanta home-improvedment retailer in December, 2000, revenues at the company have grown 12% per year, to $81.5 billion, and profits have more than doubled, to $5.8 billion.

To the ire of many investors, however, Home Depot's total return to shareholders, a key benchmark of corporate performance, is down 13%, according to Institutional Shareholder Services **(ISS)**. Still, Home Depot **(HD)** has rewarded Nardelli, 58, handsomely in that period, with some $200 million in salary, bonus, stock, stock options, and other perks. In 2005, Nardelli took home a hefty $38.1 million in total compensation.

That rich payday has attracted the attention of large institutional investors, but one lucrative element of the package is not as well-known: Nardelli's guaranteed minimum annual bonus. Of course, many CEOs are eligible for a bonus each year, usually if they hit certain financial and operating targets. Others have more limited guarantees, such as an assured payout in the first year of service. But Nardelli's employment contract shows that $3 million of his annual bonus, defined as the "target amount," is a sure thing. "For each year during the period of employment," says the agreement, "the executive will receive an annual bonus of no less than the full target amount." Last year, Nardelli earned a total bonus of $7 million.

LONG-TERM HAUL

What's more, as Home Depot prepares for its annual shareholder meeting on May 25, an analysis of CEO employment agreements by executive compensation consulting firm the Delves Group shows Nardelli's guaranteed bonus is not only lucrative, but also rare. No other chief executive among the 200 largest U.S. companies by revenue, the sample analyzed by Delves, has a comparable payout. The group also includes General Electric **(GE)**, Wal-Mart Stores **(WMT)**, and Exxon Mobil **(XOM)**.

Compensation experts say it is highly unusual for an executive to accumulate $15 million in locked-in bonus payments over five years. "It is outrageous and unspeakable to have a guaranteed bonus as long and as big as Nardelli's," says Shekhar Purohit, principal at the Delves Group.

Home Depot declined to confirm whether $3 million of Nardelli's annual bonus is guaranteed. In its 2006 proxy statement, the company says Nardelli's 2005 compensation was based on a combination of factors, including "20.4% growth in diluted earnings per share" and "net sales growth of 11.5%." It acknowledges that Home Depot's total return to shareholders has been relatively poor, vs. the Standard & Poor's 500-stock index and S&P's Retail Composite index.

BONUS OR JUST PAY?

But the proxy appears to reiterate a guarantee on Nardelli's minimum bonus. Citing compensation levels for CEOs running similarly sized companies and the need for top-notch strategic, financial, and leadership skills, the board determined "his annual bonus shall not be less than $3,000,000."

To be sure, some companies dole out smaller, one- or two-year guarantees to CEOs, usually when an executive arrives or when the company is in the middle of a turnaround, according to executive compensation specialists. Bankrupt telecom giant Worldcom, for example, assured former CEO Michael Capellas a bonus equivalent to 100% of his $1.5 million base salary in the first year after the company exited bankruptcy in 2004, according to the Delves Group. Nardelli's $3 million guarantee, however, applies every year, according to his contract, which is renewed every three years, most recently on Jan. 1. "A guaranteed bonus is no longer a bonus. It's just pay," says Charles Elson, director of the Weinberg Center for Corporate Governance at the University of Delaware.

Indeed, how Home Depot accounts for the tax deductibility of Nardelli's $3 million guaranteed bonus is an unanswered question. Under Section 162(m) of the Internal Revenue Code, which governs tax treatment for compensation to the five highest-paid executives at publicly-traded firms, no more than $1 million of an executive's pay can be deducted from corporate tax returns unless it is determined to be "performance-based" with goals that are "substantially uncertain to be met" when they are set. Home Depot guarantees Nardelli a minimum salary of $1.5 million each year. The IRS does not consider more than $1 million of a guaranteed bonus to be tax-deductible. Home Depot declined to comment on the tax issue.

FIRED-UP SHAREHOLDERS

Nardelli's bonus, with its locked-in portion, is not being showered on a slacker. The former head of General Electric's Power Systems unit who lost out in a three-way battle to replace legendary GE chief Jack Welch in 2000, Nardelli regularly puts in six-day workweeks. And he's spearheading a tricky expansion of Home Depot into the industrial supply business. But his rewards for these efforts are more than ample. Data provided by Equilar, a compensation-research firm in San Mateo, Calif., shows the median CEO bonus for the 500 largest U.S. companies last year was $1.5 million. For the largest retailers in that group, including Wal-Mart and Home Depot rival Lowe's Cos. **(LOW)**, the median was $770,849, just over one-tenth of Nardelli's total bonus.

Such outsize pay, at a time when the company's stock trades below its value when Nardelli started, is firing up shareholders. And outside pressure for change is building. In a May 22 letter to Home Depot compensation committee chairwoman Bonnie Hill, CtW Investment Group, a union-affiliated financial group, demanded that Hill personally explain her committee's pay decisions at this week's Home Depot annual meeting. Last week, the California Public Employees' Retirement System, the nation's largest pension fund and the owner of 10.3 million Home Depot shares, announced plans to support a shareholder proposal to require an advisory vote by stockholders on the company's executive compensation committee report.

Nardelli's guaranteed bonus has helped fuel the fire. In a May 12 report by ISS, a corporate governance advisory service, shareholders are advised to withhold votes for 10 of Home Depot's 12 directors up for reelection, in part, because Nardelli's employment agreement "contains egregious guarantees such as minimum cash bonuses." The Corporate Library, another governance watchdog, rates Home Depot an "F" on compensation, due partly to the guaranteed bonus. "It's representative of the whole employment agreement, which is a complete disconnect between executive compensation and company performance," says Paul Hodgson, senior research associate at the Corporate Library.

SORE SPOT

So far, Home Depot's board of directors has remained steadfastly behind Nardelli and his pay package. The company opposes all three proposals advocating more shareholder involvement in setting or disclosing Home Depot's executive compensation scheduled for a vote at the May 25 shareholder meeting. And it shows no signs of altering Nardelli's guaranteed bonus. "People who do not sit in the board room make decisions based on looking in the rear-view mirror. Directors have to make decisions based on looking forward," says Home Depot board member Hill, founder of corporate governance consulting firm B. Hill Enterprises LLC and chair of Home Depot's Leadership Development & Compensation Committee.

Still, Nardelli's hefty bonus is a sore spot with Home Depot's rank and file. At MSN's Orange Blood Bank, an Internet chat room frequented mostly by workers in Home Depot stores (orange refers to the color of the retailer's logo) complaints often erupt about their CEO's pay. And the disconnect between Nardelli and the company's retail workers is growing. Nardelli's total bonus, which Home Depot says is based on overall company performance, rose from $5.75 million in 2004 to $7 million last year. But Home Depot's Success Sharing program, which doles out bonuses primarily to Home Depot's 319,000 non-salaried employees based on store financial performance, fell from $90 million in 2004 to $44 million in 2005. The average payout to workers: $137.93. No portion of those bonuses is guaranteed.

SHAREHOLDERS TO HOME DEPOT CHIEF: YOU'RE CHICKEN

Parija Bhatnagar

Irate investors lambaste board's absence at Home Depot's annual meeting; Nardelli faces severe criticism over his "generous compensation package."

NEW YORK (CNNMONEY.COM)

Home Depot's CEO Robert Nardelli faced some very irate shareholders Thursday, who lambasted him for his "arrogance" and "excessive" pay package and the company's board for being absent from the retailer's annual shareholder meeting.

One angry shareholder berated Nardelli at the outset after learning that no other member of the company's board was present at the meeting. Others bashed his decision not to allow shareholders to ask additional questions outside of a strict one-minute time slot.

"This is outrageous that they (the board) are not willing to appear before shareholders," the shareholder, Richard Fillano, said. "I think they're too chicken to face shareholders whether to allow vote on CEO compensation or answer questions about the performance of the company. You hide behind various metrics, you won't report same-store sales, you're chicken."

The shareholder tried to continue, but was cut off.

Another attendee, Richard Ferlauto with the American Federation of State, County and Municipal Employees, which owns about four percent of Home Depot's stock in retirement plans, equated a CEO's pay to the canary in a coal mine for "both accountability and corporate governance.

"Here at the Home Depot, I'm afraid that canary has died," he said. "While you [addressing Nardelli] have been handsomely compensated, the stock price has languished. Home Depot has given you more than $200 million in compensation while the stock price is lower today than when you took over. You've got a good deal. As a long-term investor, I want you to earn your keep but we want to see pay for performance."

Home Depot (Research) angered investors last week with its surprising decision to stop reporting company sales at stores open at least a year—a key retail measure known as same-store sales—going forward. Analysts frowned on the move, calling it "strange" and "irresponsible."

The meeting, which took place in Wilmington, Del., was monitored via Web cast in New York.

Other shareholders took Nardelli to task over recent news stories on his generous pay and annual compensation package, including a *New York Times* report this week saying that Home Depot's board awarded him $245 million in his five years at the helm. During that time the stock has slid versus its main rival Lowe's and total return to shareholders has also sagged.

Another shareholder, Richard Metcalf, told Nardelli that he felt the company was facing a "crisis over questions over connecting executive compensation with company performance."

"We're in the front pages of all the newspapers. There are large shareholder groups that have recommended no votes on a lot of our directors," Metcalf said. "I think it's very bad practice not to have members of our board in attendance. It's a violation of every governance practice. When we have an elected board, they should be here to answer questions. This is really, really bad. I protest it and it needs to be corrected."

Anthony Chukumba, analyst with Morningstar, said what bothered him the most was shareholders not being allowed to ask questions. "Compared to other CEOs, I think Nardelli's compensation is excessive. The company is facing some businesses challenges. I don't understand the decision not to report same-store sales. I think Nardelli is frustrated with all the questions about what he's doing at the company."

The A.F.S.C.M.E, the government workers' union, issued a proposal that would allow investors to cast an advisory vote on executive pay packages each year. The proposal was rejected by Home Depot shareholders. Proposals seeking to separate the chairman and CEO function, greater transparency in political contributions and Home Depot's employment practices were also shot down.

The only shareholder proposal to pass was one that sought to change the voting structure for electing directors.

The meeting lasted little over 30 minutes and ended with Nardelli announcing that preliminary results showed shareholders had approved one-year terms for the director nominees.

Nardelli didn't respond directly to criticisms raised at the meeting. Phone calls to Home Depot's public relations department were not returned.

OUT AT HOME DEPOT

Behind The Flameout of Controversial CEO Bob Nardelli

In the end it came down to the headstrong CEO's refusal to accept even a symbolic reduction in his stock package. Home Depot Inc.'s (HD) board of directors wanted their controversial chief executive, Robert L. Nardelli, to amend his whopping compensation deals for recent years. After he pulled down $38.1 million from his last yearly contract, angry investors were promising an ugly fight at the company's annual meeting in May. Nardelli agreed that he would continue to receive a guaranteed $3 million bonus each year, but not more. When board members asked him to more closely tie his future stock awards to shareholder gains, he refused, according to people familiar with the matter. Nardelli has complained for years that share price is the one measure of company performance that he can't control. After weeks of secret negotiations, things came to a head at a board meeting on Jan. 2, leading to Home Depot's stunning announcement the next day that the company and Nardelli had "mutually agreed" that he would resign.

"The board loved him and hates the way this ended up," says a person familiar with the matter. But in a season of growing antipathy toward extravagantly paid executives, the directors felt they had no choice. On his way out the door, however, Nardelli negotiated another jaw-dropper: a $210 million retirement package that assures that he and his former employer will remain at the center of the swirling debate over CEO compensation. Nardelli declined to comment.

The sudden fall of one of America's best-known CEOs illustrates how perilous times have become for corporate leaders. Pointing to gargantuan pay and widespread manipulation of stock options, institutional shareholders are calling for top executives and board members to be held accountable. At Home Depot there were other points of contention: a sluggish stock price in an otherwise rising market and Nardelli's notoriously imperious manner. Judged solely by certain company financial measures, Nardelli, 58, should have enjoyed acclaim for transforming Home Depot from a faltering retail chain into an earnings juggernaut. Driven by a housing and home improvement boom, sales soared from $46 billion in 2000, the year Nardelli took over, to $81.5 billion in 2005, an average annual growth rate of 12%. Profits more than doubled, to $5.8 billion that year.

TUMULTUOUS TENURE

During the current housing slowdown, however, the financials have eroded. In the third quarter of 2006, same-store sales at Home Depot's 2,127 retail stores declined 5.1%. And with the stock price recently stuck at just over 40, roughly the same as when Nardelli arrived six years ago, he could no longer rely on other sterile metrics to assuage the quivering anger his arrogance provoked within every one of his key constituencies: employees, customers, and shareholders. Nardelli's "numbers were quite good," says Matthew J. Fassler, an analyst at Goldman Sachs Group Inc. **(GS)** But "the fact is that this retail organization never really embraced his leadership style." The CEO's reputation also suffered because of Wall Street's affection for Home Depot's smaller archrival, Lowe's Companies **(LOW)**, whose stock price has soared more than 200% since 2000, while Home Depot's shares declined 6%, according to Bloomberg data. A simmering options backdating investigation at Home Depot hasn't helped matters either, though an internal company review has thus far exonerated Nardelli.

At another time, Nardelli's impressive operating numbers might have saved him. Perhaps he would have learned to temper an ego nurtured during a long career at General Electric Co. **(GE)**. But in a prolonged season of hostility toward overweening CEOs, the former GE power systems phenom couldn't hold on. "He's not a very humble guy. He seems to have enormous energy but needs to be front and center, and that can wear on the board and the employees after a while," says Edward E. Lawler, director of the Center for Effective Organizations at the University of Southern California's Marshall School of Business.

Before the final fallout over pay, the half-hour that defined Nardelli's tumultuous tenure began at 9 a.m. on Thursday, May 28. That was the time set for the giant home-improvement retailer's 2006 annual meeting in a Wilmington (Del.) ballroom. The assembled shareholders—a sparse crowd of longtime stockholders, employees, and union representatives—expected the usual corporate routine: a presentation on the state of Home Depot's $81.5 billion business, a vote on an assortment of shareholder proposals, and plenty of time for questions aimed at Nardelli and the other 10 members of Home Depot's board.

But something strange soon became apparent: The board wasn't there. Citing time constraints and the imperative of working on important matters back home at Atlanta headquarters, the eminent overseers of Home Depot failed to show up at their own event. That left

Nardelli to handle the meeting on his own. He did that in an abrupt 30 minutes. Shareholders were limited to just one question each. A digital clock timed them: One minute, then the microphone cut off.

Nardelli spent much of last spring offering half-hearted mea culpas for the board's disappearing act. "We tried a new format. It didn't work," he said. But then, as the months unfolded, it became clear he had a problem on his hands that he couldn't just summarily dismiss. A chagrined board signaled that it planned to reduce his 2006 pay package, setting the stage for the ultimate Jan. 2 showdown on the stock plan.

"MANIACAL"

Nardelli arrived at Home Depot after losing out in 2000 in a three-way race to succeed GE's legendary Jack Welch. Despite that setback, Nardelli was anointed one of Corporate America's most talented executives, and Home Depot seemed to have scored a big victory by snaring him. Almost immediately, he embarked on an aggressive plan to centralize control of the nation's second-largest retailer after Wal-Mart Stores Inc. **(WMT)**. He invested more than $1billion in new technology, such as self-checkout aisles and inventory management systems that generated reams of data. He declared that he wanted to measure virtually everything that happened at the company and hold executives strictly accountable for meeting their numbers. All this was new at a relatively laid-back organization known for the independence of its store managers and the folksy, entrepreneurial style of retired co-founders Bernard Marcus and Arthur M. Blank. One of Nardelli's favorite sayings is: "Facts are friendly." He seemed less concerned about people being friendly. Some saw this as a strength. "This guy is maniacal about goals, objectivity, accomplishments within the boundaries of the values of the company," Kenneth G. Langone, the third co-founder of Home Depot, a member of its board of directors, and a strong Nardelli ally, said in a 2004 interview.

But among many of Home Depot's 355,000 employees, especially rank-and-file workers in its orange big-box stores, there was little sympathy as Nardelli dug himself into a deeper and deeper hole. They resented the replacement of many thousands of full-time store workers with legions of part-timers, one aspect of a relentless cost-cutting program Nardelli used to drive gross margins from 30% in 2000 to 33.8% in 2005. As the news of his resignation on Jan. 3 shot through Home Depot's white-walled Atlanta headquarters and reached stores, some employees text-messaged each other with happy faces and exclamation points. "I think that it is being received well. Most people believed that Bob was autocratic and stubborn," says an assistant manager in an Atlanta store who asked not to be named.

Possibly more devastating to his chances of a longer reign at Home Depot, Nardelli alienated customers just as thoroughly as he did employees. Staffing cuts led to persistent complaints that there weren't enough workers in Home Depot's cavernous stores to help do-it-yourself customers. That was a marked change from the era when Blank and Marcus, who started the company in 1978, preached that employees should "make love to the customer." In 2005, Home Depot slipped to last among major U.S. retailers in the University of Michigan's annual American Consumer Satisfaction Index. To try to make amends, Nardelli announced a plan in August to add 5.5 million man-hours back to stores and invest $350 million to spruce up aging outlets. "Bob Nardelli is a smart man, but he doesn't need to be in a high-profile business like retail," says a former top Home Depot executive. "He needs to be in manufacturing, a business that does not have such consumer attention."

Indeed, Nardelli's data-driven, in-your-face management style grated on many seasoned executives, resulting in massive turnover in Home Depot's upper ranks. Former chief marketing officer John H. Costello, a retailing veteran from Sears Holding Corp. **(SHLD)**, quit in late 2005, and Carl C. Liebert III, the executive vice-president who oversaw store operations, resigned last October. "He would say that you're just not leadership material, you're just not Home Depot material, you're just not the type of person we need," says a former senior executive. Managers who weren't hitting their numbers—"making plan" in Home Depot parlance—were routinely culled, their posts often filled with former executives from GE. That led some bitter insiders to dub the company "Home GEpot." In fact, since 2001, 98% of Home Depot's top 170 executives are new to their positions; 56% of the changes involved bringing new managers in from outside the company.

Nardelli's relationship with Wall Street analysts was often just as frayed. He chafed at their constant focus on "same-store sales," a standard retail measurement that tracks sales at stores open at least a year. In Nardelli's view, same-store sales was an out-of-date metric because Home Depot was diversifying away from being strictly a retail operation. Under his leadership, the company has invested more than $7.6 billion to build Home Depot Supply, which provides services to professional contractors. With $3.5 billion in revenue in the third quarter of 2006, up 159%, HDS accounted for 15% of total Home Depot sales. In Nardelli's view, this successful new arm can't be accurately measured on the basis of same-store sales.

Credit Suisse First Boston **(CS)** analyst Gary Balter says Nardelli didn't get along well with Wall Street because he was unhappy with analysts' skepticism of the move away from consumer retailing and into servicing professional contractors. "He blamed a lot of his problems on Wall Street," says Balter. "But Wall Street wanted to see results, and they just weren't there."

The lack of results, at least in terms of an improving stock price, gradually stirred anger among shareholders. Speculation mounted late last year that Home Depot could be a prime target for private equity firms hungry for retail assets. While the company spent $20.3 billion to buy back shares and issue dividends under Nardelli, investors saw almost no gains in their share value. Their frustration was exacerbated by Nardelli's eye-popping pay package: more than $200 million in salary, bonuses, stock options, restricted stock, and other perks over the last six years.

Last month, activist investor Relational Investors sharply criticized Home Depot management and called on the board to form a special committee to review the company's direction and even the possibility of a sale. Relational attributed Home Depot's difficulties to "deficient strategy, operations, capital allocation, and governance." After the announcement of Nardelli's leaving, a source familiar with Relational called the departure "a positive" but added that "the major strategy, capital, and management issues remain. Fresh new blood remains an objective."

It wasn't only activist investors like Relational who had grown tired of Nardelli's leadership. He irritated Atlanta locals, too. In a Nov. 25 letter to Nardelli, reviewed by *BusinessWeek*, A. Leigh Baier, an Atlanta attorney and Home Depot shareholder, requested that the company's board include a "non-binding" resolution in Home Depot's proxy statement allowing shareholders to vote on whether "they are in favor, or opposed to, the board of directors of Home Depot terminating your contract." Explaining his now-moot proposal, Baier says, "You can't s--t on your employees and deliver" results.

Others remain outraged, even with Nardelli gone. A group of unions whose pension funds own shares in Home Depot plans to challenge his $210 million payout at the annual meeting in May. Meanwhile, in Washington, Representative Barney Frank (D-Mass.), the incoming chairman of the House Financial Services Committee, said in a statement on Jan. 3: "The actions of Home Depot's Board of Directors to simultaneously dismiss Robert Nardelli and provide him with $210 million in severance is further confirmation of the need to deal with the pattern of CEO pay that appears to be out of control."

It's unlikely Home Depot's new chief executive, Frank Blake, will change the Nardelli-driven demand for data and centralized control. A former Deputy Energy Secretary and GE veteran, Blake played a key role in executing Nardelli's strategy at the retail chain. But company executives say he lacks Nardelli's sharp edges and prefers to build consensus rather than dictate orders. While Blake is an unknown to many Home Depot employees, the Nardelli departure was already brightening the mood at some company stores. "It's amazing the reaction of people on my floor. People are openly ecstatic. High-fiving," said an Atlanta store operations manager only hours after the Jan. 3 announcement. "There's a group talking about going to happy hour at noon."

Corporate America hasn't seen the last of Bob Nardelli, however. According to people familiar with the situation, while store workers were celebrating, the former CEO was already fielding calls from private equity firms interested in his formidable operational talents. The bright side for Nardelli in the world of privately owned corporations, of course, is that he won't have to deal with any annual meetings or shareholder questions.

ROBERT NARDELLI NAMED CEO OF CHRYSLER

Katie Benner

Under the terms of the deal for Cerberus to buy Chrysler, the ex-Home Depot chief took the helm at the struggling carmaker.

FORTUNE

(Fortune)—As the deal to sell Chrysler to Cerberus Capital Management finally came to a close on Friday, there was one rather salient fact that slipped under the radar. Robert Nardelli was appointed Chrysler's chairman and chief executive officer upon the deal's completion.

That's right. Ceberus has confirmed that the disgraced former CEO of Home Depot (Charts, Fortune 500), who became the poster child for excessive CEO compensation, has taken the reigns at Chrysler. On the day the deal was finalized, August 3, Nardelli was elected to the Chrysler board. Soon after, the directors appointed him chairman and chief executive.

However, a source inside Cerberus says that Nardelli will receive only $1 a year in base salary. This person would not go into detail regarding the rest of Nardelli's pay package, and would only add that Nardelli's pay will be directly tied to the success of Chrysler's turnaround.

Tom LaSorda, who has been CEO of the Chrysler Group since September 1, 2005, will be vice-chairman and remain president of Chrysler, reporting to Nardelli. The carmaker's chief operating officer, Eric Ridenour, has elected to leave the new company, and the COO position will not be filled. So far, no one will say why Ridenour chose to leave.

"We are excited to welcome Bob to the Chrysler family," said LaSorda in a statement. "Bob has a proven track record of success and an unwavering focus on performance, and brings deep operational experience and a broad industry background to Chrysler. His background in operations will provide valuable knowledge as we continue Chrysler's turnaround."

"I am very excited to be part of a team focused on re-establishing Chrysler as a standalone industry leader, with a renewed focus on meeting the needs of customers," said Nardelli.

Rumors have swirled since March that Cerberus was thinking of hiring Nardelli, who also worked at General Electric (Charts, Fortune 500), when CNBC reported that the private investment firm had offered him a spot as a so-called operations specialist.

Cerberus has collected a huge bench of former executives to act as advisors on deals and serve on the boards of its portfolio companies. Former GE employees who now work for Cerberus include Paul Bossidy, Michael Williams and Jeffrey Fenton. A person within Cerberus says Nardelli never officially worked for the firm.

Nardelli angered Home Depot shareholders when he refused to take questions during a shareholder meeting in May 2006 as the stock was floundering. His rich pay package drew fire; he earned $38.1 million last year. Ultimately he was forced out of the company in January 2007, but left with a $210 million golden parachute in cash and stock options that included a $20 million severance payment and retirement benefits of $32 million.

To be sure, plenty of executives before Nardelli have gotten away with big paychecks and imperious behavior. In the end, it was the stock price that got him. As Bernie Marcus, so-founder of Home Depot, told Fortune after Nardelli's departure, "If the stock had doubled, who would have cared? Instead it went nowhere, and that's what this is all about."

By the time Nardelli left the retail chain, its shares were trading at about the same price as when he arrived in 2000. Moreover, analysts said that the stock had actually lost about 40% of its value because a series of stock buybacks had reduced the amount of shares available.

But Nardelli argued that share price was just one metric used to judge the success of a corporate leader.

And it's true that other metrics improved during his tenure. Home Depot's return on capital grew to almost 20 percent, about ten percentage points above the firm's cost of capital; and sales soared from $46 billion when he arrived in 2000 to $81.5 billion in 2005. Over the same period, profits more than doubled to nearly $6 billion.

Before his rise and fall at Home Depot, Nardelli had also been a success at GE, the company where he worked for 27 years before losing the CEO spot to Jeff Immelt. Nardelli was the head of GE's Canadian appliance unit, then he moved on to the transportation systems division. He later transformed the GE Power Systems unit into one of the conglomerate's most profitable divisions.

Now that the private investment firm Cerberus owns 80.1% of Chrysler, the company will be able to implement its turnaround plan without the pressure of quarterly earnings that dogged Nardelli. Even so, his reputation as an effective leader was tarnished by his stint at Home Depot.

The recent Chrysler sale to Cerberus is high profile and risky, as is putting Nardelli in the top spot. The turnaround is considered a bellwether for both the future of U.S. auto manufacturing and the fate of labor unions. Additionally, some contend that the problems that investment banks had securitizing the loans Ceberus made to Chrysler are evidence that the heady days of private equity dealmaking are coming to a close.

Even so, a source at Cerberus says his firm is confident that Nardelli has what it takes to fix the ailing company that is weighed down by nearly $19 billion in pension and retiree healthcare costs.

CENTER FOR EDUCATION ON SOCIAL RESPONSIBILITY

PART SIX (C)

CONSUMERS

CONSUMER PRODUCT SAFETY ACT OF 1972

ENCYCLOPEDIA OF BUSINESS AND FINANCE

Congress passed the Consumer Product Safety Act in 1972 to "assist consumers in evaluating the comparative safety of consumer products; to develop uniform safety standards for consumer products and to minimize conflicting state and local regulations; and to promote research and investigation into the causes and prevention of product related death, illnesses, and injuries." The act also established the Consumer Product Safety Commission (CPSC) to "protect the public against unreasonable risks associated with consumer products." The CPSC has authority to set mandatory standards, ban products, order recalls of unsafe products, and institute labeling requirements.

The CPSC is an independent regulatory agency charged with protecting consumers from unreasonable risk of injury associated with consumer products. The most serious risks include amputation, electrocution, burns, asphyxiation, and cancer. Examples of recent product liability lawsuits in which defendant companies lost include breast implants that leaked silicone gel and football helmets that did not have enough padding. The commission has jurisdiction over about 15,000 types of consumer products, such as automatic coffee makers, toys, furniture, clothing, and lawn mowers. The CPSC works to reduce the risk of injury and death from consumer products by:

- Developing voluntary standards with industry
- Issuing and enforcing mandatory standards and banning consumer products if no feasible standard would adequately protect the public
- Obtaining the recall of products or arranging for their repair
- Conducting research on potential product hazards
- Informing and educating consumers through the media, state and local governments, and private organizations, and by responding to consumer inquiries. (CPSC, 1999).

The CPSC has three key program areas:

1. The Office of Hazard Identification and Reduction, which collects and analyzes consumer injury and death data to determine trends in consumer product hazards.
2. The Office of Compliance and Enforcement, which supervises compliance and administrative activities related to the act. This office also reviews proposed standards and rules with respect to their enforceability.
3. The Office of Information and Public Affairs, which is responsible for the development, implementation, and evaluation of a comprehensive national information and public affairs program designed to promote product safety. (Fise, 1998).

In recent years, the CPSC has been involved in actions to protect children. In 1987, for example, the commission began to examine toys that pose choking hazards. This led Congress to pass the Child Safety Protection Act of 1994. A sample of child safety issues investigated by the commission includes bicycle helmets, public play grounds, upholstered furniture, walkers, drawstrings on children's clothing, baseball protective equipment, and toys. More than 160 deaths from toys were reported between 1990 and 1997, and at least seventy-two different toys that posed a small-parts hazard were recalled between October 1996 and September 1997 by the CPSC.(Public Interest Research Group [PIRG], 2000). PIRG reports that in 1998 fewer toys posing choking hazards appeared on shelves.

In addition, the commission has also written rules to establish performance, design, composition, packaging, and construction standards for many products. Examples of products with mandatory safety standards include matchbooks, walk-behind power lawn mowers, residential garage door openers, swimming pool slides, chain-saws, home-use pesticides, and cellulose insulation (Garman, 1997).

Consumers have benefited in the areas where the CPSC has taken action. The commission is constantly challenged to keep abreast of new products and potential hazards that may be associated with them. The commission is usually able to react, however, only after a consumer has been injured or died. The CPSC has changed the way many products are designed and manufactured. Continuing education by consumer groups, the media, and the CPSE has helped increase public awareness of possible consumer safety hazards. The CPSC is an important consumer protection agency, protecting consumers by assuring that products they use every day are safe.

BIBLIOGRAPHY

Consumer Product and Safety Act (1972). Section 2051.

Consumer Product Safety Commission (CPSC). "Who Are We—What We Do for You." www.cpsc.gov/about/who.html. March 1999.

Fise, M. E. R. (1998). "Consumer Product Safety Regulation." In *Regulation and Consumer Protection: Politics, Bureaucracy and Economics*, ed. K. J. Meier, E. T. Garman, and L. R. Keiser. Houston, TX: DAME Publications.

Garman, E. T. (1997). *Consumer Economic Issues in America*, 5th ed. Houston, TX: DAME Publications.

Public Interest Research Group (PIRG). "Trouble in Toyland; Positive Signs in 1998." www.pirg.org/consumer/products/toy/98/page6.htm. March 2000

SALMONELLA OUTBREAK FUELS FOOD-SAFETY EFFORTS

Jane Zhang

WASHINGTON—The salmonella outbreak that may have killed eight people, sickened at least 575 and led to the recall of more than 1,500 peanut-related products has kick-started efforts to repair the U.S. food-safety system.

President Barack Obama cited his concerns as a public official and a father—his 7-year-old daughter eats peanut butter—when he called this past week for a complete review of Food and Drug Administration operations.

His worries were echoed by lawmakers who are pushing for an FDA food-safety overhaul, following a series of food-poisoning cases in recent years involving bagged spinach, lettuce, tomatoes, wheat flour from China and hot peppers from Mexico. Government regulation, they say, must be tightened to contend with centralization of food production, a flood of imported foods and the growing popularity of prepared meals, all of which have been blamed for outbreaks of salmonella and other ailments.

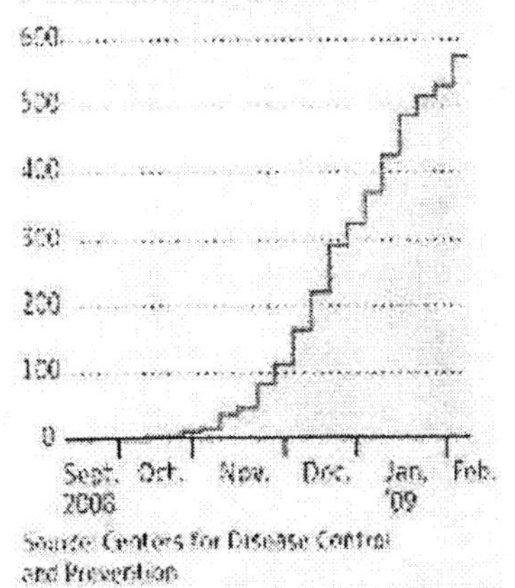

Democrats say the administration of George W. Bush underfunded federal food-safety efforts in its zeal to cut regulations. But critics cite other longstanding problems, including antiquated laws, sometimes dating back more than 100 years, that fracture responsibility for food safety among a dozen federal agencies.

The U.S. Department of Agriculture is responsible for the safety of meat, poultry and egg products. The FDA covers other foods, including vegetables. Of the two, the FDA faces bigger challenges. It doesn't have a clear mandate to set food-safety standards and lacks manpower for frequent inspections.

Both agencies rely on the U.S. Centers for Disease Control and Prevention to detect disease trends. The CDC in turn relies on understaffed state and local health departments to spot contamination outbreaks. When things go wrong, the FDA and USDA generally don't have the authority to order food recalls—producers have to voluntarily submit.

"To say that food safety in this country is a patchwork system is giving it too much credit," said Iowa Sen. Tom Harkin, chairman of the Senate Agriculture Committee, during a food-safety hearing Thursday. Waving a jar of peanut butter, he declared that U.S. food safety "has become a hit-or-miss gamble, and that is truly frightening."

Stephen Sundlof, director of the FDA's Center for Food Safety and Applied Nutrition, said Thursday that while the U.S. "food supply continues to be among the safest in the world, we look forward to working with the president and Congress to make our food even safer."

Sen. Dick Durbin (D., Ill.) plans to introduce legislation that would give the FDA authority to order food recalls and set safety standards for fresh fruits and vegetables. Rep. Bart Stupak (D., Mich.) is pushing a bill that would fund FDA inspections with fees from food companies and increase penalties for safety violations.

Rep. Rosa L. DeLauro (D., Conn.), chairman of the House Appropriations Committee panel that oversees the FDA budget, introduced legislation Wednesday to split the FDA into two agencies, one for food safety, the other regulating drugs and medical devices. "The fundamental issue is the current structure of the agency," she said.

At the FDA, consumer advocates allege, food regulation has long played second fiddle to drug regulation. The agency's food-program budget totaled $510 million in fiscal 2008, or 22% of its overall budget. That same year, there were 2,633 employees in the food program, down from 3,167 five years earlier.

Fewer field employees translates into fewer inspections. FDA food inspections have dropped 78% from 35 years ago, according to a 2007 report by an FDA advisory panel, which concluded that the agency's ability to regulate food is "severely eroded, as is its ability to respond to outbreaks in a timely manner."

Peanut Corp. of America's Blakely, Ga., facility—ground zero in the continuing salmonella outbreak—hadn't been examined by FDA inspectors since 2001. In 2006, the FDA contracted with the Georgia Department of Agriculture to conduct regular inspections of food makers, an arrangement the FDA has with 41 other states.

An FDA investigation last month turned up a leaky roof, mold, cracks in the floor and other unsanitary conditions. The agency also alleged that the plant had shipped products after samples tested positive for salmonella. The Justice Department and the FDA recently announced a criminal investigation.

Peanut Corp., which stopped work at the Blakely plant and recalled products made there since Jan. 1, 2007, has said the FDA report contained inaccuracies but hasn't elaborated. Amy Rotenberg, a Minneapolis lawyer hired by Peanut Corp., said this past week, "We are working very hard to gather and understand all of the facts."

The USDA said this past week that it would no longer buy Peanut Corp. products, and that it was tracking down what might be left of 32 truckloads of the company's goods shipped to schools in Idaho, Minnesota and California in 2007.

BUSINESS ETHICS: CONCEPTS AND CASES

Manual G. Velasquez

Consider the nature of the consumer products discussed below:

NASHVILLE, Tenn., February 26, 2004—Bridgestone/Firestone announced a recall Thursday of about 490,000 Steeltex tires linked to sport utility vehicle crashes that killed five people. . . . The tires were made for use on Ford Excursions from 2000 to 2002 and some 2003 models. The recall comes 3 years after the company began a recall of 17 million ATX, ATX II and Wilderness AT tires. More than 200 people were reported killed and hundreds more injured in rollover crashes after the tread on those tires separated. The company has spent an estimated $1.5 billion on that recall.

SAN DIEGO, Calif., June 24, 2004—Metabolife International yesterday was ordered to pay $7.46 million to a Texas woman who suffered a stroke after taking the company's ephedra diet pill . . . Metabolife 356 . . . . federal jury in Alabama awarded $4.1 million in damages to four people who suffered heart attacks or strokes after taking Metabolife 356. In April, federal regulators banned the use of ephedra supplement products after the herbal stimulant was linked to 155 deaths and numerous serious injuries.

[*Consumer Reports* in May 2004 stated it] easily purchased 12 [dangerous supplements] in February 2004 in a few days of shopping online and in retail stores. These unsafe supplements include aristolochia, an herb conclusively linked to kidney failure and cancer in China, Europe, Japan, and the U.S.; yohimbe, a sexual stimulant linked to heart and respiratory problems; bitter orange, whose ingredients have effects similar to those of the banned weightloss stimulant ephedra; and chaparral, comfrey, germander, and kava, all known or likely causes of liver failure. . . .

> WASHINGTON, D.C. April 29, 2003—Some of the hazardous products that consumers are most likely to find in their homes: *Window Blind Cords with Loops* that can strangle children. . . . the U.S. Consumer Product Safety Commission (CPSC) knows of about 160 strangulation deaths to children in looped window covering cords . . . *Halogen Torchiere Floor Lamps* that can cause fires when combustibles such as drapes come too close to the bulb. . . . CPSC knows of 290 fires and 25 deaths since 1992 related to halogen torchiere floor lamps. *Cadet Heaters* that could cause a fire. CPSC is aware of more than 320 reports of Cadet and Encore heaters that smoked, sparked, caught fire, emitted flames, or ejected burning particles or molten materials. These incidents have allegedly resulted in four deaths, two serious burn injuries and property damage claims exceeding $4.3 million. *Disposable and Novelty Lighters That Are Not Child-resistant*. . . . in a recent year there were still 2,400 fires resulting in 70 deaths and 480 injuries because of children under age 5 playing with lighters.

Americans are exposed daily to astonishingly high levels of risk from the use of consumer products. Each year some 20 million people suffer serious accidental injuries and about 100,000 are killed, more than half of them in accidents involving consumer products. After declining by more than 20 percent between 1979 and 1992 (when deaths reached a 68-year low of 86,777), accidental deaths have been rising again since 1992. The Consumer Product Safety Commission estimated that the total cost of these injuries in 2003 alone was $700 billion.

However, product injuries make up only one category of costs imposed on unwary consumers. Consumers must also bear the costs of deceptive selling practices, shoddy product construction, products that immediately break down, and warranties that are not honored. For example, several years ago, the engine of Martha and George Rose's Chevrolet station wagon began hissing and white smoke poured out of the tailpipe as she drove it 6 miles to work. Two non-Chevrolet mechanics who then checked the car later testified that the radiator and cooling system were "in satisfactory condition," that the radiator "was not boiling over," and that the temperature light on the dashboard "was not burning." Upon taking the engine apart, a mechanic found that a hair-line crack in the engine block had allowed water to enter the cylinder head, meaning that the car would need an expensive new engine. The engine was still under a "5-year or 50,000-mile" warranty, so the Roses thought the Chevrolet division of General Motors would bear the large costs of repairing what they concluded was an inherently defective engine block. However, when a Chevrolet service manager examined the dismantled car, he insisted that the problem was that the radiator thermostat had stuck shut so no coolant had reached the engine. Because the thermostat was only under a "12-month or 12,000-miles" warranty that had by then expired, and because, the Chevrolet manager claimed, the faulty thermostat had caused the engine to overheat and the engine block to crack, Chevrolet had no responsibility under the warranty. Moreover, the car had been torn down and worked on by unauthorized mechanics. Although the Roses pointed out that the other mechanics had found no evidence of overheating and that no Chevrolet mechanic had suggested replacing the thermostat at any of their regular maintenance servicings, the General Motors field manager and his superiors, both in New Orleans and Detroit, refused to honor the warranty. Without the engine, the car that General Motors had sold them was now worth only 10 percent of what they had originally paid for it. Because they could not afford an attorney for a trial they might lose, the Roses could not file suit against General Motors.

The sales practices of Pacific Bell Telephone Company (now SBC) provide another illustration of the difficulties that face consumers. In 2003, Pacific Bell paid $15 million in fines imposed by the Public Utilities Commission (PUC) of the State of California for deceptive marketing of telephone services. The charges were related to an earlier $17 million fine the PUC ordered Pacific Bell to pay 15 years earlier when sales representatives were duping phone customers into buying expensive optional features without informing them the features were optional and that cheaper basic service was available. A sales representative described her sales pitch at that time:

> I'm going to tell you that "you will get unlimited local calling, Touchtone service, our four, custom-calling services and a 20 percent discount in the Pacific Bell service area; the central office fee to turn the services on is $37.50 and I have all of these things available and it's only $22.20 a month." Most customers will say, "That's fine." It really isn't a bad deal, but how many people know they don't have to buy all those things, that they can get basic service for $9.95? The company says, "People should be intelligent enough to ask; why should it be PacBell's job to tell them?" People who don't speak English, well, they end up with those services. Sometimes they call back and say, "What is this? I didn't want this." [Pacific Telephone sales representative]

During 1998–1999, the PUC conducted a new investigation into Pacific Bell's marketing that culminated in the $15 million fine the company paid in 2003 for deceptive marketing practices similar to those the PUC had fined in 1986. The PUC found that Pacific Bell could make up to $210 million a year if enough customers could be convinced to "unblock" their numbers so that their numbers could be revealed on caller ID phones. When customers called Pacific Bell, they were offered a free "upgrade" that in fact downgraded their phone by unblocking their number. Some customers were told blocking was being discontinued or was no longer available, and others that blocking would now mean added charges, none of which was true. In addition, Pacific Bell named an expensive package of optional services "The Basics" without informing customers that "The Basics" was not its low-cost basic service, but was, in fact, a package of pricy options such as three-way calling, call forwarding, and distinctive ringing. Finally, Pacific Bell offered customers only the highest-priced insurance for inside telephone wire repair without informing them of less-expensive options and without telling them they could hire non-Pacific Bell personnel to repair their inside phone wiring.

Consumers are also bombarded daily by an endless series of advertisements urging them to buy certain products. Although sometimes defended as sources of information, advertisements are also criticized on the grounds that they rarely do more than give the barest indications of the basic function a product is meant to serve and sometimes misrepresent and exaggerate its virtues. Economists argue that advertising expenditures are a waste of resources and sociologists bemoan the cultural effects of advertising.

This chapter examines the many ethical issues raised by product quality and advertising. The first few sections discuss various approaches to consumer issues, and the last sections deal with consumer advertising. We begin with a focus on what is perhaps the most urgent issue: consumer product injuries and the responsibilities of manufacturers.

MARKETS AND CONSUMER PROTECTION

Consumer advocates point out that there were more than 500,000 injuries requiring hospital treatment inflicted on youngsters and adults using toys, nursery equipment, and playground equipment; close to 300,000 people were mangled using home workshop equipment; over 2,000,000 people needed emergency treatment for injuries involving home furnishings; and over 3,000,000 people required treatment for injuries involving home construction materials. Injuries from auto-related accidents in 2003 averaged 56,270 each week and deaths averaged 117 per day; financial losses were estimated at $479 million per day.

Many people believe that consumers automatically will be protected from injury by the operations of free and competitive markets and that neither governments nor businesspeople have to take special steps to deal with these issues. As we have seen in earlier chapters (particularly in Chapter 4), free markets promote an allocation, use, and distribution of goods that are, in a certain sense, just, respectful of rights, and efficiently productive of maximum utility for those who participate in the market. Moreover, in such markets, the consumer is said to be "sovereign." When consumers want and will willingly pay for something, sellers have an incentive to cater to their wishes. If sellers do not provide what consumers want, then sellers will suffer losses. However, when sellers provide what consumers want, they will profit. As the author of a leading textbook on economics wrote, "Consumers direct by their innate or learned tastes, as expressed in their dollar votes, the ultimate uses to which society's resources are channeled."

In the **"market" approach to consumer protection**, consumer safety is seen as a good that is most efficiently provided through the mechanism of the free market whereby sellers must respond to consumer demands. If consumers want products to be safer, they will indicate this preference in markets by willingly paying more for safer products and showing a preference for manufacturers of safe products while turning down the goods of manufacturers of unsafe products. Producers will have to respond to this demand by building more safety into their products or they risk losing customers to competitors who cater to the preferences of consumers. Thus, the market ensures that producers respond adequately to consumers' desires for safety. However, if consumers do not place a high value on safety and demonstrate neither a willingness to pay more for safety nor a preference for safer products, then it is wrong to push increased levels of safety down their throats through government regulations that force producers to build more safety into their products than consumers demand. Such government interference, as we saw earlier, distorts markets, making them unjust, disrespectful of rights, and inefficient. It is just as wrong for businesspeople to decide on their own that consumers should have more protection than they are demanding as to force on them costly safety devices that they would not buy on their own. Only consumers can say what value they place on safety, and they should be allowed to register their preferences through their free choices in markets and not be coerced by businesses or governments into paying for safety levels they may not want.

For example, an appliance selling for $100 may indicate that it will overheat if it is used for more than an hour and a half, whereas one selling for $400 may indicate that it can be run safely all day and night continuously. Some buyers will prefer the cheaper model, willingly trading the somewhat higher risk for the $300 cut in price, whereas others will prefer the more expensive one. If government regulations forced all appliance makers to make only the safer model or if manufacturers voluntarily decided to make only the safer model, then consumers who do not feel that the increase in safety is worth $300 extra to them will be out of luck. If they cannot do without the appliance, they will be forced to pay the extra $300 even if they would have preferred spending it on something else that is more valuable to them. Thus, they are unjustly forced to pay money for something they do not want, and their resources are inefficiently wasted on something that produces little utility for them.

Critics of this market approach respond, however, that the benefits of free markets obtain with certainty only when markets have the seven characteristics that define them: (a) There are numerous buyers and sellers, (b) everyone can freely enter and exit the market, (c) everyone has full and perfect information, (d) all goods in the market are exactly similar, (e) there are no external costs, (f) all buyers and sellers are rational utility maximizers, and (g) the market is unregulated. Critics of the market approach to consumer issues argue that these characteristics are absent in consumer markets, focusing especially on characteristics (c) and (f).

Markets are efficient, critics point out, only if condition (c) obtains—that is, only if participants have full and perfect information about the goods they are buying. Obviously, consumers are frequently not well informed about the products they buy simply because the sophisticated consumer products on contemporary market shelves are too complex for anyone but an expert to be knowledgeable about them. Not surprisingly, manufacturers, who are knowledgeable about their products, might not voluntarily provide information about the safety levels or defective characteristics of their products to consumers. Because gathering information is expensive, consumers may not have the resources to acquire the information on their own by, for example, testing several competing brands to determine which provides the most safety for the cost.

In theory, it would be possible for consumers who want information to turn to organizations such as the Consumers Union, which make a business of acquiring and selling product information. That is, market mechanisms should create a market in consumer information if that is what consumers want. However, for two reasons related to the nature of information, it is difficult for such organizations to cover their costs by selling information to consumers. First, as several economists have pointed out, once information is provided to one person who pays for it, it is easily leaked to many others who do not pay, especially in this age of photocopiers. Because people know they can become ***free riders*** and acquire the information compiled by others without paying for it themselves, the number of people who willingly pay for the information is too small to allow the organization to cover its costs. Second, consumers are often unwilling to pay for information because they do not know what its value to them will be until after they get it and then they no longer need to pay for it because it is already in their possession. For example, consumers may pay for the information contained in a research report and then find that they already knew what was in the report, that it is about products other than those they want to buy, or that it is irrelevant information about those products. Consumers cannot know in advance precisely what they are buying when they buy information, thus they are unwilling to pay the costs organizations must charge to gather the information. Markets alone, then, are not able to support organizations that can provide consumers with the information they need. Instead, such organizations must rely on charitable contributions or government grants.

A second criticism of the argument that free markets can deal with all consumer issues takes aim at characteristic (f) of free markets: the assumption that the consumer is a "rational utility maximizer." As one author put it, the consumer assumed by such arguments is "a budget-minded, rational individual, relentlessly pushing toward maximizing his satisfaction . . . [who is able] to think well ahead, to 'wait,' to consider. The consumer defined by the theory watches every penny." More precisely, the ***rational utility maximizer*** that the consumer is assumed to be is a person who has a well-defined and consistent set of preferences and who is certain how personal choices will affect those preferences.

Unfortunately, virtually all consumer choices are based on probability estimates we make concerning the chances that the products we buy will function as we think they will. All the research available shows that we become highly inept, irrational, and inconsistent when we make choices based on probability estimates.

First, as is obvious to any observer, few of us are good at estimating probabilities. We typically underestimate the risks of personal life-threatening activities, such as driving, smoking, or eating fried foods, and of being injured by the products we use, and we overestimate the probabilities of unlikely but memorable events such as tornadoes or attacks by grizzly bears in national parks. Studies have shown that our probability judgments go astray for a number of reasons, including the following:

1. Prior probabilities are ignored when new information becomes available, even if the new information is irrelevant.
2. Emphasis on "causation" results in the underweighing of evidence that is relevant to probability but is not perceived as "causal."
3. Generalizations are made on the basis of small sample findings.
4. Belief is placed in a self-correcting but nonexistent "law of averages."
5. People believe that they exert control over purely chance events.

Second, as a number of researchers have shown, people are irrational and inconsistent when weighing choices based on probability estimates of future costs or payoffs. For example, one set of researchers found that when people are asked to rank probable payoffs, they inconsistently will rank one payoff as being both better and worse than another. Another investigator found that when people were asked which of two probable payoffs they preferred, they would often say that they would pay more for the payoff that they least preferred. Another set of studies found that, in many cases, a majority of persons would prefer one probable payoff to another in one context but reversed their preferences in a different context although the probable payoffs were identical in both contexts.

Finally, as several critics have pointed out and as we saw in Chapter 4, markets often fail to incorporate the most fundamental characteristic of competitive markets: the presence of numerous buyers and sellers. Although buyers or consumers in most markets are numerous, still many, perhaps most, consumer markets are monopolies or oligopolies; that is, they are dominated by one or a few large sellers. Sellers in monopoly and oligopoly markets are able to extract abnormally high profits from consumers by ensuring that supply is insufficient to meet demand, thereby creating shortages that put upward pressures on prices.

On balance, then, it does not appear that market forces by themselves can deal with all consumer concerns for safety, freedom from risk, and value. Market failures, characterized by inadequate consumer information, irrationality in the choices of consumers, and concentrated markets, undercut arguments that try to show that markets alone can provide adequate consumer protection. Instead, consumers must be protected through the legal structures of government and through the voluntary initiatives of responsible businesspeople. We turn then to examining several views about the responsibilities of businesses toward consumers—views that have formed the basis of many of our consumer laws and of increased calls for greater acceptance of responsibility for consumer protection on the part of business.

It is clear, of course, that part of the responsibility for consumer injuries must rest on consumers. Individuals are often careless in their use of products. "Do-it-yourselfers" use power saws without guards attached or use flammable liquids near open flames. People often use tools and instruments that they do not have the skill, knowledge, or experience to handle.

Injuries also arise from flaws in product design, in the materials out of which products are made, or in the processes used to construct products. Insofar as manufacturing defects are the source of product-related injuries, consumer advocates claim, the duty of minimizing injuries should lie with the manufacturer. The producer is in the best position to know the hazards raised by a certain product and to eliminate the hazards at the point of manufacture. In addition, the producer's expertise makes the producer knowledgeable about the safest materials and manufacturing methods and enables it to build adequate safeguards into the design of the product. Finally, because the producer is intimately acquainted with the workings of the product, it can best inform the consumer on the safest way to use the product and on the precautions to be taken.

Where, then, does the consumers' duty to protect their own interests end, and where does the manufacturer's duty to protect consumers' interests begin? Three different theories on the ethical duties of manufacturers have been developed, each one of which strikes a different balance between the consumers' duty to themselves and the manufacturer's duty to the consumers: the contract view, the "due care" view, and the social costs view. The contract view would place the greater responsibility on the consumer, whereas the due care and social costs views place the larger measure of responsibility on the manufacturer. We examine each of these in turn.

THE CONTRACT VIEW OF BUSINESS FIRM'S DUTIES TO CONSUMERS

According to the **contract view of the business firm's duties to its customers**, the relationship between a business firm and its customers is essentially a contractual relationship, and the firm's moral duties to the customer are those created by this contractual relationship. When a consumer buys a product, this view holds, the consumer voluntarily enters into a "sales contract" with the business firm. The firm freely and knowingly agrees to give the consumer a product with certain characteristics, and the consumer in turn freely and knowingly agrees to pay a certain sum of money to the firm for the product. By virtue of having voluntarily entered this agreement, the firm then has a duty to provide a product with those characteristics, and the consumer has a correlative right to get a product with those characteristics.

The contract theory of the business firm's duties to its customers rests on the view that a contract is a free agreement that imposes on the parties the basic duty of complying with the terms of the agreement. We examined this view earlier and noted the two justifications Kant provided for the view: A person has a duty to do what the person contracts to do because failure to adhere to the terms of a contract is a practice that (a) cannot be universalized, and (b) treats the other person as a means and not as an end. Rawls's theory also provides a justification for the view, but one that is based on the idea that our freedom is expanded by the recognition of contractual rights and duties: An enforced system of social rules that requires people to do what they contract to do will provide them with the assurance that contracts will be kept. Only if they have such assurance will people feel able to trust each other's word and, on that basis, to secure the benefits of the institution of contracts.

We also noted that traditional moralists have argued that the act of entering into a contract is subject to several secondary moral constraints:

1. Both of the parties to the contract must have full knowledge of the nature of the agreement they are entering.
2. Neither party to a contract must intentionally misrepresent the facts of the contractual situation to the other party.
3. Neither party to a contract must be forced to enter the contract under duress or undue influence.

These secondary constraints can be justified by the same sorts of arguments that Kant and Rawls use to justify the basic duty to perform one's contracts. Kant, for example, easily shows that misrepresentation in the making of a contract cannot be universalized, and Rawls argues that if misrepresentation were not prohibited, fear of deception would make members of a society feel less free to enter contracts. However, these secondary constraints can also be justified on the grounds that a contract cannot exist unless these constraints are fulfilled. A contract is essentially a free agreement struck between two parties. Because an agreement cannot exist unless both parties know what they are agreeing to, contracts require full knowledge and the absence of misrepresentation. Because freedom implies the absence of coercion, contracts must be made without duress or undue influence.

Hence, the contractual theory of business firms' duties to consumers claims that a business has four main moral duties: the basic duty of (a) complying with the terms of the sales contract and the secondary duties of (b) disclosing the nature of the product, (c) avoiding misrepresentation, and (d) avoiding the use of duress and undue influence. By acting in accordance with these duties, a business respects the right of consumers to be treated as free and equal persons—that is, in accordance with their right to be treated only as they have freely consented to be treated.

The Duty to Comply

The most basic moral duty that a business firm owes its customers, according to the contract view, is the duty to provide consumers with a product that lives up to those claims that the firm expressly made about the product, which led the customers to enter the contract freely and which formed the customers' understanding concerning what they were agreeing to buy. Winthrop Laboratories, for example, marketed a painkiller that it advertised as *nonaddictive.* Subsequently, a patient using the painkiller became addicted to it and shortly died from an overdose. A court found Winthrop Laboratories liable for the patient's death because, although it had expressly stated that the drug was nonaddictive, Winthrop Laboratories had failed to live up to its duty to comply with this express contractual claim. As this example suggests, our legal system has incorporated the moral view that firms have a duty to live up to the express claims they make about their products. The Uniform Commercial Code, for example, states in Section 2-314:

> Any affirmation of fact or promise made by the seller to the buyer that related to the goods and becomes part of the basis of the bargain creates an express warranty that the goods shall conform to the affirmation or promise.

In addition to the duties that result from the express claim a seller makes about the product, the contract view also holds that the seller has a duty to carry through on any implied claims knowingly made about the product. For example, the seller has the moral duty to provide a product that can be used safely for the ordinary and special purposes for which the customer, relying on the seller's judgment, has been led to believe it can be used. Sellers are morally bound to do whatever they know the buyers understood the sellers were promising because at the point of sale sellers should have corrected any misunderstandings of which they were aware. This idea of an implied agreement has also been incorporated into the law. Section 2-315 of the Uniform Commercial Code, for example, reads:

> Where the seller at the time of contracting has reason to know any particular purpose for which the goods are required and that the buyer is relying on the seller's skill or judgment to select or furnish suitable goods, there is . . . an implied warranty that the goods shall be fit for such purpose.

The express or implied claims that a seller might make about the qualities possessed by the product range over a variety of areas and are affected by a number of factors. Frederick Sturdivant classified these areas in terms of four variables: "The definition of product quality used here is: the degree to which product performance meets predetermined expectation with respect to (1) reliability, (2) service life, (3)maintainability, and (4) safety."

Reliability Claims of reliability refer to the probability that a product will function as the consumer is led to expect that it will function. If a product incorporates a number of interdependent components, then the probability that it will function properly is equal to the result of multiplying together each component's probability of proper functioning. As the number of components in a product multiplies, therefore, the manufacturer has a corresponding duty to ensure that each component functions in such a manner that the total product is as reliable as it is implicitly or expressly claimed to be. This is especially the case when malfunction poses health or safety hazards. The U.S. Consumer Product Safety Commission lists hundreds of examples of hazards from product malfunctions in its periodic announcements.

Service Life Claims concerning the life of a product refer to the period of time during which the product will function as effectively as the consumer is led to expect it to function. Generally, the consumer implicitly understands that service life will depend on the amount of wear and tear to which one subjects the product. In addition, consumers also base some of their expectations of service life on the explicit guarantees the manufacturer attaches to the product.

A more subtle factor that influences service life is the factor of obsolescence. Technological advances may render some products obsolete when a new product appears that carries out the same functions more efficiently. Purely stylistic changes may make last year's product appear dated and less desirable. The contract view implies that sellers who know that a certain product will become obsolete have a duty to correct any mistaken beliefs they know buyers will form concerning the service life they may expect from the product.

Maintainability Claims of maintainability are claims concerning the ease with which the product can be repaired and kept in operating condition. Claims of maintainability are often made in the form of an express warranty. Whirlpool Corporation, for example, appended this express warranty on one of its products:

> During your first year of ownership, all parts of the appliance (except the light bulbs) that we find are defective in materials or workmanship will be repaired or replaced by Whirlpool free of charge, and we will pay all labor charges. During the second year, we will continue to assume the same responsibility as stated above except you pay any labor charges.

But sellers often also imply that a product may be easily repaired even after the expiration date of an express warranty. In fact, however, product repairs may be costly, or even impossible, because of the unavailability of parts.

Product Safety Implied and express claims of product safety refer to the degree of risk associated with using a product. Because the use of virtually any product involves some degree of risk, questions of safety are essentially questions of acceptable and known levels of risk. That is, a product is safe if its attendant risks are known and judged to be "acceptable" or "reasonable" by the buyer in view of the benefits the buyer expects to derive from using the product. This implies that sellers comply with their part of a free agreement if the sellers provide a product that involves only those risks they say it involves, and buyers purchase it with that understanding. The National Commission on Product Safety, for example, characterized *reasonable risk* in these terms:

> Risks of bodily harm to users are not unreasonable when consumers understand that risks exist, can appraise their probability and severity, know how to cope with them, and voluntarily accept them to get benefits they could not obtain in less risky ways. When there is a risk of this character, consumers have reasonable opportunity to protect themselves; and public authorities should hesitate to substitute their value judgments about the desirability of the risk for those of the consumers who choose to incur it. But preventable risk is not reasonable (a) when consumers do not know that it exists; or (b) when, though aware of it, consumers are unable to estimate its frequency and severity; or (c) when consumers do not know how to cope with it, and hence are likely to incur harm unnecessarily; or (d) when risk is unnecessary in that it could be reduced or eliminated at a cost in money or in the performance of the product that consumers would willingly incur if they knew the facts and were given the choice.

Thus, the seller of a product (according to the contractual theory) has a moral duty to provide a product whose use involves no greater risks than those the seller expressly communicates to the buyer or those the seller implicitly communicates by the implicit claims made when marketing the product for a use whose normal risk level is well known. If the label on a bottle, for example, indicates only that the contents are highly toxic ("Danger: Poison"), the product should not include additional risks from flammability. If a firm makes and sells skis, use of the skis should not embody any unexpected additional risks other than the well-known risks that attend skiing (e.g., it should not involve the added possibility of being pierced by splinters should the skis fracture). In short, sellers have a duty to provide a product with a level of risk that is no higher than they expressly or implicitly claim it to be and that consumers freely and knowingly contract to assume.

The Duty of Disclosure

An agreement cannot bind unless both parties to the agreement know what they are doing and freely choose to do it. This implies that the seller who intends to enter a contract with a customer has a duty to disclose exactly what the customer is buying and what the terms of the sale are. At a minimum, this means the seller has a duty to inform the buyer of any characteristics of the product that could affect the customer's decision to purchase the product. For example, if the product the consumer is buying possesses a defect that poses a risk to the user's health or safety, the consumer should be so informed. Some have argued that sellers should also disclose a product's components or ingredients, its performance characteristics, costs of operation, product ratings, and any other applicable standards.

Behind the claim that entry into a sales contract requires full disclosure is the idea that an agreement is free only to the extent that one knows what alternatives are available: Freedom depends on knowledge. The more the buyer knows about the various products available on the market and the more comparisons the buyer is able to make among them, the more one can say that the buyer's agreement is voluntary.

The view that sellers should provide a great deal of information for buyers, however, has been criticized on the grounds that information is costly and, therefore, should be treated as a product for which the consumer should either pay or do without. In short, consumers should freely contract to purchase information as they freely contract to purchase goods, and producers should not have to provide it for them. The problem with this criticism is that the information on which a person bases a decision to enter a contract is a rather different kind of entity from the product exchanged through the contract. Because a contract must be entered into freely and free choice depends on knowledge, contractual transactions must be based on an open exchange of information. If consumers had to bargain for such information, the resulting contract would hardly be free.

The Duty Not to Misrepresent

Misrepresentation, even more than the failure to disclose information, renders freedom of choice impossible. That is, misrepresentation is coercive: The person who is intentionally misled acts as the deceiver wants the person to act and not as the person would freely have chosen to act if the person had known the truth. Because free choice is an essential ingredient of a binding contract, intentionally misrepresenting the nature of a commodity is wrong.

Sellers misrepresent a commodity when they represent it in a way deliberately intended to deceive the buyer into thinking something about the product that the seller knows is false. The deception may be created by a verbal lie, as when a used model is described as new, or it may be created by a gesture, as when an unmarked used model is displayed together with several new models. That is, the deliberate intent to misrepresent by false implication is as wrong as the explicit lie.

The varieties of misrepresentation seem to be limited only by the ingenuity of the greed that creates them. A computer software or hardware manufacturer may market a product it knows contains "bugs" without informing buyers of that fact; a manufacturer may give a product a name that the manufacturer knows consumers will confuse with the brand name of a higher-quality competing product; the manufacturer may write *wool* or *silk* on material made wholly or partly of cotton; the manufacturer may mark a fictitious "regular price" on an article that is always sold at a much lower "sale" price; a business may advertise an unusually low price for an object that the business actually intends to sell at a much higher price once the consumer is lured into the store; a store may advertise an object at an unusually low price, intending to "bait and switch" the unwary buyer over to a more expensive product; and a producer may solicit paid "testimonials" from professionals who have never really used the product. We return to some of these issues when we discuss advertising.

The Duty Not to Coerce

People often act irrationally when under the influence of fear or emotional stress. When a seller takes advantage of a buyer's fear or emotional stress to extract consent to an agreement that the buyer would not make if the buyer were thinking rationally, the seller is using duress or undue influence to coerce. An unscrupulous funeral director, for example, may skillfully induce guilt-ridden and grief-stricken survivors to invest in funeral services they cannot afford. Because entry into a contract requires freely given consent, the seller has a duty to refrain from exploiting emotional states that may induce buyers to act irrationally against their own best interests. For similar reasons, the seller also has the duty not to take advantage of gullibility, immaturity, ignorance, or any other factors that reduce or eliminate the buyer's ability to make free rational choices.

Problems with the Contractual Theory

The main objections to the contract theory focus on the unreality of the assumptions on which the theory is based. First, critics argue, the theory unrealistically assumes that manufacturers make direct agreements with consumers. Nothing could be farther from the truth. Normally, a series of wholesalers and retailers stands between the manufacturer and the ultimate consumer. The manufacturer sells the product to the wholesaler, who sells it to the retailer, who finally sells it to the consumer. The manufacturer never enters into any direct contract with the consumer. How then can one say that manufacturers have contractual duties to the consumer?

Advocates of the contract view of manufacturers' duties have tried to respond to this criticism by arguing that manufacturers enter into *indirect* agreements with consumers. Manufacturers promote their products through their own advertising campaigns. These advertisements supply the promises that lead people to purchase products from retailers, who merely function as "conduits" for the manufacturer's product. Consequently, through these advertisements, the manufacturer forges an indirect contractual relationship not only with the immediate retailers who purchase the manufacturer's product but also with the ultimate consumers of the product. The most famous application of this doctrine of broadened indirect contractual relationships is to be found in a 1960 court opinion, *Henningsen v. Bloomfield Motors*. Mrs. Henningsen was driving a new Plymouth when it suddenly gave off a loud cracking noise. The steering wheel spun out of her hands and the car lurched to the right and crashed into a brick wall. Mrs. Henningsen sued the manufacturer, Chrysler Corporation. The court opinion read:

> Under modern conditions the ordinary layman, on responding to the importuning of colorful advertising, has neither the opportunity nor the capacity to inspect or to determine the fitness of an automobile for use; he must rely on the manufacturer who has control of its construction, and to some degree on the dealer who, to the limited extent called for by the manufacturer's instructions, inspects and services it before delivery. In such a marketing milieu his remedies and those of persons who properly claim through him should not depend "upon the intricacies of the law of sales. The obligation of the manufacturer should not be based alone on privity of contract [that is, on a direct contractual relationship]. It should rest, as was once said, upon "'the demands of social justice'" *Mazetti v. Armous & Co.* (1913). "If privity of contract is required," then, under the circumstances of modern merchandising, "privity of contract exists in the consciousness and understanding of all right-thinking persons. . . ." Accordingly, we hold that under modern marketing conditions, when a manufacturer puts a new automobile in the stream of trade and promotes its purchase by the public, an implied warranty that it is reasonably suitable for use as such accompanies it into the hands of the ultimate purchaser. Absence of agency between the manufacturer and the dealer who makes the ultimate sale is immaterial.

Thus, Chrysler Corporation was found liable for Mrs. Henningsen's injuries on the grounds that its advertising had created a contractual relationship with Mrs. Henningsen and this contract created an "implied warranty" about the car, which Chrysler had a duty to fulfill.

A second objection to the contract theory focuses on the fact that a contract is a two-edged sword. If a consumer can freely agree to buy a product with certain qualities, the consumer can also freely agree to buy a product without those qualities. That is, freedom of contract allows a manufacturer to be released from contractual obligations by explicitly disclaiming that the product is reliable, serviceable, safe, and so on. Many manufacturers fix such disclaimers on their products. The Uniform Commercial Code, in fact, stipulates in Section 2-316:

a. Unless the circumstances indicate otherwise, all implied warranties are excluded by expressions like "as is," "with all faults," or other language that in common understanding calls the buyer's attention to the exclusion of warranties and makes plain that there is no warranty, and
b. When the buyer before entering into the contract has examined the goods or the sample or model as fully as he desired, or has refused to examine the goods, there is no implied warranty with regard to defects that on examination ought in the circumstances to have been revealed to him.

The contract view, then, implies that if the consumer has ample opportunity to examine the product and its disclaimers and voluntarily consents to buy it anyway, the consumer assumes the responsibility for the defects disclaimed by the manufacturer, as well as for any defects the customer may carelessly have overlooked. Disclaimers can effectively nullify all contractual duties of the manufacturer.

A third objection to the contract theory criticizes the assumption that buyer and seller meet each other as equals in the sales agreement. The contractual theory assumes that buyers and sellers are equally skilled at evaluating the quality of a product and that buyers are able to adequately protect their interests against the seller. This is the assumption built into the requirement that contracts must be freely and knowingly entered into: Both parties must know what they are doing and neither must be coerced into doing it. This equality between buyer and seller that the contractual theory assumes derives from the laissez-faire ideology that accompanied the historical development of contract theory. Classical laissez-faire ideology held that the economy's markets are competitive and that in competitive markets the consumer's bargaining power is equal to that of the seller. Competition forces the seller to offer the consumer as good or better terms than the consumer could get from other competing sellers, so the consumer has the power to threaten to take business to other sellers. Because of this equality between buyer and seller, it was fair that each be allowed to try to outbargain the other and unfair to place restrictions on either. In practice, this laissez-faire ideology gave birth to the doctrine of *caveat emptor*: Let buyers take care of themselves.

In fact, sellers and buyers do not exhibit the equality that these doctrines assume. A consumer who must purchase hundreds of different kinds of commodities cannot hope to be as knowledgeable as a manufacturer who specializes in producing a single product. Consumers have neither the expertise nor the time to acquire and process the information on which they must base their purchase decisions. Consequently, consumers must usually rely on the judgment of the seller in making their purchase decisions and are particularly vulnerable to being harmed by the seller. Equality, far from being the rule, as the contract theory assumes, is usually the exception.

THE DUE CARE THEORY

The **"due care" theory of the manufacturer's duties to consumers** is based on the idea that consumers and sellers do not meet as equals and that the consumer's interests are particularly vulnerable to being harmed by the manufacturer who has a knowledge and an expertise that the consumer lacks. Because manufacturers are in a more advantaged position, they have a duty to take special care to ensure that consumers' interests are not harmed by the products that they offer them. The doctrine of ***caveat emptor*** is here replaced with a weak version of the doctrine of ***caveat vendor***: Let the seller take care. A New York court decision neatly described the advantaged position of the manufacturer and the consequent vulnerability of the consumer:

Today as never before the product in the hands of the consumer is often a most sophisticated and even mysterious article. Not only does it usually emerge as a sealed unit with an alluring exterior rather than as a visible assembly of component parts, but its functional validity and usefulness often depend on the application of electronic, chemical, or hydraulic principles far beyond the ken of the average consumer. Advances in the technologies of materials, of processes, of operational means have put it almost entirely out of the reach of the consumer to comprehend why or how the article operates, and thus even farther out of his reach to detect when there may be a defect or a danger present in its design or manufacture. In today's world it is often only the manufacturer who can fairly be said to know and to understand when an article is suitably designed and safely made for its intended purpose. Once floated on the market, many articles in a very real practical sense defy detection of defect, except possibly in the hands of an expert after laborious, and perhaps even destructive, disassembly. By way of direct illustration, how many automobile purchasers or users have any idea how a power steering mechanism operates or is intended to operate, with its "circulating work and piston assembly and its cross shaft splined to the Pitman arm"? We are accordingly persuaded that from the standpoint of justice as regards the operating aspect of today's products, responsibility should be laid on the manufacturer, subject to the limitations we set forth.

The "due care" view holds, then, that because consumers must depend on the greater expertise of the manufacturer, the manufacturer not only has a duty to deliver a product that lives up to the express and implied claims about it but also has a duty to exercise due care to prevent others from being injured by the product even if the manufacturer explicitly disclaims such responsibility and the buyer agrees to the disclaimer. The manufacturer violates this duty and is negligent when there is a failure to exercise the care that a reasonable person could have foreseen would be necessary to prevent others from being harmed by use of the product. Due care must enter into the design of the product, the choice of reliable materials for constructing the product, the manufacturing processes involved in putting the product together, the quality control used to test and monitor production, and the warnings, labels, and instructions attached to the product. In each of these areas, according to the due care view, the manufacturer, in virtue of a greater expertise and knowledge, has a positive duty to take whatever steps are necessary to ensure that when the product leaves the plant it is as safe as possible, and the customer has a right to such assurance. Failure to take such steps is a breach of the moral duty to exercise due care and a violation of the injured person's right to expect such care—a right that rests on the consumer's need to rely on the manufacturer's expertise. Edgar Schein sketched out the basic elements of the "due care" theory several years ago when he wrote:

> [A] professional is someone who knows better what is good for his client than the client himself does . . . . If we accept this definition of professionalism . . . we may speculate that

it is the *vulnerability of the client* that has necessitated the development of moral and ethical codes surrounding the relationship. The client must be protected from exploitation in a situation in which he is unable to protect himself because he lacks the relevant knowledge to do so . . . . If [a manufacturer] is . . . a professional, who is his client? With respect to whom is he exercising his expert knowledge and skills? Who needs protection against the possible misuse of these skills? . . . Many economists argue persuasively . . . that the consumer has not been in a position to know what he was buying and hence was, in fact, in a relatively vulnerable position. . . . Clearly, then, one whole area of values deals with the relationship between the [manufacturer] and consumers.

THE TOBACCO COMPANIES AND PRODUCT SAFETY

On May 24, 2004, U.S. Disrict Judge Gladys Kessler ruled the big tobacco companies—Philip Morris, Reynolds, and Liggett—would be liable for $208 billion—almost all their profits during the past 50 years—if the U.S. Department of Justice (DOJ) proved that since 1953 they knowingly conspired to deceive the public about the risks of smoking and its addictive nature, and so operated as outlaw companies in violation of the Racketeer-Influenced and Corrupt Organizations Act. The DOJ claimed that in 1953 the companies met in New York and formed a group called the Tobacco Industry Research Committee (TIRC) that began a "conspiracy to deny that smoking caused disease and to maintain that whether smoking caused disease was an 'open question' despite having actual knowedge that smoking did cause disease." In the 1950s, despite published research showing that smoking causes cancer, the group advertised "there is no proof that cigarette smoking is one of the causes" of lung cancer, and from the 1960s to the 1990s advertised that "a cause and effect relationship between smoking and disease has not been established." The DOJ alleged the tobacco companies advertised that nicotine is not addictive even as they "controlled the nicotine delivery of cigarettes so that they could addict new users." The DOJ also claimed the companies "researched how to target their marketing at children and actively marketed cigarettes to children." Finally, the DOJ stated that while the companies had a duty to test their product, to design a safe product, and to warn users of all dangers, the companies instead did no research and tried to suppress research on smoking risks, marketed a product that kills 400,000 Americans a year, designed "low tar/low nicotine" cigarettes whose risks were the same as regular cigarettees, failed before 1969 to warn of the risks and addictive nature of smoking, and targeted children who could not know the true risks of smoking.

If the DOJ claims are true, what do the three theories of manufacturers' duties imply?

The due care view, of course, rests on the principle that agents have a moral duty not to harm or injure other parties by their acts and that this duty is particularly stringent when those other parties are vulnerable and dependent on the judgment of the agent. This principle can be supported from a variety of different moral perspectives, but it is most clearly implied by the requirements of an ethic of care. The principle follows almost immediately, in fact, from the requirement that one should care for the well-being of those with whom one has a special relationship, particularly a relationship of dependence, such as a child has on its mother. Moreover, an ethic of care imposes the requirement that one should carefully examine the particular needs and characteristics of the person with whom one has a special relationship to ensure that one's care for that person is tailored to that person's particular needs and qualities. As we see, this emphasis on carefully examining the specific needs and characteristics of a vulnerable party is also an explicit and critically important part of the due care view.

Although the demands of an ethic of care are aligned with the due care principle that manufacturers have a duty to protect vulnerable consumers, the principle has also been defended from other moral perspectives. Rule utilitarians have defended the principle on the grounds that if the rule is accepted, everyone's welfare will be advanced. The principle has been argued for on the basis of Kant's theory because it seems to follow from the categorical imperative that people should be treated as ends and not merely as means—that is, that they have a positive right to be helped when they cannot help themselves. Rawls has argued that individuals in the "original position" would agree to the principle because it would provide the basis for a secure social environment. The judgment that individual producers have a duty not to harm or injure vulnerable parties, therefore, is solidly based on several ethical perspectives.

The Duty to Exercise Due Care

According to the due care theory, manufacturers exercise sufficient care only when they take adequate steps to prevent whatever injurious effects they can foresee that the use of their product may have on consumers after having conducted inquiries into the way the product will be used and after having attempted to anticipate any possibly misuses of the product. A manufacturer then is not morally negligent when others are harmed by a product and the harm was not one that the manufacturer could have possibly foreseen or prevented. Nor is a manufacturer morally negligent after having taken all reasonable steps to protect the consumer and ensure that the consumer is informed of any irremovable risks that might still attend the use of the product. For example, a car manufacturer cannot be said to be negligent from a moral point of view when people carelessly misuse the cars the manufacturer produces. A car manufacturer would be morally negligent only if it had allowed unreasonable dangers to remain in the design of the car that consumers cannot be expected to know about or cannot guard against by taking their own precautionary measures.

What specific responsibilities does the duty to exercise due care impose on the producer? In general, the producer's responsibilities would extend to the following three areas:

Design The manufacturer should ascertain whether the design of an article conceals any dangers, whether it incorporates all feasible safety devices, and whether it uses materials that are adequate for the purposes the product is intended to serve. The manufacturer is responsible for being thoroughly acquainted with the design of the item and to conduct research and tests extensive enough to uncover any risks that may be involved in employing the article under various conditions of use. This requires researching consumers and analyzing their behavior, testing the product under different conditions of consumer use, and selecting materials strong enough to stand up to all probable usages. The effects of aging and wear should also be analyzed and taken into account in designing an article. Engineering staff should acquaint themselves with hazards that might result from prolonged use and wear, and it should warn the consumer of any potential dangers. There is a duty to take the latest technological advances into account in designing a product, especially where advances can provide ways to design a product that is less liable to harm or injure its users.

Production The production manager should control the manufacturing processes so as to eliminate any defective items, identify any weaknesses that become apparent during production, and ensure that shortcuts, substitution of weaker materials, or other economizing measures are not taken during manufacture that would compromise the safety of the final product. To ensure this, there should be adequate quality controls over materials that are to be used in the manufacture of the product and over the various stages of manufacture.

Information The manufacturer should fix labels, notices, or instructions on the product that will warn the user of all dangers involved in using or misusing the item and that will enable the user to adequately guard against harm or injury. These instructions should be clear and simple, and warnings of any hazards involved in using or misusing the product should also be clear, simple, and prominent. In the case of drugs, manufacturers have a duty to warn physicians of any risks or dangerous side effects that research or prolonged use have revealed. It is a breach of the duty not to harm or injure if the manufacturer attempts to conceal or downplay the dangers related to drug usage.

In determining the safeguards that should be built into a product, the manufacturer must also take into consideration the capacities of the persons who will use the product. If a manufacturer anticipates that a product will be used by persons who are immature, mentally deficient, or too inexperienced to be aware of the dangers attendant on the use of the product, the manufacturer owes them a greater degree of care than if the anticipated users were of ordinary intelligence and prudence. For example, children cannot be expected to realize the dangers involved in using electrical equipment. Consequently, if a manufacturer anticipates that an electrical item will probably be used by children, steps must be taken to ensure that a person with a child's understanding will not be injured by the product.

If the possible harmful effects of using a product are serious or if they cannot be adequately understood without expert opinion, then sale of the product should be carefully controlled.

A firm should not oppose regulation of the sale of a product when regulation is the only effective means of ensuring that the users of the product are fully aware of the risks its use involves.

Problems with "Due Care"

The basic difficulty raised by the "due care" theory is that there is no clear method for determining when one has exercised enough "due care." That is, there is no hard-and-fast rule for determining how far a firm must go to ensure the safety of its product. Some authors have proposed this general utilitarian rule: The greater the probability of harm and the larger the population that might be harmed, the more the firm is obligated to do. However, this fails to resolve some important issues. Every product involves at least some small risk of injury. If the manufacturer should try to eliminate even low-level risks, this would require that the manufacturer invest so much in each product that the product would be priced out of the reach of most consumers. Moreover, even attempting to balance higher risks against added costs involves measurement problems; for example, how does one quantify risks to health and life?

A second difficulty raised by the "due care" theory is that it assumes that the manufacturer can discover the risks that attend the use of a product before the consumer buys and uses it. In fact, in a technologically innovative society, new products whose defects cannot emerge until years or decades have passed will continually be introduced into the market. Only years after thousands of people were using and being exposed to asbestos, for example, did a correlation emerge between the incidence of cancer and exposure to asbestos. Although manufacturers may have greater expertise than consumers, their expertise does not make them omniscient. Who, then, is to bear the costs of injuries sustained from products whose defects neither the manufacturer nor the consumer could have uncovered beforehand?

Third, the "due care" view appears to some to be paternalistic: It assumes that the manufacturer should be the one who makes the important decisions for the consumer, at least with respect to the levels of risks that are proper for consumers to bear. One may wonder whether such decisions should not be left up to the free choice of consumers, who can decide for themselves whether they want to pay for additional risk reduction.

THE SOCIAL COSTS VIEW OF THE MANUFACTURER'S DUTIES

A third theory on the duties of the manufacturer would extend the manufacturer's duties beyond those imposed by contractual relationships and beyond those imposed by the duty to exercise due care in preventing injury or harm. This third theory holds that a manufacturer should pay the costs of any injuries sustained through any defects in the product, even when the manufacturer exercised all due care in the design and manufacture of the product and has taken all reasonable precautions to warn users of every foreseen danger. According to this third theory, a manufacturer has a duty to assume the risks of even those injuries that arise out of defects in the product that no one could reasonably have foreseen or eliminated. The theory is a strong version of the doctrine of *caveat vendor*: Let the seller take care.

This third theory, which has formed the basis of the legal doctrine of ***strict liability***, is founded on utilitarian arguments. The utilitarian arguments for this third theory hold that the "external" costs of injuries resulting from unavoidable defects in the design of an artifact constitute part of the costs society must pay for producing and using an artifact. By having the manufacturer bear the external costs that result from these injuries as well as the ordinary internal costs of design and manufacture, all costs are internalized and added on as part of the price of the product. Internalizing all costs in this way, according to proponents of this theory, will lead to a more efficient use of society's resources. First, because the price will reflect all the costs of producing and using the artifact, market forces will ensure that the product is not overproduced and resources are not wasted on it. (Whereas if some costs were not included in the price, then manufacturers would tend to produce more than is needed.) Second, because manufacturers have to pay the costs of injuries, they will be motivated to exercise greater care and thereby reduce the number of accidents. Therefore, manufacturers will strive to cut down the social costs of injuries, and this means a more efficient care for our human resources. To produce the maximum benefits possible from our limited resources, therefore, the social costs of injuries from defective products should be internalized by passing them on to the manufacturer even when the manufacturer has done all that could be done to eliminate such defects. Third, internalizing the costs of injury in this way enables the manufacturer to distribute losses among all the users of a product instead of allowing losses to fall on individuals who may not be able to sustain the loss by themselves.

Underlying this third theory on the duties of the manufacturer are the standard utilitarian assumptions about the values of efficiency. The theory assumes that an efficient use of resources is so important for society that social costs should be allocated in whatever way will lead to a more efficient use and care of our resources. On this basis, the theory argues that a manufacturer should bear the social costs for injuries caused by defects in a product even when no negligence was involved and no contractual relationship existed between the manufacturer and user.

Problems with the Social Costs View

The major criticism of the social costs view of the manufacturer's duties is that it is unfair. It is unfair, the critics charge, because it violates the basic canons of compensatory justice. Compensatory justice implies that a person should be forced to compensate an injured party only if the person could have foreseen and prevented the injury. By forcing manufacturers to pay for injuries they could neither foresee nor prevent, the social costs theory (and the legal theory of "strict liability" that flows from it) treats manufacturers unfairly. Moreover, insofar as the social costs theory encourages passing the costs of injuries on to all consumers (in the form of higher prices), consumers are also being treated unfairly.

A second criticism of the social costs theory attacks the assumption that passing the costs of all injuries on to manufacturers will reduce the number of accidents. On the contrary, critics claim, by relieving consumers of the responsibility of paying for their own injuries, the social costs theory will encourage carelessness in consumers. An increase in consumer carelessness will lead to an increase in consumer injuries.

A third argument against the social costs theory focuses on the financial burdens the theory imposes on manufacturers and insurance carriers. Critics claim that a growing number of consumers successfully sue manufactures for compensation for any injuries sustained while using a product even when the manufacturer took all due care to ensure that the product was safe. Not only have the number of "strict liability" suits increased, critics claim, but the amounts awarded to injured consumers have also escalated. Moreover, they continue, the rising costs of the many liability suits that the theory of "strict liability" has created have precipitated a crisis in the insurance industry because insurance companies end up paying the liability suits brought against manufacturers. These high costs have imposed heavy losses on insurance companies and have forced many insurance companies to raise their rates to levels that are so high that many manufacturers can no longer afford insurance. Thus, critics claim, the social costs or "strict liability" theory wreaks havoc with the insurance industry, forces the costs of insurance to climb to unreasonable heights, and forces many valuable firms out of business because they can no longer afford liability insurance nor can they afford to pay for the many and expensive liability suits they must now face.

Defenders of the social costs view, however, have replied that in reality the costs of consumer liability suits are not large. Studies have shown that the number of liability suits filed in state courts has increased at a fairly low rate. Less than 1 percent of product-related injuries results in suits, and successful suits average payments of only a few thousand dollars. Defenders of the social costs theory also point out that insurance companies and the insurance industry as a whole have remained quite profitable; they also claim that higher insurance costs are due to factors other than an increase in the amount of liability claims.

The arguments for and against the social costs theory deserve much more discussion than we can give them here. The theory is essentially an attempt to come to grips with the problem of allocating the costs of injuries between two morally innocent parties: the manufacturer who could not foresee or prevent a product-related injury and the consumer who could not guard against the injury because the hazard was unknown. This allocation problem will arise in any society that, like ours, has come to rely on technology whose effects do not become evident until years after the technology is introduced. Unfortunately, it is also a problem that may have no "fair" solution.

The Contract View: The firm's moral duties to the customer are created when the firm offers a product *with certain characteristics* and the consumer agrees to pay a certain price for the product with those characteristics. Both parties fully understand the agreement, neither has intentionally misrepresented the facts and neither has been unduly influenced or forced into entering the contract. The manufacturer's correlating duties: comply with the terms of the contract; disclose the nature of the product (and any risk to health or safety); avoid misrepresentation; and avoid use of duress and undue influence (including emotional stress and taking advantage of the consumer's ignorance or immaturity). This duty to comply with express or implied claims about a product has been incorporated into the law—the Uniform Commercial Code. This includes a moral duty to provide a product that can be used safely for the ordinary and special purposes for which the customer, relying on the seller's skill and judgment, has been led to believe it can be used.

Key Questions:

The Due Care View: Because manufacturers have more knowledge and expertise, they have a duty to take special care to ensure that consumers are not harmed by their products. The manufacturer cannot effectively disclaim responsibility for the safety of its product, even if the customer were willing to agree, if a reasonable person **could have foreseen risks** and prevented harm. Due care must be used in: 1) design, including choice of materials; 2) production (manufacturing processes, quality control); and 3) information (warnings, labels and instructions attached to the product).

Key Questions:

The Social Costs/Strict Liability View: The manufacturer should pay the costs of injuries due to defects in its products, foreseen or unforeseen and despite its exercise of due care, as a matter of public policy and because injuries are an externality that should be internalized. This will incent manufacturers to work to prevent future accidents and is the most effective allocation of societal costs associated with the use of a product.

Key Questions:

COKE SUED FOR FRAUDULENT CLAIMS ON OBESITY—PROMOTING "VITAMINWATER"

vitamins + water + sugar + hype = soda - bubbles

January 15, 2009

WASHINGTON—The Coca-Cola Company has been served notice of a class action lawsuit filed over what the Center for Science in the Public Interest (CSPI) says are deceptive and unsubstantiated claims on its VitaminWater line of beverages. Coke markets VitaminWater as a healthful alternative to soda by labeling its several flavors with such health buzz words as "defense," "rescue," "energy," and "endurance." The company makes a wide range of dramatic claims, including that its drinks variously reduce the risk of chronic disease, reduce the risk of eye disease, promote healthy joints, and support optimal immune function.

In fact, according to CSPI nutritionists, the 33 grams of sugar in each bottle of VitaminWater do more to promote obesity, diabetes, and other health problems than the vitamins in the drinks do to perform the advertised benefits listed on the bottles.

CSPI's litigation department is serving as co-counsel in the suit, filed yesterday in United States District Court in the Northern District of California. The other law firms involved in the case are Reese Richman LLP and Whatley Drake & Kallas, LLC.

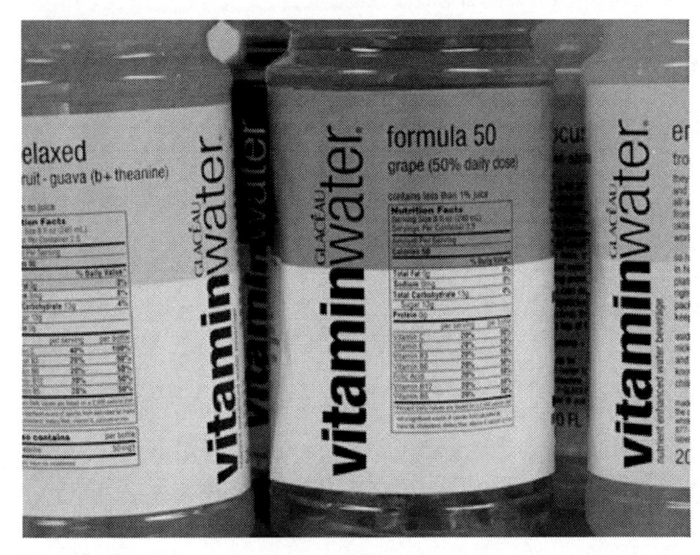

VitaminWater contains between zero and one percent juice despite product names such as "endurance peach mango" and "focus kiwi strawberry."

"When I bought VitaminWater, frankly I thought I was doing myself a favor health-wise," said the plaintiff, San Francisco, California, resident James Koh, who used to purchase and drink VitaminWater after working out at the gym. "I was attracted by the prospect of getting extra vitamins. But I had no idea that I was actually getting almost a Coke's worth of sugar and calories. There's no way I would have spent money on that, had I known."

VitaminWater's website, marketing copy, and labels claim that VitaminWater is healthy, claiming, for example, that "balance cran-grapefruit" has "bioactive components" that promote "healthy, pain-free functioning of joints, structural integrity of joints and bones" and that the nutrients in "power-c dragonfruit" "enable the body to exert physical power by contributing to the structural integrity of the musculoskeletal system."

While it is true that vitamins do play various roles in the human body, the statements on VitaminWater labels go far beyond even the loose, so-called "structure/function claims" allowed by the Food and Drug Administration and cross the line into outright fraud, according to CSPI.

Moreover, VitaminWater contains between zero and one percent juice, despite the full names of the drinks, which include "endurance peach mango" and "focus kiwi strawberry," and "xxx blueberry pomegranate acai," among others. A press release for the "xxx" drink claims its antioxidants makes the drinker "last longer" in some unspecified way; in any event, it has no blueberry, pomegranate, or acai juice, nor do the others have any cranberry, grapefruit, dragon fruit, peach, mango, kiwi, or strawberry juice.

According to documents filed in 2007 with the Securities and Exchange Commission, Coke acknowledged that "obesity and other health concerns may reduce demand for some of [its] products," and that "increasing public awareness" about health experts' concerns over sugar-sweetened beverage could affect the company's profitability. That year, Coke acquired VitaminWater's parent company, Glaceau. Also in 2007, CSPI sued Coke and its partner Nestlé over an artificially sweetened green-tea-based drink called Enviga. The companies claim Enviga burns more calories than it consumes, resulting in weight loss—a claim that CSPI says is not supported by the small number of studies on the drink's ingredients.

"Coke fears, probably correctly, that they'll sell less soda as Americans become increasingly concerned with obesity, diabetes, and other conditions linked to diets too high in sugar," said CSPI litigation director Steve Gardner. "VitaminWater is Coke's attempt to dress up soda in a physician's white coat. Underneath, it's still sugar water, albeit sugar water that costs about ten bucks a gallon." VitaminWater typically retails for about $1.49 for a 20-ounce bottle.

"My advice to consumers is to get your vitamins from real food," said CSPI executive director Michael F. Jacobson. "If you have reason to believe you have a shortcoming of one vitamin or another, perhaps take an inexpensive supplement. But don't seek out your vitamins in sugary soft drinks like Coke's VitaminWater."

Since 2005, CSPI's litigation project has, on its own or in cooperation with private law firms, negotiated settlements or voluntary changes to marketing practices with Anheuser-Busch, Airborne, Kellogg, Frito-Lay, Quaker Oats, Pinnacle Foods and others. Whatley, Drake & Kallas, LLC is a 35-lawyer firm with offices in Birmingham, New York City, and Boston which concentrates on complex class action and derivative litigation, including consumer, healthcare, insurance, employee benefits, antitrust, securities, and mass tort litigation. Reese Richman LLP handles commercial litigation with a focus on consumer, antitrust, and securities class actions.

LAWSUIT OVER DECEPTIVE VITAMIN WATER CLAIMS TO PROCEED

Court Finds Coke in Violation of Various FDA Regs and Denies Its Motion to Dismiss the Lawsuit

July 23, 2010

WASHINGTON—A federal judge has denied Coca-Cola's motion to dismiss a lawsuit over what the Center for Science in the Public Interest says are deceptive and unsubstantiated claims on the company's "vitaminwater" line of soft drinks. The company claims that vitaminwater variously reduces the risk of chronic disease, reduces the risk of eye disease, promotes healthy joints, and supports optimal immune function, and uses health buzz words such as "defense," "rescue," "energy," and "endurance" on labels.

Besides denying Coca-Cola's motion to dismiss, the ruling contains other bad omens for the company. Judge John Gleeson of the U.S. District Court for the Eastern District of New York found that the company's use of the word "healthy" violates the Food and Drug Administration's regulations on vitamin-fortified foods. The FDA's so-called "Jelly Bean" rule prohibits companies from making health claims on junk foods that only meet various nutrient thresholds via fortification. The judge also found that vitaminwater's claim on the "focus" flavor of vitaminwater that it "may reduce the risk of age-related eye disease" runs afoul of FDA regulations.

Vitaminwater is hardly a health drink with 33 grams of sugar in each 20-ounce bottle.

The judge also took note of the fact that the FDA frowns upon names of products that mention some ingredients to the exclusion of more prominent ingredients such as, in the case of vitaminwater, added sugar. The names of the drinks, along with other statements on the label, "have the potential to reinforce a consumer's mistaken belief that the product is comprised of only vitamins and water," Gleeson wrote.

"In sum, plaintiffs' allegations sufficiently state a claim that defendants have violated FDA regulations by making health claims about vitaminwater even though it does not meet required minimum nutritional thresholds, by using the word 'healthy' in implied nutrient content claims even though vitaminwater's fortification does not comply with FDA policy, and by using a product name that references only two of vitaminwater's ingredients, omitting the fact that there is a key, unnamed ingredient [sugar] in the product," Gleeson continued.

"For too long, Coca-Cola has been exploiting Americans' desire to eat and drink more healthfully by deceiving them into thinking that vitaminwater can actually prevent disease," said CSPI litigation director Steve Gardner. "In fact, vitaminwater is no more than non-carbonated soda, providing unnecessary added sugar and contributing to weight gain, obesity, diabetes, and other diseases. We look forward to representing all Americans whom Coke has deceived."

The judge also rejected Coke's argument that disclosing sugar content on Nutrition Facts labels eliminates the possibility that consumers may be misled into thinking the product has only water and vitamins, and little or no sugar. Gleeson cited a similar case involving deceptive fruit imagery on packages for Gerber's Fruit Juice Snacks, which are mostly corn syrup and sugar. That court held that "reasonable consumers should [not] be expected to look beyond misleading representations on the front of the box to discover the truth from the ingredient list in small print on the side of the box." Vitaminwater has 33 grams of sugar in each 20-ounce bottle.

The judge excluded one group of New Jersey-based plaintiffs from the case but otherwise rejected Coke's arguments to dismiss on jurisdictional grounds, paving the way for the plaintiffs' lawyers to ask to take depositions of Coca-Cola executives, to ask for discovery of key vitaminwater marketing documents, and to seek certification as a class action. Besides CSPI's litigation unit, Reese Richman LLP and Whatley Drake & Kallas, LLC are representing the plaintiffs. Michael Reese of Reese Richman and CSPI's Gardner argued in court for the plaintiffs.

CSPI is also on the verge of suing McDonald's over its use of toys to market unhealthful foods directly to young children. In previous cases, CSPI has won a major pre-lawsuit settlement agreement improving the nutritional quality of the foods Kellogg markets to children, and a settlement refunding millions of dollars to consumers who were deceived by the marketing of Airborne, a dietary supplement. CSPI is also in court in another case against Coca-Cola over deceptive claims by the company that its Enviga green-tea-flavored soft drink has "negative calories," thus promoting weight loss.

February 2, 2011

David Vladeck, Director
Bureau of Consumer Protection
Federal Trade Commission
600 Pennsylvania Ave. N.W.
Washington, DC 20580

Re: Deceptive Advertising of "vitaminwater"

Dear David:

The National Consumers League (NCL)[1] urges the Federal Trade Commission ("FTC" or the "Commission,") to promptly halt unfair and deceptive advertising by Glacéau, a subsidiary of the Coca-Cola Company, for its "vitaminwater nutrient enhanced water beverage" ("vitaminwater").

Advertising for vitaminwater deceptively claims that the beverage can reduce the chance of contracting the flu and/or the common cold. Such claims are unsubstantiated, and thus should be considered "unfair or deceptive" trade practices in violation of Section 5 of the Federal Trade Commission Act ("FTC Act"), 5 U.S.C. § 45. NCL also urges the FTC to halt the claim "vitamins + water = all you need" and the claim "nutrient enhanced water beverage" found on vitaminwater labels and promotional materials. Those statements deceptively imply that vitaminwater consists solely of vitamins and water when in fact the beverage contains substantial amounts of added sugar.

1) A point-of-sale ("POS") poster advertisement for vitaminwater states:

vitaminwater. flu shots are so last year.

The poster pictures three varieties of vitaminwater, "essential," "revive," and "multi-v." The claims "more vitamin c, more immunity, less snotty tissues" appear respectively under a picture of each variety. See Attachment A. The net impression of this POS advertisement is that vitaminwater can strengthen one's immune system to the point that administration of the flu vaccine becomes unnecessary. Such claims are unsubstantiated, and hence unfair and deceptive under the FTC Act. *Thompson Medical Co. v. FTC*, 791 F.2d 189, 193 (D.C. Cir 1986) ("in general, an advertisement is considered deceptive if the advertiser lacks a 'reasonable basis' to support the claims made in it"); *Daniel Chapter One v. FTC,* No. 10-1064, *slip op.* at 2 (D.C.

---

[1]The National Consumers League is a non-profit consumer advocacy organization. NCL is the nation's oldest consumer organization, and provides government, businesses, and other organizations with the consumer's perspective on various matters, including health-related claims for foods. NCL has a long history of filing complaints over such matters with government agencies.

Cir. Dec. 10. 2010) (denying a petition for review of an FTC Order requiring that health claims be supported by clinical trials with human subjects); *FTC v. Airborne Health,* CV 08 – 05300 *slip op.* at 6 (C.D. Cal. Aug. 13, 2008) (no credible evidence that Airborne will reduce the severity or duration of colds); *The Dannon Company,* FTC File No. 082 3158, (Dec. 15, 2010) (Dannon's ads for Dan Active deceptively conveyed to consumers that the product reduces the likelihood of getting a cold or flu); *Kellogg Company,* FTC File No. 082 3145, (June 3, 2010) (Kellogg misleadingly claimed that Rice Krispies cereal, fortified with vitamins, "now helps support your child's immunity").

The Commission should immediately take enforcement action to halt such claims because such misinformation constitutes an imminent public health hazard. Discouraging members of the public from getting a flu shot as recommended by government health authorities is not only deceptive, but dangerous. The Centers for Disease Control and Prevention (CDC), and other public health agencies, have recommended that many Americans get a vaccination to protect them from contracting the flu. *E.g.*, http://www.cdc.gov/flu/. Advertising that discourages consumers from following that advice can create substantial consumer injury, interferes with established public policy and violates the FTC Act, 15 U.S.C. § 45 (a)(1), (n).

2) A television ad for vitaminwater makes a similarly deceptive claim. The TV ad tells the story of a woman who is using a sick day to take off from work when she is perfectly healthy. The reason she has available unused sick days to do this, according to the ad, is that she drinks vitaminwater, which supports her immune system, thereby reducing her need to use sick days for legitimate reasons, and permits her to use her employer's sick leave policy to stay home with her boyfriend, watch movies, and "play hooky." The ad states:

> I love skipping work, especially when I'm feeling great. Layin' in my pj's searching Netflix for a guilty pleasure marathon. And since its Friday, I've got a nice little three-day staycation package. One of my secrets? vitaminwater power-c. It's got vitamin C and zinc to help support a healthy immune system. So I can stay home with my boyfriend – who's also playing hooky. What a coincidence.

See Attachments B and C. The implications of the ad are clear. The net impression of this advertisement is not only that the vitamin C and zinc in vitaminwater power-c help support a healthy immune system, but actually reduce the risk of contracting illnesses. The FTC Act prohibits deceptive claims, both express and implied. *Rhodes Pharmacal Co. v. FTC,* 208 F.2d 382,386 (7th Cir. 1953), *judgment modified on other grounds*, 348 U.S. 940, 75 S. Ct. 361 (1955); *see* Pridgen, D. *Consumer Protection and the Law*, §10.12 (2010). Here, the clear implication of the ad is that vitaminwater can reduce the risk of illness. Such claims are unsubstantiated and deceptive.

3) Most, if not all, varieties of vitaminwater state on the label:

> "Nutritionally enhanced water beverage" and/or "vitamins + water = all you need."

See Attachment D. These statements deceptively imply that vitaminwater consists solely of vitamins and water when the product actually contains substantial amounts of added sugar. Most varieties of vitaminwater (except vitaminwater 0, which is sugar free) contain 125 calories per bottle. The FDA has recognized that such product names and statements may mislead consumers. FDA regulations state:

> The labeling of a food which contain two or more ingredients may be misleading by reason of . . . a name which includes or suggests the name of one or more but not all such ingredients, even though the names of all such ingredients are stated elsewhere in the labeling.

21 C. F. R. § 101.18(b). The FTC has issued an enforcement policy statement indicating that it will generally follow FDA regulatory policy regarding health-related claims for food products. Enforcement Policy Statement on Food Advertising (May 1994) (available at http://www.ftc.gov/bcp/policystmt/ad-food.shtm).

The fact that the actual sugar content of vitaminwater is accurately stated in an FDA mandated nutrition label on the product does not eliminate the possibility that reasonable consumers may be misled. Ackerman v. The Coca-Cola Company, No. CV-09-0395 (JG) (RML), Slip op. (E.D.N.Y. July 21, 2010) at 33-34, citing *Williams v. Gerber Products Co.* 552 F.3d 934, 939-40 (9th Cir. 2008) ("[w]e do not think that the FDA requires an ingredient list so that manufacturers can mislead consumers and then rely on the ingredient list to correct those misinterpretations and provide a shield for liability for the deception").

The deceptive implication that vitaminwater consists only of vitamins and water is especially objectionable given the current obesity crisis in the United States. According to the CDC, about two-thirds of Americans are obese or overweight, and more than 15 percent of children are obese or overweight, *See* Childhood Overweight and Obesity (available at http://www.cdc.gov/obesity/childhood). Beverages like vitaminwater that imply they contain only vitamins and water, but in fact pack 125 calories per bottle, needlessly contribute unwelcome calories to consumers' diets. A consumer who wishes to take vitamins can take a vitamin pill and a consumer who wishes to hydrate can drink water. Neither consumer needs to, or should, consume unnecessary calories in the process.

The product labels of vitaminwater are reproduced in the form of POS display advertisements. See Attachment D. The FTC has halted deceptive health-related claims on food labels as part of its efforts to prevent unfair and deceptive trade practices. *Nestlé HealthCare Nutrition,* FTC File No. 092 3087, Complaint at page 3; Agreement Containing Consent Order at page 3 ("respondent . . . in connection with the manufacturing, *labeling,* advertising, promotion . . . or distribution of any covered product ... shall not represent, in any manner, expressly or by implication ... that such product prevents or reduces the risk of . . . cold or flu viruses" [emphasis added]).

CONCLUSION

For the reasons stated in this complaint, we urge the FTC to move quickly and halt deceptive advertising and labeling of vitaminwater. Such steps are not only necessary to protect consumers from deception, but are a public health necessity. Promotional claims that 1) dissuade consumers from getting flu shots, as recommend by U.S. public health authorities, 2) deceptively imply that vitaminwater will strengthen the immune system and protect consumers from contracting illnesses, and 3) misrepresent the sugar content of the beverage and hence contribute to the ongoing obesity crisis in America should be stopped by the Commission. The NCL further requests that the FTC require The Coca-Cola Company to run corrective advertising to dispel any lingering deceptions caused by this misleading and reckless advertising campaign.

Sincerely,

Sally Greenberg
Executive Director
National Consumers League

CASE:
PINTO FIRES

by Dennis A Gioia

On August 10, 1978, three teenage girls died horribly in an automobile accident. Driving a 1973 Ford Pinto to their church volleyball practice in Goshen, Indiana, they were struck from behind by a Chevrolet van. The Pinto's fuel tank ruptured and the car exploded in flames. Two passengers, Lynn Marie Ulrich, 16, and her cousin, Donna Ulrich, 18, were trapped inside the inferno and burned to death. After three attempts, Lynn Marie's sister, 18-year-old Judy Ann, was dragged out alive from the driver's seat, but died in agony hours later in the hospital.

They were merely the latest in a long list of people to burn to death in accidents involving the Pinto, which Ford had begun selling in 1970. By the time of the accident, the car had been the subject of a great deal of public outcry and debate about its safety, especially its susceptibility to fire in low-speed rear-end collisions. This particular accident, however, resulted in more media attention than any other auto accident in U.S. history. Why? Because it led to an unprecedented court case in which the prosecution brought charges of reckless homicide against the Ford Motor Co.—the first time that a corporation had been charged with criminal conduct, and the charge was not negligence but murder. At stake was much more than the maximum penalty of $30,000 in fines. Of immediate concern, a guilty verdict could have affected 40 pending civil cases nationwide and resulted in hundreds of millions of dollars in punitive damage awards. Of perhaps greater concern, however, were larger issues involving corporate social responsibility, ethical decision making by individuals within corporations, and ultimately, the proper conduct of business in the modern era.

How did Ford get into this situation? The chronology begins in early 1968 when the decision was made to battle the foreign competition in the small car market, specifically the Germans, but also the growing threat from the Japanese. This decision came after a hard-fought, two-year internal struggle between then-president Semon "Bunky" Knudsen and Lee Iacocca, who had risen quickly within the company because of his success with the Mustang. Iacocca strongly supported fighting the competition at their own game, while Knudsen argued instead for letting them have the small car market so Ford could concentrate on the more profitable medium and large models. The final decision ultimately was in the hands of then-CEO Henry Ford II, who not only agreed with Iacocca but also promoted him to president after Knudsen's subsequent forced resignation.

Iacocca wanted the Pinto in the showrooms by the 1971 model introductions, which would require the shortest production planning period in automotive history to that time. The typical time span from conception to production of a new car was more than three and a half years; Iacocca, however, wanted to launch the Pinto in just over two years. Under normal conditions, chassis design, styling, product planning, advance engineering, component testing, and so on were all either completed or nearly completed prior to tooling of the production factories. Yet, because tooling had a fixed time frame of about 18 months, some of these other processes were done more or less concurrently. As a consequence, when it was discovered through crash testing that the Pinto's fuel tank often ruptured during rear-end impact, it was too late (in other words, too costly) to do much about it in terms of redesign.

A closer look at the crash-test reports reveals that Ford was aware of faulty fuel tank design. Eleven Pintos were subjected to rear-end collisions with a barrier at average speeds of 31 miles per hour to determine if any fuel would be lost after impact. All eight of the Pintos equipped with the standard fuel tank failed. The three remaining cars, however, survived the test because special measures had been taken to prevent tank rupture or fuel leakage. These measures included a plastic baffle placed between the axle housing and the gas tank, a steel plate between the tank and the rear bumper, and a rubber lining in the gas tank.

It should be noted that these tests were done under guidelines established by Federal Motor Vehicle Safety Standard 301, which was proposed in 1968 by the National Highway Traffic Safety Administration (NHTSA), but not officially adopted until the 1977 model year. Therefore, at the time of the tests, the Pinto met the required standards. Standard 301 had been strenuously opposed by the auto industry, and specifically Ford Motor Co. In fact, the lobbying efforts were so strong that negotiations continued until 1976, despite studies showing that hundreds of thousands of cars burned every year, taking 3,000 lives annually; the adoption of the standard was projected to reduce the death rate by 40 percent. Upon approval of Standard 301 in 1977, all Pintos were provided with a rupture-proof fuel tank design.

But for the Pinto's 1971 debut, Ford decided to go with its original gas tank design despite the crash-test results. Because the typical Pinto buyer was assumed to be extremely price conscious, Iacocca set an important goal known as "the limits of 2,000": the Pinto could not cost more than $2,000 and could not weigh more than 2,000 pounds. Thus, to be competitive with foreign manufacturers, Ford felt it could not spend any money on improving the gas tank. Besides, during the late 1960s and early 1970s, American consumers demonstrated little concern for safety, so it was not considered good business sense to promote it. Iacocca echoed these sentiments when he said time and time again "Safety doesn't sell," a lesson he had learned after a failed attempt to add costly safety features to 1950s Fords.

Ford had experimented with placing the gas tank in different locations, but all alternatives reduced usable trunk space. A design similar to that of the Ford Capri was successful in many crash tests of speeds over 50 miles per hour, but Ford felt that lost trunk space would hurt sales too much. One Ford engineer, when asked about the dangerous gas tank said, "Safety isn't the issue, trunk space is. You have no idea how stiff the competition is over trunk space. Do you realize that if we put a Capri-type tank in the Pinto, you could only get one set of golf clubs in the trunk?"

The last of Ford's reasons for not making adjustments to the fuel tank design, however, was unquestionably the most controversial. After strong lobbying efforts, Ford and the auto industry in general convinced NHTSA regulators that cost/benefit analysis would be an appropriate basis for determining the feasibility of safety design standards. Such an analysis, however, required the assignment of a value for a human life. A prior study had concluded that every time someone died in an auto accident there was an estimate "cost to society" of $200,725 (detailed in Table 4.1: What's Your Life Worth?).

Having this value in hand, Ford calculated the cost of adding an $11 gas tank improvement versus the benefits of the projected 180 lives that would be saved (via an internal memo entitled "Fatalities Associated with Crash-Induced Fuel Leakage and Fires"). This is presented in Table 4.2: the Cost of Dying in a Pinto. As is demonstrated, the costs outweigh the benefits by almost three times. Thus, the cost/benefit analysis indicated that no improvements to the gas tanks were warranted.

Ford decided to go ahead with normal production plans, but the Pinto's problems soon surfaced. By early 1973, Ford's recall coordinator received field reports suggesting that Pintos were susceptible to "exploding" in rear-end collisions at very low speeds (under 25 miles per hour). Reports continued to indicate a similar trend in subsequent years, but no recall was initiated despite the mounting evidence. At every internal review, those responsible decided not to recall the Pinto.

Prior to the Indiana accident, the most publicized case concerning the Pinto's gas tank was that of Richard Grimshaw. In 1972, Richard, then 13, was riding with a neighbor on a road near

Table 4.1 What's Your Life Worth?

The chart below, from a 1971 study by the National Highway Traffic Safety Administration, is a breakdown of the estimated cost to society every time someone is killed in a car accident. The Ford Motor Company used the $200,725 total figure in its own cost-benefit analysis.

Component	1971 Costs
Component	
Future productivity losses	
Direct	$132,300
Indirect	41,000
Medical costs	
Hospital	700
Other	425
Property damage 1,500	
Insurance administration	4,700
Legal and court	3,000
Employer losses	1,000
Victim's pain and suffering	10,000
Funeral	900
Assets (lost consumption)	5,000
Miscellaneous accident cost	200
Total per fatality	$200,725

Table 4.2 The Cost of Dying in a Pinto

These figures are from a Ford Motor Co. Internal memorandum on the benefits and costs of an $11 safety improvement (applicable to all vehicles with similar gas tank designs) that would have made the Pinto less likely to burn.

Benefits

Savings: 180 burn deaths, 180 serious burn injuries, 2,100 burned vehicles.
Unit Cost: $200,000 per death, $67,000 per injury, $700 per vehicle.
Total Benefit (180 x $200,000) + (180 x $67,000) + (2,100 x $700) = $49.5 million.

Costs

Sales: 11 million cars, 1.5 million light trucks.
Unit Cost: $11 per car, $11 per truck.
Total Cost: (11,000,000 x $11) + (1,500,000 x $11) = $137.5 million.

San Bernardino, California, when they were hit from the rear. The Pinto's gas tank ruptured, causing the car to burst into flames. The neighbor was burned to death in a crash that would have been survivable if there had been no fire. Richard suffered third-degree burns over 90 percent of his body and subsequently underwent more than 60 operations, with only limited success. A civil suit was settled in February 1978, when a jury awarded a judgment of over $125 million against Ford, most of which consisted of punitive damages (later reduced to $6 million by a judge who nonetheless accused Ford of "callous indifference to human life"). This judgment was based on convincing evidence that Ford chose not to spend the $11 per car to correct the faults in the Pinto gas tanks that its own crash testing had revealed.

The Pinto sold well until the media called special attention to the Pinto fuel tank story. As a consequence, in June 1978, in the face of pressure from the media, the government, pending court cases, and the potential loss of future sales, Ford ordered a complete recall of all 1.5 million Pintos built between 1970 and 1976. During the 1980 Indiana trial that resulted from the fatal accident of 1978, differing views continued to be expressed about the Pinto fires case. Ford representatives argued that companies must make cost/benefit decisions all the time. They claimed that it is an essential part of business, and even though everyone knows that some people will die in auto accidents, buyers want costs held down; therefore, people implicitly accept risks when buying cars.

In a scathing article accusing Ford of criminally mismanaging the Pinto problem, investigative reporter Mark Dowie framed the case in a different and rather more sensational way, with this often-quoted speculation: "One wonders how long the Ford Motor Company would continue to market lethal cars were Henry Ford II and Lee Iacocca serving twenty-year terms in Leavenworth for consumer homicide."

QUESTIONS ON READINGS FOR PART SIX (C) (1 OF 2)

How far *must* manufacturers go to protect consumers? (legal obligations)

How can a manufacturer reduce the risk of product liability?

How far *should* they go? (ethical obligations)

The pragmatic perspective: the market approach

The principled perspective

What is the contract view?

What is the due care view?

What is the "social costs" view?

LAW AND ETHICS

Jef I. Richards

This page provides information, and links to information, about advertising law and ethics. This site is intended to supplement, not replace, the popular Advertising Law Internet Page created by Lewis Rose, at the Arent Fox Kintner Plotkin & Kahn law firm. Some of the links below are to resources on that site.

CHILDREN

Issues of advertising law and ethics often center around advertising's potential impacts on children. Since about 1970, many concerns and criticisms have been expressed about the effects of ads on kids, and many laws have been proposed to deal with those effects. In addition to the *Federal Trade Commission's* active involvement in protecting children, because much of the advertising targeting children historically has appeared on television, the *Federal Communications Commission* likewise has been heavily involved in regulating such advertising.

More recently it has become common for advertising's critics to cast otherwise unconstitutional regulatory proposals in terms of child protection. For example, after several congressional bills designed to curtail tobacco advertising failed, their sponsors began introducing bills to stop tobacco advertising that might have an impact on children. The obvious hope is that courts will be more forgiving of laws aimed at protecting kids.

For additional information, see the following: *Children's Television Act of 1990.* (47 U.S.C. Sec. 303a) Standards for children's television programming & advertising.

DECEPTION

The *Federal Trade Commission* (FTC) is the primary regulator of deceptive advertising in the U.S. It was created by the *FTC Act* in 1914.

Section 5 of the Act gave the Commission the authority to regulate "unfair methods of competition." The Act was later changed, by the Wheeler-Lea Amendment, to give the FTC authority over both "unfair methods of competition" and "unfair or deceptive acts or practices." It is through this latter power that the FTC regulates deceptive advertising.

Commissioners of the FTC act like judges, hearing cases when marketers are charged with violating the FTC Act. The Commission also publishes advertising guidelines for marketers, which are not law but merely advisory, and adopts trade regulation rules, which are law.

Basic Principles

According to its 1993 Policy Statement on Deception, the FTC considers a marketing effort to be deceptive if: (1) there is a representation, omission, act or practice, that (2) is likely to mislead consumers acting reasonably under the circumstances, and (3) that representation, omission, or practice is "material." The term "material" refers to the fact that some deceptive claims are trivial, and that the FTC will only regulate deceptions that are important to consumers, i.e., those that affect consumers' "choice of, or conduct regarding, a product."

Evidence

To prove that an ad claim is, in fact, deceptive, the FTC is not generally concerned with what the claim says, but what it conveys to consumers. If that conveyed message differs from the reality of the product attribute being advertised, the claim is considered deceptive. This requires the Commission to look at two types of evidence: (1) evidence concerning what message is conveyed to consumers, and (2) evidence concerning the product attribute's true qualities.

The former requires looking into the heads of consumers. The FTC considers surveys the best form of evidence to discover what message is conveyed by an ad, though sometimes the Commission relies on other evidence. The question of how best to unearth the inner thoughts of consumers has been an issue of significant research efforts and theoretical discussion.

The second form of evidence can require a variety of different methods of assessing a product's attributes. If, for example, the claim refers to the fuel mileage of an automobile, laboratory testing of the vehicle's fuel efficiency would normally be required. However, the FTC requires that advertisers conduct such testing prior to making the ad claim. If a claim is made without evidence in hand that the product will perform as advertised, the claim will be considered deceptive. This is known as "substantiation," and the Commission's requirements are detailed in the 1984 FTC Substantiation Policy.

Remedies

Most cases started by the FTC never require the Commission to make a final decision about the deceptiveness of an advertiser's claim. Those cases end, instead, in a "consent order," whereby the advertiser simply agrees to do what the FTC staff asks. No hearing is required.

In those cases that do end in a final FTC decision, if the claim is found deceptive, the advertiser will face one of three possible remedies: (1) a Cease and Desist Order, which requires the advertiser to stop making the claim, (2) an Affirmative Disclosure Order, which forces the advertiser to provide consumers with more information, or (3) Corrective Advertising, which is a form of affirmative disclosure that is intended to correct lingering deception that results from a long history of deceiving the consumer.

Puffery

Historically, claims that were "mere exaggerations" or "hyperbole" were considered to be puffery, and therefore not deceptive. Terms like "the best" or "the greatest" were sales talk, and the FTC would not regulate them. After all, everyone knows that "Wonder Bread" is not really a wonder, and "The Greatest Show on Earth" is not what everyone considers the greatest. Puffery, therefore, was a form of opinion statement, and considered unregulable.

Some observers have expressed concern that the "puffery defense" was a loophole through which many deceptive claims fell. The Commission has been criticized for allowing deceptive claims to slip through under the guise of puffery.

On the other hand, the FTC has defined puffery as claims that (1) reasonable people do not believe to be true product qualities, and (2) are incapable of being proved either true or false. Consequently, if deception is the creation of a "false belief" about the product in the mind of a consumer, claims that fall into the FTC definition of puffery cannot be deceptive. By definition, such claims can be neither false nor can they create belief. This means that if deceptive claims have slipped through regulation as puffs, it is because the FTC has failed to follow its own definition.

ETHICS

Law and ethics are not coterminous. All the issues discussed on this page have ethical dimensions, but not all of them implicate legal realities. The law is confined by limitations on government authority, principally through the Constitution, while ethics bear no such limitations. Ethics, therefore, should be subject to a higher standard of expectation than law. See: *bibliography of advertising ethics* and *Morality and Ethics quotes.*

FIRST AMENDMENT

The *United States Constitution*, through the First Amendment, places constraints on government repression of speech. Advertising is recognized by the courts as a form of "commercial speech." Commercial speech has been defined by the Court as speech "which does no more than propose a commercial transaction." Although the courts never have recognized it as being as valuable as some other forms of speech, commercial speech is protected by the First Amendment.

This means that many of the criticisms aimed at advertising are not regulable by government. However, the Supreme Court, in Central Hudson Gas & Electric v. Public Service Commission, declared that commercial speech can be regulated if:

- It is misleading or concerns an illegal product, OR if
- There is a substantial government interest, AND
- The regulation directly advances that government interest, AND
- The regulation is narrowly tailored to that interest.

If a regulation can pass that test, it will be held constitutional. You can read some of the *advertising-related Supreme Court decisions here*. In addition, we have provided *a bibliography of articles and books about commercial speech*, to help you learn more about this topic, along with some *quotes about advertising and free speech*.

POLITICAL

Political advertising is subject to different rules than ads for commercial products and services. Because "political speech" is widely acknowledged as the core reason behind the free speech provisions of the First Amendment, the Supreme Court treats such speech as the most valuable (and, hence, most protected) form of speech. Political advertising is both advertising and political speech, but since it does not fall within the definition of "commercial speech" it is considered political speech and receives the highest degree of protection under the First Amendment.

Political advertising is not wholly unregulated, though. It is subject to some minor restraint under the Federal Communications Commission's Equal Access law, and under the Federal Election Act. Also, most states have some laws that apply to political advertising, though most of those restrictions never have been tested for constitutionality and they are largely unenforced.

At this point little information specifically dealing with political advertising has been posted on the Internet. However, feel free to look at *Political Advertising quotes*.

PRIVACY

In marketing communications, issues of privacy have historically been the province of direct marketing. However, new technologies—particularly the Internet—have spurred an "interpersonalization" (or "demassification") of advertising. This has wrought a blurring of the lines that traditionally separated various types of marketing communication. In years past, advertising was one-way communication through a mass medium. Today, it is taking on characteristics of direct marketing, enabling two-way communication between buyer and seller. As a result, it inherits some of the legal and ethical considerations of direct marketing, which largely concern invasion of consumers' privacy. For more information, see:

Privacy in the Electronic Age. A speech by FTC Commissioner Christine A. Varney, November 1995.

SELF-REGULATION

The advertising industry has no real Code of Ethics or Code of Professional Conduct. This is largely because advertising is a profession of communication, and communication is protected by the First Amendment. While other professions can adopt a Code that is enforceable by law, any attempt to license or otherwise legally enforce an ethical code for advertising would run afoul of free speech guarantees.

The closest thing to an Advertising Code of Ethics is the Code of Advertising adopted by the Council of Better Business Bureaus (CBBB). That code applies to all Better Business Bureau members.

The CBBB also serves as the administrative parent of the advertising industry's system of self-regulation. Industry self-regulation was developed in 1971 by the three major advertising industry trade associations—the American Association of Advertising Agencies, the Association of National Advertisers, and the American Advertising Federation—along with the CBBB.

The System includes:

1. The National Advertising Division (NAD) of the CBBB, which looks for truth and accuracy in national advertising. NAD reviews advertising in response to complaints by consumers and local Better Business Bureaus. It also accepts challenges brought by competitors, which make up about half of the NAD caseload. These companies generally are seeking quick resolution from experts, while avoiding litigation. NAD chooses which cases it will open based on the merits of each case. Upon reviewing the evidence, NAD may recommend the advertiser modify or discontinue an advertising practice if the facts merit such recommendation.
2. The Children's Advertising Review Unit (CARU), which examines national advertising directed at children under 12, and privacy practices at websites directed to children under 13. CARU also pre-screens advertising to assure that it is consistent with CARU's guidelines before it reaches the marketplace.
3 The Children's Food and Beverage Advertising Initiative (Initiative), a pledge program developed for food and beverage companies. Companies participating in the Initiative account for more than 2/3 of all television advertising directed to children. This Initiative was launched in 2007.

4. The Electronic Retailing Self-Regulation Program (ERSP), which examines direct-response advertising, including infomercials, home-shopping channels and e-mail advertising. ERSP was founded in 2004.
5. The National Advertising Review Board (NARB), which serves as the appeals body for NAD and CARU cases. NARB is made up of 70 professionals from three different categories: national advertisers (40 members), advertising agencies (20 members) and individuals representing the general public (10 members). For each appealed case a panel of five—three advertiser members, one agency member, and one public member—hears the evidence and renders a decision.

Participation in the advertising industry system of self-regulation is voluntary. However, advertisers that either refuse to participate or decline to comply with the terms of an NAD, CARU, ERSP or NARB decision may be referred to the appropriate government agencies (e.g., FTC, FDA) for additional review.

SUBLIMINAL APPEALS

Subliminal stimulation has become one of the more popular advertising-related topics for students and lay-people. Popularized by Wilson Bryan Key's book, Subliminal Seduction (1973), this subject has captured the imagination of people everywhere.

The term "subliminal" means "below the limen," or below the threshold of consciousness. The idea is that certain things are heard, seen, or felt, that never reach our conscious thought processes, and that those things may still be recorded somewhere in our mind and have an impact on our decisions and behavior. Key argued that advertising professionals use this concept to hide images within advertisements, and that these images manipulate our behavior without our even realizing we have seen them.

Key uses the term "subliminal perception," which is something of a misnomer, since perception implies conscious awareness. Psychologists have studied this phenomenon since the late 1800s, and originally called it "subception." However, while this is a real psychological phenomenon, all research on this topic indicates that subliminal stimulation is incapable of affecting our purchasing behavior, contrary to the allegations of Key.

While this is a fun topic of discussion, there is no evidence that advertisers embed hidden images in advertisements, and there is ample evidence that such efforts would be a waste of time.

SWEEPSTAKES, CONTESTS & LOTTERIES

Games of chance have been popular promotional devices for nearly 500 years. In the 1500s merchants in Italy used prizes by chance as a means of increasing business. But anti-gambling laws have restricted their use as a marketing tool. Over the past century games of chance have been severely limited by both state and federal laws. In recent years, however, sweepstakes and contests have become popular marketing tools. Generally, these games of chance are permitted, so long as they do not constitute "lotteries" or "gift enterprises."

Although restrictions vary somewhat from one jurisdiction to another, a lottery, gift enterprise or similar scheme exists when:

- the distribution of a prize,
- according to chance, and
- for consideration.

So long as a sweepstake or contest does not involve all three of these elements, it normally will not run afoul of legal restrictions. Those three elements are frequently typically defined as follows:

- Prize—Anything of value offered as inducement to participate.
- Consideration—Consumers must pay some value (e.g., money, purchase of a product, etc.) . . . usually substantial value. The mere act of tuning in a TV program or paying for postage is not an act of value.
- Chance—This involves the happening of some subsequent event, incapable of ascertainment by means of known foresight or ingenuity. If skill or judgment are involved, such as betting on horse races, it is not a lottery.

Games of chance already have appeared on the Internet.

TELEMARKETING

Telemarketing has become increasingly unpopular with consumers in recent years, as the practice has become more pervasive. New technologies have made it possible for computers to place the calls, dramatically increasing the calls received by many people. It is seen by some as an invasion of their privacy, an unwanted interference, an annoyance, and when the consumer is paying for phone services by the minute (e.g., mobile telephones) sellers are costing consumers money. In effect, the marketers are seen by many as using the consumer's property (telephone) for their own purposes. This has led to numerous legal and self-regulatory measures aimed at curtailing the practice or, at a minimum, putting more control over this practice in the hands of the individual consumers.

To this end, there are many telemarketing laws that have emerged at the end of the 20th Century. Several states now require marketers to obtain lists of people who prefer not to receive telemarketing calls, and make it illegal for marketers to call anyone whose name appears on the do-not-call lists. In many cases the state's Attorney General creates and maintains such a list, in some cases they must use other lists like the one maintained by the Direct Marketing Association, and in some instances it is up to the individual marketer to establish and maintain its own list. At least two states now are requiring telemarketers to register and obtain a bond before calling consumers in that state. And some states are starting to place limits or specific requirements on calls, like prohibiting the use of automatic calling devices or requiring clear disclosures be made at the beginning of a telemarketing call. Note that many or most of these rules also apply to Unsolicited Advertising Faxes.

For additional information, see the *FTC Telemarketing Sales Rule* and other FTC Telemarketing publications and guidelines. Also see the Direct Marketing Association's State Telephone Marketing Laws and the Telephone Consumer Protection Act.

TOBACCO & ALCOHOL

Tobacco and alcohol advertisements are extremely popular targets for regulation. Both products can cause death or injury, and both are subject to attack by activist groups opposed to those products. Much debate has surrounded ad regulation proposals for these products.

Many critics have argued that ads cause consumption of these products, and that the harmful impact of these goods can be diminished by curtailing or severely restricting the ads. Others counter that there is no real evidence that the ads cause consumption and that it is the product, not the advertising, that is the danger, so it is the product that should be regulated. Central to this debate is the question of whether the First Amendment would allow such regulation.

TRADEMARK & COPYRIGHT

Trademark and copyright are part of what the legal community calls "intellectual property." These two areas of advertising law are too frequently overlooked by both scholars and practitioners. Too often, trademarks are violated, or the marketer fails to protect a mark. And, commonly, advertisements are published with no effort to protect the copyrights in the art and copy of the ads.

As a simple primer to the copyright laws, for students, I prepared How to Copyright Your Creative Work. For other information about both copyright and trademark law, see:

- *Bibliography of Copyright Issues*
- *U.S. Copyright Act*

UNFAIRNESS

In addition to its power to regulate deceptiveness, the FTC can regulate marketing practices for unfairness. It is possible for marketers to treat consumers unfairly without deceiving them.

In the past, the unfairness power enabled the FTC to reach a wide variety of marketing practices. Until 1980, the Commission defined unfairness to include "immoral, unethical, oppressive, or unscrupulous conduct." This, many business people felt, allowed the Commission too broad a range of authority. Responding to pressure from Congress, in 1980 the FTC published a *Policy Statement on Unfairness* that re-defined the scope of this authority.

After 14 years of debate, the FTC Act Amendments of 1994 incorporated a definition of "unfairness" into the Commission's enabling Act. This new definition limits the application of the FTC's unfairness power to an act or practice that:

1. or is likely to cause . . . substantial injury to consumers,
2. is not reasonably avoidable by consumers themselves,
3. is not outweighed by countervailing benefits to consumers or to competition.

How this definition will be interpreted by the Commission remains subject to speculation, until some cases of unfairness are decided.

HOW ADVERTISING PRACTITIONERS VIEW ETHICS

Moral Muteness, Moral Myopia, and Moral Imagination

Minette E. Drumwright and Patrick E. Murphy

ABSTRACT: This study examines how advertising agency personnel perceive, process, and think about ethical issues. We conducted in-depth, elite interviews with advertising practitioners at all levels in 29 agencies in eight cities. Many of our informants reported few ethical concerns in their own work or in advertising in general. They exhibited "moral myopia," a distortion of moral vision that prevents moral issues from coming into focus, and "moral muteness," meaning that they rarely talk about ethical issues. We find that the reasons for moral muteness and moral myopia are categorizable. There were, however, "seeing/talking" advertising practitioners who demonstrated "moral imagination" when responding to ethical problems. We compare the manner in which the ethically sensitive practitioners contemplate and respond to ethical issues with those characterized as having moral muteness and moral myopia. We also find that the agency context in which advertising practitioners work is important in terms of ethical sensitivity. We discuss implications for theory, research, practice, and education.

Advertising practitioners face ethical issues that are common to all professionals, but they also encounter issues related to factors unique to advertising. Despite some academic and popular discussion of ethics in advertising, ranging from its broad social consequences to consumers' perceptions of potentially objectionable ads, we know little about how advertising practitioners react to ethical issues when they arise. This paper is an attempt to address this relatively neglected area. Our focus is to examine how advertising practitioners perceive, process, and think about ethical issues. Summarizing our findings, within our sample of the advertising community, significant numbers of practitioners either do not see ethical dilemmas that arise or their vision is shortsighted. Reasons or justifications for this visual impairment can be categorized. When ethical issues are recognized, there is little communication about them. There are exceptions, however—some practitioners do see and talk about ethical issues. Finally, the type of organizational community has an impact on awareness of ethical issues and ways of dealing with them.

BACKGROUND

Cunningham (1999, p. 500) defined advertising ethics as "what is right or good in the conduct of the advertising function. It is concerned with questions of what ought to be done, not just with what legally must be done." Although ethics is considered a mainstream topic in the advertising literature (Hyman, Tansley, and Clark 1994), the amount of academic research on it has not been commensurate with its importance. Historically, the topic of ethics in advertising has been examined largely through commentary and philosophical debate (Drumwright 1993) and from a "macro" perspective of advertising's effects on society rather than at the "micro" level of the firm and the practitioners working in it (Hunt and Chonko 1987). Drumwright (1993) characterized this work as pertaining to one of two discourses: (1) a legal discourse among lawyers and regulators that focuses largely on the rights of advertisers and on what they can and cannot do vis-à-vis issues such as deception and fraud (e.g., Federal Trade Commission 1980; Preston 1994, 1996; Prosser 1984; Stern and Eovaldi 1984) and (2) a moral discourse primarily among philosophers, social critics, and ethicists that raises broad and far-reaching questions related to advertising's societal effects (e.g., Bishop 1949; Brenkert 1998; Galbraith 1958, 1967; Leiser 1979; Pollay 1986; Pontifical Council for Social Communication 1997; Santilli 1983; Waide 1987). These debates and commentaries have a long history and cut across academic disciplines. In recent studies of ethics in advertising, the emphasis has been on developing an understanding of consumers' perceptions of potentially objectionable advertising (e.g., ads with persuasive appeals, ads with idealized imagery, ads for politicians, ads for dangerous products, and ads targeting children) through empirical studies (e.g., Gulas and McKeage 2000; Latour and Henthorne 1994; Tinkham and Waver-Larisay 1994; Triese et al. 1994). Much of this work has been descriptive as opposed to normative, as has been the case for research in marketing ethics more generally (Dunfee, Smith, and Ross 1999).

Relatively few studies have examined the views of advertising practitioners. Of those that exist, most have used scenarios to assess the perceptions of respondents regarding the ethics of certain behaviors and practices (e.g., Davis 1994; Ferrell, Zey-Ferrell, and

Krugman 1983; James, Pratt, and Smith 1994; Pratt and James 1994). Moon and Franke (2000) provide a thorough review of the literature and proceed to use scenarios to collect data regarding practices that Korean advertising practitioners viewed as objectionable and compared the responses to those of American advertising practitioners in a small survey reported in *Advertising Age* (1988). They found that Koreans were more ethically sensitive in their reactions to the scenarios, on average, than were Americans. Reactions to the ethical scenarios reflected a variety of cultural influences, and Hofstede's (1980, 1983) typology of cultural dimensions helped explain certain patterns of cross-cultural differences. In another study, James, Pratt, and Smith (1994) used scenarios to identify differences in reactions of students versus those of practitioners. For example, students were more likely to apply deontology (i.e., duty-based thinking) to ethical decision making than were practitioners.

A small body of work has surveyed advertising practitioners to ascertain perceived ethical problems. For example, Rotzoll and Christians (1980) and Hunt and Chonko (1987) mailed questionnaires to advertising agency employees and asked them to describe ethical dilemmas they had encountered in response to open-ended questions. In Rotzoll and Christians' study (1980), "most respondents reported that they *did* encounter ethical decision making in their work" (p.426), and "[m]ost of the responses show a lively interest in doing the right thing" (p. 429). Rotzoll and Christians ascertained that the major areas of ethical concern involved the content and creation of advertising messages and the agency-client relationship. In Hunt and Chonko's study (1987), 85% of respondents reported ethical problems in their daily work, and 43% perceived their most difficult problem occurring with "a frequency significantly beyond the mere 'isolated incident'" (or five to seven on a seven-point scale) (p. 22). They reported that more than half of their respondents saw problems involving treating clients fairly or creating honest, non-misleading, socially desirable advertisements. In a study based on Rotzoll and Christians' and Hunt and Chonko's work, Chen and Liu (1998) surveyed Taiwanese advertising practitioners and found that 67.5% reported that ethical problems were commonplace at work. However, 74.1% said that these ethical problems affected their work "not at all" or "a little." Moon and Franke (2000) replicated Hunt and Chonko's study among advertising practitioners in Korea and found that 55% reported aspects of advertising that posed moral problems in their daily work, and 49% perceived their most difficult problem occurring frequently (five to seven on a seven-point scale). Hunt, Wood, and Chonko (1989) found that advertising agency personnel, in comparison with other marketing professionals, "perceived their companies to have the highest ethical values" (p. 84). As detailed below, our findings were considerably less encouraging.

Mail surveys and scenario analyses are effective in identifying ethical issues and determining which practices are generally accepted or rejected on ethical grounds. Yet they provide little insight into how advertising practitioners think about, approach, and deal with ethical issues—that is, the meanings that ethical issues have for them, the assumptions they make about these issues, and the paradigms from which they operate. Our goal is to examine directly how advertising practitioners perceive, process, and consider these issues.

METHOD

When the goal of research is to understand the meanings that individuals give to their actions rather than to predict their behavior, qualitative methods are often the most appropriate methodology (Braybrooke 1965). Field-based approaches, such as in-depth interviews, are particularly useful when the research objective is to understand tacit perceptions, beliefs, and values, especially when the researcher cannot be sure what interpretation, code, norm, affect, or rule is guiding the actors (Dexter 1970; Fielding and Fielding 1986; Marshall and Rossman 1989; McCracken 1988; Miles and Huberman 1994; Strauss 1990).

In-depth, elite interviews constituted our primary data source. In the social science literature, the term "elite" interviews is commonly used to refer to interviews with decision makers as opposed to consumers, an electorate, or a mass population (Dexter 1970). Elite interviews differ from highly structured survey research interviews in that the latter are useful for predicting behavior and generalizing to populations about behavior, while the former are designed to ascertain decision makers' understanding. For all their inherent benefits, behavioral reports that are produced by survey research often disregard the meaning to the actors. When one wants to know what the actors think is happening, elite interviews often provide a direct and useful tool. This type of interviewing stresses the informant's definition of the situation, encourages the informant to structure the account of the situation, and allows the informant to reveal his or her notions of what is relevant (Dexter 1970; King 1994; McCracken 1988; Schwartzman 1993). In short, the objectives of the research drove the methodology selected.

Interview Protocol

The interview protocol (see Appendix) was developed in consultation with five marketing and advertising professors and four advertising practitioners. It was pretested in personal interviews with seven advertising agency executives. In keeping with accepted practice for elite interviewing, most questions were broad and open-ended to enable informants to define the situation. The interview protocol was designed to prompt informants to engage in what Wallendorf and Brucks

(1993, p. 341) called "guided introspection." The protocol explicitly focused on ethical issues, and the purpose was made clear when setting up the interview. Advertising agency personnel were selected as informants because they occupy a critical gatekeeper role between advertisers, the media, and the public. In this role, they may perceive ethical pressures from interacting with diverse stakeholders.

Data Collection and Analysis

A total of 51 personal interviews were conducted in 29 advertising agencies in 8 cities: New York, Chicago, Philadelphia, San Francisco, Washington, DC, Minneapolis, Dallas, and Austin. The informants came from varied departments (e.g., creative, media, account services, account planning) and were at all seniority levels. Their experience spanned from 2 years to more than 40 years. (See Table 1 for demographics of the informants.) The agencies ranged in size from small privately held companies with less than 12 people and about a million dollars in annual billings, to large, publicly held, worldwide companies with thousands of employees and billions of dollars in annual billings. (See Table 2 for demographics of the agencies.)

We cycled back and forth between data collection and analysis, as is recommended in qualitative research, to provide opportunity for the interview protocol and the sample to evolve in a manner that serves the research questions (Strauss 1990). We began our study in major agencies in major markets, and we found, generally speaking, that most of our informants saw few ethical concerns in their own work or in advertising. We then broadened our sample to include a more diverse set of agencies: smaller agencies in major markets and agencies in small and mid-sized markets. When we encountered individuals who seemed to be more ethically attuned, their comments about the contexts in which they were working prompted us to interview others in those agencies to better understand the cultures, climates, and modus operandi of the agencies. Such "snowballing" techniques (Moriarity 1983) were appropriate since we were not using a random sample with a goal to predict behavior within a population. Anonymity was provided for both informants and agencies. Anonymity has obvious disadvantages, but it helps mitigate biases and demand effects related to social desirability and posturing. Absent assurances of anonymity, we likely would not have been granted many of the interviews. Widely used in the social sciences, anonymity has been employed often in qualitative field research in advertising and marketing (e.g., Arnould and Price 1993; Dougherty 1990, 1992; Drumwright 1994, 1996; Workman 1993).

TABLE 1 Demographics of Informants

	Number of informants
Job assignment	
Senior management/administration (e.g., chairman, president, executive vice president, owner, managing partner)	19
Creative	11
Account services	9
Media	6
Account planning	2
Strategic planning	2
Interactive	1
Relationship marketing	1
Total	*51*
Years of experience in advertising	
More than 25 years	9
21 to 25 years	6
16 to 20 years	9
11 to 15 years	8
6 to 10 years	15
2 to 5 years	4
Total	*51*
Gender	
Male	38
Female	13
Total	*51*
City	
Austin	8
Chicago	16
Dallas	6
Minneapolis	2
New York	14
Philadelphia	2
San Francisco	2
Washington, DC	1
Total	*51*
Ownership status of agency	
Independent	20
Holding company	31
Total	*51*

TABLE 2 Agency Demographics

	Number of agencies
Annual billings of agency office where interviews were conducted	
Less than $20 million	4
$21 million to $100 million	4
$101 million to $500 million	13
$501 million to $1 billion	3
More than $1 billion	5
Total	*29*
Number of employees in agency office where interviews were conducted	
Less than 25	6
25 to 100	7
101 to 500	10
More than 500	6
Total	*29*
Agency ownership status	
Independent	10
Holding company	19
Total	*29*
City of agency office where interviews conducted	
Austin	3
Chicago	8
Dallas	4
Minneapolis	2
New York	8
Philadelphia	2
San Francisco	2
Washington, DC	1
Total	*29*

The interviews were audiotaped and then transcribed. Data were systematically and intensively analyzed through standard procedures for qualitative analysis (Spiggle 1994; Strauss 1990). Data analysis involved several steps. First, the transcripts were reviewed individually and summarized. Second, in a phase that Strauss called "open coding," the interview transcripts were scrutinized line by line and paragraph by paragraph to suggest initial categories or themes. In the third step, which Strauss called "axial" coding, the transcripts were scrutinized again and again to consider each of the themes across the interviews and to assess the fit of each theme to the data. In a final stage, which Strauss called "selective" coding, the data were examined once again to refine the themes and findings for each.

Limitations

The limitations of this research method are well known, but attempts were made to mitigate their effects. Because some judgment is inevitably required by the analyst (Dexter 1970), a major concern is that of subjectivity in interpreting the data. To guard against subjectivity and to establish reliability, initial data analysis was undertaken by both authors working independently. Findings were identified and agreed upon. Another way to mitigate subjectivity is to be as transparent as possible; that is, we demonstrate as clearly as we can how we came to certain conclusions (Golden-Biddle and Locke 1993). Extensive use of quotations can add objectivity as well as depth of understanding. We have quoted liberally, and unless otherwise noted, quotations are representative of what was expressed by several informants. As acknowledged above, anonymity was granted to all informants to help mitigate biases and demand effects related to social desirability and posturing. Finally, the advertising practitioners chosen may not be representative of the total population, but they do vary on many dimensions, including job function, experience level, client base, agency size, and geographic location (see Tables 1 and 2). In keeping with one of the goals of qualitative research, portraying the range and depth of the phenomena is important to developing theory (Bonoma 1985; Eisenhardt 1989; Kover 1995).

FINDINGS

Generally speaking, we found two kinds of advertising practitioners with regard to ethical sensitivity, and as discussed below, generally speaking, this division was a result of where they worked. We first report our findings regarding the group that was less ethically sensitive and then contrast them with findings from the more ethically sensitive group.

We start from a normative position. We assume that ethical issues can and do arise in advertising, and that when and if they do arise, it is best if they are acknowledged and dealt with in what would be considered an ethical way. That said, we acknowledge that reasonable people can disagree over whether a particular situation poses an ethical dilemma, as well as over what the ethical response should be.

Ethical issues did not appear to be on the radar screens of our first group of informants. As one informant noted:

> Usually, ethics is something that doesn't seem to apply much. . . . You don't really think about it too much.

Even when ethical issues were noticed, they often were not discussed. As one informant put it in what was an oft-reported phenomenon:

> It's unfortunate, but it's [ethics] not a high priority. . . . This line of questioning is so interesting because it has never come up.

"Moral muteness," a term borrowed from Bird and Waters (1989), was pervasive among our first group of informants. Ethical issues did not enter into discourse at either an individual or organizational level. Bird (1996) states that people are morally mute "when they do not recognizably communicate their moral concerns in settings where such communicating would be fitting" (p. 27). When they would be expected to express themselves with respect to ethical concerns, "they either voice no moral sentiments or communicate in ways that obscure their moral beliefs and commitments" (Bird 2002, p. 16).

In addition to moral muteness, we also found what we call "moral myopia." In fact, the myopia helped explain the muteness. We define moral myopia as a distortion of moral vision, ranging from shortsightedness to near blindness, which affects an individual's perception of an ethical dilemma. Moral myopia hinders moral issues from coming clearly into focus, particularly those that are not proximate, and it can be so severe that it may render a person effectively morally blind. If moral issues are not seen at all or are somehow distorted, it is highly unlikely that sound ethical decision making will occur. The most proximate issues and those most likely to be in focus were at the workaday level of the individual, which usually were intimately tied to the individual's personal self-interest (e.g., "Is anyone stealing my ideas?"). Less proximate and more likely to be affected by myopia were issues regarding advertising messages and organizational practices of agencies and clients. Least proximate and most likely to be affected by myopia were issues referred to as "advertising's unintended social consequences." Pollay (1986, p. 19) defined the unintended social consequences of advertising as "the social byproducts of the exhortations to 'buy products,'" which tend to occur at the aggregate level of society. While we found evidences of moral myopia regarding ethical issues at all three levels—that of the individual, the organization, and society—moral shortsightedness was most acute at the societal level. We see distinct similarities between moral myopia and Levitt's (1960) marketing myopia in that both involve an inability to "see" certain important issues that are a part of the larger context in which one is working.

Not only did we find moral muteness and moral myopia; we also sought to understand the underlying assumptions, perceptions, and paradigms that support them. To do so, we examined informants' responses in more depth to understand the ways they frame and think about ethical issues. The responses ranged from a rejection of the possibility of ethical concerns in advertising at all to a variety of rationalizations that largely dismissed potential ethical concerns or responsibility. Sometimes multiple rationalizations were used simultaneously by a single individual—woven into a web of supporting rationalizations. Some informants evidenced both myopia and muteness. Indeed, these problems frequently overlapped and were reinforcing. Nevertheless, in principle, moral muteness and moral myopia are different. It is helpful to distinguish a perspective that does not really see a problem from a perspective in which the problem is seen but avoided and not discussed.

Moral Myopia

Many of our informants had difficulty seeing ethical issues or seeing them clearly. Our assessment is that people may be affected by moral myopia in varying degrees of severity, ranging from blindness to shortsightedness. While some people fail to see the moral dimension of problems at all, others have distorted moral vision that results largely from rationalization or from an unwillingness to focus on the problem so that it is seen clearly. The rationalizations contribute to and reinforce the perceptual problem. Interestingly, these responses could be categorized. We report the categories that we heard time and again. Although usually only one informant is quoted, the quotation is representative of what others expressed.

Consumers Are Smart

> Consumers are really smart, really astute. . . . I feel like I am so unpowerful that if I were unethical in my [creative] presentation [of the advertising message] and were I to oversell, I would be found out so incredibly quickly.

We heard about a strong and unwavering faith in consumers. This faith asserted that consumers are smart and therefore cannot and will not be fooled or led astray by any unethical advertising message. Since consumers will not be misled, the advertising message does not need to be ethically evaluated. This rationalization is understandable, and is certainly not unique to advertising, but in the advertising context, it seems less persuasive. It seems somewhat surprising that people whose professional raison d'être is to create advertising that works would simultaneously assert the powerlessness of their endeavors. Some informants seemed to want to have it both ways, claiming that advertising is important, worthy, and effective in selling products, but at the same time asserting that it is also relatively powerless to mislead or have any harmful effects.

Passing the Buck

> Personally I haven't thought much about this issue [negative effects of advertising], but now I think the responsibility goes back to families and the law.

Informants rationalized responsibility for the negative effects of advertising by "passing the buck." The number of potential parties to whom the buck was passed was large and included families, especially parents, peers, the media, the movies, MTV, videos, clients, the regulators, and others. Relatedly, often the buck was passed to society at large. Informants asserted that they are not creating images but merely reflecting the images that already exist in society, which is what society wants. Thus, any responsibility and/or blame should be placed on society, not on advertising. This was another iteration of the age-old debate of whether advertising creates or reflects society (Lantos 1987; Pollay 1986). As one agency president said:

> We're more sheep than we are shepherds. We follow the trends. We don't create them. We're too scared to create them; our clients are too scared to create them.

Another practitioner put it this way:

> Are you going to use an overweight, short gal with an acne problem to sell that product, or are you going to use a model with big breasts and a lot of skin? Unfortunately, that is more of a reflection of society and what society wants to see than advertisers setting out and creating this false image. . . . I think this is also what society wants to believe about itself.

One need not resolve whether advertising creates or reflects society to admit that advertising bears some responsibility. Taking an example from earlier history, advertising did not create racism, but many would say the industry contributed to it when pandering to racial stereotypes. The "sheep not shepherd" assumption enabled many advertising practitioners to avoid any responsibility for advertising's unintended consequences and for making moral judgments about them.

The buck was also passed to products and clients. The problem was with the products, not with the advertising itself. Clients, not agencies, bore responsibility for the products. Advertising professionals saw themselves as scapegoats. They and their profession were unjust recipients of blame that should be directed at other parties. Because advertising is visible and salient, it is a vulnerable, convenient, and easy target. In a slight variation of this theme with a McLuhanesque twist, one practitioner explained:

> We've become the scapegoat for things we don't even create.
> We're so easy to find on the radar screen. . . . We actually create something. We take the brunt of "Television is bad for you," which has become "Advertising is bad for you."

What Is Legal Is Moral

Related to buck passing, our informants, like many others, often equated the legal with the moral. Writers in ethics generally view the law as the "floor"—the moral minimum—but for some of our informants, if it is legal, it is ethical (Drumwright 1993; Preston 1994). A number of our informants assumed that because regulations exist and because attorneys are involved, they themselves are off the hook. As an agency president explained:

> I think this is probably one of the most ethical businesses there is. It is so regulated. Everything that we do has to go through our lawyers to make sure that it's conforming to law, and then our client's lawyers, and then we have to send it through to the networks and their lawyers. . . . It's really hard to be unethical in this business even if you wanted to.

Another senior ad agency executive framed his comments about a specific product, but his point was that the law, not ethics, should drive advertising.

> I don't feel it's ethically wrong to advertise them [cigarettes]. I don't smoke. . . . My feeling is that if they want to make it illegal, fine. But as long as it's a legal product, it should be legally sold.

The two quotes above address slightly different issues. The first is a position generally rejected as a sound basis for an ethical conclusion, that is, the contention that if it is legal, it is moral. The latter perspective is more complicated and has many adherents in advertising and beyond. Whatever one's conclusion on this matter, the potential danger is that it can buffer advertising practitioners (or any other professionals for that matter) from serious consideration of ethical issues. The worrisome thing about the perspectives exemplified by both of the quotes above is that ethical decision making is delegated to attorneys or policy-makers, and it assumes that the observance of the law or regulation is sufficient. Preston (1994, p. 128) asserted that "ethics begins only where the law ends." His logic is that "the law tells you what you must do," whereas "ethics prompts you to do things even though you don't have to." As such, Preston observed that for advertisers who believed that the law was sufficient, "ethics never really starts." The "legal is moral" approach is particularly problematic given Preston's arguments that for some advertising claims, the law ends too soon. The law is often a "blunt tool"—a cumbersome and often inefficient method with which to deal with ethical issues.

The First Amendment Misunderstanding

We heard frequent references to the First Amendment as a justification for not "censoring" advertising messages. For example, when an agency president was asked if he had considered developing a code of ethics for his agency and the advertising produced for their clients, he responded, "How could I? It would violate the First Amendment." He then pledged his allegiance to the First Amendment, suggested that everyone was attacking it, and expounded on the need to protect the First Amendment.

A naive understanding, or perhaps a misunderstanding, of the First Amendment was prevalent among some of our informants. The Supreme Court has never afforded absolute protection to speech, despite Justice Hugo Black's literal interpretation that the free speech clause of the First Amendment, "Congress shall make no law," meant that Congress should absolutely make no law that would infringe speech. Moreover, it has determined that "commercial speech" does not receive all the protection of other forms of speech. That said, the commercial speech distinction is being increasingly diminished by the Court (see *Central Hudson v. Public Service Commission* and *44 Liquormart, Inc. v. Rhode Island*).

But these doctrinal issues are not the source of the naiveté to which we refer. The First Amendment prohibits government from abridging freedom of speech; it does not stand for the proposition that all speech is equally worthy and should be uttered or encouraged, or that speakers should not be condemned for the speech that they make. To the extent that informants quoted speech maxims, they only talked about a part of the story. The part they understood was that there are desirable aspects to a "marketplace of ideas" that is free from governmental control. The justification for a "marketplace of ideas" assumes that ideas that are not currently popular should not be prohibited by the government because they may contain kernels of truth. The part informants did not understand or did not remember is that the marketplace metaphor assumes that "bad" ideas are supposed to be exposed for the lies they perpetuate and the damage that they do to the truth. Once exposed, they are to be roundly condemned. Indeed, the justification for the government allowing "bad" (i.e., false, hurtful, misleading) speech to enter the marketplace is so that it can be discredited. That the government does not prosecute those who make racial slurs does not mean that racial epithets should be encouraged. In short, some of our informants misinterpreted free speech law as meaning that they were exonerated from personal and professional responsibility, or perhaps they misunderstood the First Amendment more generally. Advertising professionals, like all speakers, have a responsibility to make judgments about speech. This becomes even more the case as the Supreme Court lessens the distinction between commercial and noncommercial speech.

Going Native

Another reported phenomenon that distorts moral vision involves becoming so close to a client's business and corporate culture that one fails to recognize or ask moral questions. We refer to this as "going native." This phenomenon is often associated with anthropologists, foreign service officers, or others who become overly immersed in foreign cultures to the point that they lose their objectivity. In advertising, going native involves overidentifying with the client's perspective to the point that one loses the ability to be critical of clients and objective in assessing their behavior and advertising. One informant elaborated on her experience:

> When you've got a group of [client] R & D people telling you this [good things about the product], and the demos . . . are showing you that maybe it's not as [good] as they make it out to be, you belive [the good things]. If you're living it every day, you believe it. . . . So, when you tell the consumer about it, you find that you're stretching the truth. This [product] is your life. It becomes your life for a year. So it doesn't feel like you're doing anything wrong.

When advertising practitioners go native, it can render them less able to make critical moral judgments.

The Ostrich Syndrome

Like the ostrich with its head in the sand, when out of sight, looming ethical issues were out of mind. Or as one informant succinctly put it: "Ignorance is bliss." A seasoned veteran with more than 15 years in the business admitted:

> I think that if I did a little bit more digging into a company's connections . . . then yes, I'd probably have a problem working on it.

Better not to dig. Again, this is not unique to advertising, but the hectic pace of the advertising business and the transient nature of projects made it easy to adopt this approach. A less experienced practitioner alluded to this:

> I don't have a lot of time to sit and think about if the people who make this thing are really evil. You just don't have time to do that. That's just the reality of it.

Moral Muteness

We now turn to moral muteness. Though moral myopia and moral muteness are often intertwined and reinforce one another, it is helpful conceptually to distinguish them. Moral muteness refers to individuals who recognize ethical issues but remain silent and avoid confronting them either personally or organizationally. Moral muteness occurs whenever people fail to communicate moral concerns that they genuinely feel, regardless of how the failure happens. Bird (2002, p. 34) identifies three forms of moral muteness: (1) negative expressions (e.g., not blowing the whistle on observed abuses, not questioning aspects of decisions thought to be morally debatable); (2) positive expressions (e.g., not speaking up for ideals), and (3) not holding others sufficiently accountable (e.g., not providing adequate feedback in supervisory relationships).

Upon examination of our informants' responses, we identified four categories of rationalizations that help to explain muteness.

Compartmentalization

One approach that contributed to moral muteness was compartmentalization. The classic form separates one's work life from one's personal life and convictions. The result is having one set of standards for work and another for nonwork matters. When asked about ethical issues at both the organizational and societal level, one young practitioner, a star creative talent, described the classic case of compartmentalization:

> I know that things go on. When I'm at home, all of these things sicken me, really. But when I'm here, it's different because I'm so into creatively what I'm doing, it's like a different picture.

Compartmentalization, which can occur for many reasons, is a complex phenomenon that can be driven by positive forces. The comment above illustrates how enjoyment of the work itself, particularly the creative aspect, encourages compartmentalization. Creativity was viewed by our informants as a chief virtue. Perhaps, and this is only speculation, when one is pursuing something that is good—being creative, entertaining the public, increasing wealth, furthering democracy, and so forth—it can serve to further compartmentalization.

Compartmentalization often involved separating one's personal standards from a client's business standards. A seasoned veteran demonstrated this approach:

> The [client] company is running a business. They can choose what they want to convey. . . . Therefore, if they want to put in these models who look like they're taking heroin or heroin chic or ultrathin models, then that is their right because it is their business, and they're running it the way that they want to. On a personal level, I find it very offensive.

The informant has a young daughter and expressed concern regarding the potential influence of advertising on children and their conceptions of beauty. Nonetheless, she compartmentalized those concerns, and as the above quote reveals, she did not make a moral judgment or exert influence on the client.

Two issues that some respondents viewed as raising ethical problems were cigarette advertising and advertising to young children, but these, too, were vulnerable to forms of compartmentalization. The informant quoted above illustrates compartmentalization with respect to advertising's effect on children. With respect to cigarettes, we observed a different variation of compartmentalization. Many agencies appeared to allow their employees substantial leeway in declining to work on controversial products, and a number of individuals said, "I'll refuse to work on cigarette advertising." This refrain was sounded often, especially by the more junior advertising practitioners, and it represents a sea change among advertising practitioners, who formerly flocked to the side of the cigarette companies (Rangan 1989). Often, however, informants appeared to ignore the connection between their personal position and their employers' institutional position. One senior executive did acknowledge the conflict:

> I personally never, would never, will never work on a cigarette ad. . . . I'm a hypocrite because . . . if the agency makes money, I get a bonus; part of that is cigarette money. I just won't work on it. I just feel better, but you want to know what it is? It's [expletive]. We shouldn't do cigarettes.

There were many ways to compartmentalize, but they all resulted in the same effect. They permitted informants to avoid taking responsibility for negative effects of advertising.

The Client Is Always Right

> Most clients come in saying they want to have really terrific advertising. . . . I found very quickly that what they want is for us to collude with them on issues. And I never can predict what it will be. We can agree to pretend to each other that they have reached excellence in some area. . . . I'm not a hardass in that I have people who want to keep their jobs. . . . I collude with them. . . . I always wish that I could be very straightforward with my clients, but they don't want it. They really don't want it. It's just annoying to them.

The client-is-always-right syndrome means that informants did not want to tell clients "no" regarding ethics or anything else. This often led informants into the role of a "please-o-holic" or "yes-person" rather than that of a trusted business collaborator with an eye toward constructive advice that may be critical at times. It reinforced the perception that advertising practitioners do not have the right to pass judgment on clients. As one young practitioner explained:

> Obviously, the last thing that you want to do is to tell your client that they're wrong. You're shooting yourself in the foot if you do that.

A senior executive had this to say:

> Obviously, agencies don't like saying "No" to a client. They don't like telling a client that he or she cannot do something, whether it's time constraints or budget constraints or it just doesn't make sense.

There were repeated claims that clients did not want to be confronted with critical questioning from their advertising agencies. In response, some informants came to believe that they should not evaluate or pass judgment on their client's ethical values:

> So the last thing that you want to do is make them [the client] feel uncomfortable about what they're doing and what their beliefs are.

Along with please-o-holic tendencies, avoidance of criticism means that an agency does not collaborate with the client as a full-fledged partner. It keeps an agency in a subordinate position, at times forcing it to censor what could be its most valuable contribution—its criticism, related to ethics or otherwise. It also reinforces the notion that advertising practitioners should not exercise the prerogative of making moral judgments about clients or exerting influence on them. These findings reinforce a description of advertisers, agencies, and the media as an "unholy trinity," in which all three parties abdicate ethical responsibility and behavior sinks to a low level (Murphy 1998b). Fiduciary responsibility then becomes equated with doing the client's bidding. To some degree, this tendency exists in other client-related businesses; however, it appears that advertising practitioners may have a special reluctance to assert their opinions. For example, lawyers must represent their clients' interests, but part of the job of a lawyer is to instruct clients in what is in their best interest.

Ethics Is Bad for Business

Cultural disincentives discouraged talking about ethical considerations. One particularly strong disincentive was that ethics was viewed as a conservative constraint, a sentence to blandness in advertising messages. What could be worse in an industry that strives for scintillating messages that "push the edge of the envelope" and are "over the top" or "edgy"? As the chief creative officer of one agency explained:

> Unfortunately, the solution [to ethical dilemmas] is often to do even less interesting advertising that's even more acceptable to the masses by offending no one.

Another significant disincentive involved inferences that were perceived to be made regarding people who would raise such concerns. For example, there was a fear that clients or co-workers would equate one who raises ethical concerns with a lack of business acumen. The chief creative officer quoted above elaborated on the reasons that advertising practitioners do not raise ethical issues with clients:

> The reason the agency doesn't want to come in and say, "Hey, this isn't ethical," is because they would be laughed out of the office. I think that they're afraid that the client would say, "Well, if you want to run a church, run a church, but if you want to make some money, you're going to have to do it our way." . . . I think there is a fear that if they were to talk about it [ethical concerns], then all of a sudden, they are taken less seriously as a business

person. And they are looked upon suspiciously as someone who has let their religious philosophies get in the way of their business acumen.

Pandora's Box Syndrome

Some expressed the view that raising any ethical issues must be avoided for fear of opening a Pandora's box. As a result, potentially harmful effects of advertising were simply not confronted or discussed since considering them could be too dangerous. It could lead one to becoming less effective at work or worse. The effects of opening a Pandora's box could ultimately prompt one to leave the industry. As one senior executive explained:

> When you start looking for ethical issues, they are everywhere. . . . You open up a can of worms that just goes on and on and on. . . . You could get so bogged down in wondering if what you are doing is right that you would end up not doing anything. . . . If you look and probe and focus the microscope, you finally get down to, "It's the darn system." . . . You pretty much get to the point, "Are we going to be in advertising or not?"

The Pandora's box syndrome seemed to block reflection and critical thinking. It caused some advertising practitioners to shy away from critically examining issues affecting the larger profession and its impact.

"Seeing, Talking" Advertising Practitioners

> I think that one of the things that would be helpful in terms of the advertising industry is to have more communication about marketing ethics. . . . I think it would make for smarter consumers and a smarter agency and smarter clients.

Notable exceptions emerged to our findings of myopia and muteness among advertising practitioners. There were "seeing, talking" advertising practitioners who typically recognized moral issues and talked about them inside the agency with their co-workers and outside the agency with their clients and potential clients. We now examine the themes that differentiated these individuals from others in our sample. We noted no systematic differences between the individuals in the first and second groups in terms of age, seniority level, gender, job assignment, or background. We did note a difference in the contexts in which these individuals worked. Almost without exception, the agencies in which the "seeing, talking" practitioners worked appeared to have organizational cultures and climates that encouraged moral seeing and talking. These agencies appeared to have some authentic norms regarding ethical behavior that were widely held and clearly articulated by members of the community. In addition, the agencies tended to be small, privately held agencies in one location or nearly autonomous units of large conglomerates typically in only one location. As mentioned earlier, we intentionally conducted additional interviews in agencies in which we found ethically sensitive informants to gain a better understanding of both this type of informant and the contexts in which they were working. The ways in which the "seeing, talking" advertising practitioners differed from the others in our sample can be likened to a decision-making process: recognition of the issue, communication about it, and the decision itself.

Recognition

The "seeing, talking" advertising practitioners appeared to recognize moral issues readily, evidencing moral discernment and understanding. For example, one informant reported that he and a colleague had recognized an unethical practice when reviewing a potential client's past advertising and had told the potential client in no uncertain terms that they were unwilling to accept the company as a client if it wanted to continue ethically problematic work of that nature. Another agency executive explained:

> Whenever we get a sense that [a promise that can't be fulfilled] is in the back of a client's mind, we point it out, and it usually goes away.

Upon recognizing unethical behavior, one individual reported that he and his colleagues ridiculed it, refusing to take it seriously.

> If, when we're getting creative, something that's unethical comes up, we laugh more than anything else. [We say,] "We can't do that; that's ridiculous." . . .
> To me, it's almost an embarrassment to take something to a client and have them say, "We can't do that. That's unethical." The agency should have felt that way before the client did.

This is in contrast to other advertising practitioners who feared that if they brought up an ethical issue, their co-workers and clients would think that they did not have business savvy. Rather than talking of "smart consumers" who cannot be deceived, these informants talked of "smart clients," who know that being unethical is not good for business. Again, this is in contrast to other informants who refrained from confronting their clients, thereby supposedly "shooting themselves in the foot." These "seeing, talking" advertising practitioners did not conceive of their roles as merely doing their clients' bidding. Instead, their roles encompassed making judgments and asserting opinions, as would be expected of a trusted partner.

There was one notable exception to the moral seeing and speaking of these informants, which frequently tended to be a blind spot. Like our other informants with moral muteness and moral myopia, they too often failed to see or be concerned about advertising's unintended social consequences. As one said:

> I don't worry about those things. I don't believe that those are the consequences [of advertising].

Another explained:

> I do not subscribe to that theory [that advertising has unintended consequences]. I do not believe it. I think that advertising is a reflection of society. . . . Maybe nobody in this business believes this. Otherwise, we'd be lawyers.

This is in keeping with Rotzoll and Christians' (1980) finding that the advertising practitioners in their sample, whom they portrayed as ethically sensitive, "generally think in terms of the closest at hand, apparently finding something like 'consequences to society' as too amorphous and involving too many results, which are simply incalculable. Social and institutional questions, therefore, receive only meager attention" (p. 429).

Some of our informants did, however, acknowledge advertising's unintended consequences:

> I'll have to be honest. There is no question that there seems to be a growing degree of expressed interest on the part of people as to advertising's unintended consequences. I guess we always need to be mindful that the communications that we create can have a ripple effect—unintended and unmeant kinds of consequences. An example is video games and the contribution that those kinds of messages have to promote the nation's undercurrent of aggressive or violent behavior. Yeah, I do think that we need to be mindful of that.

Communication

The "seeing, talking" advertising practitioners professed a strong belief in the importance of overt, direct communication, and it was not unusual for these communications to have an ethical dimension. As one senior agency executive said, "People need to talk. . . . Communication is good. We talk 15 to 20 times a day." These individuals tried to be clear in communicating their ethical values as they solicited new business, and they reported instances in which they had been direct and forthright in confronting their clients and prospective clients about their values. They even used the values of potential clients as a screening criterion in accepting new business. As one individual expressed, "We do not want to work with people who are not fair as an organization." Another informant put it even more frankly:

> And we try to be very clear with our clients, from the first time that we meet them, about what we stand for. That it's about the work, and they need to be able to not just tolerate, but welcome and encourage, bone honesty. And we're going to give them our opinion, and they're not always going to like that.

These informants often spoke of agency leaders who communicated the importance of ethics both through the examples that they set and clear statements of their values. More often than not, they reported that their agencies had an official statement that communicated a comprehensive, overarching vision of the kind of culture they wanted the agency to nurture. These visions were based on well thought out principles, and they often had been created by a group of individuals who had gone through "a lot of soul searching about what kind of community we were going to be." The visions typically were prominently featured in permanent displays within the agencies and communicated externally as well. The point is not that these agencies had statements or codes, but that the statements or codes appeared to articulate authentic norms of the agency communities and efforts were made to put them into action.

Saying No

Some advertising practitioners had the moral courage to say no to their co-workers and to their clients. For example, one agency CEO walked away from the agency's largest account when the client's COO insisted that he do something that he deemed unfair and unethical. He was widely quoted among workers in his agency as asserting, "It's OK to get fired. It's OK to resign." He not only said no, he obviously talked about it in his agency. These views were in stark contrast to prevalent sentiments described earlier that the client must be pleased at all costs. A related sentiment that these informants identified as being a part of the agency culture was, "It's OK to make mistakes." This perception enabled individuals to be straightforward about their mistakes, freeing them from the need to lie about them or cover them up.

Beyond Normal Vision: Moral Imagination

At times, the "seeing, talking" advertising practitioners demonstrated what some scholars have referred to as moral imagination (e.g., Johnson 1993; Werhane 1999). Moral imagination entails being able to see and think outside the box, envisioning moral alternatives that others do not. Our research was not designed to study moral imagination, but as we studied the real problems faced by practitioners, we saw many instances of where imaginative solutions were needed. Moreover, we believe we saw some instances in which moral imagination was employed. For example, the agency CEO who walked away from his largest account when his client insisted that he do something that he considered unethical appeared to exhibit not only moral seeing and talking, but moral imagination. He readily envisioned the implications that the unethical behavior would bring about for him, for his agency, and for his client's competitors. He also knew that resigning the account, which represented more than 25% of the agency's billings, could force him to lay off a number of agency employees, but he did not succumb to thinking he had only two alternatives—act unethically, keep the account, and avoid layoffs or act ethically and lay off a number of workers. He discussed these problems openly and at length with his client and with his co-workers. Through the discussions, the CEO envisioned a resourceful way to keep from laying people off if they lost or resigned the client. When the client refused to yield, the CEO resigned the account and implemented the alternative, avoiding layoffs. Through the combined use of moral seeing, talking, and imagination, the CEO had found an acceptable and ethical solution.

The "seeing, talking" advertising practitioners appear to have mastered the various aspects of Rest's (1994, p. 23) model of four psychological components determining moral behavior: "1) moral sensitivity (interpreting the situation), 2) moral judgment (judging which action is morally right/wrong), 3) moral motivation (prioritizing moral values relative to other values), and 4) moral character (having courage, persisting, overcoming distractions, implementing skills)." When informants demonstrated moral imagination, they also exhibited an added dimension involving unique insights, inventiveness, and resourcefulness. This enabled them to generate moral alternatives that others had not seen and uniquely equipped them to engage in moral problem solving. This dimension is somewhat akin to what Levitt (1986) identified as "marketing imagination," through which marketers make "an inspired leap from the obvious to the meaningful," reconceptualize a problem, and generate an ingenious solution to it.

DISCUSSION

Our findings differ from what we take to be the thrust of previous conclusions (e.g., Hunt and Chonko 1987; Rotzoll and Christians 1980) in that a substantial portion of informants did not see ethical issues or rationalized them away. It bears repeating that there is very little in the way of previous research that is directly relevant. In attempting to explain the differences in our findings and those of previous research, we note three factors. First, our methods differ. Personal interviews can elicit a different caliber of data that is capable of revealing thought processes that mail surveys cannot. Second, we note the passage of time from the 1980s to the twenty-first century. Time passes, and some social norms and mores change. Third, the advertising industry has undergone dramatic structural changes involving massive consolidation since the time of the previous studies. As such, agencies that historically have been privately owned have been acquired by public companies, which place much more emphasis on short-term financial performance that can work against ethical decision making. Our study was not designed to estimate the proportion of advertising practitioners in the population with moral myopia or moral muteness. What our study does do is help to elucidate the thought worlds of advertising practitioners who do not see and confront ethical issues. Moreover, it categorizes ways in which avoidance of ethical issues occurs. Some of the categories are typical of much human avoidance and rationalizing behavior; others, while not unique to advertising, are certainly exacerbated by that industry's context and demands. Our study also demonstrates, however, that there are and can be successful advertising professionals who are ethically aware and respond accordingly. Our study also finds that the context in which advertising practitioners work matters in terms of their ethical sensitivity.

We do not believe that moral myopia or moral muteness is unique to advertising or marketing. Indeed, the recent round of corporate scandals suggests that moral myopia and moral muteness are apparent in many industries. Our data were collected before the Enron debacle, and as we watched it unfold, we saw evidence of rampant moral muteness and moral myopia, which paved the way for serious ethical breaches by people of both good and ill intent. While we found moral myopia in advertising regarding issues at the individual, organizational, and societal levels, it was more acute at the organizational and societal levels. As with many issues, the first step in dealing with an ethical problem is recognition of it. Unless a problem is recognized, sound ethical decision making is highly unlikely. Thus, myopia is a serious concern. When the problem is recognized but not discussed, moral muteness is also troubling. Often when an ethical issue arises, if it is acknowledged, discussed, and debated, the "ethical" response is sometimes obvious. Other times, of course, ethical people can disagree on what constitutes the ethical response, but rarely is it a good thing to pretend that an ethical concern is nonexistent. Sometimes responses require what some have described as moral imagination (e.g., Johnson 1993; Werhane 1999), which entails being able to see and think outside the box, envisioning moral alternatives that others do not. In addition to correcting moral muteness and moral myopia, advertising practitioners—indeed all of us—should aspire to develop moral imagination.

Theoretical Implications: Individual Morality and the Importance of Community

We did not find a continuum but essentially a bifurcation of both individuals and agencies with regard to ethical sensitivity. Our findings regarding individuals resonate with cognitive theories about the development of moral reasoning by scholars such as Piaget (1965), Kohlberg (1967, 1971, 1984), and Rest (1984, 1986, 1994). We have already noted the theoretical implications of Rest's work for our findings. Drawing on Piaget's work, Kohlberg proposed a hierarchy of moral reasoning in which people move beyond individualistic, instrumental approaches to more complex problem solving that takes into account concepts such as justice, the rights of others, and the welfare of the social system. The "seeing, talking" advertising practitioners appeared to be engaged in moral reasoning characteristic of the higher stages of Kohlberg's model, while those who were myopic or mute appeared to reason in a manner representative of the lower stages.

Our findings regarding the bifurcation of agencies fit comfortably within a broader theoretical context that notes the importance of community. Moral sensitivity appeared to be nurtured and developed best in groups or communities; and the agencies in which we observed moral sensitivity have aspects that were quite different from other agencies. A number of scholars and writers in the business ethics field have noted that a corporation can be seen as a moral community (Hartman 1994, 1996; Nahser 1997; Nesteruk 1996; Solomon 1992, 1999). The agencies with talking, seeing advertising practitioners fit this description. Their employees see and reflect upon ethical issues when others do not and tend to make decisions on a set of principles and norms that are followed not only by the CEO and/or owners but others in the agency. Integrated social contract theory assumes that communities develop "authentic ethical norms . . . supported by the attitudes and behaviors of a substantial majority of the members of the community" (Dunfee, Smith, and Ross 1999). Agencies with talking, seeing advertising practitioners appear to have developed and articulated ethical norms, but it is not clear that agencies with practitioners with moral myopia and moral muteness have done so, at least not in a purposeful, premeditated manner. Moral virtues among individuals are best cultivated and sustained in communities as Woodruff (2001) expressed:

> Virtues grow in us through being used, and they are used mainly by people living or working together. . . . If you are surrounded by vice, you will find it hard to stay in tune with virtue. . . . Virtue ethics, then, deals with strengths that people develop in communities. Communities, in turn, depend on the strengths of their members. (p. 6)
> Virtues are cultivated over time, and they have the greatest lasting power in close-knit communities. (p. 24)

This concept of community draws heavily from Aristotelian ethics. Aristotle spoke of a "good community" as one where good habits are cultivated and nurtured (Aristotle 1962). Solomon (1992) and others have explicitly noted that the morals of executives, especially those most visible in the firm, are important influences on corporate morality. Equally important, he asserted, are the nature and power of institutions in shaping and sanctioning an individual's morals. It seems safe to say that only a portion of the industry falls into a moral interpretation of community.

Directions for Future Research

Our study points to a number of important directions for future research. A more thorough examination of advertising agencies that have successfully cultivated ethical sensitivity could increase our understanding of best ethical practices. If the advertising industry is to place a higher premium on ethics, more should be known about firms that appear to have ethics as a core feature. Such research is likely to glean a more thorough profile of both the leadership and the rank-and-file employees at these "talking, seeing" agencies. Examining and understanding the organizational policies, processes, cultures, and climates in which ethically aware decision makers work is at least as important as profiling the decision makers themselves. As a step toward advancing further research in advertising ethics, we offer a few research propositions that ultimately could become testable hypotheses. We leave it to future researchers to operationalize the propositions in a manner that leads to hypothesis generation.

The first proposition links the notion of community with actual ethical behavior within organizations, particularly advertising firms. The immediate leadership within the agency offices in which the interviews were conducted appeared to be central to the development of "seeing, talking" practitioners within those offices. Many of these leaders were presidents or CEOs of smaller agencies, but in larger firms, local managing directors exerted similar positive ethical influence.

P1: Leaders create a context in which moral imagination can flourish in the offices in which they work.

Several characteristics were typical of the agencies with high levels of ethical awareness. A high degree of communication typified these organizations. Furthermore, the communication between upper management and lower-level employees was frequent and dealt openly with the agency's core values and with tough ethical issues. In addition, all of these firms had a statement of values or ethics that was prominently displayed and that had been disseminated and discussed throughout the organization.

P2: Agencies with a highly communicative corporate culture demonstrate a higher level of ethical sensitivity.

P3: Agencies with frequent internal communication about core values demonstrate a higher level of ethical sensitivity.

P4: Agencies with frequent communication between upper management and lower-level employees about tough ethical issues demonstrate a higher level of ethical sensitivity.

P5: Agencies with formal ethics policies that have been widely disseminated within the organization and discussed among co-workers demonstrate a higher level of ethical sensitivity.

Moral myopia also seems to be more prevalent when there is a lack of communication with clients about values—the agency's and client's core values and the values upon which the advertising is based.

P6: Failure to communicate with clients about values leads to moral myopia.

Other questions regarding moral muteness and moral myopia must be answered. For example, how prevalent are they in the advertising profession and in marketing more generally?

Are some aspects of advertising or marketing more vulnerable to myopia and muteness? What are the antecedents of moral muteness and myopia? For instance, we did not have a large enough sample to compare whether creative, account management, or media personnel in an agency are more likely to experience muteness and/or myopia. Obviously, the specific ethical issues faced by account management (e.g., client interaction and entertaining) are somewhat different from those experienced by creatives (e.g., stealing ideas) and likewise dissimilar from people working in media (e.g., interaction with representatives of the print and broadcast media, negotiation of contracts). Upper management experiences still another level of ethical challenge (e.g., compromising organizational values to meet client demands).

P7: The position held within an agency (e.g., creative, account management, media, or senior management) is related to specific forms of moral muteness.

P8: The position held within an agency is related to specific types of moral myopia.

We found the type of community within an agency to be a correlate of myopia and muteness, but what other correlates may come into play? Does the type of educational background (e.g., liberal arts versus business majors) matter? Does it make a difference if practitioners have had formal instruction in advertising ethics as a part of a collegiate program or in workplace training programs? Are people with particular religious backgrounds more or less inclined to develop myopia or muteness than others? Is the difference between agencies with regard to ethical sensitivity better explained by something the agency does, or is it explained by the type of people who are attracted to that type of agency. We suspect there is an interactive effect. More generally, research is warranted that treats moral imagination, moral myopia, and moral muteness as dependent variables and tries to identify independent variables. Of course, this would require operationalization and specification of the dependent variables. Scenarios analysis designed to detect and examine myopia and muteness could be helpful.

More needs to be understood about enabling ethical sensitivity to take root and flourish in worldwide organizations with multiple locations. The agencies in which our talking, seeing informants worked were, almost without exception, either privately held agencies with one location or relatively autonomous units of conglomerates with one location. Because the advertising industry has undergone massive consolidation, understanding how to cultivate agency offices with talking, seeing advertising practitioners within worldwide networks composed of many different subsidiaries with offices in many far-flung locations is a particularly important endeavor. This line of inquiry would also be relevant to the marketing functions of multinational corporations. How can moral sensitivity best be cultivated in a worldwide network? What impact does the parent company have, and how can its power and influence be leveraged to encourage the development of moral sensitivity?

Our study has focused on a commercial context. Ethical sensitivity is vital to problem solving in social and nonprofit marketing. In addition, it is particularly important in corporate societal marketing (e.g., cause-related marketing, social alliances), which is at the nexus of the commercial and nonprofit or public sectors. For example, what forms does ethical sensitivity take when one is applying marketing to the complicated needs of society or trying to manage the interdependence between a company's interests and society's needs? In what ways is cultivating ethical sensitivity among social and nonprofit marketers different from encouraging it among commercial marketers? Do skills transfer directly between commercial and nonprofit or public sectors, or do they have to be adapted, depending upon the context?

Finally, we believe that it is imperative that scholars continue to examine the advertising and marketing professions critically. The advertising profession especially is one in which the positive is accentuated. In such a fast-paced, competitive, creative industry, there is little time or encouragement to focus on deep and troubling concerns to the individual, organization, or society. Nevertheless, critical examination plays a fundamentally important role in any profession. In fact, one of the characteristics of any profession is the obligation to examine, monitor, and revise its ethical standards and practices. We encourage future researchers to follow the advice of Pollay:

> Critical inquiry does not require researchers to believe that advertising will be absolved of all charges as much as it requires having faith that the institutions of advertising have some potential for self-correction and a capacity for moral action in light of new knowledge. Let us hope that marketing and advertising scholars have this faith and carry out the needed research. Let us hope that such faith is well-founded. (1986, pp. 33–34)

Pollay asserted that the institutions of advertising have potential for self-correction and the capacity for moral action. There is always "potential," but likelihood is another matter. In the final sections of this paper, we address the implications of our findings for practice and for education with the hope that such a faith is indeed warranted.

Managerial Implications

The implications of this study appear to apply not only to advertising practitioners but also to marketing practitioners more generally. They all face serious challenges if they want to make moral vision, discussion, and imagination more central to their firms. Some of our recommendations involve paradigm shifts in prevailing perspectives and conceptualization of the roles of advertising and marketing practitioners, while others involve changes in organizational cultures, policies, and practices.

A paradigm shift seems to be needed regarding what it means to serve clients well. Many of our informants generally expressed a strong sense that advertising practitioners are to do the client's bidding. Fiduciary responsibility, then, is equated with pleasing clients and doing exactly what they want done. We found this to be a norm so strong among some of our informants that it became something of a countervailing "moral" good in and of itself. The stronger the norm that the duty of advertising practitioners is to do the client's bidding, the more difficult it becomes for them to interject their own ethical judgments. To some degree this exists in other client-based businesses; however, there are often counterweights. For example, good lawyers see their job as instructing their clients as to what their best interest is, not simply doing what the client wants. Whatever the moral myopia of other professions, the more one feels obligated to defer to the client, the harder it is to assert one's own ethical judgment. Thus, one recommendation is that the conception of an advertising professional's responsibilities be reformulated and expanded, including a more sophisticated understanding of fiduciary responsibility. Undoubtedly, education and training must play a role in this paradigm shift.

The shift described above cannot occur if organizational practices and policies are not altered. For example, clients and potential clients—both their products and their business practices—should be examined and discussed with an eye toward potential ethical problems. Not all clients can be considered to be a "good" client who must be attracted to the agency and retained at all costs. Overt discussions of ethical values, both the agency's and the client's, should be initiated in the "pitch" stage and continued through the life of the relationship. Refusing to take on potential clients and dropping existing clients can and should be viewed as acceptable alternatives. When accounts are refused or resigned on ethical grounds, managers should be rewarded. Agencies also should set up procedures and systems that encourage workers to blow the whistle on questionable behavior.

Leaders, of course, play an important role. CEOs, owners, and/or managing partners should provide extensive ethical leadership, as was the case in the agencies with ethically sensitive practitioners in our sample. This role is dramatically different from the roles that self-interested CEOs with exorbitant salaries and golden parachutes often appear to play. Agency leaders should model moral seeing and speaking both individually and organizationally. Too often our respondents reported that ethical views at their agencies were implicit and not overtly expressed. Leaders should seize every opportunity to express their ethical values in face-to-face communications with employees and with clients. They also should initiate processes to formulate and articulate ethical visions and policies. The processes ideally should be participative, prompting discussion among workers at all levels and in all agency functions. If agencies have ethics statements and policies, leaders should initiate processes to revise, communicate, and promote them internally and externally (Murphy 1998a).

We recognize that paradigm shifts such as the ones that we call for are always difficult and may presently, in the context of advertising in particular and in business more generally, appear unlikely. However, when paradigm shifts do occur, they typically are undergirded by major shifts in public sentiment, cultural norms, and regulation. As an example, we cite the sea change in advertising practitioners' sentiments toward cigarette advertising that we referenced earlier. We are encouraged that in response to the recent corporate scandals, ethical behavior in business appears to be on the national agenda in a renewed way. Legislation is changing as evidenced by the Sarbanes-Oxley Act, and the public appears to be demanding that attention be given to issues of ethical behavior in business. Whether paradigm shifts occur or whether ethics concerns are a fleeting fancy remains to be seen. When public sentiment and cultural norms meaningfully change, education certainly plays a role. We turn now to the implications of our findings for educators.

Implications for Educators

We believe that educators should expose and sensitize students to ethical questions and dilemmas that they are likely to encounter as practitioners. After all, to be forewarned is to be forearmed. Forethought as to how one might deal with a situation before it occurs often leads to better decisions at the time of dilemma or crisis. This is a cardinal rule in business generally—indeed, in many of life's activities—and yet for some reason, educators shy away from this fundamental teaching goal when it comes to ethical situations. What constitutes the ethical thing to do is sometimes debatable, but it does not follow that we should therefore ignore the fact that one should be the best prepared to wrestle with it when it occurs. What constitutes the "right" action plan for a business may also be debatable, but there often is a set of helpful principles or concepts. Likewise, there are principles and concepts that can be helpful in ethical decision making. Case teaching assumes a value to forethought irrespective of whether there is a "right" answer.

Yet the educational task is even broader than simply identifying possible ethical issues. To combat moral muteness and moral myopia, students must also understand the issues of organizational culture and climate that encourage ethical behavior. Because moral myopia was most acute regarding issues related to advertising's unintended social consequences, educators must help students learn to think critically about the advertising and marketing communications industries as well as their effects on society. To accomplish this, universities should offer specialized courses dealing with advertising and marketing ethics and also integrate ethics into required courses dealing with advertising management, creative strategies, advertising campaigns, and marketing management.

The question "Can ethics be taught to undergraduate and graduate students?" is often raised. Again, that often is not the right question for the reasons stated above. Nevertheless, we assert that professors consciously or unconsciously influence their students' attitudes and values, and that adults of all ages are capable of learning that will prompt them to change their attitudes and values. The question is not "Can we influence our students' attitudes and values?" but rather "How will we influence our students' attitudes and values?" However, even if one assumes that students' values are not subject to influence in the classroom, identifying ethical issues in an unfamiliar and complex professional context can be difficult. Students with the highest values and intentions need guidance in recognizing ethical issues. Some universities do not have required or elective courses in advertising ethics or even in marketing or business ethics. When universities do have such courses, they are often upper division elective courses that students take as seniors. Because industry socialization begins early as students engage in projects and internships, we believe that exposure to ethics should ideally occur early in a student's academic career. Textbook authors should increase the coverage that they give to ethics in both textual material and in cases. Often, ethics material is relegated to a single chapter or part of a chapter at the end of a textbook, which in itself sends a signal. In the light of recent scandals, many businesses and professional corporations are realizing the need for training their employees to recognize and deal with ethical dilemmas. It would be embarrassing for the educational community to lag behind the professional one. As educators, we can help guide this effort in ways that are likely to be more productive and long-lasting after the current attention begins to fade.

CONCLUSIONS

The first step in solving a problem is identifying it and developing a better understanding of it. In this paper, we have identified moral muteness and moral myopia and tried to shed light on the rationalizations and communities that support or counteract them. We have also reported evidence of moral imagination and identified the characteristics of the communities in which it, along with moral seeing and talking, flourishes. We hope that the directions for future research that our study has produced will serve as a catalyst for improving the theory and practice of advertising and marketing ethics in academic and advertising communities.

VETERAN MARKETER PROMOTES A NEW KIND OF SELLING

Suzanne Vranica

Outgoing P&G Adman Sets Up New Shop, Hoping to Persuade Clients They Need to Show How They Can Improve People's Lives

Jim Stengel, the outgoing global marketing chief at Procter & Gamble, is moving from a big advertiser to a small start-up, hoping to remedy some of what he thinks is wrong with the industry.

Starting Monday, the 25-year P&G veteran is opening Jim Stengel LLC, which will try to persuade companies to buy into a newfangled way of selling. It's called "purpose-based marketing," which Mr. Stengel says is about defining what a company does—beyond making money—and how it can make its customers' lives better.

"Marketing is in need of a major overhaul," and "trust in brands is at an all-time low," says Mr. Stengel, who is funding the venture himself.

The well-known adman maintains that the idea of "purpose" isn't just the latest cooked-up marketing-speak. He says dozens of companies and brands have used this approach. He points to P&G's Pampers brand, which several years ago decided it had a higher purpose: helping moms develop healthy, happy babies, rather than just keeping babies' bottoms dry.

To drill home that message, the company offered parenting advice and teed up experts on an array of parenting topics. It also did research on why babies don't sleep, a study that eventually yielded a design change in Pampers to give them a more cloth-like feel. The new design keeps babies warmer, helping them sleep better.

The brand won market share. Mr. Stengel says there were several reasons for the gain. The repositioning helped inspire employees. It built trust and an emotional connection to the consumer. And it helped differentiate the brand.

Mr. Stengel is a believer in the concept: he says he is writing a book with the working title "Packaged Good," which will expand on the idea.

A similar approach, he says, worked for Safeguard in Pakistan several years ago. The antibacterial soap was floundering in the country in 2003, until P&G decided that the soap would help fight diarrhea, the cause of many early childhood deaths in the region.

P&G designed a superhero character dubbed "Commander Safeguard" to use in ads and teamed up with moms, educators and doctors to tout basic hygiene—such as hand-washing—as a way to combat the scourge. The brand's market share in Pakistan soared.

Some ad experts believe Mr. Stengel's approach is a little too touchy-feely for these tough times, when consumers are more interested in buying cheaper brands because of the economic downturn. This approach is "not going to save your bacon in this tough world," says Jack Trout, president of Trout & Partners, a marketing-strategy firm in Old Greenwich, Conn. Consumers are "going for the cheaper guy now."

Indeed, P&G on Wednesday said it would shift marketing gears, promoting the value and prices of its brands. Why? Because it "works with consumers," Chief Executive A.G. Lafley said during the company's fiscal first-quarter earnings call with analysts.

Advertising value and purpose-based marketing "are not mutually exclusive," argues Mr. Stengel. "I believe that you can communicate value and build emotional equity at the same time."

Some experts think the new approach hits an emerging sweet spot with consumers that's been building for some time. Consumers "want brands that have a purpose beyond materialism," says J. Walker Smith, president of market-research firm Yankelovich. "The rat race of having material things isn't proving to be as fulfilling for people, and they want more."

Still, the recession could hamper Mr. Stengel's ability to persuade clients to pony up money for his expertise. "I think it's a real difficult time right now for anybody to launch a business," says Russel Wohlwerth, a principal at Ark Advisors, a firm that helps marketers pick ad agencies.

Mr. Stengel says he already has signed a handful of clients but some marketers are off limits. Mr. Stengel isn't able to work for any P&G rivals because he signed a three-year noncompete agreement with his former employer.

MPG EMBRACES UNAVOIDABLE ADS

With the global economic downturn threatening to derail growth next year, MPG, a major media-buying firm, is looking to new ad venues.

The agency, owned by Havas, is launching a new division dubbed Chrysalis that will specialize in out-of-home digital media, which includes putting pitches on digital screens in places like elevators, supermarkets, gas stations and doctor's offices.

"It's a business that is exploding," says Steve Lanzano, chief operating officer at MPG North America.

Indeed, even in the troubled economic environment, the nation's digital out-of-home media industry is expected to grow 11.2% to $2.43 billion in 2008, according to PQ Media, a market-research firm in Stamford, Conn.

While that growth rate is far slower than the 20% annual growth the sector has seen over the past few years, it is more robust than growth estimates for other forms of advertising.

TV advertising, for example, is expected to increase 6.5% while spending on print ads is expected to decline 5% this year, according to Michael Morris, a media analyst with UBS.

The digital out-of-home sector is gaining steam because advertisers are under pressure to put ads where consumers can't avoid them. Wal-Mart Stores and Kellogg, for example, have bought time on Gas Station TV, which serves up a mix of entertainment and ads on fuel pumps equipped with special 20-inch liquid crystal screens.

"This is the last bastion where the consumer doesn't have control—they can't skip the ads," says Mr. Lanzano, who says Chrysalis also will offer event marketing and sponsorship services.

Still, MPG is jumping into the space a bit late. TV networks have been very aggressive in this area for some time, particularly CBS Corp., which is in the billboard business.

Rival WPP Group has an entire company dedicated to the sector.

WE'D RATHER NOT KNOW

Robert B. Reich

Robert B. Reich is professor of public policy at the University of California at Berkeley. He has published twelve books on public policy and has served in three national administrations, most recently as secretary of labor under President Bill Clinton.

Most of us are consumers who try to get the best possible deals in the market. Most of us are also moral beings who try to do the right things in our communities and societies. Unfortunately, our market desires often conflict with our moral commitments. So how do we cope with this conflict? All too often, we avoid it. We would rather the decisions we make as consumers not reflect upon our moral characters. That way we don't have to make uncomfortable choices between the products and services we want and the ideals to which we aspire.

For example, when the products we want can be made most cheaply overseas, the best deals we can get in the marketplace may come at the expense of our own neighbors' jobs and wages. Great deals also frequently come at the expense of our Main Streets—the hubs of our communities—because we can get lower prices at big-box retailers on the outskirts of town. As moral actors, we care about the well-being of our neighbors and our communities. But as consumers we eagerly seek deals that may undermine the living standards of our neighbors and the neighborliness of our communities. How do we cope with this conflict? Usually by ignoring it.

Similarly, as moral beings we want to think of ourselves as stewards of the environment, intent on protecting future generations. But as consumers, we often disregard this moral aspiration. Many of us continue to buy cars that spew carbon into the air, and some of us spend lots of time flying from one location to another in jet airplanes that have an even greater carbon footprint. And we often buy low-priced items from poor nations in which environmental standards are lax and factories spill toxic chemicals into water supplies or pollutants into the air. How do we square our moral stand on the environment with our purchasing habits? Beyond buying the occasional "eco-friendly" product, we typically don't even try.

Our market transactions have all sorts of moral consequences we'd rather not know about. We may get great deals because a producer has cut costs by setting up shop in poor nations and hiring children who work twelve hours a day, seven days a week, or by eliminating the health and pension benefits of its American employees, or by cutting corners on worker safety. As moral beings, most of us would not intentionally choose these outcomes, but as seekers of great deals we are ultimately responsible for them.

We usually avoid addressing the conflicts between our market impulses and moral ideals in two ways. First, if we learn of morally objectionable outcomes such as those I have described above, we assign responsibility for them to producers and sellers rather than to ourselves as consumers. We believe, for example, that big-box retailers are wholly responsible for giving their employees low wages and for draining business away from Main Streets, or that automakers are responsible for producing cars that emit so much carbon pollution.

Yet this logic is flawed. Producers and sellers usually have little choice but to cut costs as low if not lower than their competitors. Our own incessant demands for great deals require them to do so. They know that if they fail to offer us what we want, we're likely to take our money to their competitors. The morally objectionable outcomes we blame them for are often the inevitable side effects of their attempts to respond to our own demands for great deals.

The second way we avoid facing up to these conflicts is by compartmentalizing our market desires from our moral visions. We in effect "launder" our money through the market mechanism. When we buy from a seller who is the local franchisee of a giant retailer, and that giant retailer obtains the product through a distribution network that gets it from a manufacturer, and that manufacturer assembles specialized components from contractors who employ subcontractors all over the world, the ultimate social consequences of our purchase are so far removed from it that we can easily shield ourselves from moral responsibility. We simply don't see the connection between our consumer choices and, for example, the child laboring in a poor nation or our neighbors losing their jobs and wages.

To be sure, some consumers do shop with an eye to these far-removed moral consequences, and some companies pride themselves on selling goods and services produced in socially and morally responsible ways. But the evidence shows that most consumers want only the great deals. Even if we like to associate ourselves with responsible brands, most of us don't want to pay any extra for responsible products.

The market does not corrode our character. Rather, in these two ways it enables us to shield ourselves from any true test of our character. It thereby allows us to retain our moral ideals even when our market choices generate outcomes that would otherwise violate them.

If the market mechanism were so transparent that we could not avoid knowing the moral effects of our buying decisions, presumably we would then have to choose either to sacrifice some material comforts for the sake of our ideals or to sacrifice those ideals in order to have the comforts. That would be a true test. Absent such transparency, we don't need to sacrifice either. We can get the great deals and simultaneously retain our moral scruples without breaking a sweat.

Can and Does Consumer Activism Make a Difference: What is the Impact of Consumers as Stakeholders?*

1. Consumers influence business behavior as a group by media campaigns and through watchdog organizations. The Consumer's Union is a "watchdog" nonprofit organization that aims to provide unbiased, research-based information/education to consumers on a wide range of issues, including product safety, health care, financial services and food safety.

2. Consumers influence business behavior by influencing regulation (the consumer movement). As in all asserted market failures justifying government intervention, "market mechanisms by themselves are insufficient to promote consumer health and safety, provide social equity, protect vulnerable consumers on low or fixed incomes, or preserve the environment."(Jim Guest, President, Consumers Union of U.S., Inc., "Consumers and Consumerism in America Today," Consumer Assembly of the Consumer Federation of America, March 15, 2002). Many consumer laws were lobbied for and passed in the 1960's and 1970's. But even if the government does come to the rescue, it sometimes fails to provide adequate oversight or is underfunded. This is particularly the case today with the Consumer Product Safety Commission (CPSC) (only one toy inspector) and the Food and Drug Administration (FDA).

3. Consumers can influence business behavior by preferring to purchase goods and services of "socially responsible" businesses and by socially responsible investment. Consumers say they favor products of socially responsible firms, but there is a gap between what they say and do. One study concluded that up to 20% of customers will pay more for the products or services provided by a "good" company. There are studies that suggest an even smaller impact. However, most consumers are unaware of the CSR policies of manufacturers. Finally, consumers are more willing to avoid a "bad" product or one produced by a "bad" company than pay more for a socially responsible product or one produced by a "good" company. In fact, with respect to this asymmetry, studies have shown that consumers buy "bad" products at a greater discount than the size of the premium they will pay for "good" products.

These findings notwithstanding, 86% of CEOs surveyed by McKinsey (2008) indicated that they believe CSR is key for consumers' buying decisions!

4. Other caveats or points to consider:

(a) Some firms market their CSR activities because of activist pressures, not consumer demands.

(b) Some firms have successfully marketed CSR and made it a strategic advantage (Starbucks, Patagonia, Ben & Jerry's); however, most are small companies operating in niche markets.

(c) Few brands have been affected by the social or environmental responsibility (or the positive or negative reputation) of the firms that produce them.

(d) Some consumer boycotts have impacted sales, but most protests have had only negligible financial impact.

(e) A "good" reputation may draw more scrutiny and public pressure (e.g., British Petroleum, Starbucks, Body Shop, Nike).

(f) Less demanding alternatives for creating a good reputation, such as corporate donations and cause-related marketing, can have the same effect as adopting socially or environmentally responsible practices. These are arguably, cosmetic changes that require no significant revision of corporate policies. They may be intended to bolster a company's reputation and bottom line and do not necessarily reflect a sense of altruism or public-spirit.

Σ • **Consumers, as a stakeholder group, can have some impact...but there are limitations on this group's ability to "extract" socially desirable behavior. It is up to the firm and its management to determine how (or whether) to address the concerns of this group.**

*Summary based, in part, on "Consumers: Purity versus the Pocketbook" from *Market for Virtue* by David Vogel.

QUESTIONS ON READINGS FOR PART SIX (C) (2 OF 2)

Does advertising help or harm consumers?

What are the legal constraints on advertising?

What are the most significant ethical issues in advertising?

From the consumers' point of view

From the advertising practitioners' point of view

What impact or influence have consumers had on business with regard to safety? With regard to advertising?

CENTER FOR EDUCATION ON SOCIAL RESPONSIBILITY

CASE #5:
SUBPRIME MORTGAGES
&
PREDATORY LENDING

SUBPRIME MORTGAGES AND PREDATORY LENDING: INTRODUCTION/OVERVIEW

This case is not for purposes of representing the complexities of how the 2007 implosion of the subprime mortgage market created the widespread credit crisis and the downfall of such financial behemoths as Bear Stearns. Scrutiny here is limited solely to the description and practices of the subprime mortgage market, where some lenders acted in a predatory manner.

Subprime mortgages are a classification of real estate loans offered to individuals who do not qualify for prime rate loans (also known as "A paper" or "conventional"). Loan qualifications are based on several factors including income, assets, and credit rating (also known as a FICO [Fair Isaac Co.] score). Usually, a subprime borrower will fail to meet A paper standards in at least one of these areas.[1] Subprime borrowers often have low credit ratings, generally under 600. (The average score is 720.) Economists estimate as many as 20% of all Americans have scores under 600. Subprime lenders assume the increased risk of borrowers with less desirable credit histories, and charge those borrowers a steep premium (through increased interest rates) to obtain a loan in the same amount that an A paper borrower obtains. In essence, the lender "bets" that a particular borrower will be one of those who chooses mortgage type and loan amount wisely and will not be one of those who defaults.

Predatory lending is characterized by unscrupulous actions carried out by a lender to entice, induce, and/or assist a borrower in taking a mortgage that carries high fees, a high interest rate, strips the borrower of equity, or places the borrower in a lower credit-rated loan to the benefit of the lender. Although many subprime borrowers fail to qualify for a conventional loan and thus will automatically pay higher interest rates or fees, they are not victims of predatory lending practices unless a lender hides the additional fees/interest, the fees are excessive, the borrower would actually qualify for a conventional loan, or the lender commits other unreasonable, deceitful acts against the borrower's best interests or wishes. Many states have enacted legislation to protect borrowers and curb predatory subprime lending activities. Known as the "Homeowner Security Protection Acts" or "High Cost Home Acts," these laws make strides to help protect consumers from such predatory actions. It is important to note; however, that not all subprime lenders engage in predatory practices.

Subprime mortgages serve a societal benefit by providing loans to people who would otherwise be unable to get them. Subprime mortgages played an important role in increasing home

[1]Subprime Lending: Helping Hand or Underhanded?

ownership among racial minorities and low-income borrowers, and were highly desired by risk-tolerant investors because of their higher interest rates. Young borrowers, like recent college graduates, often have little credit history, which often means low credit ratings. Add in student loans, especially those from graduate school, and a borrower's debt-to-income ratio alone could force him/her into a subprime loan, even if he/she has never made a late payment. Another situation where subprime mortgages benefit society is when people use a subprime loan to help repair their credit rating after an unexpected job loss, an illness or injury, or just bad debt management. Regardless of whether a borrower's poor credit rating is due to financial choices or unforeseen life circumstances, he or she may find it hard to open new accounts, gain credit or be accepted for a prime rate mortgage. Subprime mortgage lenders offer an avenue for these borrowers to either begin homeownership or refinance their existing home to pay down credit cards and other debts to get their credit back on track.

Once lenders issued numerous loans, some conventional and some subprime, those loans went into investor pools and were sold in those pools to larger banks and investment funds. Each pool consisted of millions and millions of dollars of loans. A large bank like CitiGroup could hold billions of dollars of loans at a time before selling them on. Pools were broken up and resifted constantly, being sold and re-sold. Thus, the value of each pool was also constantly changing and was extremely difficult to pinpoint with any accuracy. Investment funds bought loan pools to back securities that any Joe Investor could go to places like Edward Jones to put in money. Each time a loan pool was restructured or sold, buyer and seller were "betting" that the subprime loans within the pools would not default. Pools with higher percentages of subprime loans had greater value because of the higher interest rates associated with those loans. The risk of subprime mortgages continued to be sold on to the next bidder.

Over the past few decades, the subprime mortgage market has seen significant growth as more and more people attempt to purchase homes. The subprime mortgage market grew from $35 billion in 1994 to over $401 billion in 2004.[2] This growth can be attributed to many factors, two of which were borrowers' willingness to spend more than they could afford and lenders' willingness to underwrite risky loans. Many subprime borrowers signed loan documents they didn't understand, for mortgages that were attractive in the short run but had serious long-term consequences. In addition, lenders were generally all too ready to comply with borrowers' desire to buy more house than was truly affordable.

There are several different types of subprime mortgage structures, the most common being the adjustable rate mortgage (ARM). ARMs initially charge a fixed rate, but then convert to a floating rate based on the riskiness of the borrower after the typical 2- to 5-year fixed rate expires. These types of mortgages can be misleading to borrowers, as the initial rate is usually offered at lower interest, but then resets to a higher variable rate. After the initial phase-in, payments escalate to include principal plus a margin on top of the prevailing interest rate, which often had increased dramatically in the two to five years since the inception of the loan. A borrower could start with monthly payments of $2,613.00 at 6.5% interest, but end up paying $3,345.38/month after the interest rate adjusted to 8% (a $732.38/month increase).

Another type of subprime loan is interest-only, where the borrower makes payments only on the interest for a fixed initial period, after which the payments increase to begin paying on the principal and interest together. This keeps payments low for those first few years, but does not pay down the loan or build any equity in the home. Other subprime loans include those with prepay-

[2]Business Ethics Case Studies and Selected Readings

ment penalties (which prohibit borrowers from paying the loan off early by refinancing into a lower interest rate) and those with balloon maturities. A balloon mortgage is usually rather short, with a term of five to seven years, but the payment is based on a term of 30 years. (For example, a 7-year $300,000 balloon loan at 6.25% interest would mean $1,847.15 monthly payments for 7 years, with $271,948.09 due at the end.) The risk lies in that at the end of the loan term, the outstanding balance must be paid in full. This usually means a borrower must refinance, sell the home, or convert the balloon mortgage to a traditional mortgage at the current interest rates.

As housing booms went bust and interest rates rose, borrowers with subprime mortgages found that their monthly payments had increased dramatically, and their houses were often not worth as much money as they owed. Once a borrower falls behind on payments (known as defaulting), banks initiate foreclosure proceedings. Foreclosure rates, in general, range from 20 – 50% on subprime loans, whereas only 4.5% of conventional loans went into foreclosure in 2003.[3] Foreclosures can be devastating to not only the borrowers of lost homes, but also entire neighborhoods and cities. Areas with numerous foreclosures can bring down the property values for those who have no problem paying their mortgages. The homes in foreclosure sit empty and unmaintained during foreclosure proceedings, with weeds growing, pipes bursting, and sometimes falling victim to graffiti, vandalism, and theft of appliances. In addition, once foreclosure proceedings are complete, the home is often sold at below-market rates.

For many **consumers**, subprime mortgages served as reasonable vehicles for home ownership. A subprime borrower presents the lender with a greater risk, and so pays higher fees and interest. Borrowers who were either fortunate or sensible in their choice of subprime mortgage and loan amount were greatly benefitted by the ability to own a home despite low credit scores. Those who either borrowed too much or whose payments became too great became part of the market collapse and possibly added voice to the idea that lenders could be predatory and coerce or entice subprime borrowers into damaging loans. The mortgage market (subprime or conventional) is loaded with complexities that the average borrower is unlikely to fully understand. Many subprime families reported to the ACORN study that they were not informed of alternative mortgage types available to them as subprime borrowers. Some people believe that these lenders should have disclosed extra information and homeownership counseling to help borrowers understand the full scope and consequences of their mortgage choice. Whether knowingly or through predatory lending, these borrowers entered into risky loans: "betting" that interest rates would stay low, or that they could make higher payments, or that they could refinance into a low-rate loan. Their "bets" did not pay off and they defaulted.

From the viewpoint of **lenders**, subprime mortgages were useful, and necessary, tools for offering a wide array of loans products to a wide array of borrowers. Many types of consumers desire to purchase a house. Lenders needed to be able to offer loans not just to borrowers with good credit, but also to those buying $100,000 houses or those with less-than-stellar credit. Lenders could be reasonably sure that conventional loans would not go into default and so could charge lower interest rates. They charged higher rates for the extra risk of subprime loans, then sold the risk on in loan pools. Defaulted loans either could not be sold in pools, or would bring down the value of the pool. If lenders held too many defaulted loans, they began to have difficulty selling their loans or getting a good price for them. This, in turn, meant their funds were tied in loans that couldn't be sold and they began to have liquidity troubles. Their own ability to get credit to operate their businesses and loan more money became impaired, sometimes to the

[3]Business Ethics Case Studies and Selected Readings

extent that they went bankrupt. Lenders who offered subprime loan products did so in a legal and reasonable manner were still harmed by defaults and the inability to sell loans on. Other lenders underwrote loans in a predatory manner, in which case they initially had large revenue streams and could easily hold unsold loans, but later had enormous difficulty with liquidity as their loans defaulted at much higher rates and the majority couldn't be sold.

After **investors** like large banks and investment funds purchased the loan pools, the pools were restructured and sold frequently. At first, this provided high returns on investment, because the pools with larger numbers of subprime loans carried the accompanying higher interest rates that borrowers paid. Once defaults started becoming commonplace among subprime mortgages, investors became less risk-tolerant. Loan pools with more subprime loans began to be cheaper and cheaper to buy as the defaults rose. Returns to individual investors of mortgage-backed securities decreased. Investors' perception of subprime mortgages' risk became such that they refused to buy loan pools, no matter how low the price or how high the interest. This caused a freeze of all loan pools containing any subprime mortgages whatsoever. Individual investors pulled their money out of mortgage-backed securities, which devalued entire investment funds. The freeze on loan pools with subprime loans left investors and lenders alike holding huge sums of money in loans that could no longer be sold to anyone. Without investors' desire for subprime mortgages, lenders stopped offering any subprime loan products whatsoever.

Once the housing bubbles burst and lenders had to struggle to sell their subprime loans or borrow additional funds to fund more loans of any kind, the subprime market crashed. The big banks' liquidity troubles and the subprime market collapse spread financial crisis to other credit markets. Eventually the negative ramifications of the subprime mortgage collapse have spread far beyond the lenders and credit markets; consumers like Sonia Deravedisian, with no direct ties to subprime mortgages, lost everything they invested in mutual funds or other securities backed by mortgages.[4] Owners of $100,000 houses often find they cannot sell their houses; not because no one wants to buy, but because the buyers cannot qualify for a conventional loan now that subprime products are no longer offered.

This case does not imply that predatory lending practices caused the credit market collapse, nor does it imply that all (or even most) subprime lenders used predatory techniques. Predatory lending was merely one facet of the multitude of origins for the credit markets' predicament.

Bibliography

1. Smith, Lisa. *Subprime Lending: Helping Hand or Underhanded?* 3/04/2008. http://www.investopia.com/printable.asp?a=/articles/basics/07/subprime_basics.asp

2. Jennings, Marianne M. *Subprime Lending and Marketing: From Payday to Title Loans.* "Business Ethics Case Studies and Selected Readings." Sixth Edition. South Western Cengage Learning. 2009.

3. Stecklow, Steve. *Subprime Lender's Failure Sparks Lawsuit Against Wall Street Banks.* The Wall Street Journal. April 9, 2008.

4. ACORN Fair Housing. *Foreclosure Exposure: A Study of Racial and Income Disparities in Home Mortgage Lending in 172 American Cities.* September 5, 2007. http://acorn.org/fileadmin/HMDA/2007/HMDAreport2007.pdf

[4]Subprime Lender's Failure Sparks Lawsuit Against Wall Street Banks

PREDATORY LENDING PRACTICES

There are a number of different forms that predatory lending takes. In each instance, however, a financial institution takes unfair advantage of a consumer's financial needs by charging usurious interest rates and other unconscionable fees and charges.

Predatory Mortgage Lending drains wealth from families, destroys the benefits of homeownership, and often leads to foreclosure. It is estimated that predatory mortgage lending costs Americans more than $9.1 billion each year.

Predatory mortgage lending involves a wide array of abusive practices. Here are brief descriptions of some of the most common.

Excessive fees: Points and fees are costs not directly reflected in a mortgage's interest rate. Because these costs can be financed, they are easy to disguise or downplay. On competitive loans, fees equaling less than 1% of the total loan amount are typical. On predatory loans, fees often total more than 5% of the loan amount.

Abusive prepayment penalties: Borrowers with higher-interest subprime loans have a strong incentive to refinance as soon as their credit improves. However, up to 80% of all subprime mortgages carry a prepayment penalty — a fee for paying off a loan early. An abusive prepayment penalty is often effective for more than three years and/or costs the consumer more than six months' interest. In the prime market, only about 2% of home loans carry prepayment penalties of any length.

Kickbacks to brokers (yield spread premiums): When brokers deliver a loan with an inflated interest rate (i.e., higher than the interest rate the consumer qualifies for), the lender often pays a "yield spread premium" — a kickback for making the loan more costly to the borrower. This kickback goes directly in to the pockets of the broker and consequently incentivizes the broker to put consumers in higher interest rate loans.

Loan flipping: A lender "flips" a borrower by refinancing a loan to generate fee income without providing any net tangible benefit to the borrower. Every time a loan is refinanced the consumer has to pay out fees. These fees can amount to thousands of dollars. Flipping can quickly drain borrower equity and increase monthly payments — sometimes on homes that had previously been owned free of debt.

Unnecessary products: Sometimes borrowers may pay more than necessary because lenders sell and finance unnecessary insurance or other products along with the loan.

Mandatory arbitration: Some loan contracts require "mandatory arbitration," meaning that the borrowers are not allowed to seek legal remedies in a court if they find that their home is threatened by loans with illegal or abusive terms. Because the arbitrator is often looking for the repeat business of the mortgage lender there is an automatic bias. Consequently, forced arbitration makes it much less likely that a borrower will receive a fair and appropriate remedy when they have been wronged.

Steering & Targeting: Predatory lenders may steer borrowers into subprime mortgages, even when the borrowers could qualify for a mainstream loan. Vulnerable borrowers may be subjected to aggressive sales tactics and sometimes outright fraud. Fannie Mae has estimated that up to half of borrowers with subprime mortgages could have qualified for loans with better terms. According to a government study, over half (51%) of refinance mortgages in predominantly African-American neighborhoods are subprime loans, compared to only 9% of refinances in predominantly white neighborhoods.

Short Term Predatory Lending

Payday Lending (sometimes called cash advance): is the practice of using a post-dated check or electronic checking account information as collateral for a short-term loan. To qualify, borrowers need only personal identification, a checking account, and an income from a job or government benefits, like Social Security or disability payments.

Overdraft Loans (also called "bounce protection" plans): are offered by banks to low-income consumers. In exchange for covering account overdrafts up to a set dollar limit, banks charge bounced check fees, ranging from about $20 to $35 for each transaction. Some banks also charge a per day fee of $2 to $5 until the consumer's account has a positive balance. In addition to writing checks, customers can borrow against their bounce protection limit using their debit cards and by making ATM withdrawals.

Car Title Loans: Like payday loans, car title loans are marketed as small emergency loans, but in reality these loans have extremely high annual interest rates that trap borrowers in a cycle of debt. A typical car title loan has a triple-digit annual interest rate, requires repayment within one month, and is made for much less than the value of the car. Car title loans put at high risk an asset that is essential to the well-being of working families — their vehicle.

Tax Refund Anticipation Loans (RALs): are short-term cash advances against a customer's anticipated income tax refund. But the loans are offered at high interest rates, ranging from about 40% to over 700% annual percentage rate (APR). Also, they speed up the refund process by as little as one week, compared to what consumers can expect by filing online and having their refunds deposited directly into their banking accounts.

FACES OF FORECLOSURE: A LOAN CHOICE PROVED COSTLY

The Wall Street Journal published a series of profiles of those caught in the foreclosure crisis, which has claimed more than five million American homes — about 10% of all homes with a mortgage — in the last four years. It' a crisis likely to continue in 2011: another four million people are in danger of losing their homes, according to the Mortgage Bankers Association.

WSJ's Dawn Wotapka tells the story of how the tidal wave of defaults and delinquencies caught one homeowner in Queens.

When Ghislaine Apollon emigrated from Haiti to the U.S. in 1974, she dreamed of owning a home. In 1997, after years of scraping by, she bought a fixer-upper in Queens.

Her original $147,000 mortgage was affordable on her income of about $1,600 a month from working in a hospital linen department, she said. Apollon then made some costly choices.

First, she refinanced several times and took out large amounts of cash, pushing her loan balance to nearly $400,000. And the last time she refinanced she ended up with an option adjustable-rate mortgage, which lets borrowers select from different payment choices. Apollon, like many borrowers, opted to pay the minimum, which adds to the balance.

Option ARMs have become the focus of state investigations and lawsuits by borrowers who believe they were misinformed about the loan's complicated structure.

Consumer advocates say such option ARMs have proven a problem nationwide. "Every option ARM that we've seen has been delinquent," said Farida Rampersaud, director of the Foreclosure Prevention Services Program at the Ridgewood Bushwick Senior Citizens Council Inc. in Brooklyn. "In most instances, the homeowner doesn't understand the nature of the product."

Trouble for Apollon started almost as soon as she moved into the single-story home. The ceiling leaked; the basement flooded several times. She refinanced several times to fund repairs, ratcheting up her monthly payments each time.

Apollon refinanced a final time in 2007 with Countrywide Financial Corp., which was acquired by Bank of America in 2008. This time, she wasn't looking to pull out money, but to get into a mortgage with more affordable payments. Apollon said she was stunned when she realized the consequences of her decision to make minimum payments: After a few years, "my mortgage went up and up and up" to $1,700 a month.

Realizing she would have to pay much more than that a month to start reducing her loan balance, Apollon sought a loan modification. She is being helped by Neighborhood Housing Services of Jamaica, a nonprofit. She wants a plain fixed-rate mortgage that doesn't grow.

Lenders aren't granting nearly as many loan modifications as consumer advocates would like, but Apollon has a few things in her favor. Under a 2008 settlement with several state attorneys-general over charges of predatory lending by Countrywide, Bank of America agreed to modify the terms of certain subprime and option ARM mortgages.The bank said it reviewed Apollon for that program in August 2009, but "her financial situation did not support a modification."

She was denied a modification under a government program earlier this year and stopped making payments in October. Bank of America said it was reviewing her request for a modification.

Apollon — who receives extra income by renting part of the home to a relative — has been depositing $1,600 a month into an account to get her mortgage back on track if she's granted a modification and to show that "I'm willing to pay," she said.

Apollon learned this week that her case is being reviewed. "I am excited," she said Wednesday. "So far, so good."

Of course, she added, "I have to wait until everything is finished."

SUBPRIME LENDING AND MARKETING: FROM PAYDAY TO TITLE LOANS

Marianne M. Jennings

Troubled credit history is a problem for debtors when they want to buy a home. Nonetheless, there is bad credit repentance and lender-induced redemption, and the latter can be profitable. Over the last decade there has been significant growth in the subprime mortgage market. The *subprime mortgage market* is defined to include those borrowers with a FICO (Fair Isaac Co.) score below 570. The median FICO score is 720, with a perfect score being 850. The subprime home mortgage market, from 1994 to 2004, grew from $35 billion to $401 billion. The foreclosure rates range from 20 to 50 percent on subprime loans, with the Likelihood of default higher on many of the loans because of loan structures that include high interest rates as well as balloon payments (see below for more discussion). The high default and foreclosure rates carried a secondary market impact at the beginning of 2007 as subprime lenders collapsed under the weight of their foreclosure portfolios in a soft real estate market.

"We made so much money, you couldn't believe it. And you didn't have to do anything. You just had to show up,"[14] commented Kal Elsayed, a former executive at New Century Financial, a mortgage brokerage firm based in Irvine, California. With his red Ferrari, Mr. Elsayed enjoyed the benefits of the growth in the subprime mortgage market. However, those risky debtors, whose credit histories spelled trouble, are now defaulting on their loans. Century Financial is under federal investigation for stock sales and accounting irregularities as it tries to deal with its portfolio of $39.4 billion in subprime loans. "Subprime mortgage lending was easy," mortgage brokers and analysts had commented, "until the market changes."

The subprime market is fraught with complexities that the average consumer may not fully understand as he or she realizes the dream of home ownership or a means for paying off credit card debt through a home equity loan. Some subprime borrowers are able to make payments initially because they have interest-only loans for a 3-5-year period. After that initial phase-in, their payments escalate to include principal, with the result being an inability to pay or keep current. In many subprime loans, the lender builds in very high costs for closing, appraisal, and other fees, with a result known as *equity stripping*. The loan amount is so high that the borrower owes more than 100 percent of the value of the home. The lenders often return to customers and use a practice known as *flipping*. The borrowers refinance their homes on the promise of lower payments, a lower rate, or some benefit that may actually be real. However, the costs of refinancing, known as *packing* the loan amount to increase the lender's interest in the home; the escalating interest rate; and other factors produce only a higher loan amount with a longer payment period and greater likelihood of foreclosure.

These practices, coupled with marketing techniques for subprime Senders that target the poor and elderly, have resulted in significant state and local legislation designed to curb subprime lender activities. Known as "Homeowner Security Protection Acts" or "High Cost Home Loan Acts" or "Home Loan Protection Acts," these state laws take various approaches to protecting consumers from predatory lending practices.[45] Some states limit charges or interest rates. Other states limit foreclosures or refinancings within certain time frames. Some, such as Cleveland's ordinance, simply prohibit predatory practices, making such activity a criminal misdemeanor. Cleveland's ordinance was described by a court in a successful challenge by a lender as follows:

> "Predatory loan" in Cleveland is defined as any residential loan bearing interest at an annual rate that exceeds the yield on comparable Treasury securities by either four and one-half to eight percentage points for first mortgage loans or six and one-half to ten percentage points for junior mortgages. In addition, loans are considered predatory if they were made under circumstances involving the following practices or include the following terms; loan flipping, balloon payments, negative amortization, points and fees in excess of four percent of the loan amount or in excess of $800 on loans below $16,000, an increased interest rate on default, advance payments, mandatory arbitration, prepayment penalties, financing of credit insurance, Sending without home counseling, lending without due regard to repayment, or certain payments to home-improvement contractors under certain circumstances.[46]

Cleveland's ordinance, like so many of the antipredatory statutes, ran into difficulties with judicial challenges by lenders that have argued successfully that the regulation of home, loans is preempted by the extensive federal regulation of both home mortgages and consumer credit.[47]

Companies that are having difficulty because of their subprime portfolios include New Century and Fremont General, a company whose shares have dropped 32 percent since it announced its bad loan levels in its portfolio. Also, financial companies that bought subprime loan portfolios, including H&R Block and HSBC, are suffering from the downturn and risky loans. Some of the loans are being sold back at a 25-30 percent discount. HSBC said it will take two years for it to fix its sagging portfolio.

But the mortgage brokers and lenders were not the only ones affected with the subprime loan defaults. The major Wall Street investment firms were heavily invested in financial instruments tied to these mortgage loans. When the defaults and foreclosures hit, those instruments have to be devalued. The numher of foreclosures affected real estate markets and prices, with a resulting impact on the economy and interest rates. Debtors who were facing adjustment of their initial ARMs rates on their mortgages were also unable to meet the new higher payments, something that produced even more defaults. In short, there was a tailspin, in the mortgage market, the real estate market, and the secured instruments, based on the values of both remaining steady. The result was substantial write-downs and losses as well as the removal of several CEOs for their failures to understand the risk and exposure their companies had in their ties to subprime lending. The *Fortune* cover story featured those words in a 3.5-inch headline as well as photos of Chuck Prince, Citigroup ($9.8 billion loss), Jimmy Cayne, Bear Stearns ($450 million loss), John Mack, Morgan Stanley ($3.7 billion loss), and Stan O'Neal, Merrill Lynch ($7.9 billion), with their firms' losses as of November 2007 appearing in parenthesis following their names.[48]

DISCUSSION QUESTIONS

1. Evaluate the ethics of the subprime mortgage brokers. With the subprime default rates skyracketing in 2007, there were ripple effects in the stock market. What can we learn about the isolation of individual ethical choices?
2. What are the ethical issues in subprime mortgage loans? Do the lenders fill a market niche? What could or should they have done differently?

Compare & Contrast

Consider the regulatory cycle in this situation. The story of North Carolina provides a contrast and insight into voluntary changes. North Carolina has escaped the wrath of the subprime foreclosures and resulting market downturn because of tougher lending laws it enacted in 1999. Its so-called predatory lending law, passed in a state with some of the country's largest financial institutions headquartered there, is one that has become the model for other states as well as for proposed reforms wending their way through Congress. The legislation, which helped consumers, ethical lenders, and the North Carolina economy, is perhaps a case study in how staying ahead of evolving issues and placing restraints on nefarious activities can benefit business.

North Carolina's predatory lending law includes the following protections:

- Limitations on the amount of interest that can be charged on residential mortgage loans in the amount of $300,000 or less as well as any additional fees lenders add on to the loans

- Limits on fees that may be charged in connection with a modification, renewal, extension, or amendment of any of the terms of a home loan, other than a high-cost home loan. The permitted fees are essentially the same as those allowed for the making of a new loan, with the exception of a loan application, origination, or commitment fee.
- Limits on fees to third parties involved with the processing of the loan
- Eliminates penalties for consumers who pay off their debts early
- Requires lenders to verify income of debtors
- Puts limits on fees brokers can collect for arranging mortgages

Martin Eakes, one of the business people (and a trained lawyer), who worked to get North Carolina's law in place, said, "Subprime mortgages can be productive and fruitful. We just have to put boundaries in place."

FORECLOSURE EXPOSURE: A STUDY OF RACIAL AND INCOME DISPARITIES IN HOME MORTGAGE LENDING IN 172 AMERICAN CITIES

ACORN Fair Housing

SUMMARY OF FINDINGS

Over the last two years, Americans have increasingly recognized the harm done to homeowners (both families who refinance their homes and new buyers) and neighborhoods by the sharp increase of the issuance of subprime loans. Perhaps most damaging among subprime loan products are Adjustable Rate Mortgages (ARMs), exploding ARMs, no-document loans and other products that do not require lenders to take into account the loan's long-term affordability for the borrower. ACORN's report on the 2005 Home Mortgage Disclosure Act (HMDA) data, "The Impending Rate Shock," demonstrated that unaffordable loans disproportionately impact minority and low- and moderate- income families and neighborhoods. Now these high-cost loans—many of which are exploding ARMs—have led to the foreclosure crisis that we hear about daily.

Subprime lending in 2006 continued the dangerous trends that we documented last year. In 2006, ARMs made up 80% of all subprime loans, a huge increase from 1999 when half of all subprime mortgages were ARMs.[1] These loans fall disproportionately on minority borrowers.

Problematic, unaffordable subprime loans—which this report measures through the number of high-cost loans—are more often issued to African-American and Latino homebuyers. Nationally, African-American home purchasers were **2.7 times more likely** to be issued a high-cost loan than white borrowers. Latinos were **2.3 times more likely** to be issued a high cost home purchase loan than white borrowers. Similarly, for refinance loans, African Americans were **1.8 times more likely** to be issued a high-cost loan than whites. Latinos were **1.4 times more likely** to be burdened with a high refinance cost loan than white homeowners.

Race/Ethnicity	**High Cost Home Purchase Loans**	**Disparity to White Borrowers**	**High Cost Home Refinance Loans**	**Disparity to White Borrowers**
African-American	55.3%	2.7	53.6%	1.8
Latino	46.6%	2.3	39.7%	1.4
White	20.4%		29.4%	
All Races[2]	27.5%		32.8%	

These racial disparities persist even among homeowners of the same income level. In comparative terms, upper-income[3] African-Americans were 3.3 times more likely than upper-income whites to be issued a high-cost loan when purchasing a home. Upper-income Latinos were 3 times more likely than upper-income whites to be issued a high-cost loan when purchasing a home.

High Cost Home Purchase Loans

	Low Income	**Disparities to Whites**	Moderate Income	**Disparities to Whites**	Middle Income	**Disparities to Whites**	Upper Income	**Disparities to Whites**
African-American	57.7%	**2.0**	55.1%	**2.3**	57.4%	**2.6**	54.40%	**3.3**
Latino	36.5%	**1.3**	41.0%	**1.7**	49.4%	**2.3**	48.90%	**3.0**
White	28.3%		23.6%		21.7%		16.40%	
All Races	35.0%		30.9%		30.3%		24.40%	

In 2006, upper-income African-American homeowners were 1.7 times more likely than upper-income white homeowners to receive a high-cost refinance loan. Upper-income Latinos were 1.7 times more likely to receive a high-cost loan than upper-income whites.

High Cost Home Refinance Loans

	Low Income	**Disparities to Whites**	Moderate Income	**Disparities to Whites**	Middle Income	**Disparities to Whites**	Upper Income	**Disparities to Whites**
African-American	62.50%	**2.2**	58.8%	**2.5**	55.1%	**2.5**	49.0%	**3.0**
Latino	43.00%	**1.5**	43.2%	**1.8**	41.6%	**1.9**	39.3%	**2.4**
White	39.40%		36.2%		32.9%		24.1%	
All Races	44.50%		40.5%		36.4%		27.9%	

Subprime loans have always been considered more risky than prime loans. But as interest rates rise and an the number of subprime loans that are exploding ARMs increases, subprime borrowers are struggling more than ever. Borrowers with subprime loans who are already paying higher interest rates and are disproportionately likely to be lower-income and to have fewer resources to cope with the payment increases that are built in when a mortgage is structured as an ARM. Over $1 trillion in ARMs are expected to reset to a higher interest rate in the next few years. The Center for Responsible Lending has estimated that over 2 million existing loans could be foreclosed upon in the next several years.

Borrowers in the subprime market are often steered into ARMs and other unaffordable loans without being given a choice of the fixed-rate loan for which they often qualify. Although subprime loans are intended for people who are unable to obtain a prime loan at the standard bank rate, Fannie Mae and Freddie Mac have estimated that between one-third and one-half of all borrowers in subprime loans could have qualified for a lower-cost mortgage[4]. A large number of the borrowers who have received ARMs should not have been in the subprime market at all—they would have been better off with the fixed-rate loan that they were never offered.

Borrowers in contact with ACORN have stated that they were not made aware a fixed loan was an option and that they were told that they could refinance before their monthly payments went up. Since housing prices are falling in at least one-third of metro areas, refinancing is not an option for many Americans facing foreclosure.

It is important to stem the issuing of new loans that will trap people in unaffordable payments. Measures must also be taken to help families modify unaffordable loans into affordable fixed-rate mortgages. High-cost loans, often exploding ARMs, are flooding minority neighborhoods and leading to the high numbers of foreclosures.

Summary of the 2006 Lending Data

America's lower-income and minority communities receive a disproportionate number of subprime loans and are therefore most exposed to experience default and foreclosure. Based on public data for 2006 available under the Home Mortgage Disclosure Act (HMDA), this report examines the extent of high-cost lending for 172 metropolitan areas, determines the disparities between borrowers of various races and income levels and identifies metropolitan areas that are at highest risk of facing concentrated foreclosures.[5]

1) Many more metropolitan areas are seeing high percentages of high-cost lending which is likely to lead to foreclosures.

Metropolitan areas face high numbers of foreclosures especially when more than a third of the loans in those areas are high-cost loans. ACORN's 2005 HMDA report demonstrated that in 38% of metropolitan areas studied, more than one-third of the refinance loans were high-cost.

This number almost doubled in 2006 to 65% of the metropolitan areas. In 2006, 26% of metropolitan areas studied had high-cost loans issued in at least one-third of the cases. That number was 18% in 2005.

Percentage of Metropolitan Areas where more than 1 out of 3 loans are high-cost

Type of Loan	% of Metro areas 2006	% of Metro areas 2005	Percentage increase
Refinance	**65%** (112 of 172 studied)	**38%** (49 of 130 studied)	**71%**
Purchase	**26%** (45 of 172 studied)	**18%** (23 of 130 studied)	**44%**

2) Homeowners in 68 metropolitan areas are at very high risk of foreclosure

In 68 of the 172 metropolitan areas reviewed in this report, at least one out of three loans was high-cost and likely to have its rate reset, resulting in unaffordable monthly payments for homeowners. In four (4) metropolitan areas, more than half of loans was high cost. These areas are: Detroit, MI; Laredo, TX; McAllen, TX; and Jackson, MS. In another 25 metropolitan areas at greatest risk for foreclosures, high-cost loans represented more than two of every five home-purchase and refinance loans. These 25 areas cities were largely concentrated in the South (including Texas) and in the Midwest. These cities are: El Paso, TX; Memphis, TN; Gary, IN; Brownsville, TX; Lubbock, TX; Pine Bluff, AR; Evansville, IN; South Bend, IN; Flint, MI; West Palm Beach, FL; Mansfield, OH; Macon, GA; Wichita Falls, TX; Mobile, AL; Toledo, OH; Miami, FL; Davenport, IA; Saginaw, MI; Cleveland, OH; Milwaukee, WI; Lake Charles, LA; Shreveport, LA; Springfield, MA; Baton Rouge, LA; and Tulsa, OK.

3) Even when controlling for income, minority borrowers are more likely than whites to be issued a high-cost loan and are therefore more likely to end up in foreclosure. Upper-income minority borrowers are at higher risk of foreclosure than white borrowers regardless of income.

Upper-income African Americans were at least two and a half times more likely than upper-income whites to be issued a high-cost refinance loan in 14 cities: San Francisco, Oakland, San Jose, Los Angeles and San Diego, CA; Raleigh and Durham, N.C.; Savannah, GA; New Haven and Bridgeport, CT; Philadelphia, PA; Long Island, NY; Saginaw, MI; and Bethesda, MD.

Among homebuyers, the disparities were even greater between upper-income African Americans and upper-income whites. In 13 metropolitan areas, upper-income African-Americans were at least four times more likely to receive a high-cost purchase loan than upper-income whites: Bethesda and Salisbury, MD; Des Moines, IA; Warren, MI; Anderson, SC; San Jose and San Diego, CA; Minneapolis/St. Paul, MN; Athens, GA; Bridgeport, CT; Huntsville, AL; Milwaukee, WI; and Richmond, VA.

In 13 cities, upper-income Latinos were at least twice as likely as upper-income whites to receive a high-cost refinance loan: San Francisco, San Jose, Oakland, San Diego, Santa Cruz, Los Angeles and Santa Ana, CA; Bridgeport, CT; Bethesda, MD; Warren, MI; Trenton, NJ; Cheyenne, WY; West Palm Beach, FL; Tucson, AZ; Essex County, MA; Newark, NJ; and Long Island, NY.

Among homebuyers, the disparities were even greater between upper-income Latinos and upper income whites. In nine metropolitan areas, upper-income Latinos were at least four times more likely to receive a high-cost purchase loan than upper-income whites: Bethesda, MD: Athens, GA; Warren, MI; San Jose, Santa Ana, San Francisco and Oakland, CA; and Bridgeport, CT.

UNAFFORDABLE MORTGAGES AND THE FORECLOSURE TIDAL WAVE—UNDERSTANDING THE SITUATION FOR NEIGHBOROODS AND BORROWERS

Introduction

Both communities and individual families are impacted by subprime loans that are made in a way likely to be unaffordable and the foreclosures that follow. News about the increase in foreclosures is everywhere. Many counties are reporting record numbers of foreclosure filings in 2007, often due to high-cost, subprime loans issued in 2005 and 2006. ACORN's report examines

- the effects and costs of foreclosures on communities
- the impacts of foreclosures on individual homeowners
- the characteristics of loans which are made without regard to the borrower's best interests
- what local, state and federal officials should be doing to mitigate the current problems and prevent more unaffordable loans from being written.

In the year since ACORN's report on the 2005 lending data, the number of foreclosures has continued to rise and worries about the subprime market and foreclosures have increased. In particular, we note the following facts and occurrences that show the problem and its impacts:

- The mortgage delinquency rate rose to 4.84 % of all loans in the first quarter of 2007, up from 4.41% a year before,[6] meaning more and more families are struggling to keep their homes.
- The Center for Responsible Lending estimated that starting in 2006 1.7 million subprime borrowers will lose their homes to foreclosure.[7]
- In April 2007, the number of homes on the market was 23 percent higher than the previous April, according to a June article in *The Christian Science Monitor*.[8]

- The stock market has remained jittery about the mortgage industry as shown by a sharp drop in the markets on July 24. "The drop was the [Dow] average's biggest since March 13 [2007], when the Dow tumbled 242 points, also amid concerns that the subprime woes could infect the broader lending industry."[9]
- The collapse of a highly leveraged Bear Sterns fund which had invested in subprime mortgage-backed securities is leading to possible lawsuits and fears that the market for these securities could collapse and lead to losses for Wall Street banks and other investors.
- Both the House Financial Services Committee (led by Massachusetts Rep. Barney Frank) and the Senate Banking Committee (led by Connecticut Sen. Christopher Dodd) have held hearings to look at subprime lending and its relationship to the spike in foreclosures.
- Local community members have gone to the courthouse to ask for a moratorium on foreclosures as more and more families lose their homes. Borrowers are telling state and local governments that they were not given all of the necessary and required information about their mortgages, leading the Attorneys General in Ohio and Massachusetts to implement required review periods for loans by particular lenders, halting foreclosures until the review period is over.

All indicators point to widespread anxieties about the foreclosure trend which has been caused by the large number of badly underwritten subprime loans and sometimes included misleading the borrowers. While big picture market concerns are important, the high-cost, often predatory subprime ARMs have a huge impact on certain neighborhoods as well as on the lives of the families who were given loans they can't afford and are now facing foreclosure.

The Impact of Subprime Lending and Foreclosures on Neighborhoods

Foreclosures can devastate entire neighborhoods and cities, not only the borrowers who lose their homes. High foreclosure rates occur in central cities, in established suburbs (as in the suburbs surrounding Cleveland) and in newer, fast-growing areas (such as Las Vegas and its suburbs, and the eastern parts of the Los Angeles basin). These foreclosures take a toll on neighborhoods and other homeowners, even those who have no trouble keeping pace with their mortgages. (See Appendix A for a list of the metropolitan areas with the highest foreclosure filing rates in the first six months of 2007.)

Foreclosures—and the spikes in crime and depreciating property values they cause—harm entire neighborhoods. Houses that become vacant tend not to be well maintained and detract from the neatness and feeling of well being in neighborhoods. Vacant houses have been shown to attract crime and make it more difficult for neighbors to purchase homeowners insurance. According to a study by Professor Dan Immergluck and Woodstock researcher Geoff Smith, one standard deviation increase in the foreclosure rate (about 2.8 foreclosures for every 100 owner-occupied properties in one year) corresponds to an increase in neighborhood crime of approximately 6.7%.[10] ACORN chapters across the country have spent decades fighting crime and blight associated with vacant houses and community leaders are concerned about the impact of foreclosures on their neighborhoods. Most low- and moderate-income neighborhoods cannot take an increase in crime.

Foreclosures also have been shown to decrease the value of other homes in the neighborhood. Many reports about the costs of the foreclosure crisis cite a study done on Chicago data that looks at foreclosure and single-family home sales data in Chicago in 1997 and 1998.[11] This study calculated that the foreclosure of one single-family home depresses property values within one-eighth of a mile (or one city block) by an average of 0.9 percent, and home values decrease even more in low- to moderate-income communities (1.4 percent). Because the number of houses on the market has risen sharply in the last year, housing prices are held down just by the sheer number of properties for sale. This decline in property values harms everyone in the community, even those with prime mortgages and those who own their houses outright.

Cities are also losing revenues from foreclosures. Falling property values jeopardizes crucial property taxes which fund public systems like schools, law enforcement and roads. Houses become vacant after foreclosure also increase expenses for cities. A 2005 study for the Homeownership Preservation Foundation estimated that each foreclosure generates between $430 and $19,227 in direct costs to cities.[12] These costs come from code enforcement, increased police expenses due to rises in crime, loss of utility payments and taxes and in some cases, as when a borrower walks away from a property before foreclosure, a loss of property taxes. Cities hard-hit by home foreclosures can ill afford these costs and must partner with lenders and servicers to help people keep their homes.

Subprime Lending's Impact on Individuals

Many subprime loans devastate households even before they become completely unaffordable. Unfortunately, many of these situations could have been avoided:

- Fannie Mae and Freddie Mac have estimated that between one-third and one-half of all borrowers issued subprime loans could have qualified for a lower-cost mortgage[13]. Many borrowers interviewed by ACORN say that they were not offered a fixed-rate loan.
- More than two-thirds of subprime loans are refinances[14]—that is, loans that are made to people who have already purchased a home. Many of the loan practices described below, therefore, are foisted on people who are current homeowners but now may lose their homes.
- Many families have reported to ACORN that they were not told about any other mortgage types available to them. Since these families were receiving non-standard mortgages, lenders should have provided them with extra information and homeownership counseling to help them understand the full scope and consequences of their mortgage choices. Many

families were told that they could "simply refinance" when the payments on their loans started increase, but due to the slowing housing market and tightening credit, this has often not been possible.

- Because alternative loan products (exploding ARMs with low teaser rates, interest only loans and loans made without documentation of income) became more common in 2005 and 2006, more and more families now face foreclosure because they were offered a loan that a responsible lender would have known would not be affordable in the future. Over half of loans made in 2006 were "stated income" loans[15] that did not require lenders to verify the borrower's income; brokers and lenders exaggerated borrowers' incomes to close the loan and collect the associated fees. Meanwhile, a report by analysts at Credit Suisse estimates that 80% of subprime loans made in 2006 included low "teaser" rates of as low as 1%.[16]

Families who were given an ARM often discover they cannot afford the rising payments. With many subprime ARM loans, the interest rate spike as much as three percentage points (3%) the very first time the rate changes. Therefore a subprime ARM made in March 2004 that had a starting interest rate of 7% that will got up to at 10% rate in March 2006. The difference in principal and interest alone would be over $300 a month on a 30-year mortgage of $150,000 and over $400 a month on a $200,000 mortgage, as shown in the chart below:

Sample Increase in Monthly Mortgage Payment When Adjustable-Rate Loans Reset

	$150,000	**$200,000**
Monthly Payment at 7.0%	$998	$1,331
Monthly Payment at 10.0%	$1316	$1755
Monthly Increase	**$318**	**$424**

ACORN has found that in general subprime borrowers were offered only an adjustable-rate loan and not a fixed-rate product. Many of these borrowers did not find out until closing that their mortgage included an adjustable rate. When some borrowers expressed concern about the adjustable rate, the loan officer or broker often assured them they could refinance in a year or two. None of the victims of this type said lenders explained thoroughly how adjustable-rate loans work, save indicating that rates could fluctuate without significant consequence. In fact, many of these borrowers were given an initial low teaser rate that would increase no matter what.

Once people can no longer afford their mortgages, they often lose their homes to foreclosure. With it, they lose both their equity and their good credit rating, making a future home purchase more difficult.

Some Common Types of Predatory Subprime Loans

1) *Adjustable Rate Mortgages:* Subprime ARMs have led to a jump in delinquencies and foreclosures, even compared to fixed rate subprime loans. According to the Mortgage Bankers Association's National Delinquency Survey for the first quarter of 2007 delinquency rates for subprime ARMs were up 131 basis points (from 14.44% to 15.75%), relative to the previous quarter. In contrast, the delinquency rate for subprime fixed loans was only up 16 basis points (from 10.09% to 10.25%).

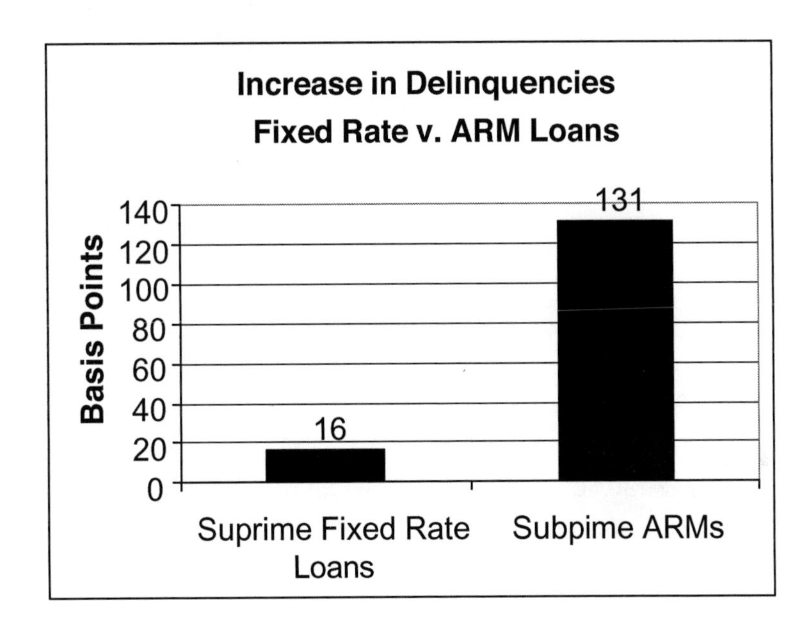

Subprime ARMs adjust can adjust even in the first year, especially if the loan started with a teaser rate. Many of the loans adjust after two years. This is a dangerous loan for homeowners because unless home prices rise rapidly, many homeowners will not have enough equity to refinance out of the higher rate. The rates on ARMs can only go up—there is no provision for the rates to fall if interest rates fall.

Over 18% of borrowers who took out ARMs from 2004 to 2006 will see a rate reset of over 50% of their starter payments and another 40% will see an increase of between 25% and 50%. These increases are almost impossible for most families to afford.[17]

One of the primary challenges for homeowners wanting to refinance their way out of their loan payments is that the value of their house will not support a new loan large enough to pay off the old one. Fully 18% of households that took out mortgages in 2006 have negative equity—and property values continue to fall in at least one-third of the country.[18] Half of American cities are experiencing declines in home prices according to the CEO of Countrywide Financial.[19] CNN reported on August 15 that housing prices fell in 46 out of 150 metro areas, or about one-third of the areas studied, during the second quarter of 2007 [20] These declining

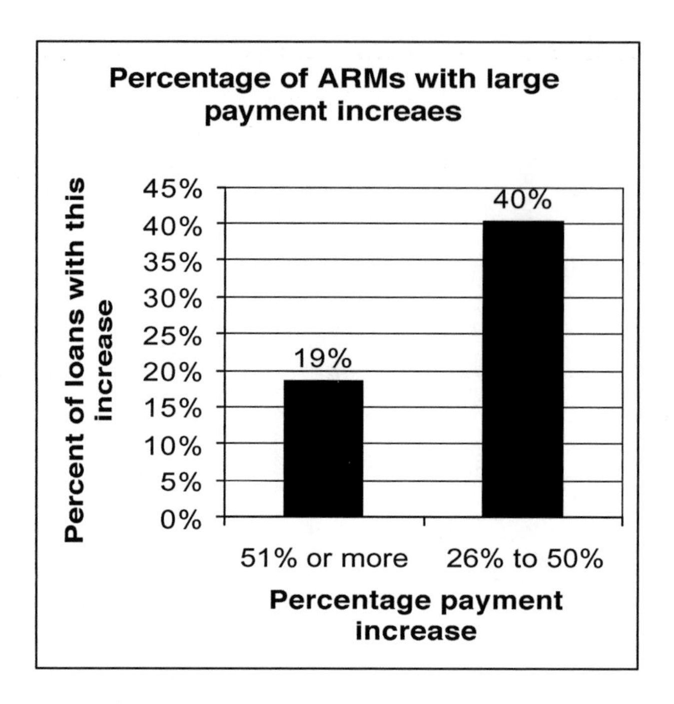

prices make it difficult for homeowners who bought or refinanced in the last couple of years to refinance their way out of a subprime loan.

Some lenders have recently announced that they will no longer make so called 2/28 loans (where there is a fixed rate for the first two years before the interest rate can rise). Unfortunately, some of these lenders are planning now to issue 3/27 loans whose teaser rates remain in effect for three years—but these still will not protect the homeowners receiving these loans.

2) *Interest-only loans:* While a prime mortgage establishes a repayment schedule over the term of the loan (normally 15 or 30 years) with payments towards both the interest and principal on the loan, interest-only loans allow payments to be made towards only the interest on the loan without making so much as a dent in the principal debt. The Federal Reserve of St. Louis estimated that almost 20% of subprime mortgages were interest-only loans.[21] These loans are being sold with initial periods of one, two or five years of interest-only payment periods, after which the loan payment schedule converts to a fully-amortized mortgage. But the longer the initial interest-only period, the shorter the time period that remains during which the full principal must be paid off—leading to a sometimes shocking jump in fully amortized monthly payments. Combined with an adjustable rate that has likely increased, the payment after the interest only period will jump upwards significantly.

In many cases, interest-only mortgages are being sold to consumers who can only afford the interest payments. Unless home values increase, homeowners will have no equity in their house. With no equity to refinance and interest rates on the rise, an adjustable rate that can only increase and skyrocketing monthly payments, these homeowners are likely to face foreclosure.

3) *Option Payment Loans:* Option payment loans are another alternative loan product that has been layered with adjustable rate mortgages. In these loans, borrowers can choose their payment level each month. They can make a payment based on a 15-year amortization (the highest amount) or based on a 30-year amortization, or they can make an interest-only payment or even choose to make the "minimum payment," which fails to cover even the interest for the month. This is also called the negative amortization payment option because it can actually add to the loan's principal debt. Borrowers who make only negative amortization payments wind up owing significantly more than the value of the home and often face an increased interest rate to compensate for the increased risk for the lender. The lack of equity means the homeowner is unable to refinance or sell the home except at a loss.

4) *Stated Income Loans:* Stated income loans do not require borrowers to document their income prior to receiving a loan. This can be useful for a self-employed individual whose income is difficult to document. But too often in the last couple of years, lenders used this product to justify a loan for which the borrower would not otherwise qualify. Usually borrowers fall quickly into default since their income it too low to cover monthly payments.

NOTES

1. Statement of Michael Calhoun, President, CRL, December 19, 2006.
2. The category ALL loans includes borrowers from other racial/ethnic groups as well as borrowers who did not self-declare their race.
3. Upper-income is defined as borrowers with incomes 120% or greater than the area median income for the metropolitan area of the borrower. Low-income borrowers have incomes below 50% of the median income, moderate-income borrowers have incomes between 50% and 79% of median income, and middle-income borrowers have incomes 80-119% of median income.
4. "Financial Services in Distressed Communities," Fannie Mae Foundation, August 2001. "Automated Underwriting," Freddie Mac, September 1996.
5. Our analysis is based on a review of first-lien conventional refinance and purchase mortgages.
6. Mortgage Bankers Association National Delinquency Survey released June 14, 2007.
7. Losing Ground study at *http://www.responsiblelending.org/pdfs/foreclosure-paper-report-2-17.pdf*
8. *http://www.csmonitor.com/2007/0618/p01s05-usec.html*
9. The New York Times, July 25, 2007, page C11
10. Dan Immergluck and Geoff Smith, "The Impact of Single-Family Mortgage Foreclosures on Neighborhood Crime," Housing Studies, Vol. 21, No. 6, November 2006.
11. Dan Immergluck and Geoff Smith, "The External Costs of Foreclosure: The Impact of Single- Family Mortgage Foreclosures on Property Values," Housing Policy Debate, Vol. 17, Issue 1.
12. Collateral Damage: The Municipal Impact of Today's Mortgage Foreclosure Boom, by William C. Apgar and Mark Duda, May 11, 2005, http://www.995hope.org/content/pdf/Apgar_Duda_Study_Short_Version.pdf
13. "Financial Services in Distressed Communities," Fannie Mae Foundation, August 2001. "Automated Underwriting," Freddie Mac, September 1996.

14. Mortgage Bankers Association Press Release, "Percentage of Subprime Loans Used by First-Time Home Buyers Up During the Second Half of 2006", 7/3/07
15. From U.S. Comptroller of the Currency John Dugan as quoted in "U.S. Bank Regulator Urges Curbing Stated-Income Subprime Loans", Bloomberg.com, May 23, 2007.
16. "Cracks in the façade", *The Economist,* March 22, 2007
17. Ibid.
18. Cagen, Christopher L., "Mortgage Payment Reset: The Issue and the Impact", First American CoreLogic, March 19, 2007.
19. The Washington Times, July 25, 2007, "Falling Home Prices Blamed for Defaults, *http://washingtontimes.com/apps/pbcs.dll/article?AID=/20070725/BUSINESS/107250066/1001*
20. *http://money.cnn.com/2007/08/15/real_estate/NAR_home_prices_lower/index.htm?*
21. *http://stlouisfed.org/publications/br/2007/a/pages/2-article.html*

BANK OF AMERICA IN SETTLEMENT WORTH OVER $8 BILLION

Ruth Simon

Nearly 400,000 Borrowers Covered in Deal With State Attorneys General Over Risky Loans Originated by Countrywide Financial

In a sweeping deal that could be worth more than $8.4 billion, Bank of America Corp. has agreed to settle claims brought by state attorneys general regarding certain risky loans originated by Countrywide Financial Corp.

The deal will cover nearly 400,000 borrowers, Bank of America announced on Monday. It will apply to borrowers who took out subprime loans with adjustable or fixed interest rates as well as those with option adjustable-rate mortgages that are serviced by Countrywide, which was acquired by Bank of America on July 1. Option adjustable-rate mortgages allow borrowers to make a minimum payment that may not even cover the interest due and can lead to a rising loan balance.

The cost of the program will be shared by Bank of America and investors who own securities composed of mortgages originated by Countrywide or by third parties who sold those loans to Countrywide. The eligible mortgages were originated prior to Dec. 31, 2007.

"With this settlement, we have the first-of-its-kind mandatory loan modification program," said Illinois Attorney General Lisa Madigan, who had filed a civil lawsuit alleging that Countrywide engaged in unfair and deceptive practices. "This program is going to help homeowners stay in their homes, which ultimately helps investors," she added. "It will shore up communities and therefore it will help with the economy."

Under the terms of the deal, Bank of America has agreed to, where possible, modify the terms of these loans where borrowers are seriously delinquent or likely to become so after their interest rate or monthly payment resets. Bank of America will first try to refinance borrowers into government-backed loans under the federal Hope for Homeowners program, which will generally require a reduction in the principal of the borrower's loan.

Another option is to reduce the borrower's interest rate to make the loan more affordable. In some cases, borrowers' interest rates may be reduced to as low as 2.5%, then rise in a stepwise fashion over time, a Bank of America spokesman said.

"We are seeking to put customers into loan modifications that are affordable and sustainable," the spokesman said. Under the program, borrowers' mortgage-related payments shouldn't exceed 34% of their monthly income. The modifications will be offered to borrowers who live in their homes and not to investors.

For borrowers with option adjustable-rate mortgages, Bank of America will reduce loan amounts so that borrowers have as much equity, if not more, than when they took out the option ARM, a Bank of America spokesman said. Bank of America won't charge borrowers for modifying the loans and will waive any prepayment penalties for those with option ARMs.

The value of the modification program is as much as $8.4 billion, according to the Bank of America spokesman. The costs of the program "have already been estimated and accounted for" by Bank of America as part of its acquisition of Countrywide, the spokesman added.

The Countrywide settlement is likely to become the largest "predatory lending" settlement in history, said California Attorney General Edmund G. Brown Jr. in a statement. The agreement would dwarf the nationwide $484 million settlement with Household Finance Corp. in 2002, he added. Countrywide has faced civil lawsuits from a number of states, including California, Florida and Illinois. Those three states played a key role in negotiating the settlement, a Bank of America spokesman said.

The Countrywide settlement "will be a good framework" for negotiations with other mortgage companies, said Florida Attorney General Bill McCollum. Mr. McCollum added that the precise details of the program are still being finalized.

In some cases, changing the terms of the loan will require the approval of investors who hold securities made up of loans that are serviced by Countrywide. Bank of America "will continue to work with investors" to get approval for the modifications, the Bank of America spokesman said. "We believe this creates a win-win for investors and for customers."

Bank of America has also set aside $150 million to provide relief for borrowers in foreclosure by, in many cases, refunding portions of closing costs and fees associated with the loan. Another $70 million has been put aside to provide financial assistance to borrowers who will lose their homes to "help them get on their feet and leave the mortgage premises in good condition," a Bank of America spokesman said. While loan modifications will be offered nationally, the additional $220 million will be made available to residents of states that ultimately sign an agreement with Bank of America.

In addition to California, Florida and Illinois, attorneys general in a number of other states, including Arizona, Connecticut, Iowa, Michigan, North Carolina, Texas and Washington, are also expected to sign the agreement, the Bank of America spokesman said.

Bank of America will begin sending offers to borrowers who qualify for a modification by Dec. 1. Bank of America won't initiate or advance foreclosure sales for borrowers who are likely to qualify for a program until a decision has been made regarding borrowers' eligibility.

Write to Ruth Simon at ruth.simon

U.S. NEWS: HOUSING BILL RELIES ON BANKS TO TAKE LOAN LOSSES; LAWMAKERS PRESSURE LENDERS TO PITCH IN TO CURB FORECLOSURES

Damian Paletta

WASHINGTON—The housing rescue bill passed by the Senate Saturday hasn't been signed into law, but top Democrats already are putting pressure on regulators and bankers to make sure a major program to prevent foreclosures doesn't fall flat.

For struggling U.S. homeowners, the success or failure of the program—which would let roughly 400,000 owners refinance into affordable, government-backed loans—depends largely on bankers' willingness to take a partial loss on the loans and to reduce the amount of money borrowers owe.

Bankers say they will do it, but it isn't clear how many loans they might be willing to restructure.

"I absolutely do believe that there will be more principal reductions," Michael Gross, Bank of America Corp.'s managing director for loss mitigation, mortgage, home-equity and insurance services, told a congressional panel Friday.

If successful, the program could put a dent in the rising foreclosure figures as interest rates on adjustable-rate loans continue to increase while house prices in many areas slip. Realty Trac Inc. reported last week that 739,714 homeowners received foreclosure warnings and other related notices in the second quarter.

Experts say the program's eventual participation could rise dramatically if home prices continue to drop—which could put more pressure on lenders to offer borrowers more assistance.

Lawmakers are already pressing regulators and lenders to prepare now so the program can begin without delay when it goes into effect Oct. 1.

The Senate approved the bill 72–13 after the House of Representatives passed it Wednesday in a 272–152 vote. Minutes after the Senate vote, Senate Banking Committee Chairman Christopher Dodd (D., Conn.) called for a prompt meeting with the Federal Reserve, the Department of Housing and Urban Development, and other regulators to determine the quickest way to get the program up and running.

House Financial Services Committee Chairman Barney Frank (D., Mass.) on Friday asked lenders to hold off on foreclosures until Oct. 1 if it is possible the borrower would qualify for the government program. He threatened legislation if loan servicers and investors don't work together to help prevent foreclosures.

Taking a loss on a loan by writing down the principal owed is one of the least desirable options for loan servicers. They typically prefer to either lower the interest rate or extend the life of the loan—from 30 years, for example, to 40 years.

"The real problem is going to be, just like with every program out there, are the banks going to take this seriously?" said Rebecca Case-Grammatico, a staff attorney at the Empire Justice Center in Rochester, N.Y., who advises clients facing foreclosure. "And if they don't, we're in the same position we've been in all along."

Whether banks embrace the program could mean the difference between foreclosure and homeownership for people like Kimberly Cox, 37 years old. Ms. Cox refinanced the $254,000 mortgage on her New Boston, Mich. house three years ago into a mortgage that had a flat interest rate for the first two years and then switched to an adjustable rate. When rates reset a year ago, her monthly payments jumped from $2,100 to $2,800, far more than she and her husband could afford.

The program will be run by the Federal Housing Administration, a division of HUD, and will insure up to $300 billion in refinanced 30-year, fixed-rate loans. The mortgages can't be for more than 90% of a home's newly appraised value. For mortgages that exceed the value of the home, the lender would have to voluntarily write down the principal to the qualifying level. If the home goes up in value, the borrower must share newly created equity with the FHA.

The program will begin Oct. 1 and end Sept. 30, 2011. Borrowers won't be able to qualify if they have intentionally defaulted on their loans or if they had a debt-to-income ratio of less than 31% as of March 1.

Karen Yule, a retired schoolteacher and counselor in Denver, hopes the program could help her save her two-story townhouse from foreclosure. She consolidated two mortgages on the home into one loan through a refinancing several years ago.

Her new adjustable-rate loan gave her multiple options each month, and she typically paid the lowest amount. Recently, her loan servicer told her she could no longer pay the lower amount she had been paying—$1,200—and her payments doubled to $2,400, well above what she was able to pay. She has tried to move into a more affordable loan, but there is a hefty prepayment penalty if she moves out of her current loan before next year.

CENTER FOR EDUCATION ON SOCIAL RESPONSIBILITY

PART SIX (D)

EMPLOYEES: DISCRIMINATION AND LAYOFFS

FEDERAL LAWS PROHIBITING JOB DISCRIMINATION

Questions and Answers

EEOC

FEDERAL EQUAL EMPLOYMENT OPPORTUNITY (EEO) LAWS

I. What Are the Federal Laws Prohibiting Job Discrimination?

- Title VII of the Civil Rights Act of 1964 (Title VII), which prohibits employment discrimination based on race, color, religion, sex, or national origin;
- the Equal Pay Act of 1963 (EPA), which protects men and women who perform substantially equal work in the same establishment from sex-based wage discrimination;
- the Age Discrimination in Employment Act of 1967 (ADEA), which protects individuals who are 40 years of age or older;
- Title I and Title V of the Americans with Disabilities Act of 1990 (ADA), which prohibit employment discrimination against qualified individuals with disabilities in the private sector, and in state and local governments;
- Sections 501 and 505 of the Rehabilitation Act of 1973, which prohibit discrimination against qualified individuals with disabilities who work in the federal government; and
- the Civil Rights Act of 1991, which, among other things, provides monetary damages in cases of intentional employment discrimination.

The U.S. Equal Employment Opportunity Commission (EEOC) enforces all of these laws. EEOC also provides oversight and coordination of all federal equal employment opportunity regulations, practices, and policies.

Other federal laws, not enforced by EEOC, also prohibit discrimination and reprisal against federal employees and applicants. The Civil Service Reform Act of 1978 (CSRA) contains a number of prohibitions, known as *prohibited personnel practices*, which are designed to promote overall fairness in federal personnel actions. 5 U. S. C. 2302. The CSRA prohibits any employee who has authority to take certain personnel actions from discriminating for or against employees or applicants for employment on the bases of race, color, national origin, religion, sex, age or disability. It also provides that certain personnel actions can not be based on attributes or conduct that do not adversely affect employee performance, such as marital status and political affiliation. The *Office of Personnel Management* (OPM) has interpreted the prohibition of discrimination based on conduct to include discrimination based on sexual orientation. The CSRA also prohibits reprisal against federal employees or applicants for whistle-blowing, or for exercising an appeal, complaint, or grievance right. The CSRA is enforced by both the *Office of Special Counsel* (OSC) and the *Merit Systems Protection Board* (MSPB).

Additional information about the enforcement of the CSRA may be found on the OPM web site at *http://www.opm.gov/er/address2/guide01.htm;* from OSC at (202) 653-7188 or at *http://www.osc.gov;* and from MSPB at (202) 653-6772 or at *http://www.mspb.gov*.

DISCRIMINATORY PRACTICES

II. What Discriminatory Practices Are Prohibited by These Laws?

Under Title VII, the ADA, and the ADEA, it is illegal to discriminate in any aspect of employment, including:

- hiring and firing;
- compensation, assignment, or classification of employees;
- transfer, promotion, layoff, or recall;
- job advertisements;
- recruitment;
- testing;
- use of company facilities;
- training and apprenticeship programs;
- fringe benefits;
- pay, retirement plans, and disability leave; or
- other terms and conditions of employment.

Discriminatory practices under these laws also include:

- harassment on the basis of race, color, religion, sex, national origin, disability, or age;
- retaliation against an individual for filing a charge of discrimination, participating in an investigation, or opposing discriminatory practices;

- employment decisions based on stereotypes or assumptions about the abilities, traits, or performance of individuals of a certain sex, race, age, religion, or ethnic group, or individuals with disabilities; and
- denying employment opportunities to a person because of marriage to, or association with, an individual of a particular race, religion, national origin, or an individual with a disability. Title VII also prohibits discrimination because of participation in schools or places of worship associated with a particular racial, ethnic, or religious group.

Employers are required to post notices to all employees advising them of their rights under the laws EEOC enforces and their right to be free from retaliation. Such notices must be accessible, as needed, to persons with visual or other disabilities that affect reading.

Note: Many states and municipalities also have enacted protections against discrimination and harassment based on sexual orientation, status as a parent, marital status and political affiliation. For information, please contact the EEOC District Office nearest you.

III. What Other Practices Are Discriminatory Under These Laws?

Title VII

Title VII prohibits not only intentional discrimination, but also practices that have the effect of discriminating against individuals because of their race, color, national origin, religion, or sex.

National Origin Discrimination

- It is illegal to discriminate against an individual because of birthplace, ancestry, culture, or linguistic characteristics common to a specific ethnic group.
- A rule requiring that employees speak only English on the job may violate Title VII unless an employer shows that the requirement is necessary for conducting business. If the employer believes such a rule is necessary, employees must be informed when English is required and the consequences for violating the rule.

The Immigration Reform and Control Act (IRCA) of 1986 requires employers to assure that employees hired are legally authorized to work in the U. S. However, an employer who requests employment verification only for individuals of a particular national origin, or individuals who appear to be or sound foreign, may violate both Title VII and IRCA; verification must be obtained from all applicants and employees. Employers who impose citizenship requirements or give preferences to U. S. citizens in hiring or employment opportunities also may violate IRCA.

Additional information about IRCA may be obtained from the Office of Special Counsel for Immigration-Related Unfair Employment Practices at 1-800-255-7688 (voice), 1-800-237-2515 (TTY for employees/applicants) or 1-800-362-2735 (TTY for employers) or at *http://www.usdoj.gov/crt/osc.*

Religious Accommodation

- An employer is required to reasonably accommodate the religious belief of an employee or prospective employee, unless doing so would impose an undue hardship.

Sex Discrimination

Title VII's broad prohibitions against sex discrimination specifically cover:

- Sexual Harassment—This includes practices ranging from direct requests for sexual favors to workplace conditions that create a hostile environment for persons of either gender, including same sex harassment. (The "hostile environment" standard also applies to harassment on the bases of race, color, national origin, religion, age, and disability.)
- Pregnancy Based Discrimination—Pregnancy, childbirth, and related medical conditions must be treated in the same way as other temporary illnesses or conditions.

Additional rights are available to parents and others under the Family and Medical Leave Act (FMLA), which is enforced by the U.S. Department of Labor. For information on the FMLA, or to file an FMLA complaint, individuals should contact the nearest office of the Wage and Hour Division, Employment Standards Administration, U.S. Department of Labor. The Wage and Hour Division is listed in most telephone directories under U.S. Government, Department of Labor or at *http://www.dol.gov/esa/public/whd_org.htm.*

Age Discrimination in Employment Act

The ADEA's broad ban against age discrimination also specifically prohibits:

- statements or specifications in job notices or advertisements of age preference and limitations. An age limit may only be specified in the rare circumstance where age has been proven to be a *bona fide* occupational qualification (BFOQ);
- discrimination on the basis of age by apprenticeship programs, including joint labor-management apprenticeship programs; and
- denial of benefits to older employees. An employer may reduce benefits based on age only if the cost of providing the reduced benefits to older workers is the same as the cost of providing benefits to younger workers.

Equal Pay Act

The EPA prohibits discrimination on the basis of sex in the payment of wages or benefits, where men and women perform work of similar skill, effort, and responsibility for the same employer under similar working conditions.

Note that:

- Employers may not reduce wages of either sex to equalize pay between men and women.
- A violation of the EPA may occur where a different wage was/is paid to a person who worked in the same job before or after an employee of the opposite sex.
- A violation may also occur where a labor union causes the employer to violate the law.

Titles I and V of the Americans with Disabilities Act

The ADA prohibits discrimination on the basis of disability in all employment practices. It is necessary to understand several important ADA definitions to know who is protected by the law and what constitutes illegal discrimination:

Individual with a Disability An individual with a disability under the ADA is a person who has a physical or mental impairment that substantially limits one or more major life activities, has a record of such an impairment, or is regarded as having such an impairment. Major life activities are activities that an average person can perform with little or no difficulty such as walking, breathing, seeing, hearing, speaking, learning, and working.

Qualified Individual with a Disability A qualified employee or applicant with a disability is someone who satisfies skill, experience, education, and other job-related requirements of the position held or desired, and who, with or without reasonable accommodation, can perform the essential functions of that position.

Reasonable Accommodation Reasonable accommodation may include, but is not limited to, making existing facilities used by employees readily accessible to and usable by persons with disabilities; job restructuring; modification of work schedules; providing additional unpaid leave; reassignment to a vacant position; acquiring or modifying equipment or devices; adjusting or modifying examinations, training materials, or policies; and providing qualified readers or interpreters. Reasonable accommodation may be necessary to apply for a job, to perform job functions, or to enjoy the benefits and privileges of employment that are enjoyed by people without disabilities. An employer is not required to lower production standards to make an accommodation. An employer generally is not obligated to provide personal use items such as eyeglasses or hearing aids.

Undue Hardship An employer is required to make a reasonable accommodation to a qualified individual with a disability unless doing so would impose an undue hardship on the operation of the employer's business. Undue hardship means an action that requires significant difficulty or expense when considered in relation to factors such as a business' size, financial resources, and the nature and structure of its operation.

Prohibited Inquiries and Examinations Before making an offer of employment, an employer may not ask job applicants about the existence, nature, or severity of a disability. Applicants may be asked about their ability to perform job functions. A job offer may be conditioned on the results of a medical examination, but only if the examination is required for all entering employees in the same job category. Medical examinations of employees must be job-related and consistent with business necessity.

Drug and Alcohol Use Employees and applicants currently engaging in the illegal use of drugs are not protected by the ADA when an employer acts on the basis of such use. Tests for illegal use of drugs are not considered medical examinations and, therefore, are not subject to the ADA's restrictions on medical examinations. Employers may hold individuals who are illegally using drugs and individuals with alcoholism to the same standards of performance as other employees.

The Civil Rights Act of 1991

The Civil Rights Act of 1991 made major changes in the federal laws against employment discrimination enforced by EEOC. Enacted in part to reverse several Supreme Court decisions that limited the rights of persons protected by these laws, the Act also provides additional protections. The Act authorizes compensatory and punitive damages in cases of intentional discrimination, and provides for obtaining attorneys' fees and the possibility of jury trials. It also directs the EEOC to expand its technical assistance and outreach activities.

EMPLOYERS AND OTHER ENTITIES COVERED BY EEO LAWS

IV. Which Employers and Other Entities Are Covered by These Laws?

Title VII and the ADA cover all private employers, state and local governments, and education institutions that employ 15 or more individuals. These laws also cover private and public employment agencies, labor organizations, and joint labor management committees controlling apprenticeship and training.

The ADEA covers all private employers with 20 or more employees, state and local governments (including school districts), employment agencies and labor organizations.

The EPA covers all employers who are covered by the Federal Wage and Hour Law (the Fair Labor Standards Act). Virtually all employers are subject to the provisions of this Act.

Title VII, the ADEA, and the EPA also cover the federal government. In addition, the federal government is covered by Sections 501 and 505 of the Rehabilitation Act of 1973, as amended, which incorporate the requirements of the ADA. However, different procedures are used for processing complaints of federal discrimination. For more information on how to file a complaint of federal discrimination, contact the EEO office of the federal agency where the alleged discrimination occurred.

The CSRA (not enforced by EEOC) covers most federal agency employees except employees of a government corporation, the Federal Bureau of Investigation, the Central Intelligence Agency, the Defense Intelligence Agency, the National Security Agency, and as determined by the President, any executive agency or unit thereof, the principal function of which is the conduct of foreign intelligence or counterintelligence activities, or the General Accounting Office.

THE EEOC'S CHARGE PROCESSING PROCEDURES

Federal employees or applicants for employment should see the fact sheet about *Federal Sector Equal Employment Opportunity Complaint Processing.*

V. Who Can File a Charge of Discrimination?

- Any individual who believes that his or her employment rights have been violated may file a charge of discrimination with EEOC.
- In addition, an individual, organization, or agency may file a charge on behalf of another person in order to protect the aggrieved person's identity.

VI. How Is a Charge of Discrimination Filed?

- A charge may be filed by mail or in person at the nearest EEOC office. Individuals may consult their local telephone directory (U. S. Government listing) or call 1-800-669-4000 (voice) or 1-800-669-6820 (TTY) to contact the nearest EEOC office for more information on specific procedures for filing a charge.
- Individuals who need an accommodation in order to file a charge (*e.g.*, sign language interpreter, print materials in an accessible format) should inform the EEOC field office so appropriate arrangements can be made.
- Federal employees or applicants for employment should see the fact sheet about *Federal Sector Equal Employment Opportunity Complaint Processing.*

VII. What Information Must Be Provided to File a Charge?

- The complaining party's name, address, and telephone number;
- The name, address, and telephone number of the respondent employer, employment agency, or union that is alleged to have discriminated, and number of employees (or union members), if known;
- A short description of the alleged violation (the event that caused the complaining party to believe that his or her rights were violated); and

- The date(s) of the alleged violation(s).
- Federal employees or applicants for employment should see the fact sheet about *Federal Sector Equal Employment Opportunity Complaint Processing.*

VIII. What Are the Time Limits for Filing a Charge of Discrimination?

All laws enforced by EEOC, except the Equal Pay Act, require filing a charge with EEOC before a private lawsuit may be filed in court. There are strict time limits within which charges must be filed:

- A charge must be filed with EEOC within 180 days from the date of the alleged violation, in order to protect the charging party's rights.
- This 180-day filing deadline is extended to 300 days if the charge also is covered by a state or local anti-discrimination law. For ADEA charges, only state laws extend the filing limit to 300 days.
- These time limits do not apply to claims under the Equal Pay Act, because under that Act persons do not have to first file a charge with EEOC in order to have the right to go to court. However, since many EPA claims also raise Title VII sex discrimination issues, it may be advisable to file charges under both laws within the time limits indicated.
- To protect legal rights, it is always best to contact EEOC promptly when discrimination is suspected.
- Federal employees or applicants for employment should see the fact sheet about *Federal Sector Equal Employment Opportunity Complaint Processing.*

IX. What Agency Handles a Charge that is also Covered by State or Local Law?

Many states and localities have anti-discrimination laws and agencies responsible for enforcing those laws. EEOC refers to these agencies as "Fair Employment Practices Agencies (FEPAs)." Through the use of "work sharing agreements," EEOC and the FEPAs avoid duplication of effort while at the same time ensuring that a charging party's rights are protected under both federal and state law.

- If a charge is filed with a FEPA and is also covered by federal law, the FEPA "dual files" the charge with EEOC to protect federal rights. The charge usually will be retained by the FEPA for handling.
- If a charge is filed with EEOC and also is covered by state or local law, EEOC "dual files" the charge with the state or local FEPA, but ordinarily retains the charge for handling.

X. What Happens after a Charge is Filed with EEOC?

The employer is notified that the charge has been filed. From this point there are a number of ways a charge may be handled:

- A charge may be assigned for priority investigation if the initial facts appear to support a violation of law. When the evidence is less strong, the charge may be assigned for follow up investigation to determine whether it is likely that a violation has occurred.
- EEOC can seek to settle a charge at any stage of the investigation if the charging party and the employer express an interest in doing so. If settlement efforts are not successful, the investigation continues.
- In investigating a charge, EEOC may make written requests for information, interview people, review documents, and, as needed, visit the facility where the alleged discrimination occurred. When the investigation is complete, EEOC will discuss the evidence with the charging party or employer, as appropriate.
- The charge may be selected for EEOC's mediation program if both the charging party and the employer express an interest in this option. Mediation is offered as an alternative to a lengthy investigation. Participation in the mediation program is confidential, voluntary, and requires consent from both charging party and employer. If mediation is unsuccessful, the charge is returned for investigation.
- A charge may be dismissed at any point if, in the agency's best judgment, further investigation will not establish a violation of the law. A charge may be dismissed at the time it is filed, if an initial in-depth interview does not produce evidence to support the claim. When a charge is dismissed, a notice is issued in accordance with the law which gives the charging party 90 days in which to file a lawsuit on his or her own behalf.
- Federal employees or applicants for employment should see the fact sheet about *Federal Sector Equal Employment Opportunity Complaint Processing.*

XI. How Does EEOC Resolve Discrimination Charges?

- If the evidence obtained in an investigation does not establish that discrimination occurred, this will be explained to the charging party. A required notice is then issued, closing the case and giving the charging party 90 days in which to file a lawsuit on his or her own behalf.
- If the evidence establishes that discrimination has occurred, the employer and the charging party will be informed of this in a letter of determination that explains the finding. EEOC will then attempt conciliation with the employer to develop a remedy for the discrimination.

- If the case is successfully conciliated, or if a case has earlier been successfully mediated or settled, neither EEOC nor the charging party may go to court unless the conciliation, mediation, or settlement agreement is not honored.
- If EEOC is unable to successfully conciliate the case, the agency will decide whether to bring suit in federal court. If EEOC decides not to sue, it will issue a notice closing the case and giving the charging party 90 days in which to file a lawsuit on his or her own behalf. In Title VII and ADA cases against state or local governments, the Department of Justice takes these actions.
- Federal employees or applicants for employment should see the fact sheet about *Federal Sector Equal Employment Opportunity Complaint Processing.*

XII. When Can an Individual File an Employment Discrimination Lawsuit in Court?

A charging party may file a lawsuit within 90 days after receiving a notice of a "right to sue" from EEOC, as stated above. Under Title VII and the ADA, a charging party also can request a notice of "right to sue" from EEOC 180 days after the charge was first filed with the Commission, and may then bring suit within 90 days after receiving this notice. Under the ADEA, a suit may be filed at any time 60 days after filing a charge with EEOC, but not later than 90 days after EEOC gives notice that it has completed action on the charge.

Under the EPA, a lawsuit must be filed within two years (three years for willful violations) of the discriminatory act, which in most cases is payment of a discriminatory lower wage.

Federal employees or applicants for employment should see the fact sheet about *Federal Sector Equal Employment Opportunity Complaint Processing.*

XIII. What Remedies Are Available When Discrimination Is Found?

The "relief" or remedies available for employment discrimination, whether caused by intentional acts or by practices that have a discriminatory effect, may include:

- back pay,
- hiring,
- promotion,
- reinstatement,
- front pay,
- reasonable accommodation, or
- other actions that will make an individual "whole" (in the condition s/he would have been but for the discrimination).

Remedies also may include payment of:

- attorneys' fees,
- expert witness fees, and
- court costs.

Under most EEOC-enforced laws, compensatory and punitive damages also may be available where intentional discrimination is found. Damages may be available to compensate for actual monetary losses, for future monetary losses, and for mental anguish and inconvenience. Punitive damages also may be available if an employer acted with malice or reckless indifference. Punitive damages are not available against the federal, state or local governments.

In cases concerning reasonable accommodation under the ADA, compensatory or punitive damages may not be awarded to the charging party if an employer can demonstrate that "good faith" efforts were made to provide reasonable accommodation.

An employer may be required to post notices to all employees addressing the violations of a specific charge and advising them of their rights under the laws EEOC enforces and their right to be free from retaliation. Such notices must be accessible, as needed, to persons with visual or other disabilities that affect reading.

The employer also may be required to take corrective or preventive actions to cure the source of the identified discrimination and minimize the chance of its recurrence, as well as discontinue the specific discriminatory practices involved in the case.

THE COMMISSION

XIV. What Is EEOC and How Does It Operate?

EEOC is an independent federal agency originally created by Congress in 1964 to enforce Title VII of the Civil Rights Act of 1964. The Commission is composed of five Commissioners and a General Counsel appointed by the President and confirmed by the Senate. Commissioners are appointed for five-year staggered terms; the General Counsel's term is four years. The President designates a Chair and a Vice-Chair. The Chair is the chief executive officer of the Commission. The Commission has authority to establish equal employment policy and to approve litigation. The General Counsel is responsible for conducting litigation.

EEOC carries out its enforcement, education and technical assistance activities through 50 field offices serving every part of the nation.

The nearest EEOC field office may be contacted by calling: 1-800-669-4000 (voice) or 1-800-669-6820 (TTY).

INFORMATION AND ASSISTANCE AVAILABLE FROM EEOC

XV. What Information and Other Assistance Is Available from EEOC?

EEOC provides a range of informational materials and assistance to individuals and entities with rights and responsibilities under EEOC-enforced laws. Most materials and assistance are provided to the public at no cost. Additional specialized training and technical assistance are provided on a fee basis under the auspices of the EEOC Education, Technical Assistance, and Training Revolving Fund Act of 1992. For information on educational and other assistance available, contact the nearest EEOC office by calling: 1-800-669-4000 (voice) or 1-800-669-6820 (TTY).

Publications available at no cost include posters advising employees of their EEO rights, and pamphlets, manuals, fact sheets, and enforcement guidance on laws enforced by the Commission. For a list of EEOC publications, or to order publications, write, call, or fax:

U.S. Equal Employment Opportunity Commission
Publications Distribution Center
P.O. Box 12549
Cincinnati, Ohio 45212-0549
1-800-669-3362 (voice)
1-800-800-3302 (TTY)
513-489-8692 (fax)

Telephone operators are available to take orders (in English or Spanish) from 8:30 a.m. to 5:00 p.m. (EST), Monday through Friday. Orders generally are mailed within 48 hours after receipt.

Information about EEOC and the laws it enforces also can be found at the following internet address: *http://www.eeoc.gov.*

DIVERSITY AND DISCRIMINATION

Joseph DesJardins

DISCUSSION CASE: FEMALE FOREMAN AND THE BROTHERHOOD

Margaret Reynolds was hired as an electrician at the Atlantic City Convention Center in 1985. Two years later she was appointed as a "sub-foreman" for the West Hall section of the Convention Center. In late September of 1987, shortly after the 1987 Miss America pageant closed, Ms. Reynolds and 16 other electricians were discharged by the Convention Center. The next day, 7 electricians were rehired and within three days 12 electricians were back working at the center. Ms. Reynolds was not among the 12. Ms. Reynolds sued both the Convention Center and her local union of the International Brotherhood of Electrical Workers claiming that she was a victim of sexual harassment while working at the Convention Center and that she was fired because she was a woman.

The United States legal system recognizes two forms of sexual harassment. Quid pro quo (Latin for "this for that") harassment occurs when granting sexual favors is made a condition of employment, as when a manager threatens an employee with dismissal unless she agrees to a sexual relationship with him or promises workplace benefits to an employee who does submit to his sexual offer. Hostile work environment occurs when a pattern of sexual harassment within the workplace prevents a woman from doing her job. Both forms of sexual harassment are understood to be forms of employment discrimination on the basis of sex, an activity prohibited by the Civil Rights Act of 1964. That law makes it illegal to deny anyone equal employment opportunities on the basis of sex.

In defining sexual harassment, the Equal Employment Opportunities Commission (EEOC) guidelines describe the kinds of workplace conduct that may be actionable under the law. These include "[u]nwelcome sexual advances, requests for sexual favors, and other verbal or physical conduct of a sexual nature." These guidelines provide that such sexual misconduct constitutes prohibited "sexual harassment," whether or not it is directly linked to the grant or denial of an economic quid pro quo, where "such conduct has the purpose or effect of unreasonably interfering with an individual's work performance or creating an intimidating, hostile, or offensive working environment." In concluding that "hostile environment" (i.e., non quid pro quo) harassment violates the law, the EEOC relied upon legal precedents developed in cases of racial and ethnic discrimination. Those precedents gave employees the right to work in an environment free from discriminatory intimidation, ridicule, and insult. If such an environment existed and interfered with the terms, conditions, and privileges of employment, courts held that unlawful discrimination had occurred. In the words of one court, "[T]he phrase 'terms, conditions or privileges of employment' in [Title VII] is an expansive concept which sweeps within its protective ambit the practice of creating a working environment heavily charged with ethnic or racial discrimination. . . . One can readily envision working environments so heavily polluted with discrimination as to destroy completely the emotional and psychological stability of minority group workers. . . ." In applying these standards to a case of alleged sexual harassment, another court concluded that: "Sexual harassment which creates a hostile or offensive environment for members of one sex is every bit the arbitrary barrier to sexual equality at the workplace that racial harassment is to racial equality. Surely, a requirement that a man or woman run a gauntlet of sexual abuse in return for the privilege of being allowed to work and make a living can be as demeaning and disconcerting as the harshest of racial epithets." [Court of Appeals for the Eleventh Circuit, in *Henson v. Dundee*, 682 F.2d 897, 902 [1982).]

Of course, not all harassment sufficiently affects the "terms, conditions and privileges of employment." For sexual harassment to be actionable, it must be sufficiently severe or pervasive "to alter the conditions of [the victim's] employment and create an abusive working environment."

Margaret Reynolds claimed that the work environment among the electricians at the Atlantic City Convention Center was both severe and pervasive enough to create an unjust barrier to her employment. According to the United States Department of Labor, women constituted just 2.3 percent of all workers in the construction trades in the year 2000. Women also held about the same percentage of supervisory positions within construction trades. Only 1 of the other 17 electricians employed by the Convention Center was a woman.

By all accounts, this workplace was normally characterized by obscene, vulgar, and crude comments and behavior. The court acknowledged that the workplace environment was "pervaded by a lexicon of obscenity" and "permeated by profanity." It was apparently normal for workers to refer to each other by obscene names and to regularly use vulgar and crude language and gestures. On only several occasions, however, was Ms. Reynolds specifically and directly targeted by such behavior and language, being called a "cunt" and "douche-bag cunt" on two occasions by co-workers. On several occasions, other co-workers would grab their crotch as they walked by her. On several other occasions some male workers refused to work with or for Ms. Reynolds. There was also some evidence that her supervisors received complaints during the Miss America pageant that pageant organizers felt uncomfortable having female construction workers present during the pageant.

In deciding the Reynolds case, a United States District Court considered whether this workplace environment was so hostile and offensive that it constituted sexual harassment. The court acknowledged that it was common for male electricians to call each other obscene names and make obscene, crude, and sexual gestures to other males. Ms. Reynolds admitted that while some of these comments seemed intended to offend her, most of the time it was just the way the male workers behaved. She also admitted that she herself had used obscene language at work and had also called male workers obscene names under her breath.

In *Margaret Reynolds v. Atlantic City Convention Center*, the District Court ruled that "in an atmosphere otherwise permeated by obscenity," the few occasions when harassment was targeted at Ms. Reynolds were not "sufficiently severe and persistent to affect seriously the psychological well-being of a reasonable employee." The court ruled that the harassment aimed at Ms. Reynolds was "isolated" rather than "pervasive" and that "these gestures and remarks were not made in church." Given the "totality of the circumstances," the harassment experienced by Ms. Reynolds did not alter the conditions of her work sufficiently to constitute an unjust denial of equal employment opportunity. It would appear, from the court's perspective, that part of the normal terms and conditions of construction work is an atmosphere of obscene and crude language and behavior. Since it was not specifically targeted at a woman and since it was not explicitly nor exclusively sexual, this normal standard of behavior did not discriminate and therefore was not illegal.

INTRODUCTION: DIVERSITY AND EQUALITY

Data from the 2000 U. S. census confirm the common observation that the American workforce is becoming increasingly diverse. Within the civilian labor force, the percentage of male workers is projected to increase by less than 10 percent between the years 1998 and 2008, while the number of women workers is projected to increase by more than 15 percent. During the same period, the percentage of African American workers will increase by almost 20 percent, the Hispanic workers by 36 percent, and Asian American workers by over 40 percent.[1]

These figures from the workforce parallel general population data. Between 1990 and 1999, the U. S. white population increased just over 7 percent. During the same period, the African American population increased 14 percent, Hispanic population increased 40 percent, and the population of Asian American and Pacific Islanders increased 44 percent. White males have not comprised the majority of the U. S. workforce since the 1970s.

Managing this changing and diverse workforce presents business management with both opportunities and challenges. Greater diversity within labor pools provides management with the opportunity to find employees with a wider range of talents, experiences, and abilities. Companies that find, recruit, hire, and retain such workers can achieve many competitive advantages in the marketplace.

Nevertheless, an increasingly diverse population in and out of the workforce creates challenges to business as well. As the Reynolds case demonstrated, what is acceptable and normal behavior with one type of worker can be offensive and a barrier to others. A diverse workforce will very likely experience similar situations in which differences among genders, ethnic groups, and cultures can create significant barriers to an efficient and peaceful workplace. Further, the workplace is but a subset of the wider society, and social concerns of equality and discrimination can be expected to appear within the workplace.

Despite decades of legal and political initiatives to bring equal opportunities to women and minorities, significant economic and social inequalities remain in the wider society. Business institutions are a prime resource for addressing these inequalities. An increasingly diverse workforce also has not yet translated into increased diversity in positions of authority, in equality of wages and benefits, and in positions of power and prestige. Evidence suggests that true equal opportunity does not yet flourish within business institutions.

Consider the mixed record on workplace equality for women. Women have made significant gains in many professional careers, for example. Between 1970 and 1990, the percentage of women physicians more than doubled from 7.6 to 16.9 percent. Between 1973 and 1993, the percentage of women lawyers and judges increased from 5.8 to 22.7 percent, and women in engineering increased from 1.3 to 8 percent. Yet women remain clustered in lower-paid and lower-status jobs, are relatively absent from higher-paying blue-collar and management positions, and continue to be paid lower wages than men. Forty percent of native-born working women fill positions classified as "administrative support" and "service" by the U.S. Bureau of Labor Statistics, while fewer than 16 percent of male workers fill such jobs. In private industry, white men comprise 65 percent of managerial positions, white women hold 25 percent, minority men 6.5 percent, and minority women less than 4 percent. Women in general hold less than 5 percent of all senior-level positions in major corporations.

Significant wage gaps correlated with gender and race also persist. Overall women still make only 75 cents to a man's dollar (up from 63 cents in 1979). White women in 1993 earned 70.8 percent of the salary of white men, while black women and Hispanic women were paid 63.7 percent and 53.9 percent, respectively. Across the board, women with the same training and educational credentials are paid less than their male counterparts. According to data from the 2000 U.S. census, native-born women with college degrees earn 74 cents for every dollar an equally educated native-born man earns, and the percentage remains very constant for all educational levels. Even the most highly educated women soon fall behind equally educated men. For example, a study of the Class of 1982 Stanford MBAs found that by 1992 the men in the class were far more likely than the women to work as CEOs, vice presidents, or directors, and, as a result, received more pay. Sixteen percent of men from this class at Stanford held CEO job titles, while only 2 percent of women were CEOs. Twenty-three percent of male 1982 Stanford MBA graduates worked as corporate vice presidents and 15 percent served as directors, compared with 10 percent of women who were vice presidents and 8 percent of women who held director positions. On average, the women Stanford MBA graduates from the Class of 1982 made 73.1 percent of the salaries of men graduates. Holding age constant also does little to eliminate the wage gap. The AMA found in 1989 that women physicians under age 40 made 66.6 percent of male salaries, women between 40 and 49 years earned 58.4 percent, and women 50 and over were paid 66.4 percent of a male physician's salary.

The situation for minority workers is at least as bleak. In 1940 black men earned on average only 40 cents for every dollar earned by white men. By 1990 black men's wages had climbed to about 75 percent of white men's, and, by 1998, to 76 percent. Real wages (wages adjusted for inflation) of black men overall have stagnated or even declined since 1975. Further, the unemployment rate of black men remains twice that of white men, and their labor force participation rate lags behind that of whites. While these rates improved dramatically with the strong economy in the period 1993 to 1999, the unemployment rate of adult black men is still in the range of 6 to 7 percent and that of black teens in the range of 25 to 30 percent. Comparable unemployment for white men was about half that for black males.

In this chapter, we shall consider what ethical responsibilities business has for addressing these challenges. We shall be guided at the start by a brief review of the early development of equal opportunity law. Before we start, perhaps a reminder about the importance of shifting perspectives within ethical controversies is worthwhile.

The majority of people reading this book will be college students, and approximately half will be male. The natural inclination will be to approach this issue as soon-to-be job applicants who will either benefit from, or be hindered by, policies of affirmative action and preferential hiring. I am willing to predict that the majority of college-aged white males will oppose preferential hiring policies, not surprising perhaps. My advice to all readers is that you try to take the point of view of different parties to these debates. Consider the legitimacy of affirmative action and preferential policies from the point of view of various job applicants, as well as business managers and democratic citizens. Consider not only how you might be affected by such policies, but also how they might contribute to, or hinder, the development of a just society.

DISCRIMINATION, EQUAL OPPORTUNITY, AND AFFIRMATIVE ACTION

An increasingly diverse workplace does present business with many challenges. Some, such as attracting and retaining skilled workers, are managerial. Others, such as insuring that workers of diverse backgrounds and expectations are treated fairly, are ethical. The following sections will examine the ethical questions raised by affirmative action and preferential hiring policies that are aimed at alleviating the racial, sexual, and ethnic inequalities sketched above.

Some might think that it is unfair or unreasonable to hold business responsible for such an intractable social problem as racial, sexual, or ethnic discrimination. From this perspective, business only has a responsibility to obey the law that prohibits discrimination in employment, but anything beyond that is asking too much of what are, after all, economic institutions. Accordingly, as long as business does not deny equal treatment and **equal opportunity**, it has fulfilled its legal and ethical responsibility concerning discrimination in work and commerce. This common view is worth considering at some length.

The first thing to note is that this view rests upon the assumed value of equality. This in itself is testimony to how far this legal and ethical debate has advanced in just a few decades. As recently as the 1960s, many state laws not only allowed but actually required racial segregation in public places and in schools. Women were also excluded from many jobs, many professions, and many schools for decades after they received the rights to vote in 1920. It is easy to forget (if in fact students of the twenty-first century ever even knew) that the Civil Rights Act of 1965 was politically a very controversial measure that required significant changes throughout American society, not the least of which was in the workplace and in commerce. (It would be interesting in this regard to consider if Margaret Reynolds's co-workers really were committed to giving women an equal opportunity to work as electricians.)

But if twentieth century history is mixed on discrimination, surely the twenty-first century is not. A commitment to equal treatment for each individual, providing each person with equal economic opportunity, is about as strong an ethical consensus as exists, at least in North America, Europe, and throughout much of the rest of the world. The ethical basis for this consensus can be found as a fundamental tenet of all major ethical theories, if not a fundamental assumption of morality itself. All individuals deserve equal moral standing. As a first approximation of business's ethical responsibility concerning discrimination, then, we can say that the commitment to equal opportunity requires business not to discriminate in any of its activities. This responsibility is sometimes referred to as requiring a policy of *passive nondiscrimination.* Business fulfills this responsibility as long as it does not do what is wrong—that is, as long as it does not discriminate. The remaining question is whether business has the further responsibility to take some positive, or "affirmative," action to counter the effects of discrimination. The question becomes, Is legal access, what is often called formal equal opportunity, a sufficient public policy for addressing the problem of discrimination? To answer this question, we need to consider in more detail exactly what this problem is.

Let us first note that discrimination itself is not necessarily a bad thing. *Discrimination* most generally refers to the ability to make distinctions, as when we describe someone as having discriminating tastes in food or music. In the workplace, we reasonably expect employers to make discrimination between employees by making distinctions between those who are hired and those who are not, between those who are promoted and those who are not, and so forth. Ethical problems arise only when the criteria used in making such discrimination are unethical or unfair.

For example, suppose I am hiring someone for a position to create and maintain a Web site for my business. It makes perfect sense to discriminate between job candidates on the basis of computer literacy and experience in working on Web sites. If I discriminate on the basis of job-relevant criteria, it would seem that I have acted in an ethically responsible way. All candidates have an equal opportunity to apply for the job, but only the person best qualified gets to be hired.

Consider a slightly different example. Suppose I have a pool of qualified candidates for this position and must discriminate between equally qualified people. Suppose also that one of the candidates graduated from my alma mater, Southern Connecticut State University. Suppose, as a loyal alumni, I like to support my school and I therefore offer the job to that candidate. I do not claim that this candidate is better qualified than others, only that I have a personal preference for SCSU graduates. Have I done anything wrong by discriminating on the basis of personal preference rather than job-relevant criterion?

Let us now change this example somewhat. Imagine that my preference was not for hiring Southern Connecticut graduates, but for hiring white males. One could imagine such a preference among Margaret Reynold's co-workers, for example. What, if anything, is the difference between hiring preferences that favor one's alma mater and those that favor white males? Or suppose, as is often done, a company gives hiring preference to family members of present employees? Is this company's desire to reward loyal employees a violation of equal opportunity?

Reflecting back on discussions in earlier chapters, we can review several general ethical perspectives on this issue. A utilitarian concern for economic efficiency would be inclined to support a narrow view of employment qualifications. Managers should make hiring decisions based primarily on the ability of the candidate to perform the job efficiently and skillfully. But as in all utilitarian calculations, other consequences (e.g., the goodwill of long-term employees whose family is given preference in hiring) must also be considered. A more libertarian approach that emphasizes property rights and managerial prerogatives would support greater latitude for managerial discretion in hiring. A general concern for justice, however, would constrain both approaches to ensure that all individuals are treated with fairness and equal respect.

Acknowledging that decisions such as the Southern Connecticut hire are often made, we might say that when all other qualifications are equal, employers should enjoy wide latitude in making hiring decisions. Of course, the degree of managerial prerogative might depend on whether or not the business was privately owned by the person making that decision or a human resource manager making the decision within a publicly traded corporation. This discretion should also depend on how the position is advertised and described. Job openings that acknowledge a preference for families of present employers won't create misleading expectations among candidates. Nevertheless, as long as the other candidates have an equal chance of being in a similar position (they could have attended Southern Connecticut, or they could just as likely have applied for a position with someone from their alma mater), and as long as they were not misled in the application process, nothing obviously unfair was done to them.

On the other hand, those candidates from other colleges might claim that there is something unfair about hiring someone based on unadvertised personal preferences rather than job-relevant qualifications. They might claim that there was something deceptive about what amounts to a hidden agenda in the process, and they might claim that while they were given legal equal opportunity, they really weren't given a fair chance at the position. To overcome the hidden advantage of a Southern Connecticut graduate, other candidates would have had to have been more qualified than the person who received the job. Thus, in effect, they were being held to higher standards and therefore, despite the appearance of a formal equal opportunity, they were not in fact being treated equally.

If it truly were a matter of random chance that they were competing with a Southern Connecticut graduate for a position being controlled by a Southern Connecticut graduate, and if they just happened to choose another school that had an equal chance of having its own active alumni hiring, then perhaps no serious unfairness has occurred. That is, if they had an equal opportunity to obtain the deciding criteria, or if there were truly other and equal opportunities open for them, then the decision might not be unfair. Given these conditions, the decision between equally qualified candidates was, in effect, made on random grounds (like flipping a coin) and thus was not unfair.

But are women and people of color in the same position as the candidates from nonfavored colleges? It seems clear that they are not. Obviously, one doesn't choose one's race, gender, or ethnic background. In this sense, individuals do not deserve whatever benefits or burdens get attached to those characteristics by society. Like the candidate from Southern Connecticut, any advantage in the job market enjoyed by white males is undeserved. Also, given the systematic inequality across society, women and people of color are less likely to have similar opportunities of being favored by someone in a position of hiring authority.

As suggested by the Margaret Reynolds case, legal access alone may not be enough to give a woman or a person of color a really fair chance to succeed in a predominately white, or predominately male, workplace. This is not to say that decisions that favor white males are the result of conscious and intentional bias. But seemingly benign factors, such as personal preference (such as the preference for certain school graduates) or criteria such as "collegiality" or whether or not someone will "fit in," can result in a hidden bias in favor of what is already established as "normal." What is often referred to as the old boys' network is a good example of such a situation. Such seemingly neutral factors in getting jobs such as having connections with someone within the company, recommendations from family friends, and having attended the right schools can turn out to have a very conservative bias, reinforcing the status quo, which turns out to be disadvantageous to women and people of color.

Consider another case in which disparate treatment can result from seemingly normal and equal treatment. Some evidence suggests that women will tend to have lower salary expectations than men. (Given the facts of wage differentials, this is not surprising perhaps.) Imagine two equally qualified candidates, one man and one woman, have been offered an entry-level position with a major corporation. Put yourself in the position of the human resource manager who will be negotiating the starting salary. You are committed to hiring both candidates and, as normal in such cases, you have a salary range within which you can operate. As a manager, your strategy is to offer the lowest starting salary that you think will get them to accept the job offer (too low and you may not get them to accept, too high and you are not doing your job to control labor costs). As often happens, you separately ask the two candidates for their salary expectations and discover that the woman is willing to accept a lower salary than the man.

Even assuming that the manager is a person of goodwill with no bias against women, there are strong institutional incentives to offer the woman a lower salary. Assume further that, as time goes on, both employees receive evaluations as having done equally good work and each gets an equal percentage pay raise. The result is an ever-widening salary gap. Occasions when disparate treatment occurs from such implicit and subtle factors (rather than from intentional bias) are sometimes referred to as institutional discrimination. To the degree that such discrimination does occur, simple legal access and passive nondiscrimination on behalf of employers will not address unequal treatment in the workplace.

Perhaps the most obvious reason why simple legal access and passive nondiscrimination are thought inadequate is the fact that, four decades after the Civil Rights Act, there remains widespread unequal treatment throughout the economy. It is fair to say that equal opportunity alone has not solved many of the problems it was designed to address. Given the facts of inequality outlined above, there seem only two options available. Either society and business can continue to rely on equal opportunity and nondiscrimination, which implies that women and people of color must continue to wait for full equality, or society and business can take more active steps to address social and economic inequality.

What I will call **affirmative action** refers to any policy or action, aimed at securing a more equal workplace, that goes beyond simple legal access or passive nondiscrimination, but that does not alter the standards or qualifications for employment. Affirmative actions policies, therefore, do provide some positive (affirmative) benefit for a previously disadvantaged group, but do so in ways that do not change or lower qualifications.

Before developing this topic, it is important to reflect on the language used in these debates. The concepts of *equal opportunity, affirmative action, preferential treatment*, and *reverse discrimination* are used very ambiguously in social debates and discussions. Those who defend policies of preference tend to identify them simply as equal opportunity of affirmative action and thus benefit from the relatively benign meaning of those terms. Critics of preferential policies will tend to call them reverse discrimination and treat them as indistinguishable from affirmative action polices, thus equating anything other than equal opportunity as unethical discrimination. For the sake of clarity, at least, I think we can offer some definitions that will not prejudge the issue rhetorically.

Equal opportunity—the opposite of segregation—refers to the commitment to legal access regardless of gender, race, or ethnic background. This is what we have called *passive nondiscrimination.* Policies described as color blind or gender blind are classic examples of equal opportunity policies. There is universal support for equal opportunity within all major ethical traditions and contemporary political philosophies.

Affirmative action refers to any positive steps taken to alleviate unequal treatment that move beyond passive nondiscrimination. For clarity's sake, we will limit affirmative action policies to those that do not change the previously existing standards or qualifications. So, for example, a human resources office that recruits women and minority candidates, encourages them to apply, advertises in media that appeal to women or minorities, and provides support for women or people of color who are hired is engaged in affirmative action. Margaret Reynolds's employer, for example, did not provide locks on the women's bathroom or shower. Because the men's bathrooms and showers did not have locks, such a decision might be consistent with a gender-blind equal opportunity. Taking such steps to provide greater security for women than what is offered to men would have been a simple example of affirmative action. Perhaps the most common example of affirmative action is the widespread practice of recruiting qualified women and minority candidates. Since this is a positive step taken to benefit women and minority candidates that is not taken for white males, this goes beyond simple equal opportunity.

Note that, in one sense, such actions do put the white male at a relatively disadvantageous position compared to where he would have been had the employer not done it. The candidate pool is larger and therefore his chances of getting the job are lowered. But few would think that the white male has been harmed in an ethically relevant sense because he has not been denied anything to which he had a legitimate ethical claim. No one's rights are violated when an employer seeks to increase the applicant pool for its positions.

Other affirmative action policies might involve hiring a minority affairs officer, or a diversity coordinator whose job is to help manage an increasingly diverse workplace by troubleshooting problems, providing support for new hires, advising and mediating disputes, and generally trying to support and retain new employees. Again, these represent affirmative steps taken to support women and minority employees, but since it does not deny white male employees anything to which they have a right, such policies are generally uncontroversial. It is very common, in fact, to find employers describing themselves as an "equal opportunity/affirmative action" employer in job postings and advertisements. The frequency of such notices testifies to the overall social consensus surrounding affirmative action policies.

More controversial, both ethically and politically, are policies that grant preference to women or people of color by affecting the qualifications for a job in a way that benefits these previously disadvantaged groups. We will reserve the phrase **preferential treatment** for policies that go beyond affirmative action by seemingly changing the job standards in an effort to hire more women and people of color. Critics of such programs tend to call them *reverse discrimination*, and since it is in dispute if such is the case, we shall avoid that phrase in favor of the more neutral preferential treatment. Defenders of these policies tend to identify them as affirmative action, perhaps more specifically as strong affirmative action to distinguish them from the "weaker" version described above. We turn now to a closer examination of these more controversial policies.

PREFERENTIAL TREATMENT IN EMPLOYMENT

On the face of it, giving "preferences" to any job applicant appears to violate the ethical commitment to equal treatment. But as the Southern Connecticut graduate example showed, not every preference in hiring is unethical. Further, if the preference is given as a means for fulfilling other ethical responsibilities, it may turn out to be ethically praiseworthy if not required. Before considering the arguments for and against preference in hiring, let us first distinguish various forms that preferential hiring might take.

Perhaps the preferential policy closest to affirmative action would, in the case of otherwise equally qualified candidates, give preference to the previously disadvantaged candidate. This is similar to how we described the case of giving preference to a graduate from your college alma mater. In such a situation, rather than rely on some personal preference or random procedure, the decision between equally qualified candidates is made in a way that addresses the social inequality. Affirmative action policies seek to increase the pool of qualified candidates, and then assume that those women and people of color who are most qualified will be hired. This initial type of preferential treatment policy goes one step further and hires those women and people of color who are equally, but not necessarily more, qualified.

A second type of preferential policy would identify members of previously disadvantaged groups in the pool of qualified applicants and give them preference in the hiring decision, even if there is another candidate, typically a white male, who is more qualified. This situation treats membership in a disadvantaged group as itself a qualification for the job.

A third type of preferential policy would simply require that members of disadvantaged groups be hired with only minimal consideration given to qualifications. Effectively, this would be the policy of those who favor hiring quotas for women and people of color. A human resources department with a quota for hiring women, for example, would be committed to hiring a certain percentage regardless of the number or qualifications of male candidates.

The first of these policies seems to raise the least serious ethical challenges. As in the college graduate case, the candidate denied a job by the first policy might claim that he was implicitly being held to higher standards than the person given preference. Like that case, there is some legitimate concern with unfairness here. Note also that such policies are least likely to effectively address the unequal treatment that women and people of color receive in the workplace. Since these policies only go slightly further than affirmative action, and since affirmative action has not advanced equality significantly over the last four decades, these policies are not likely to alter social and economic inequality noticeably.

The second and third types of preferential policy are more likely to have noticeable effects on inequalities. A quota system, in fact, would have an immediate impact by mandating equality in hiring results. One would immediately bring about equality in employment if every employer were required to meet a quota for women and minority hiring that matched the percentage of women and minorities in the general population. But these types of policies also raise the most serious ethical questions. Both policies seem to violate the white male's right to equal treatment and equal opportunity. Two fundamental ethical questions must therefore be addressed in our analysis of preferential treatment: Do preferential policies in fact violate the rights of white males, and are there other ethical considerations that would override this violation if in fact it did occur?

In July 2003 the United States Supreme Court announced a decision that addressed many of these issues. Examining a situation involving admissions policies at universities, this case established precedents for affirmative action and preferential policies in business as well. The Court's decision seems to allow the first and second types of preferential policies. The decision held that race, ethnicity, or gender can be treated as a qualification and therefore can, when all other factors are equal, determine the outcome.

The case before the Court involved the University of Michigan Law School, which relied on an admissions policy that took into account the ability of each applicant to contribute to the school's social and intellectual life. As part of this criterion, the school considered the applicant's race, on the assumption that a diverse student body would contribute to the goals of the law school, and a critical mass of minority students was required to accomplish that goal. Thus, although scores from LSAT tests, undergraduate college grades, letters of recommendation, and other traditional factors were primarily used to grant admission, an applicant's race was also a factor. Two white females who were denied admission brought the law suit, arguing that admission of minority students with lower grades and test scores violated their rights to equal treatment.

The case attracted significant attention in the corporate sector as well as in higher education. General Motors Corporation field an *Amicus Curiae* ("friend of the court") brief in support of the law school's admission policy. By doing this GM went out of its way, and at great expense to itself, to be identified as a stakeholder and to argue publicly in support of affirmative action. In its brief, GM claimed that the need to insure a racially and ethnically diverse student body was a compelling reason to support affirmative action policies. GM claimed that "the future of American business and, in some measure, of the American economy depends on it."

GM claimed that in its own business experience "only a well educated, diverse workforce, comprising people who have learned to work productively and creatively with individuals from a multitude of races and ethnic, religious, and cultural backgrounds, can maintain America's competitiveness in the increasingly diverse and interconnected world economy." Prohibiting affirmative action "likely would reduce racial and ethnic diversity in the pool of employment candidates from which the nation's businesses' own efforts to obtain the manifold benefits of diversity in the managerial levels of their work forces."

The Supreme Court ruled that diversity can be a compelling state interest in admissions to state educational institutions. Because private sector business faces a less strict standard than state institutions in this regard, this decision sets a precedent for hiring policies in the private sector as well. However, the Court offered a more ambiguous judgment on the particular admissions policies aimed at achieving this goal. By a 5–4 vote, the Court approved the Michigan Law School's policy that gave each individual candidate consideration and that would stray from race-neutral grounds only when evidence existed to show that diversity is not being produced. However, at the same time the Court also voted 5–4 against the admission policy of the undergraduate program at Michigan. That policy granted admission based on a point system in which membership in an underrepresented class received 20 out of a maximum 150 points. For comparison, academic factors counted up to 100 points, being a Michigan resident counted for 10 points, alumni children received 4 points, and notable personal achievement received 5 points. The court ruled that 20 points almost guaranteed admission and that this therefore violated the rights to equal treatment of nonminority candidates.

Thus in the Michigan case, the Supreme Court allows, but does not require, affirmative action programs that aim at creating a more diverse student body. The Court did not explicitly address the question of whether or not private employers could use similar programs. It would seem that if a private employer would connect workplace diversity to important social goals of the employer, the Court would allow these as well. GM's claims regarding the value of a diverse workforce would presumably be just this sort of connection.

A variety of philosophical arguments have been offered to support or refute the ethical legitimacy of preferential hiring. Some appeal to deontological concepts such as rights, duties, justice, and fairness. For example, some argue that preferential policies are unjust because they violate the rights of white males. Others argue that preferential policies are obligatory means for compensating people for harms they have suffered. Other arguments are more consequentialist and utilitarian, arguing that, on balance, preferential policies produce either beneficial or detrimental consequences. For example, some defend preferential hiring as a means of providing more role models for young women and people of color. Others reject these policies as likely to create more discrimination as a backlash against gender or racial preferences. For convenience sake, the following sections will examine only deontological arguments for or against. If any of these arguments are sound, if they violate rights or are required by compensatory justice, for example, then either the beneficial or detrimental consequences can legitimately be discounted.

There seem to be two general deontological arguments that the white male could make to support the claim that his rights have been violated. The first, what we shall call the merit argument, claims that by ignoring or overriding qualifications, preferential policies violate the white male's right to have hiring decisions based on merit. According to this view, the most qualified person has earned the right to the job and a denial of this is to violate a principle of merit. The second argument more simply claims that preferential treatment violates the white male's right to be treated with equal respect and given equal opportunity. From this perspective, preferential policies are a straightforward case of reverse discrimination.

Likewise there are two major deontological arguments in support of preferential policies. One claims that preference is due to women and people of color as a means for compensating them for past harms. Allowing past discrimination to go uncompensated is unfair and unjust. The second major argument claims that, properly understood, the commitment to equality and equal treatment requires that presently disadvantaged people be granted preference as a means for securing real equality in the workplace.

TEXACO: THE JELLY BEAN DIVERSITY FIASCO

Marianne M. Jennings

In November, 1996, Texaco, Inc., was rocked by the disclosure of tape-recorded conversations among three executives about a racial discrimination suit pending against the company. The suit, seeking $71 million, had been brought by 6 employees, on behalf of 1500 other employees, who alleged the following forms of discrimination:

> I have had KKK printed on my car. I have had my tires slashed and racial slurs written about me on bathroom walls. One co-worker blatantly called me a racial epithet to my face.
>
> Throughout my employment, three supervisors in my department openly discussed their view that African-Americans are ignorant and incompetent, and, specifically, that Thurgood Marshall was the most incompetent person they had ever seen.
>
> Sheryl Joseph, formerly a Texaco secretary in Harvey, Louisiana was given a cake for her birthday which occurred shortly after she announced that she was pregnant. The cake depicted a black pregnant woman and read. "Happy Birthday, Sheryl. It must have been those watermelon seeds."

The suit also included data on Texaco's workforce:

1989	Minorities as a percentage of Texaco's workforce	15.2%
1994	Minorities as a percentage of Texaco's workforce	19.4%

# of Years to Promotion by Job Classification

Minority Employees	Job	Other Employees
6.1	Accountant	4.6
6.4	Senior Accountant	5.4
12.5	Analyst	6.3
14.2	Financial Analyst	13.9
15.0	Assistant Accounting Supervisor	9.8

Senior Managers

	White	Black
1991	1,887	19
1992	2,001	21
1993	2,000	23
1994	2,029	23

Racial Composition (% of Blacks) by Pay Range

Salary	Texaco	Other Oil Companies
$ 51,100	5.9%	7.2%
$ 56,900	4.7%	6.5%
$ 63,000	4.1%	4.7%
$ 69,900	2.3%	5.1%
$ 77,600	1.8%	3.2%
$ 88,100	1.9%	2.3%
$ 95,600	1.4%	2.6%
$ 106,100	1.2%	2.3%
$ 117,600	0.8%	2.3%
$ 128,800	0.4%	1.8%

(African-Americans make up 12% of the U.S. population)

The acting head of the EEOC wrote in 1995, "Deficiencies in the affirmative-action programs suggest that Texaco is not committed to insuring comprehensive, facility by facility, compliance with the company's affirmative-action responsibilities."

Faced with the lawsuit, Texaco's former treasurer, Robert Ulrich, senior assistant treasurer, J. David Keough, and senior coordinator for personnel services, Richard A. Lundwall, met and discussed the suit. A tape transcript follows:

They look through evidence, deciding what to turn over to the plaintiffs.

Lundwall: Here, look at this chart. You know, I'm not really quite sure what it means. This chart is not mentioned in the agency, so it's not important that we even have it in there. . . . They would never know it was here.

Keough: They'll find it when they look through it.

Lundwall: Not if I take it out they won't.

The executives decide to leave out certain pages of a document; they worry that another version will turn up.

Ulrich: We're gonna purge the [expletive deleted] out of these books, though. We're not going to have any damn thing that we don't need to be in them—

Lundwall: As a matter of fact, I just want to be reminded of what we discussed. You take your data and . . .

Keough: You look and make sure it's consistent to what we've given them already for minutes. Two versions with the restricted and that's marked clearly on top—

Ulrich: But I don't want to be caught up in a cover-up. I don't want to be my own Watergate.

Lundwall: We've been doing pretty much two versions, too. This one here, this is strictly my book, your book . . .

Ulrich: Boy, I'll tell you, that one, you would put that and you would have the only copy. Nobody else ought to have copies of that.

Lundwall: O.K.?

Ulrich: You have that someplace and it doesn't exist.

Lundwall: Yeah, O.K.

Ulrich: I just don't want anybody to have a copy of that.

Lundwall: Good, No problem.

Ulrich: You know, there is no point in even keeping the restricted version anymore. All it could do is get us in trouble. That's the way I feel. I would not keep anything.

Lundwall: Let me shred this thing and any other restricted version like it.

Ulrich: Why do we have to keep the minutes of the meeting anymore?

Lundwall: You don't, you don't.

Ulrich: We don't?

Lundwall: Because we don't, no, we don't because it comes back to haunt us like right now—

Ulrich: I mean, the pendulum is swinging the other way, guys.

The executives discuss the minority employees who brought the suit.

Lundwall: They are perpetuating an us/them atmosphere. Last week or last Friday I told . . .

Ulrich: [Inaudible.]

Lundwall: Yeah, that's what I said to you, you want to frag grenade? You know, duck, I'm going to throw one. Well, that's what I was alluding to. But the point is not, that's not bad in itself but it does perpetuate us/them. And if you're trying to get away and get to the we . . . you can't do that kind of stuff.

Ulrich: [Inaudible.] I agree. This diversity thing. You know how black jelly beans agree. . . .

Lundwall: That's funny. All the black jelly beans seem to be glued to the bottom of the bag.

Ulrich: You can't have just we and them. You can't just have black jelly beans and other jelly beans. It doesn't work.

Lundwall: Yeah. But they're perpetuating the black jelly beans.

Ulrich: I'm still having trouble with Hanukkah. Now, we have Kwanza (laughter).

The release of the tape prompted the Reverend Jesse Jackson to call for a nationwide boycott of Texaco. Sales fell 8%, Texaco's stock fell 2%, and several institutional investors were preparing to sell their stock.

Texaco did have a minority recruiting effort in place and the "jelly bean" remark was tied to a diversity trainer the company had hired. The following are excerpts from Texaco's statement of vison and values:

Respect for the Individual

Our employees are our most important resource. Each person deserves to be treated with respect and dignity in appropriate work environments, without regard to race, religion, sex, age, national origin, disability or position in the company. Each employee has the responsibility to demonstrate respect for others.

The company believes that a work environment that reflects a diverse workforce, values diversity, and is free of all forms of discrimination, intimidation, and harassment is essential for a productive and efficient workforce. Accordingly, conduct directed toward any employee

> that is unwelcome, hostile, offensive, degrading, or abusive is unacceptable and will not be tolerated.

A federal grand jury began an investigation at Texaco to determine whether there had been obstruction of justice in the withholding of documents.

Within days of the release of the tape. Texaco settled its bias suit for $176.1 million, the largest sum ever allowed in a discrimination case. The money will allow a 11% pay raise for blacks and other minorities who joined in the law suit.

Texaco's chairman and CEO, Peter I. Bijur, issued the following statement after agreeing to a settlement:

> Texaco is facing a difficult but vital challenge. It's broader than any specific words and larger than any lawsuit. It is one we must and are attacking head-on.
>
> We are a company of 27,000 people worldwide. In any organization of that size, unfortunately, there are bound to be people with unacceptable, biased attitudes toward race, gender and religion.
>
> Our goal, and our responsibility, is to eradicate this kind of thinking wherever and however it is found in our company. And our challenge is to make Texaco a company of limitless opportunity for all men and women.
>
> We are committed to begin meeting this challenge immediately through programs with concrete goals and measurable timetables.
>
> I've already announced certain specific steps, including a redoubling of efforts within Texaco to focus on the paramount value of respect for the individual and a comprehensive review of our diversity programs at every level of our company.
>
> We also want to broaden economic access to Texaco for minority firms and increase the positive impact our investments can have in the minority community. This includes areas such as hiring and promotion; professional services such as advertising, banking, investment management and legal services; and wholesale and retail station ownership.
>
> To assist us, we are reaching out to leaders of minority and religious organizations and others for ideas and perspectives that will help Texaco succeed in our mission of becoming a model of diversity and workplace equality.
>
> It is essential to this urgent mission that Texaco and African-Americans and other minority community leaders work together to help solve the programs we face as a company—which, after all, echo the problems faced in society as a whole.
>
> Discrimination will be extinguished only if we tackle it together, only if we join in a unified, common effort.
>
> Working together, I believe we can take Texaco into the 21st century as a model of diversity. We can make Texaco a company of limitless opportunity. We can make Texaco a leader in according respect to every man and woman.

Even after the announcement, Texaco stock was down $3 per share, a loss of $800 million total, and the boycott was continued. Texaco's proposed merger with Shell Oil began to unravel as Shell's CEO expressed concern about Texaco's integrity. However, after the settlement, additional information about the case began to emerge.

Holman W. Jenkins, Jr. wrote the following piece for the *Wall Street Journal:*

Quietly, corporate America is debating whether Texaco's Peter Bijur did the right thing.

Mr. Bijur gets paid to make the hard calls, and with the airwaves aflame over "nigger" and "black jelly beans," Texaco took a battering in the stock and political markets. He had every reason for wanting to put a stop-loss on the media frenzy. "Once the taped conversations were revealed," he says, settling was "reasonable and honorable." So now Texaco is betting $176 million that paying off minority employees and their lawyers is the quickest way out of the news.

But as the company's own investigation showed, the truly inflammatory comments reported in the media never took place. They were purely a fabrication by opposing lawyers, and trumpeted by a credulous *New York Times*. And some digging would have shown this problem cropping up before in the career of Mike Hausfeld, lead attorney for the plaintiffs.

In an antitrust case years ago, he presented a secret recording that he claimed showed oil executives conspiring to threaten gasoline dealers. But a check by the same expert who handled the Nixon Watergate tapes showed no such thing. Says Larry Sharp, the Washington antitrust lawyer who opposed Mr. Hausfeld: "To put it generously, he gave himself the benefit of the doubt in making the transcript."

But this time the lie has been rewarded, and the broader public, unschooled in legal cynicism, heads home believing Texaco an admitted racist.

The catechism of corporate crisis management says you can't fight the media. Mr. Bijur had to consider that Jesse Jackson was threatening a boycott if Texaco failed to "regret, repent and seek renewal." Mr. Jackson pointedly added that "any attempt to shift to denial would add insult to injury"—a warning against trying to spread some egg to the faces of those who were fooled by the fake transcript.

There may have been wisdom, if not valor, in Mr. Bijur's decision to run up the white flag. But he also evinced symptoms of Stockholm Syndrome, telling CNN that Texaco was just the "tip of the iceberg" of corporate racism. Ducking this fight so ignominiously may yet prove a pennywise, pound-foolish strategy. The City of Philadelphia has decided to dump its Texaco holdings anyway, partly out of fear of more litigation.

What else could Texaco have done? It could have apologized for any offense, but stuck up for its former treasurer Bob Ulrich, who was wronged by the phony transcript and stripped of his medical benefits by Texaco. And the company could have vowed to fight the lawsuit like the dickens, arguing that Texaco is not the cause of society's racial troubles but has tried to be part of the solution.

Start with the tapes: A fair listening does not necessarily reveal a "racist" conversation by executives at Texaco, but certainly a candid conversation about the problems of race at Texaco. They spoke of "jelly beans" dividing into camps of "us" and "them," an honest representation of life at many companies, not just in the oil patch.

Mr. Bijur could have made this point, starting with the *New York Times,* which has been embroiled in its own discrimination lawsuit with Angela Dodson, once its top-ranking black female. In a complaint filed with New York City's Human Rights Commission, she claims the paper was "engaged in gender-based harassment and disability-based discrimination . . . because *The Times* no longer wanted me, as a black person, to occupy a position as Senior editor."

Her deepest ire is reserved for *Times* veteran Carolyn Lee, who is white and more accustomed to being lauded as a champion of women and minorities. Ms. Dodson told the *Village Voice:* "It got to the point that whenever I was in her presence or earshot she made remarks [about other black people] that could only be taken as negative."

This sounds remarkably like the anecdotes filed in the Texaco complaint. All an outsider can safely conclude is that race makes everything more complicated, as sensitivity begets sensitivity. Mr. Bijur would have done more for racial understanding had he used his platform to open up this subject.

Yes, the cartoonist racists are out there, he might have said, but the *Times* coverage of Texaco only found cartoonist racists. The paper could have looked to its own experience for another story—a story about how garden-variety interpersonal conflict can land even decent people in the snares of racial mistrust.

This is what affirmative action, by throwing people together, was supposed to get us past. And it may be no accident that our most quota-ridden newspaper. *USA Today,* jumped off the bandwagon on the Texaco tapes, noting the ambiguity of whether the "jelly bean" remarks were meant to be hostile or friendly to blacks.

And McPaper kept on asking intelligent questions, like whether the *New York Times* had been "used by plaintiffs in the case to promote a faulty but more inflammatory transcript?" ("Not unless the court was used," answered *Times* Business Editor John Geddes, sounding like a lawyer himself.)

So Mr. Bijur was not facing a uniformly hopeless media torrent. The truth, even a complicated truth, catches up with the headlines eventually.

In time, he might have found surprising allies drifting to his side. The *New Republic* and the *New Yorker* have run thoughtful articles arguing that businesses should be allowed to use quotas but shouldn't be subject to harassment litigation if they don't. Right now, we do the opposite: Forbid companies to promote by quota, then sue them under federal "adverse impact" rules when they don't.

In effect, liberal voices are arguing that business could do more for minorities with less conflict if freedom of contract were restored. The world is changing, and companies have their own reasons nowadays for wanting minorities around. They need input from different kinds of people on how to deal with different kinds of people. No doubt this is why McPaper feels free to thumb its nose at the conformity crowd on stories like Texaco and church-burnings. (See September's *Harvard Business Review* for what business is thinking about diversity now.)

If companies were set free to assemble the work forces most useful to them, they could sweep away a heap of excuses for recrimination. Whites couldn't feel cheated out of jobs. Blacks wouldn't end up at companies that want them only for window-dressing. And the world could go back to feeling OK about being an interesting place. We might even allow that cultural patterns other than racism may explain why so many rednecks, and so few blacks, become petroleum engineers.

Mr. Bijur may have made the best of a bad deal for his shareholders. Whether it was best for America is a different judgment.[1]

Richard Lundwall, the executive who taped the sessions with the other executives was charged with one count of obstruction of justice. Lundwall had turned over the tapes of the conversations to lawyers for the plaintiffs in the discrimination suit on October 25, 1996. Lundwall had been terminated.

Texaco hired attorney Michael Armstrong to investigate the underlying allegations. Mr. Armstrong found the tapes had not been transcribed correctly.

As part of its settlement, Texaco agreed to, at a cost of $55 million, assign a task force to police hiring and promotion as well as requiring mentors for black employees and sensitivity training for white employees.

The following interview with CEO Bijur appeared in *Business Week:*

Q: How did your legal strategy change once the news of the tapes was printed?

A: When I saw [the story], I knew that this lawsuit was pending and moving forward. I made the judgment that we needed to accelerate the settlement process. And those discussions on settlement commenced almost immediately.

Q: It has been reported that you didn't get the board of directors involved with the settlement talks and other issues. Why not?

A: You're drawing conclusions that are erroneous. The board was fully involved throughout the entire process. I talked to numerous directors personally. We had several board and executive committee meetings. The board was fully supportive of our actions.

Q: Have you met with shareholders?

A: Yes, of course. I went down to [New York] and met with the Interfaith Center on Corporate Responsibility, which is a group of religious shareholders. I expressed our position on this and listened carefully to their position and got some good counsel and guidance. But I wanted to provide our side of the issue as well. I have met with [New York State Comptroller] Carl McCall and [New York City Comptroller] Alan Hevesi about concerns that they had, and I will continue to meet with other shareholders as I normally do.

Q: Why do you think the oil industry has such a poor reputation on issues of racial diversity and gender equality? How does Texaco stack up against the others?

A: The percentage of minorities within Texaco is just about average for the petroleum industry. We have made really significant progress in the last several years in improving the percentage. But there are some very interesting points that need to be examined to place in context what may be going on in this industry. I just read a study that showed that in 1995, there were only nine petroleum engineering minority graduates that came out of all engineering schools in the United States—only nine. That's not an excuse. But it is indicative of why it is difficult for this industry to have a lot of people in the pipeline. Now, of course, that does not apply to accountants, finance people, and anybody else. But we are a very technically oriented industry.

Q: Have you personally witnessed discrimination at Texaco?

A: In the nearly 31 years I have been with Texaco, I have never witnessed an incident of racial bias or prejudice. And had I seen it, I would have taken disciplinary action. I've never seen it.

Q: Is there a widespread culture of insensitivity at Texaco?

A: I do not think there is a culture of institutional bias within Texaco. I think we've got a great many very good and decent human beings, but that unfortunately we mirror society. There is bigotry in society. There is prejudice and injustice in society. I am sorry to say that, and I am sorry to say that probably does exist within Texaco. I can't do much about society, but I certainly can do something about Texaco.

Q: What are your views on affirmative action?

A: Texaco's views on affirmative action have not changed a bit. We have supported affirmative action, and we will continue to support affirmative action.

Q: This is your first big trial since taking over. What have you learned?

A: I've learned that as good as our programs are in the company—and they really are quite good, even in this area—there's always more we can do. We've got to really drill down into the programs. We've got to make certain that they're meeting the objectives and goals we've set for them.

Q: Are there other lessons in terms of your style of management?

A: I don't think I would do anything different the next time than what I did this time.

Q: How will you make sure the spirit as well as the letter of the policy is followed at Texaco?

A: We're going to put more and more and more emphasis on it until we get it through everybody's head: Bigotry is not going to be tolerated here.[2]

Robert W. Ulrich was indicated in 1997. Mr. Lundwall entered a "not guilty" plea on July 8, 1997, and J. David Keough has sued Texaco for libel. Texaco named Mary Bush, a financial consultant, as its first black female board member.

As Lundwall's prosecution has proceeded, new discoveries have been made. For example, "purposeful erasures" have been found on the tapes.

In an interim report on its progress toward the settlement goals, Texaco revealed the following:

Polishing the Star

As part of its settlement of a discrimination lawsuit brought by black employees, Texaco has moved on a half-dozen fronts to alter its business practices.

Hiring Asked search firms to identify wider arrays of candidates. Expanded recruiting at historically minority colleges. Gave 50 scholarships and paid internships to minority students seeking engineering or technical degrees.

Career Advancement Wrote objective standards for promotions. Developing training program for new managers. Developing a mentoring program.

Diversity Initiatives Conducted two-day diversity training for more than 8,000 of 20,000 U.S. employees. Tied management bonuses to diversity goals. Developing alternative dispute resolution and ombudsman programs.

Purchasing Nearly doubled purchases from minority- or women-owned businesses. Asking suppliers to report their purchases from such companies.

Financial Services Substantially increased banking, investment management and insurance business with minority- and women-owned firms. A group of such firms underwrote a $150 million public financing.

Retailing Added three black independent retailers, 18 black managers of company-owned service stations, 12 minority or female wholesalers, 13 minority- or women-owned Xpress Lube outlets and 6 minority- or women-owned lubricant distributors.

In May 1998, the Texaco executives were acquitted of all criminal charges.

NOTES

1. Reprinted with permission of *The Wall Street Journal* © 1996 Dow Jones & Company, Inc. All rights reserved.
2. Smart, Tim. "Texaco: Lessons From A Crisis-in-Progress." Reprinted from December 2, 1996, issue of *Business Week* by special permission, © 1997 by McGraw Hill, Inc.

QUESTIONS ON READINGS FOR PART SIX (D) (1 OF 2)

What are a firm's legal obligations with regard to nondiscrimination and affirmative action?

What are its moral obligations, if any?

What are the advantages/disadvantages of a diverse workforce?

PLANNING CAN HELP REDUCE EXPOSURE TO LAYOFF-RELATED LAWSUITS

Glen Doherty

Layoffs have become an inevitable part of business survival. Layoffs, however, often come at a significant cost to employers: lawsuits by terminated workers.

Careful planning and a basic understanding of the law at issue in a reduction in force can help employers reduce this litigation exposure.

An employer considering the possibility of reducing the work force should first review company personnel policies to determine whether the policies in any way restrict its right to implement layoffs. An employer can be (and some have been) sued whenever a reduction arguably occurs in contravention of the employer's own written policies.

The typical case is where an employer's policies purport to identify the possible reasons for a layoff, and the employer bases its layoff on a reason not contained in those policies. Any such limitation must be removed and replaced with an express policy that the employer has the absolute and unfettered right to conduct layoffs.

An employer's next step may be to consider other cost-cutting measures. For example, alternatives to layoffs might include elimination of overtime or reduction in work hours. Although this analysis rarely results in layoff avoidance, its real value is that it can serve to negate the argument that the company could have avoided the reduction by implementing other cost-cutting measures, an argument often advanced by plaintiffs at trial.

Assuming the absence of these other measures, an employer should then develop its layoff plan—which must include an explanation of the business justification. An explanation will be absolutely essential to the defense of any lawsuits or other administrative proceedings challenging the layoff.

An employer should seriously consider disseminating timely and credible information to its employees about the anticipated layoffs. Effective communication is essential to minimizing rumors. Rumors often cause employees to consult with an attorney, thus setting the stage for a lawsuit in the future.

Once the layoff plan has been developed and certain information about it has been released to the work force, the employer must then develop and document the basis for selecting the positions that may be eliminated. This usually involves a determination of the positions and skills within each department, unit or work area, which must be retained to achieve the desired business goals.

An employer's next step is to establish the criteria to be used in selecting employees for inclusion in the layoff. In any litigation, the employer will need to explain its reasons for selecting certain employees for termination. Such an explanation will have credibility only if supported by a written record demonstrating the employer's objective selection criteria, and how they were applied in a uniform and even-handed manner.

Prior to notifying the affected employees, the employer should consider conducting an impact analysis of the tentative layoff list to detect patterns that may support a claim of discrimination. If such patterns are detected, adjustments should be made to minimize any unintended impact on any protected groups.

Company officials selected to meet with the affected employees and advise them of the layoff decisions should be given step-by-step instructions on what to say. Each meeting must focus on the business justification of the layoff, while providing the affected employee with general information concerning his or her selection. The absence of a reasonable and honest explanation can—and will—encourage individuals to consider litigation.

All employees who are terminated must be provided with notice under the Consolidated Omnibus Budget Reconciliation Act. Under COBRA, an employee may elect to continue his or her health care coverage for a period commonly of up to 18 months. An employer's failure to provide employees with a timely COBRA notice may result in significant liability.

Another law that must be considered by an employer is the Worker Adjustment and Retraining Notification Act. Among other things, WARN requires employers with 100 or more employees to give 60 days' notice prior to laying off 50 or more employees. Failure to follow the act's requirement may subject employers to significant damages, including 60 days' back pay plus benefits for all affected employees, $500 a day to the local government where the layoff occurred, and attorney's fees.

It is strongly recommended that an employer consider offering its affected employees severance benefits in exchange for a release and waiver of claims. A properly drafted release obtained in exchange for sufficient consideration (for example, severance pay) is a full and complete defense to a lawsuit. Unlike a general standard release, however, there are many technical and legal requirements that must be satisfied in order to obtain a valid employment release.

Because the benefits of downsizing can sometimes be negated by lawsuits from laid-off workers, employers are well advised to plan a layoff carefully and understand the laws at issue. Only with this planning and understanding can employers reduce litigation exposure inherent in a layoff.

GLEN DOHERTY is a partner in the law firm DeGraff Foy Holt-Harris Kunz & Devine LLP in Albany, N.Y.

WHEN DOWNSIZING IS UNETHICAL

William F. Roth

THE DOWNWARD SPIRAL

Downsizing in a majority of instances does not produce positive long-term results. Yet, this vehicle for improving the bottom line was very popular all through the nineties and is still used. On paper, downsizing looks good. But on paper, the calculations are done quantitatively and many of the negative changes that occur during workforce reductions and the ensuing reorganization cannot be quantified.

The reasons corporations give for downsizing include their desire to:

- Combine the responsibilities of two positions into one or eliminate a position, splitting the responsibilities amongst others.
- Eliminate functions seen as not contributing enough to the bottom line.
- Decrease the number of management layers in order to improve communication and to speed up the decision-making process.
- Eliminate duplication of responsibility.
- Get rid of bureaucratic slowdown and reduce overhead by outsourcing traditional staff responsibilities.

Downsizing is expected to enhance productivity and to cut costs, two avenues to improving the bottom line. It must be understood, however, that these two avenues are often at odds. The gains garnered by choosing one can sometimes be offset by resultant losses in the other. Production improvement efforts *do* usually include cost-cutting measures. They can also, however, necessitate additional expense. Cost-cutting efforts, in turn, can improve productivity. Too frequently, however, they instead have an extremely detrimental effect on productivity, especially when downsizing is used.

Despite this, experts are predicting that during the next decade downsizing will remain a primary choice for U.S. companies interested in improving their bottom line. Three *non-cynical* possibilities can be given for continuation of this trend:

1. Corporate heads are not paying attention to the hard lessons learned by peers.
2. Leadership believes that downsizing just hasn't been done correctly and they can devise a successful approach.
3. Due to a lack of appropriate education or training downsizing is the most appealing, or perhaps the only alternative managers can think of when trying to improve the bottom line.

HOW IT'S DONE

One of two approaches is generally used to downsize. The first is early retirement. Older employees are targeted because they usually draw larger salaries. The rationalization sometimes offered to justify this maneuver, although little data exists to support it, is that due to their age, such employees have less energy and are less productive. Financial incentives can be involved. Corporations are frequently surprised, however, by the large number of workers who try to take advantage of an early retirement offer. The problem becomes one of overkill. Too much valuable experience is lost in too many areas. Although savings are realized when slots are not refilled, and from the differential between the salaries of retirees and those of replacement workers, this approach can end up bearing a high price tag.

The second method is to fire employees. This method is less expensive and more controllable because the number of departures is preset. This method is, therefore, more popular. Employees with the largest salaries might be fired first. Or department heads might be ordered to cut their staff by a fixed percentage, say thirty percent. Or an efficiency study might be run to determine who leaves and who stays.

No matter what approach a company adopts, emphasis is on speed. Discuss the plan prior to implementation with as few managers as possible. Encourage them not to leak it. Then, when the downsizing is announced, move those departing out the door as rapidly as possible to prevent damaging the morale of remaining employees. This also allows the company to immediately start rebuilding.

SYSTEMATIC RESULTS OF DOWNSIZING

I recently asked a class of twenty-seven MBA students, all currently holding mid-level management positions, to define the effects of downsizing on key organization systems. Eighteen of these students had personally been through a downsizing. Of the remaining nine, four named a close friend who had experienced downsizing.

Concerning *access to information*, the students agreed that when a downsizing occurs, employees begin hoarding information in order to increase their value. Both intra- and interdepartmental contacts dissolve. After a downsizing, employees frequently have difficulty finding required information because the responsibility for it has been shifted. Those given control over additional files cannot gain access to them. Once access is given, they have trouble determining responsibility for the information in these files.

The students also agreed that employees have less trust in information received following a downsizing. Messages from top-level management are automatically suspect. Information gained from other areas of the organization is also viewed as questionable; reports and numbers have probably been altered to make those writing and tabulating them look more impressive.

Concerning *communication*, the key word is again mistrust. Much of what is heard is considered a smoke screen. Top-down memos are especially suspected. The rumor mill dominates. Everyone looks for hidden meaning in everything they are told.

Concerning *work design*, there is an immediate and heavy work overload for everybody. One reason for this overload is the confusion caused by people suddenly having to take on additional responsibilities without proper training. This confusion causes inefficiencies throughout the organization, because employees too frequently have to learn through trial and error.

Concerning *decision-making and problem-solving*, the students said that emphasis following a downsizing shifts to elimination of risk. Decisions are not as likely to be based on employees' best judgment. Rather, decisions are designed to please bosses. The quality of work usually deteriorates because employees frequently lack the necessary experience or training, and because a sincere effort now seems pointless due to their impression that the company believes everybody expendable. Problem-solving results are less accurate because of the difficulty in gaining access to necessary information. A lack of integration also exists because of the communication breakdown. Units tend to draw protectively inward and to focus on solving their own problems, ignoring the negative effects their solutions might have on other units. The buck is passed whenever possible.

Concerning *rewards*, while the workload and number of work hours required increases, pay often stays the same or decreases following a downsizing. The students disagreed with top-level management's rationalization that the survivors, because they still have jobs, do not mind pay cuts. The students said this added slap in the face heightens already strong feelings of resentment toward bosses. The major reward, job security, is gone. Employees no longer feel in control of their lives. Any promises by upper-level management of better days to come are viewed skeptically. People able to look for jobs with other companies frequently do so, adding to the drain on expertise.

Concerning *discipline*, due to strained relations between management and employees, and to the resultant uneasiness felt by managers, discipline following a downsizing either becomes more severe or disappears totally. Some managers use the insinuation that "You could be next" to control and drive employees. Others tolerate performance shortcomings that should not be tolerated in their efforts to regain employee trust. A "law of the jungle" attitude prevails. Both managers and employees do whatever they must to survive.

Finally, concerning *training and job-related development*, while responsibilities increase following a downsizing, there is less training. One reason offered by personnel managers is that due to the secrecy and rushed atmosphere involved they are not given enough time to plan and implement downsizing related activities. Another reason is that due to the increased workload employees have less time for training. A third reason is that training departments often suffer staff reductions during a downsizing.

The employee's perspective concerning training and job-related development also changes. The chief purpose of training frequently shifts to gaining the skills necessary to find a job elsewhere. In terms of career development, employees opt for safe, non-controversial challenges, rather than opportunities that might allow them to gain new knowledge.

IS THERE AN ALTERNATIVE?

Can these reactions be avoided or softened with better preparation? The students thought not. As one class member put it, "*When someone fires shots into a crowd and the bullets whiz by you and hit others instead, the fact that the gunner has forewarned you or apologizes afterward and promises not to fire again does not mean much.*"

Most of the literature agrees that the passage of time is the only cure for a slump in post-downsizing morale and productivity. Another factor that helps is a change in upper-level management. Employees hope the new leaders will have different agendas and that job security for workers will be one of their priorities. A third useful approach is the implementation of an intensive training effort to show employees that the company is serious in its commitment to improved performance.

Time, however, is the key ingredient for reviving morale and productivity, and we are talking about *years* rather than months in most cases. Unfortunately, while the bottom line initially improves after a downsizing, such improvements tend to taper off. Attempts to *increase productivity* are hampered by a lack of employee commitment, so that top-level management is forced back into the *cost-cutting* mode. The most convenient vehicle at its disposal for cost cutting is a second round of downsizing. However, there are now fewer resources to juggle. Also, awareness is developing that the company might be permanently alienating its work force.

A question that needs to be addressed at this point is, "*Despite their knowledge concerning the pitfalls of downsizing why do top-level executives persist?*"

Of the three reasons given earlier—lack of attention to other's experiences, a belief that they can do it better, and the perceived lack of an acceptable alternative—the last seems the most plausible. A majority of CEOs are more comfortable with quantitative solutions to corporate problems than with solutions that take into account emotional issues. Downsizing is a quantitative approach to improving the bottom line. Also, few CEOs have received the training necessary to successfully generate employee-driven productivity improvement efforts. They have not received this training on the job because a majority have been locked into their areas of expertise most of the way up the career ladder. They may have attended corporate-sponsored seminars and workshops on the subject; they may have developed some of the understanding and skills required, but not nearly enough to be effective. Those with MBAs have not received the requisite education either, because despite loud protests from a growing number of critics, emphasis in most MBA programs remains on improving specialized skills such as marketing, production, human resources, finance, and accounting. Inadequate attention has been paid to the problem of making employees more productive as individuals, as work units, and as part of a well-integrated, corporate-wide socio-technical system.

This leads to a fourth reason for the continuation of the downsizing trend, one that could be considered *cynical.* This reason also has to do with the quantitative perspective found in most companies.

THE NATURE OF THE BEAST

Companies in the United States continue to focus almost entirely on generating greater amounts of individual wealth. Because the wealth sought so avidly is measured quantitatively and because this is the *only* way to measure it, our quantitative emphasis seeps, consciously or unconsciously, into other important decisions as well. One of the most important of these decisions is how we define employees. Even though employees are different from the widgets they manufacture or the services they deliver, even though they are obviously different from the technology used, even though employees as *purposeful systems* differ from all other items taken into account when calculating ways to improve the bottom line, the tendency is to quantify them as well.

Once quantified, the nature of employees changes. It is no longer necessary to take needs and desires into consideration. With the flick of a pen, a worker can be erased with no feeling of guilt whatsoever because that person is now just part of the scheme of numbers. Downsizing is about cost cutting and costs, at least those taken into account, are defined in terms of numbers.

Sometimes business deteriorates to the point where downsizing is the best path or even the only path to follow. But while those making the decision may be forced to lay employees off when a company is stumbling into bankrupcy, when a recession hits, or when a major share of the market is being taken away by the competition, some executives downsize even when companies are doing well, when sales are increasing, and when the bottom line is improving.

One might wonder why these executives aren't hiring instead of firing?

The answer is that they are firing and not hiring because their desire is to improve efficiencies even more. They remain unsatisfied and are willing to sacrifice employees in order to further improve the value of the company's stock. The fact that by sacrificing employees, the decision-makers are probably disrupting the systemic arrangement that makes profit possible in the first place is apparently not an important consideration. The focus is totally on improving short-term value by manipulating the numbers.

Why would those at the top act in such a manner? What motivates them? The reason most frequently offered is that they are simply demonstrating allegiance to the tenets of *laissez-faire economic theory*. But this is not accurate. Once the data starts coming in, once society begins to realize that while the bottom line might improve for a month or two after an unnecessary downsizing the situation in a majority of cases deteriorates rapidly once this knowledge is in hand, if the driving force behind downsizing is truly *laissez-faire* economic theory, upper-level management would quickly realize that the benefits of downsizing are short-lived and would begin looking for another vehicle to better satisfy its interests.

But upper-level management has not begun looking for another vehicle. Instead, it sticks with downsizing, which means that short-term profit is, indeed, the goal. And, again, why are these people willing to risk so much for the possibility of an immediate improvement in the bottom line?

THE SCARCITY MENTALITY STRIKES AGAIN

In order to answer this question, it is necessary to explore briefly the history of executive compensation. Not too long ago, CEOs and others at the top received salaries set by the corporation's board of directors. Top-level executives in the United States received higher salaries than anywhere else in the world, much higher, frequently by a factor of several hundred percent. And usually, these salaries were tied in no way to the company's productivity or to its profitability. Even during hard times when profits were dropping or when employees were being laid off, salary levels on the executive levels continued to rise. An example of this phenomenon was the 75-million-dollar salary that Steven J. Ross, chairman of Time Warner Inc., took home while laying off over 600 employees because the communications/magazine industry was not doing very well that year.

Obviously, nobody needs to be paid 75 million dollars. It was a case of blatant egoism with no apologies offered. Such compensation packages were, in fact, part of a competition. People at that level were competing with each other, the objective being to earn more than other CEOs. One of the characteristics of the contest was a total lack of accountability—to stockholders, to customers, to lower-level employees. These people had created their own little world, where only the chosen were allowed to play. The situation was out of control.

A way had to be found to rein them in, to make these people accountable. The solution was to tie the compensation of top-tier executives to the company's bottom line. This was done by making stock options a large part of their package. In order for them to do well, their company had to be doing well, or at least the value of the company's stock had to be increasing, which traditionally occurs when the fortunes of the company are improving.

Problem solved.

Well, not really, for this move, in fact, created an even larger problem. *Employees, rather than simply being ignored by top-level executives, now became a target.* The stock option arrangement benefits executive management only if the value of the company's stock goes up. This happens, as has been said, when the company becomes more profitable. There are two ways to improve a company's profits. The first is to make better use of employee expertise and to encourage employees to design ways to improve productivity. The second way involves bringing efficiency experts in to cut costs. While the first way is more effective in the long run, it takes more time. The second way, especially if it results in downsizing, produces quicker results. When employees are laid off, bottom-line improvement can occur, literally, overnight. Thus, executives first began looking for "dead wood" to get rid of. Then they began looking for wood not quite dead but expendable in that the operation could probably survive without it.

Another false manifestation of the link between *laissez-faire* economic theory and egoism that made good use of downsizing was the *takeover* movement that peaked during the nineties. The men who led this movement would gain controlling interest in companies, cut the workforce, make those who remained labor harder for the same or less pay, sell off whatever assets they could, and then either let the company fall apart or sell the shell. The *only* concern in such situations was the amount of personal profit that could be squeezed out. Nothing else and nobody else mattered.

In both cases, the rationalization was that downsizing increased the efficiency of the operation, and that stockholders and society in general benefited. In reality, while some shareholders benefited, society usually did not. Most certainly company employees suffered, both those laid off and those spared. According to "Few Recover Totally from Downsizing," an article that appeared in the August 1998 edition of *U.S. Today*, the majority of workers laid off during a downsizing, when they can find another job, earn just eighty-five percent of what they would have earned if they had stayed in their original job. Those over fifty earn on average just sixty-five percent of their previous salaries.

Although our gross national product (GNP) has been steadily improving and executive compensation packages have gone through the roof, "The Downsizing of America," a *New York Times* special report published in 1998, explains that after adjusting for inflation the 1996 median wage was nearly three percent lower than what it was in 1979, and that while the *average* household income climbed ten percent during this same period, ninety-five percent of the growth was enjoyed by the wealthiest twenty percent of the population.

ETHICAL AND SYSTEMIC IMPLICATIONS

Downsizing, in most instances, is an exercise in raw egoism. *Laissez-faire* economics is used as an excuse, but egoism is the driving force. Increasingly, the media is bringing to light the hypocrisy of those who continue to use this vehicle to enhance their own wealth, showing the extent of this hypocrisy from a bottom line as well as a societal perspective. Even the *Wall Street Journal*, a bastion of *laissez-faire* economic thought that initially lauded downsizing as appropriate and necessary to maintaining the health of our corporations and of our economy, now periodically publishes pieces denouncing the motives, the shortsightedness, and the egoism of those practicing it.

When one looks at downsizing from the perspective of ethics, the results are usually negative. Downsizing satisfies utilitarian criteria only for those still advocating the economic man theory generated during the early Industrial Revolution, only for those who still believe that the sole pursuit important to improvement of the human condition is the pursuit of increased wealth. Of course, the economic man theory didn't work then, and it doesn't work now. One might suspect, based on the lessons of history, that it will never work, no matter what the economic conditions are.

Concerning the deontological approach to ethics, the only law being followed during a downsizing is the *law of the jungle*. Regarding relativism, downsizing is an example of the dark side of this school, where consensus is never really sought, where a small group forces its decision, its will on the majority. Rather than a union between *laissez-faire economic theory* and *egoism* therefore, what emerges in the case of unnecessary downsizing is a union between *egoism* and *relativism* driven by people who have never stopped competing, by people who suffer from *adolescent arrest*, people who will do whatever is necessary to win.

Concerning the universal ethical standard being offered, downsizing of course, is about as detrimental as it gets. As was said earlier, there are times when workforce reduction is the only hope left. It becomes necessary for the organization to survive. *But the decision to downsize should occur only after all else has been tried, only after everyone in the company has brought their ideas and expertise to bear on finding ways to increase efficiencies and to improve productivity.*

When this is done the organization has remained true to the universe standard. But when in order to improve the bottom line companies may downsizing their first choice, when they focus on erasing numbers, they are behaving unethically. They are not giving their most powerful resources a chance. They are acting egotistically, hoarding decision-making authority and denying the rest of the workforce the opportunity to assist. They are doing so, of course, to protect their own short-term interests.

At the same time, when such unnecessary downsizing occurs, as has been shown, the systemic nature of the operation is destroyed. Rather than a well-integrated whole the organization breaks down into an aggregate of pieces, each unit, each individual following the example of the leaders, looking out for itself, for himself with no further concern for the interactions necessary to a smooth and profitable operation.

DOING THE RIGHT THING

As an alternative to downsizing, progressive U.S. corporate leaders, along with their European and Asian counterparts, are beginning to realize that increased profitability can also be achieved by involving employees more fully in the improvement of products, manufacturing processes, management systems, and the work environment. Instead of getting rid of employees, the objective is to better utilize their expertise. Progressive CEOs understand that if organized properly, this approach starts producing positive bottom-line results almost immediately, and that these results, rather than tapering off, snowball.

How is the required level of participation orchestrated? One excellent vehicle is a quality-improvement effort. A systemic approach to quality improvement is built around an organization-wide network of teams, an adequate set of process ground rules agreed to by everyone, an ongoing familarization process, technical and management systems training, the introduction of statistical measurement techniques when applicable, and an ongoing long-and short-term planning exercise. When all these pieces are in place and properly integrated, the CEO usually has to worry about problems of expansion, rather than about layoffs.

In summary, then, downsizing has proven to be a short-term, short-sighted approach to improving the bottom line. There is no way to implement downsizing without adversely affecting employee morale and creating confusion in key management systems. Immediate savings are quickly offset by long-term systemic problems.

Powerful foreign competitors understand this. Too many corporate leaders in the United States, however, do not understand, or do not care. For those who *do* care, in order to deal with the problem, in order to change attitudes and encourage exploration of more effective alternatives, it is time to rethink the traditional approach to *training*, whether it be delivered on-site by staff and consultants or in the university classroom. Such training should focus *less* on the enhancement of quantitative and technical skills and *more* on developing management's ability to increase the contribution of employees as cost-cutters, innovators, and quality enhancers.

Before a new approach to training can be designed, however, it is necessary to deal with the second counterproductive manifestation of the marriage between the *laissez-faire* economic philosophy and egoism. This is the traditional evaluation and reward system. Evaluation and reward, according to systems theory, is the cornerstone of company culture. The effectiveness of training, along with the effectiveness of every other organization process, depends on the behaviors reinforced by evaluation and reward. If the wish is to modify an organization's culture, if the wish is to improve the results of training or of problem-solving efforts or of production efforts, if a more effective alternative to downsizing is sought, the first thing that must be addressed is the way employees are evaluated and rewarded.

SHORT-CIRCUITED: CUTTING JOBS AS CORPORATE STRATEGY

Compass Bank-Wharton

Layoffs. Downsizing. Rightsizing. Job cuts. Separations. Terminations. Workforce reductions. Off-shoring. Outsourcing.

Whatever the term, getting rid of employees can be a necessary and beneficial strategic move for companies to make. Layoffs can signal that a company is reorganizing and moving in a more profitable direction and, as a result, give Wall Street a reason to cheer and improve the morale of remaining employees. But unless job cuts are handled and explained properly—and are indeed necessary to achieve a thoughtful, overarching purpose—the solution may cause as many headaches as the ailment it was meant to cure, according to Wharton faculty members and an outplacement expert.

Consider a recent move by Circuit City Stores, a big electronics retailer based in Richmond, Va. The company announced on March 28 that it cut 3,400 jobs, or 7% of its workforce, effective that day, because the salespeople were paid "well above the market-based salary range for their role." The company did not disclose specifics, but *The Baltimore Sun* reported that the laid-off workers, known as "associates," made 51 cents more per hour above what the company had set as market wages.

Circuit City also announced that it had entered into an agreement with IBM to outsource its technology infrastructure operations, which would eliminate the jobs of 130 employees. Fifty of these workers, however, were to be hired by IBM and remain on-site to serve the Circuit City contract.

These various moves, Circuit City said in a news release, were part of a "series of changes to improve financial performance largely by realigning [the company's] cost and expense structure." The decision to terminate the 3,400 employees was disclosed in the fourth paragraph of the release and described as a "wage management initiative" that led to the "separation" of the workers.

The job cuts "focused on associates who were paid well above the market-based salary range for their role," the news release added. "New associates will be hired for these positions and compensated at the current market range for the job." The company said, however, that the people who lost their jobs received severance packages and could reapply for their old jobs, at lower pay, but had to wait 10 weeks to do so. The March 28 move, coupled with a decision made in February to realign Circuit City's retail structure by reducing the number of operating regions from 10 to eight, would save $250 million over the next two years, the company noted.

Peter Cappelli, management professor and director of the Center for Human Resources at Wharton, says Circuit City may have valid reasons for having to reduce costs, but the way it treated the 3,400 workers was highly unusual. "That's the most cynical thing I've heard about in a long time," Cappelli says. "I like to think I'm cynical, but sometimes it's hard to keep up."

According to Cappelli, Circuit City's decision to replace the terminated workers with lower-paid people is like saying: "We made a mistake in compensation by paying them more than they were worth for their performance, so we're going to get rid of them." Cappelli adds that he "had never heard of that before. Companies have always done sneaky things like getting rid of higher-wage workers with two-tier wage plans, but this . . . takes the cake."

A ONCE-RARE OCCURRENCE

There was a time in the United States when large workforce reductions were few and far between. An employee hoped—indeed expected—that his or her job would last for life, and often it did. But layoffs have become so run-of-the-mill that even news editors sometimes pay them scant attention. In an April 2 column, *New York Times* writer David Carr lamented the lack of coverage of the Circuit City job cuts. His article was headlined: "Thousands Are Laid Off at Circuit City. What's New?"

According to Michael Useem, management professor and director of the Center for Leadership and Change Management at Wharton, "After waves of large-scale layoffs among American companies, most notably in the early 1990s, but again in the early 2000s in the wake of the dotcom bust, we have learned a lot about good practices and bad practices [in eliminating jobs] by watching companies in action."

Research has shown that if a company announces a downsizing without a broader reference to a strategic plan, its stock price will, on average, drop 5% to 6% over the next several days, according to Useem. By contrast, if large-scale job cuts are announced as part of a broader restructuring, and a strategic plan is laid out, the firm's stock will rise some 4%, on average, in the days following the announcement. Useem says the research shows that, contrary to popular wisdom, Wall Street does not always welcome job cuts for their own sake.

"The tough-minded, big institutional equity market is actually skittish and worried about downsizings that are simply short-term cost-cutting measures without a broader plan described behind them," Useem notes. "Investors are not beating the drum for downsizing as much as it is sometimes said they are. It really is the restructuring they are applauding, not the particular method within it. It's helpful to think about downsizing as restoration—cutting costs as a move to restore luster and performance."

Cappelli says, however, that Wall Street does sometimes support layoffs for their own sake. "If we define layoffs as being necessary because it makes sense to keep financial analysts happy, then it may make sense for companies to lay off people because analysts have a bias toward layoffs," he says. "They love layoffs because they immediately improve the bottom line. They can't easily assess what the long-term prospects of layoffs will be, but they can see immediate benefits."

Academic research, according to Cappelli, shows that layoffs usually have negative effects on a company's performance after the cuts take place. "But in fairness to companies that feel they have to cut jobs, part of the problem with the research is how the research is done," Cappelli adds. "Companies laying off people are, by definition, already in trouble. So it's not surprising that if you select companies already in trouble [for a research study], they look in worse trouble later." It typically makes sense for a company to lay off workers only "when it has a particular problem—excess capacity. When you don't have excess capacity and you're cutting, you're cutting muscle."

SENDING SIGNALS

Wharton management professor Lawrence Hrebiniak says layoffs that are part of a restructuring can send a signal that a company is "refocusing its use of scarce resources." He likens such a move to investors who reallocate assets in their portfolios to move from poorly performing securities to more promising investments.

Downsizing can also send an important signal to customers, competitors, suppliers and Wall Street. "Years ago, Procter & Gamble cut thousands of jobs," Hrebiniak recalls. "They called it 'cost savings,' but the CEO also said P&G was sending a signal that this was a sign of a cultural revolution at P&G: to eliminate inertia, to wake people up to the focus on new markets and products and innovation, to get rid of dead wood. So layoffs can represent a refocusing."

Robert E. Mittelstaedt, dean of the W.P. Carey School of Business at Arizona State University, notes that the stock market "has more respect for [job cuts] if they are part of a broader plan. Just signaling that you're going to cut costs and not saying anything else about what you're going to do doesn't impress people a whole lot."

In fact, Wall Street respects companies for divesting themselves entirely of unprofitable or barely profitable businesses rather than trying to strengthen them through large job cuts, because jettisoning unwanted businesses can make better strategic sense, according to Mittelstaedt. "There are times companies have to say that they believe exiting a business is right," Mittelstaedt says. "That gives a better signal to the market, as opposed to trying just to cut costs."

A March 26 story in *The Wall Street Journal* that Citigroup was in the process of finishing up a restructuring plan that will result in the elimination of some 15,000 jobs appears designed to achieve both short- and longer-term goals—to juice up the company's lagging stock price and to refocus the firm, according to Hrebiniak. Citigroup reportedly wants to put more emphasis on its international operations and consolidate back-office functions.

"He's getting pressure from shareholders," Hrebiniak says of Charles Prince, Citigroup's chief executive. "He's feeling no love. He's got to show he's doing something to cut costs, improve margins, make some more money. So it may not primarily be a move to restructure at all; it could be a move to get critics off his back." If Citigroup does decide to cut 15,000 jobs, it would represent nearly 5% of its workforce of about 327,000.

Adrian Tschoegl, a Wharton management lecturer who follows the banking sector closely, says the planned Citigroup layoffs have a strategic purpose: consolidating various functions that have grown redundant over the years and have become costly and difficult to manage. He calls a 5% workforce reduction far from draconian.

"Citigroup has built up lots of bits and pieces over time, and it's a culture that tends to be combative," Tschoegl says. "Clients have been known to remark that Citibank's most tenacious competitors have been other Citibank units. So this is a case of having a lot of bits and pieces and tidying things." But cost-savings also play a big role in Citigroup's restructuring. Tschoegl says the company could benefit, for example, by moving back-office functions from high-cost locations like New York to lower-cost operations in South Dakota and India.

In general, Tschoegl says, cutting jobs makes sense when a company is not only trying to reduce costs but also complexity. One common way to achieve both goals is to outsource functions—such as security and janitorial services—to firms that specialize in such services. In these cases, outsourcing can actually benefit janitors and security guards because they will be employed by firms that can offer them an upward career path in ways that a big corporation never could.

"Where you get into trouble is if you simply cut heads across the board," Tschoegl warns. "Then you're not being sensible; you're not getting rid of things that could be done better by somebody else. . . . No company has ever gotten good by simply cutting."

Another risk is that a downsizing company can get rid of people whose knowledge and experience are vital. Wharton management professor Daniel A. Levinthal points out that Circuit City's decision to cut 3,400 veteran sales people "sounds like a massive de-skilling" of the company. Since the people who will be hired to replace the laid-off workers probably will not know the merchandise as well as the workers who were dismissed, customers who want to know how to set up a high-definition TV or why one music player is better than another might not receive the best advice.

If this is the case, Circuit City might have a hard time differentiating itself from its competitors. "These new people will be order takers and have less knowledge [about the merchandise]," says Levinthal. "Circuit City would now be competing against e-commerce because it's become similar to e-commerce and lost its differentiation as a bricks and mortar store."

As for the financial benefits associated with layoffs, Wharton accounting professor Wayne Guay says eliminating jobs can help a company financially in several ways. One benefit is that labor expenses are lower and cash flow is higher in the current and following years simply because the firm does not have to pay as many people. But layoffs do not necessarily allow a company to take a large write-off that can sharply reduce its tax liability for the year in which the job cuts take place.

BAD NEWS IN ONE BIG DOSE

Typically, it is best for a company that is downsizing to announce all the bad news "in one fell swoop" rather than in a "series of smaller, separate, sequential layoff announcements," Useem notes. "Employees don't like the sequential approach—they don't like any downsizing, of course—but they like least the suffering of a thousand cuts. The same thing is true for the stock market."

The way people are treated during a downsizing is a "testament of the values and soul of a company," according to Useem, and firms should follow several steps that demonstrate to employees and the world at large that the firms practice good management principles. First, companies should engage in as much transparency as possible, revealing as much financial information as they can to show the need for job reductions and help laid-off workers obtain retraining, outplacement assistance and resume-writing guidance.

Second, firms should work intensively with the employees who remain on the job because these people "will be shell-shocked and fearful that they could be next," Useem says. "Gloom and anxiety are exactly the opposite of what companies need when they go through downsizing because they need to get more work done with fewer people. Good morale is essential. If top and middle management works with the people who remain, it can be a vital formula for ensuring that the people who are survivors get behind the new, leaner company, and achieve the results top management wants to achieve."

Regardless of the motivation behind, and execution of, layoffs, it is clear that they will continue to occur with almost drumbeat regularity. "The use of layoffs as a management tool to cut costs is widespread," says John Challenger, chief executive of Challenger, Gray & Christmas, a Chicago-based outplacement firm. "Virtually every Fortune 500 company has done it. Only the absolutely most successful companies, [whose] profits have been consistently up, may have [avoided] them. Layoffs have come to be expected by shareholders, and we are more and more in an environment where shareholders drive company actions."

Published: April 4, 2007

RECALCULATING THE COST OF BIG LAYOFFS

by SCOTT THURM

Early in the past decade, when its sales fell 11% in two years, Honeywell International Inc. laid off 31,000 employees, one-fourth of its work force, canceled plans for new products and scaled back its global-expansion goals. Those actions "decimated our industrial base," Honeywell Chief Executive David Cote recently told the company's shareholders.

During the recent recession, Honeywell took a different tack. The company's sales fell 15% last year, and its profits shrank 23%, but the diversified manufacturer used furloughs and benefit cuts to limit layoffs to 6,000 employees, about 5% of its work force.

At the same time, Honeywell introduced 600 new products, including advanced industrial controls and fuel-efficient auto turbochargers.

Now, with the economy seemingly on the mend, Honeywell is reaping the benefits of its choice.

Last month, the company, which is based in Morristown, N.J., reported a 3% increase in first-quarter revenue and boosted its forecasts of sales and profit for the rest of the year.

That's no accident, according to some analysts and students of corporate behavior. They say companies that take a limited and more-targeted approach to layoffs tend to do better in economic recoveries than those that slash employment sharply and across the board.

"You can't shrink your way into prosperity," says Wayne Mascio, a business professor at the University of Colorado, Denver.

Mr. Mascio has studied how companies in the Standard & Poor's 500-stock index have performed over 18 years. His conclusion: those who cut deepest, relative to industry peers, delivered smaller profits and weaker stock returns for as long as nine years after a recession.

The current recovery will test those findings because many companies made unusually steep and rapid layoffs during the recession that preceded it.

Gad Levanon, a senior economist with the Conference Board, a research group, says the number of hours worked in the U.S. fell more steeply than output in 2008 and 2009, a reversal of the usual pattern during recessions.

About 100 companies in the S&P 500 reduced employment by 10% or more, according to an analysis of Securities and Exchange Commission filings by The Wall Street Journal. Thirty-nine cut more than 20% of their pre-recession jobs.

Many companies had little choice, particularly in hard-hit industries such as finance, autos, home building and some corners of technology.

Eighty-eight companies in the index, nearly a fifth of the total, saw their revenue fall 20% or more in 2009, compared with 2007, when the recession began. Such steep revenue declines create obstacles to recovery under any strategy.

Deep cuts appear to have helped some companies regain their financial footing. Ford Motor Co., for example, shed 48,000 jobs, roughly 20% of its pre-recession work force, in the past two years. Partly as a result, the auto maker has reported four consecutive profitable quarters and recently boosted output to meet increased demand for its vehicles.

Other deep cutters are still struggling. Sprint Nextel Corp. slashed its labor force by one-third, to 40,000 workers, partly by outsourcing the management of its network. But the telecommunications company posted a wider first-quarter loss, and lost an additional 75,000 net customers.

A Sprint spokesman says the company is operating more effectively and "making clear progress in turning the business around."

Some executives worry that recent cuts may have gone too far. Among 542 executives responding to a December survey by Duke University and CFO magazine, 46% said they believed their companies had taken actions during the recession that could hurt their long-term growth prospects. The most commonly cited concern: "deep cuts in work force."

Some companies continued to add jobs during the recession, though many of those positions were relatively low wage, part time or outside the U.S.

The biggest job creator in the S&P 500 was Yum Brands Inc., operator of the KFC, Taco Bell and Pizza Hut restaurant chains.

Yum added 49,000 jobs over the past two years as it expanded in China and other overseas markets. Of its 350,000 employees, 86% are part time and 79% are located abroad.

Among job cutters, how companies approach layoffs can have as much or more influence on their competitiveness as how many jobs they cut, analysts say.

Companies that used the recession to weed out weaker performers and trim bloated bureaucracies will fare better than companies that slashed across the board, they say.

Companies often vary in their responses to a downturn because of differing circumstances. Consider steelmakers Nucor Corp. and U.S. Steel Corp. Last year, both companies posted losses and saw their revenues decline roughly 53%.

Nucor, which makes steel from recycled metal at smaller, newer mills, cut about 1,300 jobs, or 6% of its work force. Its CEO, Dan DiMicco, declined to comment.

U.S. Steel, which makes steel from iron ore, idled furnaces and cut its work force by 6,000 employees, or about 12%.

A U.S. Steel spokeswoman didn't respond to requests for comment.

Honeywell executives have been frank about their choices. Mr. Cote told investors in his annual letter that the company's profit margins declined last year in part because labor costs increased as a percentage of sales.

Still, Mr. Cote said, Honeywell decided to position itself for a recovery and continue developing new products.

"We think investing in our employees is smart," he wrote.

Write to Scott Thurm at scott.thurm@wsj.com

Correction & Amplification

The last name of Wayne Cascio, a professor at the University of Colorado, Denver, was misspelled as Mascio in a previous version of this article.

THE ROLE OF BUSINESS ETHICS IN EMPLOYEE ENGAGEMENT

November 04, 2009

By Tom Monahan, CEO of the Corporate Executive Board

My focus on ethical management reminds me that I still own a box full of business cards with my name from a company that no longer exists.

My first job out of college was with Arthur Andersen. At the time, it was a single organization and I worked in a division that became Andersen Consulting, and is now Accenture. Arthur Andersen had one of the most ethical cultures I have seen; the best people, the best business systems, and a holistic commitment to performance ethics. Yet, it went from being one of the leading professional services organizations to only a Wikipedia entry in a matter of months, due to unethical behaviors in a reasonably small niche of the firm. The disappearance of my first employer due to ethical failures is a powerful lesson I bring to work everyday.

While this is a somber example of the potential downside from an ethics or compliance failure, I have the opportunity at CEB to see how much upside a manager and leader can create with a focus on this issue. One of CEB's core strengths is a voracious appetite for quantifying the drivers of corporate performance. We ask ourselves: what do the best companies do to create inordinate value? We have gathered and analyzed millions of data points about employee perceptions and behavior and rigorously tied them to key drivers of corporate productivity. What we found is a strong link between ethical cultures and employee engagement. If an employee works for a company they consider having a strong ethical culture they work harder, stay longer, and are less likely to leave. Collectively, this data points to a 9% productivity boost from ethical leadership in the management ranks. That's a stunning figure, and for me, maybe even more compelling than the business cards.

While there is a strong link, both ethical behaviors and employee engagement are at risk. What we see happening, across hundreds of thousands of employees at the world's largest companies, is a perfect storm brewing composed of three different factors.

First, we see heightened employee cynicism about commitment of management to ethical principles and compliance standards, as management teams wrestle with critical issues elsewhere in the business.

Second, unhappy employees are unable to leave their current roles. In a normal economy, if an employee does not like their boss, they can leave. However, today unsatisfied employees are unable to move because of limited opportunities. This results in what we estimate to be about a 7 percent productivity shortfall in most companies as a result of low engagement levels.

Third, employee disengagement is particularly pronounced with the highest potential employees within an organization. These employees are three times as likely to leave as a normal employee once the economy improves. Most business plans I see are built around the commitment of those employees most likely to leave.

So with a huge 9% performance boost to be had, but a "perfect storm" making it difficult for managers to seize it, what should leaders be focused on?

First, ensure consistent messages and ethical behaviors at all levels. Companies claim they employ best practices by using their CEO to reinforce ethical principals in a video or town hall meeting. Companies also need their individual managers to reinforce and demonstrate the appropriate behaviors and values of the organization. Organizations need to make sure that every layer of leadership in the company communicates the same ethically grounded priorities and then lives up to them.

Second, help employees understand how their role contributes to company strategy One of the most important things for an employee to know is how his or her behaviors and actions makes a difference, and that his or her work is connected in some way to the strategic goals of the enterprise. CEOs have spent a lot of time over the last year thinking about survival in another day, week or quarter. That has clearly been the right strategy for this past year, but now it is time to lift up again, and reinforce employees' connection to the enterprise.

Third, help employees re-forge personal networks. Having a personal network at work is a key support mechanism for ensuring ethical behaviors. These networks were certainly disrupted by the rounds of corporate downsizing this past year. And rebuilding them has become more difficult in a world where people are scattered across geographies, with work following the sun 24 hours a day. A lot of organizations are working to make sure their employees are forging connections that transcend where they are physically located.

At CEB, we serve – and learn from – the world's best companies every day. These companies have taught us that ethical behavior can drive productivity and performance in a measurable way, and needs to be managed with the same intensity as the strategic moves that have helped companies survive the economic downturn.

From an employer perspective, these actions create a much more engaged work force, and increased productivity. If you need an additional reason to implement these ideas, you can also think about this: it's no fun to have a box of business cards for positions and companies that don't exist anymore.

PINNACLE BRANDS

Gillian Flynn

When baseball struck out in 1994, Pinnacle Brands Inc., a trading card company, could have followed others' leads with layoffs. Instead, it tossed the ball to employees, challenging them to save their jobs with money-making ideas.

Downsizing in general and even single terminations present some of the greatest challenges to management in terms of emotional struggles. Companies, however, often mistakenly believe that these terminations are their only options for survival. Pinnacle thought otherwise and, in its creativity, salvaged positions and employees slated for termination. Would this work in other firms?

Are you American? Then you must love baseball. And you probably still wince a bit at the debacle of 1994, when those on-field heroes, the boys of summer, packed up their gear and headed home. The strike hit us hard. Most Americans were beyond bitter—we felt robbed, cheated out of our national pastime. There was no joy in Mudville, nor any other baseball-loving town.

If you think the average Joe was upset, consider the organizations linked to baseball because it's not just a national pastime, it's national business. Take, for instance, trading card companies. When baseball shut down, so did a huge chunk of their sales. Smaller card companies literally went bankrupt. Larger ones survived, but only after huge headcount slashes.

Of the top five trading card manufacturers, only one got through the strike with no layoffs: Pinnacle Brands Inc. It did so by issuing an intriguing challenge to its employees: If they could devise new ways to replace the $40 million of lost trading card revenue, they would keep their jobs. Pinnacle's workforce emerged from the strike victorious with a sales jump of 80% in two years. In a season without heroes on the baseball field, these employees became heroes on the business field.

ONE STRIKE CAN MEAN YOU'RE OUT (OF BUSINESS)

It was a tense spring at Pinnacle Brands. Each day the murmurs of a 1994 strike grew stronger, so did employees' fears. At that time, baseball cards represented 65% of Pinnacle's business. "Here we were getting ready for what could be a no-baseball season," remembers Carlo Frappolli, vice president of HR. "When the stars aren't hitting home runs and aren't pitching no-hitters, people don't want to buy their cards. Everyone was nervous."

Frappolli and Chairman & CEO Jerry Meyer began discussing what-ifs. A strike would all but nullify the company's need for 190 full-time employees. However, both Meyer and Frappolli strongly believed workers should be viewed as revenue producers, not expense items. Unlike executives at many companies, their first reaction wasn't to lay people off. Pinnacle's regard for its workforce is reflected in the company's operating philosophies, four of which directly address the employer-employee relationship:

- Treat all employees with dignity and respect.
- Deliver good news with grace.
- Deliver bad news quickly and with brutal honesty.
- Reward for results, not efforts.

In the first week of July, the strike ceased to be a rumor. Soon, the season was canceled. There was no good news to deliver, but the remaining three operating principles were about to come into play. Upon the official declaration of the season as null and void, Meyer convoked employees for a meeting. He delivered two messages. First, he quickly and honestly explained to employees that the company had just hit a dangerously rough patch. It was sink-or-swim time. Second and most important, he delivered the game plan: "He told the folks, 'I'm not going to save your jobs. You're going to save your jobs. You know what you can change and what you can do differently,'" says Frappolli.

Carolyn Corbin, founder of the Center for the 21st Century in Dallas, a think tank on future socioeconomic issues, believes Pinnacle's approach should serve as a role model for companies going through similar crises. "Very few companies take that risk," she says. "But in a way, it's not a risk at all because it puts the responsibility on the people to 'pay for themselves.' There isn't cash flow anymore, it's people flow: People will have to be generating, directly or indirectly, revenue for their keep or they can't stay."

The majority of Pinnacle employees remained wary at first, particularly the production people, who'd been subjected to continual cyclical layoffs under the company's former owner. Carol Anderson, an executive assistant in the finance division, recalls the workforce jitters: "Everybody sort of said, 'Uh-oh, what does this mean to us?' I think everybody went home that night a little nervous. But I thought we should give it a shot. At least it was we'd all sink or swim together, not just lay off people."

Meyer and Frappolli provided encouragement by setting up opportunities for employees to gather in informal teams and discuss ideas. Teams were deliberately cross-departmental. For instance, if employees had a new-product idea, a team would include someone from the creative end, a person from photography, people from marketing and finance. This gave employees insight into each step of a process so they didn't get blindsided halfway into a plan because they lacked the necessary perspective. It wasn't long before some amazing ideas started floating past supervisors' desks.

PINNACLE HAS A WINNING SEASON

One of the very first bright ideas came not from the COO or CFO, but someone just as in tune with the company's operations: Pinnacle's custodian. She came to Frappolli with a simple observation: The company spent approximately $50,000 a year on refrigerated sodas and bottled waters for every conference room and most executive offices, as well as personalized cups to boot. "So we stopped that," says Frappolli. "If executives feel they need to have sodas, they should go out and buy them themselves. That idea came from someone who sweeps the floors."

As soon as an employee's suggestion proved useful, Pinnacle immediately recognized him or her by printing out a big colorful poster with the person's name on it and many thanks. Some employees were spotted for a dinner with a spouse or friend at any Dallas restaurant of their choice. Others got round-trip airfare to visit nearby cities. "We tried to personalize it," says Frappolli. "Maybe we'd get them a signed football if they were a player's big fan. We tried to give things that mean something to that person."

Another simple but effective idea came in response to a newly developing area. Pinnacle had begun making pogs for Frito-Lay's division in Mexico; a 3-D pog went into every bag of chips. To understate it, the item was popular. The introduction of pogs spurred sales from 40 million bags of chips a week to 80 million and there's only 50 million people in all of Mexico. Problem was, the orders were growing so exponentially, Pinnacle couldn't keep up. In danger of losing the contract, a manufacturing supervisor set his carpentry—yes, carpentry—skills to work. On his own time, he made a "shaker table." The homemade contraption literally shakes the pogs as they come onto a ramp so they shoot down different avenues, allowing more workers to pack them. It increased Pinnacle's production capacity by tenfold—the company shipped over a billion pogs that summer. "If you looked at this table, you'd think your 10-year-old could have made it," says Frappolli. "But it's a good idea and no one had thought of it. It let us hit the order."

Employees were encouraged not just to concentrate on their own areas, but also to think outside the box. A public relations manager, for instance, was looking at the 1996 Olympics with dollar bills in his eyes. He'd been to previous Olympics and had seen how well pins had sold. He contacted one of the few companies licensed to sell Olympic pins in Atlanta, a company that lacked the distribution channels Pinnacle had established. Now that company makes the pins and Pinnacle distributes them. The venture brought in almost $20 million in revenue.

Throughout the process, Pinnacle struggled against formalizing it too much. Employees would contact either Frappolli or their supervisors with ideas. "I found from my days at large companies that programs can bog you down," says Frappolli. "With us it's if you've got a good idea that will work, let's do it. Let's quantify savings so we know it works and then reward that employee." How did the company know if an idea would work? It grabbed all the stakeholders and asked them if it was worth trying. The company tried to emphasize the positive. Maybe the first idea wasn't a home run, but if employees remained encouraged, they might hit the next one out of the ballpark.

One of the employees who scored big was Anderson. As an employee in the finance department, she was privy to the exorbitant costs of trademark searches. Every time the company came up with a new name for a trading card, it had to pay a trademark attorney to do a search and make sure it hadn't been trademarked. Anderson decided to create a database for Pinnacle, track what trademarks it owned and which ones it had searched in the past. Although she had no training in legal or intellectual-property issues, she wasn't afraid to ask a lot of questions. Anderson worked to set up the system—at home and on weekends, even on lunch breaks—for almost three months before it was up and running. It has saved more than $100,000.

Toward the close of '94, there still hadn't been even a peep about layoffs. Employees were revitalized. "Each day and each week and each month they saw we weren't laying people off and our competition was—some were laying off half their workforces, shutting entire plants down," says Frappolli. "They saw we weren't doing any of that and it really built some steam."

Pinnacle was lucky it had a tough and energized workforce, because it wasn't in the clear until fall 1995. Baseball sales are strong this spring, however, and the company is breathing a collective sigh of relief. But the message remains clear—just because we're bouncing back doesn't mean we should relax. Keep the ideas coming. Says Corbin: "What Pinnacle has done is to tell employees, 'Keep justifying your job. Earn your keep if you want to stay here.' Rather than the organization choosing who stays and who goes, the people themselves choose through their actions. What Pinnacle is doing is the most honest, empowering thing it can do."

Anderson says employees are still at it—she herself is exploring a new database. She gives much of the credit to the Pinnacle culture. "It's an atmosphere in which you can take in as much responsibility as you want." Anderson says. "If you were to leave Pinnacle—and I have no intention of doing so—you could honesty look your employer in the face and say, 'I can do anything you throw at me.'"

Truly mutual admirers, Frappolli says a lot of the credit goes to the Pinnacle workforce—a uniquely excellent group of people. "I think it would be dangerous to say that this is a template that could work across America," he says. "You need special kinds of people who believe in themselves and understand that they control their own destiny. These employees know that if they deliver results they're going to have a job and if they don't they might not. They prefer to bet on themselves rather than having a company take care of them."

Pinnacle's mission statement is "to provide unexpected delight in everything we do." In its rally against layoffs, the company certainly provided unexpected delight to a business community jaded by "unavoidable" downsizings. When the crowds cheer to the crack of the bat this week, we should reserve a portion of the adulation for the heroes off the field.

Can and Does Employee Activism Make a Difference? What is the Impact of Employees as Stakeholders?*

1. **With regard to equal employment opportunity** – Employees can take legal action, filing discrimination charges and lawsuits (including class actions, if they meet the requirements for a class). In companies with union contracts, employees' grievances, including issues related to discrimination, are handled through grievance procedures.
2. **With regard to layoffs** - Often, employees are not consulted about layoff plans. However, if management allows their input, employees can offer creative alternatives to cut costs and improve productivity and quality.

   In companies with union contracts, employees have more voice in how layoffs are conducted. The employer must bargain about the effects of a layoff (though not about the decision to lay off employees). The effects of a layoff might include, for example, the timing of the layoff, how it is conducted, severance pay and other benefits (such as training for displaced workers), how recalls/rehires will be handled, etc.

   Employees in union and non-union environments have legal remedies. For example, they can file a lawsuit alleging that a layoff was discriminatory (e.g., claiming a disproportionate number of older workers were laid off) or that the employer failed to follow the WARN Act, which, in some cases, requires advance notice.
3. **With regard to the bigger picture of CSR-**
   a. **Effect of CSR on quality and productivity of employees.** Some companies with a strong image of social responsibility (including fair treatment of employees) may enjoy a higher level of employee commitment and productivity and lower turnover than companies without such a reputation. However, other factors also affect companies' ability to attract, motivate and retain talented employees. (For example, some MBAs were attracted to Enron's financial rewards and competitive, free-wheeling, risk-oriented culture.)

      David Vogel, in *Market for Virtue*, concludes that although CSR may play a role in attracting employees, it is typically overshadowed by other business trends and opportunities. He states that there is no evidence that firms without a reputation for social responsibility have a harder time finding first-class employees or have to pay them more.

   b. **Effect employees can have on company behavior.** In some companies, CSR policies and corporate citizenship efforts have resulted from employee pressure. (Example: Merck's decision to produce the river blindness drug, partly due to pressure from its scientists.)

---

*Summary based, in part, on "Employees: You Are Where You Work?" from *The Market for Virtue* by David Vogel.

QUESTIONS ON READINGS FOR PART SIX (D) (2 OF 2)

What are a firm's legal obligations with regard to layoffs?

What are its moral obligations, if any?

How do layoffs affect firm performance?

What are the most effective downsizing strategies?

Are there creative alternatives to downsizing?

What impact or influence have employees had on discrimination? On layoffs?

CENTER FOR EDUCATION ON SOCIAL RESPONSIBILITY

CASE # 6:

WAL-MART AND WALL STREET WOMEN

WAL-MART'S WOMEN[1]

Manuel G. Velasquez

Wal-Mart Stores, the world's biggest retailer, owns more than 4,800 stores, including 1,475 discount stores, 1,750 Wal-Mart Supercenter combination discount and grocery stores, and 540 Sam's Club warehouse stores. It is the leading retailer in both Canada (236 stores) and Mexico (633), owns almost 40 percent of SEIYU, a Japanese supermarket chain, and has stores in Argentina (11), Brazil (144), China (39), Germany (92), South Korea (15), Puerto Rico (54), and the United Kingdom (270). At the end of its fiscal year, January 2004, Wal-Mart posted sales of $256.3 billion and net income of $9.1 billion. The company had over 1,500,000 employees worldwide and planned to add another 800,000 by the end of the decade.

The company is famous for its strong and distinctive corporate culture, which it actively promotes. New employees get videos, classes, and literature on Wal-Mart's culture, such as the "Three Basic Beliefs" ("Respect for the Individual," "Service to Our Customers," and "Strive for Excellence"). Employees read founder Sam Walton's personal biography and learn how his personal values became core beliefs of the company. Weekly training on company culture is mandatory for managers and employees. Managers get continuing lessons on the company's culture and impart these lessons to subordinates. Managers are evaluated on their knowledge of the culture and employees are rewarded when they demonstrate a strong commitment to it.[2] Some of the company's cultural traditions are male-oriented. Senior managers attend an annual corporate retreat, for example, that always includes fishing and quail hunting. Managers sometimes scheduled district meetings at Hooter's restaurants, and annual sales meetings sometimes featured side trips to strip clubs.

Although the staunchly antiunion company is known as a benevolent employer, its reputation has suffered recently. In July 2000, an internal audit uncovered violations of state labor laws on time for breaks and violations of federal child-labor laws. In October 2003, the INS conducted several midnight raids and discovered that the cleaning companies Wal-Mart hired to clean its stores at night had hundreds of illegal immigrants working as janitors. Wal-Mart was charged with conspiring with the cleaning companies to cheat immigrants out of their wages. In February 2004, the company was found guilty of failing to pay overtime wages to workers who claimed they had to work overtime without pay between 1994 and 1999.[3]

Wal-Mart's biggest employee headache, however, was a class action lawsuit (*Dukes et al. v. Wal-Mart Stores, Inc.*) claiming the company discriminated against female employees in promotions, pay, management training, and job assignments. The lawsuit was launched in June 2001 when six female employees accused Wal-Mart of paying women less than men and passing them over for promotions. On June 22, 2004, U.S. District Court Judge Martin Jenkins ruled that the six women could sue on behalf of all female employees of Wal-Mart who worked at its U.S. stores anytime since December 26, 1998. The women asked for back pay and compensation for all 1.6 million female employees against whom Wal-Mart had discriminated.

To support their claims, the women hired a statistical expert, Richard Drogin, a professor at California State University at Hayward, to analyze Wal-Mart's computerized employee records of 3,945,151 employees who had worked any time during 1996–2002.[4]

Drogin noted that Wal-Mart employees are divided into two main groups: hourly employees at the lower levels and salaried management employees at the higher levels. Hourly employees include store cashiers, associates, stock people, department heads, and support managers. Salaried management employees are divided into two groups: At the lower level are those who manage a single store, and at the higher level are those who manage an entire district or region or who enter corporate management. At the store level, salaried managers include store managers and assistant managers; above them are district managers, regional vice presidents, and senior vice presidents. Since Wal-Mart promotes predominantly from within, workers typically progress from being an upper hourly employee (usually a "support manager"), to management trainee, to store manager or assistant manager, and finally to district, regional, or corporate manager.

Compensation increases from one level to the next. In 2001, salaried managers made about $50,000 a year while hourly employees made $18,000. Drogin found that 65 percent of hourly employees were women, but only 33 percent of salaried managers were. At both levels, women earned less than men. The 2001 average annual earnings, for example, were as follows:

Group	%Female	Male Earnings	Female Earnings
Hourly	70.2	$18,609	$17,459
Salaried Managers	33.5	55,443	40,905

Drogin found this pattern repeated in all 41 of Wal-Mart's American regions.

Drogin also found that, on average, women earned less than men at each in-store salaried management job. During the years 1999–2001, for example, he found the following average annual salaries among salaried managers:

Job	% Female	Male Salary	Female Salary
Regional vp	10.3	$419,435	$279,772
District manager	9.8	239,519	177,149
Store manager	14.3	105,682	89,280
Comanager	23	59,535	56,317
Asst. manager	35.7	39,790	37,322
Mgmt. trainee	41.3	23,175	22,371

Drogin found a similar gap in hourly pay rates. In 2001, for example, he found that in the three largest hourly jobs average hourly wages were as follows:

Job	% Female	Male Hourly Pay	Female Hourly Pay
Dept. head	78.3	$11.13	$10.62
Sales associate	67.8	8.73	8.27
Cashier	92.5	8.33	8.05

Drogan concluded that for a single year "the total earnings paid to men is about $5,000 more than earnings paid to women, among full-time employees working at least 45 weeks, on average, in 2001."

Drogin-analyzed whether the discrepancies could be accounted for by the assumption that women left their jobs more than men, perhaps to raise children or for some other reason. This would give women higher turnover rates and men greater experience and seniority. He found that women stayed in the workforce longer than men at Wal-Mart and so had more on-the-job experience on average than men did. For example, at the end of 2001 the average number of years since their date of hire for men and women was as follows:

Job	Men	Women
All hourly	3.13 years	4.47 years
All managers	6.69	7.39
Sales associates	2.53	3.41
Dept. managers	5.29	7.49
Cashiers	1.86	2.53

Drogin discovered also that while it took women 4.38 years from their date of hire to be promoted to assistant manager, men were promoted after only 2.86 years, and while it took women 10.12 years to become store managers, it took men only 8.64 years.

Drogin next checked whether the wage and promotion discrepancies could be accounted for by the performance records of males and females. Perhaps males performed better than females. He found that, on average, women had higher performance ratings than men. In 2001, for example, the performance ratings (on a scale of 1–7, where 1 is low and 7 high) were as follows:

Job	Men's Ratings	Women's Ratings
All hourly	3.84	3.91
Sales associates	3.68	3.75
Dept. manager	4.28	4.38
Cashier	3.58	3.49

Drogin also examined whether the pay gap between male and female compensation at Wal-Mart stayed the same over the years. He found that women who were hired into, hourly jobs in 1996 were paid $0.35 less per hour than men hired into hourly jobs that same year. By 2001, the gap between the wages of these same employees had increased to $1.16 per hour. Also, women hired as sales associates in 1996 received $0.20 per hour less than men hired as sales associates that year. By 2001, the difference had grown to $1.17 per hour.

Finally, Drogin performed several statistical tests to determine whether the discrepancies in promotions and pay could be the result of women not being available (not in the "feeder pools") when promotions came up or of some other factors. He found, instead, that

- Women received 2,891 fewer promotions into Support Manager [the step before Management Trainee] than would be expected from their representation in the feeder pools.
- Women received 2,952 fewer promotions into Management Trainee than would be expected from their representation in the feeder pools.
- Women received 346 fewer promotions into Co-Manager than would be expected from their representation in the feeder pools.
- Women received 155 fewer promotions into Store Manager than would be expected from their representation in the feeder pools.
- Total earnings paid to women ranged between 5% and 15% less than total earnings paid to similarly situated men in each year 1996–2001, even when accounting for factors such as seniority, status, and store.

Drogin noted two factors that might affect women's promotion into management. First, many store managers believed that employees going into salaried management positions had to be willing to relocate geographically, and they communicated this belief to women. In practice, however, only a small proportion of managers were required to relocate their homes, and the company had programs that allowed women to opt out of this requirement. Second, while the company had a policy of posting available management positions, managers had the discrenon to not post some positions and to communicate the availability of these positions by word of mouth to potential candidates they picked.

Another expert, Marc Bendick, a labor economist, noted that Wal-Mart's top retail competitors had no trouble promoting women into management. While Wal-Mart's in-store salaried managers were 34.5 percent women, salaried managers at 20 comparable large retail chains were 56.5 percent female. If Wal-Mart had achieved the same female manager-to-non-manager ratios as comparable chains in 1999, it would have had at least 4,004 more in-store female managers, 466 more female managers at corporate headquarters, 144 more at "blue-collar" nonstore establishments, 107 more in other nonstore establishments, and 97 more in separately reporting establishments.

The six women suing Wal-Mart also hired an expert in sociology, William T. Bielby, a professor at the University of California, Santa Barbara, to analyze and report on Wal-Mart's hiring practices.[5] Based on numerous hours of testimony under oath given by Wal-Mart managers, Bielby concluded that although company guidelines stated minimum criteria for promotions, managers had no written policies to guide them in selecting among candidates who met the minimum criteria nor did they have guidelines to guide them in setting exact salaries. He noted that "a large body of social science research" showed that stereotypes of men and women were likely to influence personnel decisions when decisions were based on informal and subjective factors, because managers would then seek out and retain stereotype-confirming information while ignoring or minimizing information that defied stereotypes. "In such settings," he wrote, "stereotypes can bias assessments of women's qualifications, contributions, and advancement potential, because perceptions are shaped by stereotypical beliefs about women generally, not by the actual skills and accomplishments of the person as an individual." In his report he noted:

> For example, Store Manager Arturo Mireles testified that he was aware of no written criteria to be used in making decisions about promotion to Department Manager or Support Manager. His practice was to rely on a range of unwritten criteria, including subjective factors such as teamwork, ethics, integrity, ability to get along with others, and willingness to volunteer to come in to assist in the store or at another store outside of regular work hours. While factors like these might have common sense appeal and some might in fact be appropriate to consider in making promotion decisions, assessments will be biased [by stereotypes] unless they are assessed in a systematic and valid manner, with clear criteria and careful attention to the integrity of the decision-making process. . . . The same kind of discretion is allowed in decisions about compensation for hourly employees. . . . [A]ccording to company policy the Store Manager can pay up to two dollars an hour above the stated rate, based on

> his or her assessment of factors such as previous pay and experience. There is no company guideline and no training on when and how to adjust pay upwards and while overall payroll is monitored, there is no monitoring of these individual adjustments . . . A Store Manager can give a raise larger than the specified amount at his or her own discretion. In addition, employees can be given merit increases for "exceptional performance." . . . However, there is no guideline for assessing "exceptional performance" and no monitoring of the number of people who receive increases and how frequently they are given to any specific employee.

Bielby also noted, however, that Wal-mart's "managers testified consistently that they did not believe that women were less qualified than men for management positions in the company." Wal-Mart insisted that it explicitly prohibited any form of discriminatory behavior and that its managers all believed that women were as qualified as men.

More than 100 female Wal-Mart employees provided sworn declarations detailing their treatment in the company.[6] These experiences included:

- A female assistant manager in Utah was told by her store manager that retail is "tough" and "not appropriate" for women.
- A manager in Texas told a female employee that women have to be "bitches" to survive Wal-Mart management.
- A Sam's Club manager in California told a woman that to get promoted she should "doll up" dress a little better and "blow the cobwebs off her make up."
- Male managers in several states repeatedly told numerous women employees in virtually identical words that men "need to be paid more than women because they have families to support."
- A male manager in South Carolina told a female employee that "God made Adam first, so women will always be second to men."
- A female personnel manager in Florida was told by her manager that men were paid more than women because "men are here to make a career and women aren't. Retail is for housewives who just need to earn extra money."
- A female corporate manager in Arkansas was told by a senior U.P. that it would be better if she "were at home raising a family" and that since she did not hunt, fish, or do other typically male activities, she would not advance any further: "you aren't a part of the boy's club, and you should raise a family and stay in the kitchen."
- A female management trainee in Texas was told by her supervisor, "I don't like college graduates, and I don't like female managers" and was told by her next Manager that she should "resign and find a husband to settle down with and have children."

In the 1990s, Wal-Mart had started a number of programs to achieve diversity. The company had a written anti-discrimination policy posted everywhere. Managers got reports on the gender composition of their hourly and salaried positions. Managers were told that women's representation should "reflect the community." Managers had to set an annual goal of increasing female representation in their areas and were supposed to be evaluated on the progress they made toward reaching the goals they set for themselves. This evaluation did not affect the compensation of in-store salaried managers; however, all higher-level managers were evaluated on the progress they made toward the diversity goal they had set themselves, and this evaluation was then averaged with evaluations on three other kinds of "people" goals, and the "people average" constituted 5 percent of the final evaluation on which their compensation for the following year was based. The managers testified that they tried to set goals that were "realistic," "achievable," "made sense," and "weren't worse than the year before." A program that allowed women to enter salaried management jobs without having to relocate their homes had been begun by the late Sam Walton. After Walton's death, however, the program was not widely used nor known.

Wal-Mart management believed that if the lawsuit was successful, it could have a significant material financial impact on the company.

QUESTIONS

1. What financial impact do you think the lawsuit could potentially have on Wal-Mart?
2. What are the major moral complaints of the females suing Wal-Mart? Do you believe these moral complaints are justified? Why?
3. What factors do you think might account for the discrepancies the Drogin report uncovered?
4. What, if anything, do you think Wal-Mart should do to correct these discrepancies? Should the company institute an "affirmative action" promotion program for female employees? If so, what should this program be like?
5. Do you think the women deserve to win their lawsuit?

NOTES

1. This case is based on the documents the plaintiffs in *Dukes et al. v. Wal-Mart Stores, Inc* have made available at their "Wal-Mart Class Website" at ***http://www.walmartclass.com.*** In particular, the materials cited in notes 4, 5, and 6 are available at this website and can be accessed there.
2. See M. J. Schneider, "The Wal-Mart Annual Meeting: From Small-Town America to a Global Corporate Culture," *Human Organization,* v. 57, 1998, pp. 292–299, and "Saturday Morning Fever: Wal-Mart's Weekly Meeting," *The Economist,* December 8, 2001.
3. Wal-Mart Stores, Inc., *2004 Annual Report,* accessed August 3, 2004 at ***http://www.walmartstores.com/Files/annualreport_2004.pdf.***
4. Richard Drogin, "Statistical Analysis of Gender Patterns in Wal-Mart Workforce," February 2003, accessed August 1, 2004 on Wal-Mart Class website (see note 1); all information and quotations attributed to Drogin in this case are drawn from this report.

5. William T. Bielby, "Expert Report of William T. Bielby, Ph.D.," February 3, 2003, accessed August 1, 2004 on Wal-Mart Class website (see note 1); all information and quotations attributed to Bielby in this case are drawn from this report.
6. This summary of the 100 declarations is taken in part from the April 28, 2003 news release, "Women Present Evidence of Widespread Discrimination at Wal-Mart; Ask Judge to Expand Case to be Largest Ever Sex Discrimination Case," accessed August 2, 2004 on Wal-Mart Class website (see note 1); all 100 declarations are available on the Wal-Mart Class website and my summary includes some materials drawn from these declarations.

SUPREME COURT WILL CONSIDER WAL-MART CHALLENGE TO CLASS-ACTION SUIT

By JESS BRAVIN and ANN ZIMMERMAN

The Supreme Court agreed Monday to hear Wal-Mart Stores Inc.'s bid to block a class-action lawsuit alleging discrimination against women in a case that could have broad implications for such suits.

Filed in 2001 on behalf of as many as 1.5 million female employees, the suit says Wal-Mart paid women less than men and gave them fewer opportunities for promotions—claims that could lead to billions of dollars in back pay and punitive damages.

The issue before the Supreme Court is whether the would-be members of the class have enough in common that their claims can fairly be decided in a single action. The decision could clarify federal rules on class-action suits and perhaps establish a national standard.

Class actions aggregate multiple claims against a defendant into a single lawsuit, providing redress for wide-scale wrongdoing when it's not viable to pursue each claim individually. For instance, a class action might be filed against a company that allegedly overcharged each of a million customers $1.

The retailer's high-court petition is being supported by an array of other companies, including Bank of America Corp., General Electric Co. and Microsoft Corp. They say the lower-court ruling, if allowed to stand, could expose other companies to staggering liability by allowing unrelated discrimination claims to proceed as class action suits.

Plaintiffs' lawyers contend the class members—potentially, all women employees who have worked at Wal-Mart since Dec. 26, 1998—were all victimized by a "centralized corporate culture" and are entitled to class status.

For its part, Wal-Mart argues that personnel decisions it attributes to individual managers across its 3,400 stores cannot fairly be lumped together.

The justices will decide the class-action issue, not the merits of the discrimination claim.

The Ninth U.S. Circuit Court of Appeals authorized the suit to proceed, but it excluded from the class women who no longer worked for Wal-Mart when the original suit was filed in 2001, reducing the number covered. It left open the possibility that those plaintiffs, numbering perhaps one million, could proceed separately.

The Equal Employment Opportunity Commission backed the plaintiffs, warning the Ninth Circuit that finding for Wal-Mart could let employers escape punitive damages for systematic employment discrimination.

In asking the Supreme Court to review the issue, Wal-Mart said the appeals court misapplied the standards for defining a class of plaintiffs, exposing it to punitive damages when it should be liable only for back pay.

Federal rules provide different standards for certifying a class of plaintiffs, often depending on the type of remedy sought. For example, it's tougher to certify a class seeking monetary compensation or punitive damages than it is to certify one that just requests a court order ending a defendant's wrongdoing, said Elizabeth Chamblee Burch, a law professor at Florida State University.

Different federal appeals courts have reached different conclusions on how to define a class of plaintiffs.

"The current confusion in class-action law is harmful for everyone—employers, employees, businesses of all types and sizes, and the civil justice system," Wal-Mart said in a statement. "These are exceedingly important issues that reach far beyond this particular case."

Six women, including a greeter at the Pittsburg, Calif., store, filed the suit nine years ago on behalf of current and former Wal-Mart employees. The plaintiffs are seeking back pay, punitive damages and changes in how Wal-Mart makes its pay and promotion decisions. They charge that Wal-Mart has lagged far behind its competitors in its promotion of women and knew of discrimination against its female employees but failed to act.

The plaintiffs say the size of the class, while large, results from Wal-Mart's status as the nation's largest corporate employer. The company now employs 1.4 million people in the U.S.

The plaintiffs allege that Wal-Mart's corporate culture and employment policies fostered gender stereotyping and led to adverse treatment of women in all of the retailer's 41 domestic regions.The retailer denies it discriminated against women and says the case should not be granted class-action status because the plaintiffs' claims are too varied to proceed together, making it difficult for the company to mount a defense in a single case.

Wal-Mart also says it has improved worker treatment. After being sued repeatedly for allegedly forcing employees to work through lunch and bathroom breaks, the company installed computer systems that shut down individual cash registers when workers were scheduled for breaks. The company also began posting available job openings electronically. In December 2008, it agreed to pay up to $640 million to settle 63 state class-action overtime lawsuits.

The outcome could affect a wide swath of class action suits in areas including civil rights enforcement and tobacco litigation, says Prof. Burch. That's because class action litigation depends on the economic incentives for lawyers to file the cases.

For class-action attorneys, "the goal is to lump as many plaintiffs as possible into a class," she says.

The Supreme Court case is likely to be argued in the spring and decided by July.

Write to Jess Bravin at jess.bravin@wsj.com and Ann Zimmerman at ann.zimmerman@wsj.com.

WALL STREET'S DISAPPEARING WOMEN

Anita Raghavan

After the scandals of the 1990s, didn't investment banks put sexist employment practices behind them? Evidently not. By Anita Raghavan

Nadine Mentor, 29, had just landed in New York—and found out, she says, that she'd bagged one of the biggest gets of her career at Citigroup: a role for the bank leading a bond offering, valued at as much as $400 million, for the U.S. Virgin Islands. The deal was worth potentially more than $500,000 in fees. A day later, on Nov. 21, 2008, as she headed to a business meeting, she got an anxious call from her boss. Sensing something was up, Mentor said, "Just tell me, just tell me." Her boss gave her the bad news. Mentor, who had been lured to Citi from UBS in 2005, was included in a round of downsizing.

When her boss was laid off last summer, Amy Bartoletti, 38, says she was asked to run a Citi group that securitizes home loans through state authorities. But one of her peers in New York complained, she says, and the bank wound up making him a cohead of the group, asking both to take the Series 53 licensing test, required of managers in the municipal securities business. Bartoletti took the exam and passed in October. On Nov. 21 she was axed, told later by the bank that she was too expensive. Bartoletti contends that she and her male counterpart made the same base salary, $175,000, and that she is more qualified than he. As of late February her cohead, who now runs the group, still doesn't have his Series 53 certification. "It's the old boys' network," says Bartoletti. "It's very hard to imagine that that is what is happening in this day and age."

Mentor and Bartoletti are among five former managers and rising young stars who were cast out that day. They say that in all, 24 professionals in the public finance department lost their jobs, in roughly equal numbers of men and women. Yet the women claim they were victimized by more than economic necessity. Since the cuts, some Citi groups, like the one handling state mortgage programs, no longer have women professionals. Their lawyer, Douglas H. Wigdor, points out that just before the firings, men dominated the senior ranks in the department. He says that men had 76% of overall professional employment and two-thirds of the vice presidencies but 90% of the scarcer slots for directors and managing directors. An internal Citigroup document, dated July 20, 2006, confirms a stark disparity (*see chart, p. 78*). "We cannot confirm the authenticity of this document," says a Citi spokeswoman. The high proportion of men in public finance, coupled with the large numbers of women laid off, are a "clear indication that gender was a reason for selecting the people who were let go," says Wigdor. He recently filed charges with the U.S. Equal Employment Opportunity Commission—a first step before seeking a class action—alleging they were terminated because they were women. He calls it a case of "recessionary discrimination."

For its part, Citi says its November layoffs were "done fairly and lawfully and [were] based on legitimate business reasons unrelated to gender." Without specifying, the bank says that "many of the factual allegations from these former employees are either inaccurate or incomplete." Citi further notes that it and its municipal securities division are "disciplined, focused, consistent and vigilant in regard to our diversity-related efforts."

Still, similar claims by women who insist they were unfairly fired have been piling up recently at Merrill Lynch, Bank of America and Bank of Tokyo, as well as at Citigroup. If the claims have any merit, the mostly male club that gave rise to explosive sex discrimination lawsuits a dozen years ago against Citigroup's Smith Barney brokerage unit is back at work. This time the offenses are not the boorish behavior and outright harassment that gave rise to a total $400 million in industry settlements but something more subtle: making women bear a disproportionate share of the layoffs. In the worst financial crash since the Depression, financial services and insurance firms have cut 260,000 jobs. Seventy-two percent of the missing workers laid off have been women, even though they constituted 64% of employment before the crash began. As one plaintiff, Wan Li, bluntly puts it in a separate suit against Citigroup, which has been settled: Women "are unfairly selected for layoff over male employees with lesser merit or qualifications because of their gender." Says the bank: "Citi has a long-standing commitment to equal employment practices and to provide a professional and respectful workplace free of unlawful discrimination."

The lawsuits offer only a fractional picture. "There are plenty of women who don't sue for fear of being a pariah in the industry," says Dina Bakst, a lawyer who once worked defending employers in discrimination suits and has since switched sides and now is copresident of A Better Balance, a New York City legal advocacy group that nationally promotes women's rights in the workplace.

Nonsense, say plenty of employment specialists. How do we know, they ask, whether the women who were fired were as talented as the men who survived or replaced them? Another argument against the plaintiff's claims: Perhaps some new moms and older women have simply lost their mojo. Yet another response is that the subject of gender is irrelevant. "It is really a misguided notion to focus on whether women are victims in recessions," says Alison Fraser, director of economic policy studies at the Heritage Foundation in Washington, D.C. "What is important here is all Americans are suffering, and they are suffering at every level."

That's incontrovertible. But so is the fact that women in finance and insurance have borne a disproportionate share of the suffering. In the two years since December 2006, when employment in the sector hit a peak for the past decade, female employment has fallen 4.7% to 3.8 million, while male employment has dropped 3.2% to 2.1 million, according to the government's Current Employment Statistics survey.

On the whole, a recession hits men harder than women. That's because men tend to take more demand sensitive jobs like construction and manufacturing, and women work more in service-sector jobs like health care and education that are less cyclical. That's why, in the past 20 years, women have increased their share of total jobs from 46.6% to 49.3%. But the financial sector has its own rhythm.

For years, as the economy boomed, the financial industry was a place of seemingly limitless opportunity for women. It offered high-paying jobs and untold possibilities for advancement. Before the financial crisis hit, Zoe Cruz at Morgan Stanley, Sallie Kraw check at Citigroup and Erin Callan at now bankrupt Lehman Brothers made it to the executive suite. Now all three have been dislodged from their lofty perches (*see box, p. 78*), a story women say is being replicated at all levels in investment banking.

"I think women are just getting creamed" in the downturn, says Linda D. Friedman, the Chicago attorney who brought the case involving the infamous "Boom-Boom Room" against Smith Barney in the mid-1990s, throwing a spotlight on the frat-house-style antics that male brokers used to harass their female colleagues in the basement of Smith Barney's Garden City, N.Y. office. "There are just so few women," says Friedman, "you lose one, you lose 100%."

Indeed, none of the leading Wall Street banks—Goldman Sachs, the combined Bank of America and Merrill Lynch, JPMorgan Chase, Citigroup, UBS, Credit Suisse and Morgan Stanley—has a single woman in any of the top three jobs. Asked to provide a current breakdown of the number of female officers (managing directors, directors and vice presidents), only Goldman responded: As of today, its ranks of female vice presidents, which includes its executive directors, stand at 29.4% of the 9,244 total, up from 27.9% of 7,667 three years earlier; over the same period women increased from 15.5% of 1,236 managing directors to 16.6% of 1,796.

Part of the problem has to do with the fact that trading desks reward sharp elbows more than they value brains or managerial skills. Meanwhile, in the hushed corridors of investment banking, women are so thinly represented in the most senior positions that as securities firms shed workers, they are becoming an endangered species. The latest casuality: Ellyn McColgan, who was hired with great fanfare a year or so ago from Fidelity Investments to be the president and chief operating officer of Morgan Stanley's Global Wealth Management Group. In late January she was out of a job, the big loser in the joint venture with Citigroup's Smith Barney brokerage unit. (A male executive from Citigroup will run the combined unit with Morgan Stanley's James Gorman.) With McColgan out and Cruz and Krawcheck long gone, there are no women at the highest levels at Morgan Stanley and Citigroup. "Women are vulnerable in this kind of reduction in force" because they don't have the political clout at the highest levels, attorney Friedman argues.

For years Kathleen Bostjancic got rave reviews at Merrill Lynch. Her boss, chief North American economist David Rosenberg, gushed about her work. "Kathy continues to deliver top-caliber product," he wrote in a mid-2003 performance evaluation. "Her judgment is impeccable." Along with the high praise flowed more pay. In 2006 Bostjancic was earning $650,000 in base salary and bonus, more than twice as much as she brought home three years earlier.

Around this time Bostjancic got pregnant—and her life at Merrill, she claims, started to deteriorate. During her maternity leave Rosenberg telephoned Bostjancic and told her he wanted her to take on a role as "Washington Policy Analyst" and develop her own research studies. But when she presented a business plan for the new position upon her return in the fall of 2006, Bostjancic says, the proposal was rejected.

Over the next year tensions between her and Rosenberg grew. He was uncomfortable with an agreed-upon work-at-home arrangement in the mornings to breastfeed her son, Bostjancic says. Merrill says there was no issue. But Bostjancic claims Rosenberg asked an assistant to keep a secret log, recording when she allegedly failed to say hello to a co-worker or kept her office door closed or asked not to be interrupted for 15-minute periods. Merrill denies these allegations. Had Rosenberg asked her, Bostjancic says, she would have explained that she closed her door because she was breast-pumping milk.

In September 2007 Rosenberg gave her a memo warning that the "quality of work needs to improve dramatically." (A Merrill spokeswoman declines comment on Rosenberg's behalf.) Then in April 2008 Rosenberg notified Bostjancic that she was being terminated as part of a reduction in force. Less than two months later Merrill replaced her with Drew Matus, an economist from Lehman Brothers.

So Bostjancic alleges in a discrimination suit filed last August in federal court in Manhattan. She's seeking compensation and her old job back. Merrill denies her allegations. It adds that "in regard to Ms. Bostjancic's lawsuit, we believe Mr. Rosenberg acted appropriately."

Anita Gupta, who worked in the information technologies group at Bank of America, alleges her dismissal was characterized as a "layoff," though, she claims, "there was no downsizing in BOA's workforce. No one else was laid off." Her case, in which she sought at least $2 million in damages, offers a glimpse into the travails of working mothers on Wall Street. Gupta was fired early last year after returning from maternity leave, according to a 2008 suit against the bank and two managers, Douglas Gallager and Peter Spencer.

"Knowing she was in labor," Gupta says in her suit, she made the trek to the office after her water broke in order to explain some code to a colleague and change her laptop battery so she could be available to the group while she was out. On returning from maternity leave, Gupta claims, she was marginalized. When she finally got a meeting with Spencer, her boss, he gave her "directions that made no sense and in fact were detrimental to projects," she claims. A Bank of America spokeswoman says the allegations against Spencer and Gallager are without merit. Gupta did not receive an annual performance review for 2007 or a bonus. To make matters worse, she says, she was asked to help interview candidates for a job "that matched her job description," according to the suit. Bank of America, while admitting that it didn't give Gupta a review or bonus in 2007, denies these allegations and her version of events.

During her leave, Gupta says, the bank had agreed to provide a private room on the 43rd floor upon her return where she could breast-feed her newborn, brought to work by a nanny. When she came back to work in December 2007. Gupta claims, Spencer told her that he wanted her to share the lactation room with a Muslim employee who wanted to use it as a prayer room. That, together with her removal from work she was doing before maternity leave, led her to believe that "management . . . had no real or good faith intention of allowing her to return to work after her leave." Bank of America denies any campaign aimed at preventing Gupta from returning to work as a new mother. It says gender is not a factor in layoff decisions and that it doesn't tolerate discrimination. The bank says it settled the case for an undisclosed sum late last year in order to avoid further legal costs.

Well before Wan Li, a Citigroup banker, was laid off she was channeled into a less desirable and lucrative position over her own objections, she alleged in a lawsuit seeking class status. Filed in federal court in Manhattan in September and seeking unspecified damages, the suit claims that among Citi's discriminatory practices is a trend of "selecting women over men for layoff."

Hired in July 2001 as an assistant vice president in the Structured Trade Finance Group, Li did well in her early years, drawing reviews where she "consistently" exceeded expectations, she says in her suit. In late 2003, however, she alleges she began to hit the "proverbial glass ceiling" when she was pushed into a job with no prospect of advancement while pregnant and set to go on maternity leave. Over her opposition, Li was transferred to a support position in a newly formed Global Structured Portfolio Management Group, according to the suit. She claims she was told the move was "better" for her and would be "more manageable" for a "new mother."

Despite being told the transfer to a support role would be temporary, Li claims, her mistreatment grew worse. Returning from maternity leave in April 2004, she discovered her 2003 bonus of $75,000 was far lower than those going to her male peers and even lower than payouts given to male associates two years her junior in job rank, according to the suit.

To avoid compromising her future earnings power, Li says, she tried to transfer back to a revenue-generating role at Citigroup. But her request was denied, she claims, and she was moved to another support role in a different group. "Dismayed and dejected," Li took her concerns to several managing directors, she says in the suit. One of them advised Li to leave Citi-group altogether if she found the company's actions unacceptable, she claims.

In late June 2007, just as Li's second maternity leave was ending and she was preparing to return to work, she received a telephone call from two female officials at the bank. Her position had been eliminated in a "restructuring." Of the 40 to 50 professionals in the Asset Finance Group worldwide, Li was the only professional let go, the suit says. Citigroup declined to comment on the specific allegations of the suit.

Paula Best believes her layoff in July 2007 was payback for her decision to file a discrimination complaint against Bank of Tokyo-Mitsubishi UFJ, according to a class action she filed in October seeking unspecified damages. A 13-year veteran of Bank of Tokyo, she was terminated when the bank's securities lending business was bought by Mitsubishi UFJ Trust & Banking.

Best, an African-American, says that in 2003 her job portfolio was vastly increased when she was given oversight of international lending in addition to her existing domestic lending duties. Still, she says in the suit filed in federal court in Manhattan, she wasn't promoted to the position of vice president and was the only employee reporting directly to the department manager of securities lending who wasn't a vice president.

Answering her claim, Bank of Tokyo says Best was assigned to back-office work after another employee left. She was not given a lofty title because the bank "did not have a business need for a vice president" handling "back-office responsibilities supervising a small clerical staff."

When Best received a rating of "Achieves +" again in her performance review in May 2005, her boss told her she would be promoted to vice president. But the bump-up never materialized, and Best complained to the personnel department that she was denied the title because of her gender and race. Bank of Tokyo denies her claim, saying her boss never told her she would be made a vice president. Passed over again in 2006 and 2007 even as white male colleagues in similar roles were promoted, Best complained to the bank and contacted the EEOC. The bank's personnel department, she claims, didn't investigate her complaint but referred her to an employee assistance program for psychological counseling. The bank says that her complaint was "promptly, thoroughly and appropriately investigated" and that the counseling program was mentioned to her after she had written that she was "holding back the urge to scream from the frustration lying dormant in me."

Best says she was one of 5 employees in her department to be laid off, while 11 others were spared. Bank of Tokyo denies her allegations, pointing out that the job of Best's own supervisor was also eliminated because Mitsubishi "already had an employee performing his position."

Eleni Demetriou, a former vice president in Merrill's private client group, is convinced she was terminated because of a different sort of stink she raised. In 2005, she says in a complaint filed in New York State Supreme Court last July, she claims she witnessed two members of her group engage in activities that were of a sexual nature. The two " 'flirted' consistently with each other" and were seen wiping lipstick off their mouths and faces. Demetriou alleges. The woman, she claims, consistently dressed in a manner that "reveal[ed] that she was not wearing a bra" and presented herself with "her blouse buttoned in a fashion which appeared as though it had been unbuttoned and rebuttoned unevenly." (Merrill denies awareness of any inappropriate relationship.) Demetriou took her beef to William Kubeck, the manager of the group, and who, she says, was "close personal friends" with one of the two; he "completely ignored" her complaints, says her suit. Merrill and Kubeck deny the allegations except to concede that Kubeck did socialize on occasion with one of the two outside work.

Kubeck, she alleges, then retaliated, becoming "hostile" toward her. (Merrill and Kubeck deny that claim.) When she returned from maternity leave, Demetriou says in her suit, Kubeck blocked her bid to be promoted to director by not presenting her name for nomination—and chastised her when she was late to work because she had to care for her sick child. The comments were discriminatory because men who were late to work or simply disappeared from work were not rebuked, she alleges. Merrill and Kubeck deny all claims but concede that Kubeck did not nominate Demetriou for a promotion.

DETHRONED

Missing in action: Since the departure of these women, no female executives occupy corner offices at the leading banks. What kind of future do women have on Wall Street?

Pushed out in November 2007 as co-president of Morgan Stanley. Hasn't yet landed a job at a leading financial services company.

Demoted in June 2008 as CFO at now bankrupt Lehman Brothers. Recently took leave of absence as head of Credit Suisse's hedge fund group.

Resigned in September 2008 as chief executive of Citigroup's Global Wealth Management unit. Now sits on the board of Dell.

On Apr. 30, 2008 Demetriou was laid off. "No other individuals from the Desk were terminated as part of this layoff," she claims. Merrill disagrees. It says the firm also laid off two other employees who were part of the group managed by Kubeck. "The firm's decision on who to lay off or retain was based on a determination of who the strongest workers were, regardless of gender," says a Merrill spokesman. Demetriou is seeking $45 million in compensatory and punitive damages.

At Citigroup's public finance department some of the women let go were up-and-comers, like Brittany Sharpton, 23, and Chia, Siu, 25, analysts in, respectively, the infrastructure and the housing groups. "There was a lot of brainstorming [last summer] of what should we do to keep [Chia]," recalls Bartoletti, her former boss. Siu was promised a promotion effective January 2009. "I thought as soon as they promoted me, they'd want me to stay a year," says Siu. Instead, "I was betrayed, I was deceived." She took and passed her Series 63 exam, a license required for soliciting orders of securities. Her male counterpart—who kept his job—didn't have his Series 63 certification as of the Nov. 21 layoffs (he has since obtained it). With the layoffs, "you have taken out a whole generation of future female managing directors," says Lisa Conley, 42, the sole female director in the health care group, who was also let go in November. When Citi terminated Mentor and Bartoletti, they lost two members of the municipal securities division's "Coach for Success" program, a mentoring system for future leaders of the bank.

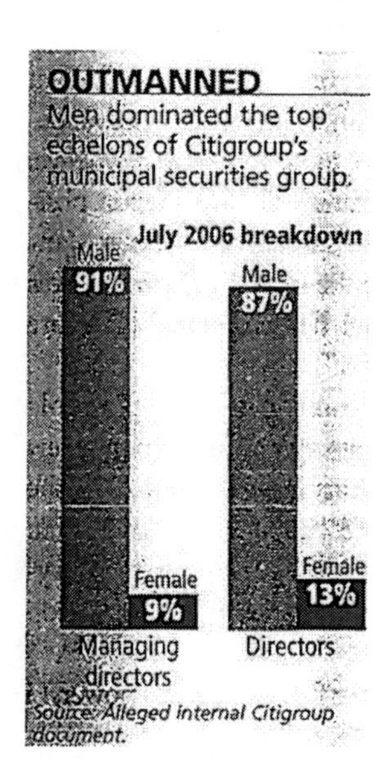

Plenty of aggrieved women are afraid of making a stir. In the summer of 2007 female employees were given the choice of cashing in on or opting out of a $46 million class-action settlement with Morgan Stanley to resolve charges of gender discrimination in its retail brokerage division. Alice Hughes, a Morgan Stanley financial adviser in Dallas, talked with several women who declined to participate—and not because they planned to pursue separate claims. "It was just sheer fear," she says, that even if they kept their jobs they might be excluded from benefits like getting a chunk of business when another broker left the firm. "They're right," says Hughes. Moreover, she claims, if they make trouble, "they will be blacklisted from working at any major firm."

CENTER FOR EDUCATION ON SOCIAL RESPONSIBILITY

PART SIX (E)

ENVIRONMENT AND A MODERN APPROACH TO SUSTAINABILITY

CENTER FOR EDUCATION ON SOCIAL RESPONSIBILITY

PART SIX (E) (I):

ENVIRONMENT-GENERAL ISSUES

BEYOND GREENING: STRATEGIES FOR A SUSTAINABLE WORLD

Stuart L. Hart

Companies need to look beyond the greening effort designed to prevent further environmental damage to a more comprehensive strategy known as sustainable global economy. This thrust aims to make the world environmentally clean for as long as civilization exists. Companies that want to chart this course of sustainability should implement activities that involve pollution prevention, product stewardship and clean technology. They should take advantage of the economic and business opportunities that clean technology offers such as the chance to develop new products to realize the goal of sustainability.

The environmental revolution has been almost three decades in the making, and it has changed forever how companies do business. In the 1960s and 1970s, corporations were in a state of denial regarding their impact on the environment. Then a series of highly visible ecological problems created a groundswell of support for strict government regulation. In the United States, Lake Erie was dead. In Europe, the Rhine was on fire. In Japan, people were dying of mercury poisoning.

Today many companies have accepted their responsibility to do no harm to the environment. Products and production processes are becoming cleaner; and where such change is under way, the environment is on the mend. In the industrialized nations, more and more companies are "going green" as they realize that they can reduce pollution and increase profits simultaneously. We have come a long way.

But the distance we've traveled will seem small when, in 30 years, we look back at the 1990s. Beyond greening lies an enormous challenge—and an enormous opportunity. The challenge is to develop a sustainable global economy: an economy that the planet is capable of supporting indefinitely. Although we may be approaching ecological recovery in the developed world, the planet as a whole remains on an unsustainable course. Those who think that sustainability is only a matter of pollution control are missing the bigger picture. Even if all the companies in the developed world were to achieve zero emissions by the year 2000, the earth would still be stressed beyond what biologists refer to as its carrying capacity. Increasingly, the scourges of the late twentieth century—depleted farmland, fisheries, and forests; choking urban pollution; poverty; infectious disease; and migration—are spilling over geopolitical borders. The simple fact is this: in meeting our needs, we are destroying the ability of future generations to meet theirs.

The roots of the problem—explosive population growth and rapid economic development in the emerging economies—are political and social issues that exceed the mandate and the capabilities of any corporation. At the same time, corporations are the only organizations with the resources, the technology, the global reach, and, ultimately, the motivation to achieve sustainability.

It is easy to state the case in the negative: faced with impoverished customers, degraded environments, failing political systems, and unraveling societies, it will be increasingly difficult for corporations to do business. But the positive case is even more powerful. The more we learn about the challenges of sustainability, the clearer it is that we are poised at the threshold of a historic moment in which many of the world's industries may be transformed.

To date, the business logic for greening has been largely operational or technical: bottom-up pollution-prevention programs have saved companies billions of dollars. However, few executives realize that environmental opportunities might actually become a major source of revenue growth. Greening has been framed in terms of risk reduction, reengineering, or cost cutting. Rarely is greening linked to strategy or technology development, and as a result, most companies fail to recognize opportunities of potentially staggering proportions.

WORLDS IN COLLISION

The achievement of sustainability will mean billions of dollars in products, services, and technologies that barely exist today. Whereas yesterday's businesses were often oblivious to their negative impact on the environment and today's responsible businesses strive for zero impact, tomorrow's businesses must learn to make a positive impact. Increasingly, companies will be selling solutions to the world's environmental problems.

Envisioning tomorrow's businesses, therefore, requires a clear understanding of those problems. To move beyond greening to sustainability, we must first unravel a complex set of global interdependencies. In fact, the global economy is really three different, overlapping economies.

The market economy is the familiar world of commerce comprising both the developed nations and the emerging economies.[1] About a billion people—one-sixth of the world's population—live in the developed countries of the market economy. Those affluent societies account for more than 75—of the world's energy and resource consumption and create the bulk of industrial, toxic, and consumer waste. The developed economies thus leave large ecological footprints—defined as the amount of land required to meet a typical consumer's needs. (See the exhibit "Ecological Footprints.")

Despite such intense use of energy and materials, however, levels of pollution are relatively low in the developed economies. Three factors account for this seeming paradox: stringent environmental regulations, the greening of industry, and the relocation of the most polluting activities (such as commodity processing and heavy manufacturing) to the emerging market economies. Thus to some extent the greening of the developed world has been at the expense of the environments in emerging economies. Given the much larger population base in those countries, their rapid industrialization could easily offset the environmental gains made in the developed economies. Consider, for example, that the emerging economies in Asia and Latin America (and now Eastern Europe and the former Soviet Union) have added nearly 2 billion people to the market economy over the past 40 years.

With economic growth comes urbanization. Today one of every three people in the world lives in a city. By 2025, it will be two out of three. Demographers predict that by that year there will be well over 30 megacities with populations exceeding 8 million and more than 500 cities with populations exceeding 1 million. Urbanization on this scale presents enormous infrastructural and environmental challenges.

Because industrialization has focused initially on commodities and heavy manufacturing, cities in many emerging economies suffer from oppressive levels of pollution. Acid rain is a growing problem, especially in places where coal combustion is unregulated. The World Bank estimates that by 2010 there will be more than 1 billion motor vehicles in the world. Concentrated in cities, they will double current levels of energy use, smog precursors, and emissions of greenhouse gas.

The second economy is the survival economy: the traditional, village-based way of life found in the rural parts of most developing countries. It is made up of 3 billion people, mainly Africans, Indians, and Chinese who are subsistence oriented and meet their basic needs directly from nature. Demographers generally agree that the world's population, currently growing by about 90 million people per year, will roughly double over the next 40 years. The developing nations will account for 90% of that growth, and most of it will occur in the survival economy.

Owing in part to the rapid expansion of the market economy, existence in the survival economy is becoming increasingly precarious. Extractive industries and infrastructure development have, in many cases, degraded the ecosystems upon which the survival economy depends. Rural populations are driven further into poverty as they compete for scarce natural resources. Women and children now spend on average four to six hours per day searching for fuelwood and four to six hours per week drawing and carrying water. Ironically, those conditions encourage high fertility rates because, in the short run, children help the family to garner needed resources. But in the long run, population growth in the survival economy only reinforces a vicious cycle of resource depletion and poverty.

Short-term survival pressures often force these rapidly growing rural populations into practices that cause long-term damage to forests, soil, and water. When wood becomes scarce, people burn dung for fuel, one of the greatest—and least well-known—environmental hazards in the world today. Contaminated drinking water is an equally grave problem. The World Health Organization estimates that burning dung and drinking contaminated water together cause 8 million deaths per year.

As it becomes more and more difficult to live off the land, millions of desperate people migrate to already overcrowded cities. In China, for example, an estimated 120 million people now roam from city to city, landless and jobless, driven from their villages by deforestation, soil erosion, floods, or droughts. Worldwide, the number of such "environmental refugees" from the survival economy may be as high as 500 million people, and the figure is growing.

The third economy is nature's economy, which consists of the natural systems and resources that support the market and the survival economies. Nonrenewable resources, such as oil, metals, and other minerals, are finite. Renewable resources, such as soils and forests, will replenish themselves—as long as their use does not exceed critical thresholds.

Technological innovations have created substitutes for many commonly used nonrenewable resources; for example, optical fiber now replaces copper wire. And in the developed economies, demand for some virgin materials may actually diminish in the decades ahead because of reuse and recycling. Ironically, the greatest threat to sustainable development today is depletion of the world's renewable resources.

Forests, soils, water, and fisheries are all being pushed beyond their limits by human population growth and rapid industrial development. Insufficient fresh water may prove to be the most vexing problem in the developing world over the next decade, as agricultural, commercial, and residential uses increase. Water tables are being drawn down at an alarming rate, especially in the most heavily populated nations, such as China and India.

Soil is another resource at risk. More than 10% of the world's topsoil has been seriously eroded. Available cropland and rangeland are shrinking. Existing crop varieties are no longer responding to increased use of fertilizer. As a consequence, per capita world production of both grain and meat peaked and began to decline during the 1980s. Meanwhile, the world's 18 major oceanic fisheries have now reached or actually exceeded their maximum sustainable yields.

By some estimates, humankind now uses more than 40% of the planet's net primary productivity. If, as projected, the population doubles over the next 40 years, we may outcompete most other animal species for food, driving many to extinction. In short, human activity now exceeds sustainability on a global scale. (See the exhibit "Major Challenges to Sustainability.")

As we approach the twenty-first century, the interdependence of the three economic spheres is increasingly evident. In fact, the three economies have become worlds in collision, creating the major social and environmental challenges facing the planet: climate change, pollution, resource depletion, poverty, and inequality.

Consider, for example, that the average American today consumes 17 times more than his or her Mexican counterpart (emerging economy) and hundreds of times more than the average Ethiopian (survival economy). The levels of material and energy consumption in the United States require large quantities of raw materials and commodities, sourced increasingly from the survival economy and produced in emerging economies.

In the survival economy, massive infrastructure development (for example, dams, irrigation projects, highways, mining operations, and power generation projects), often aided by agencies, banks, and corporations in the developed countries, has provided access to raw materials. Unfortunately, such development has often had devastating consequences for nature's economy and has tended to strengthen existing political and economic elites, with little benefit to those in the survival economy.

At the same time, infrastructure development projects have contributed to a global glut of raw materials and hence to a long-term fall in commodity prices. And as commodity prices have fallen relative to the prices of manufactured goods, the currencies of developing countries have weakened and their terms of trade have become less favorable. Their purchasing power declines while their already substantial debt load becomes even larger. The net effect of this dynamic has been the transfer of vast amounts of wealth (estimated at $40 billion per year since 1985) from developing to developed countries, producing a vicious cycle of resource exploitation and pollution to service mounting debt. Today developing nations have a combined debt of more than $1.2 trillion, equal to nearly half of their collective gross national product.

STRATEGIES FOR A SUSTAINABLE WORLD

Nearly three decades ago, environmentalists such as Paul Ehrlich and Barry Commoner made this simple but powerful observation about sustainable development: the total environmental burden (EB) created by human activity is a function of three factors. They are population (P); affluence (A), which is a proxy for consumption; and technology (T), which is how wealth is created. The product of these three factors determines the total environmental burden. It can be expressed as a formula: $EB = P \times A \times T$.

Achieving sustainability will require stabilizing or reducing the environmental burden. That can be done by decreasing the human population, lowering the level of affluence (consumption), or changing fundamentally the technology used to create wealth. The first option, lowering the human population, does not appear feasible short of draconian political measures or the occurrence of a major public-health crisis that causes mass mortality.

The second option, decreasing the level of affluence, would only make the problem worse, because poverty and population growth go hand in hand: demographers have long known that birth rates are inversely correlated with level of education and standard of living. Thus stabilizing the human population will require improving the education and economic standing of the world's poor, particularly women of childbearing age. That can be accomplished only by creating wealth on a massive scale. Indeed, it may be necessary to grow the world economy as much as tenfold just to provide basic amenities to a population of 8 billion to 10 billion.

That leaves the third option: changing the technology used to create the goods and services that constitute the world's wealth. Although population and consumption may be societal issues, technology is the business of business.

If economic activity must increase tenfold over what it is today just to provide the bare essentials to a population double its current size, then technology will have to improve twenty-fold merely to keep the planet at its current levels of environmental burden. Those who believe that ecological disaster will somehow be averted must also appreciate the commercial implications of such a belief: over the next decade or so, sustainable development will constitute one of the biggest opportunities in the history of commerce.

Nevertheless, as of today few companies have incorporated sustainability into their strategic thinking. Instead, environmental strategy consists largely of piecemeal projects aimed at controlling or preventing pollution. Focusing on sustainability requires putting business strategies to a new test. Taking the entire planet as the context in which they do business, companies must ask whether they are part of the solution to social and environmental problems or part of the problem. Only when a company thinks in those terms can it begin to develop a vision of sustainability—a shaping logic that goes beyond today's internal, operational focus on greening to a more external, strategic focus on sustainable development. Such a vision is needed to guide companies through three stages of environmental strategy.

Stage One: Pollution Prevention

The first step for most companies is to make the shift from pollution control to pollution prevention. Pollution control means cleaning up waste after it has been created. Pollution prevention focuses on minimizing or eliminating waste before it is created. Much like total quality management, pollution prevention strategies depend on continuous improvement efforts to reduce waste and energy use. This transformation is driven by a compelling logic: pollution prevention pays. Emerging global standards for environmental management systems (ISO 14,000, for example) also have created strong incentives for companies to develop such capabilities.

Over the past decade, companies have sought to avoid colliding with nature's economy (and incurring the associated added costs) through greening and prevention strategies. Aeroquip Corporation, a $2.5 billion manufacturer of hoses, fittings, and couplings, saw an opportunity here. Like most industrial suppliers, Aeroquip never thought of itself as a provider of environmental solutions. But in 1990, its executives realized that the company's product might be especially valuable in meeting the need to reduce waste and prevent pollution. Aeroquip has generated a $250 million business by focusing its attention on developing products that reduce emissions. As companies in emerging economies realize the competitive benefits of using raw materials and resources more productively, businesses like Aeroquip's will continue to grow.

The emerging economies cannot afford to repeat all the environmental mistakes of Western development. With the sustainability imperative in mind, BASF, the German chemical giant, is helping to design and build chemical industries in China, India, Indonesia, and Malaysia that are less polluting than in the past. By colocating facilities that in the West have been geographically dispersed, BASF is able to create industrial ecosystems in which the waste from one process becomes the raw material for another. Colocation solves a problem common in the West, where recycling waste is often infeasible because transporting it from one site to another is dangerous and costly.

Stage Two: Product Stewardship

Product stewardship focuses on minimizing not only pollution from manufacturing but also all environmental impacts associated with the full life cycle of a product. As companies in stage one move closer to zero emissions, reducing the use of materials and production of waste requires fundamental changes in underlying product and process design.

Design for environment (DFE), a tool for creating products that are easier to recover, reuse, or recycle, is becoming increasingly important. With DFE, all the effects that a product could have on the environment are examined during its design phase. Cradle-to-grave analysis begins and ends outside the boundaries of a company's operations—it includes a full assessment of all inputs to the product and examines how customers use and dispose of it. DFE thus captures a broad range of external perspectives by including technical staff, environmental experts, end customers, and even community representatives in the process. Dow Chemical Company has pioneered the use of a board-level advisory panel of environmental experts and external representatives to aid its product-stewardship efforts.

By reducing materials and energy consumption, DFE can be highly profitable. Consider Xerox Corporation's Asset Recycle Management (ARM) program, which uses leased Xerox copiers as sources of high-quality, low-cost parts and components for new machines. A well-developed infrastructure for taking back leased copiers combined with a sophisticated remanufacturing process allows parts and components to be reconditioned, tested, and then reassembled into "new" machines. Xerox estimates that ARM savings in raw materials, labor, and waste disposal in 1995 alone were in the $300-million to $400-million range. In taking recycling to this level, Xerox has reconceptualized its business. By redefining the product-in-use as part of the company's asset base,

Xerox has discovered a way to add value and lower costs. It can continually provide its lease customers with the latest product upgrades, giving them state-of-the-art functionality with minimal environmental impact.

Product stewardship is thus one way to reduce consumption in the developed economies. It may also aid the quest for sustainability because developing nations often try to emulate what they see happening in the developed nations. Properly executed, product stewardship also offers the potential for revenue growth through product differentiation. For example, Dunlop Tire Corporation and Akzo Nobel recently announced a new radial tire that makes use of an aramid fiber belt rather than the conventional steel belt. The new design makes recycling easier because it eliminates the expensive cryogenic crushing required to separate the steel belts from the tire's other materials. Because the new fiber-belt tire is 30% lighter, it dramatically improves gas mileage. Moreover, it is a safer tire because it improves the traction control of antilock braking systems.

The evolution from pollution prevention to product stewardship is now happening in multinational companies such as Dow, DuPont, Monsanto, Xerox, ABB, Philips, and Sony. For example, as part of a larger sustainability strategy dubbed A Growing Partnership with Nature, DuPont's agricultural-products business developed a new type of herbicide that has helped farmers around the world reduce their annual use of chemicals by more than 45 million pounds. The new Sulfonylurea herbicides have also led to a 1-billion-pound reduction in the amount of chemical waste produced in the manufacture of agricultural chemicals. These herbicides are effective at 1% to 5% of the application rates of traditional chemicals, are nontoxic to animals and nontarget species, and biodegrade in the soil, leaving virtually no residue on crops. Because they require so much less material in their manufacture, they are also highly profitable.

Stage Three: Clean Technology

Companies with their eye on the future can begin to plan for and invest in tomorrow's technologies. The simple fact is that the existing technology base in many industries is not environmentally sustainable. The chemical industry, for example, while having made substantial headway over the past decade in pollution prevention and product stewardship, is still limited by its dependence on the chlorine molecule. (Many organochlorides are toxic or persistent or bioaccumulative.) As long as the industry relies on its historical competencies in chlorine chemistry, it will have trouble making major progress toward sustainability.

Monsanto is one company that is consciously developing new competencies. It is shifting the technology base for its agriculture business from bulk chemicals to biotechnology. It is betting that the bioengineering of crops rather than the application of chemical pesticides or fertilizers represents a sustainable path to increased agricultural yields. (See "Growth Through Global Sustainability: An Interview with Monsanto's CEO, Robert B. Shapiro," by Joan Magretta.)

Clean technologies are desperately needed in the emerging economies of Asia. Urban pollution there has reached oppressive levels. But precisely because manufacturing growth is so high—capital stock doubles every six years—there is an unprecedented opportunity to replace current product and process technologies with new, cleaner ones.

Japan's Research Institute for Innovative Technology for the Earth is one of several new research and technology consortia focusing on the development and commercialization of clean technologies for the developing world. Having been provided with funding and staff by the Japanese government and more than 40 corporations, RITE has set forth an ambitious 100-year plan to create the next generation of power technology, which will eliminate or neutralize greenhouse gas emissions.

SUSTAINABILITY VISION

Pollution prevention, product stewardship, and clean technology all move a company toward sustainability. But without a framework to give direction to those activities, their impact will dissipate. A vision of sustainability for an industry or a company is like a road map to the future, showing the way products and services must evolve and what new competencies will be needed to get there. Few companies today have such a road map. Ironically, chemical companies, regarded only a decade ago as the worst environmental villains, are among the few large corporations to have engaged the challenge of sustainable development seriously.

Companies can begin by taking stock of each component of what I call their sustainability portfolio. (See the exhibit "The Sustainability Portfolio.") Is there an overarching vision of sustainability that gives direction to the company's activities? To what extent has the company progressed through the three stages of environmental strategy—from pollution prevention to product stewardship to clean technology?

Consider the auto industry. During the 1970s, government regulation of tailpipe emissions forced the industry to focus on pollution control. In the 1980s, the industry began to tackle pollution prevention. Initiatives such as the Corporate Average Fuel Efficiency requirement and the Toxic Release Inventory led auto companies to examine their product designs and manufacturing processes in order to improve fuel economy and lower emissions from their plants.

The 1990s are witnessing the first signs of product stewardship. In Germany, the 1990 "take-back" law required auto manufacturers to take responsibility for their vehicles at the end of their useful lives. Innovators such as BMW have influenced the design of new cars with their design for disassembly efforts. Industry-level consortia such as the Partnership for a New Generation of Vehicles are driven largely by the product stewardship logic of lowering the environmental impact of automobiles throughout their life cycle.

Early attempts to promote clean technology include such initiatives as California's zero-emission vehicle law and the U.N. Climate Change Convention, which ultimately will limit greenhouse gases on a global scale. But early efforts by industry incumbents have been either incremental—for example, natural-gas vehicles—or defensive in nature. Electric-vehicle programs, for instance, have been used to demonstrate the infeasibility of this technology rather than to lead the industry to a fundamentally cleaner technology.

Although the auto industry has made progress, it falls far short of sustainability. For the vast majority of auto companies, pollution prevention and product stewardship are the end of the road. Most auto executives assume that if they close the loop in both production and design, they will have accomplished all the necessary environmental objectives.

But step back and try to imagine a sustainable vision for the industry. Growth in the emerging markets will generate massive transportation needs in the coming decades. Already the rush is on to stake out positions in China, India, and Latin America. But what form will this opportunity take?

Consider the potential impact of automobiles on China alone. Today there are fewer than 1 million cars on the road in China. However, with a population of more than 1 billion, it would take less than 30% market penetration to equal the current size of the U.S. car market (12 million to 15 million units sold per year). Ultimately, China might demand 50 million or more units annually. Because China's energy and transportation infrastructures are still being defined, there is an opportunity to develop a clean technology yielding important environmental and competitive benefits.

Amory Lovins of the Rocky Mountain Institute has demonstrated the feasibility of building hypercars—vehicles that are fully recyclable, 20 times more energy efficient, 100 times cleaner, and cheaper than existing cars. These vehicles retain the safety and performance of conventional cars but achieve radical simplification through the use of lightweight, composite materials, fewer parts, virtual prototyping, regenerative braking, and very small, hybrid engines. Hypercars, which are more akin to computers on wheels than to cars with microchips, may render obsolete most of the competencies associated with today's auto manufacturing—for example, metal stamping, tool and die making, and the internal combustion engine.

Assume for a minute that clean technology like the hypercar or Mazda's soon-to-be-released hydrogen rotary engine can be developed for a market such as China's. Now try to envision a transportation infrastructure capable of accommodating so many cars. How long will it take before gridlock and traffic jams force the auto industry to a halt? Sustainability will require new transportation solutions for the needs of emerging economies with huge populations. Will the giants in the auto industry be prepared for such radical change, or will they leave the field to new ventures that are not encumbered by the competencies of the past?

A clear and fully integrated environmental strategy should not only guide competency development, it should also shape the company's relationship to customers, suppliers, other companies, policymakers, and all its stakeholders. Companies can and must change the way customers think by creating preferences for products and services consistent with sustainability. Companies must become educators rather than mere marketers of products. (See the exhibit "Building Sustainable Business Strategies.")

For senior executives, embracing the quest for sustainability may well require a leap of faith. Some may feel that the risks associated with investing in unstable and unfamiliar markets outweigh the potential benefits. Others will recognize the power of such a positive mission to galvanize people in their organizations.

Regardless of their opinions on sustainability, executives will not be able to keep their heads in the sand for long. Since 1980, foreign direct investment by multinational corporations has increased from $500 billion to nearly $3 trillion per year. In fact, it now exceeds official development-assistance aid in developing countries. With free trade on the rise, the next decade may see the figure increase by another order of magnitude. The challenges presented by emerging markets in Asia and Latin America demand a new way of conceptualizing business opportunities. The rapid growth in emerging economies cannot be sustained in the face of mounting environmental deterioration, poverty, and resource depletion. In the coming decade, companies will be challenged to develop clean technologies and to implement strategies that drastically reduce the environmental burden in the developing world while simultaneously increasing its wealth and standard of living.

Like it or not, the responsibility for ensuring a sustainable world falls largely on the shoulders of the world's enterprises, the economic engines of the future. Clearly, public policy innovations (at both the national and international levels) and changes in individual consumption patterns will be needed to move toward sustainability. But corporations can and should lead the way, helping to shape public policy and driving change in consumers' behavior. In the final analysis, it makes good business sense to pursue strategies for a sustainable world.

Related Article: Ecological Footprints

In the United States, it takes 12.2 acres to supply the average person's basic needs; in the Netherlands, 8 acres; in India, 1 acre. The Dutch ecological footprint covers 15 times the area of the Netherlands, whereas India's footprint exceeds its area by only about 35%. Most strikingly, if the entire would lived like North Americans, it would take three planet Earths to support the present world population.

Related Article: Major Challenges to Sustainability

	Pollution	Depletion	Poverty
Developed economies	greenhouse gases use of toxic materials contaminated sites	scarcity of materials insufficient reuse and recycling	urban and minority unemployment
Emerging economies	industrial emissions contaminated water lack of sewage treatment	overexploitation of renewable resources overuse of water for irrigation	migration to cities lack of skilled workers income inequality
Survival economies	dung and wood burning lack of sanitation ecosystem destruction due to development	deforestation overgrazing soil loss	population growth low status of women dislocation

Related Article: Aracruz Celulose: A Strategy for the Survival Economy

"Poverty is one of the world's leading polluters," notes Erling Lorentzen, founder and chairman of Aracruz: Celulose. The $2 billion Brazilian company is the world's largest producer of eucalyptus pulp. "You can't expect people who don't eat a proper meal to be concerned about the environment."[2] From the very start, Aracruz has been built around a vision of sustainable development. Lorentzen understood that building a viable forest-products business in Brazil's impoverished and deforested state of Espirito Santo would require the simultaneous improvement of nature's economy and the survival economy.

First, to restore nature's economy, the company took advantage of a tax incentive for tree planting in the late 1960s and began buying and reforesting cut-over land. By 1992, the company had acquired over 200,000 hectares and planted 130,000 hectares with managed eucalyptus; the rest was restored as conservation land. By reforesting what had become highly degraded land, unsuitable for agriculture, the company addressed a fundamental environmental problem. At the same time, it created a first-rate source of fiber for its pulping operations. Aracruz's forest practices and its ability to clone seedlings have given the company advantages in both cost and quality.

Aracruz has tackled the problem of poverty head-on. Every year, the company gives away millions of eucalyptus seedlings to local farmers. It is a preemptive strategy, aimed at reducing the farmers' need to deplete the natural forests for fuel or lumber. Aracruz also has a long-term commitment to capability building. In the early years, Aracruz was able to hire local people for very low wages because of their desperate situation. But instead of simply exploiting the abundant supply of cheap labor, the company embarked on an aggressive social-investment strategy, spending $125 million to support the creation of hospitals, schools, housing, and a training center for employees. In fact, until recently, Aracruz spent more on its social investments than it did on wages (about $1.20 for every $1 in wages). Since that time, the standard of living has improved dramatically, as has productivity. The company no longer needs to invest so heavily in social infrastructure.

Related Article: The Sustainability Portfolio

Clean technology

TOMORROW: Is the environmental performance of our products limited by our existing competency base?

Pollution prevention

TODAY: Where are the most significant waste and emissions streams from our current operations?

INTERNAL: Can we lower costs and risks by eliminating waste at the source or by using it as useful input?

This simple diagnostic tool can help any company determine whether its strategy is consistent with sustainability. First, assess your company's capability in each of the four quadrants by answering the questions in each box. Then rate yourself on the following scale for each quadrant: 1—nonexistent; 2—emerging; 3—established; or 4—institutionalized.

Most companies will be heavily skewed toward the lower left-hand quadrant, reflecting investment in pollution prevention. However, without investments in future technologies and markets (the upper half of the portfolio), the company's environmental strategy will not meet evolving needs.

Sustainability vision

TOMORROW: Does our corporate vision direct us toward the solution of social and environmental problems?

TODAY: Does our vision guide the development of new technologies, markets, products, and processes?

Product stewardship

What are the implications for product design and development if we assume responsibility for a product's entire life cycle?

EXTERNAL: Can we add value or lower costs while simultaneously reducing the impact or our products?

Unbalanced portfolios spell trouble: a bottom-heavy portfolio suggests a good position today but future vulnerability. A top-heavy portfolio indicates a vision of sustainability without the operational or analytical skills needed to implement it. A portfolio skewed to the left side of the chart indicates a preoccupation with handling the environmental challenge through internal process improvements and technology-development iniatives. Finally, a portfolio skewed to the right side, although highly open and public, runs the risk of being labeled a "greenwash" because the underlying plant operations and core technology still cause significant environmental harm.

Related Article: Building Sustainable Business Strategies

Stuart L. Hart is a faculty member in corporate strategy and the director of the Corporate Environmental Management Program at the University of Michigan Business School in Ann Arbor. His E-mail address is slhart@umich.edu.

NOTES

1. The terms market economy, survival economy, and nature's economy were suggested to me by Vandana Shiva, *Ecology and the Politics of Survival* (New Delhi: United Nations University Press, 1991).
2. Marguerite Rigoglioso, "Stewards of the Seventh Generation," *Harvard Business School Bulletin*, April 1996, p. 55.

A ROAD MAP FOR NATURAL CAPITALISM

Business strategies built around the radically more productive use of natural resources can solve many environmental problems at a profit.

BY AMORY B. LOVINS, L. HUNTER LOVINS, AND PAUL HAWKEN

On September 16, 1991, a small group of scientists was sealed inside Biosphere II, a glittering 3.2-acre glass and metal dome in Oracle, Arizona. Two years later, when the radical attempt to replicate the earth's main ecosystems in miniature ended, the engineered environment was dying. The gaunt researchers had survived only because fresh air had been pumped in. Despite $200 million worth of elaborate equipment, Biosphere II had failed to generate breathable air, drinkable water, and adequate food for just eight people. Yet Biosphere I, the planet we all inhabit, effortlessly performs those tasks every day for 6 billion of us.

Disturbingly, Biosphere I is now itself at risk. The earth's ability to sustain life, and therefore economic activity, is threatened by the way we extract, process, transport, and dispose of a vast flow of resources – some 220 billion tons a year, or more than 20 times the average American's body weight every day. With dangerously narrow focus, our industries look only at the exploitable resources of the earth's ecosystems – its oceans, forests, and plains – and not at the larger services that those systems provide for free. Resources and ecosystem services both come from the earth – even from the same biological systems – but they're two different things. Forests, for instance, not only produce the resource of wood fiber but also provide such ecosystem services as water storage, habitat, and regulation of the atmosphere and climate. Yet companies that earn income from harvesting the wood fiber resource often do so in ways that damage the forest's ability to carry out its other vital tasks.

Unfortunately, the cost of destroying ecosystem services becomes apparent only when the services start to break down. In China's Yangtze basin in 1998, for example, deforestation triggered flooding that killed 3,700 people, dislocated 223 million, and inundated 60 million acres of cropland. That $30 billion disaster forced a logging moratorium and a $12 billion crash program of reforestation.

The reason companies (and governments) are so prodigal with ecosystem services is that the value of those services doesn't appear on the business balance sheet. But that's a staggering omission. The economy, after all, is embedded in the environment. Recent calculations published in the journal *Nature* conservatively estimate the value of all the earth's ecosystem services to be at least $33 trillion a year. That's close to the gross world product, and it implies a capitalized book value on the order of half a quadrillion dollars. What's more, for most of these services, there is no known substitute at any price, and we can't live without them.

Some very simple changes to the way we run our businesses can yield startling benefits for today's shareholders and for future generations.

This article puts forward a new approach not only for protecting the biosphere but also for improving profits and competitiveness. Some very simple changes to the way we run our businesses, built on advanced techniques for making resources more productive, can yield startling benefits both for today's shareholders and for future generations.

This approach is called *natural capitalism* because it's what capitalism might become if its largest category of capital – the "natural capital" of ecosystem services – were properly valued. The journey to natural capitalism involves four major shifts in business practices, all vitally interlinked:

- **Dramatically increase the productivity of natural resources.** Reducing the wasteful and destructive flow of resources from depletion to pollution represents a major business opportunity. Through fundamental changes in both production design and technology, farsighted companies are developing ways to make natural resources – energy, minerals, water, forests – stretch 5, 10, even 100 times further than they do today. These major resource savings often yield higher profits than small resource savings do – or even saving no resources at all would – and not only pay for themselves over time but in many cases reduce initial capital investments.
- **Shift to biologically inspired production models.** Natural capitalism seeks not merely to reduce waste but to eliminate the very concept of waste. In closed-loop production systems, modeled on nature's designs, every output either is returned harmlessly to the ecosystem as a nutrient, like compost, or becomes an input for manufacturing another product. Such systems can often be designed to eliminate the use of toxic materials, which can hamper nature's ability to reprocess materials.
- **Move to a solutions-based business model.** The business model of traditional manufacturing rests on the sale of goods. In the new model, value is instead delivered as a flow of services – providing illumination, for example, rather than selling lightbulbs. This model entails a new perception of value,

A MacArthur Fellow, ***Amory B. Lovins*** *is the research director and CFO of Rocky Mountain Institute (RMI).*

L. Hunter Lovins *is the CEO of RMI, the nonprofit resource policy center they cofounded in 1982 in Snowmass, Colorado (http://www.rmi.org).*

Paul Hawken *is the founder of the Smith & Hawken retail and catalog company, cofounder of the knowledge-management software company Datafusion, and author of* Growing a Business *(Simon & Schuster, 1983) and* The Ecology of Commerce *(Harper Collins, 1993).*

Hawken and the Lovinses consult for businesses worldwide and have coauthored the forthcoming Natural Capitalism *(Little Brown, September 1999).*

a move from the acquisition of goods as a measure of affluence to one where well being is measured by the continuous satisfaction of changing expectations for quality, utility, and performance. The new relationship aligns the interests of providers and customers in ways that reward them for implementing the first two innovations of natural capitalism – resource productivity and closed-loop manufacturing.

- **Reinvest in natural capital.** Ultimately, business must restore, sustain, and expand the planet's ecosystems so that they can produce their vital services and biological resources even more abundantly. Pressures to do so are mounting as human needs expand, the costs engendered by deteriorating ecosystems rise, and the environmental awareness of consumers increases. Fortunately, these pressures all create business value.

Natural capitalism is not motivated by a current scarcity of natural resources. Indeed, although many biological resources, like fish, are becoming scarce, most mined resources, such as copper and oil, seem ever more abundant. Indices of average commodity prices are at 28-year lows, thanks partly to powerful extractive technologies, which are often subsidized and whose damage to natural capital remains unaccounted for. Yet even despite these artificially low prices, using resources manyfold more productively can now be so profitable that pioneering companies – large and small – have already embarked on the journey toward natural capitalism.[1]

Still the question arises – if large resource savings are available and profitable, why haven't they all been captured already? The answer is simple: scores of common practices in both the private and public sectors systematically reward companies for wasting natural resources and penalize them for boosting resource productivity. For example, most companies expense their consumption of raw materials through the income statement but pass resource-saving investment through the balance sheet. That distortion makes it more tax efficient to waste fuel than to invest in improving fuel efficiency. In short, even though the road seems clear, the compass that companies use to direct their journey is broken. Later we'll look in more detail at some of the obstacles to resource productivity – and some of the important business opportunities they reveal. But first, let's map the route toward natural capitalism.

Saving a large fraction of resources can actually cost less than saving a small fraction of resources. This is the concept of expanding returns.

Dramatically Increase the Productivity of Natural Resources

In the first stage of a company's journey toward natural capitalism, it strives to wring out the waste of energy, water, materials, and other resources throughout its production systems and other operations. There are two main ways companies can do this at a profit. First, they can adopt a fresh approach to design that considers industrial systems as a whole rather than part by part. Second, companies can replace old industrial technologies with new ones, particularly with those based on natural processes and materials.

Implementing Whole-System Design. Inventor Edwin Land once remarked that "people who seem to have had a new idea have often simply stopped having an old idea." This is particularly true when designing for resource savings. The old idea is one of diminishing returns – the greater the resource saving, the higher the cost. But that old idea is giving way to the new idea that bigger savings can cost less – that saving a large fraction of resources can actually cost less than saving a small fraction of resources. This is the concept of expanding returns, and it governs much of the revolutionary thinking behind whole-system design. Lean manufacturing is an example of whole-system thinking that has helped many companies dramatically reduce such forms of waste as lead times, defect rates, and inventory. Applying whole-system thinking to the productivity of natural resources can achieve even more.

Consider Interface Corporation, a leading maker of materials for commercial interiors. In its new Shanghai carpet factory, a liquid had to be circulated through a standard pumping loop similar to those used in nearly all industries. A top European company designed the system to use pumps requiring a total of 95 horsepower. But before construction began, Interface's engineer, Jan Schilham, realized that two embarrassingly simple design changes would cut that power requirement to only 7 horsepower – a 92% reduction. His redesigned system cost less to build, involved no new technology, and worked better in all respects.

What two design changes achieved this 12-fold saving in pumping power? First, Schilham chose fatter-than-usual pipes, which create much less friction than thin pipes do and therefore need far less pumping energy. The original designer had chosen thin pipes because, according to the textbook method, the extra cost of fatter ones wouldn't be justified by the pumping energy that they would save. This standard design trade-off optimizes the pipes by themselves but "pessimizes" the larger system. Schilham optimized the *whole* system by counting not only the higher capital cost of the fatter pipes but also the *lower* capital cost of the smaller pumping equipment that would be needed. The pumps, motors, motor controls, and electrical components could all be much smaller because there'd be less friction to overcome. Capital cost would fall far more for the smaller equipment than it would rise for the fatter pipe. Choosing big pipes and small pumps – rather than small pipes and big pumps – would therefore make the whole system cost less to build, even before counting its future energy savings.

Interface's engineer realized that two embarrassingly simple design changes would cut power requirements by 92%.

Schilham's second innovation was to reduce the friction even more by making the pipes short and straight rather than long and crooked. He did this by laying out the pipes first, *then* positioning the various tanks, boilers, and other equipment that they connected. Designers normally locate the production equipment in arbitrary positions and then have a pipe fitter connect everything. Awkward placement forces the pipes to make numerous bends that greatly increase friction. The pipe fitters don't mind: they're paid by the hour, they profit from the extra pipes and fittings, and they don't pay for the oversized pumps or inflated electric bills. In addition to reducing those four kinds of costs, Schilham's short, straight pipes were easier to insulate, saving an extra 70 kilowatts of heat loss and repaying the insulation's cost in three months.

This small example has big implications for two reasons. First, pumping is the largest application of motors, and motors use three-quarters of all industrial electricity. Second, the lessons are very widely relevant. Interface's pumping loop shows how simple changes in design mentality can yield huge resource savings and returns on investment. This isn't rocket science; often it's just a rediscovery of good Victorian engineering principles that have been lost because of specialization.

Whole-system thinking can help managers find small changes that lead to big savings that are cheap, free, or even better than free (because they make the whole system cheaper to build). They can do this because often the right investment in one part of the system can produce multiple benefits throughout the system. For example, companies would gain 18 distinct economic benefits – of which direct energy savings is only one – if they switched from ordinary motors to premium-efficiency motors or from ordinary lighting ballasts (the transformer-like boxes that control fluorescent lamps) to electronic ballasts that automatically dim the lamps to match available daylight. If everyone in America integrated these and other selected technologies into all existing motor and lighting systems in an optimal way, the nation's $220-billion-a-year electric bill would be cut in half. The after-tax return on investing in these changes would in most cases exceed 100% per year.

The profits from saving electricity could be increased even further if companies also incorporated the best off-the-shelf improvements into their building structure and their office, heating, cooling, and other equipment. Overall, such changes could cut national electricity consumption by at least 75% and produce returns of around 100% a year on the investments made. More important, because workers would be more comfortable, better able to see, and less fatigued by noise, their productivity and the quality of their output would rise. Eight recent case studies of people working in well-designed, energy-efficient buildings measured labor productivity gains of 6% to 16%. Since a typical office pays about 100 times as much for people as it does for energy, this increased productivity in people is worth about 6 to 16 times as much as eliminating the entire energy bill.

Energy-saving, productivity-enhancing improvements can often be achieved at even lower cost by piggybacking them onto the periodic renovations that all buildings and factories need. A recent proposal for reallocating the normal 20-year renovation budget for a standard 200,000-square-foot glass-clad office tower near Chicago, Illinois, shows the potential of whole-system design. The proposal suggested replacing the aging glazing system with a new kind of window that lets in nearly six times more daylight than the old sun-blocking glass units. The new windows would reduce the flow of heat and noise four times better than traditional windows do. So even though the glass costs slightly more, the overall cost of the renovation would be reduced because the windows would let in cool, glare-free daylight that, when combined with more efficient lighting and office equipment, would reduce the need for air conditioning by 75%. Installing a fourfold more efficient, but fourfold smaller, air-conditioning system would cost $200,000 less than giving the old system its normal 20-year renovation. The $200,000 saved would, in turn, pay for the extra cost of the new windows and other improvements. This whole-system approach to renovation would not only save 75% of the building's total energy use, it would also greatly improve the building's comfort and marketability. Yet it would cost essentially the same as the normal renovation. There are about 100,000 twenty-year-old glass office towers in the United States that are ripe for such improvement.

Major gains in resource productivity require that the right steps be taken in the right order. Small changes made at the downstream end of a process often create far larger savings further upstream. In almost any industry that uses a pumping system, for example, saving one unit of liquid flow or friction in an exit pipe saves about ten units of fuel, cost, and pollution at the power station.

Of course, the original reduction in flow itself can bring direct benefits, which are often the reason changes are made in the first place. In the 1980s, while California's industry grew 30%, for example, its water use was cut by 30%, largely to avoid increased wastewater fees. But the resulting reduction in pumping energy (and the roughly tenfold larger saving in power-plant fuel and pollution) delivered bonus savings that were at the time largely unanticipated.

To see how downstream cuts in resource consumption can create huge savings upstream, consider how reducing the use of wood fiber disproportionately reduces the pressure to cut down forests. In round numbers, half of all harvested wood fiber is used for such structural products as lumber; the other half is used for paper and cardboard. In both cases, the biggest leverage comes from reducing the amount of the retail product used. If it takes, for example, three pounds of harvested trees to produce one pound of product, then saving one pound of product will save three pounds of trees—plus all the environmental damage avoided by not having to cut them down in the first place.

In an experiment at its Swiss headquarters, Dow Europe cut office paper flow by about 30% in six weeks simply by discouraging unneeded information.

The easiest savings come from not using paper that's unwanted or unneeded. In an experiment at its Swiss headquarters, for example, Dow Europe cut office paper flow by about 30% in six weeks simply by discouraging unneeded information. For instance, mailing lists were eliminated and senders of memos got back receipts indicating whether each recipient had wanted the information. Taking those and other small steps, Dow was also able to increase labor productivity by a similar proportion because people could focus on what they really needed to read. Similarly, Danish hearing-aid maker Oticon saved upwards of 30% of its paper as a by-product of redesigning its business processes to produce better decisions faster. Setting the default on office printers and copiers to double-sided mode reduced AT&T's paper costs by about 15%. Recently developed copiers and printers can even strip off old toner and printer ink, permitting each sheet to be reused about ten times.

Further savings can come from using thinner but stronger and more opaque paper, and from designing packaging more thoughtfully. In a 30-month effort at reducing such waste, Johnson & Johnson saved 2,750 tons of packaging, 1,600 tons of paper, $2.8 million, and at least 330 acres of forest annually. The downstream savings in paper use are multiplied by the savings further upstream, as less need for paper products (or less need for fiber to make each product) translates into less raw paper, less raw paper means less pulp, and less pulp requires fewer trees to be harvested from the forest. Recycling paper and substituting alternative fibers such as wheat straw will save even more.

Comparable savings can be achieved for the wood fiber used in structural products. Pacific Gas and Electric, for example, sponsored an innovative design developed by Davis Energy Group that used engineered wood products to reduce the amount of wood needed in a stud wall for a typical tract house by more than 70%. These walls were stronger, cheaper, more stable, and insulated twice as well. Using them enabled the designers to eliminate heating and cooling equipment in a climate where temperatures range from freezing to 113°F. Eliminating the equipment made the whole house much less expensive both to build and to run while still maintaining high levels of comfort. Taken together, these and many other savings in the paper and construction industries could make our use of wood fiber so much more productive that, in principle, the entire world's present wood fiber needs could probably be met by an intensive tree farm about the size of Iowa.

Adopting Innovative Technologies. Implementing whole-system design goes hand in hand with introducing alternative, environmentally friendly technologies. Many of these are already available and profitable but not widely known. Some, like the "designer catalysts" that are transforming the chemical industry, are already runaway successes. Others are still making their way to market, delayed by cultural rather than by economic or technical barriers.

The automobile industry is particularly ripe for technological change. After a century of development, motorcar technology is showing signs of age. Only 1% of the energy consumed by today's cars is actually used to move the driver: only 15% to 20% of the power generated by burning gasoline reaches the wheels (the rest is lost in the engine and drivetrain) and 95% of the resulting propulsion moves the car, not the driver. The industry's infrastructure is hugely expensive and inefficient. Its convergent products compete for narrow niches in saturated core markets at commoditylike prices. Auto making is capital intensive, and product cycles are long. It is profitable in good years but subject to large losses in bad years. Like the typewriter industry just before the advent of personal computers, it is vulnerable to displacement by something completely different.

Enter the Hypercar. Since 1993, when Rocky Mountain Institute placed this automotive concept in the public domain, several dozen current and potential auto manufacturers have committed billions of dollars to its development and commercialization. The Hypercar integrates the best existing technologies to reduce the consumption of fuel as much as 85% and the amount of materials used up to 90% by introducing four main innovations.

First, making the vehicle out of advanced polymer composites, chiefly carbon fiber, reduces its weight by two-thirds while maintaining crashworthiness. Second, aerodynamic design and better tires reduce air resistance by as much as 70% and rolling resistance by up to 80%. Together, these innovations save about two-thirds of the fuel. Third, 30% to 50% of the remaining fuel is saved by using a "hybrid-electric" drive. In such a system, the wheels are turned by electric motors whose power is made onboard by a small engine or turbine, or even more efficiently by a fuel cell. The fuel cell generates electricity directly by chemically combining stored hydrogen with oxygen, producing pure hot water as its only by-product. Interactions between the small, clean, efficient power source and the ultralight, low-drag auto body then further reduce the weight, cost, and complexity of both. Fourth, much of the traditional hardware – from transmissions and differentials to gauges and certain parts of the suspension – can be replaced by electronics controlled with highly integrated, customizable, and upgradable software.

These technologies make it feasible to manufacture pollution-free, high-performance cars, sport utilities, pickup trucks, and vans that get 80 to 200 miles per gallon (or its energy equivalent in other fuels). These improvements will not require any compromise in quality or utility. Fuel savings will not come from making the vehicles small, sluggish, unsafe, or unaffordable, nor will they depend on government fuel taxes, mandates, or subsidies. Rather, Hypercars will succeed for the same reason that people buy compact discs instead of phonograph records: the CD is a superior product that redefines market expectations. From the manufacturers' perspective, Hypercars will cut cycle times, capital needs, body part counts, and assembly effort and space by as much as tenfold. Early adopters will have a huge competitive advantage – which is why dozens of corporations, including most automakers, are now racing to bring Hypercar-like products to market.[2]

In the long term, the Hypercar will transform industries other than automobiles. It will displace about an eighth of the steel market directly and most of the rest eventually, as carbon fiber becomes far cheaper. Hypercars and their cousins could ultimately save as much oil as OPEC now sells. Indeed, oil may well become uncompetitive as a fuel long before it becomes scarce and costly. Similar challenges face the coal and electricity industries because the development of the Hypercar is likely to accelerate greatly the commercialization of inexpensive hydrogen fuel cells. These fuel cells will help shift power production from centralized coal-fired and nuclear power stations to networks of decentralized, small-scale generators. In fact, fuel-

We could use wood fiber so much more productively that, in principle, the entire world's wood fiber needs could probably be met by an intensive tree farm about the size of Iowa.

cell-powered Hypercars could themselves be part of these networks. They'd be, in effect, 20-kilowatt power plants on wheels. Given that cars are left parked – that is, unused – more than 95% of the time, these Hypercars could be plugged into a grid and could then sell back enough electricity to repay as much as half the predicted cost of leasing them. A national Hypercar fleet could ultimately have five to ten times the generating capacity of the national electric grid.

As radical as it sounds, the Hypercar is not an isolated case. Similar ideas are emerging in such industries as chemicals, semiconductors, general manufacturing, transportation, water and waste-water treatment, agriculture, forestry, energy, real estate, and urban design. For example, the amount of carbon dioxide released for each microchip manufactured can be reduced almost 100-fold through improvements that are now profitable or soon will be.

Some of the most striking developments come from emulating nature's techniques. In her book, *Biomimicry*, Janine Benyus points out that spiders convert digested crickets and flies into silk that's as strong as Kevlar without the need for boiling sulfuric acid and high-temperature extruders. Using no furnaces, abalone can convert seawater into an inner shell twice as tough as our best ceramics. Trees turn sunlight, water, soil, and air into cellulose, a sugar stronger than nylon but one-fourth as dense. They then bind it into wood, a natural composite with a higher bending strength than concrete, aluminum alloy, or steel. We may never become as skillful as spiders, abalone, or trees, but smart designers are already realizing that nature's environmentally benign chemistry offers attractive alternatives to industrial brute force.

Only about 1% of all materials mobilized to serve America is actually made into products and still in use six months after sale.

Whether through better design or through new technologies, reducing waste represents a vast business opportunity. The U.S. economy is not even 10% as energy efficient as the laws of physics allow. Just the energy thrown off as waste heat by U.S. power stations equals the total energy use of Japan. Materials efficiency is even worse: only about 1% of all the materials mobilized to serve America is actually made into products and still in use six months after sale. In every sector, there are opportunities for reducing the amount of resources that go into a production process, the steps required to run that process, and the amount of pollution generated and by-products discarded at the end. These all represent avoidable costs and hence profits to be won.

Redesign Production According to Biological Models

In the second stage on the journey to natural capitalism, companies use closed-loop manufacturing to create new products and processes that can totally prevent waste. This plus more efficient production processes could cut companies' long-term materials requirements by more than 90% in most sectors.

The central principle of closed-loop manufacturing, as architect Paul Bierman-Lytle of the engineering firm CH2M Hill puts it, is "waste equals food." Every output of manufacturing should be either composted into natural nutrients or remanufactured into technical nutrients – that is, it should be returned to the ecosystem or recycled for further production. Closed-loop production systems are designed to eliminate any materials that incur disposal costs, especially toxic ones, because the alternative – isolating them to prevent harm to natural systems – tends to be costly and risky. Indeed, meeting EPA and OSHA standards by eliminating harmful materials often makes a manufacturing process cost less than the hazardous process it replaced. Motorola, for example, formerly used chlorofluorocarbons for cleaning printed circuit boards after soldering. When CFCs were outlawed because they destroy stratospheric ozone, Motorola at first explored such alternatives as orange-peel terpenes. But it turned out to be even cheaper – and to produce a better product – to redesign the whole soldering process so that it needed no cleaning operations or cleaning materials at all.

Closed-loop manufacturing is more than just a theory. The U.S. remanufacturing industry in 1996 reported revenues of \$53 billion – more than consumer-durables manufacturing (appliances; furniture; audio, video, farm, and garden equipment). Xerox, whose bottom line has swelled by \$700 million from remanufacturing, expects to save another \$1 billion just by remanufacturing its new, entirely reusable or recyclable line of "green" photocopiers. What's more, policy makers in some countries are already taking steps to encourage industry to think along these lines. German law, for example, makes many manufacturers responsible for their products forever, and Japan is following suit.

Combining closed loop manufacturing with resource efficiency is especially powerful. DuPont, for example, gets much of its polyester industrial film back from customers after they use it and recycles it into new film. DuPont also makes its polyester film ever stronger and thinner so it uses less material and costs less to make. Yet because the film performs better, customers are willing to pay more for it. As DuPont chairman Jack Krol noted in 1997, "Our ability to continually improve the inherent properties [of our films] enables this process [of developing more productive materials, at lower cost, and higher profits] to go on indefinitely."

Interface is leading the way to this next frontier of industrial ecology. While its competitors are "down cycling" nylon-and-PVC-based carpet into less valuable carpet backing, Interface has invented a new floor-covering material called Solenium, which can be completely remanufactured into identical new product. This fundamental innovation emerged from a clean-sheet redesign. Executives at Interface didn't ask how they could sell more carpet of the familiar kind; they asked how they could create a dream product that would best meet their customers' needs while protecting and nourishing natural capital.

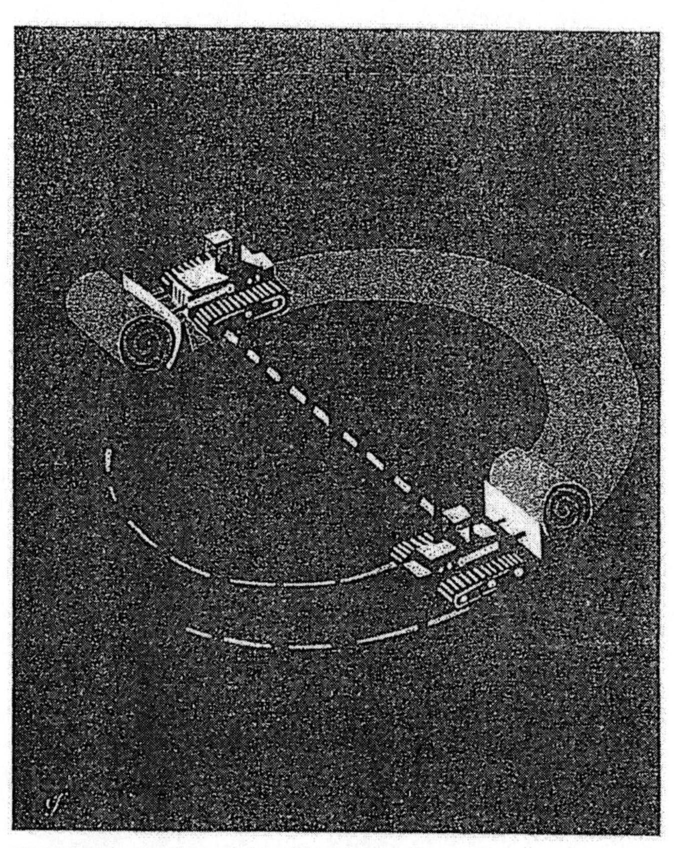

The central principle of closed-loop manufacturing is "waste equals food." *Every* output of manufacturing should either be composted into natural nutrients and returned to the ecosystem or be remanufactured into new products.

Solenium lasts four times longer and uses 40% less material than ordinary carpets – an 86% reduction in materials intensity. What's more, Solenium is free of chlorine and other toxic materials, is virtually stainproof, doesn't grow mildew, can easily be cleaned with water, and offers aesthetic advantages over traditional carpets. It's so superior in every respect that Interface doesn't market it as an environmental product – just a better one.

Solenium is only one part of Interface's drive to eliminate every form of waste. Chairman Ray C. Anderson defines waste as "any measurable input that does not produce customer value," and he considers all inputs to be waste until shown otherwise. Between 1994 and 1998, this zero-waste approach led to a systematic treasure hunt that helped to keep resource inputs constant while revenues rose by $200 million. Indeed, $67 million of the revenue increase can be directly attributed to the company's 60% reduction in landfill waste.

Subsequently, president Charlie Eitel expanded the definition of waste to include all fossil fuel inputs, and now many customers are eager to buy products from the company's recently opened solar-powered carpet factory. Interface's green strategy has not only won plaudits from environmentalists, it has also proved a remarkably successful business strategy. Between 1993 and 1998, revenue has more than doubled, profits have more than tripled, and the number of employees has increased by 73%.

Change the Business Model

In addition to its drive to eliminate waste, Interface has made a fundamental shift in its business model – the third stage on the journey toward natural capitalism. The company has realized that clients want to walk on and look at carpets – but not necessarily to own them. Traditionally, broadloom carpets in office buildings are replaced every decade because some portions look worn out. When that happens, companies suffer the disruption of shutting down their offices and removing their furniture. Billions of pounds of carpets are removed each year and sent to landfills, where they will last up to 20,000 years. To escape this unproductive and wasteful cycle, Interface is transforming itself from a company that sells and fits carpets into one that provides floor-covering services.

Under its Evergreen Lease, Interface no longer sells carpets but rather leases a floor-covering service for a monthly fee, accepting responsibility for keeping the carpet fresh and clean. Monthly inspections detect and replace worn carpet tiles. Since at most 20% of an area typically shows at least 80% of the wear, replacing only the worn parts reduces the consumption of carpeting material by about 80%. It also minimizes the disruption that customers experience – worn tiles are seldom found under furniture. Finally, for the customer, leasing carpets can provide a tax advantage by turning a capital expenditure into a tax-deductible expense. The result: the customer gets cheaper and better services that cost the supplier far less to produce. Indeed, the energy saved from not producing a whole new carpet is in itself enough to produce all the carpeting that the new business model requires. Taken together, the 5-fold savings in carpeting material that Interface achieves through the Evergreen Lease and the 7-fold materials savings achieved through the use of Solenium deliver a stunning 35-fold reduction in the flow of materials needed to sustain a superior floor-covering service. Remanufacturing, and even making carpet initially from renewable materials, can then reduce the extraction of virgin resources essentially to the company's goal of zero.

Interface's shift to a service-leasing business reflects a fundamental change from the basic model of most manufacturing companies, which still look on their businesses as machines for producing and selling products. The more products sold, the better – at least for the company, if not always for the customer or the earth. But any model that wastes natural resources also wastes money. Ultimately, that model will be unable to compete with a service model that emphasizes solving problems and building long-term relationships with customers rather than making and selling products. The shift to what James Womack of the Lean Enterprise Institute calls a "solutions economy" will almost always improve customer value *and* providers' bottom lines because it aligns both parties' interests, offering rewards for doing more and better with less.

Interface is not alone. Elevator giant Schindler, for example, prefers leasing vertical transportation services to selling elevators because leasing lets it capture the savings from its elevators' lower energy and maintenance costs. Dow Chemical and Safety-Kleen prefer leasing dissolving services to selling solvents because they can reuse the same solvent scores of times, reducing costs. United Technologies' Carrier division, the world's largest manufacturer of air conditioners, is shifting its mission from selling air conditioners to leasing comfort. Making its air conditioners more durable and efficient may compromise future equipment sales, but it provides what customers want and will pay for – better comfort at lower cost. But Carrier is going even further. It's starting to team up with other companies to make buildings more efficient so that they need less air-conditioning, or even none at all, to yield the same level of comfort. Carrier will get paid to provide the agreed-upon level of comfort, however that's delivered. Higher profits will come from providing better solutions rather than from selling more equipment. Since comfort with little or no air-conditioning (via better building design) works better and costs less than comfort with copious air-conditioning, Carrier is smart to capture this opportunity itself before its competitors do. As they say at 3M: "We'd rather eat our *own* lunch, thank you."

Elevator giant Schindler prefers leasing vertical transportation services to selling elevators because leasing lets it capture the savings from its elevators' lower energy and maintenance costs.

The shift to a service business model promises benefits not just to participating businesses but to the entire economy as well. Womack points out that by helping customers reduce their need for capital goods such as carpets or elevators, and by rewarding suppliers for extending and maximizing asset values rather than for churning them, adoption of the service model will reduce the volatility in the turnover of capital goods that lies at the heart of the business cycle. That would significantly reduce the overall volatility of the world's economy. At present, the producers of capital goods face feast or famine because the buying decisions of households and corporations are extremely sensitive to fluctuating income. But in a continuous-flow-of-services economy, those swings would be greatly reduced, bringing a welcome stability to businesses. Excess capacity – another form of waste and source of risk – need no longer be retained for meeting peak demand. The result of adopting the new model would be an economy in which we grow and get richer by using less and become stronger by being leaner and more stable.

Reinvest in Natural Capital

The foundation of textbook capitalism is the prudent reinvestment of earnings in productive capital. Natural capitalists who have dramatically raised their resource productivity, closed their loops, and shifted to a solutions-based business model have one key task remaining. They must reinvest in restoring, sustaining, and expanding the most important form of capital – their own natural habitat and biological resource base.

This was not always so important. Until recently, business could ignore damage to the ecosystem because it didn't affect production and didn't increase costs. But that situation is changing. In 1998 alone, violent weather displaced 300 million people and caused upwards of $90 billion worth of damage, representing more weather-related destruction than was reported through the entire decade of the 1980s. The increase in damage is strongly linked to deforestation and climate change, factors that accelerate the frequency and severity of natural disasters and are the consequences of inefficient industrialization. If the flow of services from industrial systems is to be sustained or increased in the future for a growing population, the vital flow of services from living systems will have to be maintained or increased as well. Without reinvestment in natural capital, shortages of ecosystem services are likely to become the limiting factor to prosperity in the next century. When a manufacturer realizes that a supplier of key components is overextended and running behind on deliveries, it takes immediate action lest its own production lines come to a halt. The ecosystem is a supplier of key components for the life of the planet, and it is now falling behind on its orders.

Failure to protect and reinvest in natural capital can also hit a company's revenues indirectly. Many companies are discovering that public perceptions of environmental responsibility, or its lack thereof, affect sales. MacMillan Bloedel, targeted by environmental activists as an emblematic clear-cutter and chlorine user, lost 5% of its sales almost overnight when dropped as a U.K. supplier by Scott Paper and Kimberly-Clark. Numerous case studies show that companies leading the way in implementing changes that help protect the environment tend to gain disproportionate advantage, while companies perceived as irresponsible lose their franchise, their legitimacy, and their shirts. Even businesses that claim to be committed to the concept of sustainable development but whose strategy is seen as mistaken, like Monsanto, are encountering stiffening public resistance to their products. Not surprisingly, University of Oregon business professor Michael Russo, along with many other analysts, has found that a strong environmental rating is "a consistent predictor of profitability."

The pioneering corporations that have made reinvestments in natural capital are starting to see some interesting paybacks. The independent power producer AES, for example, has long pursued a policy of planting trees to offset the carbon emissions of its power plants. That ethical stance, once thought quixotic, now looks like a smart investment because a dozen brokers are now starting to create markets in carbon reduction. Similarly, certification by the Forest Stewardship Council of certain sustainably grown and harvested products has given Collins Pine the extra profit margins that enabled its U.S. manufacturing operations to survive brutal competition. Taking an even longer view, Swiss Re and other European reinsurers are seeking to cut their storm-damage losses by pressing for international public policy to protect the climate and by investing in climate-safe technologies that also promise good profits. Yet most companies still do not realize that a vibrant ecological web underpins their survival and their business success. Enriching natural capital is not just a public good – it is vital to every company's longevity.

It turns out that changing industrial processes so that they actually replenish and magnify the stock of natural capital can prove especially profitable because nature does the production; people need just step back and let life flourish. Industries that directly harvest living resources, such as forestry, farming, and fishing, offer the most suggestive examples. Here are three:

- Allan Savory of the Center for Holistic Management in Albuquerque, New Mexico, has redesigned cattle ranching to raise the carrying capacity of rangelands, which have often been degraded not by overgrazing but by undergrazing and grazing the wrong way. Savory's solution is to keep the cattle moving from place to place, grazing intensively but briefly at each site, so that they mimic the dense but constantly moving herds of native grazing animals that coevolved with grasslands. Thousands of ranchers are estimated to be applying this approach, improving both their range and their profits. This "management-intensive rotational grazing" method, long standard in New Zealand, yields such clearly superior returns that over 15% of Wisconsin's dairy farms have adopted it in the past few years.

- The California Rice Industry Association has discovered that letting nature's diversity flourish can be more profitable than forcing it to produce a single product. By flooding 150,000 to 200,000 acres of Sacramento valley rice fields – about 30% of California's rice-growing area – after harvest, farmers are able to create seasonal wetlands that support millions of wildfowl, replenish groundwater, improve fertility, and yield other valuable benefits. In addition, the farmers bale and sell the rice straw, whose high silica content – formerly an air-pollution hazard when the straw was burned – adds insect resistance and hence value as a construction material when it's resold instead.
- John Todd of Living Technologies in Burlington, Vermont, has used biological Living Machines – linked tanks of bacteria, algae, plants, and other organisms – to turn sewage into clean water. That not only yields cleaner water at a reduced cost, with no toxicity or odor, but it also produces commercially valuable flowers and makes the plant compatible with its residential neighborhood. A similar plant at the Ethel M Chocolates factory in Las Vegas, Nevada, not only handles difficult industrial wastes effectively but is showcased in its public tours.

Although such practices are still evolving, the broad lessons they teach are clear. In almost all climates, soils, and societies, working with nature is more productive than working against it. Reinvesting in nature allows farmers, fishermen, and forest managers to match or exceed the high yields and profits sustained by traditional input-intensive, chemically driven practices. Although much of mainstream business is still headed the other way, the profitability of sustainable, nature-emulating practices is already being proven. In the future, many industries that don't now consider themselves dependent on a biological resource base will become more so as they shift their raw materials and production processes more to biological ones. There is evidence that many business leaders are starting to think this way. The consulting firm Arthur D. Little surveyed a group of North American and European business leaders and found that 83% of them already believe that they can derive "real business value [from implementing a] sustainable-development approach to strategy and operations."

Many executives think they already "did" efficiency in the 1970s, but with today's far better technologies, it's profitable to start over again.

A Broken Compass?

If the road ahead is this clear, why are so many companies straying or falling by the wayside? We believe the reason is that the instruments companies use to set their targets, measure their performance, and hand out rewards are faulty. In other words, the markets are full of distortions and perverse incentives. Of the more than 60 specific forms of misdirection that we have identified,[3] the most obvious involve the ways companies allocate capital and the way governments set policy and impose taxes. Merely correcting these defective practices would uncover huge opportunities for profit.

Consider how companies make purchasing decisions. Decisions to buy small items are typically based on their initial cost rather than their full life-cycle cost, a practice that can add up to major wastage. Distribution transformers that supply electricity to buildings and factories, for example, are a minor item at just $320 apiece, and most companies try to save a quick buck by buying the lowest-price models. Yet nearly all the nation's electricity must flow through transformers, and using the cheaper but less efficient models wastes $1 billion a year. Such examples are legion. Equipping standard new office-lighting circuits with fatter wire that reduces electrical resistance could generate after-tax returns of 193% a year. Instead, wire as thin as the National Electrical Code permits is usually selected because it costs less up-front. But the code is meant only to prevent fires from overheated wiring, not to save money. Ironically, an electrician who chooses fatter wire – thereby reducing long-term electricity bills – doesn't get the job. After paying for the extra copper, he's no longer the low bidder.

Some companies do consider more than just the initial price in their purchasing decisions but still don't go far enough. Most of them use a crude payback estimate rather than more accurate metrics like discounted cash flow. A few years ago, the median simple payback these companies were demanding from energy efficiency was 1.9 years. That's equivalent to requiring an after-tax return of around 71% per year – about six times the marginal cost of capital.

Most companies also miss major opportunities by treating their facilities costs as an overhead to be minimized, typically by laying off engineers, rather than as profit center to be optimized – by using those engineers to save resources. Deficient measurement and accounting practices also prevent companies from allocating costs – and waste – with any accuracy. For example, only a few semiconductor plants worldwide regularly and accurately measure how much energy they're using to produce a unit of chilled water or clean air for their clean-room production facilities. That makes it hard for them to improve efficiency. In fact, in an effort to save time, semiconductor makers frequently build new plants as exact copies of previous ones – a design method nicknamed "infectious repetitis."

In nearly every country on the planet, tax laws penalize jobs and income while subsidizing resource depletion and pollution.

Many executives pay too little attention to saving resources because they are often a small percentage of total costs (energy costs run to about 2% in most industries). But those resource savings drop straight to the bottom line and so represent a far greater percentage of profits. Many executives also think they already "did" efficiency in the 1970s, when the oil shock forced them to rethink old habits. They're forgetting that with today's far better technologies, it's profitable to start all over again. Malden Mills, the Massachusetts maker of such products as Polartec, was already using "efficient" metal-halide lamps in the mid-1990s. But a recent warehouse retrofit reduced the energy used for lighting by another 93%, improved visibility, and paid for itself in 18 months.

The way people are rewarded often creates perverse incentives. Architects and engineers, for example, are traditionally compensated for what they spend, not for what they save. Even the striking economics of the retrofit design for the Chicago office tower described earlier wasn't incentive enough actually to implement it. The property was controlled by a leasing agent who earned a commission every time she leased space, so she didn't want to wait the few extra months needed to refit the building. Her decision to reject the efficiency-quadrupling renovation proved costly for both her and her client. The building was so uncomfortable and expensive to occupy that it didn't lease, so ultimately the owner had to unload it at a firesale price. Moreover, the new owner will for the next 20 years be deprived of the opportunity to save capital cost.

If corporate practices obscure the benefits of natural capitalism, government policy positively undermines it. In nearly every country on the planet, tax laws penalize what we want more of – jobs and income – while subsidizing what we want less of – resource depletion and pollution. In every state but Oregon, regulated utilities are rewarded for selling more energy, water, and other resources, and penalized for selling less, even if increased production would cost more than improved customer efficiency. In most of America's arid western states, use-it-or-lose-it water laws encourage inefficient water consumption. Additionally, in many towns, inefficient use of land is enforced through outdated regulations, such as guidelines for ultrawide suburban streets recommended by 1950s civil-defense planners to accommodate the heavy equipment needed to clear up rubble after a nuclear attack.

The costs of these perverse incentives are staggering: $300 billion in annual energy wasted in the United States, and $1 trillion already misallocated to unnecessary air-conditioning equipment and the power supplies to run it (about 40% of the nation's peak electric load). Across the entire economy, unneeded expenditures to subsidize, encourage, and try to remedy inefficiency and damage that should not have occurred in the first place probably account for most, if not all, of the GDP growth of the past two decades. Indeed, according to former World Bank economist Herman Daly and his colleague John Cobb (along with many other analysts), Americans are hardly better off than they were in 1980. But if the U.S. government and private industry could redirect the dollars currently earmarked for remedial costs toward reinvestment in natural and human capital, they could bring about a genuine improvement in the nation's welfare. Companies, too, are finding that wasting resources also means wasting money and people. These intertwined forms of waste have equally intertwined solutions. Firing the unproductive tons, gallons, and kilowatt-hours often makes it possible to keep the people, who will have more and better work to do.

Recognizing the Scarcity Shift

In the end, the real trouble with our economic compass is that it points in exactly the wrong direction. Most businesses are behaving as if people were still scarce and nature still abundant – the conditions that helped to fuel the first Industrial

Revolution. At that time, people were relatively scarce compared with the present-day population. The rapid mechanization of the textile industries caused explosive economic growth that created labor shortages in the factory and the field. The Industrial Revolution, responding to those shortages and mechanizing one industry after another, made people a hundred times more productive than they had ever been.

The logic of economizing on the scarcest resource, because it limits progress, remains correct. But the pattern of scarcity is shifting: now people aren't scarce but nature is. This shows up first in industries that depend directly on ecological health. Here, production is increasingly constrained by fish rather than by boats and nets, by forests rather than by chain saws, by fertile topsoil rather than by plows. Moreover, unlike the traditional factors of industrial production – capital and labor – the biological limiting factors cannot be substituted for one other. In the industrial system, we can easily exchange machinery for labor. But no technology or amount of money can substitute for a stable climate and a productive biosphere. Even proper pricing can't replace the priceless.

Natural capitalism addresses those problems by reintegrating ecological with economic goals. Because it is both necessary and profitable, it will subsume traditional industrialism within a new economy and a new paradigm of production, just as industrialism previously subsumed agrarianism. The companies that first make the changes we have described will have a competitive edge. Those that don't make that effort won't be a problem because ultimately they won't be around. In making that choice, as Henry Ford said, "Whether you believe you can, or whether you believe you can't, you're absolutely right."

1. Our book, *Natural Capitalism*, provides hundreds of examples of how companies of almost every type and size, often through modest shifts in business logic and practice, have dramatically improved their bottom lines.

2. Nonproprietary details are posted at http://www.hypercar.com.

3. Summarized in the report "Climate: Making Sense *and* Making Money" at http://www.rmi.org/catalog/climate.htm.

Reprint 99309 To place an order, call 1-800-988-0086.

Amory B. Lovins, L. Hunter Lovins and Paul Hawken, *A Road Map for Natural Capitalism,* Harvard Business Review, May-June, 1999, p. 154.

QUESTIONS ON READINGS FOR PART SIX (E) (I)

What environmental challenges do we face today?

What is business' responsibility to address them or liability for not doing so?

What are the key areas of environmental laws and policies?

What is the business case for engaging in green and sustainable practices?

CENTER FOR EDUCATION ON SOCIAL RESPONSIBILITY

CASE #7: BP & DEEPWATER HORIZON

TIMELINE: BP'S WOES

from the Wall Street Journal

News that BP CEO John Browne is stepping down early amid revelations about his personal life is the latest development in a series of problems, including a refinery explosion in Texas that killed 15 people in March 2005 and an oil spill in Alaska discovered earlier this year. Below is a timeline of the energy giant's woes.

2002

June: BP agrees to a $45.8 million settlement with the state of California, resolving allegations that dozens of service stations it now owns in the state didn't make required safety upgrades.

2005

March: A deadly explosion at BP's Texas City, Texas, refinery kills 15 workers, all of them employees of contractors doing work at the plant. It was the third fatal accident at the petrochemical and refining facility in the past year and the deadliest U.S. petro-chemical accident in 15 years.

April: The U.S. Occupational Safety and Health Administration puts BP on a safety watch list.

May: BP backtracks on an earlier statement that blamed managers and other workers for the March blast at its Texas refinery.

July: BP's Gulf of Mexico Thunder Horse facility, the largest oil and gas producing platform in the world, is left listing after the passage of hurricane Dennis. Company sets aside $700 million in compensation for the families of Texas City victims.

August: The Chemical Safety and Hazard Investigation Board calls on BP to set up an independent panel to review safety across its U.S. refining operations. Former Secretary of State James Baker is eventually tapped to lead the report.

September: BP agreed to pay workplace-safety regulators $21.4 million in fines for scores of "egregious" safety violations tied to the March 23 explosion. The fine is the largest industrial-accident settlement of its kind.

December: BP says it will spend $1 billion over the next five years to improve the refinery in Texas City, including replacing equipment and beefing up maintenance programs found lacking at the facility.

2006

March: Several thousand barrels of crude spill from a ruptured pipeline at Alaska's Prudhoe Bay field.

April: U.S. environmental regulators conduct a criminal investigation into BP's management of pipelines in Alaska's North Slope. BP said it has found another pipeline break caused by corrosion at a BP-operated facility on the Alaskan North Slope. OSHA fines BP $2.4 million for alleged safety violations in its Ohio refinery. In May, the agency later opened an investigation after a contract worker suffered severe burning.

June: Robert Malone succeeds Ross Pillari as head of BP's U.S. unit. Federal investigators charge BP traders with illegally manipulating the U.S. propane market in February 2004. Simultaneous probes investigate potential manipulation cases in crude-oil and unleaded-gasoline markets.

August: BP shuts down its Prudhoe Bay oil field in Alaska following the discovery of a corroded pipeline and small leak there. Federal investigators probe changes made to a report commissioned by Alaska state officials on BP's operations there after the oil giant complained the report was overly negative.

September: BP says it had spilled about 1,000 barrels of a refined petroleum product into the port of Long Beach, Calif., the latest in a series of environmental, safety and compliance lapses in the U.S. A House committee grills BP executives on problems at Prudhoe Bay, the first of a series of harsh congressional sessions on the matter. BP will further postpone the start-up of its long-delayed Thunder Horse oil field in the Gulf of Mexico.

October: The Chemical Safety and Hazard Investigation Board, a federal agency, says cost cutting by senior executives led to the Texas refinery explosion. BP announces it is replacing Steve Marshall, the head of its Alaska division.

November: BP makes a last-minute settlement in a civil lawsuit stemming from the Texas explosion, including donating $32 million to institutions to aid health care, worker training and safety and education in Texas, Louisiana and Tennessee. The plaintiff received an undisclosed financial settlement. Indiana workplace-safety regulators propose fining BP about $384,000 for a series of violations at the company's Whiting, Ind., refinery.

December: The Commodity Futures Trading Commission informs BP it intends to bring a civil enforcement action against the company over its trading in unleaded-gasoline futures in October 2002.

2007

JAN. 12: BP names Tony Hayward CEO to succeed John Browne, who will retire at the end of July. On Jan. 16, BP is expected to release the results of an independent review of its U.S. refinery operations.

Jan. 16: An independent panel set up to review BP's refinery operations in the U.S. said company goals, such as cost-cutting, often overrode safety concerns at its plants.

March 20: The CSB issues its final report on the Texas City incident, affirming its belief that BP failed to heed safety warnings. Notable in this report is criticism of the Occupational Safety and Health Administration, which the CSB says has "an insufficient number of qualified inspectors" to guarantee safety at refineries.

April 12: Nearly a fifth of shareholders vote against an executive remuneration package that will give Mr. Browne a hefty compensation package for stepping down a year before his retirement age.

April 24: Company says first-quarter net profit fell 17% to $4.66 billion, as lower oil prices and a drop in output offset higher refining margins.

May 1: Mr. Browne resigned after a U.K. court removed an injunction that barred a newspaper group from publishing stories about his personal life and sexual orientation.

Source: WSJ.com research.

OIL GUSHES INTO ARCTIC OCEAN FROM BP PIPELINE

Leonard Doyle

Across the frozen North Slope of Alaska, the region's largest oil accident on record has been sending hundreds of thousands of litres of crude pouring into the Arctic Ocean during the past week after a badly corroded BPO pipeline ruptured.

The publicity caused by the leak in the the 30-year-old pipeline could seriously damage BP's image, which has been carefully crafted to show it as a company concerned about the environment. Unlike other major oil companies, BP boasts that it is fully signed up to the dangers of global warming and it makes a conspicuous effort to flaunt its green credentials, tackling local environmental problems and erecting wind turbines above its petrol stations.

The first indication of the spill came in early March, when an oily patch was discovered near the elevated oil transmission pipeline, but the full scale of the accident is only becoming clear with time. Environmentalists who vociferously objected to the construction of the BP pipeline may now see their worst fears realised.

Clean-up crews have removed more than 190,000 litres of crude oil and melted snow off the frozen tundra but reports indicate that the leak is the second largest crude oil spill in Alaska—second only to the 1989 Exxon Valdez disaster.

The oil gushed from the pipeline at a spot where it dips to ground level to allow caribou to cross, and has led industry critics and environmental groups to question whether BP is saving money on maintaining its network of wells, pumps and pipelines crisscrossing the tundra—a complaint the company vigorously denies.

As oil is increasingly transported through environmentally sensitive areas by pipeline, the dangers posed by poorly maintained rotting pipes has become increasingly clear.

Exploration Alaska, the BP subsidiary that operates the pipeline from which more than 910,000 litres of oil has leaked, has recently been fined more than $1.2m (£635,000) for its poor environmental safety record.

The company has now been told it cannot restart pumping oil until it the entire pipeline has been inspected and repaired. Employees claim that they repeatedly warned that money-saving cutbacks in routine maintenance and inspection had dramatically increased the chances of accidents or spills.

"For years we've been warning the company about cutting back on maintenance," Marc Kovac, a union official told the New York Times. "We know that this could have been prevented."

In the interview, Marc Kovac, an official of the United Steelworkers union which represents workers at the BP facility, said he had seen little change in BP Exploration Alaska's approach despite the warnings.

In an e-mail to a company lawyer in June 2004, Mr Kovac forwarded a collection of his earlier complaints to management. One of these, dated 28 February 2003, concerned "corrosion monitoring staffing levels". It began, "The corrosion monitoring crew will soon be reduced to six staff down from eight."

It added: "With the present staff, the crew is currently one month behind. The backlog is expected to increase with a further reduction in manpower."

Daren Beaudo, a company spokesman, said: "Whenever employees raise concerns about our operations we address them. When we inspected the line in September 2005, points of manageable corrosion were evident and all were within standards of operations integrity.

"Something happened to the corrosion rates in that line between September 2005 and the time of the spill that we don't yet fully understand."

IT'S NOT EASY BEING GREEN

Paul Roberts

This hasn't been the best year for British Petroleum. After the series of embarrassing pipeline breaks in Alaska, critics say the British energy giant can no longer claim to be an environmentally conscious oil company committed to moving "beyond petroleum." But in fact, the Alaska blunders are really just reminders that, when it comes to oil, environmental virtue is a commodity in sharp decline.

Few industries pose such challenges to corporate ethics as oil does. Extracting crude is a messy business. Burning its products produces all kinds of pollution—especially climate-warming carbon dioxide. And because oil companies must supplement their own dwindling oil fields with crude from big exporters, firms have little choice but to buy from repressive regimes like Iran, Saudi Arabia, or Russia—and worse, must often bid against India and China, which, as one analyst notes, can openly "offer bribes and arms in exchange for oil." From a purist's standpoint, oil is so problematic that a truly ethical company would abandon it completely.

BP, of course, never claimed to be leaving oil: By the company's own forecasts, alternatives won't replace oil and natural gas for 30 to 50 years. But starting in the late 1990s, CEO John Browne did argue that the transition to alternatives could be accelerated by changing industry practices today. Even as heavyweights like ExxonMobil busily denied that climate change existed—and lobbied hard to kill climate policies—BP vowed to cut its own CO2 emissions and invest heavily in solar, wind, and other alternative technologies; it even supported that oil-industry bogeyman, the Kyoto climate treaty. "Climate change is an issue which raises fundamental questions about the relationship between companies and society as a whole, and between one generation and the next," Lord Browne declared in 2002. "Companies composed of highly skilled and trained people can't live in denial of mounting evidence gathered by hundreds of the most reputable scientists in the world."

Predictably, however, BP's re-branding as the Jolly Green Energy Giant has been a hard sell. The company's actual investment in alternatives is tiny: Although BP put $500 million into solar power between 2000 and 2005, it spent $8.4 billion exploring and producing petroleum in 2004 alone. And for all the talk of a new environmental ethos, BP at one time lobbied hard to open the Arctic National Wildlife Refuge to drilling. Even its support of Kyoto is pilloried as disingenuous: BP happens to be overstocked in reserves of natural gas, a fuel that emits less CO2 than coal or oil, and whose price would rise sharply if society were forced to cut carbon emissions.

But the harshest criticism has always come from Wall Street, which worried that even a small increase in investment in non-oil alternatives would distract BP's focus from its core business—oil. After commentators and analysts ridiculed BP for moving "beyond profits," the company quietly dropped the "beyond petroleum" motto and sought to reassure markets that it was still very much an oil company. BP's spending on alternatives relative to oil and natural gas is less than 5 percent, and some environmentalists argue that, even if BP was genuinely interested in being a different kind of company, it has since chosen profit over principle.

To be fair, BP still leads the industry in green actions: Citing worrisome new data on global warming, it recently pledged to triple its production of solar panels over the next three years. Yet, ironically, some industry watchers wonder whether BP could have avoided the recent damage to its environmental image by behaving a little less green and a little more like a "normal" oil company—that is, focusing on basics such as exploration, production, and, above all, *maintenance*. ExxonMobil, a company routinely disparaged as anti-environmentalist—not least for the 1989 *Exxon Valdez* disaster—is now known for its obsessive focus on maintenance. "ExxonMobil would never have been caught with a corroded pipeline," says one industry observer. It "is a company that does everything in a gold-plated manner. It's purely a commercial decision: You never put in anything that might fail"—not for ethical reasons, but because, as BP has discovered, failure is expensive.

AT EXXON, MAKING THE CASE FOR OIL

Jad Mouawad

SIX years of relentlessly rising prices have showered the oil industry with record profits even as whipsawing energy costs have left many Americans alternately furious and baffled.

Now that the roller coaster ride appears to be screeching to a halt, one corporate giant remains confident it can weather the slowdown and uncertainty better than its rivals.

"It's not that we like lower prices, but our competitive advantage is more obvious to people in a low-price environment," says Rex W. Tillerson, the chairman and chief executive of Exxon Mobil, the world's largest, mightiest oil company. "But in a high-price environment, our competitive advantage has been quite evident as well."

However undaunted Exxon feels, it's still facing more complicated scenarios than mere price shifts. It's straining to adjust to a host of potentially seismic issues that raise pointed questions about its long-term strategy. Oil reserves are harder to find, resource-rich governments have become more assertive, and global warming concerns have spurred forceful calls to action on environmental matters.

Moreover, with the election of Barack Obama, a new chapter is about to open for the nation's energy policy. Mr. Obama says he wants to move away from oil dependence, and his policies are likely to emphasize conservation, alternative energy sources and new limits on the emissions of greenhouse gases responsible for climate change.

The question for Exxon, which Mr. Obama repeatedly singled out as an exemplar of corporate greed during the presidential campaign, is whether the model that has served the company so well for so long will keep it competitive—or whether it will still be producing hydrocarbons long after the world has moved away from dirty fuels.

Last year, Exxon, which is based in Irving, Tex., celebrated its 125th anniversary, marking a straight line that connects it to John D. Rockefeller's original Standard Oil Trust before the government broke up the enterprise. While other oil companies try to paint themselves greener, Exxon's executives believe their venerable model has been battle-tested. The company's mantra is unwavering: brutal honesty about the need for oil and gas to power economies for decades to come.

"Over the years, there have been many predictions that our industry was in its twilight years, only to be proven wrong," says Mr. Tillerson. "As Mark Twain said, the news of our demise has been greatly exaggerated."

FROM a purely financial standpoint, there's no doubt that Exxon's business strategy has paid off. Despite the broader economic turmoil, Exxon is worth around $375 billion—more than General Electric, Bank of America and Google combined—making it the world's largest corporation.

Its balance sheet is pristine and its credit rating is better than that of most governments. If Exxon's revenue were stacked against the world's G.D.P.'s, it would rank between Austria and Greece as the 26th-largest economy. As oil prices peaked this summer, the company once again set a record as the most profitable American corporation, earning $14.8 billion in the third quarter. Since 2004 alone, the company has rung up profits of about $180 billion.

Throughout its various incarnations—the Standard Oil Trust, Standard Oil of New Jersey, the Exxon Corporation, and now Exxon Mobil—the company has been an ambiguous fascination for many Americans. It is an enduring icon, as lasting as Coca-Cola or General Electric, but also a perennial corporate villain, one that reminds the nation of its dependence on hydrocarbons.

For some, the environmental impact of that earnings gusher outweighs the financial gains.

"Being Exxon is never having to say you're sorry," says Kert Davies, the research director at Greenpeace, the environmental advocacy group that has battled with Exxon for years.

On the financial front, however, Exxon's jaw-dropping results have continued to leave many analysts beaming.

"It's the world's greatest company, period," says Arjun N. Murti, a Goldman Sachs oil analyst. "I would put Exxon up against any other company at any other period of time."

"It is also the most misunderstood company in the world," he adds. "For many people, the image of Exxon is the Exxon Valdez. But there is much more to Exxon than that. Somehow, Exxon has persevered over the past 100 years with the best culture and management team any company could have."

What might be called the Exxon Way can be summed up in three ideals: discipline, patience and long-term vision. It is a formula the company drills into its managers from the moment they join Exxon, and which it keeps repeating through their careers. It explains the company's resilience and its view that it has survived, and thrived, through countless commodity cycles.

"We are all homegrown," Mr. Tillerson says. "That happens through a very deliberate and very closely managed process, and it starts the day the person walks through the door with us.

And we are the product of that system. If there is a DNA it is something you grow into after many years of working with your colleagues. It is clearly the defining strength of the company."

TAKE a room full of oil managers, and the Exxon people usually stand out, even as they try not to draw much attention to themselves. They typically band together, and often cultivate an aura of secrecy—and sometimes superiority—toward the outside world.

At Exxon, the engineers rule. From its very early days, the company has focused relentlessly on one thing: finding more ways to squeeze every penny out of each barrel of oil.

Mr. Rockefeller was an accountant who was obsessed with efficiency, and his fixations still run through the company's veins, says Joseph Allen Pratt, a historian and management professor at the University of Houston. Mr. Pratt is writing the fifth volume of Exxon's official corporate history, which the company is partly financing.

"There definitely is an Exxon way," Mr. Pratt says. "This is John D. Rockefeller's company, this is Standard Oil of New Jersey, this is the one that is most closely shaped by Rockefeller's traditions. Their values are very clear. They are deeply embedded. They have roots in 100 years of corporate history."

But the company's DNA goes well beyond the surface. Rivals acknowledge its expertise around an oil field, even as they bristle at what they call arrogance. Exxon's own executives brag that their company outperforms its peers by sticking to their playbook.

"Exxon is a very professional company," says Jeroen van der Veer, the chief executive of a leading competitor, Royal Dutch Shell.

Others say they respect the company's clarity of vision. "People know the rules when they work with Exxon," said a top oil executive who asked not to be identified in order not to jeopardize his company's relationship with Exxon. "Exxon can pick its battles. It's a pretty good strategy to have if people know that you will fight to the bitter end."

Examples of such grit abound. After a dispute with the Venezuelan government, during which Exxon persuaded a British court to briefly freeze $12 billion in government assets to fight what it considered an expropriation, the country's oil minister accused the company of "legal terrorism."

Whatever its critics might say about the company's hard-headedness, it has paid off in Exxon's bottom line. Last year, Exxon's profit per barrel was $17, exceeding BP's $12 a barrel, Shell's $14 and Chevron's $16, according to Neil McMahon, a Bernstein Research analyst.

No one is apologetic at Exxon about what it takes to get those results, especially Mr. Tillerson.

"The business model is based on a disciplined and rigorous approach to dealing with scientific data and facts," he says. "What we do is largely invisible to the public. They see the nozzle at the pump, and that's about it. They don't see the enormous level of risk that is managed very well to get that gallon of gas."

Exxon has battled powerful forces in recent years, locking horns with governments and multinational rivals from Africa to Central Asia, from Eastern Europe to South America. But last spring, the challenge struck closer to home—at the company's annual shareholder meeting in Dallas.

As oil prices zoomed above $100 a barrel, a group of investors tried to force Exxon to lay out a new strategy for developing alternative fuels and addressing global warming. While the challenge was not unprecedented—raucous shareholder meetings have been a staple for years—the dissent was led by a symbolic, if slightly quixotic, constituency: descendants of Mr. Rockefeller, who founded Standard Oil in 1882.

"Exxon Mobil needs to reconnect with the forward-looking and entrepreneurial vision of my great-grandfather," said Neva Rockefeller Goodwin, a Tufts University economist, speaking for the family. The company, she added at the time, was focused "on a narrow path that ignores the rapidly shifting energy landscape around the world."

Exxon's top managers easily brushed off the Rockefeller revolt, as they have so many obstacles over the years. Even so, Exxon and the other oil giants are facing a stark new landscape.

High prices have meant stratospheric profits, of course, but they have also led to more restrictions on access to oil fields around the world, making it harder for companies to increase their production and replace reserves.

"The largest oil companies are under tremendous pressure," said Fadel Gheit, a veteran oil analyst at Oppenheimer & Company, who worked for the Mobil Corporation before moving to Wall Street.

In the 1960s, the so-called Seven Sisters oil companies, including Exxon and Mobil, controlled most of the world's oil reserves. Today, state-owned companies, like Saudi Aramco, hold the vast majority of these reserves, while other resource holders like Russia and Venezuela have become increasingly assertive about limiting access to their reserves.

"The problem is very real," said Henry Lee, a lecturer in energy policy at Harvard University. "The oil majors are looking at a very different world than 20 years ago. That has big implications for the future of these companies. They all know it and they are all trying to figure out where they are going to be in 10 and 20 years."

The threat from state-controlled energy companies—and the larger question of tapping reserves—led to the big wave of industry mergers in the late 1990s, including Exxon's $81 billion purchase of Mobil in 1999.

"We were worried," says Lou Noto, the former chairman of Mobil. "We expected the environment to become more volatile, and more competitive, and more difficult geographically and geologically. The easy stuff had been found and we were getting into very esoteric stuff."

While the combination of Exxon and Mobil created the world's most valuable oil company, the joint entity has struggled to expand production. Exxon derives its strength from its size. But its problems are also a function of size: the company has become so large that to grow it must find increasingly big projects.

At an analyst meeting on Wall Street in March, Mr. Tillerson acknowledged the difficulty he faces: "The challenge we have today is continuing to have access to resources."

Since 1999, Exxon has spent about $125 billion foraging for new energy supplies around the globe. It expects to spend $25 billion to $30 billion each year through 2012 to seek and develop hydrocarbons. Yet the company is pumping about as much oil and gas today as Exxon and Mobil once did separately. In fact, Exxon's hydrocarbon production has been falling recently, dropping 8 percent, to 3.6 million barrels a day in the third quarter, compared with 3.9 million barrels a day in the period last year.

With about $37 billion in cash and a clean balance sheet, Exxon can afford to be picky about what prospects to explore. It has about 120 projects on its books, either in operation or in the planning stages, and it sits on up to 72 billion barrels of oil and gas reserves around the world, the most of any nonstate oil company.

To keep up momentum, Exxon plans to start up more than 60 fields or major projects by 2011, including dozens of offshore fields in West Africa, export terminals for liquefied natural gas in the Middle East, and scores of gas and oil developments in Australia, Indonesia, the United States and the Caspian Sea.

Still, despite its ability to stride the energy world like a colossus, Exxon remains more cautious than its rivals. Rather than overspend, it sows its huge returns in-house through share buybacks and large dividend payments to shareholders.

From 2003 to the third quarter of 2008, the company has paid out nearly $150 billion to shareholders—spending over $40 billion in dividends and buying back about $110 billion worth of shares.

Yet Exxon's shares are on track for their worst performance since the early 1980s, a result of the market sell-off and the drop in oil prices recently. Some analysts also said it reflected the questions hanging over the company's long-term strategy. "Exxon is a cash machine, and they could be using that cash to invest in clean technologies that would expand their base," said Andy Stevenson, an energy analyst at the Natural Resources Defense Council. "Right now, they have no growth story. They are trapped in oil and gas."

IF Exxon maintained its current buyback rate of $8 billion each quarter, it would become a private corporation between 2020 and 2030, according to a report by Bernstein Research. While that's unlikely, these payouts—$30 billion so far this year—have been criticized by some experts, who would like to see the company invest more to increase its production or expand its reserves.

"If a company is not replacing reserves, and they are spending their cash to buy back their shares, and they are not growing their production, that is called liquidating the company," says Amy Myers Jaffe, the associate director of Rice University's energy program in Houston.

Ultimately, the biggest test for Exxon's long-term business model is the fact that rising energy use—whether in the United States or in China—will eventually have to be reconciled with reducing carbon emissions and finding low-carbon energy sources. But as its contentious shareholder meeting with the Rockefeller heirs demonstrated, few topics are as touchy as Exxon's stance on climate change.

During the tenure of Lee R. Raymond, who ran the company from 1993 to 2005, Exxon became the lightning rod in the debate about climate change. Throughout the 1990s, the company was vilified by environmental groups and scientists for questioning the impact of human activities—especially the use of fossil fuels—on global warming.

Gingerly, over the last three years, Exxon has moved away from its extreme position. It stopped financing climate skeptics this year, and has sought to soften its image with a $100 million advertising campaign featuring real company executives, scientists and managers. One of the ads said the company aimed to provide energy "with dramatically lower CO2 emissions."

The company has acknowledged that climate change is a risk to the world. In a speech given before the Royal Institute of International Affairs in London last year, Mr. Tillerson said policy makers should consider setting a carbon tax or a plan that limits carbon emissions through a cap-and-trade system.

But while Exxon is slowly unshackling itself from Mr. Raymond's stance on global warming, it remains faithful to his legacy by dismissing most green alternatives and sticking with hydrocarbons. Although the company's tone has changed, its strategy has not. Despite growing pressures on oil companies to invest in alternative energy, Exxon's long-term view remains unapologetically tied to fossil fuels.

"Rex looks more approachable than his predecessor," says a rival executive who requested anonymity because he did not want to jeopardize his relationship with Mr. Tillerson, "but he is more inflexible."

Exxon's belief is that as populations expand and economies grow in developing countries, they will aspire to the comforts and amenities taken for granted in industrialized nations, and this will mean more cars on the roads—and more oil to power them.

According to Exxon's own outlook, global oil demand is set to reach 116 million barrels a day by 2030, up sharply from 86 million barrels a day today.

Meanwhile, renewable fuels, like solar, wind and biofuels, will grow at a brisk pace but they will account for just 2 percent of the world's energy supplies by then, according to Exxon, while oil, gas and coal will represent 80 percent of global energy needs by 2030.

"For the foreseeable future—and in my horizon that is to the middle of the century—the world will continue to rely dominantly on hydrocarbons to fuel its economy," Mr. Tillerson says.

For the moment, Exxon does not see much business sense in investing in solar, as BP has, or wind, like Shell, or geothermal, like Chevron. Like many oil executives, Mr. Tillerson also has little sympathy for corn-based ethanol, which he once derisively referred to as "moonshine."

Exxon does not entirely close the door to alternative investments someday. But its previous forays into renewable fuels—it was a big investor in nuclear power, synthetic fuels and solar energy in the 1970s—are seen as a costly lesson.

"Being first in something is not necessarily the best position to be in," Mr. Tillerson says. "You can be more profitable for your shareholders by coming at a later stage."

Still, Exxon sees itself as a technology-based company. Its labs are developing a thin-film battery separator and an onboard hydrogen system that could increase the range of electric cars or make the current internal combustion engines much more efficient.

The company points out that it has invested more than $1.5 billion to improve its own energy use and cut carbon emissions since 2004. And it boasts that it is spending $100 million to finance a long-term research program at Stanford University, along with General Electric, Toyota and the oilfield-services company Schlumberger, to find ways to increase energy supplies while reducing the emissions of greenhouse gases.

But to many of the company's critics, these measures look like a convenient smoke screens.

"That's kind of laughable," says Mr. Davies of Greenpeace. "What Exxon is clearly saying is that we are addicted to oil."

THE biggest area where Exxon may have an impact in tackling climate change is in what the industry calls carbon capture and sequestration. Most climate experts say that combating global warming will involve preventing heat-trapping gases like carbon dioxide from being spewed into the atmosphere by capturing them and pumping them underground.

In May, Exxon said it would invest $100 million in a demonstration plant in Wyoming to test a new cryogenic technology to capture carbon dioxide by freezing it. Managing these flows, and reducing the costs of this prohibitively expensive technology, may ultimately create a new business for Exxon if it can apply it to large emission sources, like coal-fired power plants.

But for the company to see this as a large-scale opportunity would require a "cultural leap," Ms. Jaffe says.

"Exxon may wind up being the carbon sequestration king, by accident," she says.

Whatever shape Exxon's business model takes, analysts say it is unlikely that the company will get there quietly.

"They are tough, and they have the reputation of being an unyielding company," says Michelle Michot Foss, who heads the Center for Energy Economics at the University of Texas at Austin. "But it's a tough business. They are criticized for being too conservative. But they are very patient, and probably in the long term that pays off."

WHITE HOUSE PROBE BLAMES BP, INDUSTRY IN GULF BLAST

By STEPHEN POWER and BEN CASSELMAN

January 6, 2011

The explosion that triggered last year's Gulf of Mexico oil spill was an avoidable disaster that resulted from management failures by BP PLC and its contractors, a presidential commission has concluded. But the accident also reflected systemic failures by oil companies and regulators to deal with the risks of deep-water exploration, the panel said.

A report by the National Commission on the BP Deepwater Horizon Oil Spill and Offshore Drilling castigates BP and two of the British oil giant's contractors—Transocean Ltd. and Halliburton Co.—for missteps that contributed to the worst offshore oil spill in U.S. history and the deaths of 11 rig workers.

The problems go far beyond BP, however, the report concludes—disputing oil-industry arguments that the April 20 explosion on the Deepwater Horizon rig was a one-time event caused by unusual and risky decisions by the oil company.

The panel said all three companies did a poor job of assessing the risks associated with their decisions and failed to adequately communicate, either with one another or with their own employees. Federal regulators lacked training and manpower to properly police the industry, the report finds.

The blowout "was not the product of a series of aberrational decisions made by rogue industry or government officials that could not have been anticipated or expected to occur again," according to a chapter of the report released Wednesday. "Rather, the root causes are systemic and, absent significant reform in both industry practices and government policies, might well recur."

The commission plans to issue the full report next week.

That conclusion could give regulators more ammunition to pursue tougher safety rules. At the same time, such efforts may be muted by pressure from lawmakers in both parties to allow deep-water drilling to resume.

BP said the excerpt released Wednesday, like the company's own internal investigation, concluded the accident "was the result of multiple causes, involving multiple companies."

BP added that it was working to ensure that lessons learned led to improvements in deep-water drilling, and that it had already made changes to strengthen safety and risk management.

A Transocean spokesman said procedures at the well in the final hours were directed by BP and approved by regulators. "Based on the limited information made available to them, the Transocean crew took appropriate actions to gain control of the well," he said.

Halliburton, which handled a cement seal on the well, said cement jobs "can go wrong even under optimal conditions." The company added that its cement mixture was designed to BP's specifications and passed its final laboratory test.

President Barack Obama, in setting up the seven-member panel last summer, said he wanted it to recommend safety and environmental precautions the government should take to prevent mishaps. Several other government entities, including the Justice Department, are conducting their own investigations.

A U.S. Department of Interior spokeswoman said the Obama administration had announced a slew of new safety regulations since the accident, including requirements that drilling projects meet new standards for well design, casing and cementing, and be independently certified by a professional engineer.

But the economic and political environment has changed since the summer, when images of oil fouling Gulf beaches provoked outrage toward BP and rekindled worries about the safety of offshore oil drilling.

Since then, U.S. gasoline prices have risen to an average of more than $3 a gallon, unusually high for winter. Republicans, who are generally more supportive of the oil industry and domestic exploration, have regained control of one chamber of Congress.

The report is likely to turn attention back to BP after several months in which the oil giant sought to turn the spotlight on its contractors.

In September, BP issued its own internal investigation into the disaster, which concluded that although its workers bore partial responsibility for misinterpreting a key pressure test, most of the blame for the disaster lay with its contractors. In particular, BP blamed a bad cementing job by Halliburton and the failure of Transocean workers to detect and react to signs that explosive natural gas was entering the well.

The commission's report criticizes all three companies, but focuses most heavily on BP, which owned the well and oversaw drilling operations.

The report identifies nine decisions that increased risk while potentially saving time, and said BP was responsible for at least seven of them. The report doesn't accuse BP of actively choosing cost savings over safety, but says the company failed to put in place procedures to ensure that efforts to curb costs didn't compromise safety.

The report slams BP for making repeated alterations to the well design and procedure and says the company didn't "adequately identify or address risks" created by the changes. Among the changes: delaying setting a final plug in the well, which might have stopped gas from reaching the rig.

The report also criticizes BP for its "long-string" well design, which the commission says made it difficult to get a good cement seal at the bottom of the well. BP's internal report dismissed criticisms of the design as irrelevant.

The report does echo BP's criticism of Halliburton, however, arguing that the cement seal that should have prevented gas from entering the well failed. The commission chides Halliburton over what it says was the company's failure to immediately review the cement used at the well and to alert BP after tests indicated the mixture was unstable. Halliburton has previously said a final test showed the cement would work.

The panel also criticizes Transocean for failing to detect signs of trouble and for not adequately communicating to its crew lessons learned from "an eerily similar" near-mishap on one of its rigs in the North Sea four months before the Gulf blowout.

"Given the documented failings of both Transocean and Halliburton, both of which serve the offshore industry in virtually every ocean, I reluctantly conclude we have a system-wide problem," commission co-chairman William K. Reilly said in a statement Wednesday.

Write to Stephen Power at stephen.power@wsj.com and Ben Casselman at ben.casselman@wsj.com

AS CEO HAYWARD REMADE BP, SAFETY, COST DRIVES CLASHED

By GUY CHAZAN, BENOIT FAUCON and BEN CASSELMAN

June 29, 2010

Associated Press

BP's Texas City, Texas refinery, shown after a fire in 2004, was the site of a deadly explosion in 2005.

Early on June 5, 2008, a piece of steel tubing ruptured on BP PLC's vast Atlantis oil platform in the Gulf of Mexico. The tubing was attached to a defective pipeline pump that BP had put off repairing, in what an internal report later described as "the context of a tight cost budget."

The rupture caused a minor spill, just 193 barrels of oil, but BP investigators identified bigger concerns.

They found the deferred repair was a "critical factor" in the incident, but "leadership did not clearly question" the safety impact of the delay. The budget for Atlantis—one of BP's most sophisticated facilities— was "underestimated," resulting in "conflicting directions/demands."

As investigators were questioning Atlantis' lean operation, top executives were praising it.

In an internal communication in early 2009, Neil Shaw, then-head of BP's Gulf of Mexico unit, lauded Atlantis' operating efficiency, saying it was "4% better than plan" in its first year of production. It was part of a success story that Mr. Shaw said had enabled BP to become the No. 1 oil producer in the Gulf.

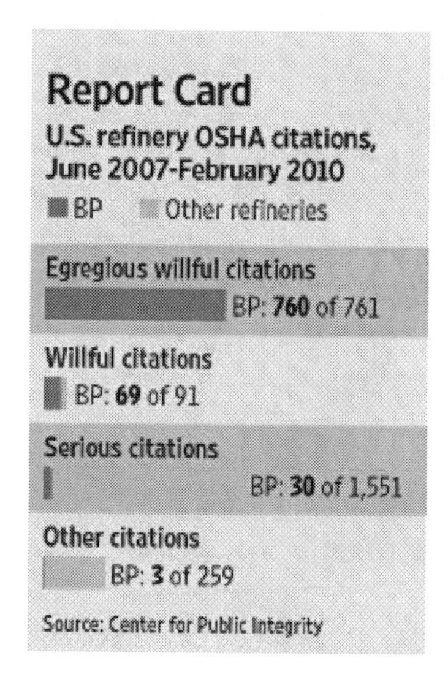

The budget squeeze on one of the British oil giant's most challenging projects underscores a tension at the heart of BP under Chief Executive Officer Tony Hayward.

Until the April 20 explosion of the Deepwater Horizon oil rig in the Gulf, Mr. Hayward repeatedly said he was slaying two dragons at once: safety lapses that led to major accidents, including a deadly 2005 Texas refinery explosion; and bloated costs that left BP lagging rivals Royal Dutch Shell PLC and Exxon Mobil Corp.

A Wall Street Journal examination of internal BP documents, legal filings, official investigations and reports by federal inspectors, as well as interviews with regulators, shows a record that doesn't always match Mr. Hayward's reports of safety improvements.

Since Mr. Hayward took over, BP has continued to spar with regulators over the same issues that got it into trouble before his tenure as CEO. Some of its refineries still get poor marks for safety. And four years after one of Alaska's worst oil spills, BP's pipelines there have continued to leak.

"They claim to be very much focused on safety, I think sincerely," says Jordan Barab, deputy assistant secretary at the Occupational Safety and Health Administration. "But somehow their sincerity and their programs don't always get translated well into the refinery floor."

BP insists it has turned a page on safety. "BP's absolute No. 1 priority is safe and reliable operations," said spokesman Andrew Gowers. In the past five years, "significant effort and investment" have been devoted to improving safety, he said, and great progress has been made on all important metrics, with reduced injury frequency and fewer incidents involving equipment breakdowns.

Savings have been achieved through "reduced corporate overheads and a simpler corporate structure," he said, not by economizing on safety. Indeed, extra dollars and staff have flowed into operations.

On Atlantis specifically, BP said it identified a problem with vibration in certain pumps but decided it "was not in itself a cause for safety or environmental concern," and deferred repairing some pumps until the following budget year."

Associated Press

A BP worker collects oil in Prudhoe Bay, Alaska, site of a 2006 spill

Mr. Hayward took the helm in May 2007, saying he would focus "like a laser" on safety and simultaneously improve BP's operations.

In October 2007, he created a management system designed to enforce safety standards consistently across the organization.

Obstacles soon emerged. A 2007 internal document setting out the safety policy spoke of an industry shortage of engineers and inspectors that could endanger plans to implement new standards for inspecting and maintaining critical equipment. An internal presentation in May 2009 cited a shortage of experienced offshore workers and said more training was required to "maintain safe, reliable and efficient operations."

The same month he revamped the safety structure, Mr. Hayward said he would streamline BP. An internal presentation to staff showed how problems such as less efficient operations had created a "growing gap between us and Shell."

Over the next three years, Mr. Hayward shed 7,500 jobs and pruned costs—$4 billion in 2009 alone. Buoyed by soaring oil prices, BP made record profits of $25.6 billion in 2008. BP soon rivaled Shell as Europe's most valuable oil company.

Mr. Hayward sought to move beyond BP's troubled past. In October 2007, the company agreed to pay $373 million to settle charges arising from the Texas City blast, oil spills in Alaska and allegations that BP traders manipulated the propane market.

BP went on to invest more than $1 billion upgrading the Texas City refinery. Earlier this year, it said its recordable injury rate there had declined every year since 2005, and that the refinery's 2009 safety performance ranked among the industry's leaders.

But OSHA, the federal overseer of workplace safety, tells a different story.

After a six-month inspection of the Texas City refinery last year, OSHA hit BP with an $87 million fine, the biggest in the agency's history. About $57 million of what OSHA describes as "failures to abate" hazards similar to those that caused the 2005 explosion, which killed 15 people. BP has contested the fines and says it is now in "constructive" discussions with OSHA.

The agency had inspected a refinery in Toledo, Ohio, which BP now jointly owns with Husky Energy, in 2006, uncovering problems with pressure-relief valves. It ordered BP to fix the valves. Two years later, inspectors found BP had carried out requested repairs, but only on the specific valves OSHA had cited. The agency found exactly the same deficiency elsewhere in the refinery. OSHA ordered more fixes and imposed a $3 million fine.

"There was clear knowledge of these problems ... and yet they hadn't been addressed" in other parts of the refinery, said Mr. Barab.

BP's Mr. Gowers said BP has "worked cooperatively with OSHA" to resolve problems at the refinery. BP said when OSHA imposed the fine that the Toledo refinery had made "measurable improvement in matters of process safety."

OSHA's Mr. Barab says because of BP's safety record, the agency scrutinized it more closely than other refiners and imposed tougher penalties because it deserved "a bit more attention on refinery safety than anyone else."

Thousands of miles to the northwest, BP was addressing safety issues on its Alaska pipelines. A corroded conduit sprang a large leak in 2006, fouling the tundra.

By the end of 2008, BP had invested $500 million to replace 16 miles of oil-transit lines at Prudhoe Bay, scene of the spill, and install a new leak-detection system.

But BP has continued to experience leaks. Last year, a civil filing by the state against BP said the company's "poor maintenance practices" have resulted in several spills since 2006. For example, some 1,000 barrels of crude oil, water and gas mixture poured onto the tundra after a 2-foot gash formed in a pipeline in November 2009.

BP said that about a third of its Alaska capital budget of between $800 million and $850 million this year is for safety and integrity projects. It said that since 2006, it has tripled the number of pipeline-corrosion inspections, to more than 100,000 a year.

Relations with Alaska's regulators remain strained, however. In September 2008, a high-pressure natural gas pipeline operated by BP ruptured, sending two segments of pipe flying 900 feet across the tundra. No one was hurt, but the official state report said the incident could have been catastrophic.

"We were able to tie it down to procedures that either were not in place or had not been fully implemented at BP in their management system," said Allison Iversen, a coordinator at Alaska's Petroleum Systems Integrity Office.

In February 2009, Ms. Iversen sent BP a letter saying it had failed to inspect the stretch of pipeline for more than a decade before it broke. A scheduled 2003 inspection was never performed because the pipe was covered in snow and the company never returned to do it. The state also said it was "deeply concerned with the timeliness and depth of the incident investigation" conducted by BP. It took four months to provide a report that other oil companies typically submit in two weeks.

BP said it is implementing a plan to address the backlog of pipeline checks and ensure any missed inspections are flagged.

In the Gulf of Mexico, BP hadn't suffered a safety disaster until the Deepwater Horizon. But there had been concerns that one might occur.

An internal BP presentation from December 2007, early in Mr. Hayward's tenure, noted that there had been 10 "high potential" incidents at BP facilities in the Gulf since the start of that year, including one December case in which a worker suffered an electric shock but survived. A common theme, the report found, was a failure to follow BP's own procedures and an unwillingness to stop work when something was wrong.

"As we enter the last two weeks of 2007, we are experiencing an unprecedented frequency of serious incidents in our operations," Richard Morrison, vice president for Gulf of Mexico production, wrote in an email to staff. "We are extremely fortunate that one or more of our co-workers has not been seriously injured or killed."

Mr. Morrison listed five near-miss incidents in November and December, including one in which natural gas escaped from a pipe aboard BP's Pompano platform, threatening an explosion.

BP said it wouldn't comment on this or any other internal communications, and declined to make Mr. Morrison available.

Meanwhile, company officials continued hammering home the message on costs. Mr. Shaw, the Gulf of Mexico head, made the point at a meeting for top managers in Phoenix in April 2008. His aim, according to an internal BP communication, was to instill a "much stronger performance culture" in the organization, based on strictly managing costs and "this notion that every dollar does matter." BP declined to make Mr. Shaw available for comment.

A former BP engineer who retired last year said the Gulf of Mexico operation under Mr. Shaw became focused on meeting performance targets, which determined bonuses for top managers and low-level workers alike. The engineer says even small costs got targeted: BP no longer provided food at lunch meetings, and eliminated the fruit bowls that were offered as part of a healthy-living drive a few years earlier.

In a statement, BP said its cost-cutting should be seen in the context of the sharp fall in oil prices in 2008, which squeezed all oil companies' profits. BP says executives are judged on the safety record of their units, not just on financial or production criteria.

The month after the Phoenix meeting, Mr. Shaw told his staff that efficiency was improving in the drilling and completing of wells.

The number of days it took to drill 10,000 feet was 6% below plan. Idle time had fallen to 24% of total rig days, from 34% in 2007. In May 2009, he said in another memo that BP's output in the Gulf had reached a record 500,000 barrels a day, a year ahead of schedule.

The improvements continued. According to an internal presentation on Gulf drilling performance dated April 13 of this year—a week before the Deepwater Horizon blast—BP's estimate for 2010 capital spending on wells in the Gulf fell by $221 million to $2.03 billion.

Some goals were more elusive. A safety steering committee worried that the "Total Recordable Incident Rate"—normally measured as total number of incidents resulting in injury or illness for every 200,000 man-hours worked—was higher than it should be.

The rate was 0.97 for the Gulf drilling unit, over the target of 0.62, say minutes of an August 2009 meeting. "In order to meet the target will need some zero months," the minutes say.

BP declined to comment on the memo's specifics but said it showed the company "continually evaluating the safety of its operations."

Some think the cost drive affected safety. Workers had "high incentive to find shortcuts and take risks," says Ross Macfarlane, a former BP health and safety manager on rigs in Australia who was laid off in 2008. "You only ever got questioned about why you couldn't spend less—never more." BP vigorously denies putting savings ahead of safety.

Risky Design

Page One: BP Relied on Cheaper Wells 06/20/10

See details on the designs of deepwter wells.

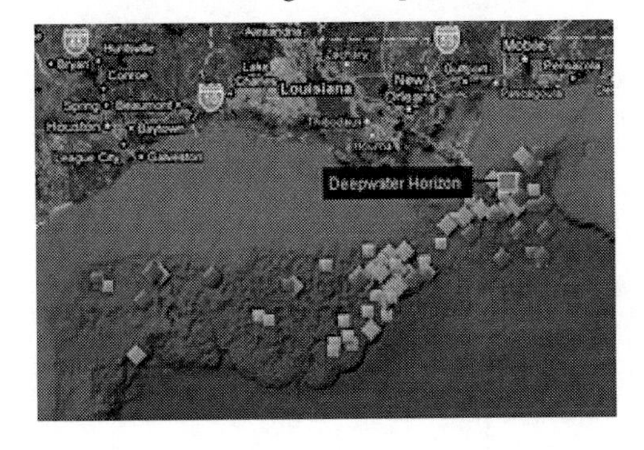

At a strategy update for investors this March, BP targeted large savings in its drilling operations. BP spends nearly $4 billion a year drilling oil wells. Management said it could slash $500 million off that figure by improving efficiency.

In that regard, the Gulf of Mexico well being drilled by the Deepwater Horizon was an outlier. Deepwater Horizon was the least efficient of the rigs working for BP in the Gulf: A BP chart showed at least 44% of its rig days were nonproductive, a much higher figure than any other vessel.

That pushed up costs, putting Horizon $29 million over budget for 2010, the largest deficit in BP's Gulf fleet.

BP says the amount of down time wouldn't have directly affected total spending on Deepwater Horizon, which was operating under a long-term, fixed-rate contract.

The April 20 explosion on the rig raised questions among congressional investigators about whether BP had cut costs too much. BP denies cost-consciousness played any role in the tragedy.

In a different context, BP had questioned the impact of its cost-cutting in the Gulf. After the 2008 incident on the Atlantis platform, BP's internal report warned of lax safety oversight and tight budgets.

It concluded: "A key question to ask, especially with apparently minor and disconnected defects, is 'What's the worst thing that could happen?'"

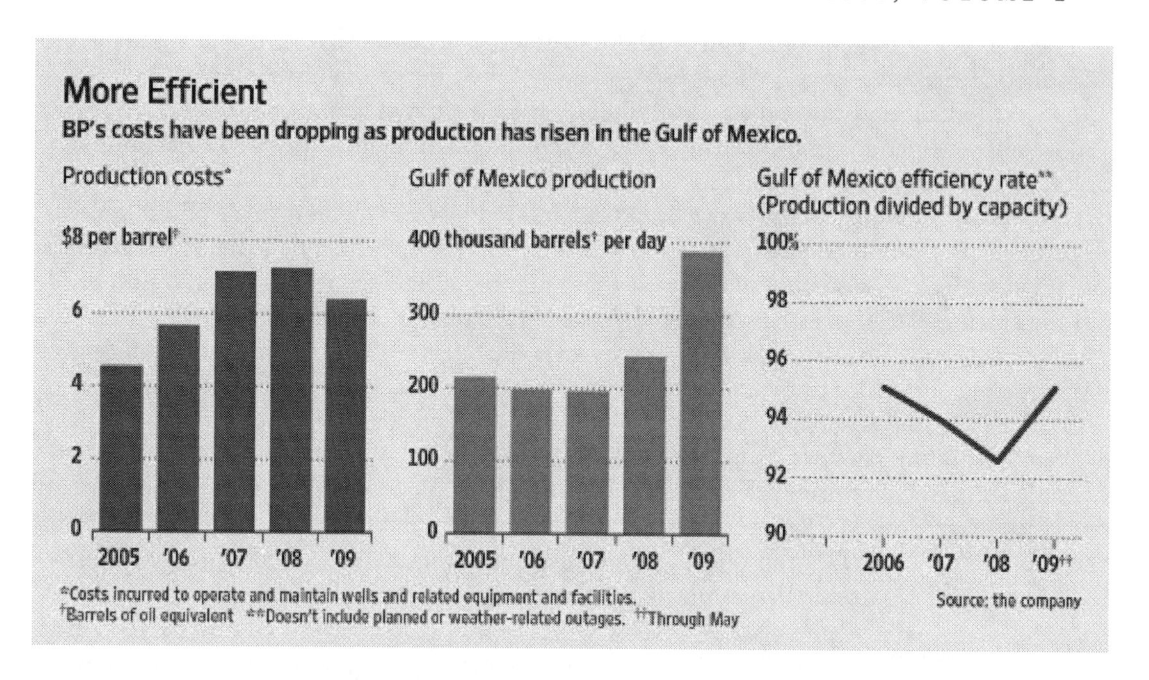

Write to Guy Chazan at guy.chazan@wsj.com, Benoit Faucon at benoit.faucon@dowjones.com and Ben Casselman at ben.casselman@wsj.com

BP'S SAFETY DRIVE FACES ROUGH ROAD

By Guy Chazan

February 1, 2011

A BP operation in the Beaufort Sea off Alaka's North Slope. Associated Press

Bob Dudley, the new chief executive of BP PLC, has vowed to change the safety culture of the accident-prone oil giant in the wake of the deadly explosion and spill at one of its wells in the Gulf of Mexico last year. But the story of a little-known BP safety official on the desolate North Slope of Alaska offers some cautions about just how difficult a job that will be.

The day after the Gulf well blew out last April, killing 11 rig workers, Phil Dziubinski was suspended from his job and escorted out of his office in Alaska. The company said he was let go as part of a broad management overhaul. In a five-month skirmish, two government agencies rejected Mr. Dziubinski's claims that he was fired as retribution for warning of safety risks. His back-and-forth with the British oil giant, though, sheds light on what Mr. Dudley is up against.

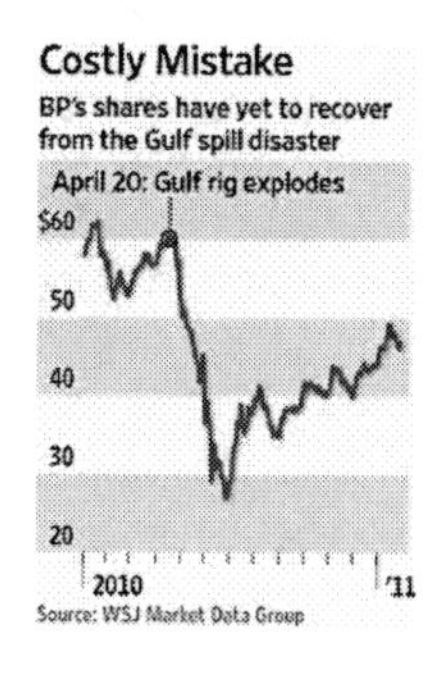

Mr. Dudley has created a new global safety division at BP, a company that also suffered a 15-fatality refinery explosion in Texas five years before the lethal Gulf accident. He has given the division power to intervene in or shut down any operation seen as too hazardous.

The safety issue goes to the heart of BP's corporate culture, say some critics, who contend that compared with its Big Oil rivals, the company has historically been focused more on deal-making and less on safety and operational excellence. "Other companies were less aggressive on growth and more focused on their safety-management systems," says John Hofmeister, a former president of Shell Oil Co. "Changing the culture is hard."

One area where safety concerns have loomed large is Alaska's North Slope, home to BP-operated Prudhoe Bay, the largest oil field in North America. Workers at the field, which opened in 1977, have long complained of aging infrastructure and a lengthy backlog of needed maintenance work.

In addition, as thousands of Alaska oil workers retired in recent years, overtime has piled up, and some workers have complained of fatigue. This is an issue Mr. Dziubinski repeatedly raised with his bosses, once referring to it in an email as an "imminent safety risk." BP technicians on the North Slope work 14 days straight and it isn't uncommon for them to put in shifts lasting 16 or 18 hours, sometimes on successive days.

BP says it has taken steps to reduce Alaskan workers' maximum hours and won't operate any facilities unless it is sure it can do so safely.

As Mr. Dudley tackles the BP safety culture, he will be under pressure, not least from U.S. authorities, to show improvements. A U.S. presidential commission's report last month on the Gulf disaster said decision-making processes by BP and its contractors "did not adequately ensure that personnel fully considered the risks created by time- and money-saving decisions." BP says the report supports its own view that the accident was "the result of multiple causes, involving multiple companies."

BP "is working with regulators and the industry to ensure that the lessons learned from [the Gulf well] lead to improvements in operations and contractor services in deep-water drilling," the company said. Even before the report, BP said, it was taking steps such as changing its pay structure to better reward safety performance and risk management. BP reports fourth-quarter financial results on Tuesday.

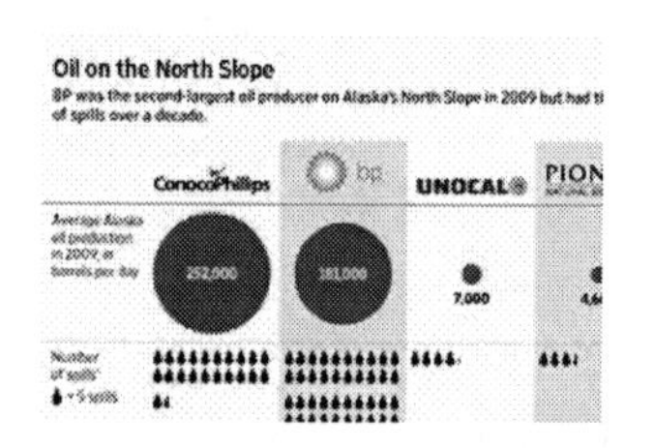

Mr. Dziubinski became BP's ethics and compliance leader for Alaska operations in mid-2006, shortly after the company suffered a 4,000-barrel oil spill on the North Slope. That happened a year after the refinery explosion in Texas City, Texas, an accident that led a federal agency called the Chemical Safety Board to suggest BP managers didn't listen enough to what workers were telling them.

"Reporting bad news was not encouraged," the report said, "and often Texas City managers did not effectively investigate incidents or take appropriate corrective action."

Promising change, BP in 2006 appointed an ombudsman, retired federal judge Stanley Sporkin, to receive and act on concerns raised by workers throughout the company. For BP

Alaska, the company set up a program to allow employees and contractors to raise issues without fear of retribution, placing Mr. Dziubinski, a veteran safety official, in charge.

At first, workers were skeptical. "I thought, 'Here's another supervisor from Anchorage...I'm going to have to be on guard with this guy,'" says Marc Kovac, a steward of United Steelworkers' Alaska Local 4959.

Suspicions faded, and employees soon began turning to Mr. Dziubinski with their grievances. Mark McCarty, a technician who sat on a BP health, safety and environment committee, says, "Phil was a bulldog in terms of making sure our concerns were addressed."

In 2006, BP decided to survey its Alaska workers. It had done this several years earlier and heard concerns about equipment such as fire- and gas-detection systems in need of upgrading, and complaints that cuts in staffing and training had made operations less safe. So BP re-interviewed several hundred workers to see if these issues had been addressed.

The review team, consisting of Mr. Dziubinski, three other managers and a few workers, found progress on some things, like pipeline inspections, but concluded that other matters, such as staffing levels and upgrades to fire- and gas-detection systems, still "need work."

BP's plan was to share the detailed survey results with the work force, according to the USW. Instead, BP decided not to. It declined to say why or discuss the issue.

At a meeting in March 2007, Mr. Dziubinski disagreed with a supervisor's assessment that the company was on track to fix all safety issues. Mr. Dziubinski said that several problems flagged by workers in the past still hadn't been addressed, and that BP was taking too long to deal with workers' current concerns.

Abraham Lustgarten/ProPublica
Union steward Marc Kovac sat in on safety meetings.

"We tend not to listen to the workers," Mr. Dziubinski said, according to notes of the meeting taken by the USW's Mr. Kovac, who was there.

Mr. Dziubinski also was frustrated that BP had decided against releasing the report, according to Mr. Kovac. "That was the beginning of the decline of Phil's relationship with upper management," he says.

Phil Dziubinski for State Senate
Phil Dziubinski warned of safety risks

In 2009, Mr. Dziubinski engaged his bosses about staffing levels and the length of work shifts. North Slope workers' normal schedule was two weeks of 12-hour days and seven-day weeks followed by two weeks off. But overtime was common, and some workers told their company safety committees that people were showing signs of fatigue. "You had walking zombies up here," says Mr. McCarty, the BP technician.

The USW asked BP in 2008 how much overtime had been logged over three years. It turned out to be double the industry average, according to Glenn Trimmer, a North Slope technician who is secretary-treasurer of the union's Alaska local.

BP added several dozen people to its work force of about 2,000 in Alaska and changed its rules so that for all shifts of longer than 16 hours, approval was needed from what is known as an area manager.

Later, BP stiffened this requirement for managerial approval, following a complaint to its ombudsman that some technicians were working consecutive 18-hour shifts.

Mr. Dziubinski, who had access to overtime records, informed his bosses about situations that concerned him, including one employee who had worked 36 consecutive days without proper managerial approval and who had logged 320.5 hours of overtime in a single month.

He told his superiors that at three "gathering centers"—facilities that separate crude into oil, gas and water—some workers "have excessive overtime rates that may require leadership intervention to decrease a safety risk."

His emails to his bosses, which were contained in the OSHA complaint he later filed and have been reviewed by The Wall Street Journal, said the rule requiring area-manager approval for shifts of 16 hours or more was followed only about half of the time.

In an Oct. 30, 2009, email, Mr. Dziubinski described the overtime situation as "an imminent safety risk." Citing shift patterns, he wrote to his bosses that "allowing the continuation of the 16+ hour work shifts would be seen by internal and external stakeholders as putting production ahead of safety."

Asked about the overtime issue, a BP spokesman said it "is being managed at the highest levels" of the company's Alaska unit. "We have taken measurable steps to reduce the maximum allowable hours," the spokesman said, adding that the company will "not operate facilities unless we are sure we can do so safely."

A facility called the Lisburne Production Center suffered a small spill in autumn 2009, which Mr. Dziubinski came to regard as symptomatic of a larger malaise. A worker there emailed BP two months later with a long list of equipment the worker described as out of service or not working well. Mr. Dziubinski investigated and later told the USW's Mr. Kovac, "The maintenance condition of [that facility] is in a poor state and BP management was not paying attention to it."

After he started emailing his bosses about the overwork issue, some of his responsibilities were shifted to others, Mr. Dziubinski asserted in his later OSHA filing. He also said a website where employee concerns were logged was changed, and he no longer received email notification of new complaints.

BP disputed these claims. A company lawyer told OSHA that "no effort was made to preclude" Mr. Dziubinski from access to new complaints and that Mr. Dziubinski remained "the single point of contact for roughly 52% of all concerns filed between January 2009 and May of 2010."

By May he was gone. On March 15, 2010, BP told Mr. Dziubinski, then 59 years old, that he wouldn't have a position in the Alaska operation after it was reorganized.

On April 21, while Mr. Dziubinski was still coming to work at his Anchorage office, management accused him of trying to contact other staffers who were being let go. Security guards escorted him out.

His suspension came two months after BP's ombudsman, Mr. Sporkin, had written to BP Alaska saying "we are concerned that the contractor work force has not received adequate assurances of non-retaliation for raising concerns about BP's operations."

BP says that "we expect and encourage our employees to raise safety concerns" and "have a zero tolerance policy regarding retaliation." Mr. Sporkin declined to be interviewed.

The company, in denying to OSHA that Mr. Dziubinski had been dismissed because of his safety activism, said he was terminated as part of a wholesale reorganization of the U.S. business that would shed 200 managers in all, including 30 in Alaska. A BP lawyer told OSHA Mr. Dziubinski's job performance didn't "reflect the level of competency or effectiveness" BP sought for the new organization it was forming.

Mr. Dziubinski's lawyer countered that his client had several years of consistently positive job evaluations and had received a bonus in 2008 and pay increase in 2009. His 2009 performance review described the numerous appeals workers sent to him as "a testament to his reputation and expertise."

"Phil did a fantastic job during a tough time for the company" and "had [my] fullest confidence," says a former BP Alaska executive who supervised him.

In July, an OSHA investigator ruled in BP's favor, finding insufficient evidence for Mr. Dziubinski's claim he was punished for pushing the safety issue. The Alaska labor department declined to disturb the ruling.

Subsequently, as Mr. Dziubinski was preparing a wrongful-termination suit, in the midst of the furor over the Gulf spill, he and BP reached a settlement, which is confidential.

BUSINESS AND NGOS: REACHING FOR A LONGER SPOON

June 3, 2010

The disaster in the Gulf of Mexico is straining ties between companies and activists

IT IS not just Barack Obama and Tony Hayward, BP's boss, who are under fire because of the environmental catastrophe unfolding in the Gulf of Mexico. In the decade or so since BP acknowledged the need to slow climate change and signalled its commitment to investing in cleaner sources of energy with the slogan "Beyond Petroleum", many environmental activists and NGOs have laid down their placards and helped the firm execute its green strategies. They are now facing intense criticism of that collaboration from their own supporters, who say the oil spill has left BP's (always contentious) green claims "Beyond Parody" and the company "Beyond the Pale".

The website of one such NGO, the Nature Conservancy, has been bombarded with complaints from donors horrified by the discovery (although it had never hidden the fact) that over the years it had received around $10m in gifts of cash and land from BP, and had even given the oil giant a seat on its "International Leadership Council". Another, Conservation International, has accepted over $2m from BP, advised the firm on its oil extraction methods, and from 2000 to 2006 included on its board John Browne, BP's boss at the time and the moving force behind the firm's conversion to greenery. The Environmental Defense Fund, another big NGO, had helped BP develop its internal carbon-trading system, and more recently campaigned alongside it for a law to cap America's emissions of greenhouse gases through the US Climate Action Partnership (USCAP), an alliance of NGOs and big businesses. Other prominent NGO members of USCAP include the Nature Conservancy, the Pew Center on Global Climate Change, the Natural Resources Defense Council and the World Resources Institute.

The scrutiny of these ties to BP is intensifying the perennial debate about how long a spoon NGOs should use when supping with corporate devils. The failure of governments to make progress on a new climate deal in Copenhagen last December had already prompted some debate among activists about whether a more confrontational style of campaigning was needed to stir the world from its torpor.

The renewed debate comes when relations between business and NGOs (environmental and otherwise) are closer than ever before. In 1990, when Environmental Defense announced an agreement to help McDonald's reduce the environmental impact of its packaging, there was shock and dismay from activists and business alike. Environmental Defense was accused of selling out, while the fast-food retailer, which had previously had a reputation for hostility to green causes, was chided by some of its peers for allowing tree-huggers into the boardroom. "At the time, it was heresy to say that companies and NGOs could work together; now it is dogma, at least for the Fortune 500," says Gwen Ruta, who oversees Environmental Defense's corporate partnerships. Its current collaborators include such frequent targets of activists' ire as Wal-Mart, a giant retailer with no time for unions, and Kohlberg Kravis Roberts (KKR), a private-equity firm often depicted as a financial predator.

The spill seems certain to prompt NGOs to review their ties to business. Lenny Mendonca of McKinsey, one of the authors of a new report, "Shaping the Future: Solving Social Problems through Business Strategy", sees a "risk of heading into a vicious circle of antagonism." But he believes that would be a mistake.

The report, published by a group called the Committee Encouraging Corporate Philanthropy, whose members include dozens of corporate bigwigs, argues that various factors will encourage firms to embrace worthy causes more warmly in future: the likelihood of government action on climate change, the growing importance of a firm's reputation when it comes to recruiting and the emphasis that the governments of booming emerging markets place on good corporate citizenship. All this, the report optimistically argues, could drive a "self-reinforcing state of trustworthy, pro-social corporate behaviour that simultaneously delivers bottom-line results and community benefits."

Collaboration between business and NGOs, if well designed, can certainly yield significant mutual benefit. This week Environmental Defense and KKR reported that the first two years of their partnership, which aims to cut costs in KKR's portfolio of companies through energy efficiency and other green measures, had already generated savings of $160m. The same approach has now been adopted by at least one of KKR's rivals, the Carlyle Group.

The efforts of McDonald's to address NGOs' concerns, starting with its partnership with Environmental Defense, have been "as important to the company's success as the Happy Meal", says Walter Massey, a director who chairs the firm's committee on corporate social responsibility. He was particularly delighted by a partnership with Greenpeace to exclude soyabeans grown on deforested land in the Amazon from the company's supply chain, which "led to the Greenpeace campaign director issuing a statement congratulating McDonald's for pushing 'a multi-million-dollar industry towards a more sustainable future'."

For several years Mr Massey has also been on the board of BP, which he believes benefited from its work with NGOs after a deadly accident at a refinery in Texas in 2002. "The company's reservoir of goodwill, built up over years of committed corporate stewardship, was of critical aid in helping us to weather the storm," he said in March. The latest crisis suggests that the reservoir is not bottomless, however.

BP's travails illustrate the limits of enthusiastic corporate citizenship. However much BP works with NGOs, it will find it impossible to move beyond petroleum, with all its attendant environmental problems. Likewise, PepsiCo will struggle to live up to the spirit of its pledge to promote healthier living while the bulk of its profits comes from fattening drinks and snacks.

Partnerships that address NGOs' misgivings about a firm's supply chain are likely to prove much more successful. That has certainly been the case at Wal-Mart, which has demanded higher environmental standards from its suppliers, to widespread acclaim. Efforts by firms such as Coca-Cola to work with NGOs to conserve water and increase access to it in the developing world have promise since they should make it easier for the firm to secure a reliable supply of the main ingredient of its drinks.

The spill also highlights the question of whether NGOs should accept money for the advice they give to companies. For organisations such as the Nature Conservancy, which protects ecologically sensitive spots by buying them or persuading others to set them aside, businesses are a big source of income. But partnerships with grubby firms risk turning off its million-odd individual donors.

Campaigning NGOs, which rely on a reputation for righteousness, are particularly at risk. The website of Greenpeace, whose activists like to chain themselves to things, is full of reminders that it never accepts money from companies. Similarly, there has been relatively little criticism of Environmental Defense because, from its first dealings with McDonald's, it has never accepted any corporate dollars. Ironically, this policy had prompted grumbles from some big individual donors, who asked why firms as rich as Wal-Mart and KKR should be the ultimate recipients of their charity.

The spill has presumably squelched such talk. Firms on the lookout for ways to improve their image and NGOs hoping to bring about meaningful change seem like natural partners. Most of the time the benefits of co-operation outweigh the risks. But whenever money changes hands, suspicions are bound to arise. The NGOs which accepted BP's largesse presumably now wish that they had brought a longer spoon to the feast.

BP OFFERS FINANCIAL AID TO STATION OWNERS

By NAUREEN S. MALIK

June 29, 2010

NEW YORK—BP PLC is expanding financial incentives to its branded fuel marketers facing reduced sales and boycotts related to the Gulf of Mexico oil spill.

In addition to covering the marketing costs for distributors and filling-station owners, the oil giant is cutting credit-card fees and offering a cash refund for BP-branded fuel sold, according to the BP Amoco Marketers Association, an independent organization representing 10,000 BP stations.

The fee for BP cards will be suspended outright while fees owed to BP for other Visa and MasterCard Inc. card fees will be cut by a fifth, benefiting gas-station owners directly. BP will also offer a one-cent-a-gallon refund to its distributors for some fuel sold during the summer.

BP suffers little direct impact from consumer protests or boycotts of its branded stations because the vast majority of them are owned by independent entrepreneurs. These include 10,000 retail stations that fly the BP flag and another 1,000 or so that carry the Arco and "ampm" names. There are roughly 475 distributors, known as jobbers, who supply these stations and sometimes own them outright.

The new incentives, plus advertising support, would total about $50 million to $70 million, but it is unclear how much will be allocated for each particular facet of the plan, said John Kleine, executive director of BP Amoco Marketers Association. The board's 21 members met with BP marketing executives in Chicago last week. BP spokesman Scott Dean confirmed the moves in an email, adding the company was rolling out a marketing package tied to a "Locally Owned, Locally Operated" message.

In recent weeks, distributors and gas station owners carrying the BP brand have stepped up marketing campaigns as oil continues to gush into the Gulf 10 weeks after the explosion and sinking of the Deepwater Horizon rig. BP has backed their efforts by covering marketing expenses and providing templates for radio, television and on-site advertising campaigns.

The impact from boycotts has varied widely at retail stations within a single city depending on demographics. Some sites haven't been affected at all while others have seen sales drop anywhere from 5% to 30%, according to reports Mr. Kleine has received.

"We are all very anxious," said Mark Oil Co. President Bill Tome, based on conversations with other distributors. His firm operates 35 stations in the Charlotte, N.C., area. As the oil spill drags on, "people become more anxious and frustrated," and fears are customers will start avoiding stations even more, he said.

In a letter to distributors, BP said it would drop the fixed 13-cent charge for the BP proprietary card to zero and lower the fee for Visa and MasterCard cards to 1.4% from 1.75%, Mr. Tome said. All card transactions across the BP-branded retail sites are executed through a company system, a common practice in the fuel distribution business. BP estimated the savings will come to about half a cent a gallon for the retailer, Mr. Tome said.

BP is also offering a special, volume-based refund to retailers this summer. Once a retailer sells 85% of the total average volume of fuel it purchased from BP during the first four months of the year, it will collect a refund of a penny a gallon in June, July and August—the peak summer driving months.

Distributors in the Gulf region have been hardest hit by the fallout from the spill, with sales down by an average of 10%, compared with a drop of 5% elsewhere in the U.S. Some of the retailers and marketers in the Gulf already receive a penny-a-gallon refund from BP and the new program could double their refund, Mr. Tome said.

The Gulf area's retailers and marketers also have the option to try to offset some of their losses through the broad $20 billion fund BP set up to compensate for business lost because of the spill. Mr. Kleine said he didn't know if any of them had applied.

BP-OUR VALUES

WHAT WE STAND FOR

BP wants to be recognised as a great company – competitively successful and a force for progress. We have a fundamental belief that we can make a difference in the world.

We help the world meet its growing need for heat, light and mobility. We strive to do that by producing energy that is affordable, secure and doesn't damage the environment.

BP is progressive, responsible, innovative and performance driven.

Progressive
We believe in the principle of mutual advantage and build productive relationships with each other, our partners and our customers.

Responsible
We are committed to the safety and development of our people and the communities and societies in which we operate. We aim for no accidents, no harm to people and no damage to the environment.

Innovative
We push boundaries today and create tomorrow's breakthroughs through our people and technology.

Performance driven
We deliver on our promises through continuous improvement and safe, reliable operations.

These values guide us in the conduct of our business. In all our business we expect high ethical standards and act in accordance with our Code of Conduct.

CENTER FOR EDUCATION ON SOCIAL RESPONSIBILITY

PART SIX (E) (II):

THE GLOBAL ENVIRONMENT—CLIMATE CHANGE

BRIEFING: GREEN AMERICA

From *The Economist*

Belatedly, and for many reasons, America is embracing environmentalism.

When Jim Webb, the new Democratic senator from Virginia, replied to George Bush's state-of-the-union message, he could bear to endorse only one of the president's proposals. This was the idea of cutting America's petrol (gasoline) consumption by 20% in ten years, by increasing ethanol production to 35 billion gallons a year and raising fuel efficiency standards for cars.

Such a plan would reduce America's dependence on imported oil from dangerous places (as would Mr Bush's plan to double the country's petroleum reserves). But it would address global warming only tangentially. The Democrats in Congress are weighing much more dramatic measures, including across-the-board cuts to the greenhouse gases that are heating up the planet. At the state level, politicians of all stripes are already taking more radical steps. Even big business is coming round. Mr Bush may be dragging his feet, but America is greening fast.

The Democrats' victory in last year's elections means that Congress's stance on environmental issues has changed dramatically. In one race for the House of Representatives, a Democratic consultant on wind power defeated a Republican ally of the oil industry. Barbara Boxer, an ardent advocate of firm action on climate change, has taken over the chairmanship of the Senate Environment Committee from James Inhofe, who often described global warming as "the greatest hoax ever perpetrated on the American people".

Since Congress convened earlier this month, the Democrats have got to work fast. The House has passed a bill that would eliminate a tax break for oil production in America, and would impose penalties on firms that refuse to renegotiate the absurdly generous leases the government accidentally granted them in the late 1990s. The proceeds—perhaps $15 billion over the next decade—would be used to fund renewable energy schemes.

Nancy Pelosi, the new speaker of the House, is now turning her attention to global warming. She is setting up a committee to address both that issue, and America's dependence on imported fuel. She wants to see legislation before July 4th, so that she can declare "energy independence" on the same day that the founding fathers severed political ties with Britain.

Meanwhile, some half-dozen bills on global warming are circulating in the Senate. Several propose cap-and-trade schemes, whereby the government would create a fixed number of permits to produce greenhouse gases and then auction them or allocate them to businesses. Firms without enough permits to cover their emissions would either have to pollute less, or buy up spare ones from firms that had managed to cut back.

John McCain, a leading Republican presidential candidate, and Joe Lieberman, a former Democratic one, are behind the most prominent cap-and-trade scheme. Barack Obama, one of the Democrats' current presidential aspirants, is a co-sponsor. It is the most ambitious of the bills with serious backing: it would cut carbon emissions to 2004 levels by 2012 and then mandate further reductions of 2% a year until 2020. Although these targets are less onerous than those of the Kyoto protocol, the United Nations' treaty on climate change, most analysts reckon they will prove too exacting for Congress.

An alternative cap-and-trade scheme, sponsored by Jeff Bingaman, chairman of the Senate Energy Committee, suffers from the opposite problem: excessive modesty. His plan would aim to slow the growth of emissions, and ultimately stabilise them at their 2013 level by 2020. It includes a safety valve, under which the government would automatically issue more permits to pollute if the price of those permits rose too far. The economic impact would be much smaller than under the McCain-Lieberman plan but so, too, would the reductions in emissions.

Dianne Feinstein, a Democratic senator from California, is proposing a third approach. She wants to create cap-and-trade mechanisms within industries rather than across the economy as a whole. She has, for instance, proposed legislation that would cut power companies' emissions by 25% of their projected levels by 2020.

All these initiatives face an uphill battle. The previous Senate rejected the McCain-Lieberman plan twice—by a bigger margin the second time around. Any bill that involves mandatory caps on greenhouse-gas emissions would need 60 of the chamber's 100 votes to succeed, since Mr Inhofe has pledged to filibuster all such measures. In the House the Energy Committee is chaired by John Dingell, a Democrat from the carmaking hub of Detroit who has long opposed mandatory caps. Mr Dingell, who says Ms Pelosi's new committee is "as useful as feathers on a fish", will still have a big say in any legislation. And even if a bill overcomes all these obstacles, it would risk a presidential veto.

A MATTER OF SECURITY

But whatever the fate of these proposals, the political climate is changing faster than the weather. Almost all the leading presidential candidates favour emissions caps. One of them, Hillary Clinton, has condemned the Bush administration's failure to act as "unAmerican". That is a remarkable change since 2000, when Al Gore toned down his environmental rhetoric during his presidential campaign for fear of sounding pious and obsessive. Indeed, activists are so convinced that the next president will be greener than Mr Bush that they are debating whether to settle for immediate but modest measures on global warming, or wait for a new administration to take bolder steps.

The Democrats have always been the greener party, but environmentalism is budding among Republicans too. Take Saxby Chambliss, a moderate senator. He voted against the McCain-Lieberman bill in 2005, but changed his mind after visiting Greenland to view the melting ice cap. "There really is something to it," he now says.

Many factors lie behind the party's shift. Most have to do not with sudden sentimentality in the face of Nature, but with national security (a motivation that lies, too, behind Ms Pelosi's new committee and Mrs Clinton's patriotic posturing). Fiscal hawks fret about the impact of growing oil imports on the dollar. Military types fear global conflict for dwindling resources in the event of catastrophic global warming. Neoconservatives worry about America's dependence on oil imports from unstable if not openly hostile countries in Latin America and the Middle East. Some think the solution is simply to pump more oil at home, but others argue that America needs to move away from oil altogether. One such figure, Jim Woolsey, a former director of the Central Intelligence Agency, pointedly drives a Toyota Prius, a famously fuel-efficient car.

At the same time, a growing number of evangelical Christians are beginning to see global warming as a moral issue. They argue that mankind, as steward of God's creation, has a duty to protect the environment. One outfit, the Evangelical Climate Initiative, encourages prominent pastors and theologians to sign a "Call to Action". Another group, the Evangelical Environmental Network, runs a website called "What would Jesus drive?" Last year Pat Robertson, a prominent televangelist, told his flock "We really need to address the burning of fossil fuels."

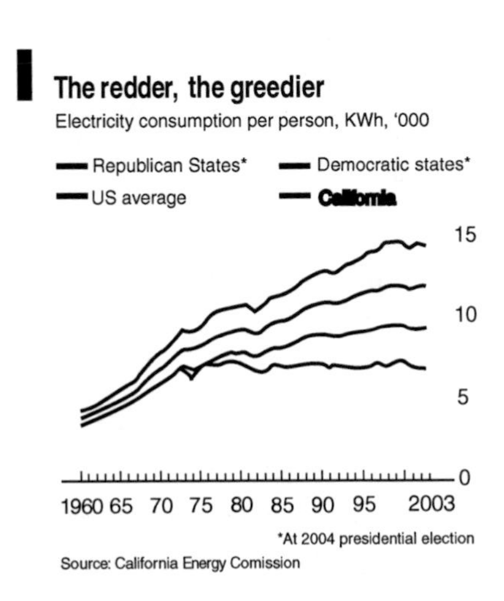

The Republican Party has a strong, albeit fitful, tradition of environmentalism. Teddy Roosevelt expanded America's national parks. Richard Nixon created the Environmental Protection Agency (EPA). Mr. Bush's father, when he was president, signed off on America's first nationwide cap-and-trade scheme to control emissions of the gases that cause acid rain.

But the strongest force propelling environmentalism among Republicans is self-preservation. Arnold Schwarzenegger, the decidedly green governor of California, was one of the few luminaries in the party unaffected by last year's electoral meltdown.

Republicans in other western states, where a Democratic tide is rising and a pristine landscape is a major tourist attraction, are following Mr Schwarzenegger's moves with interest. They fear the party may lose ground with moderate middle-class types who dislike urban sprawl and unfettered oil-drilling.

The destruction wrought by Hurricane Katrina in 2005 had a big influence on voters, according to Jonathan Lash of the World Resource Institute. Americans seem to view the increasing incidence of freakish weather as proof that climate change is real. Many of them paid to see Mr Gore's film on the subject, making it the third-most-successful documentary of all time (and now a candidate for an Oscar). Polls show that Americans are gradually growing more exercised about global warming, although they are still less anxious than Europeans or Japanese.

THE BUSINESS VIEW

Even big business, which stands to lose most from stricter environmental regulation, is beginning to accept that change is in the air. Exxon Mobil, led until recently by a fierce sceptic of global warming, now concedes that there is a problem, and that its products are contributing to it. Last year four-fifths of utility executives polled by Cambridge Energy Research Associates, a consultancy, expected mandatory emissions caps within a decade.

If regulation is indeed on its way, many firms would like Congress to fix the rules sooner rather than later, to help them plan investments in factories and power plants with long lifespans. Earlier this week ten companies, including Alcoa, Caterpillar and DuPont, called for Congress to set up a cap-and-trade system for greenhouse gases as quickly as possible. Since most of the firms involved produce clouds of emissions, they would obviously like to influence future legislation.

But the firms' bosses claim to see emissions caps as an opportunity, not a threat. GE, a member of the group, wants its executives to use their "ecomagination". By the same token Rick Wagoner, the head of GM, the world's biggest carmaker, recently hoped aloud that oil prices would remain high, so that his firm would keep its incentive to develop fuel-efficient cars. Wal-Mart, America's biggest retailer, hopes to double its sales of low-watt lightbulbs.

Lots of firms are growing healthily on the back of America's sudden enthusiasm for alternative energy. Americans invested almost $30 billion in the sector in 2006, according to New

Energy Finance, a research firm. American venture capitalists lavish seven times more on greenery than their counterparts in Europe. Ethanol production was expected to double in the next few years, even before the latest boost from Mr Bush. Wind and solar power are also booming. And the bigger green firms become the more influence they will have over politicians.

STATES TO THE FORE

At the very least, business want to avoid a patchwork of conflicting local regulations on environmental matters in general, and greenhouse-gas emissions in particular. There is already a bit of a muddle, since several states have taken much bolder and more experimental steps than the federal government. California, the boldest of all, has taken on carmakers, electricity companies and the EPA, to name a few. Its politicians vie to out-green one another. Some 40 of its legislators drive hybrid cars. Mr Schwarzenegger, not to be bested, has converted one of his fuel-swigging Hummers to run on hydrogen.

Congress may be thinking about tackling greenhouse-gas emissions, but California has already done it. Its Global Warming Solutions Act, which was passed last year, aims to cut them to 1990 levels by 2020—an ambitious target for a state that has grown rapidly in the past 15 years and will probably continue to do so. The details have yet to be fleshed out, but the reductions will come from both a cap-and-trade scheme for industry and regulations of various sorts.

Mr Schwarzenegger issued the first such regulation earlier this month, obliging producers of petrol and other fuels to cut the emissions of carbon dioxide from their products by 10% by 2020—presumably by mixing in more ethanol and other biofuels. It is not California's first attempt to reduce emissions from transport: its legislature voted for stringent cuts in 2002. That move has become snarled in a court battle over whether states have the right to set fuel-economy standards. Meanwhile, the politicians keep trucking. In September, the state showily sued six car manufacturers, alleging they had damaged its climate. It is also suing the EPA, for failing to regulate greenhouse-gas emissions.

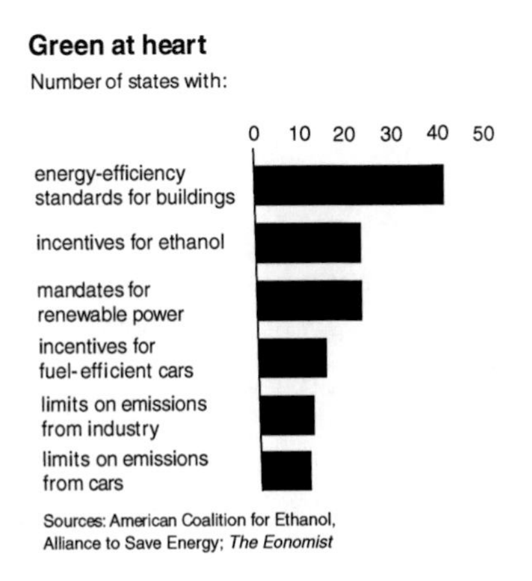

California's politicians are keen on renewables too. State law requires utilities to generate 20% of the power they sell from sources such as windmills and biomass plants by 2010, and 33% by 2020. Solar power has won even greater favour: under the "million solar roofs" scheme, the state plans to spend more than $3 billion over the next decade subsidising the installation of solar-power panels.

California has also pioneered the practice of "decoupling", which deprives power firms of their incentive to sell as much electricity as possible. Instead, the local regulator has devised a formula to reward firms whose sales are lower than expected, and to allow the recovery of the costs of energy-efficiency schemes.

Such measures (along with high power prices to pay for them) have helped California rein in its electricity consumption—although lovely weather and a relative lack of heavy industry have also played a part. Power use per person has remained roughly stable in the state since the 1970s, even as it has doubled in the rest of the country (see chart on following page). As a result, California's greenhouse-gas emissions per person are on a par with those of Denmark. Relative to the size of its economy, they are lower.

But California is not America's only green enclave. Nine states in the north-east have combined to reduce emissions from power generation through a cap-and-trade scheme. Two of them plan to auction all the permits, unlike the countries in the European Union's Emissions Trading Scheme, which handed them out for nothing. Ten states have signed up to follow California's standards on car exhaust, including its requirements on greenhouse gases. Many more promote ethanol, or renewables, or energy-efficient buildings (see chart).

On the whole, left-leaning states are keener on greenery than right-wing ones, which tend to be more energy-intensive. But politicians of all stripes in the Midwest are keen to promote ethanol for the sake of local farmers, who grow the corn from which it is made. And Texas recently overtook California as the country's biggest generator of wind power.

Greenery is also popular at the local level. Almost 400 cities have devised plans to curb or reduce their greenhouse gas emissions. Many buy only fuel-efficient cars for their municipal fleets. Laura Miller, the mayor of Dallas, has spoken out against the plans of local utilities to build 17 new coal-fired power plants. What is the point of her city buying police cars fuelled by natural gas, she asks, when they will soon be overshadowed by clouds of soot?

Despite all this grassroots environmentalism, America remains the biggest contributor to global warming, accounting for roughly a fifth of all the world's emissions. The federal government's recalcitrance on the subject remains the biggest obstacle to an effective global scheme to tackle the problem. But whereas in Europe or Asia new ideas often flow from the centre to the regions, in America the states are the incubators of big shifts in policy. This means that change is coming—fast.

A FREE ECONOMY IS A CLEAN ECONOMY: HOW FREE MARKETS IMPROVE THE ENVIRONMENT

Ben Lieberman

Environmental protection has become synonymous with big government: massive environmental statutes and global treaties, volumes of expansive and expensive regulations, and armies of bureaucrats micromanaging the private sector in an effort to reduce pollution. This certainly describes nearly all of the existing policies for addressing environmental concerns as well as most pending proposals dealing with global warming.

However, the *Index of Economic Freedom* strongly suggests that this command-and control approach to "going green" is a fundamentally misguided one. It is the nations whose economies are ranked as most free that do the best to protect the environment, while the least free ones do the worst. Thus, the same free-market principles that have proven to be the key to economic success can also deliver environmental success and point the way to an approach that advances both concerns.

THE CORRELATION BETWEEN ECONOMIC FREEDOM AND ENVIRONMENTAL PERFORMANCE

While the *Index* ranks 179 economies based on 10 measures of economic freedom, others have tried to gauge nations' environmental performance. Such evaluations are subjective— likely more so than measures of economic freedom—and limited by the availability of reliable data. However, one well-regarded effort sis the 2010 Environmental Performance Index (EPI), conducted by Yale University's Center for Environmental Law and Policy and other organizations.[1]

The EPI ranks 163 nations based on 10 categories of environmental public health and ecosystem measures. Among the former are access to safe drinking water and sanitation, and among the latter are protection of forests and fisheries as well as efforts to address global warming. Drawing on data from 2007 and

[1] Yale Center for Environmental Law & Policy and Center for International Earth Science Information Network in collaboration with the World Economic Forum and Joint Research Centre of the European Commission, *2010 Environmental Performance Index*, January 2010, at *http://www.epi.yale.edu/file_columns/0000/0157/epi2010_report.pdf*, and "2010 Environmental Performance Index: Summary for Policymakers," at *http://ciesin.columbia.edu/repository/epi/data/2010EPI_summary.pdf* (cited hereafter as "2010 EPI Summary").

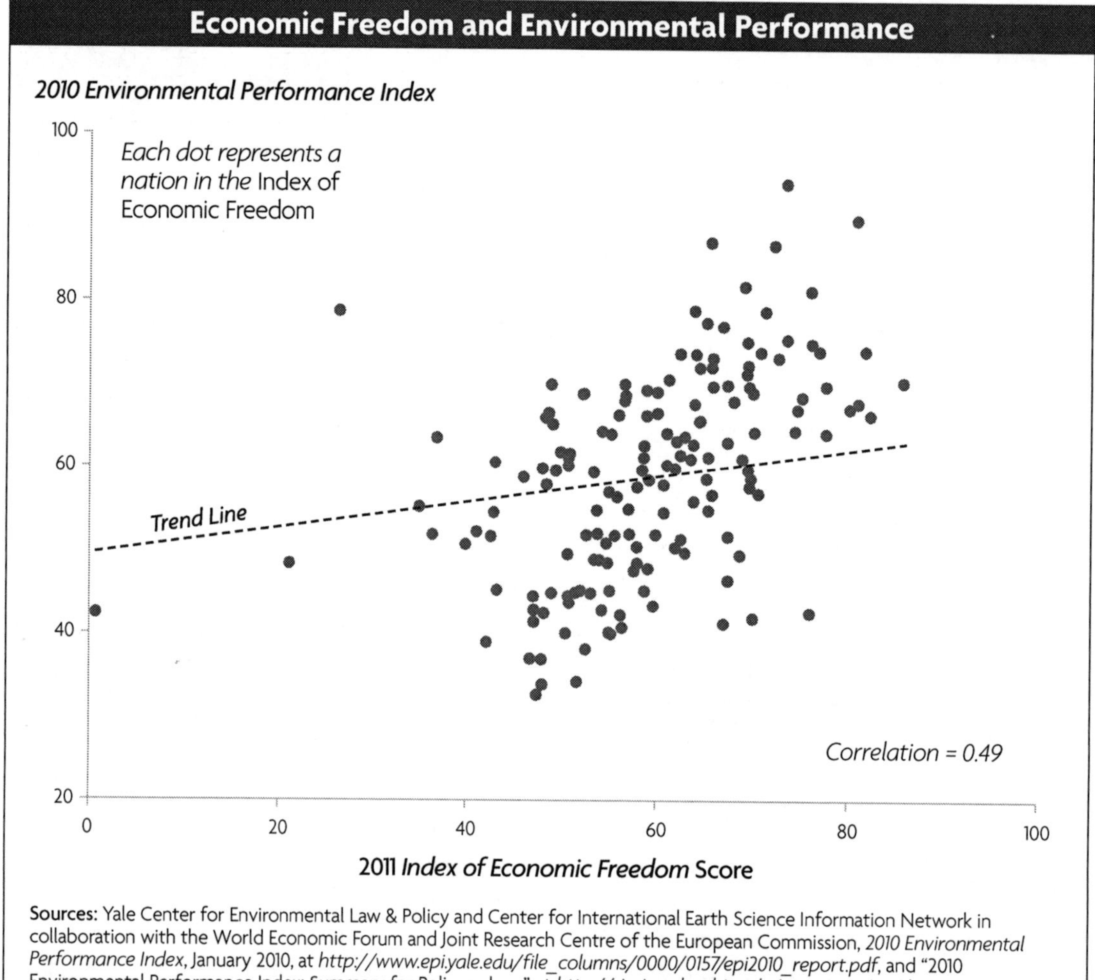

Sources: Yale Center for Environmental Law & Policy and Center for International Earth Science Information Network in collaboration with the World Economic Forum and Joint Research Centre of the European Commission, *2010 Environmental Performance Index*, January 2010, at *http://www.epi.yale.edu/file_columns/0000/0157/epi2010_report.pdf*, and "2010 Environmental Performance Index: Summary for Policymakers," at *http://ciesin.columbia.edu/repository/epi/data/2010EPI_summary.pdf*; Terry Miller and Kim R. Holmes, *2011 Index of Economic Freedom* (Washington, D.C.: The Heritage Foundation and Dow Jones & Company, Inc., 2011), at *www.heritage.org/index*.

Chart 1 heritage.org

2008, the best performers include Iceland, Switzerland, Sweden, and Costa Rica. Among the worst are Mauritania, the Central African Republic, Turkmenistan, and Haiti.

The EPI is not without its flaws, such as the excessive weight it gives to global warming relative to other environmental concerns. Furthermore, America's sharp drop in the rankings over a short span—28th in 2006, 39th in 2008, and 61st in 2010—raises methodological questions, especially given that, by most measures, America's environment was improving over this same period. Overall, however, the EPI is a useful gauge of national environmental performance.

Correlating the two indices, one finds a positive relationship between a nation's level of economic freedom and its environmental performance. (See Chart 1.) In other words, free economies tend to be clean economies. This pattern can be seen regionally as well. (See Chart 2.) Recognition of this relationship points to a number of significant policy lessons that can be drawn as nations seek to improve their approach to protecting the environment.

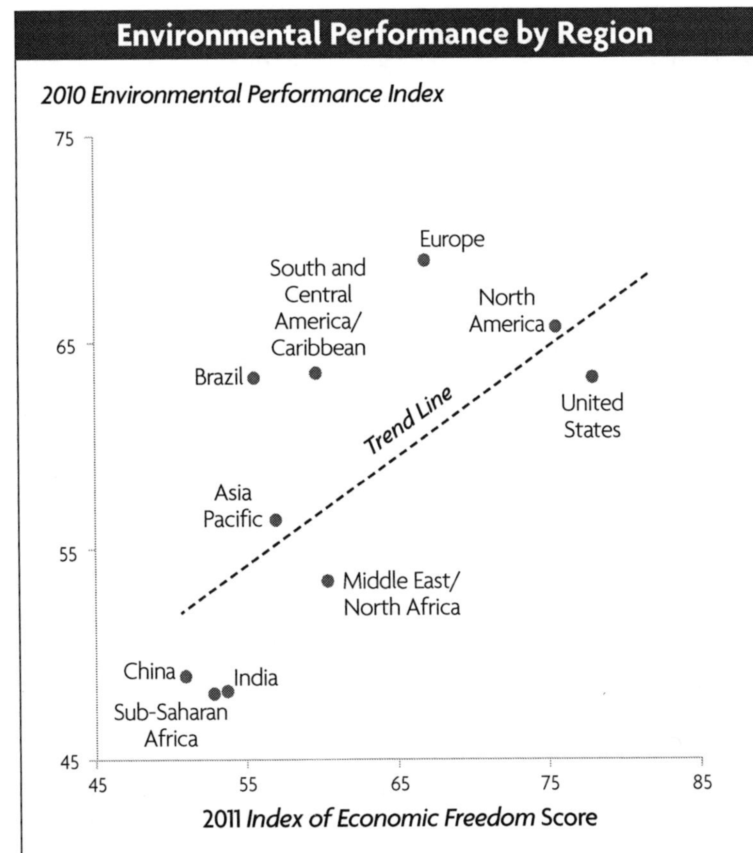

Sources: Yale Center for Environmental Law & Policy and Center for International Earth Science Information Network in collaboration with the World Economic Forum and Joint Research Centre of the European Commission, *2010 Environmental Performance Index*, January 2010, at *http://www.epi.yale.edu/file_columns/0000/0157/epi2010_report.pdf*, and "2010 Environmental Performance Index: Summary for Policymakers," at *http://ciesin.columbia.edu/repository/epi/data/2010EPI_summary.pdf*; Terry Miller and Kim R. Holmes, *2011 Index of Economic Freedom* (Washington, D.C.: The Heritage Foundation and Dow Jones & Company, Inc., 2011), at *www.heritage.org/index*.

FREE = WEALTHY = CLEAN

The *Index of Economic Freedom* finds a very clear association between economic freedom and prosperity.[2] The EPI similarly finds that "[w]ealth correlates highly with EPI scores."[3]

There are simple reasons for the association between wealth and environmental performance. One can think of environmental protection as a good that only prosperous societies can afford. People who lack the necessities do not have the luxury of worrying about endangered species or the health of forests, and even if they did, they would not have the wherewithal to do much about it. However, as economies develop, a point is reached at which there is both the willingness and the means to address environmental concerns. Most countries show increasing levels of environmental harm over time until a certain level of per capita wealth is achieved, and then the environment begins to improve.[4] The exact level of wealth needed before things start to become cleaner varies across countries and among different environmental concerns, but the general trend is clear. This is often referred to as the environmental transition or the environmental Kuznets curve. (See Chart 3.)

Many mistakenly believe that rising wealth harms the environment as per

---

[2] See Chart 3, "Economic Freedom Promotes Greater Prosperity," in Terry Miller and Kim R. Holmes, *2010 Index of Economic Freedom* (Washington: The Heritage Foundation and Dow Jones & Company, Inc., 2010), p. 49.

[3] "2010 EPI Summary," p. 3.

[4] Indur M. Goklany, *The Improving State of the World: Why We're Living Longer, Healthier, More Comfortable Lives on a Cleaner Planet* (Washington: Cato Institute, 2007) pp. 103–116; Bruce Yandle, Madhusudan Bhattarai, and Maya Vijayaraghavan, "Environmental Kuznets Curves: A Review of Findings, Methods, and Policy Implications," Property and Environment Research Center *Research Study* No. 02-1 Update, April 2004, at http://www.perc.org/pdf/rs02_1a.pdf

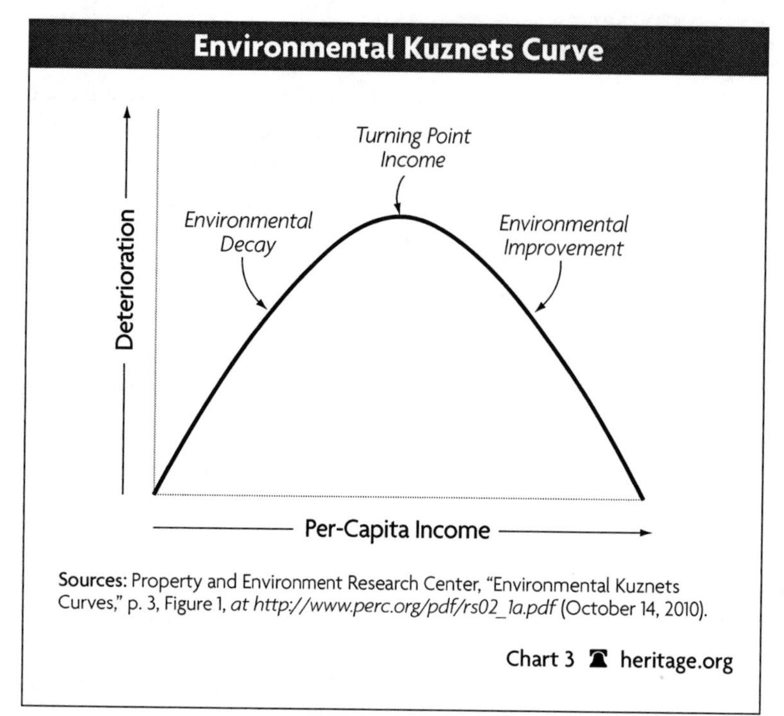

capita usage of energy and other resources increases. Indeed, some activists and academics pursue environmentalism as if it were a crusade against materialism.[5] However, such views are out of step with the empirical evidence. In reality, anything that jeopardizes continued economic growth likely also jeopardizes continued environmental improvement.

Another common assumption is that the environment improves only after national laws and regulations are imposed, but this is not the case. For example, air pollution in America actually reached its peak and began improving before the enactment of the federal Clean Air Act and creation of the Environmental Protection Agency to implement it in 1970.[6] To the extent that governments took the lead, it was state and local governments. In effect, Americans reached a level of prosperity (as well as accompanying technological advancement) that enabled progress in air quality at the state and local levels as the public began to demand it. The private sector also played a role, as the profit motive leads to improvements in energy and resource efficiency, which drive down emissions per unit of output.

Similarly, improvements in America's water quality began decades before enactment of the Clean Water Act and Safe Drinking Water Act in the early 1970s, and similar trends have occurred in many other nations.[7] Once again, state and local governments and private-sector innovation led the way. If anything, national laws were a lagging indicator, and to the extent that they were unnecessarily expensive or interfered with ongoing efforts, they may even have been counterproductive.[8]

Nor are environmental laws of any value without the wealth to implement them. Many developing nations have tough laws on the books that are simply underenforced or ignored in practice. For example, Mexico has stringent air and water pollution statutes not unlike the American statutes, but air and water quality are worse south of the border.

National laws are only one (and not necessarily the best) means by which a society committed to addressing environmental concerns can do so. But it is the underlying wealth that makes any chosen means feasible, and a

---

[5] See Anne H. Ehrlich and Paul R. Ehrlich, *Healing the Planet: Strategies for Resolving the Environmental Crisis* (Reading, Pa.: Perseus Publishing, 1991).

[6] Goklany, *The Improving State of the World*, pp. 137–139, 232–234.

[7] *Ibid.*, pp. 153–158, 232–234.

[8] Steven F. Hayward, "The United States and the Environment: Laggard or Leader?" American Enterprise Institute *Environmental Policy Outlook* No. 1, February 2008, at *http://www.aei.org/outlook/27548*; Jonathan H. Adler, "Free and Green: A New Approach to Environmental Protection," *Harvard Journal of Law & Public Policy*, Vol. 24, No. 2 (Spring 2001), at http://www.thefreelibrary.com/Free+and+green:+a+new+approach+to+environmental+protection-a074802881.

free economy is the best way to generate that necessary wealth.

NON-WEALTH FACTORS THAT MAKE FREE ECONOMIES CLEAN

Most significantly, a well-developed system of private property rights, enforced through an effective legal system, provides for better stewardship of natural resources than is provided by a system that is characterized by no clear ownership or overwhelming government ownership.[9] In fact, measures of property rights (one of the 10 equally weighted factors that comprise the *Index of Economic Freedom*) correlate more closely with environmental performance than do measures of overall economic freedom. (See Chart 4.)

A property owner with the three d's—defined, defensible, and devisable rights—is uniquely incentivized to take care of his own property and actively discourage others from harming it. We see this all around us. Consider a typical homeowner's yard, which is better maintained and kept freer of trash than an unclaimed lot or a public park.

This phenomenon turns out to be true on a larger scale as well, and with environmental implications.[10] For example, the devastating forest fires that have become common in the western U.S. in recent years have originated primarily on federally controlled lands, not in privately owned forests, which tend to be much better managed against such risks.[11] Around the world, nations that lack well enforced private property rights—corrupt states like Zimbabwe, where farmland is routinely confiscated and it is uncertain who really owns what, or Communist states like North Korea where the central government controls nearly every acre—score low in both economic freedom and environmental performance.[12]

Environmental measures that infringe on property rights often backfire, as evidenced in the United States by the Endangered Species

Environmental Performance and Property Rights

In the chart below, nations are placed into four equal-sized groups based on their Property Rights score in the 2011 Index of Economic Freedom.

Average Score of the Environmental Performance Index

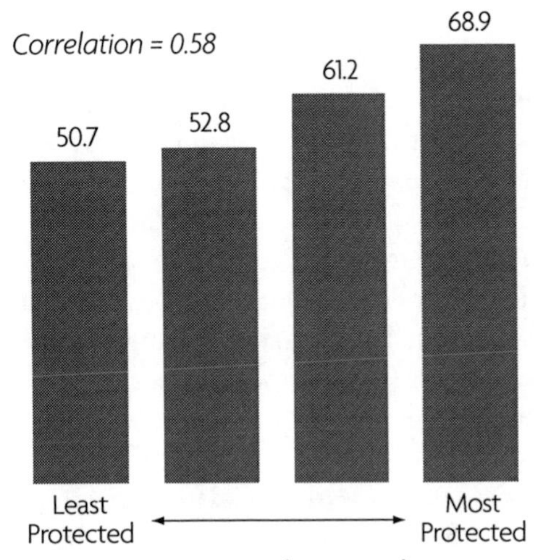

Property Rights Quartile

Sources: Yale Center for Environmental Law & Policy and Center for International Earth Science Information Network in collaboration with the World Economic Forum and Joint Research Centre of the European Commission, *2010 Environmental Performance Index*, January 2010, at *http://www.epi.yale.edu/file_columns/0000/0157/epi2010_report.pdf*, and "2010 Environmental Performance Index: Summary for Policymakers," at *http://ciesin.columbia.edu/repository/epi/data/2010EPI_summary.pdf*; Terry Miller and Kim R. Holmes, *2011 Index of Economic Freedom* (Washington, D.C.: The Heritage Foundation and Dow Jones & Company, Inc., 2011), at *www.heritage.org/index*.

Chart 4 heritage.org

---

[9] Robert J. Smith, "Privatizing the Environment," *Policy Review*, Spring 1982, pp. 11–50; Terry L. Anderson and Donald R. Leal, *Free Market Environmentalism* (Boulder, Colo.: Westview Press, 1991).

[10] Robert J. Smith," Resolving the Tragedy of the Commons by Creating Private Property Rights in Wildlife," *Cato Journal*, Vol. 1, No. 2 (Fall 1981), at http://cei.org/pdf/4420.pdf.

[11] Robert Nelson, *A Burning Issue: A Case for Abolishing the U.S. Forest Service* (Lanham, Md.: *Rowman & Littlefield, 2000).*

[12] *Miller and Holmes,* 2010 Index of Economic Freedom, *pp. 255–256 and 447–448; "2010 EPI Summary," p. 4.*

Act.[13] The statute has a very poor record of actually helping listed species, in part because it punishes farmers, ranchers, and other property owners with onerous restrictions if such species appear on their land. The application of this law forces landowners—many, if not most, of whom would otherwise be predisposed toward helping species—to preemptively make their land unsuitable for endangered animals (for example, by cutting down trees before they become big enough to serve as nesting sites for certain listed birds) and thus avoid the act's potentially ruinous burdens.[14]

Free trade, another component of the *Index of Economic Freedom*, also correlates strongly with environmental performance. (See Chart 5.) The reasons go beyond the wealth created by the mutually beneficial exchange of goods and services. Perhaps more important, trade encourages the development and widespread deployment of cleaner and more efficient technologies regardless of their nation of origin.[15] It also allows nations to specialize, enhancing efficiencies that are both economically and environmentally beneficial. Of course, to the extent that nations restrict trade, they forgo some or all of these benefits. For example, some countries impose strict tariffs on tech nologies that could reduce greenhouse gas emissions and air pollutants.[16]

Environmental Performance and Trade Freedom

In the chart below, nations are placed into four equal-sized groups based on their Trade Freedom score in the 2011 Index of Economic Freedom.

Average Score of the Environmental Performance Index

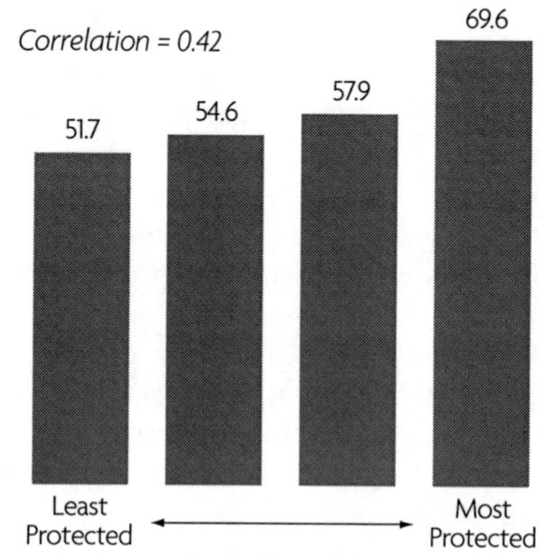

Sources: Yale Center for Environmental Law & Policy and Center for International Earth Science Information Network in collaboration with the World Economic Forum and Joint Research Centre of the European Commission, *2010 Environmental Performance Index*, January 2010, at *http://www.epi.yale.edu/file_columns/0000/0157/epi2010_report.pdf*, and "2010 Environmental Performance Index: Summary for Policymakers," at *http://ciesin.columbia.edu/repository/epi/data/2010EPI_summary.pdf*; Terry Miller and Kim R. Holmes, *2011 Index of Economic Freedom* (Washington, D.C.: The Heritage Foundation and Dow Jones & Company, Inc., 2011), at *www.heritage.org/index*.

Chart 5 heritage.org

Free economies also encourage social stability, which is necessary in dealing with environmental challenges. This is especially true of environmental problems with costly and complex solutions that require a longterm commitment. Economic freedom is also correlated with democratization and freedom from corruption: The governments that are most responsive to the popular will are the ones that

---

[13] Implementation of the Endangered Species Act of 1973, *Report to the House Committee on Resources, Majority Staff, 109th Congress, May 2005, at http://www.waterchat.com/Features/Archive/050517_ESA_Implementation_Report.pdf.*

[14] *Charles C. Mann and Mark L. Plummer,* Noah's Choice: The Future of Endangered Species *(New York: Alfred A. Knopf, 1995).*

[15] *Daniella Markheim, "Opportunity at Copenhagen—Nations Should Promote Free Trade at the Climate Conference," Heritage Foundation* Copenhagen Consequences, *No. 7, December 4, 2009, pp. 3–5, at* http://s3.amazonaws.com/thf_media/2009/pdf/CC7.pdf; *Sallie James, "A Harsh Climate for Trade: How Climate Change Proposals Threaten Global Commerce," Cato Institute* Trade Policy Analysis No. 41, September 9, 2009, pp. 14–17, at http://www.cato.org/pub_display.php?pub_id=10520.

[16] Tim Wilson, "Undermining Mitigation Technology: Compulsory Licensing, Patents and Tariffs," Institute of Public Affairs *Backgrounder* 21/1, August 2008, at http://www.ipa.org.au/library/publication/1219192134_document_wilson_mitigationtechnology.pdf.

deal most effectively with their environmental concerns.

In sum, the very same principles that make people freer and unleash economic progress also serve to advance environmental improvement.

FREEDOM'S TECHNOLOGICAL EDGE

The role of technology is also critical to environmental protection. Many environmental challenges await the technologies that can address them effectively and affordably, and free economies foster such innovation. This is partially due to the wealth effect, as stronger economies invest more in research and development and can more readily afford to deploy new technologies.17[17] In addition, free economies reward successful entrepreneurs, including those who find ways to improve efficiency or reduce waste.18 [18]Intellectual property rights also help to incentivize the development of new technologies, as do tax policies that encourage the replacement of older and dirtier plant and equipment with newer and cleaner production processes. On the other hand, governments that prop up inefficient state-run entities or impose burdensome environmental regulations on new facilities while grandfathering less efficient older ones impede the benefits of capital turnover.

There are many examples of free economies leading the way with advances that provide both economic and environmental benefits. For example, American agriculture has become much more efficient by incorporating improvements in crop varieties as well as advances in farming methods and machinery. This has enabled a nearly threefold increase in the amount of food grown in the U.S. since 1930 while actually decreasing the acreage needed to grow it.[19] Needless to say, the many experiments in state-run agriculture over this span did not do nearly as well. Improvements in yield per acre have allowed other land to be left in its natural state; in fact, the extent of American forests and other natural habitat has increased along with rising farm productivity.[20]

The agriculture example also demonstrates how technology and trade can intersect to extend the environmental benefits around the world. American food production currently exceeds domestic demand, and the surplus is exported to countries that are less able to produce it as efficiently. In other instances, the technological advances themselves have been exported, allowing farmers in other nations to achieve similar yield gains using the breakthroughs pioneered in the U.S. Either way, the environment benefits by reducing the amount of global habitat destruction from conversion to cropland. Of course, such benefits can accrue only to the extent allowed by trade policy.

Just as farmers operating in a free economy have dramatically improved productivity and efficiency by incorporating new technologies, so have manufacturers. Over time, every ton of steel, ream of paper, or new car requires less energy and other resource inputs to produce and thus causes less pollution to be emitted. In other words, technological advancement allows for a shrinking environmental impact per unit of production.[21] Though the motive is cost reduction and increased profits, the end result is good for the environment.

Manufacturing in Germany provides a good example of the technological and environmental benefits of economic freedom. During the Cold War, West Germany had more freedom and a cleaner environment than East Germany. It produced energy and goods with considerably lower emissions per unit of output. With the collapse of Communism,

---

[17] Goklany, *The Improving State of the World*, p. 108.

[18] Indur Goklany, "Richer Is Cleaner: Long-Term Trends in Global Air Quality," in *The True State of the Planet: Ten of the World's Premier Environmental Researchers in a Major Challenge to the Environmental* Movement, *ed. Ronald Bailey (New York: Free Press, 1995), pp. 343–345.*

[19] *Goklany, The Improving State of the World, pp. 117–121, 190.*

[20] *Dennis Avery, "Saving the Planet with Pesticides: Increasing Food Supplies While* Preserving the Earth's Biodiversity," in *The True State of the Planet*, pp. 72–73.

[21] Goklany, "Richer Is Cleaner," in *The True State of the Planet*, pp. 344–345.

superior West German technology flooded into the former East Germany, and environmental quality has been improving there ever since. Today, North Korea and South Korea are in the same situation as East and West Germany before the Berlin Wall came down, with disparities in economic freedom leading to disparities in technological progress and environmental performance.

The benefits of technology are likewise significant when it comes to global warming policy, as they can achieve reductions in carbon dioxide emissions from fossil fuel use. Carbon intensity, defined as carbon dioxide emissions per unit of gross domestic product (GDP), has been declining globally.[22]

There is a correlation between carbon intensity trends and economic freedom: The freest of the major economies have generally led the way in reducing carbon intensity.[23] In other words, free economies encourage finding ways to improve energy efficiency or utilize alternative energy sources, and this minimizes the increases in carbon dioxide emissions that are created by each additional dollar of GDP.

The carbon intensity declines point the way to a rational market-based global warming policy that has been ignored in the rush to expand the role of government. The 1997 Kyoto Protocol global warming treaty and national laws and regulations restricting greenhouse gas emissions—one form or another of centralized control over energy use—are all costly departures from economic freedom that show little promise.[24] For example, the Kyoto Protocol has been remarkably ineffective, and the United States has done a better job of reducing emissions as a treaty outsider than have many signatory nations.[25] Further, unlike these expensive and heavy-handed restrictions on energy use, economic freedom makes sense whether or not global warming actually turns out to be a real crisis.

In effect, free economies spur technological advances that allow us to meet human needs while treading ever more lightly on the Earth.

POLICY LESSONS

The correlation between economic freedom and environmental protection and the reasons behind it offer two important lessons as the world addresses environmental concerns.

The first is that the same principles that make societies wealthy—free markets, property rights, rule of law, free trade, limited government— can also make them clean. Thus, the potential for environmental improvement offers yet another good reason for nations to pursue an agenda that raises their score in the *Index of Economic Freedom.*

The second is that environmental measures that take nations in a direction away from economic freedom—for example, by destroying wealth or undercutting the workings of the free market—can be ineffective if not counterproductive and should be avoided.

---

[22] U.S. Department of Energy, Energy Information Administration, *International Energy Annual 2006*, Table H.1pco2, "World Carbon Intensity—World Carbon Dioxide Emissions from the Consumption and Flaring of Fossil Fuels per Thousand Dollars of Gross Domestic Product Using Purchasing Power Parities, 1980–2006," at *http://www.eia.doe.gov/pub/international/iealf/tableh1pco2.xls*.

[23] Todd Wynn, "Economic Freedom: A No-Regrets Strategy for Reducing Global Energy Consumption," Cascade Policy Institute, April 2010, at *http://www.cascadepolicy.org/pdf/041310_Freedom_on_Energy.pdf.*

[24] See Ben Lieberman, "What Americans Need to Know About the Copenhagen Global Warming Conference," Heritage Foundation *Special Report* No. 71, November 17, 2009, at *http://www.heritage.org/Research/Reports/2009/11/What-Americans-Need-to-Know-About-the-Copenhagen-Global-Warming-Conference*; David W. Kreutzer, Karen A. Campbell, William W. Beach, Ben Lieberman, and Nicolas D. Loris, "What Boxer–Kerry Will Cost the Economy," Heritage Foundation *Backgrounder* No. 2365, January 26, 2010, at *http://www.heritage.org/Research/Reports/2010/01/What-Boxer-Kerry-Will-Cost-the-Economy*; Ben Lieberman, "Proposed Global Warming Bills and Regulations Will Do More Harm Than Good," Heritage Foundation *WebMemo* No. 2665, October 23, 2009, at *http://www.heritage.org/Research/Reports/2009/10/Proposed-Global-Warming-Bills-and-Regulations*-Will-Do-More-Harm-Than-Good.

[25] See Lieberman, "What Americans Need to Know About the Copenhagen Global Warming Conference," p. 2.

TIME FOR A SMARTER APPROACH TO GLOBAL WARMING

Investing in energy R&D might work. Mandated emissions cuts won't.

By BJØRN LOMBORG

December 15, 2009

Copenhagen

The saddest fact of climate change—and the chief reason we should be concerned about finding a proper response—is that the countries it will hit hardest are already among the poorest and most long-suffering.

In the run-up to this month's global climate summit in Copenhagen, the Copenhagen Consensus Center dispatched researchers to the world's most likely global-warming hot spots. Their assignment: to ask locals to tell us their views about the problems they face. Over the past seven weeks, I recounted in these pages what they told us concerned them the most. In nearly every case, it wasn't global warming.

Everywhere we went we found people who spoke powerfully of the need to focus more attention on more immediate problems. In the Bauleni slum compound in Lusaka, Zambia, 27-year-old Samson Banda asked, "If I die from malaria tomorrow, why should I care about global warming?" In a camp for stateless Biharis in Bangladesh, 45-year-old Momota Begum said, "When my kids haven't got enough to eat, I don't think global warming will be an issue I will be thinking about." On the southeast slopes of Mt. Kilimanjaro in Tanzania, 45-year-old widow and HIV/AIDS sufferer Mary Thomas said she had noticed changes in the mountain's glaciers, but declared: "There is no need for ice on the mountain if there is no people around because of HIV/AIDS."

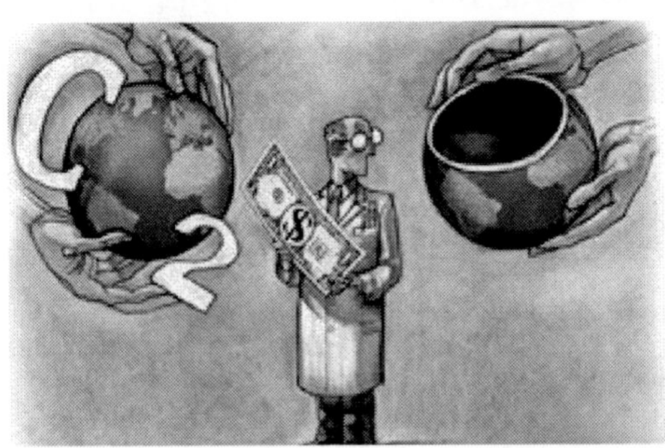

David Klein

There is no question that global warming will have a significant impact on already existing problems such as malaria, malnutrition, and water shortages. But this doesn't mean the best way to solve them is to cut carbon emissions.

Take malaria. Most estimates suggest that if nothing is done, 3% more of the Earth's population will be at risk of infection by 2100. The most efficient global carbon cuts designed to keep average global temperatures from rising any higher than two degrees Celsius above pre-industrial levels (a plan proposed by the industrialized G-8 nations) would cost the world $40 trillion a year in lost economic growth by 2100—and have only a marginal impact on reducing the at-risk malaria population. By contrast, we could spend $3 billion a year on mosquito nets, environmentally safe indoor DDT sprays, and subsidies for new therapies—and within 10 years cut the number of malaria infections by half. In other words, for the money it would take to save one life with carbon cuts, smarter policies could save 78,000 lives.

Many well-meaning people argue that we do not need to choose between tackling climate change and addressing these more immediate problems directly. We can, they say, do both. If only that were true. Just last week, activists from the international aid agency Oxfam reported evidence that European countries were planning to "cannibalize" existing development aid budgets and repackage them as climate-change assistance. According to Oxfam, if rich nations diverted $50 billion to climate change, at least 4.5 million children could die and 8.6 million fewer people could have access to HIV/AIDS treatment. And what would we get for that $50 billion? Well, spending that much on Kyoto-style carbon-emissions cuts would reduce temperatures by all of one-thousandth of one degree Fahrenheit over the next hundred years.

Money spent on carbon cuts is money we can't use for effective investments in food aid, micronutrients, HIV/Aids prevention, health and education infrastructure, and clean water and sanitation. This does not mean that we should ignore global warming. But it does raise serious questions about our dogmatic pursuit of a strategy that can only be described as breathtakingly expensive and woefully ineffective.

As I write this in the Bella Center in Copenhagen, I am surrounded by delegates, politicians and activists engaged in negotiating a successor to the Kyoto Protocol. Almost every one of them is singing from the same hymn-book: The world's nations must commit themselves to drastic, immediate carbon cuts if we are to avoid the worst of global warming.

The tune may be seductive, but the lyrics don't make any sense. Even if every major government were to slap huge taxes on carbon fuels—which is not going to happen—it wouldn't do much to halt climate change any time soon. What it would do is cost us hundreds of billions—if not trillions—of dollars, because alternative energy technologies are not yet ready to take up the slack.

Over the last several centuries, the world economy has exploded and the human condition has improved immeasurably because of cheap fossil fuels; we're not going to end that connection in just a few decades. Just before the summit convened, political leaders from a number of major nations were lauded for announcing carbon-reduction targets that are in fact economically, technically, and politically impossible to achieve. We saw the same thing at the 1992 "Earth Summit" in Rio de Janeiro and then again a decade later in Kyoto. And just like the promises made back then, the vows being made now in Copenhagen are sure to be broken by future administrations. Pretending otherwise is fraudulent.

There was one positive sign in Copenhagen last week. Someone leaked a draft text of a proposed climate agreement that would break away from the deeply flawed Kyoto model (which exempted the developing world from having to promise anything) and compel both rich and poor nations alike to agree to specific carbon cuts. The leak caused great dissension and infighting among delegates, reflecting a realization—at last—that cutting carbon emissions is not going to be easy.

Of course, I would like to see the politicians move even further away from the Kyoto approach. Instead of making far-fetched promises about greenhouse gases, how about a concrete commitment to green energy research and development? Specifically, we should radically increase spending on R&D for green energy—to 0.2% of global GDP, or $100 billion. That's 50 times more than the world spends now—but still twice as cheap as Kyoto. Not only would this be both affordable and politically achievable, but it would also have a real chance of working.

In order to make this kind of shift, leaders will have to stop papering over a consistent record of failure and instead recognize that the Kyoto approach is going nowhere. In this sense, the likely failure of the Copenhagen summit could end up being a blessing in disguise. If we are serious about helping the world's worst-off inhabitants, we are going to need to rethink our approach completely.

Mr. Lomborg is director of the Copenhagen Consensus Center, a think tank, and author of "Cool It: The Skeptical Environmentalist's Guide to Global Warming" (Knopf, 2007).

DOES HELPING THE PLANET HURT THE POOR?

No, if the West Makes Sacrifices

By PETER SINGER

January 22, 2011

All of us who are middle class or above in the U.S. and other industrialized nations spend money on many things we do not need. We could instead donate that money to organizations that will use it to make a huge difference in the lives of the world's poorest people—people who struggle to survive each day on less than we spend on a bottle of water. For decades, that is what I've been advocating we should do.

But this concern for the poor appears to be in tension with the need to protect our environment. Is there any point in saving the lives of people who will continue to have more children than they can feed? Don't rising populations in developing countries increase the pressure on forests and other ecosystems? Then there is climate change. How would the world cope if everyone were to become affluent and match our per capita rate of greenhouse gas emissions?

I take these questions very seriously. My first popular book, "Animal Liberation," published in 1975, argued that we should extend our ethical concerns beyond the boundary of our species. In Australia, my country of birth, I was a founding member of the Australian Greens. So balancing poverty reduction and environmental values is important to me. The problem is how to do it.

Part of the answer—the easy part—is that poverty reduction and environmental values often point in the same direction. It is simplistic to assume that helping more children to survive to reproductive age is bound to increase population in poor countries. Poor parents often have large families so that at least some of their children will survive to take care of them in old age. As parents grow more confident that their children will live to adulthood, they have fewer children. And if reducing poverty makes it possible for families to send their children (especially their daughters) to school, all the evidence indicates that their children will have smaller families.

But we shouldn't pretend that there is bound to be this kind of harmony between economic development and environmental protection. Some development projects provide employment opportunities for the poor but at a high cost to wilderness. From Indonesia to Brazil, vast areas of tropical rainforest have been cleared to grow palm oil and soybeans or to graze cattle, thus destroying entire ecosystems and releasing huge quantities of carbon.

What should we do? Sometimes we should choose to protect the environment and the nonhuman animals that depend on it, even if that denies economic opportunities to some people living in extreme poverty. Areas rich in unique biodiversity are part of the world's heritage and ought to be protected. We should, of course, try to find alternative environmentally sustainable opportunities for those living in or near these areas. But there is no single currency by which we can measure the benefit of saving human lives against the cost of destroying forests that provide the last remaining refuges for free-living chimpanzees, orangutans or Sumatran tigers.

Cost-benefit analysis certainly can't handle this task. Even when economists ignore environmental concerns, their usual method of assigning a value to human lives leads to the ethically embarrassing conclusion that the poor count for less because they earn less and cannot pay as much to reduce life-threatening risks.

Economists also tend to trip up on the issue of whether to discount the future. Suppose we believe that in 200 years, people would be prepared to pay $1 million (in current dollars) to have a virgin forest in their region. Today, however, we can profit by cutting down the forest. If we discount the future value of the forest by 5% per annum, how large a present-day profit would be necessary to cover the loss of a million dollars in 2211? Just $60. Such a discount rate cannot be justified on the basis of the real rate of return on capital. It implies a pure time discount—that is, it implies that the future matters much less than the present.

Giving equal weight to the interests of future generations provides us with strong reasons to be concerned about environmental preservation, as well as about the more immediate concern of reducing global poverty. We should help today's global poor, but not at the expense of tomorrow's global poor. To preserve the options available to future generations, we should aim at development that does no further damage to wilderness or to endangered species.

It is clear, though, that the planet cannot sustain six billion people at the level of the most affluent billion in the world today, especially in terms of greenhouse gas emissions. The failure of the major industrialized nations to reduce their emissions to a level that will not cause serious adverse effects to others is moral wrongdoing on a scale that exceeds the wrongdoing of the great imperial powers during the era of colonialism.

According to the World Health Organization, the rise in temperature that occurred between the 1970s and 2004 is causing an additional 140,000 deaths every year (roughly equivalent to causing, every week, as many deaths as occurred in the terrorist attacks of Sept. 11, 2001). The major killers are climate-sensitive diseases such as malaria, dengue and diarrhea, which is more common when there is a lack of safe water. Malnutrition resulting from crops that fail because of high temperatures or low rainfall is also responsible for many deaths. Fertile, densely settled delta regions in Egypt, Bangladesh, India and Vietnam are at risk from rising sea levels.

In 2007 the UN's Intergovernmental Panel on Climate Change found that a temperature rise in the range of 2 to 2.4 degrees Celsius by 2080 would put stress on water resources used by 1.2 billion people. Rising sea levels would expose, each year, an additional 16 million people to coastal flooding. A temperature rise limited to two degrees by 2080 now seems about the best we can hope for, and recently there have been alarming indications that sea level rises could be much greater than the IPCC anticipated.

Perhaps a technological miracle is just around the corner, one that will enable everyone in the world to consume energy at something like the levels at which we consume it, without bringing about disaster for everyone. It isn't ethically defensible, however, to do nothing while hoping for a miracle, given that it will be others, not us, who suffer the gravest consequences if that miracle never arrives.

Some argue that there is little point in the older industrialized nations cutting back on their emissions when China has already overtaken the U.S. as the world's leading emitter of greenhouse gases; India's emissions are also growing rapidly. The problem is that someone has to take the lead. Otherwise, everyone will hold back to see who goes first, and no one will act.

All the ethical arguments point to the industrialized Western nations taking the lead. On the familiar rule that "if you broke it, you fix it," there is no doubt that these nations bear historical responsibility for most of the greenhouse gases now in the atmosphere. Several Chinese think tanks recently produced a report titled "Carbon Equity." They calculated that from 1850 to 2004, the average American put 21 times as much carbon dioxide into the atmosphere as the average Chinese, and 53 times as much as the average Indian.

Granted, until the 1980s, no one really knew the effect of putting carbon dioxide into the atmosphere, but we definitely knew about it in 1992 when the "Earth Summit" was held in Rio de Janeiro. The U.S. and other major nations signed a declaration promising to keep greenhouse gas emissions below the level that would cause "dangerous anthropogenic interference with the climate system." That's a promise that has manifestly not been kept.

Even if newly emerging major emitters like China, India and Brazil were prepared to forget about the past and share the burden of major reductions in greenhouse gases, the only fair long-term basis for such a distribution would be equal per capita shares. On that basis, the U.S. is still emitting four or five times as much as China and at least 12 times as much as India.

There is also a strong moral case for saying that rich nations should cut back on their "luxury emissions" before poor nations have to cut back on "subsistence emissions." India still has more than 450 million people living in extreme poverty, and China over 200 million. No one with any concern for human welfare could ask the world's poor to refrain from increasing their greenhouse gas emissions in order to put more food on the table for their families, when we think little of flying down to the tropics for a winter vacation, emitting more in a week than the typical family in a developing country does in a year. Needs should always take precedence over luxuries.

All of us living comfortably in industrialized nations should use more energy from sources other than fossil fuels, use less air-conditioning and less heat, fly and drive less, and eat less meat. And we ought to start doing these things now, for our own sake, for the sake of the global poor and for the sake of future generations everywhere.

A Reply to Bjørn Lomborg

Contrary to what Mr. Lomborg suggests, my essay does not focus exclusively or primarily on green issues, nor do I accept en bloc the green agenda that he criticizes. I am not opposed to the genetic modification of plants, for example, as long as there is proper oversight.

I can't see how my opposition to discounting the future would leave us eating only porridge, as Mr. Lomborg says. We can take our fair share of the abundance that the world is capable of producing, but we should not indulge in luxuries that require the emission of high levels of greenhouse gases, thus imperiling the lives of hundreds of millions of less fortunate people.

Mr. Lomborg doesn't reject the idea that we have an ethical obligation to future generations. Nor does he defend cost-benefit analyses that value a human life in proportion to the person's income. On both issues, he just says that we are too selfish to do what is right. Mr. Lomborg is a technological optimist but an ethical pessimist. I'm all for sustainable technology and economic growth, but I also think we should do what we can to encourage people to take a more ethical approach to global issues.

I wish that Mr. Lomborg were right that $100 billion a year could provide the world's poor with clean drinking water, sanitation, food, health and education, but that figure is wildly optimistic. By using this very low figure, and by ignoring the very real risk that climate change will turn out to be a disaster on an unprecedented scale, Mr. Lomborg can misleadingly claim that trying to slow climate change is a bad investment.

Let me end by agreeing with Mr. Lomborg on the need for more investment in research and development for green energy. Such investment could be funded by a carbon tax or, under a cap-and-trade scheme, by the sale of quotas to emit carbon. Either of these methods of putting a price on carbon would in itself create further economic incentives for the development of green energy.

—Mr. Singer is professor of bioethics at Princeton University and laureate professor at the University of Melbourne. His books include "Animal Liberation," "Practical Ethics" and "The Life You Can Save."

DOES HELPING THE PLANET HURT THE POOR?

Yes, if We Listen to Green Extremists

By BJØRN LOMBORG

January 22, 2011

Peter Singer poses an interesting and important question: Can we afford to both reduce poverty and clean up the environment? From an empirical standpoint, the answer is definitely yes. The developed world is sufficiently rich that doing both should be well within our means.

The key, of course, is being smart about how we tackle these big problems. Right now, the only legally binding climate policy, the European Union's 20-20 policy, will cost its members $250 billion in lost economic growth every year over the next century (according to research by the noted climate economist Richard Tol). Yet the net effect will be an almost immeasurable reduction in global temperatures of just 0.1 degrees Fahrenheit by 2100. If spent smartly, the same resources really could fix both global warming and poverty.

In a curious way, Mr. Singer's essay is an example of one of the stumbling blocks to making smarter policy decisions. He starts out saying we want to do a variety of good things, but almost reflexively he ends up focusing on green issues—and doing so in a very predictable way: The developed world has sinned and needs to atone.

Mr. Singer correctly points out that concerns over the environment and poverty are often linked. But he thinks about this only in terms of how poverty is bad for the environment, since poorer, less educated people tend to have more children, which puts more pressure on such things as forests and biodiversity.

But his argument can—and should—be taken further. As we get richer and such immediate concerns as water, food and health become less of an issue, we become more open to environmental concerns. Among other things, we become more willing to pay extra for technology that pollutes less and to accept more costly regulations to limit pollution.

We've already seen the results of this "greening" of society in the developed world, where for a number of decades air and water pollution has been dropping steadily. In London, which keeps the best statistics, air pollution maxed out in 1890 and has been declining ever since—to the point where the air is now cleaner than it has been at any time since 1585. In similar fashion, in some of the better-off developing countries, the focus has shifted from creating to cleaning up pollution. Today the air in both Mexico City and Santiago, Chile, is getting healthier.

Mr. Singer also evades the awkward point that an excessively green approach can actually make the environment more imperiled. Consider the fate of the world's forests. As we get richer and more environmentally conscious, our growing passion for organic farming and antipathy to genetically modified crops inevitably leads us to accept decreased agricultural yields. An obvious consequence is that we end up converting more wilderness to agricultural use.

We've seen similar unintended consequences from the use of inefficient first-generation biofuels such as ethanol. As a result of pressure from environmentalists and lobbying by agricultural interests, use of these fuels was made mandatory by many governments in the industrialized world. Diverting farm products into our gas tanks has driven up food prices, resulting in more starvation and wasted resources and causing still more forests to be razed.

Mr. Singer criticizes the use of cost-benefit analysis because it doesn't value human lives at the same rate in developed and developing countries. As uncomfortable as it may be, the reality is that we don't actually think of all people as equal. If we did, we would be building all of our new hospitals in developing countries. Mr. Singer may regard this fact as shameful, but ignoring the ethical judgment of nearly everyone makes his analysis less helpful.

Similarly, Mr. Singer criticizes the way that discounting is used by economists to make future costs comparable to values in the present. He argues that we should give "equal weight to the interests of future generations." Once again, this may sound admirable. But think about the consequences of heeding Mr. Singer's advice. By choosing a discount rate close to zero, we effectively say that the desires of infinite numbers of future generations are vastly more important than our own, meaning that we should save the great bulk of our resources for the future and consume just enough to survive. Essentially, our generation should eat porridge, while we leave virtually all benefits to the future.

This was what the economist Nicholas Stern concluded in the controversial 2006 review of climate change that he conducted for the British government. Mr. Stern said, in effect, that we should be saving 97.5% of all our wealth for future generations. The silliness of this view becomes apparent when we realize that, by this logic, our children and grandchildren also would be expected to continue the cycle of bowing to future generations, leaving almost everything to their progeny and pushing forward an ever larger mountain of resources that are never to be consumed.

We don't behave this way. Partly because we are selfish and partly because we expect that future generations are likely to be much better off than we are. Compared with the future, we

Cost-Benefit Analysis

In 2008, Mr. Lomborg's Copenhagen Consensus Center convened some of the world's top economists to evaluate how $75 billion could be best used to solve global problems.

At the top:

Micronutrient supplements for children (vitamin A and zinc)

For an annual cost of $60.4 million, the economists projected a yield of more than $1 billion in benefits.

Tuberculosis management

In 22 countries with a high incidence of TB, diagnosis and treatment would yield $1.7 trillion in benefits for a cost of $18.3 billion.

At the bottom:

Global-warming mitigation

Spending $800 billion on carbon taxes was found to generate only $685 billion worth of benefit.

are the poor generation, and it is hardly moral to have the poor generation pay the most. Rather, it makes sense to leave generalized assets, such as knowledge and technology, to future generations. This gives them a much greater capacity to tackle problems that come their way. Our actual financial savings for the future tend to be about 15% of income. We could debate whether the number should be 10% or 20%, but it is far-fetched to suggest that it should be 97.5%. We all recognize that we should care for the future, but at the same time we should care for ourselves.

Mr. Singer falls into the trap of saying that global warming is so terrible that dealing with it should take priority over all other concerns. This is simply wrong. Global warming is a problem that we must confront, but according to economic modeling by Carlo Carraro of the University of Venice, its damage is likely to cost something on the order of 2% to 5% of GDP by the end of the century.

At the same time, it is helpful to recall that our fossil-fuel economy has created amazing opportunities for almost everyone in the world, lifting hundreds of millions of people out of poverty. The United Nations climate panel estimates that economic growth will enable an increase per capita GDP in developing countries by some 2,400% over the course of the century.

Mr. Singer claims that problems related to climate change (such as an increased incidence of malaria) cause 140,000 deaths a year. Let's put aside for the moment the fact that rising temperatures are likely do more good than harm on this score, preventing so many cold-related fatalities that the net effect of global warming is likely to be a total of about 200,000 fewer people dying each year.

Even if we accept Mr. Singer's concerns, is fighting global warming through drastic carbon cuts really the best way to help people with malaria? By implementing the Kyoto protocol (at a cost of $180 billion a year), we could reduce the number of annual malaria deaths by 1,400. But we could prevent 850,000 malaria deaths a year at a cost of just $3 billion simply by providing adequate supplies of mosquito nets and medicine. For every potential malaria victim saved through climate policy, we could save 36,000 people through smarter, cheaper remedies for malaria.

From Mr. Singer's initial question of whether we can afford to both reduce poverty and clean up the environment, he ends up focusing on global warming and arguing that we simply need to "use less air-conditioning and less heat, fly and drive less, and eat less meat." This is a poor prescription, not only for those of us in developed nations but for developing countries and for future generations as well. It is an incredibly expensive way to achieve very little—and it won't happen.

Fortunately, there is a more sensible way forward that could use the same $250 billion that the European Union is expecting to waste annually on ineffective global warming policies. First, we should spend about $100 billion a year on research and development to make green energy cheaper and more widely available. Mr. Singer argues that it is not ethically defensible just to hope for a "technological miracle" that will allow us to end our reliance on fossil fuels. He is right. We must invest much more in green energy research and development, and it is the most politically realistic and economically efficient way to combat global warming.

This would leave $50 billion a year to develop adaptations for dealing with the impact of global warming and $100 billion a year for the world's poor, a sum that, according to the U.N., would go a long way toward providing them with clean drinking water, sanitation, food, health and education.

We are perfectly capable today of tackling the problems of both poverty and environmental pollution. But to do so, we must think clearly and rationally, and we must carefully weigh the costs and benefits of the approaches available to us.

—Mr. Lomborg is the author of "The Skeptical Environmentalist" and "Cool It." He directs the Copenhagen Consensus Center and is an adjunct professor at Copenhagen Business School.

U.N. CLIMATE TALKS END

Rich Nations Agree to Help Poorer Ones but Put Off Figuring Out Who Will Pay

By JEFFREY BALL And CASSANDRA SWEET

December 13, 2010

World leaders at a climate-change conference in Cancun, Mexico, made clear that addressing the issue will be all about money, agreeing that rich countries would spend potentially trillions of dollars to help poor countries develop on a greener path.

But the diplomats postponed hashing out which rich countries would pay how much, and exactly what the poor countries would have to do to get the checks.

The two-week United Nations climate conference in the resort city of Cancun underscored that future global efforts to address climate change will likely depend more on economic incentives than on environmental mandates.

Countries often seek to curb emissions by raising taxes on fossil-fuel consumption and raising subsidies for energy-efficient and renewable-energy technologies.

That is why international negotiations over climate policy amount to a game of economic chicken, with the world's major economies—notably China and the U.S.—trying to ensure they aren't stuck with the bulk of the cost of emission cuts.

The Cancun talks, which ended Saturday morning after an all-night negotiating session, committed rich countries to "the goal" of creating a fund that starting in 2020 would spend $100 billion a year to help poor countries develop on a cleaner path. That would be on top of the money that rich countries would spend to curb their own emissions. Diplomats also agreed that the World Bank would administer the developing countries' fund, but they left the details—such as where the money would come from—for another day.

"It's really complicated stuff, talking about trying to regulate entire economies, trying to get economies onto lower-carbon paths," Todd Stern, the top U.S. climate negotiator, said in a news conference after the conclusion of the meeting Saturday. "If you can take good steps every year, that's a better way to make progress" than trying to solve the climate problem in a single agreement, he said.

The talks also left in doubt the future of the Kyoto Protocol, a 1997 international treaty that obligates the rich countries that ratified it to start cutting their emissions.

The conference averted a collapse of the diplomatic groundwork laid out in the Kyoto agreement. Despite the continuing disagreements over who will foot the bill, diplomats and many observers hailed the Cancun talks simply for keeping alive the international effort to curb greenhouse-gas emissions. A year ago, after a U.N. climate conference in Copenhagen failed to achieve a global agreement, many predicted such efforts were dead.

The Cancun document urged rich countries to sign up for a tougher round of emissions reductions after 2012, when the Kyoto treaty's current mandates are set to expire.

But Japan, one of the largest economies to have ratified the Kyoto agreement, indicated it doesn't intend to take on deeper emission-cutting obligations under a future treaty unless China and the U.S., too, pledge to shoulder a big chunk of the cost of a climate cleanup.

China and the U.S., the world's biggest economies and biggest emitters, say they are moving to slow their emissions growth voluntarily, through such moves as ramping up energy efficiency and the use of renewable energy. Neither country is subject to a requirement under the Kyoto Protocol to cut its emissions by a specific amount.

It would be "neither fair nor effective" for Japan to pledge deeper emissions cuts without more action by the world's largest emitters, Shinsuke Sugiyama, Japan's top climate negotiator, said Saturday in a news conference following the Cancun talks' conclusion.

China said rich countries must move first. In a statement following the close of the talks, the Chinese government said rich countries should agree to a deeper round of emission cuts under the Kyoto treaty at the next round of U.N. climate talks, to be held at the end of 2011 in South Africa. Rich countries also should provide more money "to support developing countries' efforts in addressing climate change," China said.

Over the past year, many countries have said they're implementing domestic programs to curb emission growth voluntarily. But the International Energy Agency said recently that those pledges aren't enough to prevent global temperatures from rising to a level that many national scientific academies say could trigger dangerous consequences from climate change.

"We have a long, challenging road ahead of us," Connie Hedegaard, the European commissioner for climate action, said Saturday. "A lot remains to be done."

—Jason Dean contributed to this article.

Write to Jeffrey Ball all jeffrey.ball@wsj.com and Cassandra Sweet at cassandra.sweet@wsj.com

THE CAP-AND-TRADE BAIT AND SWITCH

The climate bill in Congress is not the market solution the president promised.

By DAVID SCHOENBROD AND RICHARD B. STEWART

August 24, 2009

As a candidate for president in April 2008, Barack Obama told Fox News that "a cap-and-trade system is a smarter way of controlling pollution" than "top-down" regulation. He was right. With cap and trade the market decides where and how to cut emissions. With top-down regulation, as Mr. Obama explained, regulators dictate "every single rule that a company has to abide by, which creates a lot of bureaucracy and red tape and often-times is less efficient."

It's no wonder that the House advertises its American Clean Energy and Security Act of 2009 (also known as the Waxman-Markey bill) as "cap and trade." And last Thursday a coalition of environmental groups and unions launched a "Made in America Jobs Tour" to sell it as a ticket to "long-term economic prosperity." But the House bill would, if passed by the Senate this autumn, fail the environment and fail the test of economic efficiency.

Waxman-Markey is largely top-down regulation dressed in cap-and-trade clothing. It purports to set a cap on greenhouse gases, but the cap is so loose in the early years that through the use of cheap offsets the U.S. need not significantly reduce its fossil-fuel emissions until about 2025. Then the bill would require a nosedive in fossil-fuel emissions. This balloon mortgage pledge of big cuts later is unlikely to be kept.

The top-down directives come in three forms. First, electric utilities, auto makers and states get free allowances on the condition that they comply with regulations requiring coal sequestration, alternative energy sources, energy conservation, advanced auto technology and more. Second, many other provisions of the 1,428 page bill mandate outright regulation on subjects ranging from how electricity is generated to off-road vehicles and household lighting. Third, still other provisions provide subsidies for government-chosen technology "winners" such as alternate energy sources, plug-in vehicles and weatherization of old buildings.

Progress on most or all such fronts will be needed, but when, where and how should be decided principally by a cap-driven market, not the "red tape" that candidate Obama deplored.

This government dictation of technology would undermine President Obama's March 19 pledge that, by addressing climate change, we would become "the world's leading exporter of renewable energy." That requires coming up with better, lower-cost technologies than the rest of the world. This won't happen if the government picks the technologies. Recall that, in the 1980s, government established the Synfuels Corporation that spent billions to produce energy alternatives and came up with nothing. More recently, government required refiners to put corn-based ethanol into gasoline on the theory that it's good for the environment. Yet we've learned that wide-scale ethanol production can do more harm than good in regard to air quality and climate change, turn wildlife habitat into corn fields, and raise food prices.

By contrast, the cap-and-trade legislation that Congress applied to acid rain in 1990 produced big dividends for the environment and the economy. It cut the acid-rain causing emissions from power plants by 43% and saved electricity consumers billions of dollars compared to top-down regulation.

A cap and trade can be used to tackle carbon emissions more efficiently than top-down micromanagement of technology. Indeed, cap and trade should be used to regulate major conventional pollutants such as sulfur dioxide and nitrogen oxides. It is not only the smarter way to regulate such pollutants, as Mr. Obama recognized, but it is also necessary because key greenhouse gases and many conventional pollutants come from the same fuel-burning processes. Systems for regulating both kinds of pollutants should work together rather than at cross purposes, as detailed in our recent report for the New York Law School and NYU School of Law: "Breaking the Logjam: Environmental Reform for the New Congress and Administration."

Why has the House turned its back on the cap-and-trade approach? Both parties have played to their bases so that the only way for the Democrats to pass Waxman-Markey was to buy swing votes by picking among technologies such as coal sequestration to please critical constituencies.

While the House represents constituencies, the president must keep the focus on the broad national interest. Candidate Obama's comments on cap and trade came when asked to back up his claim that he would be a "uniter" by naming "a hot-button issue where you would be willing to buck the Democratic Party line and say, 'You know what? Republicans have a better idea here?'" President Obama needs to lead on the principles on which he campaigned and the Republicans in the Senate need to listen. Otherwise, Congress will pass something like the House bill or, worse still, won't legislate at all.

In that case, the Environmental Protection Agency would regulate greenhouse gases under the Clean Air Act. This would involve even more top-down control than Waxman-Markey. Regulators would be required, for example, to impose source-specific emission limits on every major new or modified source. Government would decide who cuts emissions through a complicated process that would undoubtedly produce the very red tape and inefficiency Mr. Obama warned about. Congress should instead apply to climate change the market-based solution that it successfully applied to acid rain nearly 20 years ago.

Mr. Schoenbrod teaches law at New York Law School, is a visiting scholar at American Enterprise Institute, and was a staff attorney at the Natural Resources Defense Council. Mr. Stewart teaches law at New York University and was chairman of Environmental Defense Fund.

CHILLING EFFECT

Global warmists try to stifle debate

John Fund

John McCain, Barack Obama and Hillary Clinton all promise bold action on climate change. All have endorsed a form of cap-and-trade system that would severely limit future carbon emissions. The Democratic Congress is champing at the bit to act. So too is the Climate Action Partnership, a coalition of companies led by General Electric and Duke Energy.

You'd think this would be a rich time for debate on the issue of climate change. But it's precisely as sweeping change on climate policy is becoming likely that many people have decided the time for debate is over. One writer puts climate change skeptics "in a similar moral category to Holocaust denial," another envisions "war crimes trials" for the deniers. And during the tour for his film "An Inconvenient Truth," Al Gore himself belittled "global warming deniers" as unworthy of any attention.

Take the reaction to Danish statistician Bjorn Lomborg's latest book, "Cool It," which calls for a reasoned debate on global warming. Mr. Lomborg himself leans left, and he opens his book by declaring his belief that "humanity has caused a substantial rise in atmospheric carbon-dioxide levels over the past centuries, thereby contributing to global warming." But he has infuriated environmentalists by saying it is necessary to debate "whether hysterical and head-long spending on extravagant CO_2-cutting programs at an unprecedented price is the only possible response." To do so, he says, it will be necessary to cool the doomsday rhetoric, allowing a measured discussion about the best ways forward. "Being smart about our future is the reason we have done so well in the past. We should not abandon our smarts now."

Mr. Lomborg's solution is to avoid discredited cap-and-trade programs, in which developing nations limit economic growth while they fruitlessly try to convince booming economies such as India and China to do the same. His alternative: "Let's focus on research and development. Let's focus on noncarbon-emitting technologies like solar, wind, carbon capture, energy efficiency and also, let's realize the solution may come from nuclear fission and fusion." He laments that the climate change issue has been demagogued by ideological groups on both sides, "and the ones who are making panicky or catastrophic claims simply have better press." At the end of the day, he ruefully acknowledges that potential progress and the sorts of solutions he advocates "are just boring things."

Let's hope Mr. Lomborg is wrong in his fear that the media are uninterested in showcasing a real debate on climate change. The proof may be found next week, when hundreds of scientists, economists and policy experts who dissent from the "consensus" that climate change requires radical measures will meet in New York to discuss the latest scientific, economic and political research on climate change. Five tracks of panels will address paleoclimatology, climatology, global warming impacts, the economics of global warming and political factors. It will be keynoted by Czech President Vaclav Klaus, who has argued that economic growth is most likely to create the innovations and know-how to combat any challenges climate change could present in the future. (Information on the conference is here.)

The conference is being organized by the free-market Heartland Institute and 49 other co-sponsors, including a dozen from overseas. Heartland president Joseeph Bast says its politically incorrect purpose is to "explain the often-neglected 'other side' of the climate change debate. This will be their chance to speak out. It will be hard for journalists and policy makers to ignore us."

I wonder. Already, environmental groups have sent out their opinion to their media friends that the conference is simply a platform for corporate apologists and can safely be ignored. One group alleges the conference will have "no real scientists" present despite an impressive array of speakers such as Patrick Michaels, a past president of the American Association of State Climatologists, and Willie Soon, an astrophysicist at the Harvard-Smithsonian Center for Astrophysics.

Critics point out that ExxonMobil gave nearly $800,000 to Heartland between 1998 and 2005 and that the group's board of directors include several people with ties to energy companies. The authors of the blog Real Climate don't engage the issues raised by the conference but instead attack it as stuffed with shills. When Heartland experts tried to respond to those charges, they were blacklisted from the comments section of the Real Climate Web site.

All this has led the Western Standard, a Canadian magazine sympathetic to the global warming skeptics, to predict that "the gathering will be completely ignored, even though it's being held in the news media capital of the world." Let's hope not. Global warming is too important a subject not to debate, and we in the U.S. may rue the day we rushed pell-mell into expensive and shortsighted solutions when much more rational and cost-effective ones were readily available.

CLEANING UP: A SPECIAL REPORT AND CLIMATE CHANGE

Business is Getting Down to Cutting Carbon, but Needs More Incentives to Make Much Difference to Climate Change, argues Emma Duncan

from The Economist

When the notion of global warming first seeped into public consciousness in the 1980s, business took a dim view of it. Admitting that human activity was changing the climate would involve accepting some responsibility, which was likely to mean coughing up cash. So, in 1989, shortly after the establishment of the Intergovernmental Panel on Climate Change, the

body set up under UN auspices to establish a scientific consensus on the issue, the big carbon emitters set up the Global Climate Coalition (GCC). It cast doubt on the science and campaigned against greenhouse-gas reductions.

The GCC folded in 2002. Its line of argument enjoyed a final flowering last year, in a startlingly inane television commercial put out by the business-funded Competitive Enterprise Institute (CEI). It showed pictures of trees (breathing in carbon dioxide) and a happy little girl blowing dandelion seeds (breathing out carbon dioxide). The punchline was: "Carbon dioxide: they call it pollution; we call it life."

These days very few serious businessmen will say publicly either that climate change is not happening or that it is not worth tackling. Even Exxon Mobil, bête noire of the climate-change activists, has now withdrawn funding from the CEI and appears to accept the need for controls on carbon emissions.

Businesses in every sector boast about their greenness. Annual reports elaborate on investments to offset companies' emissions. Of course the companies that do this tend to be those with few emissions, such as banks and retailers. Some oil companies do it too, but they offset only the greenhouse gases that they emit in producing petrol, not the emissions from the petrol itself. Power generators, which emit CO_2 on a huge scale, do not do it.

Yet the corporate world's sudden conversion to greenery is not just fluff. Big emitters are beginning to price carbon into their investment plans, and to alter them accordingly. As a result, wind and solar energy are getting an enormous boost, the price of electricity produced from renewable sources is dropping fast and flurry of projects to sequester carbon emissions from power generation is beginning to get under way. On the transport side, money is flowing into biofuels and electric cars.

Energy has become the hot new area for venture capitalists and universities. MIT's president, Susan Hockfield, has started an "energy initiative" to promote research into alternative sources, storage and cleaning up conventional sources; and student enrolment into energy-related courses has tripled over the past five years. In 2003, the most recent year for which figures are available, America's power-generation industry spent less on R&D as a proportion of turnover than did the country's pet-food industry, which suggests there is scope for more investment.

What is driving this shift towards cleaner energy? First, moral pressure.

EVERYBODY'S GREEN NOW

How America's big companies got environmentalism

Meetings of the Edison Electric Institute, the trade association for the American power utilities, do not normally make waves. But the one that took place at Scottsdale, Arizona, on January 10th of this year was different.

Up until then, the EEI had been split between the companies arguing for carbon constraints—

usually those, like Exelon, PG&E and Entergy, with more gas and nuclear energy than coal—and those arguing against—usually those, like TXU and Southern, with lots of coal. Since coal provides 50% of America's power, the coal utilities had mostly had the upper hand, and the organisation had advocated only voluntary restraint.

But this year the new chairman, Jim Rogers of Duke Energy, asked each of the 50 chief executives present what they thought the government should do about carbon. "It was pretty clear going round the table that the vast majority wanted to move on," says Mr Rogers. Afterwards the EEI announced that it was calling for "regulation." It balked at the word "mandatory," but the implication hung in the air.

Power generation is the biggest source of CO_2 in America. America is the biggest source of CO_2 in the world. If America continues to refuse to control its carbon-dioxide emissions at the federal level, there is no chance that countries such as China and India, whose emissions will soon overtake America's, will control theirs. The EEI's turnaround was therefore significant.

Similar things have been going on in other industries. Companies that once pooh-poohed the idea of climate change have gone quiet; others have come out loudly in support of emissions controls. The shift culminated, in January this year, in the establishment of the United States Climate Action Partnership calling for "strong" federal action to combat climate change. The initiative was launched by ten blue-chip companies, along with four NGOs. Membership has now doubled, and includes GM, GE, BP, Alcan and Alcoa.

Attitudes in corporate America have changed in part because a federal system of controls has come to look like the lesser of two evils. America's states have already started to legislate to cut emissions. California is leading the charge. Last September it passed Assembly Bill 32, under which carbon emissions are to be cut to 1990 levels by 2020 and to 80% below 1990 levels by 2050. It will probably be implemented through a European-style cap-and-trade scheme. And California has adopted a low-carbon fuel standard that will require oil companies to cut the carbon content of their petrol. Other state governments have been watching California's initiative carefully and seem likely to follow its lead.

For companies, a diverse patchwork of state-wide systems is much harder to cope with than a single nationwide system. According to Ken Cohen, vice-president of public affairs at Exxon Mobil, "we need a uniform and predictable system. If the states are left to their own devices, we won't get that. It needs to be a federal system." And since the Democrats took over Congress last November, the chances of America adopting federal controls have risen sharply. Bills are proliferating. Dan Kammen, of the Energy and Resources Group at the University of California at Berkeley, says he has never had so many calls along the lines of: "I'm Congressman X and I need to write a high-profile bill on climate change. What should it say?"

But in accepting the idea of federal regulation, companies are not just bowing to the inevitable. There is money in it, too. If the American government adopts a cap-and-trade system (see next article), it will hand out permits to pollute. They are, in effect, cash. According to Paul Bledsoe of the National Commission on Energy Policy, those allowances are likely to be worth in the region of $40 billion. Companies therefore want to be involved in designing those regulations. As Mr Rogers explains: "There's a saying in Washington: if you're not at the table, you're on the menu."

The process has become self-reinforcing. In order to be seen to be green, companies have to lobby for emissions controls. That increases the pressure for emissions controls, which in turn increases the need to be seen to be green.

The more that American businessmen examine the European system, the less alarming the prospect of carbon constraints begins to look. Not only has it resulted in a lot of cash being handed over, but it has also created a whole new business: the carbon market.

Easy options—HFC-23 and other fabulously dirty (ie, profitable) industrial gases—will soon run out. Guy Turner at New Carbon Finance reckons that the days of the CER that costs less than €1 to produce are over, and that the range is now more like €1-5. But there is plenty of scope at that level. China's industrialisation is a fast and dirty business, and there will be no shortage of greenhouse gases produced there for rich-country money to clean up.

That is part of the problem. Of the 65% of companies surveyed by Point Carbon earlier this year which claimed that the ETS had led them to abate their emissions (up from 15% the previous year), most were planning to buy credits rather than cut their own emissions. Yet the ETS was intended to cut European emissions as well as Chinese ones.

This is happening on a small scale. At times the carbon price has made it worth power companies' while to switch from dirty fuels to cleaner gas. "We massively reduced our lignite production when the CO_2 price was at its height," says Alfred

IRRATIONAL INCANDESCENCE

People can't be bothered to make easy energy savings

Some ways of cutting carbon are cheaper than others. So, at different carbon prices, different sorts of methods of abatement become worthwhile. Vattenfall, a Swedish power utility, has tried to quantify which ones would be worth undertaking at what price (see chart 3).

The result is a testament to economic irrationality. The measures below the horizontal line have a negative abatement cost—in other words, by carrying them out, people and companies could both cut emissions and save money. At a macroeconomic level they would boost, rather than reduce, economic growth.

Lighting, for instance, accounts for some 19% of the world's electricity use. A standard incandescent light bulb costs around €1, says Theo van Deursen, chief executive of Philips Lighting, and uses €15-worth of electricity a year. A low-energy one costs €5-6 and uses €3-worth. The payback on investing in a compact fluorescent bulb, therefore, is less than a year. Yet low-energy lighting makes up only 30% of Philips's sales. Mr van Deursen admits to being disappointed. Sales are rising faster in the developing world: there, people pay more attention to electricity bills than they do in the rich world.

Economists trying to explain this apparent irrationality suggest that the savings are too small and the effort involved in change too large. People find their electricity bills too boring to think about; within companies, those responsible for keeping bills down may not have the authority to spend the necessary capital. Another explanation is the agency problem: that the developer who would have to pay higher capital costs up front will not be forking out for the electricity bills. Besides, people buy houses not because they have good insulation but because they have pretty views.

Compared with pursuing greater energy efficiency, the abatement measures into which so much money is now being poured look rather expensive. Carbon capture and storage and wind and solar power, for instance, all have positive, and relatively high, abatement costs.

But the cheapest sources of abatement are diffcult for policymakers to get at. Billions of different actors are involved. They cannot be targeted in the way that a few hundred factories can. What is more, amoderate carbon price is not likely to be effective, since people clearly do not care enough about cost.

One policy option is to decouple the utilities' revenues from the amount of electricity they sell. That gives them an incentive to increase the effciency of power usage rather than to produce and sell extra power. California is already doing this, which is presumably why electricity prices there are among the highest in America, while consumption is relatively low.

Energy-efficiency standards, such as building regulations, are another option. Economists generally prefer to avoid rules that specify what companies can produce and how, because they require governments, rather than markets, to allocate resources, and markets tend to do a better job. But if, as in this case, a public as well as a private good is involved, and the market does not seem to be doing its job properly, there is an argument for governments giving it a

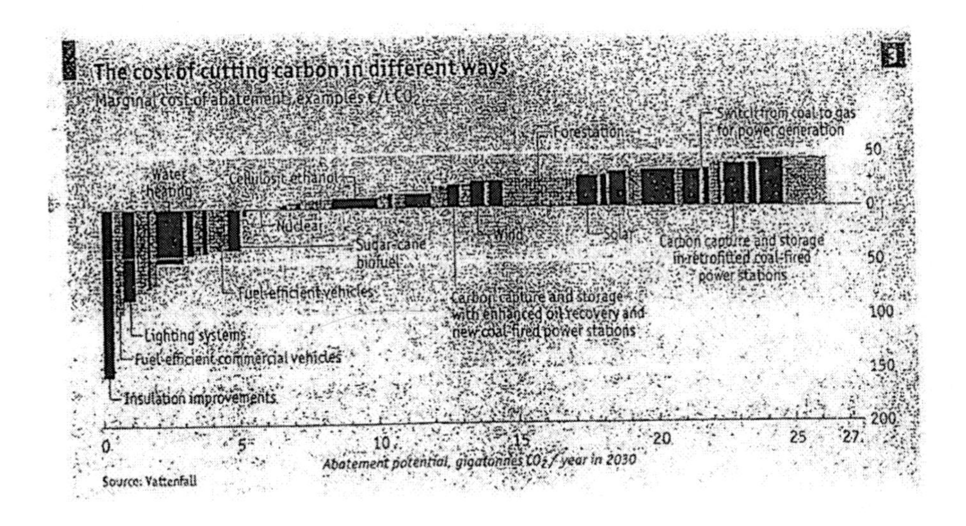

nudge.

There are lots of energy-efficiency regulations in place already, and they are being tightened. Incandescent light bulbs are the top target at the moment. Both the European Union and Australia said earlier this year that they are planning to ban them. But the man in the vanguard of this green revolution is Fidel Castro, who started phasing them out two years ago.

Mr Khosla is backing some 27 companies in four clean-energy areas: replacing oil, replacing coal, developing new materials and energy efficiency. His model is the usual one: he finds an inventor or a good piece of intellectual property, adds some money and an experienced manager and waits for it to flourish or fail.

Bud Klepper, for instance, had been working for years on a process to make cellulosic ethanol without anybody paying much attention. But then he met Mr Khosla, who liked his scheme, introduced him to Mitch Mandich, a former Apple employee, added some money and stirred. In February the resulting company, Range Fuels, announced that it would build a commercial-scale cellulosic ethanol plant in Georgia, using the state's abundant wood cuts off as feedstock.

The VCs who used this model to transform the computer business reckon that they can do the same for the energy business. "The investments we're making are like those we made in the internet," says Mr Doerr. "They're based on technological and scientic innovation, they're driven by entrepreneurs, and they're distributed, in the way that the internet was distributed." The VCs also reckon that they can topple incumbents, as they did in the information and communications business. "Look at voice telephony," says Mr Khosla. "These days, it's basically free. Ten years ago, people told me that would never happen. AT&T believed that—and look what happened to them."

At the other end of the scale is Mr Immelt. "When I was looking at the growth potential of our businesses three years ago," he says, "I saw an emphasis on clean energy and energy efficiency, on scarcity and the rise of regulatory pressure. And I thought—we've got something here. And so he developed the theme, making GE the big company best known for espousing greenness. "Green is green" has become a company mantra. And GE was among the ten companies that launched the United States Climate Action Partnership.

Green synergies

The vehicle that Mr Immelt settled on for promoting green products was Ecomagination. This brings together products from GE's different businesses that are either intrinsically green—like wind turbines—or have been certified as being more competitive and producing fewer emissions than whatever else of that sort is on the market. Not all GE's products get through. The GEnx aero engine, which powers Boeing 747s and 787s, did, but the new-generation CFM engine for narrow-bodied jets did not, because its emission levels are no lower than the competition's. Ecomagination's sales have been rising slightly faster than GE's, by 12% a year rather than 9%. Its energy products have been rattling along.

To a large extent, Ecomagination is a marketing device. GE was selling all those aero and power-generation engines long before Ecomagination was invented, and "fuel efficiency has always been the number one criterion for airline-engine economics," says Tom Brisken, general manager of the GEnx programme. But Mr Immelt has also made sizeable clean-energy investments. He bought Enron's wind-turbine business out of bankruptcy for $358m. Sales rose from $200m in 2002 to around $4 billion last year. His purchase of Chevron's integrated gasification combined-cycle technology—a potentially cleaner but costlier coal-burning technology for power stations—has still to prove itself, because GE has not yet sold a plant.

GE's enthusiasm for greenery is informing its R&D effort. The company is, for instance, looking at radical ways of making aero engines cleaner. "Suppose we used a totally different fuel. Suppose we used a bio-derived fuel." says Sanjay Correa, GE's global technology leader for energy and propulsion. Biofuels are widely believed to be out of the question for aero engines because they are less energy-intensive, so more is needed to travel the same distance. But Mr Correa points out that aeroplanes these days have such a long range that they can cross the Atlantic with their tanks only one-third full. "We've done tests. We've studied this pretty hard. It works."

So who is best placed to win in the clean-energy stakes: the VC who helped transform the computer business or the chief executive of one of the great incumbents? The VCs point out that the energy business is becoming more friendly to small companies. Electricity generation is becoming more distributed as wind farms and solar panels feed into grids. Ethanol can be produced in backyard plants.

True; but that is happening at the margin. The big companies still dominate. According to Michael Liebreich of New Energy Finance, only around $2 billion of the $71 billion that went into the clean-energy investment last year was VC money.

The VC model is an excellent way of generating innovation, and fine for the early stages of clean-energy companies, but ultimately does not suit the energy business as well as it suits computing. Moving molecules around takes far more capital investment than moving bits of information around. Shipping fuel from fineries to petrol stations and running electricity grids are operations best done at scale; and the energy business's hunger for capital ensures a measure of protection for incumbents. Mr Khosla may very well produce some exciting new technologies and thus generate some valuable intellectual property; but it is Mr. Immelt who will exploit them.

Not even 1% of passengers have taken up BA's very reasonably priced offer to offset the carbon emissions of their flights (£5 for LondonMadrid, £13.50 for London-Johannesburg). That may be because people are selfish—or it may be because they are rational enough to know that their individual economic choices are not going to make a blind bit of difference to the future of the planet. Nobody is going to save a polar bear by turning off the lights.

As voters, however, people can make a difference. Climate change is a collective problem, which can be dealt with only collectively. Voters can encourage that by electing governments committed to changing the rules to encourage companies to behave differently.

There are three ways for governments to persuade companies to constrain carbon: subsidies, standards and a carbon price. Subsidies are popular with recipient companies; with greens, who reckon that any money used to combat climate change is well spent; and with governments, which like handing out taxpayers' money. Taxpayers tend not to notice. Some economists also advocate subsidies to particular technologies because they need a kickstart to get them to market. That may be true in the case of big, risky processes such as CCS. But subsidies tend to be inefficient because they require governments to pick technologies. And, once in place, they are hard to abolish.

A second way for governments to discourage emissions is by setting standards for products and processes (such as imposing energy-efficiency requirements for buildings, or banning incandescent lightbulbs). Such standards are usually a bad idea, for they require governments to tell the private sector how to allocate resources, and the private sector tends to be better at that than governments are. But given the market's inability to eliminate energy waste from buildings, and society's interest in doing so, they are probably worth having in this case.

Still, a carbon price is likely to be the best way to cut emissions. That can be established through either a tax or a cap-and-trade system of the sort Europe has.

A tax would be the better option. Unlike a cap-and-trade system, which stipulates the amount of CO_2 that may be emitted and allows the price to vary, a tax sets a price and lets it determine the quantity emitted. The volatility of the carbon price in Europe, which has variously risen above €30 and dropped to close to zero, is blamed in part for the lack of investment in clean energy, so there is a lot to be said for setting a price. But the prospects for a tax are not good. Business—particularly in America—is allergic to the very word; and the allowances which companies tend to be handed in the early stages of a cap-and-trade system have an obvious appeal to companies concerned about rising costs.

Whichever way a carbon price is established, the big question remains: can it be set at a level high enough to make a difference to climate change without derailing the world economy?

Probably. According to Richard Newell of Duke University, economists' estimates of the carbon price needed to stabilise CO_2 concentrations at 550 parts per million (widely reckoned to be a safeish level) range from $5 to $30 per tonne by 2025 and from $20 to $80 per tonne by 2050. The Intergovernmental Panel on Climate Change came out with fairly similar figures in its fourth report earlier this year—$20-50 per tonne by 2020-30. Mr Newell reckons that, in

America, $20 per tonne would raise petrol prices by an average of 18 cents (or 6%) per gallon, and electricity prices by 14%. A $50 price would raise petrol prices by an average of 45 cents (or 15%), and electricity prices by 35%.

At the bottom end of the range these costs are not huge. Even at the top end they are manageable. The IPCC's estimates of what a $20-50 carbon price would do to world GDP by 2050 range from a slight increase on what it otherwise would have been to 4% less. The average is 1.3% less, which would mean that average annual growth would be around 0.1% lower than it might otherwise have been.

Those prices assume that the entire world adopts a carbon price. That is a heroic assumption. Persuading developing countries to do so will be very hard.

It cannot be done unless all rich countries take the first step. They need to set an effective carbon price, and show the developing world that they can do so without ruining their economies. It wouldn't be a solution to climate change, but it would be a start.

CEOS CAN HAVE A 'HUGE IMPACT' ON CLIMATE CHANGE

Multinationals have both the responsibility and reach to make a difference.

Jeff Swartz

As leaders around the world grapple with how to craft policies to protect the environment, a new report from the United Nations shows what's at stake for Asia. Recently, the U.N. Environment Program released a study of the effects of "black clouds"—particulate matter and other pollutants released by industry—and the results are sobering.

According to the U.N., this type of smog blocks between 10% and 25% of the natural sunlight that would otherwise shine on Beijing's crowded streets. Wind and rain "washes" a portion of that smog onto the surface of the Himalayan glaciers, the water source for billions of people in China, India and Pakistan. Respiratory and cardiovascular diseases are on the rise; rice harvests are declining. Billions of people are living their lives literally and figuratively under a pervasive brown cloud. This is an environmental crisis with no bailout plan in sight.

This situation poses a serious challenge to policy makers and businessmen alike. If we expect the government or the self-regulating global business community to address the problem alone, we will be disappointed. Everyone has an oar to pull here.

Rather than necessarily being the "enemy," for-profit business can be a force for good in the effort. Not only are many polluting activities directly under their control, but many businesses today buy and sell along a value chain stretching from developed economies to developing economies—giving every company the responsibility to contribute to a solution and also the reach to do so.

I'm not an environmental scientist or a meteorologist. I'm a third-generation, U.S.-based bootmaker. Why does an American bootmaker care about black clouds and deteriorating environmental conditions in China? I care because my company directly and indirectly employs about 160,000 people in stores, offices and factories in China, and we continue to expand our presence there by opening more and more stores. Environmental degradation negatively affects the lives of our employees, vendors and consumers.

CEOs can and do have a huge impact on climate change, in the way they run their businesses, in the choices they make about materials, energy use, chemical use and transportation. A few years ago, Timberland helped to convene a multicompany working group to address pollution from tanneries. Together we developed a streamlined method for auditing their environmental effects and created a forum for sharing data and best practices. Over the past five years, Timberland has also planted more than 700,000 trees in the Horqin Desert in Inner Mongolia in an effort to slow the rate of desertification and restore the barren area to the grassland it once was. The erosion of desert is causing severe drought and sand storms every spring, affecting hundreds of millions of people in northern China, some of whom are our customers.

Consumers also have a role to play here. "Citizen consumers"—individuals who vote with their dollars, every day—are in the best position to influence companies' environmental choices. Consumers need to demand tangible change by holding the business community accountable using their wallets.

This is all a tall order at a tough time, when people are losing their homes, their jobs and their optimism. Understandably, the focus is largely on needs much more immediate than solving the climate crisis. However, the need to act for common good doesn't go away when we're facing multiple disasters, because the hovering smog and brown cloud over Asia won't stop growing while we tend to other issues.

Mr. Swartz is chief executive of the Timberland Company.

EXCERPTS FROM TODAY'S CLIMATE-CHANGE REPORT

from the Wall Street Journal

Excerpts from the U.N. International Panel on Climate Change's fourth assessment report, released Friday.

—"Most of the observed increase in globally averaged temperatures since the mid-20th century is very likely due to the observed increase in anthropogenic greenhouse gas concentrations. This is an advance since the Third Assessment Report's conclusion that 'most of the observed warming over the last 50 years is likely to have been due to the increase in greenhouse gas concentrations.'"

—"Global atmospheric concentrations of carbon dioxide, methane and nitrous oxide have increased markedly as a result of human activities since 1750 and now far exceed pre-industrial values determined from ice cores spanning many thousands of years. The global increases in carbon dioxide concentration are due primarily to fossil fuel use and land-use change, while those of methane and nitrous oxide are primarily due to agriculture."

—"The primary source of the increased atmospheric concentration of carbon dioxide since the pre-industrial period results from fossil fuel use, with land use change providing another significant but smaller contribution."

—"Warming of the climate system is unequivocal, as is now evident from observations of increases in global average air and ocean temperatures, widespread melting of snow and ice, and rising global mean sea level."

—"The observed widespread warming of the atmosphere and ocean, together with ice mass loss, support the conclusion that it is extremely unlikely that global climate change of the past fifty years can be explained without external forcing, and very likely that it is not due to known natural causes alone."

—"Anthropogenic forcing is likely to have contributed to changes in wind patterns, affecting extra-tropical storm tracks and temperature patterns in both hemispheres."

—"Temperatures of the most extreme hot nights, cold nights and cold days are likely to have increased due to anthropogenic forcing. It is more likely than not that anthropogenic forcing has increased the risk of heat waves."

—"Since the Third Assessment Report (in 2001), progress in understanding how climate is changing in space and in time has been gained through improvements and extensions of numerous datasets and data analyses, broader geographical coverage, better understanding of uncertainties, and a wider variety of measurements."

—"Eleven of the last 12 years (1995-2006) rank among the 12 warmest years in the instrumental record of global surface temperature (since 1850)."

EXXON SOFTENS CLIMATE-CHANGE STANCE

Hoping to Shape Policy, Oil Giant Joins Dialogue On Curbing of Emissions

By Jeffrey Ball

In one of the strongest signs yet that U.S. industry anticipates government curbs on global-warming emissions, Exxon Mobil Corp., long a leading opponent of such rules, is starting to talk about how it would like them to be structured.

Exxon, the world's largest publicly traded oil company by market value, long has been a lightning rod in the global-warming debate. Its top executives have openly questioned the scientific validity of claims that fossil-fuel emissions are warming the planet, and it has funded outside groups that have challenged such claims in language sometimes stronger than the company itself has used. Those actions have prompted criticism of the company by environmentalists and by Democrats in the U.S., who now control the Congress.

Now, Exxon has cut off funding to a handful of those outside groups. It says climate-science models that link greenhouse-gas concentrations to global warming are getting more reliable. And it is meeting in Washington with officials of other large corporations to discuss what form the companies would prefer a possible U.S. carbon regulation to take.

WORDS ARE NUANCED

The changes in Exxon's words and actions are nuanced. The oil giant continues to note uncertainties in climate science. It continues to oppose the Kyoto Protocol, the international global-warming treaty that limits emissions from industrialized countries that have ratified it. It also stresses that any future carbon policy should include developing countries, where emissions are rising fastest. (See related article.)

Still, the company's subtle softening is significant and reflects a gathering trend among much of U.S. industry, from utilities to auto makers. While many continue to oppose caps, these companies expect the country will impose mandatory global-warming-emission constraints at some point, so they are lining up to try to shape any mandate so they escape with minimum economic pain.

Exxon has stopped funding the Competitive Enterprise Institute, a Washington-based think tank that last year ran television ads saying that carbon dioxide, the main greenhouse gas, is helpful. After funding them previously, Exxon decided in late 2005 not to fund for 2006 CEI and "five or six" other groups active in the global-warming debate, Kenneth Cohen, Exxon's vice president for public affairs, confirmed this week in an interview at Exxon's headquarters in Irving, Texas. He declined to identify the groups beyond CEI; their names are expected to become public in the spring, when Exxon releases its annual list of donations to nonprofit groups.

Myron Ebell, director of CEI's energy and global-warming program, declined to comment about why Exxon didn't fund CEI last year. But he added: "Like any company, they are concerned about both policies and image.

"We're not at the mercy of our funders for what we believe. But we are dependent on them for funding to help promote our programs," he said. "Obviously, we would like to find a lot more funding on energy and global warming than we've had."

More significant are the meetings between executives from Exxon and other companies to discuss the potential structure of a U.S. carbon regulation. Several parallel tracks of discussions are under way, some sponsored by Washington think tanks, including the Brookings Institution and Resources for the Future.

The meetings underscore the view within much of U.S. industry that the science and the politics of global warming are changing. "The issue has evolved," Mr. Cohen said.

Exxon says important questions remain about the degree to which fossil-fuel emissions are contributing to global warming. But "the modeling has gotten better" analyzing the probabilities of how rising greenhouse-gas emissions will affect global temperatures, Mr. Cohen said. Exxon continues to stress the modeling is imperfect; it is "helpful to an analysis, but it's not a predictor," he said. But he added, "we know enough now—or, society knows enough now—that the risk is serious and action should be taken."

The question is what kind of action. The economic reality is that some companies will win from a carbon constraint and some companies will lose, depending on how the regulation is written.

QUESTION OF A CAP

One question is whether a carbon tax or cap should be imposed upstream—on producers of fossil fuels—or downstream, on the industries, and perhaps even the individual consumers, who use those fuels. Another question is whether such a constraint should target just a few industries or should be applied across the economy.

Such questions already are sparking fierce lobbying fights among industries in Europe. There, countries have slapped carbon caps on several heavily emitting industries. Now the countries are toughening those constraints.

A similar zero-sum fight appears increasingly likely in the U.S. California adopted a broad global-warming cap last year, and now it has to decide which companies, and perhaps which consumers, to stick with the responsibility for meeting the targets. Other states say they plan to follow California's lead.

In Washington, meanwhile, Democratic congressional leaders say they will push for some sort of federal carbon constraint.

"By all indications, we'll certainly see much more legislative activity at the state and federal level going forward," Exxon's Mr. Cohen said. Among the broad options being debated, he said, "some look more favorable to us than others."

Exxon wants any regulation to be applied across "the broadest possible base" of the economy, said Jaime Spellings, Exxon's general manager for corporate planning. Exxon says avoiding a ton of carbon-dioxide emissions is, with certain exceptions, less expensive in the power industry than in the transportation sector. Though solar energy remains expensive, reducing a ton of emissions by generating electricity from essentially carbon-free sources such as nuclear or wind energy is cheaper than reducing a ton of emissions through low-carbon transportation fuels such as ethanol.

Exxon, like the U.S. government, also argues that any regulation should take into account rising emissions from developing countries, too. Both Exxon and the federal government oppose the Kyoto Protocol.

The fact that Exxon officials are beginning to lay out even these generalities is significant, said Philip Sharp, president of Resources for the Future. "They are taking this debate very seriously," said Mr. Sharp, a former Democratic congressman long active in energy-policy debates. "My personal opinion of them has changed by watching them operate."

Can and Does Environmental Activism Make a Difference? What is the Impact of Environmental Advocates as Stakeholders?*

The standards for corporate environmental responsibility are often unclear and "environmental sustainability" is generally difficult to define or measure. Nonetheless, environmental advocates attempt to influence corporate practices related to natural resource management, waste generation and recycling, production and marketing of "green" products and pollution prevention and control. Two of the most visible environmental issues today are climate change and forestry.

CLIMATE CHANGE, REGULATION AND SELF-REGULATION

At some level it can be argued that the inevitability of national and international regulation, including adoption of a new version of the Kyoto treaty (including or not including developing countries) is a testament to the efforts of environmental advocates. However, the likelihood of increasing restriction on greenhouse gases at the state, national and international levels is not due solely to the efforts of these environmental activists; diverse groups have provided a ground swell of support for climate change regulation.

In *The Market for Virtue,* David Vogel concludes that public pressure (by NGO's, activist investors and shareholders) on business to reduce (and disclose) emissions of carbon and other greenhouse gases has made a difference in the U.S. and Europe. However, it is difficult to measure the impact of civic pressure on the emergence of voluntary standards and agreements; one must also consider the impact of the threat of government regulation and litigation, the possibility of new markets, and potential cost savings due to reduced emissions and increased production efficiency. Vogel also argues that government regulation has been a far greater influence than business self-regulation, given the additional costs of greenhouse gas reductions and limited consumer demand for environmentally-sensitive products.

FORESTRY AND SELF-REGULATION

Among the most highly publicized areas of stakeholder activism, tropical deforestation has led to voluntary codes in forestry. NGO boycott campaigns against importation of wood from tropical and old-growth forests and protests against large corporations led by NGO's such as the Rainforest Action Network have led to changes in policies at Home Depot, Kinko's, etc. Staples, also a target of NGO's, has since tried to make its environmental practices a competitive advantage. Forest Stewardship Council (FSC) - certification that forestry products are from sustainable

---

*Summary based, in part, on "Corporate Responsibility for the Environment" from *The Market for Virtue* by David Vogel.

managed forests—has led some retailers and construction companies to purchase FSC wood. Impact has been mostly in Europe.

Vogel's conclusion on stakeholder influence in this area: voluntary corporate purchasing practices have reduced destruction of old-growth forests in North America but there is little impact on tropical deforestation and loss of biodiversity because social pressures and the market for eco-friendly products are not so effective in developing countries.

THE INFLUENCE OF ENVIRONMENTAL ADVOCATES: MIXED RESULTS

If we try to zero in on the influence of environmental advocates, we find that business' response to public criticism has produced mixed results. For example, Shell's response to media exposure, NGO criticism and consumer boycott related to deep-sea disposal of its Brent Spar platform led to questionable net social benefit. (Deep-sea disposal was not proven to be environmentally hazardous and land disposal, which Shell finally agreed to, was far more costly.) In other words, environmental advocates have had effective influence, at times, but produced questionable results. Also, as noted above, their influence has been mostly in developed countries; they have had little impact on air and water pollution, for example, in developing countries.

THE RISKS OF ENVIRONMENTAL ADVOCACY

Business' response to environmental issues, particularly climate change, is not without risks if you consider the problem from a purely pragmatic (aprincipled) perspective. An Economist article points out that these risks include the "fad" nature of the challenge (stakeholder concerns abate); the volatility of oil prices (if they crash, investments in renewables look less wise); the fact that the financial incentives for energy efficiency, on which business is banking, may not come to fruition; and consumer demand to buy ethically sound products doesn't include their willingness to pay more for them.

QUESTIONS ON READINGS FOR PART SIX (E) (II)

What are the likely causes and effects of climate change?

Is government regulation the answer, at state, national, or international levels?

What laws (U.S. and international) are in place to deal with climate change? What more could/should governments do?

Who should pay to solve the problem?

What has business done to address climate change? What should it do?

What impact have environmental advocates had?

CENTER FOR EDUCATION ON SOCIAL RESPONSIBILITY

PART SIX (F)

THE COMMUNITY:
LOCAL AND GLOBAL

CORPORATIONS AND THE PUBLIC INTEREST: GUIDING THE INVISIBLE HAND

Steven Lydenberg

As a first step in addressing the current dilemma about corporations' relationship to society, this chapter defines and examines the public interest that corporations can best serve—what I call the creation of long-term wealth. Five companies that integrate this concept into their daily operations are described to illustrate its benefits. These profiles also highlight the ongoing challenges of long-term wealth creation, which can require astute management skills and undivided focus. This chapter also discusses why government, before it can create a transparent market that values and rewards such exceptional efforts, must first ensure, through legislation and regulation, that uncontrolled business does not abuse public wealth. At the same time, it must distinguish those services that it can best deliver as public goods from those that may be best delivered through the private markets.

DEFINING LONG-TERM WEALTH

A definition of the public interest that corporations can best serve in today's world is the starting point for this discussion. I define that public interest here as: *the creation of value that will continue to benefit members of society even if the corporation were dissolved today.*

This definition builds on the familiar concept that corporations can create economic wealth that benefits society through productivity gains. As corporations innovate and increase efficiency, they generate wealth that raises overall prosperity to new levels. Having demonstrated their worth in the marketplace, corporations' technological and managerial innovations can transcend the life of the company to become part of society's wealth-generating capabilities.

Today, however, many investors, consumers, public policymakers, employees, and communities increasingly expect corporations to provide value that goes beyond simple efficiency increases. Their new definition of value qualifies the ways in which profits should be generated, and once generated, put to use. I call this value *long-term wealth*. Long-term wealth encompasses productivity gains and technological advances, but it also demands that the profits generated not be made at the expense of society or the environment and that they be productively reinvested for the benefit of the corporation's stakeholders.

As formulated here, this concept of long-term wealth is a variation on many of the ideas developed in a rich literature over the past three decades. Approaching the same idea from varying perspectives, advocates of the development of increasingly prosperous societies that can endure have promoted the concepts, among others, of sustainability (for example, John Elkington), natural capitalism (Paul Hawken), natural economics (Jane Jacobs), total wealth creation (Margaret Blair), social entrepreneurship (David Bornstein), blended value (Jed Emerson), civic stewardship (Marcy Murninghan), the open enterprise (Don Tapscott and David Ticoll), moral capitalism (Stephen Young), and the moral economy (William Greider).

These and other authors have talked of the importance of developing human capital, community capital, and environmental capital (Jon Gunneman, for example) and have drawn analogies between the values of societal and financial wealth. They also share many of the concerns of economists such as Amartya Sen, who stress society's obligation to provide citizens with crucial qualities of life in addition to raising income levels.

My particular formulation of long-term wealth creation includes three expectations that proponents of SRI and CSR have come to consider as part of the corporation's obligations to society. They are that corporations:

- Do not externalize costs onto society.
- Do not deplete natural resources irretrievably.
- Do not impoverish stakeholders.

Or, to put it positively, corporations should do the following:

- Address and minimize the public costs they incur before they declare private profits.
- Preserve and renew resources so that they remain available for future generations.
- Invest in stakeholder relations, including, but not limited to, their stockowners.

In concrete terms, corporations that pursue long-term wealth creation might, for example, do these things: invest in employee training that prepares workers not only for their current jobs but for future employment as well; develop a community's capacity to provide child care not only for their own employees but for other community members; pay their fair share of taxes so that local governments can provide infrastructure and education in their communities, even if that means reduced profits for stockowners; educate employees on retirement planning, even if they are not required to do so by law; preserve biodiversity and implement energy efficiency programs, even if the payback may be difficult to justify in the short run; require vendors and suppliers to implement credible quality or environmental management systems, even if that means increased prices; and ensure access to capital for underserved communities or entrepreneurs, even if they may ultimately become new competitors. Although not necessarily in corporations' narrowly defined, short-term interests, these initiatives create lasting societal value.

Conversely, corporations that destroy long-term wealth might do the following: compensate management excessively, asserting that the marketplace demands such salaries and bonuses; fail to provide adequate pensions for their employees, pointing out that their peers do no better; extract tax breaks that exceed the quantifiable benefits that their presence provides local communities simply because they have the power to do so; refuse to implement a comprehensive environmental management system on the grounds that they have no such legal obligation; encourage consumption of "supersized" portions of unhealthy food or promote the sale of unnecessarily expensive, patent-protected drugs because these marketing opportunities are irresistible; provide products or services that are potentially addictive, such as tobacco and gambling, without confronting their harmful effects; or ignore the potentially adverse long-term effects of burning fossil fuels in the face of overwhelming evidence of global harm. Although not illegal, such corporate actions leave society the poorer.

The definition of long-term wealth as conceived here can be expressed as a formula: start with the value of a company's contributions to society through productivity gains and innovation (less any costs it imposes through anticompetitive practices), add to it the value of the company's internalization of social costs (less its externalized costs), plus the value of its sustainable management of environmental resources (less the costs of its environmental harms), plus the value created through its investments in stakeholder relations (less any costs created by mismanagement or neglect of these relations).

Expressing this concept through such a formula raises a number of important questions, however. What does it mean for a company to internalize costs, manage for sustainability, or invest in the value of its stakeholders? How easily can companies achieve these goals? To what extent can these efforts be meaningfully quantified? What is the proper role of government in supporting these efforts? What is the role of the marketplace in their cultivation? Why are these issues of crucial importance today?

FIVE EXAMPLES OF LONG-TERM WEALTH CREATION

To answer the first of these questions, let's begin by looking at five corporations, each of which exemplifies one element of the preceding equation: Organic Valley (internalization of costs), Patagonia (commitment to environmental sustainability), and Springfield Remanufacturing, Wainwright Bank, and Timberland (investments in stakeholders—employees, customers, and communities, respectively).

Organic Valley Family of Farms

Organic Valley Family of Farms is a cooperative of dairy and other farmers headquartered in rural LaFarge, Wisconsin, with over six hundred participating members in eighteen states around the country. The co-op was founded in 1988 by George Siemon who, after fifteen years as a farmer devoted to organic principles, joined with a half-dozen of his peers to create the Coulee Region Organic Produce Pool. From this modest beginning grew Organic Valley Family of Farms, which in 2003 had $156 million in revenues (and projected 2004 revenues of over $200 million) and whose farmers managed ninety-five thousand acres of land organically.

Organic Valley has taken the exceptional step of internalizing some of the costs that large-scale, chemical-dependent agribusiness often imposes on society. The food products that today's agribusiness brings to the supermarket shelves at low cost to consumers can come at a high cost to society in the form of an increasingly contaminated water supply, deteriorating soil quality, and wetlands damaged by overuse of fertilizers and pesticides. Moreover, these giant firms' economies of scale make small-scale, local land ownership increasingly difficult. To avoid this externalization of costs onto society, Organic Valley promotes the adoption of small-scale organic farming techniques.

A major challenge for its small farmers, however, is that in a volatile commodity market, where conventional milk is often priced more cheaply than its organic counterpart, those who adopt organic farming practices run the risk of being priced out of business. Organic Valley has developed a two-pronged solution to this problem. First, the co-op's elected board of directors meets annually to set a fair and stable price for their products—that is, a predictable, minimum price that the co-op will pay for the year, independent from the swings of the commodity market. With the assurance of this stable price, the co-op's farmers can continue their organic practices and manage their farms at a reasonable profit. In recent years that price at times has been as much as 40 percent above that of the commodity market.

An additional benefit to co-op members is their ability to market their products collectively under the Organic Valley brand name, which offers a guarantee to the consumer on product quality, environmental values, and local land ownership. Through an extensive distribution network, the co-op's products are available throughout the United States, as well as in Canada and Japan. These policies and practices help insulate small-scale organic farmers from the pressures of the commodity markets created by large-scale agribusiness that would otherwise not allow them to serve consumers committed to sustainable agriculture. Meanwhile, their organic farms create a long-term societal wealth in the form of enriched soil, clean water, and a network of independent agricultural entrepreneurs.

Patagonia, Inc.

Founded in the early 1970s and headquartered in Ventura, California, Patagonia, Inc., is a high-profile outdoor apparel company with approximately $230 million in revenues in 2003.

The company is a rare example of a firm that has been willing to gamble its financial future on a company-wide commitment to environmental sustainability. It made this gamble most dramatically in 1996 when its founder, Yvon Chouinard, recognized that his commitment to the environment was being undercut by the company's use of conventionally grown cotton, one of the most chemically dependent of crops. At that time, the company decided to convert the cotton in its entire product line to organic. Its commitment to do so, however, forced it to cut its sportswear line by one-third because of limitations on the amount of high-quality organic cotton then available, at a cost of approximately $20 million in lost sales.

Patagonia has since gone on to become a highly successful promoter of organic cotton throughout the sports apparel industry, even among its competitors such as Nike and Mountain Equipment Co-op. In addition, its Beneficial T's program produces T-shirt "blanks," as well as tote bags and hats, with 100 percent organic cotton content. The company makes these items available to clothing designers throughout the apparel industry. As of 2004 the Beneficial T's program was using about five hundred thousand pounds of organic cotton annually.

The switch to organic cotton was one of the boldest steps in the firm's company-wide efforts to implement environmental programs, but not the only one. In 1993 Patagonia worked with one of its suppliers to develop technology that could produce fleece fabric from recycled plastic soda bottles. In a similar initiative in 2004, it introduced a filament partially made from recycled plastic into the yarns used in clothing such as running shorts and rain shells. Similarly in the energy area, in constructing its distribution center in Reno, Nevada, it incorporated energy-efficient lighting systems that provide 30 percent savings on energy bills and radiant heating systems that generate savings of approximately 15 percent. Its Reno outlet store uses solar panels to generate electricity. Its thirteen buildings in California purchase electricity from renewable energy plants.

Through two exceptional policies, Patagonia also supports the environmental movement more generally. Today, employees who have been with the firm for two years can take an eight-week paid leave (with benefits) to work with environmental organizations. In addition, the company donates 1 percent of its sales to environmental causes, a generous and highly unusual approach to charitable giving. (Most companies pledge a percentage of profits, rather than sales, to charity.) Through this program, Patagonia has made $20 million in gifts to environmental organizations to date. To promote similar environmental giving programs, Yvon Chouinard was instrumental in the founding of 1 Percent for the Planet, an alliance of thirty-three businesses, mostly small firms that have made similar pledges, which through December 2003 had donated $1.7 million to environmental causes.

Springfield Remanufacturing Corporation

A manufacturing firm headquartered in Springfield, Missouri, Springfield Remanufacturing Corporation (SRC) has survived and thrived in large part because of its willingness to invest in its employees. In the mid-1980s, this remanufacturer of automotive components was a division of International Harvester, then on the brink of bankruptcy. Rather than see his division close down, its manager, Jack Stack, persuaded corporate headquarters to sell the business to its employees. Stack then began the painstaking process of educating the new owners about the business of running a business. They were taught financials, budgeting, cost management, and operations. They learned to grapple with difficult decisions about allocation of resources to debt repayment, investments in technology, and payouts to owners.

Today, with a total of some eight hundred employee-owners at twelve principal subsidiaries and revenues of approximately $200 million in 2003, SRC is a profitable holding company operating multiple related firms. Upon joining the firm, each new employee participates in a two-day workshop on open book management and subsequently takes part in weekly "huddles"; in these staff meetings, the financials of the subsidiary's operations, as well as the financials of other subsidiaries, are shared and discussed. In addition, the management teams of all the subsidiaries meet every two weeks to share financial information that they then communicate back to their teams. SRC also holds quarterly financial literacy workshops, which were attended by approximately 120 company members annually as of 2004. Most recently, SRC has invested in educating its employees on the issue of health care costs. As part of this program, it has hired a part-time fitness instructor and a part-time wellness coordinator. These efforts resulted in a 33 percent reduction in health care costs for the firm in the first six months of 2004.

SRC believes that investments in open book management, with its ability to empower employees, can have long-term benefits for other firms as well. Consequently, it has established a subsidiary called the Great Game of Business, named after Stack's book on the subject.[5] This consulting and training firm provides a range of assessment, training, and coaching services on open book management to approximately three hundred companies each year. Its annual National Gathering of Games, a three-day conference dedicated to open book management, had approximately 350 attendees in 2004.

Wainwright Bank & Trust Company

Wainwright Bank & Trust Company is a Boston-based bank with approximately $625 million in assets as of 2003. It has chosen to focus its business particularly on strengthening those in need in its local community, where it is the bank of choice for many social service organizations. From the early 1990s through 2004, it lent $11 million to organizations providing housing for persons with AIDS and $15 million to those serving the homeless, as well as $75 million to affordable housing agencies. During that time, it made some $350 million in community development loans. Wainwright maintains a four-person team in its lending department; this team specializes in loans to community service organizations.

Wainwright has also invested in its customer base in ways that go beyond simply providing a needed service at a reasonable price. The bank includes on its own Web site a section called CommunityRoom.net. There, local nonprofit clients can maintain individual Web pages (over one hundred as of 2004) describing their activities. The Web site is set up so that through it individuals can make donations directly to these organizations, and in 2003 the site generated approximately $250,000 in donations for these groups. (Donations were running at double that rate as of mid-2004.) The bank's brick-and-mortar branches also have rooms set aside for use by community groups that are accessible at all times. The bank's most recent branch features a "cybercafe" in the lobby, with a fireplace, a plasma-screen TV, free coffee and doughnuts, and Internet access available at no cost to members of the community, whether or not they are bank customers.

Wainwright has also made an exceptional commitment to the local gay and lesbian community. It was one of the original sponsors of Boston's Gay Pride parade in 1993 and the lead sponsor in 2004. It was among the first publicly traded companies in the United States to have an openly lesbian member on its board of directors. Its top management has frequently spoken out on gay and lesbian rights, and for many years the bank offered an affinity credit card (such cards donate a percentage of revenues to charitable causes) that gave a portion of the amounts charged to organization serving gay and lesbian communities and organizations working with the homeless.

The Timberland Company

Many companies have employee volunteer programs, but few have worked to make a spirit of service to the community a part of the corporate culture as thoroughly as the Timberland Company. Founded in 1918 and headquartered in Stratham, New Hampshire, this manufacturer of footwear and apparel had approximately $1.3 billion in 2003 revenues. Through a program called Path of Service, employees can spend up to 40 hours each year volunteering with social service organizations on company time. Since the inception of this program, employees have logged over 250,000 hours in volunteer time.

The company has focused its volunteering particularly on City Year, a Boston-based urban Peace Corps–style organization for the young (between seventeen and twenty-four years of age) that served as a model for President Clinton's Americorps national service program. Founded in Boston in 1988, City Year now has programs in fourteen communities around the country. Its diverse pool of 750 participants take part each year in programs of community service, leadership development, and civic engagement. In 2001, City Year launched its Clinton Democracy Fellowship program, which brings to the United States young leaders from other countries who are committed to citizen service and social entrepreneurship.

Since 1992, Timberland has been a major supporter of City Year, identifying itself publicly with the organization. During that time, it has donated some $20 million in goods and services to City Year, including employee volunteer time and clothing in the form of a City Year uniform. Timberland's CEO, Jeffrey Swartz, serves on the organization's board of directors, and the City Year New Hampshire Corps is housed at the company's headquarters. In addition, Timberland regularly contracts with City Year staff for training in volunteerism and diversity awareness. Timberland's commitment to civic involvement also sets the tone for the company's strong initiatives on environmental and overseas labor issues throughout its operations.

I have chosen these five smaller companies here to illustrate how a firm's identity can be bound up in exceptional commitments to creating long-term wealth. But many larger companies are also committed to creating long-term wealth that transcends technological innovation or increases in efficiency. For example, since the early 1990s, through its funding for dependent care, International Business Machines Corporation (IBM) has invested in the child care and elder care infrastructures of communities where its plants are located. IBM was also instrumental in the formation of the American Business Collaborative for Quality Dependent Care in 1992, through which it and a coalition of other companies—including Abbott Laboratories, ExxonMobil, General Electric, Johnson & Johnson, and Texas Instruments—have invested over $135 million in these infrastructures around the country. The purpose of this program is not only to create long-lasting solutions to the dependent care needs for company employees but also to help solve this problem for their surrounding communities.

In another example of the kind of long-term wealth that large firms can create, Starbucks Corporation, in partnership with Conservation International, developed a set of coffee-sourcing guidelines in 2001 that define a category of preferred suppliers to which Starbucks turns first for its purchases and from which it is willing to accept higher prices. To qualify, these preferred suppliers must meet certain quality, social, and environmental criteria. The greater their verifiable commitments to set goals in these areas, the higher their status as preferred vendors. This program supports coffee farmers who are part of a sustainable society.

Organizations such as San Francisco-based Business for Social Responsibility, which is dedicated to promoting responsible business practices, and recent books such as *Profits with Principles* by Ira Jackson and Jane Nelson have documented and continue to encourage similar efforts by many larger corporations.

ENCOURAGING AND ASSESSING WEALTH CREATION

These examples illustrate both the appeal of wealth creation and its challenges. As we have seen, companies that look to the long term can create value that would persist even if they went out of business tomorrow: Organic Valley would leave a legacy of enriched farmland, Patagonia would leave a strengthened organic cotton industry, Springfield Remanufacturing would leave workers who are trained to understand and manage a business, Wainwright Bank would leave a strengthened customer base of social service organizations, and Timberland would leave a broadly shared sense of service and community. These are valuable assets that have strong appeal.

These examples are also helpful in making several broader points that illustrate the challenges of long-term wealth creation. These are initiatives at companies that today enjoy reasonable profitability. But integrating long-term wealth creation into business operations is not an automatic guarantee of rewards in the marketplace. It is a complicated task that requires good business sense, strong management skills, and financial resources. One of the favorites of the SRI community in the mid-1980s was Digital Equipment Corporation, whose employee and community relations were in many senses exemplary. Through various business missteps it fell on hard financial times and was eventually acquired by Compaq Computer (in turn acquired by Hewlett-Packard Company). More recently, AstroPower, one of the few publicly traded corporations focused on the commercialization of solar power technologies, appealed to many social investors. However, it suffered financially and in October 2004 declared bankruptcy and agreed to be acquired by General Electric. Astute business judgments and effective management skills are necessary to make these often complicated and groundbreaking efforts pay off in the marketplace.

These examples also illustrate the point that the generation of long-term wealth, when executed throughout a firm, requires single-minded focus. Internalizing even a single societal cost, such as Organic Valley has done, can be a challenging business proposition that pays off only if the market is persuaded that the resulting product carries additional value. Attempting to sustain a single natural resource, as Patagonia has done, can require a company to gamble its financial future as it ventures into untried territory. Empowering workers to understand the basics of business and financial decision making, as Springfield Remanufacturing has done, is a costly, ongoing effort that will bring rewards only if employees are motivated to apply their newfound skills productively. The demands of even a single effort may mean—as the authors of the book *Built to Last* and other works on the characteristics of enduring and successful corporate cultures point out—that these companies "tend to have only a few core values" on which they build their business and which remain central to their identity over time.

One of the implications of this need to focus is that companies engaged in long-term wealth creation should not necessarily be expected to excel in everything they do. There is a tendency among those approaching the concept of socially responsible business to want to find only angels—or devils—when it comes to CSR records. The fact that a company with an exceptional commitment in one area chooses not to make extraordinary efforts in all others is not a cause for alarm. Companies' stories are multifaceted, and finding excellence in one or two areas is difficult enough in and of itself. Moreover, companies change, new issues emerge, and difficult situations arise. Thinking of companies as either all good or all bad is often an approach that fails to comprehend the complexities of business and its relationship to society, a fact that is as true for small companies with limited resources as for large companies with their multiple management challenges.

These general observations will inform our discussion further in part 2 when we examine the difficulties of the current financial and consumer marketplaces in quantifying and judging the value of these considerable efforts in wealth creation and in rewarding them consistently. However, before we turn to the question of how today's marketplace can be transformed to achieve these goals, we need to address briefly government's role outside the marketplace in ensuring that the fundamentals of societal wealth are not destroyed or abused by unscrupulous corporations. These steps are necessary to create the level playing field that corporations need to compete fairly and transparently in these areas.

RELATIVE ROLES OF GOVERNMENT AND THE MARKETPLACE

The first step that government must take, before it attempts to create a marketplace that directs the private sector toward the public interest, is to enact and enforce laws and regulations that prevent the most blatant destruction of long-term wealth. Today's governments make many corporate activities illegal because they impose unacceptable costs. Engaging in price fixing, marketing unsafe products, operating unsafe work environments, manufacturing ozone-depleting chemicals, publishing inaccurate financial statements, and discriminating in the workplace are all illegal because they impose unacceptably high costs on society. Their costs are unacceptably high no matter how beneficial they might be to individual company profits. Government cannot wait for the marketplace to prevent or correct such abuse, nor can it rely on the marketplace to do so.

A second duty of government is to distinguish between public and private goods. A detailed discussion of this important subject is beyond the scope of this book—but I will observe that long-term wealth creation, as I use the term, is provided by the private sector, whereas the term *public goods* refers to what the public sector delivers. Corporations' ability to generate long-term wealth should not be confused with governments' obligations to provide public goods.

This distinction can be confusing, because the further out one looks, the more long-term wealth can resemble public goods. The two, however, are not the same. There are activities for which government will judge the for-profit sector ill-suited. For example, few would argue that corporations should provide basic public goods such as the legal system, public safety, national defense, or roads, sewers, and other infrastructure. Yet as the pendulum has swung in recent years from government toward the private sector, corporations have begun increasingly to experiment with supplying services that were traditionally in the public domain, such as prison management, primary education, and military support services. Moreover, it is often a matter of ongoing debate as to what role government should play in such areas as providing health care, supporting postsecondary education, maintaining cultural institutions, assuring the availability of public utilities, and so on.

Debates about these issues are a sign of a healthy and open society. These debates may be played out through experimentation in the marketplace, but ultimately it is government's role to determine which goods and services should be public and which should be private. Where one national government or another draws the line will vary, but once that line has been drawn, the concept of long-term wealth generation can be usefully applied to activities that are allocated to the private sector and should not be confused with government-provided public goods. Indeed, the debate about whether particular corporate activities can create long-term wealth can be a help as government grapples with issues of which activities belong in the public sphere and which in the private.

Once government has established a level playing field and distinguishes the public from the private, the marketplace then can be particularly useful—but currently isn't constructed to be particularly effective—in encouraging positive and innovative initiatives that create long-term wealth. Encouraging corporations to pay increased attention to energy efficiency and conservation, to balance work and family considerations for their employees, to shift to organic agriculture, to support local communities and help them create strong infrastructures, to monitor the labor practices of their foreign vendors—all are examples of areas of clear benefit to society, but for which direct regulations can be problematic and for which rewards through the marketplace can consequently be particularly useful.

In addition, the marketplace can play a catalytic role where corporate activities are not illegal but there is debate about their benefit or harm, or when government has chosen not to act to correct such harm. Tobacco products are legal, but even when used as intended and in moderation can impose health care costs on society. When pharmaceutical companies lobby to extend patent protections on their drugs or to prevent the marketing of cheaper versions of HIV/AIDS medications, they are acting legally but make health care unnecessarily expensive or deprive those without resources of much-needed care. Aggressive marketing of sports utility vehicles is legal but can increase fatal crashes because of their design and contribute to health and environmental problems for the general public because of their fuel inefficiency. Paying a minimum wage that is not a living wage is legal but can create a class of the working poor, for whom society must bear the cost of social services.

Similarly, there are often profound debates in a society about whether new technologies and business practices are creating or destroying long-term wealth. For example, as agribusinesses aggressively pursue genetically modified plants and foods, corporations generally see little potential for harm while many governments, scientists, and individuals around the world are not sure whether genetically altered hormones, food crops, and cotton will feed and clothe the poor or threaten the viability of agriculture for future generations. Similarly, the success of

Wal-Mart and other "big box" stores raises a divisive issue as to whether the unrelenting drive to provide goods at the lowest possible price is providing poor communities with exactly what they need at prices they can afford or destroying communities and impoverishing workers.

In these cases, a fully informed, properly constructed marketplace has the potential to play a valuable role by airing issues publicly, assessing the potential for future costs or liabilities, and generally pushing corporations to reform or pushing government to further action. It will take a special effort by government along with investors, consumers, and corporations themselves to transform today's marketplaces into new vehicles that can reasonably and successfully analyze issues of long-term wealth and encourage its creation. Transfers of assets and power from government to corporations can capitalize on business's efficiency and innovation, but only if the marketplaces are set up to influence them where government chooses not to, or is ill-suited to apply systematic pressure.

By 2050, in a world of nine billion technologically advanced people, the margins for error will be considerably slimmer than they are today. Only if government and the marketplaces coordinate to work in an effective and balanced manner toward an enduring society will social and environment crises of substantial proportions be avoided. When and how best to use the marketplace so that corporations can be directed to these ends as part of that effort is a question that the SRI and CSR movements have explored from various angles in recent years.

TEAMING UP TO BRAND AND BOND: TIMBERLAND PARTNERS WITH CITY YEAR, SOS, AND SKILLSUSA

The Center for Corporate Citizenship at Boston College

CORPORATE CITIZENSHIP is fast becoming an essential business competency. Many companies are coming to find that developing the economic assets and social and human capital of low-income communities pays dividends to the bottom line. In the short and long term, this kind of strategy develops untapped markets, new labor pools, effective suppliers, and new operating sites. Leading businesses find that integrating business and community development creates new pathways to achieve long-term sustainable success—a "win-win" proposition for the business and the community.

In this series we profile examples of this integrated approach across a range of industry sectors.

Timberland strengthens its brand identity through partnerships that promote social justice and a service ethic worldwide.

In 1989, the nonprofit youth service corps City Year asked Timberland to donate 50 pairs of work boots for young adults serving their communities. That request sparked a relationship based on a shared vision of making a difference in the community, and set Timberland on a trajectory of a growing commitment to community service.

THE BUSINESS CHALLENGE

In the 1980s, Timberland was an entrepreneurial, high-growth company aspiring to grow into a larger-scale enterprise. Accomplishing that transition would require radical reform.

Concurrently, but in a separate initiative, Timberland forged a strong partnership with City Year. "When we went into the communities we served," notes Timberland CEO Jeffrey Swartz, "we saw our potential in a different context. We saw that serving the community was central to our identity—it was who we are, not just what we do." Timberland was determined to grow as a values-centered company and provide consumers with value in its products' utility, innovation, and quality and imbue the values of service and social justice throughout the organization.

By the mid-1990s, after creating a successful relationship with City Year, Timberland sought to further embed service into its corporate identity and products. But when the company faced a liquidity crisis in 1995, its bankers demanded that Timberland get out of the service business. Swartz's response: "As long as I'm running the company, values are central to who we are." Despite the fiscal difficulties, the company doubled the number of paid community service hours offered to employees. That, according to Swartz, is in part what saved Timberland.

THE SOLUTION

Timberland's strength was rooted in its commitment to value, both commercial and societal. Based on that principle, Timberland aimed to inextricably join the concepts of commerce and social justice in a number of different ways. For example, the company instituted closer oversight of the labor practices of its suppliers, especially those in developing countries; wrote a code of conduct for its contractors and licensees; and expanded its monitoring of those facilities by internal teams and independent nongovernmental organizations.

Timberland is a global leader in the design, engineering, and marketing of premium-quality footwear, apparel, and accessories for consumers who value the outdoors and their time in it. Timberland products are sold worldwide through leading department and specialty stores as well as Timberland retail stores. Timberland's dedication to making quality products is matched by the company's commitment to "doing well and doing good"—forging powerful partnerships among employees, consumers, and service partners to transform the communities in which they live and work. To learn more about Timberland, please visit www.timberland.com. For more information about Timberland's commitment to corporate social responsibility, including a searchable database of thousands of volunteer opportunities, please visit www.timberlandserve.com.

To further signal that the tenets that guide the company are not distinct from the products it offers, in 2001 Timberland moved its social enterprise department, which oversees community service and social justice initiatives, under the direction of the chief marketing officer. While joining social enterprise and marketing may carry a veneer of cause-related marketing, Timberland made the shift to ensure that social enterprise is part of the company's brand in a fundamental way. Social enterprise at Timberland is not an adjunct to brand building—it's central to it.

Internally, Timberland raised the bar for community service with policies and programs that bring employees worldwide into their communities. When Timberland sales associates convene for meetings, they don't bring their golf clubs. They bring rugged work clothes for community service programs built into the agenda.

Timberland extended that community service credo to its retail customers. The company involved retail buyers in service projects that transformed the community, concomitantly strengthening Timberland's relationships with those key accounts. Serving together is a powerful way to spark common vision, which translates back to the boardroom or office. In 2003, Timberland expanded its service program again, going directly into the marketplace to engage consumers in community service programs. "We humbly and respectfully ask people to give back to the community," says Carolyn Casey, Timberland's director of social enterprise. "We invite them to change the landscape or social fabric of where they live."

EXPANDING PARTNERSHIPS

The success of the partnership with City Year spurred Timberland to broaden its strategic partnerships to include other nonprofit organizations. Timberland's social enterprise department oversees the company's partnerships, facilitating communications and events. To achieve strategic cogency with its nonprofit partners, however, Timberland gave each strategic business unit the responsibility of developing its own social justice platform. The manager of each brand— such as women's shoes, outdoor performance, and men's apparel— works with the social enterprise department and the strategic nonprofit partner to develop programs to carry out that business unit's social justice platform.

Timberland's children's and women's divisions, for example, have forged a strong partnership with Share Our Strength, which fights hunger. Timberland's PRO brand, catering to consumers who work in construction, trades, and factories, partners with SkillsUSA, which promotes excellence for students in vocational trades. Timberland's outdoor performance line, including hiking and trail running shoes, has aligned with the Student Conservation Association, which provides conservation services in national parks, forests, refuges, and urban areas. That partnership is active in Earth Day activities sponsored by Timberland's retail stores in the United States, Europe, and Asia. Timberland's other nonprofit partners include Clean Air-Cool Planet, which helps fight global warming and find energy solutions, and the Harlem Children's Zone, a community-building initiative in New York City. International partners include Unis City in France, City Team in The Netherlands, and City Year Democracy Fellows in Johannesburg, South Africa.

For each partnership, Timberland has created innovative, customized engagement strategies. These partnerships have become integral to Timberland's market approach, helping the company meet two of what its calls its bold goals—to be a global values brand, and to be a reference company for a socially accountable business globally.

City Year is a national youth service corps that unites over 1,000 diverse 17- to 24-year-olds for a challenging year of leadership development, civic engagement, and full-time service. Corps members invest over 1 million hours of service to transform communities and build a stronger future. Timberland proudly serves as a National Leadership Sponsor; in addition, Timberland President and CEO Jeff Swartz served as chair of the National Board of Trustees for eight years.

EXPANDING SERVICE

In 1996 Timberland sought to share its service ethic with its international distributors to consistently represent the company's brand and values. City Year organized a service day at a group home for troubled 12- to 17-year-old boys near Timberland's New Hampshire headquarters. More than 90 Timberland distributors, some Timberland staff, and a group from City Year worked for six hours at the home alongside its residents repairing, painting, and cleaning up the house and yard. That outpouring of care was a new experience for many of the boys, some of whom had been abused or neglected. "We'd asked the distributors to bring a small item from their countries, which they left in the group home," recalls Gordon Peterson, Timberland's vice president of operations. "By the end of the day, half the distributors had tears in their eyes. And for the boys in the residential home, that day was so powerful that they started attending our service events as part of their treatment regime."

Through such events, City Year taught Timberland that service is a vehicle to teach leadership as well as promote justice. Timberland's Social Enterprise director Casey describes service as "part science, which involves the technical work, and part art, where the heart and mind undergo transformation." Over their 15-year partnership, City Year has helped Timberland implement service days and lead team-building and mentoring programs, while Timberland invests $1 million annually in City Year, including furnishing City Year's uniforms and housing City Year offices in the firm's corporate headquarters in New Hampshire and its retail store in Chicago.

As service became a Timberland hallmark, the company constructed a broader infrastructure for employees' community service. The Path of Service employee volunteer program, instituted in 1992, contains several components.

Timberland employees are given 40 hours of paid time annually for community service—up from 16 hours when the program began. Some of those hours are devoted to company-organized projects such as Earth Day and Serv-A-Palooza. During Serv-A-Palooza, launched in 1998, Timberland closes its traditional work operations one day each year to bring together its employees, vendors, and community partners for community service projects worldwide. In 2001, Timberland created the service sabbatical, enabling up to four employees annually to spend three to six months working at nonprofits that support civic issues.

The hours employees commit to service promote not only internal branding but also employee retention. The ethic of teamwork quickly and powerfully deemphasizes hierarchy while promoting involvement and creativity. Although the vision and passion for service unquestionably grew from Timberland's CEO, the service initiatives now emanate from all corners of the organization.

Employee engagement in service was the first of several concentric circles in Timberland's branding efforts. The next circle reached to Timberland's retail customers—though that sometimes meant blazing new trails. For instance, at the annual sales meeting of a major national account, the client asked a Timberland associate what entertainment Timberland would be providing, explaining that one large sneaker manufacturer was sponsoring a golf tournament and another was hosting a dinner cruise. The Timberland representative responded that Timberland would host a day of service. The client, laughing, asked, "Seriously, what event are you going to host?" Ultimately, the client's CEO, corporate team, and top store managers from across the country joined Timberland's CEO Jeff Swartz and company associates in community service. Surveyed after the week-long meeting, the client's team said the service day was the best part of the event. Timberland had conveyed its brand identity while helping a client become involved in its own community.

TIMBERLAND AND SHARE OUR STRENGTH

While Timberland successfully extended its reach, the company's business needs continued to expand, including a need to sharpen the focus on evolving product lines. Serving on the board of City Year, Timberland CEO Swartz met Bill Shore, founder and CEO of Share Our Strength (SOS), which fights hunger and poverty by mobilizing the culinary industry to organize events and teach cooking and nutrition to low-income families. While Share Our Strength, an organization that fights hunger and poverty, might not seem like a natural partner for a footwear and apparel company, Swartz was compelled by Shore's model of community service—to generate community wealth rather than redistribute it.

Swartz considered Share Our Strength's problem-solving, market-based strategy to be entrepreneurial and impressive. He recognized the potential for synergy between Share Our Strength, with its mission to equip people to make a difference in the world, and Timberland. Thus, in 1996 Timberland's second major nonprofit partnership was born. Timberland became a local sponsor for SOS's Taste of the Nation events in Boston and New Hampshire, a signature food-sampling benefit that features top chefs and restaurateurs.

Meanwhile, Timberland was considering adding more mission-related messages to its products. At the time, the company was developing a children's leather crib bootie. Timberland decided that this new product line was the perfect vehicle for its message. Since crib booties are early footwear, the company chose to imbue the product with a mission to support children, deciding that a portion of the proceeds from every crib bootie sold would go to Share Our Strength to fight children's hunger. To help with marketing, Timberland provided kits to retailers who wished to add a local angle to the promotion. The kit contained Timberland's powerful graphics as well as guidelines and graphics that enabled retailers to highlight local food banks that SOS supports.

Share Our Strength works toward ending hunger and poverty in the United States and around the world. By supporting food assistance, treating malnutrition and other consequences of hunger, and promoting economic independence among people in need, Share Our Strength meets immediate demands for food while investing in long-term solutions to hunger and poverty.

While Timberland had a strong heritage in the suburban market because many consumers wore Timberland products in their youth, the company was relatively new to the children's business. SOS was instrumental in introducing Timberland to young parents through media such as parenting magazines, where SOS conveyed a meaningful message about the company's values. To date, the sales of Timberland's booties have raised $150,000 for SOS.

To keep the partnership running smoothly, Timberland's crib bootie marketing manager talks monthly with her liaison at SOS. They evaluate the impact of their efforts and address any challenges. SOS reviews the tools it can offer Timberland, such as upcoming meetings with various media; public relations efforts led by SOS cast a different tone and lend legitimacy to Timberland's programs. With the monthly discussions, the contract between the two organizations, and facilitation by Timberland's social enterprise director, the partnership has become institutionalized.

Other Timberland divisions work with SOS as well. When the women's casual business sought to weave social values into its line in a branding effort similar to that of the children's division, the group brainstormed with the Social Enterprise director about causes that would have particular resonance for women. They decided to leverage the company's existing partnership with SOS, but broadened the purpose to fighting hunger in families. The women's casual business partnered specifically with SOS's Operation Frontline, a program that offers a series of cooking and nutrition classes for low-income women and their families.

Despite the success of the relationship, however, it has posed some challenges. For Timberland, a soft retail environment forces a sharp look at how marketing dollars are spent. "That's when I pull out the list of how much SOS has done for us," says Helen Kellogg, former marketing director for the Timberland Kids category. "The return directly correlates with the effort both partners put into the relationship. It goes beyond corporate philanthropy. SOS works hard to make sure we get a return on our investment." At times, one partner nets greater returns than the other—booties may not be selling well, or SOS invests time-consuming efforts on Timberland's behalf. Taking a long view can help offset the short-term imbalance.

SkillsUSA is a national nonprofit that annually serves more than one-quarter of a million high school and college students—and their instructors—enrolled in training programs in technical, skilled, and service occupations, including health occupations. SkillsUSA has more than 13,000 chapters in 54 state and territorial associations. SkillsUSA provides quality education experiences for students in leadership, teamwork, citizenship and character development. It builds and reinforces self-confidence, work attitudes, and communications skills. It emphasizes total quality at work, high ethical standards, life-long education, pride in the dignity of work, and community service. The SkillsUSA association is a partnership between education and business and industry. More than 1,000 corporations, trade associations, and labor unions actively support SkillsUSA on a national level through financial aid, in-kind contributions, and involvement of their people in SkillsUSA activities. Many more work directly with state associations and local chapters.

Timberland's partnership with SOS is integrated throughout the company's business. For instance, Timberland takes its retail customers to restaurants in the SOS network. When Timberland sponsors corporate events, SOS chefs cater. In February 2003 at the World Shoe Association trade show in Las Vegas, Timberland sponsored The Taste of Timberland—an extension of SOS's Taste of the Nation—in which 15 SOS chefs catered a dinner for Timberland customers, reinforcing Timberland's commitment to community.

These events, known as Justice Dinners, are built into the annual contract between Timberland and SOS. The contract articulates events scheduled for the year, itemizes costs, and builds in Timberland's community wealth venture—its extra donation. The contract encompasses all the scheduled joint efforts, including crib booties, and lays out other planned projects, such as an editorial that the organizations' CEOs will co-author. A fee-for-service structure formalizes the relationship: SOS provides a service for Timberland, Timberland pays for that service and rewards SOS with incremental donations. Beyond financial donations to SOS, Timberland broadens SOS's brand awareness and credibility. It's a partnership based on mutual needs.

TIMBERLAND AND SKILLS USA

The target market for Timberland's PRO brand is very different from those of the women's and children's divisions. The company launched its PRO brand in 1999 to reconnect with Timberland's consumers in service, factory, and construction work. The brand grew well, and in fall 2002 the company introduced its first work apparel line. That made Timberland PRO the first truly integrated work brand at the retail level, unlike its competitors, which focus either on footwear or apparel.

Seeking to move outside of traditional marketing tactics, Timberland PRO's brand manager sought to align the brand with its target market in the realm of community service. In its search,

Timberland PRO found SkillsUSA-VICA (SkillsUSA), an organization of more than 250,000 secondary and post-secondary students who have chosen careers in the vocational trades. SkillsUSA's mission is "to help its members become world-class workers and responsible American citizens." Timberland PRO saw a partnership with SkillsUSA as an opportunity to drive brand loyalty with younger consumers while helping communities.

SkillsUSA holds competitions at the local, state, and national level for students in a variety of fields. Timberland PRO's brand manager visited the championships in 2001, and his meeting with the director of SkillsUSA's partnerships laid the groundwork for Timberland PRO's involvement in the 2002 national championships. Timberland CEO Swartz presented the keynote address to the 12,000 students at the 2002 opening ceremonies, addressing the concepts of doing well and doing good. The speech sparked great enthusiasm for the planned Timberland service day during the championships, and more students signed up to work than could be used in the planned projects.

In 2003, Timberland PRO expanded its involvement into SkillsUSA's state level. At a New York women's shelter, construction students built shelves and cosmetology students provided makeovers. In Virginia, a group cleaned up the grounds of a camp for disadvantaged children. And in Oregon, Timberland PRO and SkillsUSA students spent a day working with Habitat for Humanity helping a young mother build a home. The Timberland PRO brand manager invests his time building relationships with SkillsUSA's state directors and participating in each service day, then teams with City Year to coordinate the logistics for each service event. City Year's involvement in turn prompts the students to consider initiating their careers with a year of service for City Year.

Working with its partners to promote social justice, Timberland has helped transform the communities it serves. Significantly, this work has also transformed Timberland as a company.

HUMILITY AND PERSISTENCE

Through its partnerships, Timberland has transformed itself along with the communities it serves. While the company is passionate about social justice— beginning with its visionary and charismatic CEO—it approaches these endeavors with humility. The company tells stories of people in local organizations who have inspired Timberland's ethic. "We're careful not to over-commercialize those messages," emphasizes Social Enterprise Director Casey. "We would never trade on these partnerships."

Timberland's partnerships operate on two-way streets. The partners base their arrangements not on writing a check but on mutual benefits for both the company and the nonprofit. Nonetheless, it's difficult to put a price tag on the richness and power derived from performing service. The process of transformation begins several months prior to the service day, when participants receive information that provides the context for their upcoming service experience. By the time they've put away their paintbrush, they haven't just painted a room, they've created a music room and opened up a child's imagination to the performing arts.

It's easy to wax poetic about service. It's tougher when one must answer to Wall Street. Swartz's response is all business: "As long as the results are what we expect, I support this notion independent of whether the cynics think it's a good idea. Someone has to go first—that's the job of the entrepreneur."

The IN PRACTICE series is supported by the Ford Foundation's Corporate Involvement Initiative. The series captures the process by which companies work to increase the economic assets and social and human capital of low-income communities and individuals. The Center focuses on companies that aim to accomplish this through regular business operations and investment of core business resources. By sharing both successes and challenges, these profiles offer practical insights that our members can use to influence their own efforts. These are stories of partnership, integration, communication and commitment.

THE CENTER FOR CORPORATE CITIZENSHIP at Boston College provides leadership in establishing corporate citizenship as a business essential, so that all companies act as economic and social assets to the communities they affect.

CENTER FOR EDUCATION ON SOCIAL RESPONSIBILITY

CASE #8:

OKLAHOMA LEAGUE FOR THE BLIND (NEW VIEW) AND GREYSTON BAKERY

NEW VIEW (FORMERLY THE OKLAHOMA LEAGUE FOR THE BLIND): INTRODUCTION/OVERVIEW

New View is a private non-profit organization that provides employment for the visually impaired. Centered in Oklahoma City, this organization cultivates independence for, and currently employs, over one hundred blind or visually impaired people. New View was created in 1949 by six blind men to provide training and vocational opportunities for the blind people of Oklahoma. By starting this organization, they saw to the needs for blind employment, awareness, and improved quality of life for blind people. With the employment rate for people with disabilities at only 38.8% in Oklahoma, (Cornell University 2005 Disabilities Status Report) and an estimated 75% unemployment rate for the blind nationwide, it is hard for vision impaired people to find jobs. At New View, workers are provided with premium vocational, rehabilitative and educational training. They receive both life skills as well as vocational skills.

New View operates under the supervision of the Javits-Wagner-O'Day Program. This program, based on the **Wagner-O'Day Act** passed by Franklin D. Roosevelt in 1938, coordinates government purchases of products and services from nonprofit organizations that employ blind and severely disabled workers. (History of JWOD Program) The idea behind the organization is to provide opportunities for employment for blind and disabled workers through services and products to the Federal Government. With the help of the JWOD Program, New View is able to have government contracts for various products. And in accordance to the JWOD guidelines, at least 75% of the employees at New View are blind or vision impaired.

Manufacturing and contract operations account for 98 percent of New View's income. They supply goods and services to government organizations, manufacture commercial and residential products, and perform specific services to organizations. New View products include wooden chocks for air planes, fire hoses for the U.S. Forestry Service, first aid kits for government agencies, and vinyl home products. Foam cups are another long standing New View product. New View also operates through service contracts like the ones it has with Tinker Air Force Base and McConnell Air Force Base for switchboard operations, mail sorting, and janitorial services. New View also offers services for teaching skills to people with deteriorating eyesight. They produce Braille and large print products to schools and provide intern programs for blind students.

Aside from providing employment for disabled workers, New View offers a wide variety of social services to the Oklahoma community. As Leah Wall, Director of Development for New View, put it, "There are two sides to our organization; an opportunity employment side and a social service side." New View holds training sessions to teach living skills development for local blind people, including how to calibrate and use an oven. The organization provides transportation at a fee for blind residents of the state. Using a fourteen passenger bus, they transport people to and from work and even take blind people to their doctors' appointments. New View also extends its outreach to the vision-impaired youth of Oklahoma by hosting summer youth camps. They offer summer internships for blind youth, by taking them to New View and helping them gain valuable work experience that they couldn't find elsewhere. Oklahoma is celebrating its state centennial in 2007, and New View is working alongside the city to provide Braille on all the signs during the celebration.

When asked about the future of New View, Leah Wall stated; "We are hoping to increase our service contracts so that we can increase employment and provide more opportunities for the blind." She went on to say that New View is seeking to improve health awareness in order to combat blindness. In the future, New View aims to increase independence and quality of life for the blind people of Oklahoma.

New View has the following mission statement: "The mission of New View is to facilitate independence and improve the quality of life for people who are blind or vision-impaired by providing employment opportunities and services." This organization follows through on its goal by providing rehabilitative training and services for people who are blind both inside and outside of the organization. New View serves as a front runner for blind education and equality in the community by entitling capable blind people with independence and work.

BIBLIOGRAPHY

1. "About Oklahoma League for the Blind." 2004 OLB. http://www.olb.org/about_us.php. 2/5/07.
2. "Disability Statistics." Cornell University 2003-2007. http://www.ilr.cornell.edu/edi/disabilitystatistics/index.cfm?n=1. 2/5/07.
3. "Oklahoma League for the Blind Provides Unique Opportunities." Page, David. March 20, 2006. http://www.findarticles.com/p/articles/mi_qn4182/is_20060320/ai_n16153005. 2/7/07.
4. Interview with Leah Wall, Director of Development. Feb 19, 2007.
5. "A Brief History of the JWOD Program." January 4, 2007. http://www.jwod.gov/jwod/about_us/about_us.html. 2/18/07.

United States Summary

These statistics indicate the social and economic status of non-institutionalized people with disabilities in the United States, using data from the 2008 American Community Survey (ACS). Comparisons to the 2007 Disability Status Report should not be made due to changes in the 2008 ACS questions.

Age: In 2008, the prevalence of disability in the US was:

- 12.1 percent for persons of all ages
- 0.7 percent for persons ages 4 and under
- 5.1 percent for persons ages 5 to 15
- 5.6 percent for persons ages 16 to 20
- 10.4 percent for persons ages 21 to 64
- 26.6 percent for persons ages 65 to 74
- 51.5 percent for persons ages 75+

Gender: In 2008, 12.4 percent of females of all ages and 11.7 percent of males of all ages in the US reported a disability.

Hispanic/Latino: In 2008, the prevalence of disability among persons of all ages of Hispanic or Latino origin in the US was 8.4 percent.

Race: In the US in 2008, the prevalence of disability for working-age people (ages 21 to 64) was:

- 10.2 percent among Whites
- 14.3 percent among Black / African Americans
- 4.6 percent among Asians
- 18.8 percent among Native Americans
- 9.8 percent among persons of some other race(s)

Employment: In 2008, the employment rate of working-age people (ages 21 to 64) with disabilities in the US was 39.5 percent.

Looking for Work: In the US in 2008, the percentage actively looking for work among people with disabilities who were not working was 8.7 percent.

Full-Time/Full-Year Employment: In the US in 2008, the percentage of working-age people with disabilities working full-time/ full-year was 25.4 percent.

Annual Earnings: In 2008, the median annual earnings of working-age people with disabilities working full-time/full-year in the US was $35,600.

Annual Household Income: In the US in 2008, the median annual income of households with working-age people with disabilities was $39,600.

Poverty: In the US in 2008, the poverty rate of working-age people with disabilities was 25.3 percent.

Supplemental Security Income: In 2008, the percentage of working-age people with disabilities receiving SSI payments in the US was 17.7 percent.

Educational Attainment: In 2008, the percentage of working-age people with disabilities in the US:

- with only a high school diploma or equivalent was 34.0 percent
- with only some college or an associate degree was 29.7 percent
- with a bachelor's degree or more was 12.3 percent.

Veterans Service-Connected Disability: In 2008, the percentage of working-age civilian veterans with a VA determined Service-Connected Disability was 16.9 percent in the US.

Health Insurance Coverage: In 2008 in the US, 81.8 percent of working-age people with disabilities had health insurance.

Prevalence of disability among non-institutionalized people of all ages in the United States in 2008*

Chart

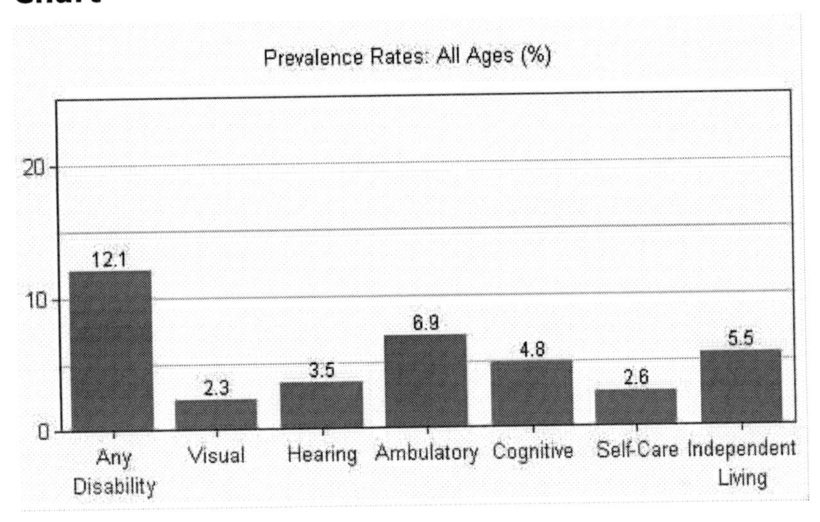

Table

Disability Type	%	MOE	Number	MOE	Base Pop.	Sample Size
Any Disability	12.1	0.05	36,169,200	157,070	299,852,800	2,949,415
Visual	2.3	0.02	6,826,400	71,880	299,852,800	2,949,415
Hearing	3.5	0.03	10,393,100	88,160	299,852,800	2,949,415
Ambulatory	6.9	0.04	19,203,700	118,020	278,976,400	2,770,321
Cognitive	4.8	0.04	13,462,900	99,810	278,976,400	2,770,321
Self-Care	2.6	0.03	7,195,600	73,750	278,976,400	2,770,321
Independent Living	5.5	0.04	13,179,300	98,800	238,826,000	2,384,789

* **Note:** Children under the age of five were only asked about Vision and Hearing disabilities. The Independent Living disability question was only asked of persons aged 16 years old and older.

Employment

Introduction

This section examines the employment rates of non-institutionalized working-age people (ages 21 to 64) with disabilities in the United States, using data from the 2008 American Community Survey (ACS). For definitions of terms, see Glossary. Comparisons to the 2007 Disability Status Report should not be made due to changes in the 2008 ACS disability questions.

Quick Statistics

Employment: with disability
39.5%

Employment: without disability
79.9%

- In 2008, the employment rate of working-age people with disabilities in the US was 39.5 percent.
- In 2008, the employment rate of working-age people without disabilities in the US was 79.9 percent.
- The gap between the employment rates of working-age people with and without disabilities was 40.4 percentage points.
- Among the six types of disabilities identified in the ACS, the highest employment rate was for people with a "Hearing Disability," 56.0 percent. The lowest employment rate was for people with a "Self-Care Disability," 18.7 percent.

Annual Earnings (Full-Time / Full-Year workers)

Introduction

This section examines the median annual earnings of non-institutionalized working-age people (ages 21 to 64) with disabilities who work full-time/full-year in the United States, using data from the 2008 American Community Survey (ACS). For definitions of terms, see Glossary. Comparisons to the 2007 Disability Status Report should not be made due to changes in the ACS disability questions.

Quick Statistics

Earnings: with disability
$35,600

Earnings: without disability
$40,700

- In 2008, the median earnings of working-age people with disabilities who worked full-time/full-year in the US was $35,600.
- In 2008, the median earnings of working-age people without disabilities who worked full-time/full-year in the US was $40,700.
- The difference in the median earnings between working-age people with and without disabilities who worked full-time/full-year was $5,100.
- Among the six types of disabilities identified in the ACS, the highest annual earnings was for people with "Hearing Disability," $40,700. The lowest annual earnings was for people with "Cognitive Disability," $30,600.

Median annual earnings of non-institutionalized working-age people (ages 21 to 64) who work full-time/full-year by disability status in the United States in 2008

Chart

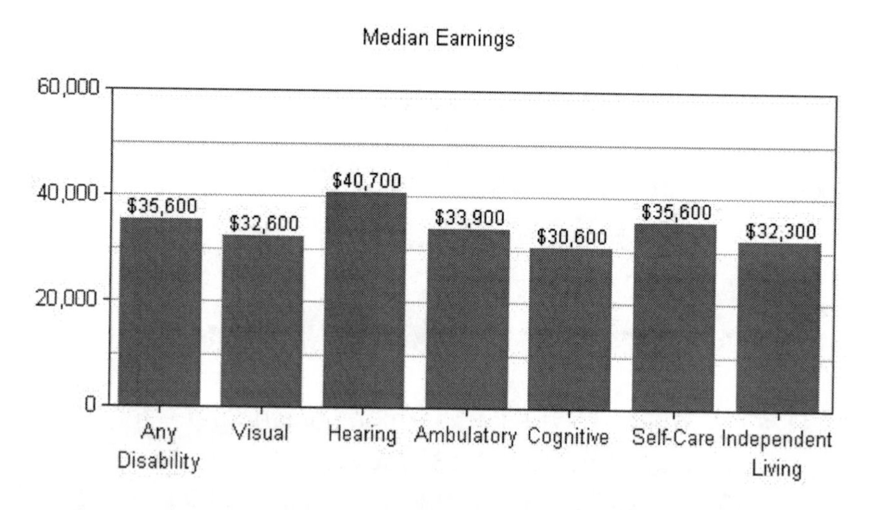

Table

Disability Type	Median Earnings	MOE	Base Pop.	Sample Size
No Disability	$40,700	$100	94,829,000	914,570
Any Disability	$35,600	$370	4,645,000	46,353
Visual	$32,600	$790	960,000	8,812
Hearing	$40,700	$720	1,632,000	17,103
Ambulatory	$33,900	$570	1,703,000	17,011
Cognitive	$30,600	$670	1,011,000	9,515
Self-Care	$35,600	$1,380	338,000	3,155
Independent Living	$32,300	$1,070	554,000	5,460

Poverty

Introduction

This section examines the poverty rates † of non-institutionalized working-age people (ages 21 to 64) with disabilities in the United States, using data from the 2008 American Community Survey (ACS). For definitions of terms, see Glossary. Comparisons to the 2007 Disability Status Report should not be made due to changes in the 2008 ACS disability questions.

Quick Statistics

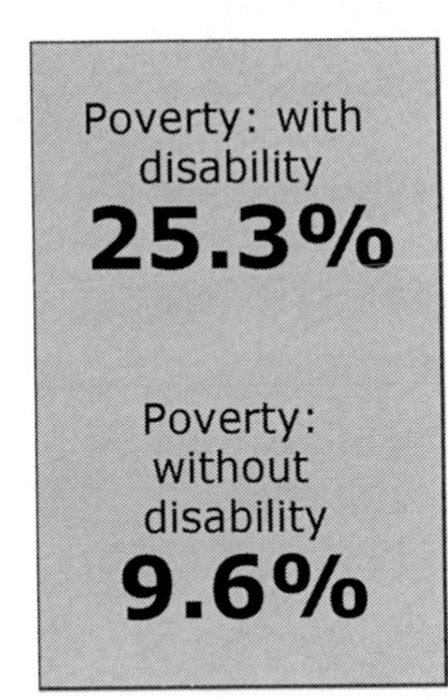

- In 2008, the poverty rate of working-age people with disabilities in the US was 25.3 percent†.
- In 2008, the poverty rate of working-age people without disabilities in the US was 9.6 percent †.
- The difference in the poverty rate between working-age people with and without disabilities was 15.7 percentage points†.
- Among the six types of disabilities identified in the ACS, the highest poverty rate was for people with "Cognitive Disability," 32.4 percent. The lowest poverty rate was for people with "Hearing Disability," 18.0 percent.

† **Note**: The Census Bureau does not calculate poverty status for those people living in military group quarters or college dormitories.
† **Caution:** Estimate based on small sample size (less than 40 individuals).

Education

High School Diploma/Equivalent

Introduction

This section explores the percentage of non-institutionalized working-age people (ages 21 to 64) with disabilities with only a high school diploma or equivalent in the United States, using data from the 2008 American Community Survey (ACS). Comparisons to the 2007 Disability Status Report should not be made due to changes in the 2008 ACS disability questions. For definitions of terms, see Glossary.

Quick Statistics

High School Only: with disability
34.0%

High School Only: without disability
26.2%

- In 2008, the percentage of working-age people with disabilities with only a high school diploma or equivalent in the US was 34.0 percent.
- In 2008, the percentage of working-age people without disabilities with only a high school diploma or equivalent in the US was 26.2 percent.
- The difference in the percentage with only a high school diploma or equivalent between working-age people with and without disabilities was 7.8 percentage points.
- Among the six types of disabilities identified in the ACS, the highest percentage with only a high school diploma or equivalent was for people with "Independent Living Disability," 35.2 percent. The lowest percentage with only a high school diploma or equivalent was for people with "Visual Disability," 31.7 percent.

THE AMERICANS WITH DISABILITIES ACT

Susan Campbell
Matt Rita

BACKGROUND

The Americans with Disabilities Act ("ADA") was signed into law by the first President Bush on July 26, 1990. By its terms, the statute was (and is) intended "to provide a clear and comprehensive national mandate for the elimination of discrimination against individuals with disabilities." 42 U.S.C. § 12101(b).

In its early years, Title I of the ADA (the portion of the statute dealing with employment) spawned considerable litigation, as many employees with medical conditions or other physical limitations claimed to be covered by its anti-discrimination protections.

In recent years, however, federal courts—including the United States Supreme Court—have interpreted the ADA somewhat narrowly. Thus, it is perhaps not surprising that the numbers of disability discrimination charges filed with the Equal Employment Opportunity Commission ("EEOC") have gone from a high of 19,798 in fiscal year 1995, down to a low of 14,893 in fiscal year 2005.

WHICH EMPLOYERS ARE COVERED BY THE ADA?

The ADA covers all employers, including state and local governments, who have "**15 or more employees** for each working day in each of 20 or more calendar weeks in the current or proceeding calendar year." 42 U.S.C. § 12111(5)(A).

Employers who do not fall within the above definition still must be mindful of the ADA's requirements and prohibitions. Most states (including Colorado) have enacted similar antidiscrimination laws which apply even to small employers. On April 20, 2006, in the case of *Tesmer v. Colorado High School Activities Association*, the Colorado Court of Appeals stated that "[w]henever possible, the [Colorado Anti-Discrimination Act] should be interpreted consistently with the Americans with Disabilities Act."

WHICH EMPLOYEES ARE PROTECTED BY THE ADA?

The general rule of the ADA is that "[n]o covered entity shall discriminate against a **qualified individual with a disability** because of the disability of such individual in regard to . . . terms, conditions and privileges of employment." 42 U.S.C. § 12112(a). The terms "qualified" and "disability" have specific *legal* definitions under the ADA, and should not be used or interpreted in a colloquial (or even medical) sense.

(a) Under the ADA, the term "**qualified** individual with a disability" means "an individual with a disability who, with or without reasonable accommodation, can perform the essential functions of the employment position that such individual holds or desires." 42 U.S.C. § 12111(8).

(b) With respect to an individual, the statute defines "**disability**" to mean:

- a physical or mental **impairment** that
- **substantially limits** on or more of
- the **major life activities** of such individual

In the January 8, 2002 case of *Toyota Motor Manufacturing, Kentucky, Inc. v. Williams*, the United States Supreme Court made it clear that this is "a demanding standard," and that "[m]erely having an impairment does not make one disabled for purposes of the ADA." The Court went on to write that "[i]t is insufficient . . . to merely submit evidence of a medical diagnosis . . ."

(c) The ADA covers not only individuals who are *currently* and *actually* disabled (within the meaning of the above definition), but also individuals who:

- have **a record of** a substantially limiting impairment, and/or
- are **regarded as** having such an impairment

(d) In evaluating whether or not an individual has a "disability" under the ADA, one must take into account "mitigating measures," such as medication or other aids. For example, if an individual has poor eyesight, then his limitations in the major life activity of seeing must be assessed when he is using corrective lenses. This common-sense approach was adopted by the United States Supreme Court in a June 22, 1999 opinion written by (now retired) Justice Sandra Day O'Connor in the case of *Sutton v. United Air Lines, Inc.*

WHO IS EXCLUDED FROM THE ADA'S PROTECTIONS?

When Congress enacted the ADA, it expressly excluded certain conditions and behaviors from the statute's protections. *See* 42 U.S.C. § 12210–12211. Those exclusions include:

- *current* illegal drug use or resulting psychoactive disorders
- homosexuality, bisexuality, transvestism or transsexualism
- sexual behavior disorders
- compulsive gambling, kleptomania and pyromania

DIRECT THREAT

The ADA provides that "[i]t may be a defense to a charge of [disability] discrimination . . . that . . . application of qualification standards, tests, or selection criteria that screen out . . . an individual with a disability . . . [is] **job-related** and consistent with **business necessity**. . . ." 42 U.S.C. § 12113(a).

The text of the statute goes on to state that such qualification standards "may include a requirement that an individual shall not pose a **direct threat** to the health or safety of other individuals in the workplace." 42 U.S.C. § 12113(a). Elsewhere, the ADA defines the term "direct threat" to mean "a significant risk to the health or safety of others that cannot be eliminated by reasonable accommodation." 42 U.S.C. § 12111(3).

The EEOC, which is the federal agency charged with enforcing Title I of the ADA, has promulgated a regulation that carries the "direct threat" defense one step further, by allowing an employer to screen out a disabled worker not only for risks that he would pose to *others* in the workplace, but also for risks on the job to *his own* health or safety. *See* 29 C.F.R. § 1630.15(b). That regulation was challenged in court but upheld by the United States Supreme Court on June 10, 2002 in the case of *Chevron U.S.A. Inc. v. Echazabal.*

DISABILITY-RELATED INQUIRIES AND MEDICAL EXAMINATIONS

The ADA permits an employer to "require a medical examination **after** an offer of employment has been to a job applicant and prior to the commencement of the employment duties of such applicant," 42 U.S.C. § 12112(d)(3), so long as:

- *all* entering employees are subjected to such an exam
- medical information about the applicant is kept confidential
- the results of the exam are used only for non-discriminatory purposes

Otherwise, a covered employer "shall not conduct a medical examination or make inquiries of a job applicant as to whether such applicant is an individual with a disability or as to the nature or severity of such disability." 42 U.S.C. § 12112(d)(2).

REASONABLE ACCOMMODATION

What is the covered employer's duty to provide reasonable accommodation?

(a) When a disabled employee (who is otherwise qualified for the job) is unable to perform the job because of the mental or physical limitations of his disability, the employer is required to provide a "reasonable" accommodation of the limitations.

(b) Employer should engage in an interactive "dialogue" with employee about his limitations and reasonable accommodation options. (Failure of employee to cooperate in dialogue can provide a defense to employee's ADA claim.) The employer is not required to implement the employee's requested accommodation if there are other reasonable accommodations that enable employee to perform the job.

(c) Reasonable accommodations may include (whether they are "reasonable" in a specific case depends on the circumstances):

- acquiring or modifying equipment or devices;
- job restructuring;
- part-time or modified schedules;
- reassignment to a vacant position;
- adjusting or modifying exams, training materials, or policies;
- making the workplace accessible; and
- leave to recover from effects of disability—but not indefinite leave.

(d) An employer is required to provide a reasonable accommodation unless doing so would cause the employer "undue hardship."

- "Undue hardship" means the accommodation would be unduly costly, extensive or disruptive, or that it would fundamentally alter the nature or operation of the business;
- Factors to be considered in determining whether an accommodation causes undue hardship include: cost of the accommodation; employer's size and financial resources; nature and structure of employer's operation; technical feasibility; administrative burden; whether funding can be obtained from outside source; whether costs can be offset by tax credits or deductions.

(e) When is an accommodation <u>not</u> a "reasonable" accommodation?

- eliminating an <u>essential</u> job function
- fundamentally altering or restructuring an essential job function
- creating a new job
- creating a modified duty or part-time job (unless required by policy, contract, etc.)
- leave for indefinite period

(f) What is an "essential function"?

- A duty or function critical or fundamental to accomplishment of the job.
- Factors that determine whether function is "essential":
  - employer's judgment
  - written job description prepared before advertising or interviewing for job
  - time spent performing job function
  - consequence of not performing the job function
  - collective bargaining agreement
  - work experience of past and present incumbents
- Is a job analysis necessary to determine essential functions?

(g) Examples of reasonable accommodation decisions:

Regular Attendance Regular attendance at work is an essential function of a job. EEOC v. Yellow Freight Systems, 253 F.3d 943 (7th Cir. 2001) (upholding discharge of dock worker for excessive absenteeism).	**Full-Time Employment** Employer did not have to agree to a reduced work schedule as an accommodation where the position in question required full-time work. DeVito v. Chicago Park District, 270 F.3d 532 (7th Cir. 2001).
Physical Presence at Work Disabled employees do not have a right to work from home where physical presence is an essential function of the job because they must interact with others in the workplace. Heaser v. Toro Company, 247 F.3d 826 (8th Cir. 2001).	**Mandatory Overtime** The employer was not required to excuse a utility worker from overtime work because of his back problems where overtime was an essential function of the job. Davis v. Florida Power & Light Company, 205 F.3d 1301 (11th Cir. 2000).
Inability to Accept Criticism Employee with an anxiety disorder could not perform the essential functions of his job because he could not deal with stressful situations or accept negative performance evaluations without experiencing anxiety and stomach pain. Gonzagowski v. Widnall, 115 F.3d 744 (10th Cir. 1997) ("It is unreasonable to require an employer to create a work environment free of stress and criticism.")	**Answering Customer Calls** Power company was justified in terminating employee who suffered unpredictable panic attacks at work because she could not consistently answer customer calls about electric or gas emergencies. Emerson v. Northern States Power Company, 856 F.3d 506 (7th Cir. 2001).

Pushing Wheelchairs	**Heavy Lifting**
Discharge of a nurse who needed a motorized cart because of her arthritis did not violate the ADA because she was unable to push wheelchairs and perform other job functions. Stafne v. Unicare Homes, 266 F.3d 771 (8th Cir. 2001).	EEOC lawsuit against United Airlines for failing to accommodate a customer service representative, who could not perform heavy lifting necessary to move passenger baggage, was rejected because lifting and moving baggage was an essential function of the job. EEOC v. United Airlines, 1999 U.S. App. LEXIS 13347 (10th Cir.).
Operating Equipment	**Travel**
The discharge of an employee with epilepsy who could not work near or operate heavy equipment for at least three months was upheld, because operating the equipment was an essential function of the job. Matthews v. *The Denver Post*, 263 F.3d 1164 (10th Cir. 2001) (*The Denver Post* represented by HRO).	Court dismissed constructive discharge claim of an auditor who could not travel for extended periods, because the ADA does not require restructuring a job's essential functions and the employer proved that travel was an essential function of the plaintiff's job. Wells v. Shalala, 228 F.3d 1137 (10th Cir. 2000).

(h) Reasonable accommodation checklist:

1. What is the original job?
2. What are the essential functions of the job?
3. Will a job analysis be necessary to determine essential functions?
4. What effect does disability have on job performance?
5. What accommodations in original job are possible and/or requested by employee to minimize effect of disability?
6. Has employer engaged in interactive dialogue with disabled employee? Has employer conducted a reasonable accommodation "thought process" considering the possible options?
7. Is there an accommodation that would enable employee to perform essential functions of original position?
8. Is the accommodation "reasonable"?
9. Does the accommodation produce "undue hardship"?
10. Has employer thought through other options? If no reasonable accommodation in original position, can employee be reassigned to a vacant position he/she is qualified to perform (consider pay grade, compensation, seniority).
11. Other considerations:
    - If employee's disability causes a direct threat to health or safety, can the threat be minimized by a reasonable accommodation?
    - How has employer treated disabled and non-disabled employees in the past?
    - What do employer's policies say?
    - Does employer need to consult expert re essential functions or possible accommodations?

AN ENTREPRENEURIAL APPROACH TO WELFARE TO WORK PROGRAMS

Carolyn Brown

Welfare-to-work programs are provided in different forms from state to state. These programs, mandated by congressional welfare reform legislation, link welfare recipients to an active transitioning to unsubsidized work.

The number of people receiving welfare subsidies is the lowest it has been since 1967. A variety of factors have contributed to the success of the program such as innovative local programs by government institutions and businesses, flexible hiring practices by corporations, and the participation of small businesses in hiring and training welfare recipients. State governments, community colleges, large corporations, coalitions of small business, and even university students are finding ways throughout the country to get people off welfare and into the work force.

State human service agencies are developing innovative delivery systems for welfare-to-work programs that use existing state agency resources as well as resources of local communities and businesses. Wisconsin Works, known as W-2, which boasts a stunning percent decrease in people receiving cash payment since the mid 1980s relies on an integrated series of services provided by the State of y has helped make W-2 one of the most successful welfare-to-work programs in the country (Stephenson 1999).

Having reached a pinnacle of achievement, W-2 is now turning resources and creative energy to finding ways of solving problems of the chronically unemployed and disabled poor as well as problem solving for ways to decrease the number of working former welfare recipients who live below the poverty line without benefits or adequate child care (Stephenson 1999).

Iowa, Washington, Oregon, and Maryland have developed training and employment coordination programs administered through their community college systems which provide both specific skills development training and training in "soft skills" such as work place behavior, dependability, and dealing with domestic problems that interfere with job attendance. Programs in Iowa and Washington recruit employers, provide human services and place program participants (Pierce 1998).

Two students at Yale started a service that reaches out to welfare recipients in the community to help them find work, fill out forms, write resumes, find pro-bono legal services, and improve their English. These students also provide transportation, problem solve and "stop at nothing" to help their clients. (Meckler 1999). The founders, Brian Kreiter and Kirsten Lodal have recruited students throughout the country to get involved with welfare recipients looking for work, and have prompted the creation of six chapters at universities around the country (Meckler 1999).

While large corporations are usually the first ones contacted to hire welfare recipients because of their ability to hire large numbers of employees, early research on welfare-to-work programs indicate that small businesses are invaluable players in the process of putting welfare recipients to work. "The national Welfare to Work Partnership, a nonprofit founded by leviathans such as United Parcel Service and Burger King to encourage private sector participation, now has a membership dominated by small firms, according to spokesman Luis Vizcaino (Dickerson 1998).

Coalitions of small businesses that have organized to participate in welfare-to-work programs are active in San Francisco and Los Angeles. The California Small Business Association collaborated with San Francisco's Small Business Network to "survey more than 300 small business owners to find out how they felt about hiring welfare recipients and what they would need to do so" (Torres 1999). Employers are reluctant to hire welfare recipients because they wanted employees with "good work attitudes who would show up on time and be trainable" (Torres 1999). Generally employers perceive welfare recipients to lack the "soft skills" needed to be dependable employees. In addition, the small firms lack human resource departments and "need someone to handle issues such as child care or transportation, worker's compensation and unemployment, and paperwork." (Torres 1999)

San Francisco's Small Business Network joined forces with Juma, a nonprofit human services program, to provide employment services to small businesses that hire welfare recipients. The services include five weeks of training in customer service, communication skills and dealing with domestic issues such as child care and family violence. Counseling to set short and long term employment goals, job placement, and long-term support and mentoring for employees are also important components of the program. At the same time, Juma recruits small business employers, provides them with information about the program and the candidates, prescreens candidates for suitability for each position, and completes the paperwork for the employers. Juma seeks positions that pay at least $8 per hours and provide benefits and upward mobility (Torres 1999).

In Los Angeles, the GAIN program recruits small and large employers for welfare recipients and provides screening, placement, follow up, and paperwork services for small businesses that hire welfare recipients. GAIN has positive feedback from small business owners like Kim DeVane "It used to take me a week to hire a warehouse worker. Now it's a couple of hours. Quite frankly, I prefer hiring someone they've recommended than someone who has walked in off the street." (Dickerson 1998)

Skepticism about the long term willingness and ability of small businesses to absorb the welfare recipients prompted the formation of the Welfare-to-Work Leadership (WWL), a group of 24 California Southland CEOs whose mission it is to "mobilize the Los Angeles business community to take an active role in getting residents off the dole" (Dickerson 1998). A major thrust of the group will be "stumping for welfare reform, explaining its bottom-line benefits, dispensing information and linking emplyers to agencies that can get them started" (Dickerson 1998). One of the "bottom-line benefits' for businesses hiring welfare recipients is a federal tax credit that allows employers to take up to $8500 in tax credits over two years (Szabo 1999). The greatest difficulty facing WWL is convincing employers that welfare recipients are not "damaged goods" and that former welfare recipients are developing good employment records in many businesses (Dickerson 1998).

Good employment records for former welfare recipients are frequently achieved in settings where the employer is willing to provide personal contact and individual coaching on the skills the employees lack. This personal attention is best met in a small business environment, and small businesses continue to show success in hiring former welfare recipients (Stipe 1998). Sarian Bouma was honored as the US Small Business Administration National Welfare to Work Entrepreneur of the Year for her employment of former welfare recipients. Bouma is herself a former welfare recipient who started a commercial building maintenance business in Washington, D.C. in 1987 and currently employs 165 people (Stipe 1998). Rena Burns, chief executive officer of a technology and communications firm in Santa Monica, California was honored with the Small Business Association Welfare to Work Small Business Owner of the Year Award for her personal work with former welfare recipients. She coaches each employee personally on office demeanor and professional behavior. She also works with the teams in each department to maintain open communication and mutual respect. "I was surprised at how easy it was to hire welfare-to-work employees and how responsive they were to the job demands," says Burns (Klein 1999).

Small business are joining large corporations, colleges, university students, and state-funded human service agencies to make the welfare reform legislation linking government benefits to employment a success. Some obstacles still stand in the way of declaring the welfare reform legislation an inarguable success. President Clinton has proposed an increase in the minimum wage because many employed former welfare recipients still receive government subsidies for day care and medical benefits and/or continue to live below the poverty line while working full time. Affordable day care continues to be an obstacle for welfare mothers becoming employed full time. Day care providers require a rate of pay that, in many cases, exceeds the total monthly income of women working in low wage jobs. Advocacy groups continue to lobby federal and state governments for increased day care subsidies (Wilson 1998).

While it may be too soon to declare the welfare reform initiative a total success, the variety of innovative programs and business efforts throughout the country have begun to make a significant contribution to getting people off welfare.

REFERENCES

Dickerson, M. (1998, June 24). Putting people to work. *Los Angeles Times Online.* Available http://www.latimes.com/HOME/ARCHIVES. *c981504**

Klein, K.E. (1999, May 12). Technology firm owner involved in hiring former welfare recipients says mentoring, equitable treatment are keys. *Los Angeles Times,* p.2. *c2002342*

Meckler, L. (1999, September 24). Students work to get people off welfare. *The Detroit News.* Available www.detnews.com/1999/classrooms/9909/25/09240185.html *c2001287*

Pierce, D. (1998, March 16). Welfare to work: State community college models. AACC Letter, p.2. *c990510*

Stephenson, C. (1990, December 12). With welfare rolls down dramatically, W-2 faces new standard for success-evolving with its clientele. Milwaukee Journal Sentinel, p.9. *c2002344*

Stipe, S. (1998, May 4). Bouma turned her life around to start firm. Baltimore Business Journal. Available http://www.amcity.com/baltimore/stories/050498/smallbll.html. *c990289*

Szabo, J. (1999, March). Extra credit. *Entrepreneur,* 3. *c991608*

Torres, V. (1999, February 24). Small firms prepare welfare recipients for hire ground. *Los Angeles Times,* l. *c991465*

Wilson, Y. (1998, Janury 28). Day care costs test welfare-to-work plan. *San Francisco Chronicle,* p.1. *c991553*

*CELCEE document number

CELCEE is an adjunct ERIC Clearinghouse funded by the Kauffman Center for Entrepreneurial Leadership. The opinions expressed herein do not necessarily reflect those of the sponsoring institutions, and no official endorsement should be inferred.

IS IT ALL ABOUT THE BROWNIES?

Taking Less As Opposed To Giving Back

by Beth Parish

Beth Parish is Program Manager for the John J. Sullivan Endowed Chair for Free Enterprise at Regis University in Denver, Colorado. The mission of the Sullivan Chair is to help forge multi-sector partnerships that use Free Enterprise solutions to address social needs. To learn more about how you can partner with the Sullivan Program, please contact Beth at bparish @ regis.edu

Most of us have heard about businesses on a mission to give back to the community, or a business with a double or triple bottom line that looks at social mission, environmental impact and profit. While there is no right way to look at the business of doing good, another model to consider can be described by the philosophy of Julius Walls Jr., CEO of Greyston Bakery; last spring when Julius visited Regis University in Denver he challenged business students to think about "taking less, as opposed to giving back."

Even though you might not have heard of Greyston Bakery in Yonkers, New York you have probably enjoyed their delicious brownies during a late night indulgence, on top of your favorite birthday cake or after eating dinner with your family. In addition to making the great tasting Do Goodie brownie, Greyston Bakery makes the brownies for Ben and Jerry's and Haagen Dazs ice cream.

As told by *Denver Post* columnist Al Lewis, "Those tasty little brownie chunks are not baked by elves, but often by felons, drug addicts, social misfits and people who are otherwise deemed unemployable. Greyston is their only hope in a "hood where the unemployment rate exceeds 30 percent." As the company website says, "We don't hire people to bake brownies; we bake brownies to hire people." The unique practice of hiring the traditionally "unemployable" is not the only thing that separates Greyston from other large commercial bakeries. Through its profits, Greyston Bakery is a "source of revenue for the Greyston Mandala, a West Chester County, New York organization, supporting affordable childcare for the community, affordable housing for the homeless and low income families, and affordable health care for persons with HIV."

Greyston Bakery can be described as a Social Enterprise. According to the Social Enterprise Alliance a social enterprise is, "any non-profit, for-profit or hybrid corporate form that utilizes market-based strategies to advance a social mission."

While Julius Walls did not found Greyston Bakery, he is largely responsible for the business leadership and vision that has made the organization into what it is today—a $6 million business. Furthermore, Greyston has an industry-leading rate of employee retention at 80%, a bakery with several significant ice cream partners, a brand new gourmet brownie that is available through Vitamin Cottage and Whole Foods, and an enterprise with a growing online brownie gift business in the Do Goodie Brownie.

Those tasty little brownie chunks are not baked by elves, but often by felons, drug addicts, social misfits and people who are otherwise deemed unemployable.

Throughout his journey, Julius Walls has learned some valuable lessons on what can lead to the success of a social enterprise and how to maximize the positive impact a business can have on a community.

Lesson number one is that **you have to have a great product.** Consumers don't often buy a brownie because it has a great social mission. If the brownie isn't, as my son says, "to die for," why eat it? While I would love to support the Greyston mission, am I going to give up the calories on a "so so" brownie?

Furthermore, ice cream partner Haagen Dazs, is not going to add Greyston's brown sugar cake to the *Sticky Toffee Pudding Ice Cream* unless the quality is superior. Consider Greyston's first vision statement, "Greyston Bakery is the nationally leading Brownie Company. We produce Do Goodie, the best tasting highest quality brownies at a great value to the consumer." This company knows product quality comes first.

Even their brownie partner Ben and Jerry's realizes that product quality comes first when they talk about selling flavor, Chocolate Fudge Brownie, which ". . . combines our great ice cream with chunks of chewy, fudgy brownies. These brownies are baked by Greyston Bakery, which provides employment and training to economically disadvantaged residents of Yonkers, NY. We are glad to have Greyston as a business partner because we get great tasting brownies and we also get to support the good work they do to create economic opportunities in their community."

The great product leads to the next learning—**you have to make a profit.** When Julius Walls spoke to MBA students at Regis University in July 2007 he noted, "failure is not an option" because so many segments of the community are dependent on Greyston Bakery. The bakery employs the hard to employ, delivers funds to the Greyston Foundation, and serves as a model for other social enterprises. To do all of these things, Greyston Bakery must make a profit. As noted in their guiding principles "The bakery should consistently achieve an operating profit. Achieving operating profit is the best route to long-term survival of the organization, and the best inducement for others to follow the bakery's model."

In the United States, with the talk of corporate greed and excessive profits, often for-profit businesses are seen as evil, while the not for-profit sector is seen as good. Under Julius Walls leadership, Greyston Bakery is an excellent example of a for-profit business that is delivering jobs, workforce development, low-income housing, supportive services, childcare, after-school programs, comprehensive HIV community health programs, and community gardens to the greater Yonkers, New York area.

One tough lesson Julius passes on is that as an employer who needs to make a profit, he **cannot do everything at once.** To meet its financial goals, Greyston Bakery is able to offer its employees a fair wage, but often not a living wage. As the bakery's guiding principles say, "The bakery will pay employees fair wages for their skills. While for some employees this salary may not currently constitute a 'living wage,' the bakery is committed to working with these individuals to improve their skill set and value." Walls argues that given the opportunity, his employees can succeed beyond their dreams and societies dreams. He says, "We all have equal value, just different skill sets." In fact, Walls is a partner in a New York restaurant with one of his former employees.

To assist the employees, the bakery offers mentoring and training and encourages the workforce to seek outside educational opportunities. While Julius hopes to be able to offer all employees a living wage, he has been able to offer profit sharing, so all members of the work team are rewarded when the company is successful. Mentoring and advancing within the organization can be seen through the story of Dieulane Philogene, who began working at Greyston Bakery putting together boxes, almost nine years ago. Greyston gave Dieulane steady employment, the opportunity to provide for her children, and the chance to further her education. After working for Greyston for several years, Dieulane went back to school for her associates degree in accounting - she will graduate early in 2009 and has worked her way up within the organization. She is now a member of the accounting department. When it came to studying T accounts, she admits she struggled; Julius saw some of the difficulty she was having and took time out of his schedule to tutor Dieulane and offer her encouragement. After spending an hour with Julius, the mysterious T accounts seemed "clear as day."

Dieulane's situation is not unique in the *promote from within* environment at Greyston, and Julius sets the tone with his desire to see all succeed.

Another significant principle that Julius has brought to Greyston Bakery is **transparency.** Julius has many talents and strengths and has a background in accounting, so looking at financial statements comes as second nature. Julius encourages an open door policy and wants all the Greyston employees to understand the business; what he did not realize is that when he shared the organization's financials, no one knew what they were looking at. After offering education on financial statements, the workforce could see the positive financial results of the effort and work they put into the bakery.

Purpose fills each day at Greyston. Employees begin their day with a moment of silence – whether to pray, regroup, or just stand there. Julius admits he quietly prays each day, before the bakery fires up, for strength, wisdom, and courage – believing in himself and his entire team that they all can make a difference. He says, "success and failure are not solely dependent on me." He regularly quotes Langston Hughes' *Mother to Son* where a mother speaks to her son about life experiences and says, *"Life for me ain't been no crystal stair. It's had tacks in it, and splinters and boards torn up . . . But all this time I's been a-climbin' on . . . Don't you set down on the steps 'cause you finds it's kinder hard. Don't you fall now."*

"Failure is not an option" because so many segments of the community are dependent on Greyston Bakery.

As we look at Greyston Bakery, a question we should consider is "Why is the Greyston model so unique?" In the world of for-profit businesses, are there other examples of corporations that are "taking less and giving more?" Greyston Bakery is not just giving back, but through the Greyston Foundation, they are fundamentally changing the Yonker's approach to collaborative community development. The challenge that for-profit businesses in the United States need to take up is how can we give more in terms of employment, profit sharing, community impact and take less from society, the environment and the consumer.

The Greyston Bakery model demonstrates how we could challenge our thinking on the role of for–profit businesses in the delivery of social goodwill.

IN DEFENSE OF INTERNATIONAL SWEATSHOPS

Ian Maitland

The critics' charges are undoubtedly accurate on a number of points: (1) There is no doubt that international companies are chasing cheap labor. (2) The wages paid by the international sweatshops are—by American standards—shockingly low. (3) Some developing country governments have tightly controlled or repressed organized labor in order to prevent it from disturbing the flow of foreign investment. Thus, in Indonesia, independent unions have been suppressed. (4) It is not unusual in developing countries for minimum wage levels to be lower than the official poverty level. (5) Developing country governments have winked at violations of minimum wage laws and labor rules. However, most jobs are in the informal sector and so largely, outside the scope of government supervision. (6) Some suppliers have employed children or have subcontracted work to other producers who have done so. (7) Some developing country governments deny their people basic political rights. China is the obvious example; Indonesia's record is pretty horrible but had shown steady improvement until the last two years. But on many of the other counts, the critics' charges appear to be seriously inaccurate. And, even where the charges are accurate, it is not self-evident that the practices in question are improper or unethical, as we see next.

WAGES AND CONDITIONS

Even the critics of international sweatshops do not dispute that the wages they pay are generally higher than—or at least equal to—comparable wages in the labor markets where they operate. According to the International Labor Organization (ILO), multinational companies often apply standards relating to wages, benefits, conditions of work, and occupational safety and health that both exceed statutory requirements and those practised by local firms. The ILO also says that wages and working conditions in so-called Export Processing Zones (EPZs) are often equal to or higher than jobs outside.[1] The World Bank says that the poorest workers in developing countries work in the informal sector where they often earn less than half what a formal sector employee earns. Moreover, "informal and rural workers often must work under more hazardous and insecure conditions than their formal sector counterparts."[2]

The same appears to hold true for the international sweatshops. In 1996, young women working in the plant of a Nike supplier in Serang, Indonesia, were earning the Indonesian legal minimum wage of 5,200 rupiahs or about $2.28 each day. As a report in the *Washington Post* pointed out, just earning the minimum wage put these workers among higher-paid Indonesians: "In Indonesia, less than half the working population earns the minimum wage, since about half of all adults here are in farming, and the typical farmer would make only about 2,000 rupiahs each day."[3]. . . Also in 1996, a Nike spokeswoman estimated that an entry-level factory worker in the plant of a Nike supplier made five times what a farmer makes. Nike's chairman, Phil Knight, likes to teasingly remind critics that the average worker in one of Nike's Chinese factories is paid more than a professor at Beijing University. There is also plentiful anecdotal evidence from non-Nike sources. A worker at the Taiwanese-owned King Star Garment Assembly plant in Honduras told a reporter that he was earning seven times what he earned in the countryside.[4] In Bangladesh, the country's fledgling garment industry was paying women who had never worked before between $40 and $55 a month in 1991. That compared with a national per capital income of about $200 and the approximately $1 a day earned by many of these women's husbands as day laborers or richshaw drivers.[5]. . .

There is also the mute testimony of the lines of job applicants outside the sweatshops in Guatemala and Honduras. According to Lucy Martinez-Mont, in Guatemala the sweatshops are conspicuous for the long lines of young people waiting to be interviewed for a job.[6] Outside the gates of an industrial park in Honduras . . . "anxious onlookers are always waiting, hoping for a chance at least to fill out a job application [for employment at one of the apparel plants]."[7]

The critics of sweatshops acknowledge that workers have voluntarily taken their jobs, consider themselves lucky to have them, and want to keep them. . . . But they go on to discount the workers' views as the product of confusion or ignorance, and/or they just argue that the workers' views are beside the point. Thus, while "it is undoubtedly true" that Nike has given jobs to thousands of people who wouldn't be working otherwise, they say that "neatly skirts the fundamental human-rights issue raised by these production arrangements that are now spreading all across the world." Similarly, Charles Kernaghan says that "[w]hether workers think they are better off in the assembly plants than elsewhere is not the real issue." Kernaghan, and Jeff Ballinger of the AFL-CIO, concede that the workers desperately need these jobs. But "[t]hey say they're not asking that U.S. companies stop operating in these countries. They're asking that workers be paid a living wage and treated like human beings."[8]

Apparently these workers are victims of what Marx called false consciousness, or else they would grasp that they are being exploited. According to Barnet and Cavanagh, "For many workers . . . exploitation is not a concept easily comprehended because the alternative prospects for earning a living are so bleak."[9]

IMMISERIZATION AND INEQUALITY

The critics' claim that the countries that host international sweatshops are marked by growing poverty and inequality is flatly contradicted by the record. In fact, many of those countries have experienced sharp increases in living standards—for all strata of society. In trying to attract investment in simple manufacturing, Malaysia and Indonesia and, now, Vietnam and China are retracing the industrialization path already successfully taken by East Asian countries such as Taiwan, Korea, Singapore, and Hong Kong. These four countries got their start by producing labor-intensive manufactured goods (often electrical and electronic components, shoes, and garments) for export markets. Over time they graduated to the export of higher value-added items that are skill-intensive and require a relatively developed industrial base.

As is well known, these East Asian countries have achieved growth rates exceeding eight percent for a quarter-century. . . . The workers in these economies were not improverished by growth. The benefits of growth were widely diffused: These economies achieved essentially full employment in the 1960s. Real wages rose by as much as a factor of four. Absolute poverty fell. And income inequality remained at low to moderate levels. It is true that in the initial stages the rapid growth generated only moderate increases in wages. But once essentially full employment was reached, . . . the increased demand for labor resulted in the bidding up of wages as firms competed for a scarce labor supply.

Interestingly, given its historic mission as a watchdog for international labor standards, the ILO has embraced this development model. It recently noted that the most successful developing economies, in terms of output and employment growth, have been "those who best exploited emerging opportunities in the global economy."[10] An "export-oriented policy is vital in countries that are starting on the industrialization path and have large surpluses of cheap labour." Countries that have succeeded in attracting foreign direct investment (FDI) have experienced rapid growth in manufacturing output and exports. The successful attraction of foreign investment in plant and equipment "can be a powerful spur to rapid industrialization and employment creation.". . .

According to the World Bank, the rapidly growing Asian economies (including Indonesia) "have also been unusually successful at sharing the fruits of their growth."[11] In fact, while inequality in the West has been growing, it has been shrinking in the Asian economies. They are the only economies in the world to have experienced high growth *and* declining inequality, and they also show shrinking gender gaps in education. . . .

PROFITING FROM REPRESSION?

What about the charge that international sweatshops are profiting from repression? It is undeniable that there is repression in many of the countries where sweatshops are located. But economic development appears to be relaxing that repression rather than strengthening its grip. The companies are supposed to benefit from government policies (e.g., repression of unions) that hold down labor costs. However, as we have seen, the wages paid by the international sweatshops already match or exceed the prevailing local wages. Not only that, but incomes in the East Asian economies, and in Indonesia, have risen rapidly. Moreover, even the sweatshops' critics admit that the main factor restraining wages in countries like Indonesia is the state of the labor market. . . . The high rate of unemployment and underemployment acts as a brake on wages: Only about 55 percent of the Indonesian labor force can find more than thirty-five hours of work each week, and about two million workers are unemployed.

The critics, however, are right in saying that the Indonesian government has opposed independent unions in the sweatshops out of fear they would lead to higher wages and labor unrest. But the government's fear clearly is that unions might drive wages in the modern industrial sector *above* market-clearing levels—or, more exactly, farther above market. . . . I think we can safely take at face value its claims that its policies are genuinely intended to help the economy create jobs to absorb the massive numbers of unemployed and underemployed.

LABOR STANDARDS IN INTERNATIONAL SWEATSHOPS: PAINFUL TRADE-OFFS

Who but the grinch could grudge paying a few additional pennies to some of the world's poorest workers? There is no doubt that the rhetorical force of the critics' case against international sweatshops rests on this apparently self-evident proposition. However, higher wages and improved labor standards are not free. After all, the critics themselves attack companies for chasing cheap labor. It follows that, if labor in developing countries is made more expensive (say, as the result of pressure by the critics), then those countries will receive less foreign investment, and fewer jobs will be created there. Imposing higher wages may deprive these countries of the one comparative advantage they enjoy, namely low-cost labor. . . .

By itself that may or may not be ethically objectionable. But these higher wages come at the expense of the incomes and the job opportunities of much poorer workers. As economists explain, higher wages in the formal sector reduce employment there and (by increasing the supply of labor) depress incomes in the informal sector. The case against requiring above-market wages for international sweatshop workers is essentially the same as the case against other measures that artificially raise labor costs, such as the minimum wage. In Jagdish Bhagwati's words: "Requiring a minimum wage in an overpopulated, developing country, as is done in a developed country, may actually be morally wicked. A minimum wage might help the unionized, industrial proletariat, while limiting the ability to save and invest rapidly which is necessary to draw more of the unemployed and nonunionized rural poor into gainful employment and income."[12] The World Bank makes the same point: "Minimum wages may help the most poverty-stricken workers in industrial countries, but they clearly do not in developing nations. . . . The workers whom minimum wage legislation tries to protect—urban formal workers—already earn much more than the less favored majority. . . . And inasmuch as minimum wage and other regulations discourage formal employment by increasing wage and nonwage costs, they hurt the poor who aspire to formal employment."[13]

The story is no different when it comes to labor standards other than wages. If standards are set too high they will hurt investment and employment. The World Bank report points out that "[r]educing hazards in the workplace is costly, and typically the greater the reduction the more it costs. Moreover, the costs of compliance often fall largely on employees through lower wages or reduced employment. As a result, setting standards too high can actually lower workers' welfare. . . ." Perversely, if the higher standards advocated by critics retard the growth of formal sector jobs, then that will trap more informal and rural workers in jobs that are far more hazardous and insecure than those of their formal sector counterparts. . . .

Of course it might be objected that trading off workers' rights for more jobs is unethical. But, so far as I can determine, the critics have not made this argument. Although they sometimes implicitly accept the existence of the trade-off (we saw that they attack Nike for chasing cheap labor), their public statements are silent on the lost or forgone jobs from higher wages and better labor standards. At other times, they imply or claim that improvements in workers' wages and conditions are essentially free: According to Kernaghan, "Companies could easily double their employees' wages, and it would be nothing."

In summary, the result of the ostensibly humanitarian changes urged by critics are likely to be (1) reduced employment in the formal or modern sector of the economy, (2) lower incomes in the informal sector, (3) less investment and so slower economic growth, (4) reduced exports, (5) greater inequality and poverty. . . .

CONCLUSION: THE CASE FOR NOT EXCEEDING MARKET STANDARDS

. . . The business ethicists whose views I summarized at the beginning of this essay—Thomas Donaldson and Richard De George—objected to letting the market alone determine wages and labor standards in multinational companies. Both of them proposed criteria for setting wages that might occasionally "improve" on the outcomes of the market.

Their reasons for rejecting market determination of wages were similar. They both cited conditions that allegedly prevent international markets from generating ethically acceptable results. Donaldson argued that neoclassical economic principles are not applicable to international business because of high unemployment rates in developing countries. And De George argued that, in an unregulated international market, the gross inequality of bargaining power between workers and companies would lead to exploitation.

But this essay has shown that attempts to improve on market outcomes may have unforeseen tragic consequences. We saw how raising the wages of workers in international sweatshops might wind up penalizing the most vulnerable workers (those in the informal sectors of developing countries) by depressing their wages and reducing their job opportunities in the formal sector. . . . As we have seen, above-market wages paid to sweatshop workers may discourage further investment and so perpetuate high unemployment. In turn, the higher unemployment may weaken the bargaining power of workers vis-à-vis employers. Thus, such market imperfections seem to call for more reliance on market forces rather than less. Likewise, the experience of the newly industrialized East Asian economies suggests that the best cure for the ills of sweatshops is more sweatshops. But most of the well-intentioned policies proposed by critics and business ethicists are likely to have the opposite effect.

Where does this leave the international manager? If the preceding analysis is correct, then it follows that it is ethically acceptable to pay market wage rates in developing countries (and to provide employment conditions appropriate for the level of development). That holds true even if the wages pay less than so-called living wages or subsistence or even (conceivably) the local minimum wage. The appropriate test is not whether the wage reaches some predetermined standard but whether it is freely accepted by (reasonably) informed workers. The workers themselves are in the best position to judge whether the wages offered are superior to their next-best alternatives. (The same logic applies *mutatis mutandis* to workplace labor standards.)

Indeed, not only is it ethically acceptable for a company to pay market wages, but it may be ethically unacceptable for it to pay wages that exceed market levels. That will be the case if the company's above-market wages set precedents for other international companies that raise labor costs to the point of discouraging foreign investment. Furthermore, companies may have a social responsibility to transcend their own narrow concern with protecting their brand image and to publicly defend a system that has improved the lot of millions of workers in developing countries.

CORPORATIONS

Nearly fifty years ago the vice president of Ford Motor Company described the modern business corporation as the dominant institution of American society. Today few observers would disagree. As one of them puts it, "The modern corporation is *the* central institution of contemporary society." As an aggregate, corporations wield awesome economic clout, and the 500 largest U.S. companies constitute at least three-quarters of the American economy. But the dominant role of corporations in our society extends well beyond that. Not only do they produce almost all of the goods and services we buy, but also they and their ethos permeate everything from politics and communications to athletics and religion. And their influence is growing relentlessly around the world—even if the reach of multinational corporations and the negative consequences of globalization are sometimes exaggerated.

By any measure, the biggest corporations are colossi that dominate the earth. Many of them employ tens of thousands of people, and the largest have hundreds of thousands in their ranks. PepsiCo, for example, has about 116,000 employees worldwide, a figure that pales beside General Electric's approximately 340,000 and General Motors's 388,000—not to mention the 1.2 million people who work for Wal-Mart, the world's largest private-sector employer. And their revenues are dazzling. In 2002, for example, General Motors took in more than $177 billion, Wal-Mart $220 billion, Ford $162 billion, and IBM $86 billion. By comparison, the gross domestic product (GDP) of Norway (that is, the total market value of all the goods and services produced there) was around $37 billion; that of Portugal $44 billion. The state of California, which has far and away the largest annual revenue of any U.S. state, makes about what General Motors makes. But Kansas takes in only around $12.8 billion and Vermont less than a third of that.

And corporations are growing larger and wealthier every year. For example, in 1989 Time Inc. merged with Warner Communications to form Time Warner. Seven years later Time Warner combined with Turner Broadcasting. Then in January 2001, in a move that shook up Wall Street, Time Warner and America Online merged. At a stroke, the new company they created was valued at $350 billion. What does $350 billion mean? It is equivalent to the GDP of India, the fifteenth highest in the world. It is more than the combined GDPs of Hungary, Ukraine, the Czech Republic, New Zealand, Peru, and Pakistan. And it is more than the industrial output of the United Kingdom or the manufacturing output of China.

Like any other modern corporation, in principle AOL Time Warner is a three-part organization, made up of stockholders, who provide the capital, own the corporation, and enjoy liability limited to the amount of their investments; managers, who run the business operations; and employees, who produce the goods and services. However, a corporate giant like AOL Time Warner is less like a single company and more like "a fabulously wealthy investment club with a limited portfolio." Such companies invest in subsidiaries, whose heads, writes business analyst Anthony J. Parisi, "oversee their territories like provincial governors, sovereigns in their own lands but with an authority stemming from the power center. . . . The management committee exacts its tribute (the affiliate's profits from current operations) and issues doles (the money needed to sustain and expand those operations)." In the best-run organizations the management system is highly structured and impersonal. It provides the corporation's overall framework, the formal chain of command, that ensures that the company's profit objectives are pursued.

The emergence of corporate behemoths like AOL Time Warner is one of the more intriguing chapters in the evolution of capitalism. Certainly the political theory of John Locke and the economic theory of Adam Smith admitted no such conglomerates of capital as those that originated in the nineteenth century—as late as 1832 hardly any private firms had ten or more employees—and today dominate America's, even the world's, economic, political, and social life. This book isn't the place to analyze why a people committed to an individualistic social philosophy and a free-competition market economy allowed vast oligopolistic organizations to develop. Rather, the concern here is with the problem of applying moral standards to corporate organizations and with understanding their social responsibilities. After a brief review of the history of the corporation, this chapter looks at the following specific topics:

1. The meaning of *responsibility* and the debate over whether corporations can be meaningfully said to have moral responsibility.
2. The controversy between the narrow and the broad views of corporate social responsibility
3. Four key arguments in this debate: the invisible-hand argument, the hand-of-government argument, the inept-custodian argument, and the materialization-of-society argument
4. The importance of institutionalizing ethics within corporations and how this may be done

NOTES

1. International Labor Organization, *World Employment* 1995 (Geneva: ILO, 1995), 73.
2. World Bank, *Workers in an Integrating World Economy*, 5.
3. Keith B. Richburg and Anne Swardson, "U.S. industry overseas: Sweatshop or job source? Indonesians praise work at Nike factory," *Washington Post*, July 28, 1996.
4. Larry Rohter, "To U.S. critics, a sweatshop; for Hondurans, a better life," *New York Times*, July 18, 1996.
5. Marcus Brauchli, "Garment industry booms in Bangladesh," *Wall Street Journal*, August 6, 1991.
6. Lucy Martinez-Mont, "Sweatshops are better than no shops," *Wall Street Journal*, June 25, 1996.
7. Rohter, "To U.S. critics, a sweatshop."
8. William B. Falk, "Dirty little secrets," *Newsday*, June 16, 1996.
9. Richard J. Barnet and John Cavanagh, "Just undo it: Nike's exploited workers," *New York Times*, February 13, 1994.
10. ILO, *World Employment* 1995, 75.
11. World Bank, *The East Asian Miracle* (New York: Oxford University Press, 1993), 2.
12. Jagdish Bhagwati and Robert E. Hudec, eds., *Fair Trade and Harmonization* (Cambridge: MIT Press, 1996). vol. 1, p. 2.
13. World Bank, *Workers in an Integrating World Economy*, 75.

CAN MULTINATIONAL CORPORATIONS PROTECT WORKERS RIGHTS?

Auret Van Heerden and Dorothee Baumann

Globalization has produced global markets for capital, labour, goods and information. Investors, retailers and brand-name companies can move around the world in search of the best economic opportunities with greater freedom and flexibility than ever before. They can source goods from an agent in Hong Kong who in turn places the order with a manufacturer in Korea who has them produced in an export processing zone (EPZ) in Bangladesh for delivery directly to a retail store in the United States or the UK. In this complex sourcing arrangement the buyer (a brand-name company or a retailer or an agent) may not even know in which country the actual production is taking place, nor how many contractors or sub-contractors are involved.

Even more serious is the fact that the buyer probably has no idea of the labour conditions at those production sites. In many cases, the labour laws are not being applied and none of the actors involved, from the USA to Hong Kong to Korea to Bangladesh, is assuming the responsibility for applying any agreed-upon labour standards. Even if they did agree to apply Bangladeshi Labour Law, the EPZs are exempted from the provisions of the Labour Relations Ordinance that provides for freedom of association and collective bargaining, so the parties involved would have to decide what to do about that glaring violation of the ILO's core labour standards. Should they simply accept the Bangladeshi situation as it is, with its built-in denial of freedom of association, or should they try to make up for that deficiency by taking some private initiative to restore or repair workers rights? Even if they did agree that they needed to ensure that workers have the freedom to form or join organizations of their own choosing, should a Multinational Corporation (MNC) and its business partners promote and protect workers rights, and are they capable of doing so?

Many companies respond by saying that it is not their place to enforce labour laws and that they cannot be held responsible for the actions or failings of government. Others go further and say that it would not be appropriate for a MNC to step in to fill the gap left by the lack of government enforcement. The upshot of this is that popular consumer goods, from computers to sneakers to underwear, are frequently made under unregulated conditions in which we have no way of knowing whether child labour, forced labour or harassment (to name just three code elements) may have been employed to meet the demands of production in an increasingly competitive environment.

On the contrary, the regular series of exposés in the media leave us with considerable concerns as to the social, labour and environmental conditions under which our favorite brand-name goods were produced. How can concerned workers, consumers, policy-makers and the rest of civil society know whether a company had conducted its international operations in a socially responsible way? Who sets the standards that they should respect, who monitors their performance against those standards, and what sanctions should apply in cases of non-compliance?

In this article we will pose two questions—should MNCs promote and defend labour rights, and can they? In a brief response to the first question we will argue that MNCs should assume responsibility for labour standards throughout their global supply chains, and that wherever those fall short of generally accepted ILO standards, the MNC should take appropriate steps to ensure the application and maintenance of the ILO standard or the equivalent local law. The argument behind that reasoning is a pragmatic one. In many regions, state actors are either unable (e.g. failed or failing states) or unwilling (e.g. for political reasons) to enforce the rule of law and MNCs remain the only actors that have the expertise and the resources to restore lawful conditions and implement labor rights. This means that an MNC, in jurisdictions where there is inadequate enforcement of labour law, often fulfill functions that would normally be performed by state actors like the Department of Labour or other enforcement agencies. There are manifold empirical examples that demonstrate that MNCs assume such responsibility. However, such enforcement of global rules through private actors poses the question of legitimacy. It is therefore essential that the labour standards performance of MNCs is monitored and measured and reported to key stakeholders.

It has long been accepted that the financial systems and performance of a company should not only respect the law, but be shown to do so. That is why they are obliged to be audited by external auditors and why those audits are available to the relevant authorities, investors and other interested parties. The controversies surrounding the abuse of workers rights in the global supply chains of brand-name companies have raised the same concerns regarding company performance on labour standards and they have responded by having their facilities socially audited, often by the same firms who do their financial audits.

Our argument is that such social auditing must meet certain criteria for it to be a valid means of promoting and defending labour rights, particularly when it is substituting for the lack of government enforcement, and those criteria include—

- Brand accountability—the brand-name company must accept responsibility for its entire supply-chain and must agree to ensure application of the code of conduct throughout that supply-chain. The brand (or buyer) cannot shift that responsibility onto the supplier and in so doing wash their hands of the ultimate responsibility. The brand must also accept responsibility for all of its suppliers and not cherry-pick some of them for monitoring or reporting.

- Monitoring—the auditing or inspection of supplier facilities must be according to internationally accepted standards and benchmarks and should not ratchet-down those standards or performance benchmarks.
- Remedies—the non-compliance identified in inspections must be remedied in a timely and lasting manner. Too many audit-based approaches lay the emphasis on the audit and obscure the remedial component.
- Verification—the internal audits conducted by the brand must be verified by a credible and independent third party in order to serve as a reality check for the brand and to provide assurance to the public that the program is being implemented.
- Transparency—the concerned public must be able to see enough detail of the code implementation and monitoring process to satisfy them as to the integrity of the program.
- Multi-stakeholder engagement—industry- or company-based initiatives obviously contain serious conflicts of interest (the fox guarding the henhouse) and for this reason alone it is necessary to involve other stakeholders in the governance and implementation of such programs. In addition, any private system that assumes state-like functions would have to have legitimating processes such as democracy or transparency for it to limit the inherent danger of abuse of power.

In recent years we have seen an increase in the number of initiatives to monitor the labour standards of MNCs. This sometimes consists only of the MNC adopting a code of conduct and doing its own internal monitoring, but there are also initiatives that involve third-party verification of the MNCs suppliers around the world. A brief survey of the world of codes of conduct and monitoring shows that there are different species of initiative, and different levels within those species. The broad species are monitoring initiatives on the one hand and learning forums on the other. The former will always involve performance criteria but the levels vary greatly. The latter may not require any performance other than agreement on a model code or principles and then some participation in the activities of the forum (pilot projects, seminars etc). The monitoring initiatives can then be divided into those who hold the brand accountable and those that are supplier certification systems.

We would argue that most of the approaches fall short of the legitimating criteria we listed above. Too many of the monitoring efforts do not hold the MNC accountable, do not involve remedial action or independent verification, do not engage stakeholders and are not transparent.

The second question we posed at the start of this article remains then—can MNCs effectively promote labour rights? We have argued that they should, but can they get it right and is auditing the way to do it?

In the program of the Fair Labor Association (FLA) companies sign onto a Code of Conduct and then agree to implement and monitor it throughout their supply-chains. Non-compliance issues must be remedied. The FLA then conducts unannounced, external audits of 5% of those factories to verify whether the company has implemented the code. The results of the external audits are published, as is an annual report on the compliance programs of FLA companies. Each year the strengths and weaknesses of the code implementation and monitoring program are reviewed and improvements are made to the next years' program.

One of the key conclusions the FLA reached was that auditing does not bring about compliance. Applying greater pressure on suppliers through increased audits is more likely to lead to evasion than to compliance, for the simple reason that the original reasons for the non-compliance are seldom identified and dealt with through audits. Therefore, the FLA decided to conduct more root cause analysis and to stress the need for capacity building to address those causes. The aim is to achieve sustainable compliance by developing the capacity of managers and workers to manage code elements in a self-sufficient manner.

Sustainable compliance involves a factory having a policy and procedure on each code element and trained staff to implement them. Those policies and procedures must necessarily be communicated to workers who must not only understand them but be able to use them. To achieve these levels FLA companies are working with suppliers in a longer term capacity building effort, often through joint programs initiated by the FLA. This approach requires that workers be aware of the code standards and it works best when workers are involved in defining the policies and procedures and in their implementation.

This means that FLA companies are not simply acting as enforcers of labour standards, they are also engaging in the development work required to make labour standards compliance a reality in supplier factories. Not many MNCs can make that statement. In fact, not many MNCs can claim to be implementing a code of conduct throughout their supply chains. Most of those who even have a code of conduct are only implementing it on a selective basis without any independent verification, multi-stakeholder engagement or transparency.

FLA companies go further by acknowledging that external pressure can never be a substitute for labour-management interaction on terms and conditions of work. Company monitors, and labour inspectors for that matter, can never visit factories frequently enough to ensure that labour rights are respected in practice. The only way to promote respect for labour rights on an ongoing basis is to cultivate a labour-management relationship through which code elements from freedom of association to hours of work to occupational safety and health can be addressed. If labour and management agree the necessary policies and procedures required to ensure compliance, and jointly monitor the implementation of those, we have the elements necessary to achieve sustainable compliance. Our answer to the question of whether MNCs can promote and defend labour rights is therefore yes, provided the appropriate criteria apply to the monitoring initiative and that the approach is based on achieving sustainable compliance.

A Thumbnail Sketch of the Foreign Corrupt Practices Act

Summary created from Michael V. Seitzinger, J.D., "Foreign Corrupt Practices Act", *CRS Report to Congress* (March 3, 1999), *http://usinfo.org/enus/government/branches/crs_fcpa.html* and U.S. Department of Justice, "Lay-Person's Guide to FCPA", *http://www.usdoj.gov/criminal/fraud/docs/dojdocb.html.*

Before the enacting of the Foreign Corrupt Practices Act (FCPA) in 1977, the practice of making questionable or illegal payments by United States corporations to foreign government officials existed to some extent within the American business community. Congress believed that the existence of slush funds and secret payments by American corporations adversely affected American foreign policy, damaged abroad the image of American democracy, and impaired public confidence in the financial integrity of American corporations. Prior to the FCPA, the only action the US government took against these types of payments were lawsuits filed by the Securities and Exchange Commission (SEC) against public corporations for concealing the payments from required public disclosures made by the firms and the potential for an antitrust action for restraints of trade, or fraud prosecutions by the Justice Department.

Government officials and administrators contended that more direct prohibitions on foreign bribery and more detailed requirements concerning corporate record keeping and accountability were needed to deal effectively with the problem. Thus, Congress enacted the FCPA.

The principal purpose of the 1977 Act was to prevent corporate bribery of foreign officials. It has three basic provisions to accomplish this purpose.

1. Any entity that issues securities must be registered with the SEC. The FCPA amended section 13(b) of the Securities Exchange Act to require these issuers of securities to keep detailed books, records, and accounts which accurately record corporate payments and transactions. These requirements are in addition to the SEC filing and reporting requirements that were already in existence.
2. SEC registered issuers must institute and maintain an internal accounting control system to assure management's control, authority, and responsibility over the firm's assets.
3. Domestic corporations, whether or not registered with the SEC, are prohibited from corruptly bribing a foreign official, a foreign political party, party official, or candidate for the purpose of obtaining or maintaining business.

In 1997, thirty-four other countries enacted similar anti-bribery legislation, through the Organization for Economic Cooperation and Development (OECD). These countries are Argentina, Austria, Australia, Belgium, Brazil, Bulgaria, Canada, Chile, Czech Republic, Demark, Finland, France, Germany, Greece, Hungary, Iceland, Ireland, Italy, Japan, Korea, Luxembourg,

Mexico, New Zealand, The Netherlands, Norway, Poland, Portugal, Slovak Republic, Spain, Sweden, Switzerland, Turkey, United Kingdom, and the United States. Potentially noteworthy for US companies after 2000, as the rise of the "Asian Tiger" economies continues and the US increases trade and job outsourcing with Asia, is the utter lack of Asian participants in the 1997 OECD agreement.

POTENTIAL CONSEQUENCES FOR VIOLATING THE ACT:

Before the FCPA, fraud prosecutions by the Justice Department were rare, and so the worst penalties a business could be subjected to were monetary, if the business lost lawsuits filed by the SEC. Companies could merely run a cost-benefit analysis of the price of the bribe and considerations of the potential for increased revenue, versus the potential cost of getting caught and losing lawsuits. Now; however, there are provisions in the FCPA that create criminal penalties for corrupt payments, which businesses must now consider along with potential financial penalties. The person who actually made the payment, and potentially any person who sanctioned or knew of the payment could be held criminally liable.

There are additional criminal penalties for any person who knowingly circumvents or knowingly fails to implement a system of accurate and reasonable accounting controls.

ALLOWED BEHAVIOR AND DEFENSES TO VIOLATIONS OF THE FCPA:

Under the 1977 Act, not all payments to employees of foreign governments were intended by Congress to be considered illegal bribes. For example, the definition of "foreign official" excluded employees of a foreign government "whose duties are essentially ministerial or clerical." Also, the legislative history of the Act specifically states that it was not intended to cover "grease payments" to foreign officials, explained as "payments for expediting shipments through customs or placing a transatlantic telephone call, securing required permits, or obtaining adequate police protection, transactions which may involve even the proper performance of duties." The legislative history also suggests that extortions of money by foreign officials may be used as a defense against bribery charges by a business if its property or lives of its employees have been threatened. An example used to illustrate acceptable payments was the payment to a foreign official to prevent the dynamiting of an oil rig.

An issuer which holds 50% or less of the voting power of a domestic or foreign firm is required to use its influence only in good faith to cause the domestic or foreign firm to devise and maintain a system of acceptable accounting controls. The House Report states that this amendment is intended to recognize that it is unrealistic to expect a minority owner to exert a disproportionate degree of influence over the accounting practices of a subsidiary.

The first of the enumerated affirmative defenses is that the payment was lawful under the written laws and regulations of the foreign official's, political party's, party official's, or candidate's country. Another affirmative defense is that the payment was a reasonable and bona fide expenditure, such as travel and lodging expenses which were incurred by or on behalf of a foreign official, party, party official, or candidate, and was directly related to the promotion, demonstration, or explanation of products or services or the execution or performance of a contract with a foreign government or agency. This defense would not apply, however, if a payment or gift is corruptly made in return for an official act or omission because it would then not be a bona fide, good faith payment.

OTHER LEGISLATION COVERING INTERNATIONAL BUSINESS OPERATIONS:

- Statutes such as the mail and wire fraud statutes, 18 U.S.C. § 1341, 1343, and the Travel Act, 18 U.S.C. § 1952, which provides for federal prosecution of violations of state commercial bribery statutes, may also apply to corrupt payments to foreign officials for the purpose of obtaining or keeping business.
- Bilateral and multilateral trade agreements (such as the World Trade Organization and NAFTA)
- Bilateral investment treaties

A special report on forests

THE LONG ROAD TO SUSTAINABILITY

September 23, 2010

Western consciences can do only so much to conserve forests

In June last year Daniel Avelino, the public prosecutor of Brazil's state of Pará, the home of most of the Amazon cattle-herd, probably saved more rainforest than many conservation groups ever will. He identified 20 big ranches operating on illegally cleared land and traced the slaughterhouses buying their cattle. He then established that some of the world's best-known retailers, including Wal-Mart and Carrefour, were buying meat from them. He fined the ranchers and abattoirs 2 billion reais ($1.2 billion) and told the retailers that unless they cleaned up their supply chains he would fine them, too.

The response was dramatic. Overnight, the retailers stopped buying meat from Pará and the slaughterhouses closed. To get themselves off the hook, and cows back on it, the abattoirs vowed that in future they would deal only with ranchers who had registered their names and property details and promised not to deforest illegally. Over 20,000 have done so. In the absence of a reliable land registry, Mr Avelino says this will make it much easier to bring illegal deforesters to book. "Once I know who owns the farm, I can send the fine through the post," he says.

Around the same time Greenpeace waded in with a report on the role of Amazon beef in deforestation. That, too, hit at the rich end of the industry's supply chain, linking beef and leather from the Amazon to companies such as Adidas, Nike, Toyota, Gucci and Kraft. Many have since agreed to work with Greenpeace against illegal deforestation. And Wal-Mart has promised to trace its products from the manger to the refrigerator.

That is the upside of growing global demand for tropical food, timber and biofuels: pressure for Western standards to be adopted up the supply chain. This is driven by the eco-worries of Western consumers—and the activists who play on them. Having been long since given the brush-off by rainforest governments, they are finding companies that operate in tropical countries and sell to Western markets much more responsive.

Nestlé, a giant food company, is another of Greenpeace's recent targets. The environmentalists made a spoof advertisement for one of the company's chocolate bars, KitKat, which contains palm oil, and published it on the internet. The ad shows an office worker munching on a chocolate bar which turns out to be the bloody severed finger of an orang-utan. This scored more than

1.5m online hits and put Nestlé in a panic. It stopped buying palm oil from its main Indonesian supplier, Sinar Mas, a big conglomerate with a reputation for chewing up rainforest, and said it would purge from its supply chain any producer linked to illegal deforestation. It has since promised to get 50% of its palm oil from sustainable sources next year. And unconvinced by the standard of most of this "sustainable" oil, Nestlé is setting its own.

Three reasons for pessimism

But there are three black clouds over this sunny scene. The first is financial: eco-concerned consumers may want sustainable products, but they do not want to pay more for them. That does not matter much to Nestlé because it buys only 320,000 tonnes of palm oil a year, just 0.7% of global output. It is a bigger problem for Wal-Mart, which deals in bulk and has tight margins. It expects to charge no more for its green beef than for its current offering. That will raise questions about how green it really is. To track an animal efficiently in the Amazon might well involve expensive technologies. Uruguay, for example, has a system of microchipping calves that costs about $20 a head. That may be beyond Wal-Mart's budget.

The same problem haunts the main forest-related certification scheme, for timber. It dates back to 1993, when the Forest Stewardship Council, an alliance of greens and loggers, drew up a list of rules for sustainable forestry. The hope was that consumer demand for FSC-certified wood products would force logging companies to adopt the scheme. But only about 15% of timber globally, and less than 2% of tropical timber, is covered by it. Getting certified is expensive, costing about $50,000 per concession, and the returns are often meagre. Tests by the Home Depot, America's biggest purveyor of FSC-stamped products, suggest that barely a third of customers would pay a premium of 2% for a certified product, not enough to green even Western retailers.

The second cloud over tropical certification schemes, as Wal-Mart may find, is doubt about their reliability. Some also say that sustainable tropical logging is impossible. Remove 200-year-old Amazon mahogany or Congolese sapele trees and the species may go locally extinct. And although it is true, as loggers argue, that extracting old, slow-growing trees and preserving their carbon in expensive furniture may represent a net sequestration opportunity, high levels of wastage make the argument less convincing. So does the fact that a logged forest can be much less permanent than a mahogany table.

Loggers do most harm to forests not by removing trees but by building roads that give land-grabbers access to them. To get FSC certification, companies need to prevent such trespass. But logging roads remain long after loggers have moved on. In Africa they represent a particular threat to precious forest fauna, including chimpanzees, bonobos and gorillas, by connecting forests to the fast-growing cities where bushmeat is prized. Along a fresh logging road in southern Cameroon, your correspondent once saw many hunters—and the half-eaten remains of two gorillas.

In messy countries like Cameroon, certification schemes get corrupted. At best, certifiers may struggle to examine vast concessions on brief visits, as the guests of loggers who are also paying their fee. Further down the supply chain, timber-dealers and factories are often certified largely on the strength of documents which may be illegally bought. This also allows inventories to be inflated and illegal wood to enter the supply chain. And there is still plenty about, despite the recent reduction reported in Cameroon and elsewhere.

Who cares?

The third factor undermining certification schemes is the most important: the majority of tropical commodities are not consumed in eco-sensitive markets. Most rainforest timber is used locally. In Brazil, for instance, the proportion is 80%. And the biggest importers of tropical timber, China and India, show scant concern for its provenance (though China, the biggest exporter of wood-based products to Western markets, has recently seemed to care a bit more). China and India are also the biggest importers of palm oil. Brazilian beef goes mainly to Russia, Iran, Hong Kong and Egypt. They are not tree-huggers.

This highlights one of the biggest problems in forest conservation. Most of the changes it requires, such as rational land-use planning, law enforcement and the rest, have to be led by governments. Market-led schemes can succeed up to a point, as Greenpeace has often shown, but without government support they soon hit their limits. On the other hand, when governments put their weight behind conservation, a fair bit of progress is possible.

Western governments are starting to do their bit. A 2008 amendment to America's Lacey act has made it an offence to import illegal timber. This puts the onus on federal authorities to prove illegality, which can be difficult, especially when the wood is from a dodgy place, like Cameroon, and processed by a less dodgy one, like China. Nor is legality the same as sustainability, but often they are close. Gibson Guitar, an iconic American company, is at risk of becoming the first victim of this reform. It is being investigated on suspicion of knowingly importing illegal Madagascan rosewood.

In July the EU also passed a law criminalising the import of illegal timber. Its strict rules on beef imports, which demand traceability in producer countries, could one day help reform Brazil's cattle practice. But it would be far better if Brazil were to decide to take such steps itself.

BUILDING THE RIGHT MODEL FOR BUSINESS IN CHINA

BY Jeff Swartz

July 13, 2009

Like it or not, for most major shoe manufacturers, China is the place to be. Pretty much whatever you need to make shoes—from factories with trained and available labor, to the largest concentration of leather tanneries on earth, to component suppliers of the mundane and the exotic—you can find in Guangzhou Province. As a "one-stop shop," China offers efficiency both in time and resources—scarce commodities from any CEO's point of view. And not just efficiency—our Chinese suppliers meet our quality standards consistently and deliver on time, as promised. They have the knowledge and the infrastructure to support the business, make quality product and meet our expectations. It makes for a pretty compelling case to do business in China.

Of course, competing in the global economy is not about simple choices—and sourcing from China, with issues of environmental practice and respect for the dignity and human rights of workers, serves as a prime example of how brands like ours must struggle to balance the demands of the marketplace with the demands of the civic square. How does the CEO of a publicly traded company, responsible to shareholders every 90 days, balance the allure of high quality and low cost with substantive concerns about human rights and environmental consequences? My view, 15+ years after we first began working in South East Asia is that the CEO's answer to the question, "Commerce or justice?" needs to be "Yes." High quality, low cost ... accountability for decent working conditions, fair pay, high standards of environmental practice ... this is not a pipe dream, rather, a reality that can be delivered—if you're willing to do the work.

Stella International facilities in Guangdong Province

Doing the work means not checking your principles at the door; sometimes that's surprisingly easy and sometimes it's just plain hard...and expensive. For Timberland in China, this has meant engaging from the beginning with factory owners on an explicit set of performance outcomes demanded from our "code of conduct." Over 15 years, we've learned—getting the performance we expect requires clear standards, a regular measurement and management process, and equal parts commitment from the brand and the factory. We've seen this model of principles + passion + hard work yield real progress—as with Stella International, one of the premier manufacturers anywhere in the world, and a longtime Timberland factory partner. Stella makes high quality shoes and believes, from founder / CEO down through their ownership team, in the model of brand + principles + factory + hard work = a sustainable relationship. Stella gets it. With other partners, we've seen the same inputs yield very different outcomes—including one where we invested years of effort only to conclude that the factory owners were mouthing the words but not living the principles. Leaving that factory group cost us millions.

Even with leaders like Stella, who get it, what worked before—a mutual commitment to a code of conduct—doesn't suffice any longer. As activists insisted, so our entire industry grew more accountable for human rights in the supply chain. Increased accountability led to more codes of conduct, more frequent audits ... and greater frustration. Faced with any number of brands operating in the same factory, each with their own codes, audits and expectations, factories became overwhelmed with "human rights inspection fatigue." And while brand after brand clamored for "compliance," NGOs and activists continued to insist that for all the activity, the outcome from a worker's perspective was not good enough. To live our principles effectively, we've learned that high quality, low cost, on time, with respect for human rights and accountability for environmental footprint now demands engaged collaborative networks—brand, factory, workers, activists. Compliance is no longer a high standard, it's merely table stakes.

15+ years into doing business in China, I believe a responsible CEO can sign up to the challenges of the global supply chain without selling out principles or disappointing shareholders. Commerce or justice? I'll take both.

Read more of Jeff Swartz's blog For the Greener Good

Jeff Swartz is the third generation of the Swartz family to lead Timberland. His grandfather Nathan started the predecessor company to Timberland in 1952. Jeff's father Sidney and his uncle Herman launched the Timberland brand in the early 1970s. Jeff was promoted to President and CEO in 1998, after working in virtually every functional area of the company since 1986. Under Jeff's leadership, Timberland has grown rapidly.

Timberland today competes in countries around the world, designing, manufacturing and marketing footwear, apparel and accessories for men, women and children. Timberland has been listed on Business Ethics *magazine's list of 100 Best Corporate Citizens and in 2002, Timberland received the Ron Brown Award, a Presidential award recognizing outstanding corporate leadership in social responsibility. Follow Jeff Swartz on Twitter @ Timberland Jeff.*

Can and Does Community Activism Make a Difference? What is the Impact of the Local and Global Community as Stakeholders?*

In response to "civil regulation"/community pressure, more than 1,000 companies have adopted codes that set standards for working conditions and for the environment (e.g., use of pesticides and water pollution), establish monitoring and auditing of suppliers, etc. These companies usually require that wages be paid at the local industry prevailing wage or the local minimum wage.

In the United States, Nike, Hewlett Packard, IBM, GE and Dupont, for example, set standards for and audit working conditions in their contract factories. In Europe, major retailers (Carrefour, Marks & Spencer and Ikea) have adopted company codes and audit suppliers for compliance with labor standards and practices. Some companies, particularly natural resource companies, have incorporated reference to human rights in their business principles or codes of conduct.

Various industries have adopted codes/norms (both national and international), including: the **toy industry**, the **computer industry** –the Electronics Industry Code of Conduct (health, safety, labor and human rights standards), and the **chemical industry** – the Responsible Care initiative that sets standards on and audits emissions and worker safety. The **extractive industry**(with some NGO's) has adopted the "Voluntary Principles on Security and Human Rights" (guidelines for maintaining security of operations while respecting human rights in the local community) which pledges to improve environmental performance and combat corruption/bribe-paying to local governments. **But there is a lack of standards in agriculture**, the poorest sector, with the exception of the fair trade movement in the coffee industry.

In the United States, certain NGO's, such as such as the Fair Labor Association (FLA) and the Workers' Rights Consortium, set standards, and monitor and certify manufacturers. Internationally, **The International Labor Organization (ILO)** sets out standards for collective bargaining, forced labor, child labor, equal opportunity and treatment, wages, working time, occupational health and safety, human rights, etc. **Voluntary code SA8000** for toy manufacturers and retailers, including Timberland, goes beyond the ILO standards in requiring a living wage and facilitation of unionization.

The UN Global Compact, which was formed in 1999, is the world's largest voluntary corporate citizenship initiative. It has 8000 participants including more than 5300 companies within 130 countries and sets global norms for corporate citizenship. The Compact consists of 10 core principles of corporate behavior (but has no certification standards) covering human and workplace rights (including the right to a "living wage"), corruption and environmental responsibility. Companies that sign the Compact commit to incorporating these principles into their operations and to report on their progress. In 2009 UN Secretary-General Ban Ki-moon called for a new phase of the program - which he dubbed Global Compact 2.0. The key, according to Mr. Ban, is credibility - which Compact participants would have to earn and maintain through annual Communication on Progress reports.

Finally, the **International Organization for Standardization (ISO)** has established a Working Group on Social Responsibility and is developing **ISO 26000** (guidance on social responsibility, including human rights, labor practices and community involvement/social development).

Have these efforts made a difference?

Child Labor: There has been some impact on child labor, because the cost of compliance is lower than for compliance with other working-condition standards (on pay, overtime and safety). We have witnessed some progress in manufacturing (production of soccer balls, rugs, textiles and footwear, etc.), but not in agriculture, where 70% of children are employed. It appears that the net impact of these efforts may be that some children are forced into lower-paying and more dangerous occupations (in the informal sector, where no standards apply).

Working Conditions: There have been some improvements in working conditions, including health and safety standards, but attempts (all voluntary) are least effective with regard to pay and overtime limitations and freedom of association. Why? MNC's do not believe consumers will pay more to cover the increased production costs, it is hard to monitor working hours and pay, and there is pressure on MNC's from Asian competitors (who are not subject to the same public criticism) to keep costs low. This has resulted in MNC's putting the financial burden of responsible labor practices (e.g., audits and other costs of certification of compliance) on their developing-country suppliers...who then must reduce wages or increase overtime in order to keep costs low and retain MNC business.

It is also worth noting that voluntary standards related to working conditions have been adopted only by Western manufacturers and retailers and they primarily govern only the manufacture of products for the U.S. and Europe.

Human Rights: Voluntary standards and public pressure not to invest (or to divest operations) in countries that do not respect human rights have had limited effect because: they are vague and poorly defined; they often impose few real obligations or monitoring or reporting requirements; and they tend to be industry-specific (for example, related to the extractive industry).

*Summary based, in part, on "Corporate Responsibility for Working Conditions in Developing Countries" and "Corporate Responsibility for Human Rights and Global Corporate Citizenship" from *The Market for Virtue* by David Vogel.

"Overview." *United Nations Global Compact.* Web. 25 May 2011. <http://www.unglobalcompact.org/ParticipantsAndStakeholders/index.html>.

QUESTIONS ON READINGS FOR PART SIX (F)

How has globalization changed what it means for a company to be a good corporate citizen?

From a legal perspective? (e.g. The Foreign Corrupt Practices Act)

From an ethical perspective?

What are the types of labor and environmental problems associated with multinational corporations' (MNC) operations in developing countries?

What responsibility do MNC's have for working conditions in their supply chains? For human rights in the countries where they operate?

What standards should MNCs follow when operating in developing countries?

What is the importance of auditing, monitoring and disclosure of conditions in MNC supply chains?

What are the limitations of these control mechanisms?

What efforts have been made by the global community to help MNC's self-regulate?

Have these efforts made a difference?

CENTER FOR EDUCATION ON SOCIAL RESPONSIBILITY

CASE #9:

THE FUTURE OF MICROFINANCE: THE ACCION INTERNATIONAL MODEL

V.

THE GRAMEEN BANK MODEL

MICROFINANCE'S SUCCESS SETS OFF A DEBATE IN MEXICO

Elisabeth Malkin

VILLA DE VÁZQUEZ, Mexico—Carlos Danel and Carlos Labarthe turned a nonprofit that lent money to Mexico's poor into one of the country's most profitable banks.

But not all of their colleagues in the world of microlending—so named for the tiny loans it grants—are heaping praise on the co-executives of Compartamos. Some are vilifying them as "pawnbrokers" and "money lenders."

They are the center of a fractious debate: how far should microfinance go toward becoming big business?

At one end stand traditional microlenders, like the economist Muhammad Yunus, founder of the most famous microlender, the Grameen Bank, and winner of the 2006 Nobel Peace Prize. At the other are the Two Carloses, as they are widely known in this tight-knit world that gave them their start as starry-eyed idealists.

Microlenders, the original and still the most common type of microfinance organization, help the poor start or expand businesses in places most banks shun, like the slums of Calcutta or these impoverished hills in Mexico's sugar cane country, three hours south of Mexico City. Their efforts are widely considered successful in transforming the lives of developing-world entrepreneurs, particularly women, and their families.

Many microlending advocates, including Mr. Yunus, say that success is threatened by Mr. Danel and Mr. Labarthe's market-oriented model, with its emphasis on investor returns.

"Microfinance started in the 1970s with a focus on using this breakthrough to help end poverty," said Sam Daley-Harris, director of the Microcredit Summit Campaign, a nonprofit endeavor that promotes microfinance for families earning less than $1 a day. "Now it is in great danger of being how well the investors and the microfinance institutions are doing and not about ending poverty." He said the situation posed the danger of "mission drift."

Mr. Danel and Mr. Labarthe say microfinance will help more poor people by tapping the boundless pool of investor capital rather than the limited pool of donor money.

"It's marvelous to have one creditor but it's marvelous to have one million creditors," Mr. Labarthe said, "and that's where we really start to change the face of opportunity."

Compartamos ("let's share" in Spanish) expects to reach one million borrowers this year. Its profits are healthy, some $80 million last year, and its portfolio has grown to almost $400 million. Since it went public nearly a year ago, return on equity has been more than 40 percent.

Both sides agree that there is a need for capital, too great to be met by the donor groups that initially financed microlending. Deutsche Bank estimates the global demand for microfinance loans at about $250 billion, 10 times the amount that has been lent.

But Compartamos's decision to go public last April became a flashpoint in what had been a genteel debate over how microfinance could tap into the financial markets' vast resources. The initial public offering gets special mention at every microfinance conference, and has been condemned by Mr. Yunus, the Nobel laureate.

Alex Counts, president of the Washington-based Grameen Foundation, said Compartamos's poor clients "were generating the profits but they were excluded from them."

Lynne Patterson, a founder of Pro Mujer, a nonprofit microfinance group with branches in several Latin American countries, agrees. "We use the profit to reinvest in the service of the clients," she said, referring to loan repayment profits.

Since lack of access to credit is just one of the problems the poor face, Pro Mujer also offers services like breast cancer screenings, advice on dealing with domestic violence and financial education.

Still, in three decades microfinance has evolved—from small nongovernmental organizations lending $50 to women to buy sewing machines or fruit to sell at market to, in some cases, formal banks that cover costs and grow through profits, like any business.

On Wall Street, investment banks package microfinance loans to sell to institutional investors, many of them "socially responsible" and looking for steady returns rather than trading profits. A few equity funds have even taken stakes in microfinance institutions.

Critics say that Compartamos manages its business to benefit its investors, not its borrowers. The bank began as a nongovernmental organization in 1990, started by a Catholic social action group called Gente Nueva, whose inspiration was a visit by Mother Teresa to Mexico.

After Compartamos became a for-profit company in 2000, costs fell as efficiencies increased, but the bank kept interest rates high. On average, customers pay an annual interest rate of almost 90 percent, which includes 15 percent in government tax. In much of the world, microfinance interest rates range from 25 to 45 percent. But in Mexico, high costs, inefficiency and limited competition keep interest rates much higher. Compartamos's rates are only a few percentage points higher than Pro Mujer's, for example.

Like microfinance businesses around the world, Compartamos makes loans without collateral. Its borrowers, who are nearly all women, are organized in groups, which guarantee the loans. Stop paying and your friends must pay for you: the system keeps default rates down.

Historically, microlenders point out, such borrowers are excellent risks. For instance, Compartamos's nonperforming loans were just 1.36 percent of its portfolio at the end of last year.

Servicing those loans takes labor and that pushes up rates on such small amounts. A Compartamos collection agent visits each group every week, riding public buses out to villages.

Compartamos is more efficient than other Mexican microfinance institutions and its own borrowing costs are lower, thanks to its strong credit rating. Critics charge that it has not passed those savings on to its customers.

The numbers seem to bear that out. A study last year by the Consultative Group to Assist the Poor, known as CGAP, a microfinance industry group based at the World Bank, estimated that 23.6 percent of Compartamos's interest income went to profits. Its return on average equity is more than triple the 15 percent average for Mexican commercial banks.

Profit is not a dirty word in the microfinance world. The question is how much is appropriate. CGAP estimates the average return on assets for self-sufficient organizations to be 5.5 percent. The figure for Compartamos was 19.6 percent in the fourth quarter.

Mr. Danel said Compartamos's interest rates have fallen 30 percentage points over the last five years. "They go down based on efficiencies, and we pass this benefit on to the customer," he said.

Compartamos grew to 840,000 customers last year, from 60,000 in 2000.

Last April, Compartamos' owners sold 30 percent of their stock on the Mexican stock market in an initial public offering. The public offering brought in $458 million. Private Mexican investors, including the bank's top executives, pocketed $150 million from the sale. More than half of the public offering proceeds went back to development institutions that had invested in Compartamos when it moved from being a nonprofit to a commercial venture in 2000.

One of them was Acción International, a Boston-based nongovernmental organization that helps build microcredit institutions and provides them with technical assistance. Acción invested $1 million in Compartamos in 2000. It sold half its 18 percent stake at the time of the public offering for $135 million.

"This is one strategy to address poverty that doesn't remain small and beautiful," said María Otero, president of Acción.

Charles Waterfield, a microfinance consultant who has been among the most vocal critics of Compartamos's model, disagrees. "Not only are they making obscene profits off poor people, they are in danger of tarnishing the rest of the industry," he said. "Compartamos is the first but they won't be the last."

There has not been a rush to market yet. In part, the subprime mortgage debacle and the ensuing selloff on global markets has made this a poor time for initial public offerings.

Compartamos has not escaped the turmoil; its stock price is up nearly 17 percent since the offering, but down 32 percent from its high last July.

Those who argue for more such public offerings say that Compartamos set the right example.

"Boy, you got a lot of people's attention with that I.P.O.," said Bob Pattillo, who runs Gray Ghost, a fund that invests in microfinance. "This has got Wall Street's eye, London's eye, Geneva's eye—to have one out there to say that if all the dots got connected this can be quite profitable."

Mr. Danel and Mr. Labarthe argue that successful microlenders in a middle-income country like Mexico should use the capital markets, instead of crowding out donations.

As part of their defense, they argue that Compartamos's success has prompted a number of institutions, including traditional banks and retailers, to start offering financial products to the poor. "We don't only see ourselves as a specialist in microfinance but also as the builder of an industry," Mr. Danel said.

Compartamos estimates that its target market is 14 million households, more than half of the country's population, most of them with little or no access to banking services.

At the recent weekly meeting of a group of Compartamos borrowers in the village of Valle de Vázquez, the interest rate was not a great concern. Indeed, several women said they had left another microfinance institution because it charged more.

The group was well established, 35 strong and well into its third year of borrowing. The meeting, which took place in the living room of one borrower's home, was the start of a new four-month borrowing cycle.

A Compartamos manager, Claudia Ayala, began with a pep talk, pointing to a house plant set on a chair beside her. "This plant grows and this group can grow," she said to the women, who were listless in the afternoon heat. "How? By inviting more compañeras," or friends. "By fertilizing it with responsibility," she said.

Though the village depends largely on remittances sent by relatives in the United States, the Compartamos loans have helped some women become self-sufficient.

Silvina Martínez started a little restaurant in her house a year ago to sell her homemade snacks to students at a nearby high school. It has grown steadily since then. With this cycle, she was going to borrow about $1,100 to paint the restaurant and expand her menu. "It's my own business," she said. "You are a slave to it, but at least it's mine."

Other women were successful entrepreneurs to start with, but the Compartamos credit gives them a push, allowing them to hire an employee or help ease their cash flow.

Alejandra Abúndez, 57, keeps pigs and cattle, and produce 330 pounds of cheese a day, which she sells in the local market. She and her daughter, Micaela Rivera, were borrowing $3,550 from Compartamos to buy animal feed and to stock the tiny store in her front entryway.

"Everything I have, I invest," said Ms. Abúndez, who has left a widow with five children at 35. "No gadding about for me."

FREQUENTLY ASKED QUESTIONS AND MICROFINANCE GLOSSARY

International Year of Microcredit 2005

Microcredit and microfinance have changed the lives of people and revitalized communities in the world's poorest and also the richest countries. We have seen the enormous power that access to even modest financial services can bring people. With access to a range of financial tools, families can invest according to their own priorities—school fees, health care, business, nutrition or housing.

However, studies have shown that of the 4 billion people who live on less than $1400 a year, only a fraction have access to basic financial services.

With this huge unmet demand, the Year of Microcredit 2005 calls upon us to build inclusive financial sectors and strengthen the powerful, but often untapped, entrepreneurial spirit existing in impoverished communities.

FREQUENTLY ASKED QUESTIONS

- **What is the difference between microfinance and microcredit?**
  Microcredit is a small amount of money loaned to a client by a bank or other institution. Microfinance refers to loans, savings, insurance, transfer services, microcredit loans and other financial products targeted at low-income clients. Microcredit has been changing the lives of people and revitalizing communities worldwide since the beginning of time.
- **Who are the clients of microfinance?**
  The clients of microfinance are generally poor and low-income people. They may be female heads of households, pensioners, artisans or small farmers. The client group for a given financial organization depends on that organization's mission and goals.

- **How do financial services help poor and low-income people?**
  Anyone who has access to savings, credit, insurance and other financial services is more resilient and better able to deal with everyday demands. Microfinance helps poor and low-income clients deal with their basic needs. For example, with access to microinsurance, poor people can cope with sudden expenses associated with serious illness or loss of assets. Merely having access to formal savings accounts has also proved to be an incentive to save. Clients who join and stay in microfinance programmes have better economic conditions than non-clients.
- **What is a microfinance institution?**
  A microfinance institution (MFI) is an organization that provides financial services targeted to the poor. While every MFI is different, all share the common characteristic of providing financial services to a clientele poorer and more vulnerable than traditional bank clients.
- **What is an inclusive financial sector?** An inclusive financial sector allows poor and low-income people to access credit, insurance, remittances and savings products. In many countries, the financial sectors do not provide these services to the lower income people. An inclusive financial sector will support the full participation of the lower income levels of the population.
- **If microfinance is about serving the poor, why does the provision of financial services need to be profitable?**
  Microfinance institutions need to be profitable in order to cover the costs of reaching out and meeting the demand of underserved segments of the population over a sustained period of time. Additionally, after a series of very small loans, a microentrepreneur often wants to expand her business; a microfinance institution must keep up with the demand for larger loan amounts so businesses can grow into small enterprises.
- **How can poor people afford such high interest rates?**
  Microcredit interest rates are set to provide viable, long-term financial services on a large scale, while subsidized interest rates generally benefit only a small number of borrowers for a short period. Studies conducted in India, Kenya and the Philippines found that the average annual return on investments by microbusinesses ranged from 117 to 847 per cent. These high returns are commonplace among microentrepreneurs, and while the interest rates seem high, they usually represent only a small portion of microentrepreneurs' total returns. Interest rates charged by informal moneylenders are overwhelmingly higher than those of MFIs.
- **Do poor people save?**
  Poor people save all the time, although mostly in informal ways. They invest in assets such as jewelry, domestic animals, building materials and things that can be easily exchanged for cash.

Access to secure, formal savings services provides a cushion when families need more money for seasonal expenses and in tough times. Secure savings accounts allow people to guard against unexpected expenses associated with illnesses, build assets, prepare for old age or pay for school fees, marriages and births.

- **Why is microfinance so important for women?**
  In a world where most poor people are women, studies have shown that access to financial services has improved the status of women within the family and the community. Women have become more assertive and confident. Furthermore, as a result of microfinance, women own assets, including land and housing, play a stronger role in decision-making, and take on leadership roles in their communities.
- **When is microcredit NOT appropriate?**
  Microcredit may be inappropriate where conditions pose severe challenges to loan repayment. For example, populations that are geographically dispersed or have a high incidence of disease may not be suitable microfinance clients. In these cases, grants, infrastructure improvements or education and training programmes are more effective. For microcredit to be appropriate, the clients must have the capacity to repay the loan under the terms by which it is provided.

back to top

- **Microfinance Glossary**
  Bankable people are those deemed eligible to obtain financial services that can lead to income generation, repayment of loans, savings, and the building of assets.
  Microcredit is a small amount of money loaned to a client by a bank or other institution. Microcredit can be offered, often without collateral, to an individual or through group lending.
    - **Group lending,** also known as solidarity lending, is a mechanism that allows a number of individuals to provide collateral or guarantee a loan through a group repayment pledge. The incentive to repay is based on peer pressure; if one person in the group defaults, the other group members make up the payment amount.
    - **Individual lending,** in contrast, focuses on one client and does not require other people to provide collateral or guarantee a loan.
- **Microentrepreneurs** are people who own small-scale businesses that are known as **microenterprises**. These businesses usually employ less than 5 people and can be based out of the home. They can provide the sole source of family income or supplement other forms of income. Typical microentrepreneur activities include retail kiosks, sewing workshops, carpentry shops and market stalls.
- **Microfinance** refers to loans, savings, insurance, transfer services and other financial products targeted at low-income clients.

- **Microinsurance** is a system by which people, businesses and other organizations make payments to share risk. Access to insurance enables entrepreneurs to concentrate more on growing their businesses while mitigating other risks affecting property, health or the ability to work.
- **Microsavings** are deposit services that allow people to store small amounts of money for future use, often without minimum balance requirements. Savings accounts allow households to save small amounts of money to meet unexpected expenses and plan for future investments such as education and old age.
- **Remittances** are transfers of funds from people in one place to people in another, usually across borders to family and friends. Compared with other sources of money that can fluctuate depending on the political or economic climate, remittances are a relatively steady source of funds.
- **Unbanked** describes people who have no access to financial services (services that include savings, credit, money transfer, insurance, or pensions) through any type of financial sector organization such as banks, non-bank financial institutions, financial cooperatives and credit unions, finance companies, and NGOs. Implicit in this definition is that financial services are usually available only to those individuals termed "economically active" or "bankable".

REIMAGINING MICROFINANCE

Alex Counts

Critics of microfinance institutions (MFIs) ask them to choose between helping the poor or making money for investors, but this is a false choice. MFIs can have their impact and profit, too, says the author, the CEO of the Grameen Foundation. He sketches a new vision of microfinance as a platform, not a product; one that relies on high volumes, not high margins, and that uses limits on private benefit, holistic performance standards, and third-party certification to help MFIs meet both their bottom lines.

Despite the fact that most microfinance institutions (MFIs) were established to reduce poverty, many are starting to look like traditional financial institutions. To expand their outreach and loan portfolios, they tap into commercial and quasi-commercial sources of finance, which require them to demonstrate consistent profitability to their investors. When the Mexican MFI Banco Compartamos went public in 2007, for example, its existing shareholders earned returns of approximately 100 percent compounded annually over an eight-year period.

This trend toward commercialization has led critics to ask whether MFIs will continue to serve the world's poorest people. They point out that many profit-minded MFIs have either raised their interest rates or failed to lower them when reductions in costs allowed them to do so. They note that some MFIs have cut back on social service programs, infrastructure, and staff training to reduce costs and increase short-term profitability. They show that a growing number of MFIs are not tracking their social impact even though they have the tools to do so.

At the same time, other critics worry that MFIs are not commercial enough. They say that MFIs' commitment to social justice keeps these organizations from becoming profitable. Lack of profitability in turn prevents MFIs from attracting the investment they need to meet the estimated $300 billion demand for their services. (MFIs currently supply an estimated $15 billion to $25 billion in loans.) And when MFIs attempt to lower interest rates and offer nonfinancial services, some observers decry these nonprofit-minded measures.

Yet I believe that the dichotomy between commercial microfinance and pro-poor microfinance is a false one. In its place, I propose a new model that could make microfinance both more relevant to the world's poor and more profitable in the long term. This model views microfinance not as a mere financial product, but as a platform for delivering a host of products and services to the world's poorest, most isolated people.[1] The model relies on high volumes, not high margins. And it uses private benefit limits, holistic performance standards, and third-party certification to make sure that MFIs meet both of their bottom lines. All MFIs—nonprofits, for-profits, nonbank finance companies, and any other institutional form—can adopt and adapt this model.

If MFIs can take up these practices, they can avoid making a false choice between serving the poor and acting businesslike. In addition, they may have a longer-term impact on poverty while generating profits up and down the value chain—from poor families to multinational corporations. Finally, by reimagining microfinance MFIs may regain the public's trust, avoiding the regulatory backlash that would put the industry into a defensive stance from which it might never recover.

Platform, Not Product

MFIs' most important assets are not their loan portfolios, but their high-quality relationships with the world's poor.[2] In this new model of microfinance, MFIs use these relationships as a platform from which to develop and distribute a range of products and services—not just financial ones.

Although some of these nonfinancial products can be quite profitable, not every new product or service needs to be. As in many commercial spheres, some products are "loss leaders" that exist to attract clients, to strengthen relationships with existing clients, or to help clients take advantage of other, profitable products. For example, an educational loan to a client's child may enable that student to use profitable financial products in the future. Likewise, MFIs that use the platform approach to educate, strengthen, and win the loyalty of clients can generate long-term profits for investors and customers alike.

One example of an MFI that views microfinance as a platform and not a product is Grameen Bank. Established as a pilot project in 1976. Grameen Bank transformed into the world's first commercial microfinance bank in 1983. In its first 15 years, the bank experimented with everything from organizing client-run preschools, to partnering with local government agencies to organize immunization days, to distributing vegetable seeds and saplings at cost.

By the early 1990s, the bank decided to turn most of its nonfinancial initiatives into separate companies. That way, individual CEOs could have more control over their operations, and the bank could reduce the effect of failed enterprises on other Grameen initiatives. Most of these companies use bank resources, such as staff, knowledge, relationships, and facilities, to take on poverty-reduction opportunities that microfinance alone could not adequately address. For example, GrameenPhone, Bangladesh's largest and most profitable telecom company, has helped 300,000 Grameen Bank clients establish profitable mobile pay phone businesses.

Grameen has likewise created nonprofit organizations to address other issues affecting the poor, such as health care. For instance, Grameen Kalyan has set up more than 30 health clinics located alongside Grameen Bank branches. The organization uses a health insurance model in which Grameen clients and other poor families pay a yearly insurance premium and receive preventive and curative services for a small co-payment. They can also buy medicine at a discounted rate. Because health crises are the primary reason microfinance clients default on their loans, the clinics' successes redound to the success of Grameen Bank. Another thriving initiative is Grameen Shakti, a profitable yet nonprofit renewable energy company that sells, finances, and services solar power systems for families and businesses, thus providing clean power without subsidy. To date, the organization has installed more than 120,000 solar power systems.

The Haitian nonprofit MFI Fonkoze similarly partners with its for-profit sister, Sèvis Finansye Fonkoze (SFF), to integrate innovative financial products with social service delivery. Together, Fonkoze and SFF offer a growing number of their more than 160,000 clients an outstanding adult education program with modules on basic literacy, business management, human rights, agriculture, and reproductive health. The program is voluntary, but the MFI strongly encourages its clients—especially those who cannot read or write—to participate. World-class experts designed the program, and cost-effective local field staff implement it. Philanthropic donations currently fund the program, but over time, as it grows and achieves economies of scale, interest rates should cover its cost. In this way, the commercial enterprise will both invest in and benefit from the long-term health and business savvy of clients. Preliminary data on a group of clients who had access to both financial and educational services show an 8 percent reduction in the percentage of people living below $1 a day and a 9 percent reduction in those living below $2 a day. Fonkoze is already generating surplus revenue, and the more recently established SFF is on course to earn a profit in 2008.

The African microfinance community likewise boasts an MFI that both contributes to and profits from its network of relationships. Called Jamii Bora, this Kenyan nonprofit is the shining star of African MFIs. Like Grameen, Jamii Bora observed that the most common reason that its clients failed to repay their loans was illness. To prevent illness-related loan defaults, the organization attempted in 2001 to develop a health insurance program by partnering with insurance companies. But the companies' rates—an average of $80 per year—were too expensive for many of Jamii Bora's clients.

Not giving up, the organization next approached missionary hospitals that were on the brink of bankruptcy to explore the possibility of partnering. Jamii Bora agreed to help keep the hospitals open by paying them for its clients' health care. To finance this plan, the MFI charged clients a $12 annual insurance premium for five family members and $2 for each additional family member. Clients pay the premium in weekly installments—a schedule that poor clients can handle—to trusted loan officers at borrower meetings. The program has not only stabilized the finances of several participating hospitals—a boon for the communities—it has also made Jamii Bora's clients healthier. And loan defaults have fallen as a result. The health program has never received donor funding, and Jamii Bora recorded its first profit in the first quarter of 2004. As of mid-2007, the MFI has served 170,000 clients with an outstanding loan portfolio of more than $5.7 million. Despite recent political upheaval in Kenya, Jamii Bora remains profitable.

MFIs that view microfinance as a platform are not necessarily the ones that earn the greatest profits in the short term. Creating divisions or sister companies that deliver social services can be expensive, even when these organizations are profitable. Nevertheless, the long-term social *and* financial viability of this new model of microfinance makes it superior to a more narrowly focused approach.

High Volume, Not High Margins

Microfinance has survived by charging relatively high interest rates, with average APRs falling between 25 percent and 70 percent. Interest rates are high in part because servicing unsecured small loans in remote locations is a costly business. Yet many MFIs keep charging high interest rates even after their gains in efficiency and profitability have lowered the cost of servicing loans.

High interest rates have exacted a real cost. For many MFIs, client dropout rates remain unacceptable, sometimes exceeding 40 percent per year. And in Ecuador, Nicaragua, and India, populist politicians have cracked down on MFIs that allegedly charge exorbitant rates, collect payments unethically, and hide rates from clients. The most infamous of these cases took place in India in March 2006. Local government officials in the state of Andhra Pradesh padlocked the entrances to some 50 branch offices of two microfinance institutions and imprisoned their loan officers. The national and especially local press stoked the flames of this dispute, which lasted six months.

An uneasy truce has allowed the MFIs to return to business, but conflict could reemerge, as some of the underlying reasons for the flare-up—such as competition between state-run and private MFIs—remain largely unresolved. Ironically, Indian MFIs charge some of the lowest rates in the world, trailing only Bangladesh and Bolivia in the affordability of their loan products.

To calm regulators and policymakers and enhance their antipoverty impact, MFIs should view themselves as high-volume businesses, rather than as high-margin ones. In other words, MFIs should aim to conduct many marginally profitable transactions, rather than fewer highly profitable ones. The microfinance markets in Bangladesh and Bolivia are examples of high-volume, low-margin models. In Bangladesh, where more than 20 million people receive microfinance services, rates have been low all along, ranging from 15 percent to 30 percent. In Bolivia, interest rates were initially much higher than in Bangladesh, but have come down dramatically, falling from 50 percent in the mid-1990s to just over 20 percent today. During the same period, the Bolivian microfinance industry grew from some 200,000 clients to more than 600,000.

From its inception, Grameen Bank has conceived of its business as one based on volume, not margin. In its early years, the bank could have taken advantage of its near-monopoly and charged much higher interest rates. Experience has shown that in many countries without competition, clients are willing to pay rates of 30 percent to 60 percent (client attrition is usually very high above that level). Instead, Grameen Bank fixed its interest rates for commercial loans at 20 percent, offering lower rates for housing and student loans. Perhaps this business model is why Grameen Bank has enjoyed a reasonably good relationship with policymakers and regulators in Bangladesh.

The commercial MFI Amhara Credit and Savings Institution (ACSI) has likewise adopted a high-volume, low-margin business model. As of 2007, ACSI was one of Ethiopia's largest and most successful MFIs, with a total clientele of almost 840,000 people (including clients who only save and do not borrow), an outstanding loan portfolio of $102 million, and more than $53 million in savings. This market leader in Ethiopia has achieved one of the leanest cost structures in Africa, even in the absence of competition and despite operating in a remote region of the country. Founded in 1995, its clients pay interest rates ranging from 16 percent to 20 percent, which is some 41 percent less than the average microloan APR in sub-Saharan Africa. ACSI's default rate is less than 1 percent, compared to 4.7 percent for African MFIs overall.

ACSI also serves as a platform for other products and services. Through its collaboration with the regional government, it distributes products and services to enhance food security. As a result, its borrowers—who are among the poorest served by any large African MFI—are better able to withstand food shortages and to become increasingly productive and profitable citizens—not to mention ACSI clients.

Limits on Private Benefit

Seemingly excessive executive pay has become a major issue for both multinational corporations and nonprofit organizations. MFIs are especially sensitive to issues of private benefit because of their overarching social objectives, reliance on philanthropy, and periodic requests for special regulatory consideration. Microfinance executives who have received windfalls from public offerings are especially controversial, potentially undermining the public's positive perception of microfinance.

The leaders of some MFIs anticipated these issues and adopted policies that limit how much employees and investors can benefit from their activities. For instance, Grameen Bank adopted the Bangladeshi government's pay scale, which keeps salaries quite modest. (A reasonably generous early retirement package ensures that new blood is always coming into the organization and that those who have served for more than a decade can move into second careers with a cushion.)

The bank's founder, Nobel laureate Muhammad Yunus, has a simple lifestyle and owns no shares in Grameen companies, setting an example for the rest of the microfinance community.

From its inception, Grameen borrowers could purchase shares in the bank and today own more than 90 percent of the bank. For this reason, if the Grameen Bank ever held an IPO, most of the profits would go to clients. Many Indian MFIs have adopted some form of this ownership structure.

Cashpor, a commercial MFI in northern India, has taken an additional measure to stay true to its antipoverty mission: It uses at least one-quarter of its district-level profits to endow scholarships for the children of clients and to provide health care services. This use of profits made more sense than, say, giving bonuses to field officers or executives.

As Cashpor recently learned, limiting private benefit not only advances MFIs' social missions, but also gives them political cover. After Cashpor fired a politically well-connected loan officer for embezzlement, local elites filed a court case against the MFI. The lawsuit claimed that Cashpor was taking advantage of the poor because the organization charges interest. Because Cashpor uses part of its profits to fund health and education programs, though, local police say that the plaintiffs are likely to drop the case.

Holistic Performance Standards

Over the last decade, the microfinance movement has developed benchmarks for assessing efficiency and financial performance. The Microfinance Information Exchange (MIX) and the *Microbanking Bulletin* are constructive efforts to accelerate this important trend. Yet practitioners and investors still have no way to measure and compare the poverty-reduction track records of MFIs. Using indicators such as average loan size and repayment rates as proxies for poverty alleviation impact may be nearly useless, if not misleading. (For more on these metrics, see "In Microfinance, Clients Must Come First" in the winter 2008 issue of the *Stanford Social Innovation Review.*)

If microfinance is going to live up to its billing as a double bottom line business—that is, a business that charts both financial and social returns—MFIs must develop and agree upon robust measures of and standards for their social impacts. Social performance standards will also redound to MFIs' first bottom line by assuring that clients and their businesses are healthy in every sense of the term. Moreover, regularly measuring client progress will help MFIs focus innovation on lagging groups and regions.

The most straightforward measure of microfinance's social impact is clients' economic status. A relatively new tool for measuring this important outcome is the Progress out of Poverty Index (PPI), which the Grameen Foundation, the Consultative Group to Assist the Poor, and the Ford Foundation all champion. The PPI is a statistically robust, easily used tool that assesses the poverty levels of groups and individuals within and across nations. Using existing data from either national household surveys or the World Bank Living Standards Measurement Survey, the PPI allows MFIs to divide their clients into distinct poverty bands (very poor, moderately poor, and above the poverty line). MFIs can then use this baseline to monitor client progress. To date, almost 20 countries have PPIs, including Bolivia, Haiti, India, Mexico, Morocco, Pakistan, and the Philippines. (See p. 50 for Peru's PPI.)

Grameen Bank has always encouraged researchers to test its poverty-reduction performance. In the late 1990s the bank began using a 10-point checklist of easily observable indicators to measure its own progress. Among other outcomes, the checklist assesses whether a family has winter clothing for all members, saves money at a good rate, and sends all its children to school regularly. When families meet all 10 criteria, the bank considers them to have crossed the poverty threshold and be "nonpoor." Using this checklist, Grameen has tracked how many families with more than four years of borrowing experience have escaped poverty. For one cohort, the bank found that poverty rates dropped from 85 percent in 1997 to 37 percent in 2006.

Tracking outcomes and aiming to alleviate poverty have not prevented Grameen Bank from turning profits while operating in perhaps the most competitive microfinance market in the world. The bank's profits have allowed it to make higher education and housing loans widely available despite the fact that it charges interest rates—5 percent and 8 percent, respectively—that do not even cover the cost of capital. Profits have also let the bank offer beggars a subsidized loan program, which was reaching some 86,000 clients by late 2007.

Third-Party Certification

For many years, confusion reigned as consumers tried to figure out which products were organic or fairly traded. Once organizations developed credible certification criteria and companies adhered to them, consumers readily discerned their desired products—and paid premiums for them. Both companies and nonprofits then reaped the rewards of third-party certification.

A similar situation exists in microfinance. Investors have no way of knowing whether an MFI is actively and effectively working to alleviate poverty. When MFIs chart record-breaking returns, people question whether individual MFIs or even the entire sector is drifting away from its mission. Investors wonder whether they should continue offering resources, and governments wonder whether they should continue their regulatory support.

I propose that MFIs must receive objective third-party certification before claiming to be double bottom line organizations. Only groups with this third-party certification would have access to subsidized capital. I imagine that MFIs earning this certification would enjoy improved public relations, as well as financial and regulatory benefits. I also believe they would do a better job of pursuing, monitoring, and delivering social returns.

Designing certification criteria and organizing an overseeing body will require much thought and dialogue. But from Grameen's experience, I've identified four areas that merit inclusion: social performance, private benefit, consumer protection, and reinvestment of profits.

Social performance. A growing criticism of MFIs is that their pursuit of investment capital is leading them not only to offer fewer services to their clients, but also to exclude the world's poorest people from their client base. To curb this tendency, MFIs should agree to track and publish data on the percentage of the poor and the poorest among their entering clients, in addition to tracking poverty-reduction outcomes in the ways described above.

In the new model of microfinance, merely reporting on target clientele and impact trends would not be enough to retain certification. Instead, MFIs would have to ensure that a certain percentage of entering clients are below the poverty line, and that a certain percentage of clients overcome poverty within, say, five years. Of course, certifying agencies would take into account extenuating circumstances such as recent natural disasters, as well as regional variability.

Cashpor already measures its social performance with its housing index. This index uses the condition of borrowers' houses—usually their most important asset—to measure their financial well-being. The index first assigns scores based on a house's size, structural condition, and quality of walls and roof. It then uses cutoff scores to distinguish between the poor and those above the poverty line. With this index, the organization can easily exclude people who have assets above a defined threshold.

Private benefit. As discussed above, limiting private benefit would help make sure that profits mainly benefit clients directly (through lower rates) and indirectly (through product development). More importantly, it would enhance the public trust in microfinance and MFIs. MFIs seeking third-party certification would be required to cap overall compensation for senior staff and directors, as well as to limit the returns that IPOs or other liquidity-generating events would yield for executives. Furthermore, when organizations realize windfalls, such as through an IPO, they would have to divert a meaningful amount of these resources to qualified clients—say, those in good standing who have been involved for more than two years. Linking staff and director benefits to client benefits is another idea worth exploring.

Consumer protection. Accusations of MFIs expressing their fees in misleading ways or using unscrupulous collection practices are surfacing more often and undermining the public trust in microfinance. Most of these charges are untrue or exaggerated, but they point to the need to establish a clear code of conduct and reasonable monitoring and enforcement mechanisms. Although the Microfinance Network and other national bodies have made progress down this path, their efforts are not enough.

To be certified, MFIs would have to implement measures to protect consumers, such as disclosing interest rates and fees. They would also have to eschew unethical debt collection practices, such as seizing the assets of borrowers who are behind on their payments without providing reasonable means for rescheduling loan payments.

Profit reinvestment. When MFIs generate profits, they should have an obligation to allocate some portion of their surplus in a manner consistent with their overarching social purpose. Otherwise, they open themselves up to charges of maximizing profits at the expense of their social missions.

Certified MFIs would be required to reduce their interest rates when profits go beyond an agreed-upon threshold—even in the absence of competition. Alternatively, MFIs earning more than a specified level of profits could provide new products and services that address poor clients' needs, particularly those related to accumulating assets, promoting education, and social empowerment. Or as a third option, MFIs could refund profits to clients in the form of non-voting shares, which would make clients minority owners of the organizations from which they borrow.

Ahead of the Curve

Some microfinance observers have argued that when MFIs rigorously pursue their social impacts, they put themselves at a competitive disadvantage because they sacrifice the short-term profits that many financiers expect. But this argument is misguided: Maximum poverty reduction and long-term business considerations are not only consistent, but also reinforcing. From a purely commercial perspective, the long-term viability of the microfinance business model requires political and regulatory support. If MFIs would protect consumers, limit benefits to staff and investors, and share their windfalls with the poor clients who arguably generated them, they would more likely win the support of politicians and government agencies. Moreover, increased competition with other MFIs will ultimately drive microfinance to be a high-volume business, rather than high-margin business. Encouraging MFIs to shift to that business model now will put them ahead of the curve.

Implementing this new model will not be easy. Increasingly, many MFIs want to strip down their product offerings to achieve higher levels of return on assets and to attract large amounts of capital. MFI executives who have received paltry salaries for years are tempted by the prospect of becoming wealthy in the wake of public offerings. Some investors in microfinance are loath to acknowledge the trade-offs between short-term profit maximization and social impact. And the public is willing to accept anecdotes in place of data as evidence of microfinance's relevance. "In social change, the easiest person to deceive is yourself," says Paul Maritz, a former senior executive at Microsoft Corp. and board chair of the Grameen Foundation.

Still, the benefits of microfinance realizing its two bottom lines are real, and the pathway to doing so is reasonably clear. A first step is to see past the false choice between pro-poor and commercial microfinance. Whether in the economic, political, or scientific spheres, false dichotomies lead to stale debates and suppress creative thinking and action. Looking to the founding principles of microfinance, but reimagining them according to the principles of all successful, long-term commercial endeavors, will lead this important and ever-improving antipoverty strategy to be a major force in creating a more just world. Microfinance will not by itself put "poverty in a museum," as Yunus once said. But with a forward-looking strategy that builds on these promising new ideas and practices, microfinance will play a major role in realizing this breathtaking vision.

1 For an excellent description of this approach, see Marge Magner's paper "Microfinance: A Platform for Social Change," which is available in English and Spanish on the Grameen Foundation Web site. Magner headed Citigroup's consumer bank until her retirement in 2005.
2 "Poor" generally refers to those who make less than their country's national poverty line, and "poorest" to those in the bottom half of those under the poverty line.

ALEX COUNTS is the president and CEO of the Grameen Foundation, a Washington, D.C.–based organization that combines microfinance, technology, and innovation to fight poverty through a network of partners in 25 countries.

Source URL: http://www.ssireview.org/articles/entry/937/

MICROFINANCE
TIME TO TAKE THE CREDIT

Aid donors have shown microfinance can work. They should now leave their successes behind.

SUCCESS has many fathers. No wonder, then, that paternity suits are flying in microfinance—lending small amounts to help the poor pull themselves out of poverty. Thanks first to charities and, later, international financial institutions (IFIs) like the World Bank, microfinance has been shown to work. Now philanthropists such as Bill Gates and Pierre Omidyar, the founder of eBay, are using their own charities to pour money into the field. So, increasingly, is the for-profit sector, including "socially responsible" investors and capitalists more interested in the bottom line than the poverty line.

Microfinance is a promising way to get credit to parts of the economy that are starved of capital. So it is a pity that all these lenders are competing to support the same, small group of microfinance institutions that cater to the most creditworthy borrowers. It would be better for the poor if the IFIs and donors left the best credit risks to profit-seeking lenders and concentrated instead on those still stuck outside the system.

Micromanagement

No doubt that sounds ungrateful. Microfinance is in vogue thanks partly to the IFIs, which provided grants, loans and training to untested microcredit institutions. The private sector shunned the risk—out of ignorance, a lack of expertise and fears that making money from the poor would look predatory. The pioneering work of donors means there are now some 10,000 microfinance institutions lending an average of less than $300 to 40m poor borrowers worldwide.

As a result, microfinance has become profitable. Top-tier microlenders no longer need subsidies or even commercial loans from IFIs or philanthropists. ProCredit, made up of 19 microfinance banks in countries from Moldova to Ecuador, was established in 1998 by some IFIs. Now wildly successful, it boasts over 2.2m customer accounts and arrears by volume of a minuscule 1.2%. So many of its banks make money that it could even list its shares on the stockmarket.

The Inter-American Development Bank has acknowledged that the best microlenders can finance themselves either by gathering deposits to finance loans or by attracting commercial investors. It is busily selling equity stakes in its portfolio of microfinance investments. But other development groups are less willing to cut the apron strings. They continue to devote scarce aid dollars to the microlenders that need them least. Having nurtured these outfits when for-profit groups would not, they now want to bask in their successes. Some philanthropists, too, prefer to take the safe route and invest in stable, profitable top-tier microfinance groups.

This trophy lending is harmful. By subsidising microfinance groups that do not need it, aid bodies and philanthropists discourage private money, which cannot compete with their soft terms. In the long run, this harms microfinanciers, because it slows their integration into the financial-services industry and thus hampers their transformation into lenders able to stand alone.

Aid money is better spent where commercial cash fears to tread—such as on the next generation of microfinance institutions. Subsidies are often needed to lend to the rural poor, where small, scattered populations make it hard for commercial lenders to cover their costs. Donor funds could be used to invest in technology such as mobile payments, which promise to cut the cost of providing microcredit. Top microfinance institutions themselves may need help in expanding into insurance and other financial products for the poor, as well as in tapping the capital markets. IFIs, in particular, can press foreign governments to get rid of interest-rate caps and other misguided regulations that impede microlending.

Only a fraction of the world's 500m impoverished "micro-entrepreneurs" have access to the financial system. There is not enough donor or "socially responsible" money in the world to meet the demand. That's why microfinance needs private-sector capital. Aid agencies, philanthropists and well-meaning "social" investors can help attract it by investing only where commercial outfits will not. When the children come of age, the best parents step aside.

MICROLENDERS, HONORED WITH NOBEL, ARE STRUGGLING

By VIKAS BAJAJ

MUMBAI, India—Microcredit is losing its halo in many developing countries.

Microcredit was once extolled by world leaders like Bill Clinton and Tony Blair as a powerful tool that could help eliminate poverty, through loans as small as $50 to cowherds, basket weavers and other poor people for starting or expanding businesses. But now microloans have prompted political hostility in Bangladesh, India, Nicaragua and other developing countries.

In December, the prime minister of Bangladesh, Sheik Hasina Wazed, who had championed microloans alongside President Clinton at talks in Washington in 1997, turned her back on them. She said microlenders were "sucking blood from the poor in the name of poverty alleviation," and she ordered an investigation into Grameen Bank, which had pioneered microcredit and, with its founder, was awarded the Nobel Peace Prize in 2006.

Here in India, until recently home to the world's fastest-growing microcredit businesses, lending has slowed sharply since the state with the most microloans adopted a strict law restricting lending. In Nicaragua, Pakistan and Bolivia, activists and politicians have urged borrowers not to repay their loans.

The hostility toward microfinance is a sharp reversal from the praise and good will that politicians, social workers and bankers showered on the sector in the last decade. Philanthropists and investors poured billions of dollars into nonprofit and profit-making microlenders, who were considered vital players in achieving the United Nations' ambitious Millennium Development Goals for 2015 that world leaders set in 2000. One of the goals was to reduce by half the number of people in extreme poverty.

The attention lavished on microcredit helped the sector reach more than 91 million customers, most of them women, with loans totaling more than $70 billion by the end of 2009. India and Bangladesh together account for half of all borrowers.

But as with other trumpeted development initiatives that have promised to lift hundreds of millions from poverty, microcredit has struggled to turn rhetoric into tangible success.

Done right, these loans have shown promise in allowing some borrowers to build sustainable livelihoods. But it has also become clear that the rapid growth of microcredit — in India some lending firms were growing at 60 percent to 100 percent a year — has made the loans much less effective.

Most borrowers do not appear to be climbing out of poverty, and a sizable minority is getting trapped in a spiral of debt, according to studies and analysts.

"Credit is both the source of possibilities and it's a bond," said David Roodman, a senior fellow at the Center for Global Development, a research organization in Washington. "Credit is often operating at this knife's edge, and that gets forgotten."

Even as the results for borrowers have been mixed, some lenders have minted profits that might make Wall Street bankers envious. For instance, investors in India's largest microcredit firm, SKS Microfinance, sold shares last year for as much as 95 times what they paid for them a few years earlier.

Meanwhile, politicians in developing nations, some of whom had long resented microlenders as competitors for the hearts and minds of the poor, have taken to depicting lenders as profiteering at the expense of borrowers.

Nicaragua's president, Daniel Ortega, for example, supported "movimiento no pago," or the no-pay movement, which was started in 2008 by farmers after some borrowers could not pay their debts. Partly as a result of that campaign, a judge recently ordered the liquidation of one of the country's leading microlenders, Banco del Exito, or Success Bank.

"These crises happen when the microfinance sector gets saturated, when it grows too fast, and the mechanisms for controlling overindebtedness is not very well developed," said Elisabeth Rhyne, a senior official at Accion International, a organization in Boston that invests in microlenders. "On the political side, politicians or political actors take advantage of an opportunity. When they see grievances, they go, 'Wow, we can make some hay with this.' "

While a broad thread of resentment and disenchantment runs across the globe, the hostility toward microcredit stems from different circumstances in each nation.

In Bangladesh, Ms. Hasina appears to have become embittered with Grameen after its founder, Muhammad Yunus, who shared the Nobel, announced in 2007 that he would start a political party. At that time, the country was ruled by a caretaker government appointed by the military. Though Mr. Yunus later gave up on the idea, analysts say Ms. Hasina and Mr. Yunus have not made amends.

Ms. Hasina's recent comments about microcredit were prompted by a Norwegian documentary that accused Grameen of improperly transferring to an affiliate $100 million that Norway had donated to it more than a decade ago. Ms. Hasina said Grameen, 3.4 percent of which is owned by the government, might have transferred the money to avoid taxes.

The bank, which has denied that accusation, reversed the transfer after Norwegian officials objected to it. Norway recently issued a statement clearing Grameen of wrongdoing.

The prime minister's press secretary did not return calls seeking comment.

In India, leaders in the southern state of Andhra Pradesh, which accounts for about a third of the country's microloans, have accused lenders of impoverishing customers. Stories proliferated in the local news media about women who had amassed debts of $1,000 or more as loan officers cajoled them into borrowing more than they could afford and then browbeat them to

repay. Many had used the money to pay for televisions or health care or to softer
failed crops, rather than as seed money for businesses.

Microcredit firms in India were also accused of siphoning borrowers from go
"self-help groups" — women's organizations that can borrow small amounts at su
est rates from government-owned banks.

The movement against microcredit was started by opposition politicians, who have encouraged borrowers not to repay their loans and have accused senior leaders of the ruling Congress Party of being in cahoots with lenders. The Congress-led state government made the cause its own and passed a tough new law in December to cap interest rates and regulate collections.

The crisis has had ripples across the nation. Banks, the primary source of money for microlenders, have turned off the tap because they are worried about the industry's future. As a result, microlenders have slowed or stopped lending nationwide.

Grameen Financial Services, a microlender in Bangalore that is not related to Grameen Bank, has idled 600 new employees it hired just a few months earlier with plans to expand into western and central India. The firm does not lend in Andhra Pradesh.

"This is frustrating," said Suresh K. Krishna, managing director of Grameen Financial. "This is not what we set out for. The whole objective of floating this was to support entrepreneurs and support people in the rural areas and people below the poverty line."

Industry leaders say they hope the issues will be resolved soon. The federal government and the Reserve Bank of India, the country's central bank, are working on new federal regulations to oversee microcredit, said Alok Prasad, chief executive of the Microfinance Institutions Network.

Still, some industry officials acknowledge that the sector needs to reform itself to overcome political opposition and live up to its promise. They say organizations that now offer only loans need to diversify into microsavings accounts, which many specialists assert are much better than loans at easing poverty.

The industry, they say, also needs to speed up efforts to build a credit bureau that would reduce overlending. And organizations need to measure their success not just by growth and profits, but by how fast their customers are getting out of poverty, experts say.

"We at microfinance have a job to do to make it easier for politicians to support us," said Alex Counts, the chief executive of the Grameen Foundation, a nonprofit in Washington that is not part of Grameen Bank. "Rather than make claims that get out in front of the research, we need to impose on ourselves the discipline of transparency about poverty reduction."

SUICIDES IN INDIA REVEALING HOW MEN MADE A MESS OF MICROCREDIT

By YOOLIM LEE and RUTH DAVID – Dec 28, 2010

BLOOMBERG MARKETS MAGAZINE

Tanda Srinivas was lounging in the yard of his two-room house in the southern Indian village of Mondrai shortly after noon on Oct. 28 when his wife, Shobha, burst out of the door covered in flames and screaming for help.

The 30-year-old mother of two boys had poured 2 liters of kerosene on herself and lit a match. The couple had argued bitterly the day before over how they would repay multiple loans, including those from microlenders who had lent small sums to dozens of villagers, says Venkateshwarlu Masram, a doctor who called for the ambulance.

Shobha, head of several groups of women borrowers, was being pressured to pay interest on her 12,000 rupee ($265) loan. Lenders also were demanding that she cover for the other women, even though the state had restricted microfinance activities two weeks earlier, Bloomberg Markets magazine reports in its February issue.

When Srinivas, 35, tried to snuff out the flames with a blanket, his polyester clothes caught fire. Within three days, both parents were dead, leaving their sons orphans.

Now, on this November morning, the boys' ailing 70-year-old grandfather and blind grandmother say they are caring for Aravind, 10, and Upender, 13, in the farming village where many men earn a living gathering palm extract to make alcoholic beverages.

None of the boys' relatives can support them full time, says their 60-year-old grandmother, Saiamma, breaking into tears.

India's Microlending Hub

The horrific scene in Mondrai, 80 kilometers (50 miles) from the city of Warangal, has played out in dozens of ways across Andhra Pradesh, India's fifth-largest state by area and the site of about a third of the country's $5.3 billion in microfinance loans as of Sept. 30.

More than 70 people committed suicide in the state from March 1 to Nov. 19 to escape payments or end the agonies their debt had triggered, according to the Society for Elimination of Rural Poverty, a government agency that compiled the data on the microfinance-related deaths from police and press reports.

Andhra Pradesh, where three-quarters of the 76 million people live in rural areas, suffered a total of 14,364 suicide cases in the first nine months of 2010, according to state police.

A growing number of microfinance-related deaths spurred the state to clamp down on collection practices in mid-October, says Reddy Subrahmanyam, principal secretary for rural development.

"Every life is important," he says.

Perverse Turn

On Nov. 8, police arrested two managers of lender Share Microfin Ltd. on allegations of abetting another suicide, this one of a 22-year-old mother. Share Microfin didn't respond to requests for comment on this story.

As India struggles to provide decent education, health care and jobs to millions still locked in poverty, microlending — the loaning of small sums to the world's neediest people to help them earn a living — has taken a perverse turn.

Microcredit has become "Walmartized" by unrestrained selling of cheap products to the poor, says Malcolm Harper, chairman of ratings company Micro-Credit Ratings International Ltd. in Gurgaon, India.

"Selling debt is like selling drugs," says Harper, 75, the author of more than 20 books on microfinance and other topics. "Selling debt to illiterate women in Andhra Pradesh, you've got to be a lot more responsible."

Opposite Effect

K. Venkat Narayana, an economics professor at Kakatiya University in Warangal, has studied how microfinance lenders persuaded groups of women to borrow.

"Microfinance was supposed to empower women," he says. "Microfinance guys reversed the social and economic progress, and these women ended up becoming slaves."

India's booming microlending industry is part of a global phenomenon that began as a charitable movement but now attracts private capital seeking growth and high returns.

Banco Compartamos SA, a former nonprofit that's now the largest lender to Mexico's working poor, raised about $467 million in its 2007 initial public offering. The August IPO of SKS Microfinance Ltd., India's biggest microlender, drew further attention to the industry.

SKS began operating in 1998 as a nongovernmental organization led by Vikram Akula, 42, an Indian-American with a Ph.D. in political science from the University of Chicago.

The company raised 16.3 billion rupees by selling 16.8 million shares at 985 rupees each. SKS shares peaked at 1,404.85 rupees on Sept. 15. As of Dec. 28, they'd fallen to 652.85 rupees.

Andhra Pradesh Crisis

On Oct. 15, the government of Andhra Pradesh imposed restrictions that bar microlenders' collection agents from visiting borrowers and required companies to get local authorities' approval for new loans. The rules have crippled lending and repayments. Loan collection levels in the state have dropped to less than 20 percent from 98 percent previously, according to an industry group.

The upheaval in Andhra Pradesh is a long way from the vision of Muhammad Yunus.

The former economics professor won the Nobel Peace Prize in 2006 for his pioneering work in Bangladesh providing small sums to entrepreneurs too poor to get bank loans.

Yunus, 70, discovered more than three decades ago that when you lend money to women in poverty, they can begin to earn a living, and most of them will pay you back.

Yunus started the Grameen Bank Project in 1976 to extend banking services to the poor. Since then, it has lent $9.87 billion and recovered $8.76 billion; 97 percent of its 8.33 million borrowers are female.

'Wrong Direction'

Yunus says he's not against making a profit. But he denounces firms that seek windfalls and pervert the original intent of microfinance: helping the poor.

The rule of thumb for a loan should be the cost of funds plus 10 percent, he says.

"Commercialization is the wrong direction," Yunus says, speaking in a telephone interview from Bangladesh's capital of Dhaka. "An initial public offering is the triggering point for making a lot of money personally as well as for the company and shareholders."

David Gibbons, chairman of Cashpor Micro Credit, a nonprofit microlender to the poorest women in India's Uttar Pradesh and Bihar states, says public, for-profit lenders face a conflict.

"They have to decide between the interests of their customers and interests of their investors," he says.

'Can't Be Done'

Gibbons, 70, says he learned that lesson when he tried to raise 4 million pounds ($6.2 million) from two wealthy London-based nonresident Indian investors in November 2006.

Talks failed because of differences over expectations for returns on equity and other contract terms, he says.

"That's what made me think this just can't be done," he says.

Indian microlenders differ from Yunus's Grameen Bank in key ways. To protect depositors' money after bankruptcies among nonbanking financial companies in the early 1990s, India's Reserve Bank in 1997 made it more difficult for them to meet the requirements needed to take deposits from the public. Only 36 microlenders are registered as nonbank financial companies, according to information supplied by the Reserve Bank.

ɔ Sad'

Indian microlenders themselves borrow from banks at 13 percent or more on average and extend credit to the poor. They charge interest rates that can rise to 36 percent, says Alok Prasad, chief executive officer of the Microfinance Institutions Network, which represents 44 microlenders. He says all 44 firms are registered with the Reserve Bank.

SKS Microfinance gets funds at about 12 percent interest and lends at 24.52 percent in Andhra Pradesh, spokesman Atul Takle says.

In Bangladesh, Grameen Bank got a banking license in 1983, which allowed it to take deposits. It charges 5 percent for education loans and 8 percent for housing loans. Beggars can borrow for free, and interest on major loans is capped at 20 percent, Yunus says.

"Microfinance has been abused and distorted," he says. "I feel so sad because that's not the microcredit I have created."

Indian microfinance has roots in decades-old informal community financing.

Nongovernmental organizations pioneered cooperative lending, known today as self-help groups, with seed money from the National Bank for Agriculture and Rural Development. Encouraged by these projects, the state-backed bank worked to tie borrowing groups to local bank branches in 1992.

For-Profit Companies

Nonprofit organizations subsequently got involved as middlemen between the banks and the borrowers. By 2005, nonprofits such as SKS and Share Microfin had turned themselves into profit-making enterprises.

Akula's SKS attracted investors such as Khosla Ventures, Sun Microsystems Inc. co-founder Vinod Khosla's venture capital firm.

Capital flowed into the new industry from commercial banks, venture firms and private equity.

Sequoia Capital, in Menlo Park, California, and Bangalore- based Infosys Technologies Ltd. Chairman N.R. Narayana Murthy were among the backers. George Soros's Quantum Fund has a 0.37 percent stake in SKS.

Private-equity investors alone have put $515 million into Indian microfinance companies since 2006, research service Venture Intelligence says.

'Explosive Growth'

More than half of the 66 Indian microlenders tracked by Micro-Credit Ratings are for-profit firms. Some 260 microlenders had 26.7 million borrowers and 183.44 billion rupees of loans outstanding as of March, according to the Microfinance India State of the Sector Report 2010.

"Over the last two years, we've been seeing explosive growth," says N. Srinivasan, who wrote the report. "Microfinance institutions found that it's easy to make money. Not that making money is bad, but when you go overboard and say you require money for growth, you get into problems."

Polelpaka Pula, a mother of two, says she saw microlenders rushing into her village of Pegadapalli to compete for business — with tragic results.

Her husband, Prakash, a painter who made 250 rupees on a good day, first borrowed from a group of villagers to build a house. Each participant of the so-called chit fund contributed 1,000 rupees a month and took a turn collecting the entire sum.

Microfinance officers from L&T Finance Ltd., Spandana Sphoorty Financial Ltd., Share Microfin and SKS began offering loans in the village starting in 2004, she says.

The couple, already contributing to their village fund, took five more loans totaling 64,000 rupees. That saddled them with payments of 7,300 rupees a month, more than Prakash's 5,000 rupee maximum monthly income.

Loan Shark

When Prakash ran out of microlenders to borrow from, he went to a village loan shark, who charged 100 percent interest.

With no way out and debt from multiple lenders ballooning, Prakash hanged himself in November 2009, his wife says.

The small house he'd dreamed of was never completed. Only the foundation stands next to the home of his parents, a tiny structure with a roof of palm leaves.

Spandana says that neither of the couple's names is in its database. The company says the media wrongly attribute harassment cases to microfinance, especially when Spandana is mentioned.

"The trigger factors for suicide are manifold, such as stressful situations at home," the company said in an e-mail response to questions about the death.

Subprime Parallel

SKS spokesman Takle says its staff has practiced responsible lending for the past 12 years. Its employees are not paid based on the loan size or repayment percentage.

"This ensures against giving out larger loans than what a borrower can repay," Takle says. A spokesman for L&T Finance declined to comment.

Overlending in Andhra Pradesh calls to mind the U.S. subprime crisis, says Lakshmi Shyam-Sunder, director of corporate risk at International Finance Corp. in Washington, which invests in microlenders.

"Subprime lending was initially seen as extending homeownership to poorer people, doing good," Shyam-Sunder says.

As the industry expanded, making a profit became more important to some lenders, she says. "Tension arises when you work on activities with both social goals as well as commercial interests," she says, adding that it's important to strike the right balance.

Companies chasing profits amid poor corporate governance are undermining the intent of microfinance, Cashpor's Gibbons says.

'Lending Gone Wild'

During the past five years, the number of microloans in India has soared an average of 88 percent a year and borrower accounts have climbed 62 percent annually, giving India the world's largest microfinance industry, Micro-Credit Ratings says.

"This is unrestrained consumer lending gone wild," Gibbons says. "It's not about poverty reduction anymore."

Sumir Chadha, managing director at Sequoia Capital India Advisors Pvt., says that without a profit motive it's hard to find anyone who will lend to the poor.

"Capitalism doesn't have to be a bad thing," says Chadha, whose firm has a 14 percent stake in SKS. "If you can't profit off the poor, it means that no companies will service the poor—and then they will be worse off than earlier."

Chand Bee's Tale

For Chand Bee, a 50-year-old who led three borrowing groups in Andhra Pradesh, too many loans almost became her undoing.

She says she ran away from home after collectors began harassing her. She took out multiple loans beginning in 2005, and she names Spandana as one of the lenders.

Some of the money paid for the funeral of her eldest son. When she fell behind on payments, she says loan officers threatened to humiliate her in front of neighbors and pressed her to sell her small grandchildren into prostitution.

She left her slum in Warangal, where she lived with her deaf husband, some of her eight grown children and more than a dozen grandchildren.

After living as a beggar for a year, Chand Bee returned home in early November when family members told her that the state ordinance that went into effect on Oct. 15 had suspended some collections. A Spandana spokeswoman says none of the company's four customers in the district with the name Chand Bee has had trouble repaying.

Almost every household in the slum of 250 people—where barefoot children play in lanes between rows of dilapidated shacks—has taken several loans. So many microlenders ply their trade that residents refer to them by the days they collect: Monday company, Tuesday company and so on.

Debt Free

Rabbani, a widow with four children, is one of the few women who are debt-free. She started a spice shop with two loans, which she repaid with her small profit. After seeing her neighbors' pains, she vowed never to seek another microloan.

SKS says 17 of its clients have committed suicide, none because of loans being in arrears or harassment.

"Suicide is a complex issue," Akula says.

Sitting in the second-floor conference room of SKS's seven- story headquarters in Hyderabad, where posters of smiling women running handicraft and tailor shops decorate the doors of elevators, Akula says there's nothing wrong with seeking profits.

"What does it matter to a poor woman how much an investor makes?" says Akula, dressed in his trademark knee-length kurta shirt from Fabindia, a seller of ethnic clothes made by rural craftsmen. "What matters to her is that she gets a loan on time at a reasonable rate that allows her to earn higher income."

Commercial Venture

Turning SKS into a commercial venture allowed the firm to tap an unlimited pool of funds from private investors. That, in turn, let the company grow and reduce rates, Akula says.

"Interest rates have come down over time," he says. "Because it works, she comes back year after year," he says of his customers.

His autobiography, "A Fistful of Rice" (Harvard Business Review Press, 2010), provides a glimpse of the expansion drive.

Akula, a former McKinsey & Co. consultant, studied McDonald's Corp. and Burger King Holdings Inc. in 2005 to learn about their speedy training of unskilled workers. He devised a two-month course to train as many as 1,000 new loan officers a month.

"I now had one goal for SKS; to grow, grow, grow as fast as we could," he writes. "We could practice microfinance in a way that would serve more poor people than anyone had ever thought possible."

Akula says the commercial model of microfinance isn't the only way.

Returning to 'Roots'

"It's an important complement to other forms of finance," he says. New microfinance companies don't spend time to build trust, Akula says. "As an industry, we need to go back to our roots," he says.

The Reserve Bank is scheduled to report on the industry in January. The finance ministry is planning new rules.

Sequoia Capital's Chadha says he's concerned about "regulatory uncertainty" created by the state ordinance and prefers federal regulation. Nationwide rules would prevent individual states from damaging credit discipline by waiving loans, Microfinance Institutions' Prasad says.

"It is no different than needing good regulation for stock investing or starting a manufacturing facility," SKS investor Khosla says.

'People, Not Profit'

From Yunus's perspective, it's essential that the industry move away from seeking maximum profits and get back to focusing on the poor.

"If not, you are not helping poor people's lives," he says. "You are not patient. You are not restrained. You don't have empathy for the people. You are just using them to make money. That's what blinds you when you are in the profit-making world. We need to see the people, not profit."

Any such changes would be too late for Atthili Padma and Shivalingam, a young couple in Andhra Pradesh's cotton-farming village of Chennampalli.

Padma, a 22-year-old mother of two, walked out of her house on Oct. 7 with her 18-month-old son and 4-year-old daughter, according to Maruthi Prasad, a superintendent at the police station in Shankarampet.

Padma's Death

Instead of heading to her parents' house as she often did, she walked 2 kilometers in the opposite direction. She came to an old Hindu temple where villagers worship Lord Shiva, the god of destruction. Padma continued until she stood in front of a well once used to irrigate crops, her father-in-law, Pochaiah, says. There, with no one to dissuade her, she jumped into the well with her children.

The day before she died, Padma had visited her parents after arguing with her husband over loans they couldn't repay, according to Mangamma, the couple's neighbor.

Their marriage five years ago was arranged by their parents and the couple had become close and hadn't fought before that day, Mangamma says. The loans totaled 20,000 rupees, Pochaiah says.

Padma's death is recorded as a microfinance-related suicide in the list by the Society for Elimination of Rural Poverty.

'Sad Day for Microfinance'

Police arrested Padma's husband, Shivalingam, on Oct. 13 for allegedly abetting Padma's suicide. They also alleged that he'd harassed her to provide money to marry him, which is illegal in India, according to Narayana, a constable at the Shankarampet police station.

Police made two further arrests on Nov. 8: Share Microfin managers Sriram Raghavender, 27, and Polapalli Kumaraswami, 22, also for allegedly abetting the suicide, according to superintendent Prasad. The two managers and Shivalingam have been released on bail and are awaiting a court hearing, Prasad says.

Advocates and investors such as Khosla say microfinance—when it works correctly—is the best way to give the rural poor a shot at better lives.

The tragedies in India present the worst possible outcome, says Cashpor's Gibbons, whose Nov. 15 speech opened a morning session of the annual Microfinance India Summit in New Delhi.

"This is a sad day for microfinance," said Gibbons, who has promoted the movement for the past two decades.

"Often people asked me, 'What are you doing here?'" he told the audience. "I've been always proud to say, 'I'm doing microfinance.' Now, when people ask, I feel embarrassed. I feel like hiding somewhere."

To contact the reporters on this story: Yoolim Lee in Singapore at yoolim@bloomberg.net; Ruth David in Mumbai at rdavid9@bloomberg.net

To contact the editors responsible for this story: Michael Serril at mserril@bloombern.net; Phillip Lagerkranser at lagerkranser@bloomberg.net

THE CLIENT PROTECTION PRINCIPLES IN MICROFINANCE

The Client Protection Principles for microfinance and the accompanying Smart Campaign are part of a collaborative initiative endorsed and led by a broad coalition of microfinance institutions (MFIs), networks, funders, and practitioners. The purpose of the Campaign, which is housed at the Center for Financial Inclusion, and the Principles is to ensure that providers of financial services to low-income populations take concrete steps to protect their clients from potentially harmful financial products and ensure that they are treated fairly. There is now broad consensus that it is critical for the industry to join together and proactively safeguard the interests of microfinance clients through appropriate policies, practices, and products. As the Campaign gains momentum, MFIs that have embedded the principles into their core business activities will have a competitive advantage—not just with clients but with investors, donors, governments, and policy makers.

What are the Client Protection Principles?

Client Protection Principles describe the minimum protection microfinance clients should expect from providers. These Principles are distilled from the path-breaking work of providers, international networks, and national microfinance associations to develop pro-consumer codes of conduct and practices. While the Principles are universal, meaningful and effective implementation will require careful attention to the diversity within the provider community and conditions in different markets and country contexts. Over the past several years, consensus has emerged that providers of financial services to low-income clients should adhere to the following six core principles:

- ***Avoidance of Over-Indebtedness.*** Providers will take reasonable steps to ensure that credit will be extended only if borrowers have demonstrated an adequate ability to repay and loans will not put borrowers at significant risk of over-indebtedness. Similarly, providers will take adequate care that only appropriate non-credit financial products (such as insurance) are extended to clients.

- ***Transparent and Responsible Pricing.*** The pricing, terms, and conditions of financial products (including interest charges, insurance premiums, all fees, etc.) will be transparent and will be adequately disclosed in a form understandable to clients. Responsible pricing means that pricing, terms, and conditions are set in a way that is both affordable to clients and sustainable for financial institutions.
- ***Appropriate Collections Practices.*** Debt collection practices of providers will not be abusive or coercive.
- ***Ethical Staff Behavior.*** Staff of financial service providers will comply with high ethical standards in their interaction with microfinance clients and such providers will ensure that adequate safeguards are in place to detect and correct corruption or mistreatment of clients.
- ***Mechanisms for Redress of Grievances.*** Providers will have in place timely and responsive mechanisms for complaints and problem resolution for their clients.
- ***Privacy of Client Data.*** The privacy of individual client data will be respected in accordance with the laws and regulations of individual jurisdictions, and such data cannot be used for other purposes without the express permission of the client (while recognizing that providers of financial services can play an important role in helping clients achieve the benefits of establishing credit histories).

What does endorsement mean?

Institutions and individuals that endorse the Client Protection Principles are committing to be a part of an industry-wide process to translate the Principles into standards, policies, and practices appropriate for different types of microfinance clients, products, providers, and country contexts.

By endorsing these Principles, **providers of financial services, networks, and individuals working in microfinance** are committing to a process of implementation of the principles into their own organization's operations and institutional culture. For MFIs, it begins with an examination of their own practice to identify areas for improvement and active promotion of the principles to staff. For networks, endorsement is a commitment to engage with its affiliated organizations to promote and support the Campaign and Coalition and to implement the principles. Individuals endorsing the Campaign are signaling their intention to honor the principles personally and to work within their own organizations to implement them.

Donors and investors also play an important role in ensuring the success of this initiative. By endorsing the principles, investors and donors commit to work to support providers that adequately protect their low-income clients, and to identify practical ways of incorporating the Client Protection Principles into their due diligence, monitoring, and governance roles.

CENTER FOR EDUCATION ON SOCIAL RESPONSIBILITY

PART SEVEN

VALUES REVISITED: ENTER COURAGE

MORAL COURAGE CHECKLIST

Rushworth Kidder

Like most good things, moral courage is hedged about with imitations, counterfeits, and challenges. What keeps me from being distracted as I seek the morally courageous path? How can I circumvent the detours that would inhibit or quench my moral courage?

Here are a dozen inhibitors to avoid:

1. **Overconfident cultures** that seep into organizations and cut off discussion, tolerate unethical acts, or refuse to hear new ideas from me or anyone else
2. **Compromises** engendered by my desire to be liked, to win promotion or election, or to duck tough but right demands
3. **Foolhardiness** as I forge ahead with chutzpah and quixotic derring-do but without a proper assessment of risk
4. **Timidity** that urges me to flee from situations demanding bold forwardness—a cowardly unwillingness to endure the discomfort that moral courage often requires
5. **Raw courage** that ignores the principled heart of moral courage, substituting instead a misplaced sense of honor or a merely physical bravery
6. **Tepid ethics,** lacking sufficient intensity and breadth to rise above the merely dutiful and tolerant, keeping me from the resounding vision and clarity that often characterize true moral courage
7. **Overreflection,** leading me to rationalize my way out of an expression of moral courage that may have been my first instinct
8. **Bystander apathy** that dilutes my responsibility in the presence of others, letting me excuse my lack of courage because no one else is being courageous, either
9. **Groupthink** that huddles around and staunchly defends a bad collective decision that no one in the group, acting alone, would have countenanced
10. **Normalized deviancy,** leading me to redefine some wrong behaviors as acceptable rather than take a morally courageous (though perhaps unpopular) stand against them

11. **Altruism,** which can challenge my moral courage when expressed in excess (as with manipulative generosity) or when misapplied (as with well-intentioned meddling)
12. **Cultural differences,** persuading me that the boundaries of my moral concern need not extend to include *those people* who are so radically different from me

If I avoid all these, am I home free? Not necessarily. There's a courage of denial needed to escape these pitfalls. But there's also a courage of affirmation that requires proactive, engaged, and positive steps. Avoiding detours doesn't necessarily prove I chose the best road in the first place.

VALUES IN TENSION

Ethics Away from Home

Thomas Donaldson

What should managers working abroad do when they encounter business practices that seem unethical? Should they, in the spirit of cultural relativism, tell themselves to do in Rome as the Romans do? Or should they take an absolutist approach, using the ethical standards they use at home no matter where they are?

According to Thomas Donaldson, the answer lies somewhere in between. Some activities are wrong no matter where they take place. Dumping pollutants for unprotected workers to handle is one example of a practice that violates what Donaldson calls core human values: respect for human dignity, respect for basic rights, and good citizenship. But some practices that are unethical in one part of the world might be ethical in another. What may feel like bribery to an American, for example, may be in keeping with Japan's longstanding tradition of gift giving. And what may seem like inhumane wage rates to citizens of developed countries may be acceptable in developing countries that are trying to attract investment and improve standards of living.

Many business practices are neither black nor white but exist in a gray zone, a moral free space through which managers must navigate. Levi Strauss and Motorola have helped managers by treating company values as absolutes and insisting that suppliers and customers do the same. And, perhaps even more important, both companies have developed detailed codes of conduct that provide clear direction on ethical behavior but also leave room for managers to use the moral imagination that will allow them to resolve ethical tensions responsibly and creatively.

When we leave home and cross our nation's boundaries, moral clarity often blurs. Without a backdrop of shared attitudes, and without familiar laws and judicial procedures that define standards of ethical conduct, certainty is elusive. Should a company invest in a foreign country where civil and political rights are violated? Should a company go along with a host country's discriminatory employment practices? If companies in developed countries shift facilities to developing nations that lack strict environmental and health regulations, or if those companies choose to fill management and other top-level positions in a host nation with people from the home country, whose standards should prevail?

Even the best-informed, best-intentioned executives must rethink their assumptions about business practice in foreign settings. What works in a company's home country can fail in a country with different standards of ethical conduct. Such difficulties are unavoidable for businesspeople who live and work abroad.

But how can managers resolve the problems? What are the principles that can help them work through the maze of cultural differences and establish codes of conduct for globally ethical business practice? How can companies answer the toughest question in global business ethics: What happens when a host country's ethical standards seem lower than the home country's?

COMPETING ANSWERS

One answer is as old as philosophical discourse. According to cultural relativism, no culture's ethics are better than any other's; therefore there are no international rights and wrongs. If the people of Indonesia tolerate the bribery of their public officials, so what? Their attitude is no better or worse than that of people in Denmark or Singapore who refuse to offer or accept bribes. Likewise, if Belgians fail to find insider trading morally repugnant, who cares? Not enforcing insider-trading laws is no more or less ethical than enforcing such laws.

The cultural relativist's creed—When in Rome, do as the Romans do—is tempting, especially when failing to do as the locals do means forfeiting business opportunities. The inadequacy of cultural relativism, however, becomes apparent when the practices in question are more damaging than petty bribery or insider trading.

In the late 1980s, some European tanneries and pharmaceutical companies were looking for cheap waste-dumping sites. They approached virtually every country on Africa's west coast from Morocco to the Congo. Nigeria agreed to take highly toxic polychlorinated biphenyls. Unprotected local workers, wearing thongs and shorts, unloaded barrels of PCBs and placed them near a residential area. Neither the residents nor the workers knew that the barrels contained toxic waste.

We may denounce governments that permit such abuses, but many countries are unable to police transnational corporations adequately even if they want to. And in many countries, the combination of ineffective enforcement and inadequate regulations leads to behavior by unscrupulous companies that is clearly wrong. A few years ago, for example, a group of investors became interested in restoring the SS *United States*, once a luxurious ocean liner.

Before the actual restoration could begin, the ship had to be stripped of its asbestos lining. A bid from a U.S. company, based on U.S. standards for asbestos removal, priced the job at more than $100 million. A company in the Ukranian city of Sevastopol offered to do the work for less than $2 million. In October 1993, the ship was towed to Sevastopol.

A cultural relativist would have no problem with that outcome, but I do. A country has the right to establish its own health and safety regulations, but in the case described above, the standards and the terms of the contract could not possibly have protected workers in Sevastopol from known health risks. Even if the contract met Ukranian standards, ethical businesspeople must object. Cultural relativism is morally blind. There are fundamental values that cross cultures, and companies must uphold them. (For an economic argument against cultural relativism, see "The Culture and Ethics of Software Piracy" at the end of this article.)

At the other end of the spectrum from cultural relativism is ethical imperialism, which directs people to do everywhere exactly as they do at home. Again, an understandably appealing approach but one that is clearly inadequate. Consider the large U.S. computer-products company that in 1993 introduced a course on sexual harassment in its Saudi Arabian facility. Under the banner of global consistency, instructors used the same approach to train Saudi Arabian managers that they had used with U.S. managers: the participants were asked to discuss a case in which a manager makes sexually explicit remarks to a new female employee over drinks in a bar. The instructors failed to consider how the exercise would work in a culture with strict conventions governing relationships between men and women. As a result, the training sessions were ludicrous. They baffled and offended the Saudi participants, and the message to avoid coercion and sexual discrimination was lost.

The theory behind ethical imperialism is absolutism, which is based on three problematic principles. Absolutists believe that there is a single list of truths, that they can be expressed only with one set of concepts, and that they call for exactly the same behavior around the world.

The first claim clashes with many people's belief that different cultural traditions must be respected. In some cultures, loyalty to a community—family, organization, or society—is the foundation of all ethical behavior. The Japanese, for example, define business ethics in terms of loyalty to their companies, their business networks, and their nation. Americans place a higher value on liberty than on loyalty; the U.S. tradition of rights emphasizes equality, fairness, and individual freedom. It is hard to conclude that truth lies on one side or the other, but an absolutist would have us select just one.

The second problem with absolutism is the presumption that people must express moral truth using only one set of concepts. For instance, some absolutists insist that the language of basic rights provide the framework for any discussion of ethics. That means, though, that entire cultural traditions must be ignored. The notion of a right evolved with the rise of democracy in post-Renaissance Europe and the United States, but the term is not found in either Confucian or Buddhist traditions. We all learn ethics in the context of our particular cultures, and the power in the principles is deeply tied to the way in which they are expressed. Internationally accepted lists of moral principles, such as the United Nations' Universal Declaration of Human Rights, draw on many cultural and religious traditions. As philosopher Michael Walzer has noted, "There is no Esperanto of global ethics."

The third problem with absolutism is the belief in a global standard of ethical behavior. Context must shape ethical practice. Very low wages, for example, may be considered unethical in rich, advanced countries, but developing nations may be acting ethically if they encourage investment and improve living standards by accepting low wages. Likewise, when people are malnourished or starving, a government may be wise to use more fertilizer in order to improve crop yields, even though that means settling for relatively high levels of thermal water pollution.

When cultures have different standards of ethical behavior—and different ways of handling unethical behavior—a company that takes an absolutist approach may find itself making a disastrous mistake. When a manager at a large U.S. specialty-products company in China caught an employee stealing, she followed the company's practice and turned the employee over to the provincial authorities, who executed him. Managers cannot operate in another culture without being aware of that culture's attitudes toward ethics.

If companies can neither adopt a host country's ethics nor extend the home country's standards, what is the answer? Even the traditional litmus test—What would people think of your actions if they were written up on the front page of the newspaper?—is an unreliable guide, for there is no international consensus on standards of business conduct.

BALANCING THE EXTREMES: THREE GUIDING PRINCIPLES

Companies must help managers distinguish between practices that are merely different and those that are wrong. For relativists, nothing is sacred and nothing is wrong. For absolutists, many things that are different are wrong. Neither extreme illuminates the real world of business decision making. The answer lies somewhere in between.

When it comes to shaping ethical behavior, companies must be guided by three principles.

- Respect for core human values, which determine the absolute moral threshold for all business activities.
- Respect for local traditions.
- The belief that context matters when deciding what is right and what is wrong.

Consider those principles in action. In Japan, people doing business together often exchange gifts—sometimes expensive ones—in keeping with long-standing Japanese tradition. When U.S. and European companies started doing a lot of business in Japan, many Western businesspeople thought that the practice of gift giving might be wrong rather than simply different. To them, accepting a gift felt like accepting a bribe. As Western companies have become more familiar with Japanese traditions, however, most have come to tolerate the practice and to set different limits on gift giving in Japan than they do elsewhere.

Respecting differences is a crucial ethical practice. Research shows that management ethics differ among cultures; respecting those differences means recognizing that some cultures have obvious weaknesses—as well as hidden strengths. Managers in Hong Kong, for example, have a higher tolerance for some forms of bribery than their Western counterparts, but they have a much lower tolerance for the failure to acknowledge a subordinate's work. In some parts of the Far East, stealing credit from a subordinate is nearly an unpardonable sin.

People often equate respect for local traditions with cultural relativism. That is incorrect. Some practices are clearly wrong. Union Carbide's tragic experience in Bhopal, India, provides one example. The company's executives seriously underestimated how much on-site management involvement was needed at the Bhopal plant to compensate for the country's poor infrastructure and regulatory capabilities. In the aftermath of the disastrous gas leak, the lesson is clear: companies using sophisticated technology in a developing country must evaluate that country's ability to oversee its safe use. Since the incident at Bhopal, Union Carbide has become a leader in advising companies on using hazardous technologies safely in developing countries.

Some activities are wrong no matter where they take place. But some practices that are unethical in one setting may be acceptable in another. For instance, the chemical EDB, a soil fungicide, is banned for use in the United States. In hot climates, however, it quickly becomes harmless through exposure to intense solar radiation and high soil temperatures. As long as the chemical is monitored, companies may be able to use EDB ethically in certain parts of the world.

DEFINING THE ETHICAL THRESHOLD: CORE VALUES

Few ethical questions are easy for managers to answer. But there are some hard truths that must guide managers' actions, a set of what I call *core human values*, which define minimum ethical standards for all companies. The right to good health and the right to economic advancement and an improved standard of living are two core human values. Another is what Westerners call the Golden Rule, which is recognizable in every major religious and ethical tradition around the world. In Book 15 of his *Analects*, for instance, Confucius counsels people to maintain reciprocity, or not to do the others what they do not want done to themselves.

Although no single list would satisfy every scholar, I believe it is possible to articulate three core values that incorporate the work of scores of theologians and philosophers around the world. To be broadly relevant, these values must include elements found in both Western and non-Western cultural and religious traditions. Consider the examples of values in the insert "What Do These Values Have in Common?"

At first glance, the values expressed in the two lists seem quite different. Nonetheless, in the spirit of what philosopher John Rawls calls *overlapping consensus*, one can see that the seemingly divergent values converge at key points. Despite important differences between Western and non-Western cultural and religious traditions, both express shared attitudes about what it means to be human. First, individuals must not treat others simply as tools; in other words, they must recognize a person's value as a human being. Next, individuals and communities must treat people in ways that respect people's basic rights. Finally, members of a community must work together to support and improve the institutions on which the community depends. I call those three values *respect for human dignity, respect for basic rights, and good citizenship.*

Those values must be the starting point for all companies as they formulate and evaluate standards of ethical conduct at home and abroad. But they are only a starting point. Companies need much more specific guidelines, and the first step to developing those is to translate the core human values into core values for business. What does it mean, for example, for a company to respect human dignity? How can a company be a good citizen?

I believe that companies can respect human dignity by creating and sustaining a corporate culture in which employees, customers, and suppliers are treated not as means to an end but as people whose intrinsic value must be acknowledged, and by producing safe products and services in a safe workplace. Companies can respect basic rights by acting in ways that support and protect the individual rights of employees, customers, and surrounding communities, and by avoiding relationships that violate human beings' rights to health, education, safety, and an adequate standard of living. And companies can be good citizens by supporting essential social institutions, such as the economic system and the education system, and by working with host governments and other organizations to protect the environment.

What Do These Values Have in Common?

Non-Western	Western
Kyosei (Japanese): Living and working together for the common good.	Individual liberty
Dharma (Hindu): The fulfillment of inherited duty.	Egalitarianism
Santutthi (Buddhist): The importance of limited desires.	Political participation
Zakat (Muslim): The duty to give alms to the Muslim poor.	Human rights

The core values establish a moral compass for business practice. They can help companies identify practices that are acceptable and those that are intolerable—even if the practices are compatible with a host country's norms and laws. Dumping pollutants near people's homes and accepting inadequate standards for handling hazardous materials are two examples of actions that violate core values.

Similarly, if employing children prevents them from receiving a basic education, the practice is intolerable. Lying about product specifications in the act of selling may not affect human lives directly, but it too is intolerable because it violates the trust that is needed to sustain a corporate culture in which customers are respected.

Sometimes it is not a company's actions but those of a supplier or customer that pose problems. Take the case of the Tan family, a large supplier for Levi Strauss. The Tans were allegedly forcing 1,200 Chinese and Filipino women to work 74 hours per week in guarded compounds on the Mariana Islands. In 1992, after repeated warnings to the Tans, Levi Strauss broke off business relations with them.

CREATING AN ETHICAL CORPORATE CULTURE

The core values for business that I have enumerated can help companies begin to exercise ethical judgment and think about how to operate ethically in foreign cultures, but they are not specific enough to guide managers through actual ethical dilemmas. Levi Strauss relied on a written code of conduct when figuring out how to deal with the Tan family. The company's Global Sourcing and Operating Guidelines, formerly called the Business Partner Terms of Engagement, state that Levi Strauss will "seek to identify and utilize business partners who aspire as individuals and in the conduct of all their businesses to a set of ethical standards not incompatible with our own." Whenever intolerable business situations arise, managers should be guided by precise statements that spell out the behavior and operating practices that the company demands.

Many companies don't do anything with their codes of conduct; they simply paste them on the wall.

Ninety percent of all *Fortune* 500 companies have codes of conduct, and 70% have statements of vision and values. In Europe and the Far East, the percentages are lower but are increasing rapidly. Does that mean that most companies have what they need? Hardly. Even though most large U.S. companies have both statements of values and codes of conduct, many might be better off if they didn't. Too many companies don't do anything with the documents; they simply paste them on the wall to impress employees, customers, suppliers, and the public. As a result, the senior managers who drafted the statements lose credibility by proclaiming values and not living up to them. Companies such as Johnson & Johnson, Levi Strauss, Motorola, Texas Instruments, and Lockheed Martin, however, do a great deal to make the words meaningful.

Johnson & Johnson, for example, has become well known for its Credo Challenge sessions, in which managers discuss ethics in the context of their current business problems and are invited to criticize the company's credo and make suggestions for changes. The participants' ideas are passed on to the company's senior managers. Lockheed Martin has created an innovative site on the World Wide Web and on its local network that gives employees, customers, and suppliers access to the company's ethical code and the chance to voice complaints.

Codes of conduct must provide clear direction about ethical behavior when the temptation to behave unethically is strongest. The pronouncement in a code of conduct that bribery is unacceptable is useless unless accompanied by guidelines for gift giving, payments to get goods through customs, and "requests" from intermediaries who are hired to ask for bribes.

Motorola's values are stated very simply as "How we will always act: [with] constant respect for people [and] uncompromising integrity." The company's code of conduct, however, is explicit about actual business practice. With respect to bribery, for example, the code states that the "funds and assets of Motorola shall not be used, directly or indirectly, for illegal payments of any kind." It is unambiguous about what sort of payment is illegal: "the payment of a bribe to a public official or the kick-back of funds to an employee of a customer. . . ." The code goes on to prescribe specific procedures for handling commissions to intermediaries, issuing sales invoices, and disclosing confidential information in a sales transaction—all situations in which employees might have an opportunity to accept or offer bribes.

Codes of conduct must be explicit to be useful, but they must also leave room for a manager to use his or her judgment in situations requiring cultural sensitivity. Host-country employees shouldn't be forced to adopt all home-country values and renounce their own. Again, Motorola's code is exemplary. First, it gives clear direction: "Employees of Motorola will respect the laws, customs, and traditions of each country in which they operate, but will, at the same time, engage in no course of conduct which, even if legal, customary, and accepted in any such country, could be deemed to be in violation of the accepted business ethics of Motorola or the laws of the United States relating to business ethics." After laying down such absolutes, Motorola's code then makes clear when individual judgment will be necessary. For example, employees may sometimes accept certain kinds of small gifts "in rare circumstances, where the refusal to accept a gift" would injure Motorola's "legitimate business interests." Under certain circumstances, such gifts "may be accepted so long as the gift inures to the benefit of Motorola" and not "to the benefit of the Motorola employee."

***Many activities are neither good nor bad but exist in* moral free space.**

Striking the appropriate balance between providing clear direction and leaving room for individual judgment makes crafting corporate values statements and ethics codes one of the hardest tasks that executives confront. The words are only a start. A company's leaders need to refer often to their organization's credo and code and must themselves be credible, committed, and consistent. If senior managers act as though ethics don't matter, the rest of the company's employees won't think they do, either.

CONFLICTS OF DEVELOPMENT AND CONFLICTS OF TRADITION

Managers living and working abroad who are not prepared to grapple with moral ambiguity and tension should pack their bags and come home. The view that all business practices can be categorized as either ethical or unethical is too simple. As Einstein is reported to have said, "Things should be as simple as possible—but no simpler." Many business practices that are considered unethical in one setting may be ethical in another. Such activities are neither black nor white but exist in what Thomas Dunfee and I have called *moral free space*. In this gray zone, there are no tight prescriptions for a company's behavior. Managers must chart their own courses—as long as they do not violate core human values.

Consider the following example. Some successful Indian companies offer employees the opportunity for one of their children to gain a job with the company once the child has completed a certain level in school. The companies honor this commitment even when other applicants are more qualified than an employee's child. The perk is extremely valuable in a country where jobs are hard to find, and it reflects the Indian culture's belief that the West has gone too far in allowing economic opportunities to break up families. Not surprisingly, the perk is among the most cherished by employees, but in most Western countries, it would be branded unacceptable nepotism. In the United States, for example, the ethical principle of equal opportunity holds that jobs should go to the applicants with the best qualifications. If a U.S. company made such promises to its employees, it would violate regulations established by the Equal Employment Opportunity Commission. Given this difference in ethical attitudes, how should U.S. managers react to Indian nepotism? Should they condemn the Indian companies, refusing to accept them as partners or suppliers until they agree to clean up their act?

Despite the obvious tension between nepotism and principles of equal opportunity, I cannot condemn the practice for Indians. In a country, such as India, that emphasizes clan and family relationships and has catastrophic levels of unemployment, the practice must be viewed in moral free space. The decision to allow a special perk for employees and their children is not necessarily wrong—at least for members of that country.

How can managers discover the limits of moral free space? That is, how can they learn to distinguish a value in tension with their own from one that is intolerable? Helping managers develop good ethical judgment requires companies to be clear about their core values and codes of conduct. But even the most explicit set of guidelines cannot always provide answers. That is especially true in the thorniest ethical dilemmas, in which the host country's ethical standards not only are different but also seem lower than the home country's. Managers must recognize that when countries have different ethical standards, there are two types of conflict that commonly arise. Each type requires its own line of reasoning.

In the first type of conflict, which I call a *conflict of relative development*, ethical standards conflict because of the countries' different levels of economic development. As mentioned before, developing countries may accept wage rates that seem inhumane to more advanced countries in order to attract investment. As economic conditions in a developing country improve, the incidence of that sort of conflict usually decreases. The second type of conflict is a *conflict of cultural tradition*. For example, Saudi Arabia, unlike most other countries, does not allow women to serve as corporate managers. Instead, women may work in only a few professions, such as education and health care. The prohibition stems from strongly held religious and cultural beliefs; any increase in the country's level of economic development, which is already quite high, is not likely to change the rules.

To resolve a conflict of relative development, a manager must ask the following question: Would the practice be acceptable at home if my country were in a similar stage of economic development? Consider the difference between wage and safety standards in the United States and in Angola, where citizens accept lower standards on both counts. If a U.S. oil company is hiring Angolans to work on an offshore Angolan oil rig, can the company pay them lower wages than it pays U.S. workers in the Gulf of Mexico? Reasonable people have to answer yes if the alternative for Angola is the loss of both the foreign investment and the jobs.

Consider, too, differences in regulatory environments. In the 1980s, the government of India fought hard to be able to import Ciba-Geigy's Entero Vioform, a drug known to be enormously effective in fighting dysentery but one that had been banned in the United States because some users experienced side effects. Although dysentery was not a big problem in the United States, in India, poor public sanitation was contributing to epidemic levels of the disease. Was it unethical to make the drug available in India after it had been banned in the United States? On the contrary, rational people should consider it unethical not to do so. Apply our test: Would the United States, at an earlier stage of development, have used this drug despite its side effects? The answer is clearly yes.

If a company declared all gift giving unethical, it wouldn't be able to do business in Japan.

But there are many instances when the answer to similar questions is no. Sometimes a host country's standards are inadequate at any level of economic development. If a country's pollution standards are so low that working on an oil rig would considerably increase a person's risk of developing cancer, foreign oil companies must refuse to do business there. Likewise, if the dangerous side effects of a drug treatment outweigh its benefits, managers should not accept health standards that ignore the risks.

When relative economic conditions do not drive tensions, there is a more objective test for resolving ethical problems. Managers should deem a practice permissible only if they can answer no to both of the following questions: Is it possible to conduct business successfully in the host country without undertaking the practice? and is the practice a violation of a core human value? Japanese gift giving is a perfect example of a conflict of cultural tradition. Most experienced businesspeople, Japanese and non-Japanese alike, would agree that doing business in Japan would be virtually impossible without adopting the practice. Does gift giving violate a core human value? I cannot identify one that it violates. As a result, gift giving may be permissible for foreign companies in Japan even if it conflicts with ethical attitudes at home. In fact, that conclusion is widely accepted, even by companies such as Texas Instruments and IBM, which are outspoken against bribery.

Does it follow that all nonmonetary gifts are acceptable or that bribes are generally acceptable in countries where they are common? Not at all. (See "The Problem with Bribery" at the end of this article.) What makes the routine practice of gift giving acceptable in Japan are the limits in its scope and intention. When gift giving moves outside those limits, it soon collides with core human values. For example, when Carl Kotchian, president of Lockheed in the 1970s, carried suitcases full of cash to Japanese politicians, he went beyond the norms established by Japanese tradition. That incident galvanized opinion in the United States Congress and helped lead to passage of the Foreign Corrupt Practices Act. Likewise, Roh Tae Woo went beyond the norms established by Korean cultural tradition when he accepted $635.4 million in bribes as president of the Republic of Korea between 1988 and 1993.

GUIDELINES FOR ETHICAL LEADERSHIP

Learning to spot intolerable practices and to exercise good judgment when ethical conflicts arise requires practice. Creating a company culture that rewards ethical behavior is essential. The following guidelines for developing a global ethical perspective among managers can help.

Treat corporate values and formal standards of conduct as absolutes. Whatever ethical standards a company chooses, it cannot waver on its principles either at home or abroad. Consider what has become part of company lore at Motorola. Around 1950, a senior executive was negotiating with officials of a South American government on a $10 million sale that would have increased the company's annual net profits by nearly 25%. As the negotiations neared completion, however, the executive walked away from the deal because the officials were asking for $1 million for "fees." CEO Robert Galvin not only supported the executive's decision but also made it clear that Motorola would neither accept the sale on any terms nor do business with those government officials again. Retold over the decades, this story demonstrating Galvin's resolve has helped cement a culture of ethics for thousands of employees at Motorola.

Design and implement conditions of engagement for suppliers and customers. Will your company do business with any customer or supplier? What if a customer or supplier uses child labor? What if it has strong links with organized crime? What if it pressures your company to break a host country's laws? Such issues are best not left for spur-of-the-moment decisions. Some companies have realized that. Sears, for instance, has developed a policy of not contracting production to companies that use prison labor or infringe on workers' rights to health and safety. And BankAmerica has specified as a condition for many of its loans to developing countries that environmental standards and human rights must be observed.

Allow foreign business units to help formulate ethical standards and interpret ethical issues. The French pharmaceutical company Rhône-Poulenc Rorer has allowed foreign subsidiaries to augment lists of corporate ethical principles with their own suggestions. Texas Instruments has paid special attention to issues of international business ethics by creating the Global Business Practices Council, which is made up of managers from countries in which the company operates. With the overarching intent to create a "global ethics strategy, locally deployed," the council's mandate is to provide ethics education and create local processes that will help managers in the company's foreign business units resolve ethical conflicts.

In host countries, support efforts to decrease institutional corruption. Individual managers will not be able to wipe out corruption in a host country, no matter how many bribes they turn down. When a host country's tax system, import and export procedures, and procurement practices favor unethical players, companies must take action.

Many companies have begun to participate in reforming host-country institutions. General Electric, for example, has taken a strong stand in India, using the media to make repeated condemnations of bribery in business and government. General Electric and others have found, however, that a single company usually cannot drive out entrenched corruption. Transparency International, an organization based in Germany, has been effective in helping coalitions of companies, government, officials, and others work to reform bribery-ridden bureaucracies in Russia, Bangladesh, and elsewhere.

Exercise moral imagination. Using moral imagination means resolving tensions responsibly and creatively. Coca-Cola, for instance, has consistently turned down requests for bribes from Egyptian officials but has managed to gain political support and public trust by sponsoring a project to plant fruit trees. And take the example of Levi Strauss, which discovered in the early 1990s that two of its suppliers in Bangladesh were employing children under the age of 14—a practice that violated the company's principles but was tolerated in Bangladesh. Forcing the suppliers to fire the children would not have ensured that the children received an education, and it would have caused serious hardship for the families depending on the children's wages. In a creative arrangement, the suppliers agreed to pay the children's regular wages while they attended school and to offer each child a job at age 14. Levi Strauss, in turn, agreed to pay the children's tuition and provide books and uniforms. That arrangement allowed Levi Strauss to uphold its principles and provide long-term benefits to its host country.

Many people think of values as soft; to some they are usually unspoken. A South Seas island society uses the word *mokita*, which means, "the truth that everybody knows but nobody speaks." However difficult they are to articulate, values affect how we all behave. In a global business environment, values in tension are the rule rather than the exception. Without a company's commitment, statements of values and codes of ethics end up as empty platitudes that provide managers with no foundation for behaving ethically. Employees need and deserve more, and responsible members of the global business community can set examples for others to follow. The dark consequences of incidents such as Union Carbide's disaster in Bhopal remind us how high the stakes can be.

THE CULTURE AND ETHICS OF SOFTWARE PIRACY

Before jumping on the cultural relativism bandwagon, stop and consider the potential economic consequences of a when-in-Rome attitude toward business ethics. Take a look at the current statistics on software piracy: In the United States, pirated software is estimated to be 35% of the total software market, and industry losses are estimated at $2.3 billion per year. The piracy rate is 57% in Germany and 80% in Italy and Japan; the rates in most Asian countries are estimated to be nearly 100%.

There are similar laws against software piracy in those countries. What, then, accounts for the differences? Although a country's level of economic development plays a large part, culture, including ethical attitudes, may be a more crucial factor. The 1995 annual report of the Software Publishers Association connects software piracy directly to culture and attitude. It describes Italy and Hong Kong as having "'first world' per capita incomes, along with 'third world' rates of piracy." When asked whether one should use software without paying for it, most people, including people in Italy and Hong Kong, say no. But people in some countries regard the practice as *less* unethical than people in other countries do. Confucian culture, for example, stresses that individuals should share what they create with society. That may be, in part, what prompts the Chinese and other Asians to view the concept of intellectual property as a means for the West to monopolize its technological superiority.

What happens if ethical attitudes around the world permit large-scale software piracy? Software companies won't want to invest as much in developing new products, because they cannot expect any return on their investment in certain parts of the world. When ethics fail to support technological creativity, there are consequences that go beyond statistics—jobs are lost and livelihoods jeopardized.

Companies must do more than lobby foreign governments for tougher enforcement of piracy laws. They must cooperate with other companies and with local organizations to help citizens understand the consequences of piracy and to encourage the evolution of a different ethic toward the practice.

THE PROBLEM WITH BRIBERY

Bribery is widespread and insidious. Managers in transnational companies routinely confront bribery even though most countries have laws against it. The fact is that officials in many developing countries wink at the practice, and the salaries of local bureaucrats are so low that many consider bribes a form of remuneration. The U.S. Foreign Corrupt Practices Act defines allowable limits on petty bribery in the form of routine payments required to move goods through customs. But demands for bribes often exceed those limits, and there is seldom a good solution.

Bribery disrupts distribution channels when goods languish on docks until local handlers are paid off, and it destroys incentives to compete on quality and cost when purchasing decisions are based on who pays what under the table. Refusing to acquiesce is often tantamount to giving business to unscrupulous companies.

I believe that even routine bribery is intolerable. Bribery undermines market efficiency and predictability, thus ultimately denying people their right to a minimal standard of living. Some degree of ethical commitment—some sense that everyone will play by the rules—is necessary for a sound economy. Without an ability to predict outcomes, who would be willing to invest?

There was a U.S. company whose shipping crates were regularly pilfered by handlers on the docks of Rio de Janeiro. The handlers would take about 10% of the contents of the crates, but the company was never sure which 10% it would be. In a partial solution, the company began sending two crates—the first with 90% of the merchandise, the second with 10%. The handlers learned to take the second crate and leave the first untouched. From the company's perspective, at least knowing which goods it would lose was an improvement.

Bribery does more than destroy predictability; it undermines essential social and economic systems. That truth is not lost on businesspeople in countries where the practice is woven into the social fabric. CEOs in India admit that their companies engage constantly in bribery, and they say that they have considerable disgust for the practice. They blame government policies in part, but Indian executives also know that their country's business practices perpetuate corrupt behavior. Anyone walking the streets of Calcutta, where it is clear that even a dramatic redistribution of wealth would still leave most of India's inhabitants in dire poverty, comes face-to-face with the devastating effects of corruption.

NEW ETHICS IN THE OFFICE

Robert A. Giacalone

Most of the ethics violations that catch the public attention these days are related to loss of money, loss of power, and loss of esteem. When a society considers ethics violations only in materialistic terms, the response is to create laws like Sarbanes-Oxley, which are designed to protect against financial misconduct.

Unfortunately, that's not the whole story. There is evidence that, around the globe, people are becoming relatively less interested in materialistic values and more interested in an emerging set of post-materialistic values. I say *relatively*, because there's no expectation that people are going to live in mud houses and give up their cars. But people whose basic security needs have been met are shifting their attention to post-materialistic values that revolve around community connectedness, interpersonal relationships, quality of life, and family.

The numbers of people adopting these values are staggering. In 1970, for every four materialists, there was one post-materialist; by the mid-1990s, the ratio was four to three. These values are changing in industrialized countries throughout the world.

As one might imagine, post-materialistic people are interested in working at companies whose values match their own. They want to know if their organization is socially responsible and ecologically sound. They're interested in issues of community well-being. In my work with companies, I have heard stories about senior-level executives who won't accept positions if the job will require them to spend too much time away from their families. I know of companies that are losing well-paid employees because workers are more interested in quality of life than money. It isn't just that these individuals have different values than traditional materialist employees, but that they increasingly are redefining their values preferences in moral terms.

As more post-materialists join the workforce, we will see a change in what's considered ethically acceptable behavior in the workplace—a shift toward concern with unethical actions that harm people in nonfinancial ways. One current example is the increased interest in bullying. There have always been mean kids on the playground and abusive bosses in the corner office, so why is there an interest in the topic now? There's been no change in the law—what has changed is people's sensitivity. We also see more companies wrestling with environmental issues or making provisions for employees who need child care or elder care services. As time goes on, companies that ignore these issues will be seen as ethically cavalier or socially irresponsible.

At the moment, we as a society haven't quite sensitized organizations to these types of ethics violations. Years ago, in a similar fashion, society slowly became aware of the mistreatment of women and minorities. Long before any laws were instituted, people had a sense that such mistreatment was occurring. The first step toward correcting a problem is for a significant percentage of the population to agree that one exists.

Very few business schools are teaching their students about these post-materialistic values, yet I think it's important that we train business students to consider them. In my classes, I'm enlarging the scope of ethical concerns to include issues that have little financial implication. I talk about trends in society that business has instigated and ask students about the impact of these trends on people. I have students look at what is and isn't acceptable in the workplace, including issues of supervisor abuse and long hours. Many students are familiar with these issues from their own life experiences, but never considered them from an ethical stance. More and more are beginning to understand that issues such as quality of work life are not simply about profitability, but about human dignity and ethics.

Students need to see that the competitive edge will go to the first companies to figure out how to deal with these new kinds of ethical issues. From a practical standpoint, managers are going to have to rethink their definitions of what is ethical in the workplace. Of course, no one is asking companies to ignore those ethical issues with financial implications. But as more and more employees with post-materialist values enter the workforce, employers who fail to consider the changing ethical standards that accompany these values will suffer the consequences of their choices.

GET AGGRESSIVE ABOUT PASSIVITY

Judith Samuelson and Mary Gentile

In *Conspiracy of Fools: A True Story*, Kurt Eichenwald relates how Enron's leaders engaged in massive book-cooking with little interference from the dozens of managers, lawyers, and advisers who had a pretty good idea of what was going on. Similarly, at Parmalat, employees not involved in the Italian dairy giant's fraud apparently were aware of it because they often joked about fictitious milk sales to Cuba long before those became a public scandal. Tolerance of organizational bad behavior has become so expected that, in 2002, *Time* magazine named Enron's Sherron Watkins, the FBI's Coleen Rowley, and WorldCom's Cynthia Cooper "Persons of the Year" for going public with stories of organizational failure. Why should simply speaking out about outrageous conduct be so difficult–and so rare?

Psychologists have studied the "bystander effect" and other theories of why people who are aware of wrongdoing fail to intervene. Passivity, it seems, is epidemic, cutting off oxygen to corporate consciences everywhere. Managers and executives generally have the right "values"—that is, they know what they should do when circumstances call on them to take a stand or make a hard choice. If managers acted on those values, and if they applied the same skills they draw on when making a tough sell or marshaling resources for a new business venture, then the misconduct might never escalate to the point where heroic whistle-blowing is required.

But people usually don't act on their values, our research show, because they don't consider such action to be part of their jobs. Businesspeople view moral and ethical dilemmas as exceptions—and human beings don't deal with exceptions terribly well. In extensive interviews with dozens of managers who had confronted ethical quandaries, we heard repeatedly how they considered such questions—even the classic ones case studies often address—to be "extraordinary" or an "intrusion." They talked about being derailed by these issues, not because they felt morally ambivalent but because dealing with these sorts of problems is simply not what they do.

Confronting such dilemmas, managers feel as though they are stepping out of their competent, action-oriented work identities to expose a more personal part of themselves. So they try to swiftly put the problem aside or behind them in order to get back to their "real" work. As a result, they choose paths that present the least friction—the fewest channels to go through and people to persuade, the easiest case to present. One manager described the experience of being forced to choose between standing up to his employer and taking advantage of a client: "In retrospect, the problem I faced really wasn't that overwhelming—that is, once I figured out what I wanted to do. But at first I just tried to get out of it or get beyond it as quickly as I could. In fact, I lied. I instinctively lied to get out of the situation, hoping it wouldn't happen again."

Such conflicts are greatest for employees who define their jobs narrowly: as simply closing the next deal or making the numbers. Managers who view their professional purpose in broad terms—delivering customer value, say, or building a sustainable enterprise—have an easier time with ethical questions, our research suggests. The broader scope encompasses more kinds of decisions, more types of concerns, and so ethical questions can become just another part of the landscape. As a result, those employees are less likely to lay low or obfuscate or even lie to avoid a tricky situation.

Most organizations want workers who don't just think the right thing but also do it. Managers have a responsibility to help employees over their mental hurdles. Leaders who act ethically themselves are necessary but not sufficient—they must also make clear that correctly resolving ethical and moral questions is part of everyone's job and that time spent doing so does, in fact, serve the business. And they should make it easier for employees to seek mentors who will guide them across difficult terrain and to build coalitions among like-minded colleagues willing to share the journey. Some companies are having success with programs in which people practice arguing ethical positions in front of respected leaders and peers.

Luigi Zingales, an entrepreneurship and finance professor at the University of Chicago Graduate School of Business, has suggested making whistle-blowing more common by offering monetary incentives. But whistle-blowing isn't a desirable end; it is a last resort. When we reach that stage, it means we have failed, both as organizations and as people. Rather than lionizing the exception, let us make the contemplation of moral and ethical questions the stuff of everyday work.

JUDITH SAMUELSON *(judy.samuelson@aspeninst.org) is the executive director of the Business and Society Program of the Aspen Institute, a nonprofit organization headquartered in Washington, DC, that is devoted to improving leadership.* **MARY GENTILE** *(mcgentile@aol.com) is the research director of the institute's most recent leadership development initiative, Giving Voice to Values.*

THE COURAGE TO BE MORAL

Rushworth Kidder

If humanity is to survive and avoid new catastrophes, then the global political order has to be accompanied by a sincere and mutual respect among the various spheres of civilization, culture, nations, or continents, and by honest efforts on their part to seek and find the values or basic moral imperatives they have in common.

—Václav Havel

Though she's now the chief executive of a financial services firm, Valerie would be the first to tell you she comes from a modest family background. She has no personal wealth behind her. No trust funds cushioned her upbringing. No family business spun off profits in her direction. She didn't grow up at country clubs or on yachts, nor did she rub shoulders with friends whose parents sat on boards or dispensed charitable largesse throughout the community. Quite the opposite.

"When I was twelve, my father lost our home and family business in a bankruptcy," she recalls. "He walked out, discouraged and angry, never helping in any way through the years." She and her mother "moved from two new cars, fancy schools and clothes, and household help to a small farming town where we were clearly poor." Smart and hardworking, she learned money management as a vocation, picking it up not from well-heeled family members but through careful study in academic and professional circles.

Given her current line of work, those are important points. Her business has only one client: a large, multigenerational family of substantial wealth. As head of the Family Office, Valerie's task is to manage more than fifty employees in a variety of professions—law, accounting, auditing, financial planning—who provide whatever services the hundreds of family members need as they grow and sustain their many-faceted fortunes.

In the eight years Valerie has been in this position, she's done exceedingly well by her clients. Her contract, which pays her nicely but not extravagantly, reflects their satisfaction with her work. She's happy with her job. She respects the family. She has found plenty to keep her professionally satisfied. Which is why she was surprised by the moral courage she suddenly had to display not long ago in the face of a powerful temptation.

She was approached by the founder of another financial services firm, whom she thought of as a reputable man. His search for a new chief executive had led him to her doorstep. Being content where she was, Valerie had no difficulty initially deflecting the offer. Soon a sweeter deal was on the table. It multiplied her salary considerably and provided the potential for significant additional benefits. No longer quite so sure of her position, she struggled with the offer, hesitating to take it. The longer she stalled, the more the offer continued to rise, until she could no longer resist discussing it with the founder of the firm.

The more he talked, the more she found him persuasive. It was, indeed, a most attractive job. It would properly reward her for a record of excellent work. It would crown an already exemplary career with a satisfying sense of accomplishment. And although she never set out to be a "textbook case" of anything, this job could catapult her into a category she'd always admired: the self-made American success story.

So the negotiations moved forward to a final offer. In it, the founder stipulated that she should begin work immediately. Under Valerie's Family Office contract, however, she had a clear obligation to give the family six months' notice that she was leaving. The only way to avoid that requirement would be for her to indicate that she was dissatisfied with her current employer, or that she needed to move on for the sake of her professional growth and had initiated the conversation with the other company herself, neither of which was true. The founder of the offering firm, anticipating this problem, included the text of a letter from Valerie to the Family Office asserting these very things. All that was needed was Valerie's signature.

Taken aback by that request, she told the founder she could not do such a thing. She saw it as fundamentally dishonest under the law, irresponsible to her prior commitments, and disrespectful to a family she liked very much. The founder, however, had anticipated that response as well. His counteroffer was immediate: an additional $1 million to secure her signature.

Valerie never wavered. Something deep in her nature—call it conscience, conviction, principles, values, integrity—gave her the courage to refuse. Her explanation was simple. She told the founder she could not work for someone who requested her to lie or break a promise made in good faith to her employer. While the request itself concerned her mightily, she was even more troubled by what it told her about her prospective employer—and, by extension, the organizational culture he was probably creating at his firm. Rejecting an offer that was extraordinary by every measure, Valerie remained at the Family Office. Nor did she use that incident as a source of leverage with the family to increase her compensation. She remains well paid, though she has never become rich.

Does that matter? Given her background, she admits that "a really good income was probably more of a temptation to me than most people. I remember on my thirteenth birthday deciding that this was a valuable experience, being really poor, but *once* was enough."

She learned, she said, that "girls had to get educations and make good livings to support themselves and their families. And if they want to get married they shouldn't marry flashy and high maintenance, like Dad, they should marry steady and true and committed."

The qualities identified by that thirteen-year-old—steady and true and committed—were still there decades later when this temptation arose. So was something else. "I have learned to think financial *serenity*," she says, "not financial *security*." Taken together, those values undergirded her courage to resist that temptation. Today, she's sure enough of her decision that she can still look herself in the mirror and know she did the right thing.

But what if, like the witch's mirror in the fable of Snow White, hers could talk back? What would it tell her?

Maybe it would say, "Foolish girl! You had a promise of immense future wealth right in your hands, and you walked away. You know you've never had much, and this was your chance to make it *really* big. Call that moral courage? I call it stupidity."

Or maybe it would say, "Good for you. You resisted one of the most subtle temptations that life can toss up. Even if he hadn't turned out to be a wholesale prevaricator, even if he didn't start deceiving you as well as others, even if that were the last lie he'd ever been party to—you couldn't have accepted those terms and still lived by your values. You'd have compromised the most important thing about yourself—your character. You stood up to that lie. That took real moral courage."

At its simplest, then, moral courage is *the courage to be moral.* But what, the mirror might ask, does *moral* mean? Valerie's experience reveals her reliance on three values: *honesty, responsibility,* and *respect.* That's not surprising. Those are three of the core values that define our sense of the word *moral.* With two others—*fairness* and *compassion*—they make up the five-fingered hand that appears to constitute humanity's common moral framework.

Humanity's common moral framework. Can there be such a thing? Given the global diversity of culture, ethnicity, race, religion, gender, political persuasion, economic disparity, and educational attainment, is it possible to discover a core of shared values operating across all these variations? Is it possible that the moral relativism so vigorously espoused in the twentieth century is simply a hypothesized intellectual convenience rather than an empirical fact? Is there really a deep ethic, a substrate of moral values that provides constant aspirational direction to human endeavor throughout the world?

Or is morality simply a set of personal and fungible guidelines for behavior, shifting with each situation, varying widely from culture to culture, and easily negotiable on occasions where, as in Valerie's case, an extra $1 million suddenly appears on the table?

Based on our research at the Institute for Global Ethics, the former appears to be true. It's becoming clear that, wherever we go in the world and ask, "What do you think are the core moral and ethical values held in highest regard in your community?" we hear the same five answers: *honesty, responsibility, respect, fairness*, and *compassion*. As the following sections indicate, the evidence for this five-fingered hand of values—drawn from global interviewing, facilitated discourse, survey research, and textual analysis—goes very deep.

GLOBAL INTERVIEWING

In the early 1990s, I conducted face-to-face interviews with twenty-four people from sixteen countries. Each interviewee, in the eyes of his or her peers, was something of an ethical standard-bearer—"a keeper of the conscience of their community," as I described them at the time, "a center of moral gravity." To each I put a common question: If you could help create a global code of ethics, what would be in it? What moral values would you bring to the table from your own culture and background?

The resulting interviews came together in 1994 in my book *Shared Values for a Troubled World: Conversations with Men and Women of Conscience*. If the interviewees could have addressed these questions together in the same room rather than in the pages of a book, they would have emerged, I felt, with the following list of common values:

- Love
- Truthfulness
- Fairness
- Freedom
- Unity
- Tolerance
- Responsibility
- Respect for life

This list is not in priority order. And the words are less important than the ideas: "Love," for example, might have been reported as *compassion, caring, kindness*, or *empathy*, while "truthfulness" could have appeared as *integrity* or *honesty*. Yet however diverse their backgrounds, these interviewees appeared to hold in common these eight major moral ideas.

These interviews were, of course, examples of journalism. As such, they depended on a relationship of trust between writer and reader regarding some key questions. Why were these interviewees selected? What were they asked? How were their responses interpreted? Which of their comments were reported, and which were not? Only when the reader believes the reporter has worked hard to achieve objectivity will that trust be created.

At its best, then, journalism is flawed. It typically gets the story first and tells it in compelling ways. But it doesn't always get it right. For that, three other methodologies are helpful: facilitated discourse, survey research, and textual analysis. Each of these methods seeks to extend the pool of participants, ensure greater levels of objectivity, and impose higher standards of validity. If, as has been noted, "the plural of *anecdotes* is *data*," these methods seek to move from storytelling to social science, building from narratives to numbers in an effort to create other kinds of arguments.

HOTLINES HELPFUL FOR BLOWING THE WHISTLE

Paul Sweeney

Question: What is the No. 1 deterrent to corporate fraud? If you guessed "tips"—and if this had been a TV game show—you'd have hit the jackpot.

Most studies consistently show that about a third of the instances of business and workplace fraud that eventually come to light were first disclosed by employees or other key informants blowing the whistle. Most recently, this was confirmed in 2006 by the Association of Certified Fraud Examiners (ACFE) in its biennial, in-depth survey. The fraud-busting group found that 34.2 percent of "occupational fraud"—defined essentially as misusing one's position at an organization for personal economic gain—was first detected by tipsters.

Tips, according to ACFE's survey, work better at detecting white-collar larceny than a whole panoply of formalized legalistic procedures. Disclosure of fraud from informants outpaces internal audits (20.2 percent), internal controls (19.2 percent) and external audits (12 percent).

None of those more orthodox constraints, moreover, qualified for the second-most-common way that rip-offs are uncovered. A quarter of occupational fraud (25.4 percent) was detected "by accident," according to ACFE.

Together, tips and accidental discovery account for nearly 60 percent of all fraud detection, which speaks to the capricious and serendipitous nature of combating thievery that is often elaborate and technologically sophisticated. Unlike an old-fashioned bank embezzler, who stuffs cash into a valise and blows town, modern defalcation schemes typically involve adding or removing accounting entries into a computer or remitting payments to spurious addresses.

In cases where top company executives or owners concocted a scam, ACFE reports, the percentage of frauds first uncovered by tips alone rises still further—up to 48 percent, or nearly half. That is especially significant because, ACFE notes, dollar losses resulting from conniving top executives and owners "tend to be larger than for any other group."

All told, ACFE reports, fraud in 2006 accounted for losses of roughly $652 billion in the U.S., or 5 percent of annual corporate revenues.

The fact that tips are the No. 1 fraud detection method and that whistleblowers played a key role in uncovering the multi-billion-dollar scandals earlier this decade at Enron Corp. and WorldCom Inc. has not been lost on lawmakers. The Sarbanes-Oxley Act, enacted in 2002, requires that publicly traded companies maintain reporting mechanisms, including a toll-free whistleblower hotline, and that oversight is lodged with the audit committee.

Today, according to the Security Executive Council's 2007 report, some 81 percent of public and private companies have instituted whistle-blower hotlines. Companies employing "best practices," says Ron Durkin, a forensic accountant at KPMG and a former FBI agent, have added "robust" training and education programs that encourage not only employees but vendors and customers to call the hotline if they see anything that looks amiss.

"People need awareness training," he says, "so that if they see that a particular vendor is always getting contracts or that it seems like he's being paid more than other vendors, it could, indicate an improper relationship and misappropriation of company assets."

Increasingly, companies are taking such concerns to heart. At Molson Coors Brewing Co., for example, "Just about every speech our chief executive makes is about doing business according to our ethics and values," says spokesman Paul de la Plante. "It's an important topic, and it's embedded in our culture."

Warren Buffett, the celebrated billionaire chairman at Berkshire Hathaway, announced in 2005 that his holding company would implement a whistleblower hotline. "Berkshire would be more valuable today if I had put in a whistleblower line decades ago," he wrote in his letter to stockholders.

Paul Regan, president of the forensic *accounting firm* Hemming Morse in San Francisco, says that he regularly gets involved in fraud investigations first uncovered by tips. A typical recent case that owed its discovery to a company hotline, Regan says, involved a ruse contrived by the controller at a trucking company. Essentially, the executive—who is now in jail—was billing the company for "maintenance repairs at facilities [that were] never done," a scheme that cost the company a half-million dollars before it was halted.

The controller-turned-scam artist, Regan says, devised a scheme to generate phony invoices from a nonexistent truck repair business and approve checks that were mailed to a post office box. "And then he just took the money," Regan says, adding: "Checks mailed to P.O. boxes can be a red flag."

The ACFE reports that "asset misappropriation"—such as the falsifying of invoices, payroll fraud and revenue-skimming that Regan was describing—accounted for 90 percent of occupational fraud. Yet it was the least costly, resulting in median losses of $150,000. "Corruption," which includes engaging in bribery or conflicts of interest, was the next most common fraud, with 38 percent of the cases, resulting in median losses of $538,000.

Financial fraud ranks third in frequency, accounting for just 10.6 percent of the reported fraud cases. It typically entails such practices as booking fictitious sales or inflating inventory and expenses. But, the ACFE reports, it is arguably the most pernicious, creating median losses of $2 million per instance. Falsified documents may also be among the hardest of frauds to detect.

To be fair, some observers say the importance of hotlines is debatable. Stuart Stein, a partner in the Washington law office of Hogan & Hartson, says: "I really haven't seen that much in terms of hotline utilization that rises to a senior level of concern. Typically, if a more senior officer in the company believes financial malfeasance or misdeeds are occurring or that the direction management is taking is incorrect, that person will go to the treasurer or chief financial officer or chief executive—or take (the issue) directly to the audit committee."

Nonetheless, says Cathy Fleming, a law partner at Nixon Peabody in New York, the Sarbanes-Oxley compliance environment has made "whistleblowers a hotter topic. And auditors and the general counsel have become more attuned to their concerns and are paying more attention. It's easier to fix problems internally than to have outsiders come in and tell you that you have to fix it."

Despite the high visibility of whistleblowers' salutary role in keeping organizations honest and the encomiums they've earned in recent years—most notably, Time magazine named Enron's Sherron Watkins, WorldCom's Cynthia Cooper and the FBI's Coleen Rowley its "Persons of the Year" in 2002 for their bravery in combating corporate and governmental corruption—it remains a precarious calling. Cooper, who was interviewed in the midst of a book tour touting her WorldCom memoir, Extraordinary Circumstances: The Journey of a Corporate Whistleblower, says she is regularly approached these days by whistleblowers sharing stories of rough treatment after being labeled as troublemakers or disgruntled employees.

"Two people recently came up to me in tears, reliving what they had gone through," Cooper said in a telephone interview. "They told about being isolated in the workplace and pushed out of their organizations and struggling to find new employment."

Donna Sockell, a business ethics and industrial relations expert at the University of Colorado, says: "It worries me that there's a presumption against the motivation of a whistleblower and that you can be blackballed. How do you tell a someone in a job interview, 'Well, I discovered the employer was diverting funds and I couldn't live with that.'"

Under Sarbanes-Oxley, whistle-blowers are granted legal protections enabling them to report financial and accounting irregularities without fear that they will suffer demotion, harassment, threats or retribution. The Occupational Safety and Health Administration, a division of the U.S. Department of Labor, hears and adjudicates charges of retaliation.

The agency has the ability to find in favor of whistleblowers and impose such remedies as reinstatement, back wages and "expungement" of negative material from personnel files. But, while those protections look good on paper, says Thomas Devine, legal director at the Government Accountability Project, "The reality of Sarbanes-Oxley is that few whistleblowers prevail."

Richard Moberly, a law professor at the University of Nebraska, testified to Congress during hearings on whistle-blower protection in May 2007, reporting that the current process provides "many but not sufficient protections." His exhaustive review of 700 decisions in whistleblower cases heard by OSHA under Sarbanes-Oxley found that only 3.6 percent won relief, and only 6.5 percent won appeals in front of a Department of Labor administrative law judge.

Deloitte's Bishop acknowledges that whistleblowers have a tough row to hoe. But, ever the optimist, he believes that can change if society just rethinks its attitudes toward whistleblowers. He would like to see more organizations commending tipsters much in the way that the Austin, Texas-based ACFE salutes whistleblowers with the "Cliff Robertson Sentinel Award."

Robertson, the Oscar-winning actor and the first recipient of the award, was made a persona non grata in Hollywood when he discovered that a Tinseltown mogul had improperly cashed an $11,000 check.

For now, whistleblowers will do well to familiarize themselves with hotlines run by such companies as Allegiance Inc., a Salt Lake City-based vendor. A competitor, The Network, based in Atlanta, offers Report-Line and EthicsLine products that are recommended by the fraud examiners group. It also boasts half the Fortune 500 companies as clients.

Both promise anonymity—so much so that Allegiance brands its proprietary product "SilentWhistle"—as well as day-long and year-long global access and skilled professional operators, familiar with securities laws and whistleblowing statutes, who are trained to get to the bottom of a tipster's story. Increasingly, hotlines are adding an online capability as well.

Clay Osborne, director of Silent-Whistle, notes that its annual service costs as little as 50 cents an employee. Its 2,200 clients include more than 200 banks and credit unions. For their money, they also get a service with the capability to understand a whistle-blower's tale in 173 languages.

If companies can save just a fraction of that $650 billion a year that fraud costs Corporate America, chances are hotlines programs pay for themselves.

PAUL SWEENEY (easysween@aol.com) is a freelance writer in Austin, Texas, and a frequent contributor to Financial Executive.

QUESTIONS ON READINGS FOR PART SEVEN

A review of ethical relativism . . . what is it?

What are Donaldson's and Kidder's views on ethical relativism? On the universality of certain values?

Donaldson: "Values in Tension: Ethics away from home"

What principles does Donaldson recommend we use as a guide when doing business in foreign countries?

What are the two types of conflicts in values across borders?

What kinds of problems have whistleblowers reported?

What are some of the difficulties that whistleblowers face?

Do you think you would blow the whistle on corporate wrongdoing? Why or why not?

CENTER FOR EDUCATION ON SOCIAL RESPONSIBILITY

CASE # 10:
WHISTLE BLOWING

CRITICS BLOW WHISTLE ON LAW

By ASHBY JONES And JOANN S. LUBLIN

November 1, 2010

Costly Cases

Some large whistleblower cases:

Settling company	Settlement amount*	Year deal reached	Main charge that was settled
Pfizer	$2.3 billion	2009	Improper marketing of Bextra
Eli Lilly	$1.4 billion	2009	Improper marketing of Zyprexa
Tenet Healthcare	$900 million	2006	Improper Medicare billing
TAP Pharmaceutical	$875 million	2001	Improper marketing of Lupron
GlaxoSmithKline	$750 million	2010	Defective drugs
Columbia/HCA Healthcare	$745 million	2000	Improper Medicare billing

* Settlement reached between company and government, includes any criminal penalties
Source: Taxpayers Against Fraud; Justice Department; WSJ Research

A new law that provides financial incentives for employees to tell regulators about securities fraud and other wrongdoing threatens to increase costs for companies and undermine internal fraud detection efforts launched under the 2002 Sarbanes-Oxley law, corporate lawyers and advisers say.

The incentives add to existing whistleblower laws that regulators use to investigate companies. One such law, the False Claims Act, helped secure a $750 million settlement between drugmaker GlaxoSmithKline PLC and the Justice Department last week. Cheryl Eckard, a whistleblower and former Glaxo quality assurance manager, stands to get $96 million.

The sweeping Dodd-Frank financial reform law passed in July will apply similar types of financial rewards to a much larger universe of wrongdoing, including many types of securities or accounting fraud or bribery allegations, not covered by prior whistleblowing laws.

The "bounty" provision "runs in direct opposition" to internal fraud-detection efforts put in place or beefed up under the Sarbanes-Oxley law that passed after a wave of accounting scandals, says Richard Crist, chief ethics and compliance officer at Allstate Insurance Co. "It undermines a lot of work that a lot of us have done."

In the past, companies typically attempted to address certain fraud allegations internally by setting up confidential hotlines through which employees report alleged ethical misdeeds and illegal behavior. But the Dodd-Frank provision offers a financial incentive to ignore a company's own process and run straight to the government, management lawyers say.

Corporate whistleblowers who take original evidence of financial fraud under the Dodd-Frank law directly to the U.S. Securities and Exchange Commission or the Commodity Futures Trading Commission stand to get between 10% and 30% of a penalty that is over $1 million.

Meanwhile, plaintiffs lawyers eager to handle complaints on behalf of whistleblowers are getting the word out, issuing press releases and publishing articles about the new law and in some instances, running ads soliciting work.

"We're gearing up, we're going to be very devoted to this topic," said Rebecca Katz, a lawyer at Bernstein Liebhard LLP, a plaintiffs firm based in New York. Ms. Katz said the calls to the firm from potential whistleblowers have "gone up tenfold" since the law was passed, but that the firm has been judicious in passing information to the SEC. "I don't want to throw something at the SEC without having analyzed it, looked at it, made sure it's going to get taken seriously," Ms. Katz said.

Whistleblower claims under the False Claims Act largely target fraud perpetrated on the government. But Dodd-Frank opens a broad new arena for possible complaints: violations of the securities laws. The SEC said it has already received hundreds of whistleblower tips since the passage of the law, some of which it is investigating.

"Which do you think is going to win—an internal whistleblower program that relies on trust or one that offers a huge financial bounty?" asks Kenneth Grady, the general counsel at Wolverine World Wide Inc., the owner of Hush Puppies, Merrell and other shoe brands. "For a whistleblower, it's a no brainer."

Some corporate-governance experts say financial incentives are needed to draw out more whistleblowers, especially since internal programs sometimes don't work. Ms. Eckard, who blew the whistle on GSK, raised concerns internally before being terminated, according to her lawyer.

"She raised the issue internally first, which is the way it should work," said Allstate's Mr. Crist, although the example doesn't alleviate his fears that some employees might report to the government first.

The SEC, which under the law must come up with specific rules to handle tips, is expected to release proposed rules by the end of the year and ask for public comment. Companies and their directors are lobbying regulators to minimize the impact of the provision on the private sector.

Kenneth Daly, president of the National Association of Directors, says he hopes to meet with SEC officials this week and suggest the agency avoid investigating a complaint unless the individual already has gone through his or her employer's complaint system.

Kathleen Edmond, the chief ethics officer at retailer Best Buy Co., says her company doesn't plan to offer financial rewards to internal whistleblowers, but will continue to lavish attention and recognition on employees that "do the right thing," and tell the company of wrongdoing first.

Last summer, the company feted an employee who blew the whistle on a scheme that defrauded the company some $41 million between June 2003 and August 2007. "We lauded him and publicized what he did," recalled Ms. Edmond. "We think it strengthened our culture."

"We hope that blowing the whistle internally is so comfortable that people won't go outside," she says.

Other labor experts say more companies should offer small incentives to encourage employees to come forward. "You can give spot financial awards—$1,000 here and $1,000 there—to people who keep their concerns inside the company," said Dan Westman, a labor and employment lawyer at Morrison & Foerster LLP in McLean, Va.

Compared with the likely bigger government incentives, corporate whistleblowing rewards "need to be more timely" to be effective, adds Michael Brozzetti, CEO of Boundless LLC, a Philadelphia internal-audit consultancy.

—Kara Scannell contributed to this article.

Write to Ashby Jones at ashby.jones@wsj.com and Joann.lublin@wsj.com.

MERCK TO PAY $650 MILLION IN MEDICAID SETTLEMENT

Carrie Johnson

Merck agreed yesterday to pay more than $650 million to settle charges that it routinely overbilled the government for its most popular medicines, the arthritis drug Vioxx and the cholesterol drug Zocor, cheating Medicaid out of millions of dollars in discounts over eight years.

Prosecutors say the drugmaker gave pills to hospitals at virtually no cost to hook poor patients on expensive medicine. When the patients left the hospital, they often continued taking the drugs, but with the government footing the higher bill.

The Merck settlement culminates an investigation that began in 2000 and is one of the first in a series of cases centering on whether drugmakers used unfair pricing practices to bilk the government. The Justice Department is looking into 630 health-care whistleblower claims.

H. Dean Steinke, a district sales manager for Merck, set off the investigation after he noticed his company was using questionable sales tactics. Steinke complained to his supervisors, who brushed him off, so he turned to federal authorities.

Steinke, a 51-year-old Michigan native, will receive about $68 million from the settlement as a whistleblower reward. He said he was prompted to go to authorities after his direct supervisor told him: "I don't care how you do it, but get the damn business," when he questioned the sales practices. "There comes a time when you just dig in your heels and say, 'You know what? They're not going to get away with it,'" Steinke said.

The agreement yesterday, one of the largest health-care fraud recoveries, also closes a related case about Merck overcharging for the antacid Pepcid. William St. John LaCorte, a doctor in New Orleans who questioned the Pepcid charges, will receive a yet-to-be-determined share of the settlement proceeds.

Merck did not admit wrongdoing. The country's third-largest drugmaker stood by its pricing strategies but wanted to resolve the disputes, executives said in a statement. Merck agreed to heightened oversight by regulators for five years as part of the deal. The company remains the focus of a separate grand jury investigation related to Vioxx marketing and is striving to execute another multibillion-dollar settlement of thousands of lawsuits filed by people who had heart attacks after taking the painkiller.

The whistleblowing case centered on Merck's giving hospitals across the country 92 percent discounts on Vioxx, an arthritis drug pulled from the market three years ago for safety concerns; Zocor, a popular cholesterol-lowering medicine that drew intense competition from rivals; and Pepcid, an antacid tablet now sold over-the-counter. Merck offered the pills at the discount under a legal loophole, known as nominal pricing, that Congress created a generation ago to give poor patients access to medicine.

Merck and industry experts had argued that the pricing strategy fell within the law and helped reduce costs for many government-funded hospitals. But prosecutors said the Whitehouse Station, N.J., drugmaker used the discounts to outflank its competition, offering massive markdowns to hospitals that agreed to put its medicines on a list of preferred drugs or to prescribe them for as many as three-quarters of eligible patients. In some cases, hospitals favored Merck's drugs over cheaper generics. This practice conflicted with the law because Merck did not offer Medicaid the same discounts, authorities said. The law requires the government be charged no more than other customers.

"The company perceived a loophole and tried to drive through that loophole," said L. Timothy Terry, who leads Nevada's Medicaid Fraud Control Unit and who played a central role in the case. "I think they were exploiting these programs."

The pricing allegations cover bills paid by federal Medicaid plans and plans for states from California to New York. Patrick Burns, a spokesman for Taxpayers Against Fraud, a nonprofit group that supports the pursuit of such cases, said the settlement calls attention to an improper business strategy that has been used by as many as a dozen other drug companies.

"It's heroin-dealer economics," he said. "Your first shot is for free, and after that it becomes more expensive . . . not to the hospital but to Medicaid, which is paying the bill."

Congress tightened the nominal pricing loophole at issue in the Merck case, but prescription drug costs continue to rise steadily, a major issue for presidential candidates jockeying to present health-care reform plans. Meanwhile, on Capitol Hill, such key lawmakers as Sen. Charles E. Grassley (R-Iowa) and Rep. Henry A. Waxman (D-Calif.) are pressing government administrators for better oversight of drug spending.

But, as the Merck investigation underscores, the road to financial recovery for the government and for the whistleblower is not always clear, or direct.

The Merck case had been quietly proceeding under court seal since December 2000, after Steinke came forward in Michigan. He initially worried that Merck's sales campaigns ran afoul of laws that prohibit kickbacks to doctors and hospitals. Over time, the case expanded into a deeper examination of whether Merck had complied with rules requiring manufacturers to offer federal and state agencies their "best price" on drugs.

Steinke took his case to Steven H. Cohen, of Chicago, and Mark Allen Kleiman of Santa Monica, Calif., lawyers who regularly handle whistleblower cases. Together, they filed a lawsuit and waited to see whether federal prosecutors in Philadelphia would intervene, which would have strengthened their case and potentially offered a big financial reward under the False Claims Act. More than three years passed with no clear word from government officials in Philadelphia or Washington about the Justice Department's interest in the case. Then Cohen and Kleiman learned that personnel changes in the U.S. attorney's office meant they needed to introduce new officials to the complex issues and the 10,000 pages of documents Steinke had compiled.

Sitting down with a new, skeptical lead prosecutor in 2004 marked a low point, the lawyers recalled. The allegations were too complicated, the prosecutor said, and the case was too difficult to prove. The lawyers reluctantly agreed with her.

"It was gut-wrenching," said Kleiman, a former health-care executive who attended law school after his own negative experience with corporate corruption.

"This will be called the worst day in our life," added Cohen, a former congressional staff member and the son-in-law of retired D.C. federal appeals court judge Abner Mikva.

Their mood lifted weeks later, when they bumped into a Nevada health-care official at a conference and he invited them to discuss their case. Steinke and the lawyers traveled to Carson City, Nev., where Deputy Attorney General Tim Terry told them he was interested. "Tim was a real advocate for us, immediately," Steinke said. By then he had left Merck and joined another pharmaceutical company. Eventually, he got out of the business.

Steinke's thick brown hair turned gray as he spent weeks of vacation time sitting in conference rooms in Philadelphia and Carson City, poring over 440 boxes of documents to help prosecutors make sense of the scheme. To decompress, he built a wooden deck in his backyard. The construction project consumed seven years.

Steinke, who has an undergraduate degree in fisheries and wildlife biology, said he has not drafted a blueprint for his future. He has a notion, though, to start a rehabilitation center for wounded animals with some of his settlement proceeds. For him, he said, the issue was not one of money but of principle.

"Sometimes you just get so frustrated about things that are wrong," he said. "These are the things that drive you, and you're not going to stop until things are resolved."

2ND WSJ UPDATE: MERCK SETTLES SALES, MARKETING PROBES

by Peter Loftus

PHILADELPHIA (Dow Jones)—Merck & Co. (MRK) has agreed to pay more than $650 million to resolve government investigations and lawsuits related to the drug maker's pricing programs and marketing efforts.

The settlements resolve allegations that Merck underpaid rebates to the Medicaid health program for the poor, in connection with drugs Zocor, Vioxx and others. Also, the settlement resolves accusations that Merck paid improper inducements to doctors and other health-care professionals.

The Merck settlements are the latest examples of heightened government scrutiny of the pharmaceutical industry, which has stemmed from increased drug prices, questionable marketing and advertising practices and drug safety concerns. What's more, Merck recently agreed to a $4.85 billion settlement of product-liability litigation surrounding Vioxx.

"When a big drug company like Merck takes extraordinary and excessive measures to artificially sustain higher prices the government must pay for drugs, or engages in kickbacks to increase market share, higher costs to all of us are the bottom line." Patrick Meehan, U.S. Attorney for the Eastern District of Pennsylvania, said at a press conference here Thursday.

Merck shares rose 3 cents to $45.74 in recent trading.

(This story and related background material will be available on The Wall Street Journal Web site. WSJ.com)

Costs of the settlement will be covered by a $670 million charge that Merck booked for the fourth quarter of last year. Merck, Whitehouse Station, N.J., said Thursday the settlements don't constitute an admission of any liability or wrongdoing.

"Merck believes its pricing and sales and marketing policies and practices were consistent with all applicable regulations and contracts during the relevant time," the company said in a press release.

The settlements stem partly from whistleblower lawsuits filed against the company. In one case filed in 2005, former Merck sales representative Dean Steinke alleged that Merck violated a Medicaid rebate law in connection with its marketing of the Zocor cholesterol-lowering drug and Vioxx, a pain drug that Merck pulled from the market in 2004 after it was linked to increased risk of cardiovascular disease.

Merck allegedly offered deep discounts for Zocor and Vioxx to hospitals if they used large quantities of the drugs in place of rival products, according to the Justice Department. The prices, known as "nominal pricing," amounted to less than 10% of the average manufacturers' price, the government said.

The government alleged Merck improperly excluded such discounts from prices it reported to the government. Medicaid is supposed to get the best price available for a drug, but the government argued that Merck's improper price calculations deprived Medicaid of the best price.

Federal law requires drug makers to give Medicaid the best price they offer any customer. But an exception in the 1990 law says medicines sold at a discount of 90% or more don't have to be disclosed or included in the best-price calculation. That steep discount was meant to let companies make inexpensive medicines available to charitable organizations.

The law doesn't specifically say who can receive the special pricing. But federal and state regulators alleged that Merck's pricing for the hospitals didn't qualify for such an exception, because it came in exchange for the hospitals agreeing to boost the share of Merck's drug they prescribed at the expense of rival drugs. In essence, the government said, the low price was offered for marketing rather than charitable purposes. Patients would likely stay on these drugs once they left the hospital, the suit said, further boosting Merck's sales.

Steinke's lawsuit also alleged that from 1997 to 2001, Merck had various sales programs designed to induce physicians to prescribe its products. The inducements were allegedly "excess payments" disguised as fees for training, consultation and market research. The government characterized these fees as illegal kickbacks.

Meehan said examples of the inducements included all-expense paid trips to Florida and payments of up to $1,500 to individual doctors. Since 2001, Merck has taken steps to rectify the sales programs and has cooperated with investigators, Meehan said.

Steinke worked for Merck from 1995 to 2001, first as a sales rep then as a manager for the Michigan sales region, according to court documents. Under laws designed to encourage whistleblowers, he will receive $44.7 million from the federal government's share of the settlement that was announced in Philadelphia, plus $23.5 million from the states' share.

The settlement announced in Philadelphia totaled $399 million, comprising $218 million to be paid to the federal government and $181 million for 49 states and the District of

Columbia, plus interest. Meehan's office investigated the matters with attorneys general from various states including Nevada.

In a separate settlement, Merck agreed to pay $250 million plus interest to settle allegations from a New Orleans physician, William St. John LaCorte. In a lawsuit filed in federal court in 1999, he accused Merck of using a discount pricing scheme to encourage hospitals to use the Pepid heartburn drug, but not reporting the discounts to the government for purposes of calculating best prices. The state of Louisiana had filed its own complaint against Merck incorporating these allegations.

LaCorte also will receive a share of proceeds from the federal and state settlements related to his lawsuit, but the Justice Department didn't say how much.

Merck also agreed to enter into a corporate integrity agreement with the Office of Inspector General of the U.S. Department of Health and Human Services. This incorporates the company's existing comprehensive compliance program, which was enhanced in 2001, governing its pharmaceutical sales and marketing activities in the U.S. Merck's compliance program includes specific policies and procedures for its interactions with healthcare professionals and is designed to help prevent, detect and resolve potential violations of company policy or the law.

MERCK WHISTLEBLOWER WINS $68M AWARD

Associated Press

PHILADELPHIA (AP)—A sales manager who 'just couldn't abide' by the way Merck wanted him to market the drugs Vioxx and Zocor to doctors took the lonely step of filing a whistleblower suit against his employer.

Seven years later, Merck & Co. will pay $671 million to settle complaints it overcharged government health programs and gave doctors improper inducements to prescribe its drugs.

And whistleblower H. Dean Steinke, the Michigan sales manager whose lawsuit led to about $400 million of the recovery, gets a $68 million reward.

'He did it because he really, truly thought that Merck was doing the wrong thing and he just couldn't abide by it, even though he was putting his career on hold,' said Steinke's lawyer, Steven Cohen of Chicago. His small firm, which specializes in such cases, will receive an undisclosed share of the award.

Steinke, who through his lawyer declined an interview, had climbed the sales ladder at Merck for about 12 years and was a district sales manager when he filed the lawsuit. He made the move only after his internal complaints were ignored, Cohen said.

Steinke believed that Merck, as it introduced the much-anticipated painkiller Vioxx and tried to ward off competition for Zocor, an anti-cholesterol drug, had crossed the line when it came to inducements to physicians.

The government investigated his sealed lawsuit, which also alleged that Merck overcharged government health plans, under the Federal False Claims Act.

Prosecutors ultimately alleged that Merck paid physicians, hospitals and others excess fees to run supposed educational programs, from lunches to speaking engagements to visiting professorships, in hopes they would favor their products.

Prosecutors also accused Merck of giving doctors and hospitals steep volume-based discounts on Vioxx, Zocor and Pepcid, in the hope that patients would come to rely on them. The company failed to offer Medicare and other government agencies the same price, as required by law, they said.

'It's heroin-dealer economics. Your first shot of dope is free and then it's more expensive,' said Pat Burns, a spokesman for the whistleblower group Taxpayers Against Fraud.

As part of the agreement, Merck denied any wrongdoing.

Steinke left Merck a month after he filed his lawsuit in December 2000 and went to work for a small pharmaceutical company that shared his values, Cohen said. He made repeated trips to Philadelphia to help government investigators.

'The whistleblower is stuck in a very lonely and isolated circumstance while the government's investigation is proceeding,' Cohen said.

His award includes $44.7 million from federal agencies—roughly 20 percent of the government's recovery—and about $23.5 million from various states, Cohen said.

The remainder of the settlement announced Wednesday stems from a lawsuit filed by a New Orleans doctor, William St. John LaCorte. His award had not yet been determined.

Cohen described Steinke, who is married with no children, as a reserved man from 'good midwestern stock.'

He recently left his drug-company job.

THE CURIOUS CASE OF LEHMAN'S WHISTLEBLOWER

By CESAR BACANI, 21 March 2010

A week after the release of a report on Lehman Brothers' 2008 bankruptcy, another piece of the puzzle has fallen into place. The *Wall Street Journal* has unearthed a letter written by Matthew Lee, a senior vice president in charge of the bank's global balance sheet and legal entity accounting.

A summary of Lee's May 18, 2008 letter is actually footnoted in the report on Lehman's bankruptcy by Alex Valukas, the chairman of U.S. law firm Jenner & Block LLP who was tasked by the Bankruptcy Court of the Southern District of New York to examine the bank's demise. Reading the actual document, though, gives a more complete picture of what transpired at Lehman as Lee saw it.

To my mind, what is equally interesting is how Lee's actions illuminate the various options available to potential whistleblowers everywhere. Lee was fired a few days after writing the letter. According to the Wall Street Journal, he considered filing a complaint for age discrimination – he is now 56 – but ended up with a severance agreement that, says his lawyer, prevented him from going to court or filing a whistleblower complaint under the Sarbanes-Oxley Act.

I'm not making a moral judgement on the personal decisions that were made in this case. Could things have gone differently had Lee not negotiated a severance agreement and filed a whistleblower's complaint instead? I'm not sure. It may be that the problems Lee flagged within Lehman combined with the toxic external environment of sub-prime and derivatives losses would have brought the bank to bankruptcy regardless of what Lee decided to do.

What appears to have happened is that a hard-headed personal choice was made and someone walked off with what I assume was a substantial severance package. (According to the *Guardian* newspaper, Lehman collapsed before Lee received the full amount of the severance.) Lehman then managed to hang on for several more months until the house of cards finally fell apart in September 2008.

Litany of Complaints

Suggestions have been made that Lee had seen the writing on the wall for himself professionally early on. Quoting his lawyer, Erwin Shustak, the *Wall Street Journal* said that Lee had been demoted two months before writing his letter. The reasons for the demotion have not been made clear, but Shustak wrote in a letter to a member of Lehman's general counsel staff that a company-wide decision appears to have been made "to replace more senior, higher paid employees, such as Mr. Lee . . . with younger, less experienced and less expensive employees."

According to Shustak, says the *Journal*, Lee had raised the issues contained in his May 18 letter to Martin Kelly, Lehman's global controller, several months earlier. (Kelly, who now works for Barclays, declined to comment.) He finally decided to write a formal letter with his attorney's help.

In that letter addressed to Kelly as controller, Gerard Reilly as head of capital markets product control, Erin Callan as CFO and Christopher O'Meara as chief risk officer, Lee said he was compelled to bring to their attention "conduct and actions on the part of the Firm that I consider to possibly constitute unethical or unlawful conduct."

Lee made six allegations. The first was that he believed Lehman's books and records "contain approximately five (5) billion dollars of net assets in excess of what is managed on the last day of the month." Second, Lee said Lehman had "tens of billions of dollars of unsubstantiated balances, which may or may not be 'bad' or non-performing assets or real liabilities." Third, the bank has "tens of billions of dollars of inventory that it probably cannot buy or sell in any recognized market, at the currently recorded current market values."

Fourth, Lee said that he did not believe that Lehman had "invested sufficiently in the required and reasonably necessary financial systems and personnel to cope with [its] increased balance sheet." Fifth, he singled out the finance functions and department in Mumbai, India, as not having "sufficient knowledgeable management in place" and warned of a "very real possibility of a potential misstatement of material facts being efficiently distributed by that office."

Finally, said Lee, "certain senior level internal audit personnel do not have the professional expertise to properly exercise the audit functions they are entrusted to manage, all of which have become increasingly complex as [Lehman Brothers] as undergone rapid growth in the international marketplace."

'Victim of Retaliation'

Lee's letter was cited as a key piece of evidence in Valukas's voluminous report in the determination that Ernst & Young, as Lehman's external auditor, had been professionally negligent. [16] The auditors had read Lee's letter, but did not alert the board's audit committee about it when they met, said Valukas. Ernst & Young interviewed Lee about a month later, when he had already been terminated from his job. In a statement, says the *Wall Street Journal*, Ernst & Young said that Lehman's management had determined that the "allegations were unfounded."

Why didn't Lee file a whistleblower's report under Sarbanes Oxley? It appears that he was hoping for a settlement with Lehman. In his letter to the bank, Shustak said that his client was considering an age discrimination suit against Lehman. "Mr. Lee believes he has been the victim of retaliation for bringing what he believed, in good faith, to have been ethical and securities law violations by Lehman to Lehman's management's attention," the lawyer wrote.

Curiously, instead of threatening to sue Lehman as a "victim of retaliation," Shustak indicated that Lee was considering an age discrimination suit. "At the same time," the lawyer wrote, "Mr. Lee would prefer to resolve his dispute with Lehman amicably." A settlement was indeed reached – that's the previously mentioned severance agreement that precluded Lee from filing a lawsuit or a whistleblower complaint. In effect, both parties got what they wanted.

Whistleblower Lessons

It is not clear to me whether Lee has any legal liability under Sarbanes-Oxley. As I understand it, the law requires the CEO and CFO to certify that the company's financial statements comply with the standards and regulations issued by the appropriate U.S. authorities and that the company has adequate internal controls in place. As the executive officer in charge of global balance sheet and legal entity accounting, Lee had presumably signed off internally to the correctness of Lehman's accounting, which is partly the basis, I assume, for the certification by the CEO and CFO.

But Lee's 2008 letter makes clear that he believes Lehman's accounting and internal controls have serious shortcomings. If his lawyer's account is true, he had also raised the issue with his supervisor before he wrote it. Whether all these will inoculate him from legal liability, if indeed he is exposed to such liability, is still to be determined. But Lee can at least plausibly say that he had done all that he could do.

Some may say that he could have done more by going public. This is, of course, easy for outside observers to say. There are many professional and personal reasons that must be taken into account before going that route. Even Sherron Watkins, the celebrated Enron "whistleblower," did not actually go public – she wrote an internal email warning of misstatements in the company's financial statements, a message that came to public attention five months after she sent it, when the Enron scandal had already come to light.

It is true that we now have Sarbanes-Oxley to theoretically protect whistleblowers. [17] Section 301 of Sarbanes-Oxley requires U.S. listed companies to establish a whistleblower's system that protects the anonymity of internal complainants. Section 806 of the same Act imposes civil liability on public companies that retaliate against employees who files a whistleblower's report. Still, the decision to actually blow the whistle on company wrongdoing is a personal one that rests with each individual employee.

For would-be whistleblowers, there is at least one important takeaway from Matthew Lee's decision-making, and that is to lawyer up. A good attorney, as Erwin Shustak apparently is, can lay out all the legal options and implications for one's contemplated action. It is well and good to do one's civic duty by exposing wrongdoing at one's company. But you must also make sure to protect yourself, your job and your family against the negative effects of being a good Samaritan.

About the Author

Cesar Bacani is senior consulting editor at CFO Innovation.

THE LEHMAN WHISTLEBLOWER'S LETTER

By MICHAEL CORKERY

In May 2008, former Lehman Senior Vice President Matthew Lee wrote a letter to senior management warning that the New York securities firm may have been masking the true risks on its balance sheet. A month later, he had been ousted.

His warning was revealed for the first time in a report by a U.S. bankruptcy-court examiner and showed that Lehman's auditors knew of potential accounting irregularities and allegedly failed to raise the issue with Lehman's board. Here is the letter that placed the little-known Lehman executive at the center of allegations that Lehman manipulated its numbers and misled investors.

Gentlemen and Madam:

I have been employed by Lehman Brothers Holdings, Inc. and subsidiaries (the "Firm") since May 1994, currently in the position of Senior Vice President in charge of the Firm's consolidated and unconsolidated balance sheets of over one thousand legal entities worldwide. During my tenure with the Firm I have been a loyal and dedicated employee and always have acted in the Firm's best interests.

I have become aware of certain conduct and practices, however, that I feel compelled to bring to your attention, as required by the Firm's Code of Ethics, as Amended February 17, 2004 (the "Code") and which requires me, as a Firm employee, to bring to the attention of management conduct and actions on the part of the Firm that I consider to possibly constitute unethical or unlawful conduct. I therefore bring the following to your attention, as required by the Code, "to help maintain a culture of honesty and accountability". (Code, first paragraph).

The second to last section of the Code is captioned "FULL, FAIR, ACCURATE, TIMELY AND UNDERSTANDABLE DISCLOSURE". That section provides, in relevant part, as follows:

"It is crucial that all books of account, financial statements and records of the Firm reflect the underlying transactions and any disposition of assets in a full, fair, accurate and timely manner. All employees...must endeavor to ensure that information in documents that Lehman Brothers files with or submits to the SEC, or otherwise disclosed to the public, is presented in a full, fair, accurate, timely and understandable manner. Additionally, each individual involved in the preparation of the Firm's financial statements must prepare those statements in accordance with Generally Accepted Accounting Principles, consistently applied, and any other applicable accounting standards and rules so that the financial statements present fairly, in all material respects, the financial position, results of operations and cash flows of the Firm.

Furthermore, it is critically important that financial statements and related disclosures be free of material errors. Employees and directors are prohibited from knowingly making or causing others to make a materially misleading, incomplete or false statement to an accountant or an attorney in connection with an audit or any filing with any governmental or regulatory entity. In that connection, no individual, or any person acting under his or her direction, shall directly or indirectly take any action to coerce, manipulate, mislead or fraudulently influence any of the Firm's internal auditors or independent auditors if he or she knows (or should know) that his or her actions, if successful, could result in rendering the Firm's financial statements materially misleading"

In the course of performing my duties for the Firm, I have reason to believe that certain conduct on the part of senior management of the Firm may be in violation of the Code. The following is a summary of the conduct I believe may violate the Code and which I feel compelled, by the terms of the Code, to bring to your attention.

1. Senior Firm management manages its balance sheet assets on a daily basis. On the last day of each month, the books and records of the Firm contain approximately five (5) billion dollars of net assets in excess of what is managed on the last day of the month. I believe this pattern indicates that the Firm's senior management is not in sufficient control of its assets to be able to establish that its financial statements are presented to the public and governmental agencies in a "full, fair accurate and timely manner". In my opinion, respectfully submitted, I believe the result is that at the end of each month, there could be approximately five (5) billion dollars of assets subject to a potential write-off. I believe it will take a significant investment of personnel and better control systems to adequately identify and quantify these discrepancies but, at the minimum, I believe the manner in which the Firm is reporting these assets is potentially misleading to the public and various governmental agencies. If so, I believe the Firm may be in violation of the Code.

2. The Firm has an established practice of substantiating each balance sheet account for each of its worldwide legal entities on a quarterly basis. While substantiation is somewhat subjective, it appears to me that the Code as well as Generally Accepted Accounting Principles require the Firm to support the net dollar amount in an account balance in a meaningful way supporting the Firm's stated policy of "full, fair, accurate and timely manner" valuation. The Firm has tens of billions of dollars of unsubstantiated balances, which may or may not be "bad" or non-performing assets or real liabilities. In any event, the Firm's senior management may not be in a position to know whether all

of these accounts are, in fact, described in a "full, fair, accurate and timely" manner, as required by the Code. I believe the Firm needs to make an additional investment in personnel and systems to adequately address this fundamental flaw.

3. The Firm has tens of billions of dollar of inventory that it probably cannot buy or sell in any recognized market, at the currently recorded current market values, particularly when dealing in assets of this nature in the volume and size as the positions the Firm holds. I do not believe the manner in which the Firm values that inventory is fully realistic or reasonable, and ignores the concentration in these assets and their volume size given the current state of the market's overall liquidity.

4. I do not believe the Firm has invested sufficiently in the required and reasonably necessary financial systems and personnel to cope with this increased balance sheet, specifically in light of the increased number of accounts, dollar equivalent balances and global entities, which have been created by or absorbed within the Firm as a result of the Firm's rapid growth since the Firm became a publicly traded company in 1994.

5. Based upon my experience and the years I have worked for the Firm, I do not believe there is sufficient knowledgeable management in place in the Mumbai, India Finance functions and department. There is a very real possibility of a potential misstatement of material facts being efficiently distributed by that office.

6. Finally, based upon my personal observations over the past years, certain senior level internal audit personnel do not have the professional expertise to properly exercise the audit functions they are entrusted to manage, all of which have become increasingly complex as the Firm has undergone rapid growth in the international marketplace.

I provide these observations to you with the knowledge that all of us at the Firm are entrusted to observe and respect the Code. I would be happy to discuss any details regarding the foregoing with senior management but I felt compelled, both morally and legally, to bring these issues to your attention. These are, indeed, turbulent times in the economic world and demand, more than ever, our adherence and respect of the Code so that the Firm may continue to enjoy the investing public's trust and confidence in us.

Very truly yours,

MATTHEW LEE

CENTER FOR EDUCATION ON SOCIAL RESPONSIBILITY

PART EIGHT

VALUES AND A JOB: BUILDING A CULTURE OR FINDING A FIT: THE ROLE OF CONSCIENCE

50 CODES OF CONDUCT BENCHMARKED—Q3 2008

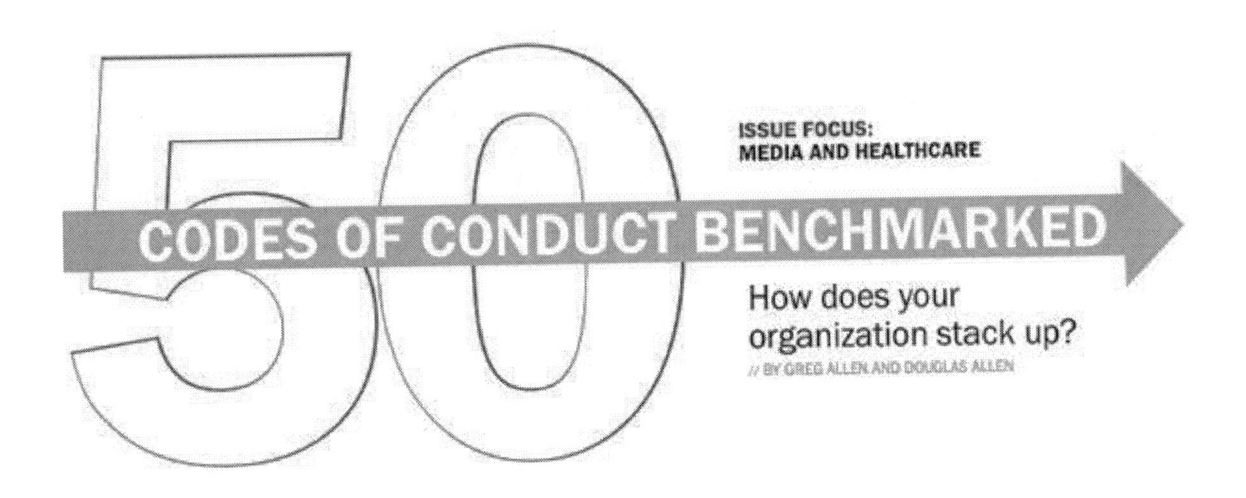

BY GREG ALLEN AND DOUGLAS ALLEN

An organization's Code of Conduct, alternatively referred to as Code of Ethics or Code of Business Standards, is the stated commitment of the behavioral expectations that an organization holds for its employees and agents. Such Codes are now commonplace for most corporations, increasingly shared not only with employees, but with customers and the public at large as well. To be successful, a Code must be believable by all stakeholders to which it applies. Certainly the subject corporation's commitment in action has significant impact. However, how the Code itself is written, what it contains, omits and how it is communicated all play instrumental underlying roles in whether it has the power to influence not only perceptions, but actions. Having reviewed over 800 Codes of Conduct, the Ethisphere editorial team has revised its methodology to more accurately reflect the most up-to-date best practices.

OVERALL GRADE METHODOLOGY

Each Code is rated by a panel of experts from the Ethisphere Institute and an aggregate score is derived through application of the following sub-scores: Public Availability (5%); Tone From the Top (15%); Readability & Tone (20%); Non-Retaliation & Reporting (10%); Values & Commitments (10%); Risk Topics (20%); Comprehension Aids (5%); Presentation & Style (15%).

BENCHMARKING DEFINED

A complete Code of Conduct analysis using Ethisphere Institute methodology typically examines 57 elements. This benchmarking analysis focuses on eight of the more critical components:

Public Availability A Code should be made readily available to all stakeholders. What is the availability and ease of access to the Code?

Tone from the Top Level at which the leadership of the organization is visibly committed to the values and topics covered in the Code.

Readability and Tone What is the style and tone of the language used in the document? Is it easy to read and reflective of its targeted audience?

Non-Retaliation & Reporting Is there a stated and explicit non-retaliation commitment and dedicated resources available for making reports of code violations? If so, is it presented clearly?

Commitment & Values Does the Code embed corporate values or mission language? Does it identify the ethical commitments held to its stakeholders (e.g. customers, vendors, communities)?

Risk Topics Does the Code address all of the appropriate and key risk areas for the company's given industry?

Comprehension Aids Does the Code provide any comprehension aids (Q&As/FAQs, checklists, examples, case studies) to help employees and other stakeholders understand key concepts?

Presentation and Style How compelling (or difficult) is the Code to read? This depends on layout, fonts, pictures, taxonomy and structure.

MEDIA	Public Availability	Tone from the Top	Readability and Tone	Non-Retaliation	Commitment to Stakeholders	Risk Topics	Learning Aids	Presentation and Style	OVERALL	KEY TAKEAWAYS
	AREAS OF BENCHMARKING									
APN NEWS AND MEDIA	A	F	D	F	D	D-	F	F	D-	There's nothing nice to say about this Code, except that it's very easy to find. Bonus points for just barely breaking the 500 word threshold. Allow us to extend the same courtesy APN has given their complia-
BERTELSMANN AG	C+	C+	B-	B-	B	A-	F	D+	C+	The language throughout this Code is very halting. Most of the time, each risk section comes off as more of a list of rules and definitions than a coherent paragraph. Kudos for addressing almost all major risk topics without going overboard on length.
CBS CORP	A	A-	B	A	B	A-	C-	C+	B	Like devious high school students, CBS and Viacom took their Codes home and compared notes. The two are nearly identical with only minor phrase changes. We're not crying plagiarism, but the façade of two separate companies could be better maintained. (See Viacom for more critique.)
CTVGLOBEMEDIA	A	B+	C	C+	B	A	B+	D	B-	CTV's catch phrase is "Our Moral Compass" and, after the cover page, presentation quickly goes south. Though the content is solid, with good coverage of risk topics and pertinent comprehension aids.
DISCOVERY HOLDING COMPANY	B+	D-	C	C+	F	D	F	F	D	When Discovery Holding spun off of Liberty Media like some astronomical body no longer held in orbit by its larger celestial parent, they took a souvenir with them: The Code. The two could be identical twins. (See Liberty Media for more commentary.)
EMI GROUP PLC	B	F	D+	F	F	D	F	F	D-	Was Don McLean mourning a plane crash or EMI's awful Code when he sang about "the day the music died?" Major point lossage for not mentioning reporting or non-retaliation in ANY capacity.
GANNETT COMPANY	B+	D	D	D	F	D-	F	D-	D-	The Code talks about how some relationships need to be kept at "arms' length" to avoid conflict of interest. Whose arms are we talking here, Shaquille O'Neal's or Danny DeVito's? Anyways... this Code needs a few more writers/editors to work on it to get past the press check.
INTERACTIVECORP (IAC)	A	D	D+	D	F	D	F	F	D	More like InActive! But seriously... how InterActive can you be if you've got a four year-old Code collecting dust? We're sure they wouldn't go that long without updating one of their websites.
ITV PLC	A	F	B	F	B	F	F	D-	D+	Simply put: If they condense all of the equally available policy documents into the "Code of Conduct," ITV's grade will quickly shoot up. The writing is pleasant, but the content is lacking.
LIBERTY MEDIA CORP	B+	D-	C	C+	F	D	F	F	D	We discovered a friendly Code under the beastly introduction. Explicitly stating that the Code applies to all companies of which Liberty Media owns "more than 50% of the voting power" is overkill.
LIONS GATE ENTERTAINMENT	A	D	C	A-	C	C-	F	F	C-	Drudging through large paragraphs of risk information is never pleasant, so we hated to do it twice. Large chunks of text can be found verbatim in Univision's Code. We're not sure which Code came first, but you might want to consider throwing this one to the lions.
MEDIA GENERAL	A	D	D+	D	C-	D+	F	D-	D	A demotion is in order until this Code is improved, something like Media Lieutenant would suffice. The Code chugs through a weak list of risk topics that lack in-depth information. Drop and give us 20 for pinning on a "this should meet all SOX requirements" badge as a last ditch effort.
MEDIASET SPA	A	D	D+	F	C	D-	F	D	D	This Code is tough to read. The candidly subordinating reference to "covered persons" as "Subjects" had one of our more sadistic editors in stitches. But it might be smart to include something about harassment and discrimination in future revisions.
NEWS CORPORATION	A	D-	C-	C+	C-	C	F	B	C-	These standards need some editing. Start by interrupting Rupert's asset-buying bonanza to write an introduction and follow that up by explicitly protecting employee privacy. Sprinkle some comprehension aids on top and you'll have taken a giant step towards a better grade.
QUEBECOR	A	F	D+	C	F	C-	F	D-	D	Vive Quebec! Though when the Quebecois get a chance to write their own constitution, we hope it ends up a bit better than this Code—a dreary document straight from the legal department. Give it some sincerity by focusing on stakeholders.
SCHOLASTIC CORP	A	D+	D+	C+	C	C+	D-	F	D+	By listing "discounts not available to the general public" as an acceptable business courtesy, Scholastic has opened up an unethical playground of reciprocating "discounts."
TIME WARNER	A	A	B	A-	B	A-	B	B-	B+	We get the ethical vibe Time Warner is emanating, but they need to rein it in a bit. Almost too many comprehension aids and heaps of risk information will bury readers. Bonus points for reiterating non-retaliation and reporting.
TRANSCONTINENTAL	A	B	B-	D	B	C+	F	C	C+	Transcontinental has set the type for a good Code, it just needs a little more follow-through. Spoiler alert: Did you know that "a bankruptcy" is considered important inside information? Stop the presses!
TRINITY MIRROR PLC	B	C-	D	F	D	D	F	D	D	Trinity's Code is only three pages. While we love the symbolism there (not really), we suggest making the Code comprehensive instead of trying to address only a handful of risk topics. And is the term "onus" really necessary?
UNIVISION COMMUNICATIONS	B+	A-	C	A-	B-	C-	F	D	C	Joe Uva personally "assures" that there will be no retaliation for good faith reports. We've got triple bonus points for any CEO who personally GUARANTEES there will be no retaliation.
VIACOM	A	A-	B	A	B	A-	C-	C	B	This Code is well-branded and easy to read. Excellent use of the qualifier "generally" to create policy grey areas. "Viacom generally does not extend credit to directors or executive officers." Whether or not a judge will think so is a different story. (See CBS for more critique.)
VIVENDI	B	D+	C	C-	B	B-	F	C	C	Vivendi, vidi, vici! Only, it seems they forgot the "vici." This Code is headed in the right direction, but still needs some work. To improve this Code, start with an executive introduction, keep non-retaliation language fresh and add some learning aids.
WALT DISNEY COMPANY	B	A	D	D+	A	A	F	F	C+	Disney's Code lacks their trademark magic. The Code does a great job addressing all major stakeholders, but the dense text and boring presentation probably aren't a walk in the Park for "Cast Members."
WASHINGTON POST COMPANY	A	B+	D	B-	C	B+	D-	F	C	We lost three writers after reading that they "generally prohibit except with the explicit prior approval" use of company computers for gambling or pornography in pursuit of "legitimate...journalistic activity."
YAHOO! INC	B+	C	C-	C+	B-	A	F	F	C	A fairly dense Code, but does well with risk topics. We can't help but wonder why they redacted "the Hotline" number. Thumbs up for mentioning that this Code applies to all "Yahoos." If the Code is any indication, there may be a few "Yahoos" in the compliance department.

AREAS OF BENCHMARKING

HEALTHCARE	Public Availability	Tone from the Top	Readability and Tone	Non-Retaliation	Commitment to Stakeholders	Risk Topics	Learning Aids	Presentation and Style	OVERALL	KEY TAKEAWAYS
AETNA	A	A	B	A	A-	A-	A	B+	B+	With its heavy usage of the second-person "you," the health care behemoth takes on a severely bossy tone in its Code. Lay off the power trip and dress down the flowery text layout. Say some nice things, and call it a day. Or an "A."
AMERIGROUP	A	D-	D	B	D-	C	F	F	D+	If Caps Lock were cruise control for cool, then this code would be as hip as Will Smith. Unfortunately, when AMERIGROUP capitalizes AMERIGROUP whenever they mention AMERIGROUP, it takes away from the message the Code was trying to make to employees.
APRIA HEALTHCARE	A	D-	C+	B+	B-	B+	F	F	C	Wonderful attention to industry-specific risk areas. Apria's code is obviously centered around home health care issues. Tweak a few things and give us some kind of presentation and this Code will be great.
BAXTER INTERNATIONAL	A	A	B	A	A-	A	D	B	B+	An attractive Code that covers risk topics pertinent to all businesses and the health care industry specifically. It's a little long for our tastes, but there's plenty of triangles to make up for it. Wait...what? Look up their Code to get our last joke.
BAYER GROUP	A	C-	C-	C	C	C+	F	B-	C	I've had sneezes that lasted longer than the executive statement. Just like their eponymous aspirin, the Code may prevent a legal headache, but it won't miraculously cure Bayer's ethical health.
BRISTOL-MYERS SQUIBB	A	A-	C-	A	A+	A+	A	B	B+	Informative and thorough as any emergency room visit, but about as readable as a pharmacist's handwriting. Excellent coverage of risk topics, and how could it not be at 51 pages?
CATHOLIC HEALTHCARE WEST	A	A-	D+	B	C	A-	F	D-	C+	If this Code is any indication, the Pope's got it all wrong about Western Catholics. This Code doesn't summarize their beliefs (or ANYTHING, for that matter), and it certainly doesn't glamorize its tenets. Tone down the legalese and invest in some design.
CIGNA CORPORATION	A	D	C-	C+	D-	C-	F	F	D+	As boring as any waiting room pamphlet. Although, it is nice to see CIGNA getting into the spirit of the election season by encouraging employees to register to vote and stay on top of issues.
COMMUNITY HEALTH SYSTEMS	A	D-	C+	C-	C	C+	F	F	C-	On the first page of its Code, Community Health Systems, Inc. says it doesn't have any employees. Who exactly is reading this besides us?
COVENTRY HEALTH CARE	A	D	D	B	C-	B	F	F	C-	This Code is for the birds. Though it's got all of the substance it needs, it's got such a lackluster, legalese tone that it needs to be completely overhauled, stat.
CVS CAREMARK	A	C	A-	A-	A+	A-	C+	A-	B+	It's like the ubiquitous drugstore—by the time you leave the store, you're struggling to decide what to put back on the shelf. Or you're hooked on a lot of pills. We were really pulling for this one—if only the Code had an executive statement and a few more comprehension aids.
DAVITA	A	B-	C-	C+	C	B-	F	F	C-	In-a-gadda-DaVita, honey, don'tcha know that I'll always be true? And the truth might hurt because this Code is in serious need of some some color, or at the very least some use of the bold or underline functions.
GENTIVA HEALTH SERVICES	A	B	B	B	D	C+	D	F	C	Let me respond in a way that your code writer will understand. XII. Your Code [A.] Needs improvements 1. so that readers think (a) you care ii. about what you're saying.
HCA	A	B+	C	C	A	B+	F	C-	B-	This Code was 38 pages, but felt like 60. Nice job on discussing commitments to stakeholders, however the Code goes overboard when it insists the wallet cut-out to be kept with you at ALL TIMES.
HEALTH NET	A	A-	D+	B-	C-	C-	F	F	C-	The company netted some points (and held onto some staplers) by listing "office machinery" in the protection of business assets section. Otherwise, this Code is lacking a ton of key risk areas (harassment, anyone?)
IASIS HEALTHCARE	B+	F	B	D	A	D+	F	D	C-	We found the "We will: -Do such and such" format very pleasant for the commitments and values at the beginning, but once Iasis gets into actual content, it becomes a bit condescending.
JOHNSON AND JOHNSON	B+	F	C	C-	D-	C	F	D-	D+	Forget the bandage and gauze jokes here. This Code needs a major operation—or better yet, a new team of writers.
LABCORP	A	D	C	C+	D	B+	F	F	C-	Good coverage of risk topics. However, according to this Code, all employees should exercise due diligence in taking care of their personal finances. So... LabCorp employees, mail that car payment... TODAY!
MEDCO	A	A-	B+	A	C	A-	D	C+	B	Solid Code. Symptoms include a rash of what appears to be stock photos, bland comprehension aids and multiple text walls. Our prescription? Spread out the text and insert (yikes) pictures throughout the document.
MOLINA HEALTHCARE	A	D	D	D-	F	C	F	F	D	If the success of the company is truly tied to employees' ability to follow the high standards of the Code, please get a new one.
NOVARTIS	B-	A-	B-	B-	B+	B-	F	B	B-	Solid Code. We'd like to point out that since 2001 (when this Code was written) the price of digital cameras has fallen dramatically. I know you're busy making vaccines, but are photos and comprehension aids too much to ask for?
OMNICARE	A	D	D-	D	F	D	F	F	D-	According to them, the elusive "Omnicare Code of Integrity" will guide business decisions with respect to ethics. Hmm... we thought that's what the "Code of Business Conduct and Ethics" would cover. Weird.
QUEST DIAGNOSTICS	A	C-	D	C+	D	D	F	C	D+	We know you have to be pretty intelligent to work at Quest Diagnostics, but writing at a graduate school level doesn't really jive with Code best practices. Why not fix up the Code with some of the compelling compliance language from your website?
SUN HEALTHCARE GROUP	B+	B+	C+	B	A-	C	C-	C+	C+	We were nearly lulled to sleep by all of the friendly, smiling faces and the soft lighting that peppered this Code. Particularly heartbreaking was the section dedicated to employees' reactions to patients with dementia who try to give precious heirlooms as gifts.
TENET HEALTHCARE	A	A	A+	A	A+	B-	C-	A-	A-	This Code really is at the head of the class. The stated commitments to the community are impressive, especially the list of yearly charity events. We appreciate the pun of a subtitle, "the tenets we live by."

BEYOND THE CODE: INSPIRING ETHICAL CONDUCT

Steve Henn

November 2007—Although Sarbanes-Oxley has required public companies to adopt a Code of Conduct and take other measures to deter unethical behavior, the adoption of such Codes has had no demonstrable positive impact on corporate conduct (as evidenced by the decline in positive outcomes of ethics programs in the 2005 Ethics Resource Center™ National Business Ethics Survey). This has led some organizations to take a hard look at their workplace cultures to try to ascertain what motivates employees to comply with or disregard the standards of conduct that the organization promotes.

While Boards and the C-suite have started to recognize that their actions, attitudes and decisions have a direct influence on the cultures of their organizations, the truth is that corporate conduct is not shaped solely by the few people at the top of the corporate ladder.

While no company can expect to be "ethical" with an apathetic (or worse, unethical) CEO or other C-level executives, an ethical culture needs to be embedded into all levels of a company's personnel. It is likely that most employees take their cues about what is and is not acceptable practice in their company from those immediately around them: their manager and their peers, rather than directly emulating senior management. Therefore, if a company is serious about effecting positive change in its corporate culture, it should explore methods of influencing peer-to-peer behavior.

How can a company promote positive role modeling and high standards of conduct within the ranks, rather than just at the top? One option is to complement company-wide ethics education programs with smaller-scale unit/team culture building and training programs that connect the corporate mission and values to the day-to-day work and challenges of the individual teams. Such programs, which encourage teams to articulate their own missions and goals that connect to the values of the company, show employees how corporate values come into play in their daily tasks and force employees to think about the impact that any misconduct may have on their co-workers and the reputation of their entire team.

The objective of such an approach is to set a high standard for conduct and accountability within a work group, but it is a standard set and agreed upon by members of the group. It is also a standard that is encouraged by an employee's peers and, if necessary, enforced by those same peers. The team charter and mission statement ultimately arrived at should clearly dovetail with the company's Code of Conduct, mission and values, but at the same time provide an individual articulation of how a team is contributing to that mission and upholding the corporate values at a "local" level.

Of course this approach will invariably result in differences between one team/department's values and the next. But by allowing the tailoring of the corporate values to the department's mission, a deeper sense of connection and commitment to the overarching goals of the organization is fostered. Furthermore, in the foreign offices of multi-national organizations, where the resident employees may have a harder time connecting the corporate values to the local culture and customs, the local culture building approach helps a company bridge that gap.

"Tone at the Top", "Message in the Middle" are extremely important, but "Behavior at the Bottom" is critical in fostering an ethical culture and preventing a crisis.

In future newsletter articles, we will discuss more specific programs based on the team/unit culture-building model.

MAKING THE TOUGH CALL

Great leaders recognize when their values are on the line.

Noel M. Tichy and Warren G. Bennis

Great leaders are celebrated for their judgment. But what is good judgment and how do the best leaders sustain it? It's not a matter of intellect or of the ability to make the right decision in an instant, but of character. Character provides the moral compass—it tells you what you must do. Then there's courage. It produces results, ensuring that you follow through on the decision you've made. No matter what processes you follow, no matter how hard you try, without character and courage, no one can clear the high bar that is judgment. You may luck into making some good decisions and sometimes obtain good results, but without character and courage, you will falter on the most difficult and most important questions.

Jim Hackett, the CEO of Steelcase (NYSE:SCS), the office furniture company, has spent much of his career thinking about what it means to be a leader who operates based on a clear set of values. He began to develop this way of thinking, he says, after a meeting with the hotelier Bill Marriott. The men met at a pivotal moment in Hackett's business career. He was 39 and had become president of Steelcase only six months earlier. Marriott, meanwhile, was then in his seventies and had been running the Marriott (NYSE:MAR) hotel empire for decades. Despite the gap in their ages, the two men had some things in common and they hit it off. "I was young, trying to change an old family business and he was old, trying to change an old family business," Hackett recalls.

Much of their conversation focused on values, with Marriott encouraging Hackett to build for himself and for his company a reputation of "unyielding integrity." On the plane trip back from Washington, D.C., to his home in Grand Rapids, Michigan, Hackett couldn't stop thinking about that conversation. A few months later, he gave a talk to his management team on the subject of integrity. It's important to develop these points of view within an organization before trouble occurs, Hackett says, and to ask your team, "How are we going to act when we get in trouble because I can guarantee you in business, you will."

Ten years after that meeting with Bill Marriott, Jim Hackett was faced with a business judgment that had far greater implications than he could have known at the time.

The issue was fire retardant. Steelcase had begun selling a new line of products, designing panels that could be used either for waist-high office cubicles or to cover floor-to-ceiling walls. Building managers embraced the product because it made their lives easier. Instead of buying, storing, and repairing two different products, they could use only one.

With a successful new product launched, what could possibly go wrong? As it turned out, Steelcase, which had a lot of experience in the cubicle business but none in the wall business, soon discovered that the rules governing fire standards for floor-to-ceiling walls were stricter than those for cubicles, and the product might not be up to the higher standards. When the first inkling of a problem arose, however, there was an impulse on the part of some people within the company to ignore it. "We had not had one damaged installation," Hackett recalls. "I was getting the crap beaten out of me by the analysts. Our customers even called us and said 'Oh, don't worry about it. What you're worried about—no one will ever have a problem.'" Despite these reassurances, Hackett sensed that this was a volatile situation, and one that required careful consideration. So he told his managers to look into it further.

As Steelcase executives began to focus on the problem, a numbers of rationales for inaction were developed. It was a new product after all, and there was no track record to suggest how customers would install it. Fire codes vary by municipality, so there was no one standard that Steelcase had to live up to. Nobody could say definitively just how fire-retardant would be fire-retardant enough or how far off the mark Steelcase's panels were. Within the company, some managers wondered if customers in places with stricter fire codes had already exchanged the panels for a more fire-retardant product.

Still, Hackett felt that if Steelcase's standard of unyielding integrity was to mean anything, he had to act. So he made the call to quietly recall the panels through Steelcase dealers and replace them with ones that met stricter fire codes. Implementing the decision was time consuming and expensive. Steelcase took a $40 million write-off. Along the way Hackett and all of his executives lost their annual performance bonuses.

Soon after, however, Hackett's decision was vindicated. One of Steelcase's customers for the surface panel product line was the Department of Defense. Panels with the added fire-retardant material were installed in the perimeter walls of the Pentagon, coincidentally in the part of the building that was destroyed on 9/11. After the attack, Hackett recalls, "it was determined, with all the jet fuel and fire, if the new fire-retardant material was not there, the fire would have spread in a far more disastrous outcome." Character and courage are the bedrock of good judgment, and Jim Hackett displayed them both in this instance.

Judgment is a complicated subject, of course. It is about more than decision making or having high standards. And it is too intertwined with luck and with the vicissitudes of history, too influenced by personal style, to pin down entirely. Sir William Osler, one of the fathers of modern medicine, ruefully lamented at the end of the 19th century: "If there were not so much variability among individuals, medicine would be a science, not an art." The same can be said for the study of leadership.

But one thing is striking: When you ask people, as an exercise, to make a list of bad decisions they've made in their lives, an alarming number of them will include a statement to the effect of "I really knew in my gut what I should do, but I didn't do it." Having a set of standards or values isn't enough. Even character isn't enough. Having the courage to act on your standards is an integral part of the bundle of what it takes to exercise good judgment and to be a good leader.

ETHICS AND ORGANIZATIONAL CULTURE

March 26, 2010

CHARLES HARRINGTON, CHAIRMAN AND CEO, PARSONS

A major league baseball team is playing its last regular season game of the year: win this game and they advance to the play-offs; lose, and they watch the play-offs on TV. In the bottom of the 9th, one of its star players steps to the plate, the score tied, a man on first, no outs. The right thing for him to do is to lay down a sacrifice bunt to move the runner into scoring position. This player happens to have an incentive clause in his contract, however, that would be triggered if he gets one more hit for the season, and that incentive clause would bring him a big bonus and a contract extension. The player lays down the sacrifice bunt, and his team goes on to win the game and advance to the post season.

After the game, a reporter who was aware of what was at stake for that star player in his last at-bat asked the team's manager how he convinced the player "to do what was right." The manager replied, "We try to create an atmosphere here where the question doesn't even arise."

I heard this true story from one of our executives, and I often use it when talking to our employees about the way we "play the game" at Parsons. Our strong commitment to our six Core Values – Safety, Quality, Integrity, Diversity, Innovation and Sustainability – governs everything we do at Parsons. Our Core Values are the very beliefs that form the culture of our organization, that make us who we are, that form the basis for all of our decisions. We strive hard to create an atmosphere where the question of deviating from those Core Values, from doing what is right, whether for perceived individual or corporate gain, never even gets raised.

Each of our Core Values has a goal, and for Integrity our goal is ZERO deviations from our Corporate Ethics Policy. We have performance metrics that we have developed to track composite leading and lagging indicators of our performance against this goal and to report to management, and to our Board of Directors, on our progress on a quarterly basis.

To achieve this goal requires constant communication. All new employees receive training in Parsons' Ethics Policy, including watching a video from me discussing the importance of a commitment to ethics for our company, our employees, our customers and our suppliers. All employees are required to be re-trained in our Ethics Policy on a regular basis, and our employees participate in Ethics Challenges on our internal website several times a year. Additionally, each of our quarterly Executive Committee meetings addresses an Ethics/Integrity Moment.

A company should seek constant improvement in the way it conducts business, and commitment to integrity is no exception. We are always looking for ways to improve our ethics program, both in terms of the message itself and the way we communicate that message. As an example, in the past Parsons issued periodic Ethics Bulletins to employees, highlighting particular ethics issues in each Bulletin, but that was a static communication. Over the past year, we have instituted Ethics Challenges on our internal website, describing a certain fact scenario in which our employees could well find themselves, and asking our employees to vote and comment on how the person in the Challenge should respond. We then compile the responses and publish them on our internal website, along with a sampling of the comments submitted and with an analysis from our Ethics Committee.

We've gone from a static communication to an interactive dialog, and we've had tremendous responses, both in terms of the number of people who participate and in the depth of the comments we've received. Most importantly, it has our employees talking and debating about ethics, and that's really what any company hopes to achieve.

In the short term, a corporation's commitment to integrity may cost it a project, or result in an individual employee, or the corporation, missing certain financial targets. Parsons has in the past walked away from potential projects or teaming partners when questionable ethics issues have surfaced, and we will continue to do so in the future. The end results of such short-term losses, however, are virtually always long-term gains: gains in reputation as a company that doesn't cut ethical corners; gains in attracting employees who already have their own personal commitment to integrity and want to work for a company which is similarly committed; and gains in attracting the right kind of suppliers, subcontractors and teaming partners with whom to work.

In my baseball example at the beginning of this article, the star player did "what was right," laid down a sacrifice bunt, and the team won the game and went to the play-offs. But suppose, despite the bunt, the team had gone on to lose the game? In my mind, laying down the bunt, playing the game the right way, was still the right thing to do. And conducting our business with integrity in everything we do, playing the game "the right way" even if it means losing a potential project or customer or partner, is always the right way to play the game.

PINTO FIRES AND PERSONAL ETHICS: A SCRIPT ANALYSIS OF MISSED OPPORTUNITIES

by DENNIS A. GIOIA

Dennis A. Gioia is Associate Professor of Organizational Behavior in the Department of Management and Organization, The Smeal College of Business Administration, Pennsylvania State University. Professor Gioia's primary research and writing focus of the nature and uses of complex cognitive processes by organization members and the ways that these processes affect sensemaking, communication, influence and organizational change. His most recent research interests have to do with the less rational, more intuitive, emotional, and political aspects of organizational life — those fascinating arenas where people in organizations tend to subvert management scholars' heartfelt attempts to have them behave more rationally. Prior to this ivory tower career, he worked in the real world as an engineering aide for Boeing Aerospace at Kennedy Space Center and as vehicle recall coordinator for Ford Motor Company in Dearborn, Michigan.

ABSTRACT. This article details the personal involvement of the author in the early stages of the infamous Pinto fire case. The paper first presents an insider account of the context and decision environment within which he failed to initiate an early recall of defective vehicles. A cognitive script analysis of the personal experience is then offered as an explanation of factors that led to a decision that now is commonly seen as a definitive study in unethical corporate behavior. The main analytical thesis is that script schemas that were guiding cognition and action at the time precluded consideration of issues in ethical terms because the scripts did not include ethical dimensions.

In the summer of 1972 I made one of those important transitions in life, the significance of which becomes obvious only in retrospect. I left academe with a BS in Engineering Science and an MBA to enter the world of big business. I joined Ford Motor Company at World Headquarters in Dearborn Michigan, fulfilling a long-standing dream to work in the heart of the auto industry. I felt confident that I was in the right place at the right time to make a difference. My initial job title was "Problem Analyst"—a catchall label that superficially described what I would be thinking about and doing in the coming years. On some deeper level, however, the title paradoxically came to connote the many critical things that I would *not* be thinking about and acting upon.

By that summer of 1972 I was very full of myself. I had met my life's goals to that point with some notable success. I had virtually everything I wanted, including a strongly-held value system that had led me to question many of the perspectives and practices I observed in the world around me. Not the least of these was a profound distaste for the Vietnam war, a distaste that had found me participating in various demonstrations against its conduct and speaking as a part of a collective voice on the moral and ethical failure of a democratic government that would attempt to justify it. I also found myself in MBA classes railing against the conduct of businesses of the era, whose actions struck me as ranging from inconsiderate to indifferent to simply unethical. To me the typical stance of business seemed to be one of disdain for, rather than responsibility toward, the society of which they were prominent members. I wanted something to change. Accordingly, I cultivated my social awareness; I held my principles high; I espoused my intention to help a troubled world; and I wore my hair long. By any measure I was a prototypical "Child of the '60s."

Therefore, it struck quite a few of my friends in the MBA program as rather strange that I was in the program at all. ("If you are so disappointed in business, why study business?") Subsequently, they were practically dumbstruck when I accepted the job offer from Ford, apparently one of the great purveyors of the very actions I reviled. I countered that it was an ideal strategy, arguing that I would have a greater chance of influencing social change in business if I worked behind the scenes on the inside, rather than as a strident voice on the outside. It was clear to me that somebody needed to prod these staid companies into socially responsible action. I certainly aimed to do my part. Besides, I liked cars.

INTO THE FRAY: SETTING THE PERSONAL STAGE

Predictably enough, I found myself on the fast track at Ford, participating in a "tournament" type of socialization (Van Maanen, 1978), engaged in a competition for recognition with other MBA's who had recently joined the company. And I quickly became caught up in the game. The company itself was dynamic; the environment of business, especially the auto industry, was intriguing; the job was challenging and the pay was great. The psychic rewards of working and succeeding in a major corporation proved unexpectedly seductive. I really became involved in the job.

Market forces (international competition) and government regulation (vehicle safety and emissions) were affecting the auto industry in disruptive ways that only later would be common to the wider business and social arena. They also produced an industry and a company that felt buffeted, beleaguered, and threatened by the changes. The threats were mostly external, of course, and led to a strong feeling of we-vs-them, where we (Ford members) needed to defend ourselves against them (all the outside parties and voices demanding that we change our ways). Even at this time, an intriguing question for me was whether I was a "we" or a "them." It was becoming apparent to me that my perspective was changing. I had long since cut my hair.

By the summer of 1973 I was pitched into the thick of the battle. I became Ford's Field Recall Coordinator — not a position that was particularly high in the hierarchy, but one that wielded influence for beyond its level. I was in charge of the operational coordination of all of the recall campaigns currently underway and also in charge of tracking incoming information to identify developing problems. Therefore, I was in a position to make initial recommendations about possible future recalls. The most critical type of recalls were labeled "safety campaigns" — those that dealt with the possibility of customer injury or death. These ranged from straight-forward occurrences such as brake failure and wheels falling off vehicles, to more exotic and faintly humorous failure modes such as detaching axles that announced their presence by spinning forward and slamming into the startled driver's door and speed control units that locked on, and refused to disengage, as the car accelerated wildly while the spooked driver futilely tried to shut it off. Safety recall campaigns, however, also encompassed the more sobering possibility of on-board gasoline fires and explosions . . . .

THE PINTO CASE: SETTING THE CORPORATE STAGE

In 1970 Ford introduced the Pinto, a small car that was intended to compete with the then current challenge from European cars and the ominous presence on the horizon of Japanese manufacturers. The Pinto was brought from inception to production in the record time of approximately 25 months (compared to the industry average of 43 months), a time frame that suggested the necessity for doing things expediently. In addition to the time pressure, the engineering and development teams were required to adhere to the production "limits of 2000" for the diminutive car: it was not to exceed either $2,000 in cost or 2,000 pounds in weight. Any decisions that threatened these targets or the timing of the car's introduction were discouraged. Under normal conditions design, styling, product planning, engineering, etc., were completed prior to production tooling. Because of the foreshortened time frame, however, some of these usually sequential processes were executed in parallel.

As a consequence, tooling was already well under way (thus "freezing" the basic design) when routine crash testing revealed that the Pinto's fuel tank often ruptured when struck from the rear at a relatively low speed (31 mph in crash tests). Reports (revealed much later) showed that the fuel tank failures were the result of some rather marginal design features. The tank was positioned between the rear bumper and the rear axle (a standard industry practice for the time). During impact, however, several studs protruding from the rear of the axle housing would puncture holes in the tank; the fuel filler neck also was likely to rip away. Spilled gasoline then could be ignited by sparks. Ford had in fact crash-tested 11 vehicles; 8 of these cars suffered potentially catastrophic gas tank ruptures. The only 3 cars that survived intact had each been modified in some way to protect the tank.

These crash tests, however, were conducted under the guidelines of Federal Motor Vehicle Safety Standard 301 which had been proposed in 1968 and strenuously opposed by the auto industry. FMVSS 301 was not actually adopted until 1976; thus, at the time of the tests, Ford was not in violation of the law. There were several possibilities for fixing the problem, including the option of redesigning the tank and its location, which would have produced tank integrity in a high-speed crash. That solution, however, was not only time consuming and expensive, but also usurped trunk space, which was seen as a critical competitive sales factor. One of the production modifications to the tank, however, would have cost only $11 to install, but given the tight margins and restrictions of the "limits of 2,000," there was reluctance to make even this relatively minor change. There were other reasons for not approving the change, as well, including a widespread industry belief that all small cars were inherently unsafe solely because of their size and weight. Another more prominent reason was a corporate belief that "safety doesn't sell." This observation was attributed to Lee Iacocca and stemmed from Ford's earlier attempt to make safety a sales theme, an attempt that failed rather dismally in the marketplace.

Perhaps the most controversial reason for rejecting the production change to the gas tank, however, was Ford's use of cost-benefit analysis to justify the decision. The National Highway Traffic Safety Association (NHTSA, a federal agency) had approved the use of cost-benefit analysis as an appropriate means for establishing automotive safety design standards. The controversial aspect in making such calculations was that they required the assignment of some specific value for a human life. In 1970, that value was deemed to be approximately $200,000 as a "cost to society" for each fatality. Ford used NHTSA's figures in estimating the costs and benefits of altering the tank production design. An internal memo, later revealed in court, indicates the following tabulations concerning potential fires (Dowie, 1977):

Costs: $137,000,000

(Estimated as the costs of a production fix to all similarly designed cars and trucks with the gas tank aft of the axle (12,500,000 vehicles x $11/vehicle))

Benefits: $49,530,000

(Estimated as the savings from preventing (180 projected deaths x $200,000/death) + (180 projected burn injuries x $67,000/injury) + (2,100 burned cars x $700/car))

The cost-benefit decision was then construed as straightforward: No production fix would be undertaken. The philosophical and ethical implications of assigning a financial value for human life or disfigurement do not seem to have been a major consideration in reaching this decision.

PINTOS AND PERSONAL EXPERIENCE

When I took over thee Recall Coordinator's job in 1973 I inherited the oversight of about 100 active recall campaigns, more than half of which were safety-related. These ranged from minimal in size (replacing front wheels that were likely to break on 12 heavy trucks) to maximal (repairing the power steering pump on millions of cars). In addition, there were quite a number of safety problems that were under consideration as candidates for addition to the recall list. (Actually, "problem" was a word whose public use was forbidden by the legal office at the time, even in service bulletins, because it suggested corporate admission of culpability. "Condition" was the sanctioned catchword.) In addition to these potential recall candidates, there were many files containing field reports of alleged component failure (another forbidden word) that had led to accidents, and in some cases, passenger injury. Beyond these existing files, I began to construct my own files of incoming safety problems.

One of these new files concerned reports of Pintos "lighting up" (in the words of a field representative) in rear-end accidents. There were actually very few reports, perhaps because component failure was not initially assumed. These cars simply were consumed by fire after apparently very low speed accidents. Was there a problem? Not as far as I was concerned. My cue for labeling a case as a problem either required high frequencies of occurrence or directly-traceable causes. I had little time for speculative contemplation on potential problems that did not fit a pattern that suggested known courses of action leading to possible recall. I do, however, remember being disquieted by a field report accompanied by graphic, detailed photos of the remains of a burned-out Pinto in which several people had died. Although that report became part of my file, I did not flag it as any special case.

It is difficult to convey the overwhelming complexity and pace of the job of keeping track of so many active or potential recall campaigns. It remains the busiest, most information-filled job I have ever held or would want to hold. Each case required a myriad of information-gathering and execution stages. I distinctly remember that the information-processing demands led me to confuse the facts of one problem case with another on several occasions because the tell-tale signs of recall candidate cases were so similar. I thought of myself as a fireman—a fireman who perfectly fit the description by one of my colleagues: "In this office everything is a crisis. You only have time to put out the big fires and spit on the little ones." By those standards the Pinto problem was distinctly a little one.

It is also important to convey the muting of emotion involved in the Recall Coordinator's job. I remember contemplating the fact that my job literally involved life-and-death matters. I was sometimes responsible for finding and fixing cars NOW, because somebody's life might depend on it. I took it *very* seriously. Early in the job, I sometimes woke up at night wondering whether I had covered all the bases. Had I left some unknown person at risk because I had not thought of something? That soon faded, however, and of necessity the consideration of people's lives became a fairly removed, dispassionate process. To do the job "well" there was little room for emotion. Allowing it to surface was potentially paralyzing and prevented rational decisions about which cases to recommend for recall. On moral grounds I knew I could recommend most of the vehicles on my safety tracking list for recall (and risk earning the label of a "bleeding heart"). On practical grounds, I recognized that people implicitly accept risks in cars. We could not recall all cars with *potential* problems and stay in business. I learned to be responsive to those cases that suggested an imminent, dangerous problem.

I should also note, that the country was in the midst of its first, and worst, oil crisis at this time. The effects of the crisis had cast a pall over Ford and the rest of the automobile industry. Ford's product line, with perhaps notable exception of the Pinto and Maverick small cars, was not well-suited to dealing with the crisis. Layoffs were imminent for many people. Recalling the Pinto in this context would have damaged one of the few trump cards the company had (although, quite frankly, I do not remember overtly thinking about that issue).

Pinto reports continued to trickle in, but at such a slow rate that they really did not capture particular attention relative to other, more pressing safety problems. However, I later saw a crumpled, burned car at a Ford depot where alleged problem components and vehicles were delivered for inspection and analysis (a place known as the "Chamber of Horrors" by some of the people who worked there). The revulsion on seeing this incinerated hulk was immediate and profound. Soon afterwards, and despite the fact that the file was very sparse, I recommended the Pinto case for preliminary department-level review concerning possible recall. After the usual round of discussion about criteria and justification for recall, everyone voted against recommending recall — including me. It did not fit the pattern of recallable standards; the evidence was not overwhelming that the car was defective in some way, so the case was actually fairly straightforward. It was a good business decision, even if people might be dying. (We did not then know about the pre-production crash test data that suggested a high rate of tank failures in "normal" accidents (cf., Perrow, 1984) or an abnormal failure mode).

Later, the existence of the crash test data did become known within Ford, which suggested that the Pinto might actually have a recallable problem. This information led to a reconsideration of the case within our office. The data, however, prompted a comparison of the Pinto's survivability in a rear end accident with that of other competitors' small cars. These comparisons revealed that although many cars in this subcompact class suffered appalling deformation in relatively low speed collisions, the Pinto was merely the worst of a bad lot. Furthermore, the gap between the Pinto and the competition was not dramatic in terms of the speed at which fuel tank rupture was likely to occur. On that basis it would be difficult to justify the recall of cars that were comparable with others on the market. In the face of even more compelling evidence that people were probably going to die in this car, I again included myself in a group of decision makers who voted not to recommend recall to the higher levels of the organization.

CODA TO THE CORPORATE CASE

Subsequent to my departure from Ford in 1975, reports of Pinto fires escalated, attracting increasing media attention, almost all of it critical of Ford. Anderson and Whitten (1976) revealed the internal memos concerning the gas tank problem and questioned how the few dollars saved per car could be justified when human lives were at stake. Shortly thereafter, a scathing article by Dowie (1977) attacked not only the Pinto's design, but also accused Ford of gross negligence, stonewalling, and unethical corporate conduct by alleging that Ford knowingly sold "firetraps" after willfully calculating the cost of lives against profits (see also Gatewood and Carroll, 1983). Dowie's provocative quote speculating on "how long the Ford Motor Company would continue to market lethal cars were Henry Ford II and Lee Iacocca serving 20 year terms in Leavenworth for consumer homicide" (1977, p. 32) was particularly effective in focusing attention on the case. Public sentiment edged toward labeling Ford as socially deviant because management was seen as knowing that the car was defective, choosing profit over lives, resisting demands to fix the car, and apparently showing no public remorse (Swigert and Farrell, 1980–81).

Shortly after Dowie's (1977) expose, NHTSA initiated its own investigation. Then, early in 1978 a jury awarded a Pinto burn victim $125 million in punitive damages (later reduced to $6.6 million, a judgment upheld on an appeal that prompted the judge to assert that "Ford's institutional mentality was shown to be one of callous indifference to public safety" (quoted in Cullen *et al.*, 1987, p. 164)). A siege atmosphere emerged at Ford. Insiders characterized the mounting media campaign as "hysterical" and "a crusade against us" (personal communications). The crisis deepened. In the summer of 1978 NHTSA issued a formal determination that the Pinto was defective. Ford then launched a reluctant recall of all 1971–1976 cars (those built for the 1977 model year were equipped with a production fix prompted by the adoption of the FMVSS 301 gas tank standard). Ford hoped that the issue would then recede, but worse was yet to come.

The culmination of the case and the demise of the Pinto itself began in Indiana on August 10, 1978, when three teenage girls died in a fire triggered after their 1973 Pinto was hit from behind by a van. A grand jury took the unheard of step of indicting Ford on charges of reckless homicide (Cullen *et al.*, 1987). Because of the precedent-setting possibilities for all manufacturing industries, Ford assembled a formidable legal team headed by Watergate prosecutor James Neal to defend itself at the trial. The trial was a media event; it was the first time that a corporation was tried for alleged *criminal* behavior. After a protracted, acrimonious courtroom battle that included vivid clashes among the opposing attorneys, surprise witnesses, etc., the jury ultimately found in favor of Ford. Ford had dodged a bullet in the form of a consequential legal precedent, but because of the negative publicity of the case and the charges of corporate crime and ethical deviance, the conduct of manufacturing businesses was altered, probably forever. As a relatively minor footnote to the case, Ford ceased production of the Pinto.

CODA TO THE PERSONAL CASE

In interviewing years since my early involvement with the Pinto fire case, I have given repeated consideration to my role in it. Although most of the the ethically questionable actions that have been cited in the press are associated with Ford's intentional stonewalling after it was clear that the Pinto was defective (see Cullen *et al.*, 1986; Dowie, 1977; Gatewood and Carroll, 1983) — and thus postdate my involvement with the case and the company — I still nonetheless wonder about my own culpability. Why didn't I see the gravity of the problem and its ethical overtones? What happened to the value system I carried with me into Ford? Should I have acted differently, given what I knew then? The experience with myself has sometimes not been pleasant. Somehow, it seems I should have done *something* different that might have made a difference.

As a consequence of this line of thinking and feeling, some years ago I decided to construct a "living case" out of my experience with the Pinto fire problem for use in my MBA classes. The written case description contains many of the facts detailed above; the analytical task of the class is to ask appropriate questions of me as a figure in the case to reveal the central issues involved. It is somewhat of a trying experience to get through these classes. After getting to know me for most of the semester, and then finding out that I did *not* vote to recommend recall, students are often incredulous, even angry at me for apparently not having lived what I have been teaching. To be fair and even-handed here, many students understand my actions in the context of the times and the attitudes prevalent then. Others, however, are very disappointed that I appear to have failed during a time of trial. Consequently, I am accused of being a charlatan and otherwise vilified by those who maintain that ethical and moral principles should have prevailed in this case no matter what the mitigating circumstances. Those are the ones that hurt.

Those are also the ones, however, that keep the case and its lessons alive in my mind and cause me to have an on-going dialogue with myself about it. It is fascinating to me that for several years after I first conducted the living case with myself as the focus, I remained convinced that I had made the "right" decision in not recommending recall of the cars. In light of the times and the evidence available, I thought I had pursued a reasonable course of action. More recently, however, I have come to think that I really should have done everything I could to get those cars off the road.

In retrospect I know that in the context of the times of my actions were *legal* (they were all well within the framework of the law); they probably also were *ethical* according to most prevailing definitions (they were in accord with accepted professional standards and codes of conduct); the major concern for me is whether they were *moral* (in the sense of adhering to some higher standards of inner conscience and conviction about the "right" actions to take). This simple typology implies that I had passed at least two hurdles on a personal continuum that ranged from more rigorous, but arguably less significant criteria, to less rigorous, but more personally, organizationally, and perhaps societally significant standards:

X	X	?
Legal	Ethical	Moral

It is that last criterion that remains troublesome.

Perhaps these reflections are all just personal revisionist history. After all, I am still stuck in my cognitive structures, as everyone is. I do not think these concerns are all retrospective reconstruction, however. Another telling piece of information is this: The entire time I was dealing with the Pinto fire problem, I owned a Pinto (!). I even sold it to my sister. What does that say?

WHAT HAPPENED HERE?

I, of course, have some thoughts about my experience with this damningly visible case. At the risk of breaking some of the accepted rules of scholarly analysis, rather than engaging in the usual comprehensive, dense, arms-length critique, I would instead like to offer a rather selective and subjective focus on certain characteristics of human information processing relevant to this kind of situation, of which I was my own unwitting victim. I made no claim that my analysis necessarily "explains more variance" than other possible explanations. I do think that this selective view is enlightening in that it offers an alternative explanation for some ethically questionable actions in business.

The subjective stance adopted in the analysis is intentional also. This case obviously stems from a series of personal experiences, accounts, and introspections. The analytical style is intended to be consistent with the self-based case example; therefore, it appears to be less "formal" than the typical objectivist mode of explanation. I suspect that my chosen focus will be fairly nonobvious to the reader familiar with the ethical literature (as it typically is to the ethical actor). Although this analysis might be judged as somewhat self-serving, I nonetheless believe that it provides an informative explanation for some of the ethical foibles we see enacted around us.

To me, there are two major issues to address. First, how could my value system apparently have flip-flopped in the relatively short space of 1–2 years? Secondly, how could I have failed to take action on a retrospectively obvious safety problem when I was in the perfect position to do so? To begin, I would like to consider several possible explanations for my thoughts and actions (or lack thereof) during the early stages of the Pinto fire case.

One explanation is that I was simply revealed as a phony when the chips were down; that my previous values were not strongly inculcated; that I was all bluster, not particularly ethical, and as a result acted expediently when confronted with a reality test of those values. In other words, I turned traitor to my own expressed values. Another explanation is that I was simply intimidated; in the face of strong pressure to heel to company preferences, I folded—put ethical concerns aside, or at least traded them for a monumental guilt trip and did what anybody would do to keep a good job. A third explanation is that I was following a strictly utilitarian set of decision criteria (Valasquez *et al.*, 1983) and, predictably enough, opted for a personal form of Ford's own cost-benefit analysis, with similar disappointing results. Another explanation might suggest that the interaction of my stage of moral development (Kohlberg, 1969) and the culture and decision environment at Ford led me to think about and act upon an ethical dilemma in a fashion that reflected a lower level of actual moral development than I espoused for myself (Trevino, 1986 and this issue). Yet another explanation is that I was co-opted; rather than working from the inside to change a lumbering system as I had intended, the tables were turned and the system beat me at my own game. More charitably, perhaps, it is possible that I simply was a good person making bad ethical choices because of the corporate milieu (Gellerman, 1986).

I doubt that this list is exhaustive. I am quite sure that cynics could match my own MBA students' labels, which in the worst case include phrases like "moral failure" and "doubly reprehensible because you were in a position to make a difference." I believe, however, on the basis of a number of years of work on social cognition in organizations that a viable explanation is one that is not quite so melodramatic. It is an explanation that rests on a recognition that even the best-intentioned organization members organize information into cognitive structures or schemas that serve as (fallible) mental templates for handling incoming information and as guides for acting upon it. Of the many schemas that have been hypothesized to exist, the one that is most relevant to my experience at Ford is the notion of a script (Abelson, 1976, 1981).

My central thesis is this: *My own schematized (scripted) knowledge influenced me to perceive recall issues in terms of the prevailing decision environment and to unconsciously overlook key features of the Pinto case, mainly because they did not fit an existing script. Although the outcomes of the case carry retrospectively obvious ethical overtones, the schemas driving my perceptions and actions precluded consideration of the issues in ethical terms because the scripts did not include ethical dimensions.*

Script schemas

A *schema* is a cognitive framework that people use to impose structure upon information, situations, and expectations to facilitate understanding (Gioia and Poole, 1984; Taylor and Crocker, 1981). Schemas derive from consideration of prior experience or vicarious learning that results in the formation of "organized" knowledge—knowledge that, once formed, precludes the necessity for further active cognition. As a consequence, such structured knowledge allows virtually effortless interpretation of information and events (cf., Canter and Mischel, 1979). A *script* is a specialized type of schema that retains knowledge of actions appropriate for specific situations and contexts (Abelson, 1976, 1981). One of the most important characteristics of scripts is that they simultaneously provide a cognitive framework for *understanding* information and events as well as a guide to appropriate *behavior* to deal with the situation faced. They thus serve as linkages between cognition and action (Gioia and Manz, 1985).

The structuring of knowledge in scripted form is a fundamental human information processing tendency that in many ways results in a relatively closed cognitive system that influences both perception and action. Scripts, like all schemas, operate on the basis of prototypes, which are abstract representations that contain the main features of characteristics of a given knowledge category (e.g., "safety problems"). Protoscripts (Gioia and Poole, 1984) serve as templates against which incoming information can be assessed. A pattern in current information that generally matches the template associated with a given script signals that active thought and analysis is not required. Under these conditions the entire existing script can be called forth and enacted automatically and unconsciously, usually without adjustment for subtle differences in information patterns that might be important.

Given the complexity of the organizational world, it is obvious that the schematizing or scripting of knowledge implies a great information processing advantage—a decision maker need not actively think about each new presentation of information, situations, or problems; the mode of handling such problems has already been worked out in advance and remanded to a working stock of knowledge held in individual (or organizational) memory. Scripted knowledge saves a significant amount of mental work, a savings that in fact prevents the cognitive paralysis that would inevitably come from trying to treat each specific instance of a class of problems as a unique case that requires contemplation. Scripted decision making is thus efficient decision making but not necessarily good decision making (Gioia and Poole, 1984).

Of course, every advantage comes with its own set of built-in disadvantages. There is a price to pay for scripted knowledge. On the one hand, existing scripts lead people to selectively perceive information that is consistent with a script and thus to ignore anomalous information. Conversely, if there is missing information, the gaps in knowledge are filled with expected features supplied by the script (Bower *et al.*, 1979; Graesser *et al.*, 1980). In some cases, a pattern that matches an existing script, except for some key differences, can be "tagged" as a distinctive case (Graesser *et al.*, 1979) and thus be made more memorable. In the worst case scenario, however, a situation that does not fit the characteristics of the scripted perspective for handling problem cases often is simply not noticed. Scripts thus offer a viable explanation for why experienced decision makers (perhaps *especially* experienced decision makers) tend to overlook what others would construe as obvious factors in making a decision.

Given the relatively rare occurrence of truly novel information, the nature of script processing implies that it is a default mode of organizational cognition. That is, instead of spending the predominance of their mental energy thinking in some active fashion, decision makers might better be characterized as typically *not* thinking, i.e., dealing with information in a mode that is akin to "cruising on automatic pilot" (cf., Gioia, 1986). The scripted view casts decision makers as needing some sort of prod in the form of novel or unexpected information to kick them into a thinking mode—a prod that often does not come because of the wealth of similar data that they must process. Therefore, instead of focusing what people pay attention to, it might be more enlightening to focus on what they do *not* pay attention to.

PINTO PROBLEM PERCEPTION AND SCRIPTS

It is illustrative to consider my situation in handling the early stages of the Pinto fire case in light of script theory. When I was dealing with the first trickling-in of field reports that might have suggested a significant problem with the Pinto, the reports were essentially similar to many others that I was dealing with (and dismissing) all the time. The sort of information they contained, which did not convey enough prototypical features to capture my attention, never got past my screening script. I had seen this type of information pattern before (hundreds of times!); I was making this kind of decision automatically every day. I had trained myself to respond to prototypical cues, and these didn't fit the relevant prototype for crisis cases. (Yes, the Pinto reports fit a prototype—but it was a prototype for "normal accidents" that did not deviate significantly from expected problems). The frequency of the reports relative to other, more serious problems (i.e., those that displayed more characteristic features of safety problems) also did not pass my scripted criteria for singling out the Pinto case. Consequently, I looked right past them.

Overlooking uncharacteristic cues also was exacerbated by the nature of the job. The overwhelming information overload that characterized the role as well as its hectic pace actually forced a greater reliance on scripted responses. It was impossible to handle the job requirements *without* relying on some sort of automatic way of assessing whether a case deserved active attention. There was so much to do and so much information to attend to that the only way to deal with it was by means of schematic processing. In fact, the one anomaly in the case that might have cued me to gravity of the problem (the field report accompanied by graphic photographs) still did not distinguish the problem as one that was distinctive enough to snap me out of my standard response mode and tag it as a failure that deserved closer monitoring.

Even the presence of an emotional component that might have short-circuited standard script processing instead became part of the script itself. Months of squelching the disturbing emotions associated with serious safety problems soon made muffled emotions a standard (and not very salient) component of the script for handling *any* safety problem. This observation, that emotion was muted by experience, and therefore de-emphasized in the script, differs from Fiske's (1982) widely accepted position that emotion is tied to the top of a schema (i.e., the most salient and initially–tapped aspect of schematic processing). On the basis of my experience, I would argue that for organization members trained to control emotions to perform the job role (cf., Pitre, 1990), emotion is either not a part of the internalized script, or at best becomes a difficult-to-access part of any script for job performance.

The one instance of emotion penetrating the operating script was the revulsion that swept over me at the sight of the burned vehicle at the return depot. That event was so strong that it prompted me to put the case up for preliminary consideration (in theoretical terms, it prompted me cognitively to "tag" the Pinto case as a potentially distinctive one). I soon "came to my senses," however, when rational consideration of the problem characteristics suggested that they did not meet the scripted criteria that were consensually shared among members of the Field Recall Office. At the preliminary review other members of the decision team, enacting their own scripts in the absence of my emotional experience, wondered why I had even brought the case up. To me this meeting demonstrated that even when controlled analytic information processing occurred, it was nonetheless based on prior schematization of information. In other words, even when information processing was not automatically executed, it still depended upon schemas (cf., Gioia, 1986). As a result of the social construction of the situation, I ended up agreeing with my colleagues and voting not to recall.

The remaining major issue to be dealt with, of course, concerns the apparent shift in my values. In a period of less than two years I appeared to change my stripes and adopt the cultural values of the organization. How did that apparent shift occur? Again, scripts are relevant. I would argue that my pre-Ford values for changing corporate America were bona fide. I had internalized values for doing what was right as I then understood "rightness" in grand terms. The key is, however, that I had not internalized a *script* for enacting those values in any specific context outside my limited experience. The insider's view at Ford, of course, provided me with a specific and immediate context for developing such a script. Scripts are formed from salient experience and there was no more salient experience in my relatively young life than joining a major corporation and moving quickly into a position of clear and present responsibility. The strongest possible parameters for script formation were all there, not only because of the job role specifications, but also from the corporate culture. Organizational culture, in one very powerful sense, amounts to a collection of scripts writ large. Did I sell out? No. Were my cognitive structures altered by salient experience? Without question. Scripts for understanding and action were formed and reformed in a relatively short time in a way that not only altered perceptions of issues but also the likely actions associated with those altered perceptions.

I might characterize the differing cognitive structures as "outsider" versus "insider" scripts. I view them also as "idealist" versus "realist" scripts. I might further note that the outsider/idealist script was one that was more individually-based than the insider/realist script, which as more collective and subject to the influence of the corporate milieu and culture. Personal identity as captured in the revised script became much more corporate than individual. Given that scripts are socially constructed and reconstructed cognitive structures, it is understandable that their content and process would be much more responsive to the corporate culture, because of its saliency and immediacy.

The recall coordinator's job was serious business. The scripts associated with it influenced me much more than I influenced it. Before I went to Ford I would have argued strongly that Ford had an ethical obligation to recall. After I left Ford I now argue and teach that Ford had an ethical obligation to recall. But, *while I was there,* I perceived no strong obligation to recall and I remember no strong *ethical* overtones to the case whatsoever. It was a very straightforward decision, driven by dominant scripts for the time, place, and context.

WHITHER ETHICS AND SCRIPTS?

Most models of ethical decision making in organizations implicitly assume that people recognize and think about a moral or ethical dilemma when they are confronted with one (cf., Kohlberg, 1969 and Trevino's review in this issue). I call this seemingly fundamental assumption into question. The unexplored ethical issue for me is the arguably prevalent case where organizational representatives are not aware that they are dealing with a problem that might have ethical overtones. If the case involves a familiar class of problems or issues, it is likely to be handled via existing cognitive structures or scripts—*scripts that typically include no ethical component in their cognitive content.*

Although we might hope that people in charge of important decisions like vehicle safety recalls might engage in active, logical analysis and consider the subtleties in the many different situations they face, the context of the decisions and their necessary reliance on schematic processing tends to preclude such consideration (cf., Gioia, 1989). Accounting for the subtleties of ethical consideration in work situations that are typically handled by schema-based processing is very difficult indeed. Scripts are built out of situations that are normal, not those that are abnormal, ill-structured, or unusual (which often can characterize ethical domains). The ambiguities associated with most ethical dilemmas imply that such situations demand a "custom" decision, which means that the inclusion of an ethical dimension as a component of an evolving script is not easy to accomplish.

How might ethical considerations be internalized as part of the script for understanding and action? It is easier to say what will *not* be likely to work than what will. Clearly, mere mention of ethics in policy or training manuals will not do the job. Even exhortations to be concerned with ethics in decision making are seldom likely to migrate into the script. Just as clearly, codes of ethics typically will not work. They are too often cast at a level of generality that can not be associated with any specific script. Furthermore, for all practical purposes, codes of ethics often are stated in a way that makes them "context-free," which makes them virtually impossible to associate with active scripts, which always are context-bound.

Tactics for script *development* that have more potential involve learning or training that concentrates on exposure to information or models that explicitly display a focus on ethical considerations. This implies that ethics be included in job descriptions, management development training, mentoring, etc. Tactics for script *revision* involve learning or training that concentrate on "script-breaking" examples. Organization members must be exposed either to vicarious or personal experiences that interrupt tacit knowledge of "appropriate" action so that script revision can be initiated. Training scenarios, and especially role playing, that portray expected sequences that are then interrupted to call explicit attention to ethical issues can be tagged by the perceiver as requiring attention. This tactic amounts to installing a decision node in the revised scripts that tells the actor "Now think" (Abelson, 1981). Only by means of similar script-breaking strategies can existing cognitive structures be modified to accommodate the necessary cycles of automatic and controlled processing (cf., Louis and Sutton, 1991).

The upshot of the scripted view of organizational understanding and behavior is both an encouragement and an indictment of people facing situations laced with ethical overtones. It is encouraging because it suggests that organizational decision makers are not necessarily lacking in ethical standards; they are simply fallible information processors who fail to notice the ethical implications of a usual way of handling issues. It is an indictment because ethical dimensions are not usually a central feature of the cognitive structures that drive decision making. Obviously, they should be, but it will take substantial concentration on the ethical dimension of the corporate culture, as well as overt attempts to emphasize ethics in education, training, and decision making before typical organizational scripts are likely to be modified to include the crucial ethical component.

REFERENCES

Abelson, R. P.: 1976, 'Script Processing in Attitude Formation and Decision-Making', in J. S. Carroll and J. W. Payne (eds.), *Cognition and Social Behavior* (Erlbaum, Hillsdale, NJ), pp. 33–45.

Abelson, R. P.: 1981, 'Psychological Status of the Script Concept', *American Psychologist* **36**, pp. 715–729.

Anderson, J. and Whitten, L.: 1976, 'Auto Maker Shuns Safer Gas Tank', *Washington Post* (December 30), p. B–7.

Bower, G. H., Black, J. B. and Turner, T. J.: 1979, 'Scripts in Memory for Text', *Cognitive Psychology* **11**, pp. 177–220.

Cantor, N. and Mischel, W.: 1979, 'Prototypes in Person Perception', in L. Berkowitz (ed.), *Advances in Experimental Social Psychology* **12** (Academic Press, New York), pp. 3–51.

Cullen, F. T., Maakestad, W. J. and Cavender, G.: 1987, *Corporate Crime Under Attack* (Anderson Publishing Co., Chicago).

Dowie, M.: 1977, 'How Ford Put Two Million Firetraps on Wheels', *Business and Society Review* **23**, pp. 46–55.

Fiske, S. T.: 1982, 'Schema-Triggered Affect: Applications to Social Perception', in M. S. Clark and S. T. Fiske (eds.), *Affect and Cognition* (Erlbaum, Hillsdale, NJ), pp. 55–78.

Gatewood, E. and Carroll, A. B.: 1983, 'The Anatomy of Corporate Social Response: The Rely, Firestone 500, and Pinto Cases', *Business Horizons,* pp. 9–16.

Gellerman, S: 'Why "Good" Managers Make Bad Ethical Choices,' *Harvard Business Review* (July–August), pp. 85–90.

Gioia, D. A.: 1989, 'Self-Serving Bias as a Self-Sensemaking Strategy', in P. Rosenfeld, and R. Giacalone (eds.), *Impression Management in the Organization* (LEA, Hillsdale, NJ), pp. 219–234.

Gioia, D. A.: 1986, 'Symbols, Scripts, and Sensemaking: Creating Meaning in the Organizational Experience.' in H. P. Sims, Jr. and D. A. Gioia (eds.), *The Thinking Organization: Dynamics of Organizational Social Cognition* (Jossey-Bass, San Francisco), pp. 49–74.

Gioia, D. A. and Manz, C. C.: 1985, 'Linking Cognition and Behavior: A Script Processing Interpretation of Vicarious Learning', *Academy of Management Review* **10**, pp. 527–539.

Gioia, D. A. and Poole, P. P.: 1984, 'Scripts in Organizational Behavior', *Academy of Management Review* **9**, pp. 449–459.

Graesser, A. C., Gordon, S. G. and Sawyer, J. D.: 1979, 'Recognition Memory for Typical and Atypical Actions in Scripted Activities: Test of Script Pointer and Tag Hypothesis', *Journal of Verbal Learning and Verbal Behavior* **18**, pp. 319–332.

Graesser, A. C., Woll, S. B., Kowalski, D. J. and Smith, D. A.: 1980, 'Memory for Typical and Atypical Actions in Scripted Activities', *Journal of Experimental Psychology* **6**, pp. 503–515.

Kohlberg, L.: 1969, 'Stage and Sequence: The Cognitive-Development Approach to Socialization', in D. A. Goslin (ed.), *Handbook of Socialization Theory and Research* (Rand-McNally, Chicago), pp. 347–480.

Louis, M. R. and Sutton, R. I.: 1991, 'Switching Cognitive Gears: From Habits of Mind to Active Thinking', *Human Relations* **44**, pp. 55–76.

Perrow, C.: 1984, *Normal Accidents* (Basic Books, New York).

Pitre, E.: 1990, 'Emotional Control', working paper, the Pennsylvania State University.

Swigert, V. L. and Farrell, R. A.: 1980–81, 'Corporate Homicide: Definitional Processes in the Creation of Deviance', *Law and Society Review* **15**, pp. 170–183.

Taylor, S. E. and Crocker, J.: 1981, 'Schematic Bases of Social Information Processing', in E. T. Higgins, C. P. Herman, and M. P. Zanna (eds.), *Social Cognition* **1** (Erlbaum, Hillsdale, NJ), pp. 89–134.

Trevino, L.: 1986, 'Ethical Decision Making in Organizations: A Person-Situation Interactionist Model', *Academy of Management Review* **11**, pp. 601–617.

Trevino, L.: 1992, 'Moral Reasoning and Business Ethics: Implications for Research, Education and Management', *Journal of Business Ethics* **11**, 445–459.

Valasquez, M., Moberg, D. J. and Cavanaugh, G. F.: 1983, 'Organizational Statesmanship and Dirty Politics: Ethical Guidelines for the Organizational Politician', *Organizational Dynamics* (Autumn), pp. 65–80.

Van Maanen, J.: 1978, 'People Processing: Strategies of Organizational Socialization', *Organizational Dynamics* (Summer), pp. 19–36.

Pennsylvania State University,
Smeal College of Business Administration,
University Park, PA 16802,
U.S.A.

QUESTIONS ON READINGS FOR PART EIGHT

What values would you build into the culture of a company you create?

How would you ensure the culture is implemented?

What forces might place pressure on your firm's culture?